Ambrose Macaulay,
27 March 1971. X

SACRAMENTUM MUNDI

VOLUME ONE: ABSOLUTE — CONSTANTINIAN ERA

SACRAMENTUM MUNDI

An Encyclopedia of Theology

Edited by

KARL RAHNER SJ, Münster
and
JUAN ALFARO SJ, Rome
ALBERTO BELLINI, Bergamo
CARLO COLOMBO, Venegono
HENRI CROUZEL SJ, Toulouse
JEAN DANIÉLOU SJ, Paris
ADOLF DARLAP, Munich
CORNELIUS ERNST OP, Oxford
JOSÉ FONDEVILLA SJ, Barcelona
PIET FRANSEN, Louvain
FERGUS KERR OP, Oxford
PIET SCHOONENBERG, Nijmegen
KEVIN SMYTH, Paris
† GUSTAVE WEIGEL SJ, Woodstock

Published by Herder and Herder New York · Burns & Oates London · Palm Publishers
Montreal · Herder Freiburg · Éditions Desclée de Brouwer Bruges · Editorial Herder
Barcelona · Edizioni Morcelliana Brescia · Paul Brand Hilversum

SACRAMENTUM MUNDI

AN ENCYCLOPEDIA OF THEOLOGY

VOLUME ONE

ABSOLUTE AND CONTINGENT
TO
CONSTANTINIAN ERA

BURNS & OATES

HERDER AND HERDER NEW YORK
232 Madison Avenue, New York, N. Y. 10016

BURNS & OATES LIMITED
25 Ashley Place, London S. W. 1

1st Edition 1968
2nd Impression 1968
3rd Impression 1969
4th Impression 1969

General Editor: Adolf Darlap

First published in West Germany © 1968, Herder KG
Printed in West Germany by Herder
SBN 223 29384 9

GENERAL PREFACE

"Sacramentum Mundi" is an international theological encyclopedia which is being published simultaneously in six languages (English, Dutch, French, German, Italian and Spanish). It is an attempt to formulate present-day developments of the understanding of the faith, basing itself on modern theological investigations of the key-themes of the theological disciplines, in the hope that they will thus be fruitful for personal reflection in faith and in practice. The developments in question may be characterized as a thinking which takes fully into account the conditions of past and present historical growth in the understanding of faith. It has therefore a strongly marked orientation to the future — its historical dimension — and is also marked by its openness for the other Christian Churches, the non-Christian religions and for the world in general — its social dimension.

To make what is hoped to be a Summa of modern theology easily accessible to the enquiring and open-minded reader of today, both clerics and lay people, the encyclopedia is presented in alphabetical order. While normally an encyclopedia is supposed to offer matters to be looked up and used on occasion, but precisely not what one needs to remember permanently, here the opposite goal is aimed at. The fundamental effort is to furnish the truths which should be the constant and vital possession of the believer as he tries to answer for his faith and his hope and the promise which it contains (1 Pet 3:15).

It should be clear that such an undertaking cannot be carried out in the same way for all the terms and concepts of the theological sciences and that as a first effort in this direction it may not be equally successful in dealing with all relevant themes. In some cases it was possible to adopt the findings of earlier discussion of certain themes, which only needed to be pin-pointed and completed in view of the purpose of this work.

The work is the product of an international editorial board, which collectively assumes responsibility for all the editions in the various languages. The contributors are also drawn from many countries. The international character of the team of collaborators was meant to provide an example of the co-operation between theologians of many lands which is so necessary in the post-conciliar epoch, and was also considered a means of avoiding one-sided emphases. The editors also recognized, however, that such international co-operation would inevitably demand from all a certain patience and openness with regard to what might seem alien. The differences in the articulation of the various themes, due to the various theological backgrounds and hence thought-forms of the authors, have not been smoothed out by the editors, but deliberately left standing.

The six editions are substantially identical; but this does not mean that the various national editors have not made some adaptations to suit the *genius loci* of each region.

THE EDITORS

PREFACE TO THE ENGLISH EDITION

In the present state of Catholic theological writing in English no one could doubt the usefulness of a comprehensive survey of central theological topics conducted by a group of writers in basic sympathy with each other, whose theological views have emerged from a serious and disciplined study of the relevant sources and from an awareness of the problems posed by life and thought in the modern world. The views expressed are of course authoritative only in the sense that they are put forward by serious theological authors; they are not offered as definitive, and the highly selective bibliographies supplied are meant to be used not only as a guide to further reflection but also as a means of testing the well-foundedness of the views proposed. The fact that this work is appearing simultaneously in several languages should contribute to the reintegration of Catholic theology, no longer on the basis of an artificially preserved scholasticism, but of a wider tradition of theology in which the creative scholastic thinkers find their proper place: this living tradition is not closed but open to every valid original development.

After the premature death of Fr. Gustave Weigel, S.J., the original editor of the English edition, responsibility for the English edition was assumed by the present writer and Fr. Fergus Kerr, O.P. Mr. Kevin Smyth, who had already done so much for the encyclopedia, finally assumed editorial responsibilities, and it is to him that the English edition in its present form is due. Of the numerous translators who have made this edition possible, apart from Mr. Smyth (philosophical, biblical and other articles), special thanks are due to Mr. W. J. O'Hara (articles by Fr. Karl Rahner and others), Mr. Richard Strachan and Fr. T. Hamilton, S.J. (historical and socio-political questions), Mr. A. David Lewis (Church history), and Dr. David J. Bourke (biblical exegesis).

In its English edition, the encyclopedia will be complete in six volumes; a detailed index will be found at the end of the last volume.

CORNELIUS ERNST, O.P.

ABBREVIATIONS

The following list does not include biblical and other well-known abbreviations.

Whenever an author, not listed below, is cited in an article by name only, followed by page number(s), the reference is to a work listed in the bibliography at the end of the article.

AAS	*Acta Apostolicae Sedis* (1909 ff.)
ACW	J. Quasten and J. C. Plumpe, *Ancient Christian Writers* (1946 ff.)
Billerbeck	(H. L. Strack and) P. Billerbeck, *Kommentar zum Neuen Testament aus Talmud und Midrasch,* I–IV (1922–28; reprint, 1956), V: rabbinical index, ed. by J. Jeremias and K. Adolph (1956)
CBQ	*Catholic Biblical Quarterly* (1939 ff.)
Chalkedon	A. Grillmeier and H. Bacht, eds., *Das Konzil von Chalkedon, Geschichte und Gegenwart,* 3 vols. (1951–54; 2nd enlarged ed., 1962)
CIC	*Codex Iuris Canonici*
CIO	*Codex Iuris Canonici Orientalis* (Unless stated otherwise, the references are to the law relating to persons.)
Collectio Lacensis	*Collectio Lacensis: Acta et Decreta Sacrorum Conciliorum Recentiorum,* ed. by the Jesuits of Maria Laach, 7 vols. (1870–90)
CSEL	*Corpus Scriptorum Ecclesiasticorum Latinorum* (1866 ff.)
D	H. Denzinger, *Enchiridion Symbolorum, Definitionum et Declarationum de Rebus Fidei et Morum* (31st ed., 1957); see also *DS*
DB	F. Vigouroux, ed., *Dictionnaire de la Bible,* 5 vols. (1895–1912)
DBS	L. Pirot, ed., *Dictionnaire de la Bible, Supplément,* continued by A. Robert (1928 ff.)
DS	H. Denzinger and A. Schönmetzer, *Enchiridion Symbolorum, Definitionum et Declarationum de Rebus Fidei et Morum* (33rd ed., 1965); see also *D*
DSAM	M. Viller, ed., *Dictionnaire de Spiritualité ascétique et mystique. Doctrine et Histoire* (1932 ff.)
DTC	A. Vacant and E. Mangenot, eds., *Dictionnaire de théologie catholique,* continued by É. Amann, I–XV, *Table analytique* and *Tables générales,* XVI ff. (1903 ff.)

ABBREVIATIONS

Enchiridion Biblicum	*Enchiridion Biblicum. Documenta Ecclesiastica Sacram Scripturam Spectantia* (3rd ed., 1956)
ETL	*Ephemerides Theologicae Lovanienses* (1924 ff.)
GCS	*Die griechischen christlichen Schriftsteller der ersten drei Jahrhunderte* (1897 ff.)
Hennecke-Schneemelcher-Wilson	E. Hennecke, W. Schneemelcher and R. McL. Wilson, eds., *New Testament Apocrypha*, 2 vols. (1963–65)
HERE	J. Hastings, ed., *Encyclopedia of Religion and Ethics*, 12 vols. + index (1908–26; 2nd rev. ed., 1925–40)
JBL	*Journal of Biblical Literature* (1881 ff.)
JTS	*Journal of Theological Studies* (1899 ff.)
LTK	J. Höfer and K. Rahner, eds., *Lexikon für Theologie und Kirche*, 10 vols. + index (2nd rev. ed., 1957–67)
Mansi	J. D. Mansi, *Sacrorum Conciliorum Nova et Amplissima Collectio*, 31 vols. (1757–98); reprint and continuation ed. by L. Petit and J. B. Martin, 60 vols. (1899–1927)
NRT	*Nouvelle Revue Théologique* (1879 ff.)
NTS	*New Testament Studies* (1954 ff.)
PG	J.-P. Migne, ed., *Patrologia Graeca*, 161 vols. (1857 ff.)
PL	J.-P. Migne, ed., *Patrologia Latina*, 217 vols. + 4 index vols. (1844 ff.)
Pritchard	J. B. Pritchard, ed., *Ancient Near Eastern Texts relating to the Old Testament* (1950; 2nd revised and enlarged ed., 1955)
RGG	K. Galling, ed., *Die Religion in Geschichte und Gegenwart*, 6 vols. + index (3rd rev. ed., 1957–65)
RHE	*Revue d'histoire ecclésiastique* (1900 ff.)
RHPR	*Revue d'histoire et de philosophie religieuse* (1921 ff.)
RSPT	*Revue des sciences philosophiques et théologiques* (1907 ff.)
RSR	*Recherches de science religieuse* (1910 ff.)
RSV	Revised Standard Version of the Bible
TS	*Theological Studies* (1940 ff.)
TWNT	G. Kittel, ed., *Theologisches Wörterbuch zum Neuen Testament*, continued by G. Friedrich (1933 ff.); E. T.: *Theological Dictionary of the New Testament* (1964 ff.)
ZAW	*Zeitschrift für die alttestamentliche Wissenschaft* (1881 ff.)
ZKT	*Zeitschrift für Katholische Theologie* (1877 ff.)

A

ABSOLUTE AND CONTINGENT

I. The Absolute. II. The Contingent.

I. The Absolute

1. The notion of the absolute is that of the unconditioned in general. The opposite notion is that of the relative. The absolute excludes entirely any dependence in its existence from anything else. This substantive use of the word means absoluteness of being, not merely an unconditioned validity or concept, which latter is called absolute if it does not imply a relation to something else. The absolute in general, being a *singulare tantum,* is more than the independence which may to a certain extent be attributed to substances (and "absolute accidents"), which are absolute in so far as they have independent being or at least cannot be entirely subsumed in relationship or relativity.

2. The real existence of the absolute, understood in this way, seems to result at once (granted that anything at all exists), from the nature of the concept. The concepts "absolute" and "relative" are contradictory: there is no other alternative, which would be neither dependent nor independent in being. But the relative, of its nature, points on to that from which it depends, and ultimately to that which is itself not relative and, therefore, to the absolute. And the assumption that the relative exists in a series without a beginning, in a *regressus in infinitum,* would not silence the allusion to the absolute which proceeds from the relative as such, though the imagination, linked to space and time, fails to do justice to this effort of thought.

Above all, a closed circle of relative beings, that is, one without a beginning or end, would be simply impossible: for A must have helped B to exist, though A itself would be dependent for its existence on B, via C, D, etc. If any thing at all exists, it cannot be merely relative, that is, something existing by reference to something else and hence ultimately by reference to that which is absolutely other: therefore the absolute necessarily exists.

3. The obviousness with which the absolute presents itself as that which exists as necessarily as it is thought of, corresponds to the philosophical tradition of the last two thousand years. The universal religious experience of the "Other", the wielder of ultimate, unconditioned power, becomes in the reflection of India the Universal One, of which this world is the illusory manifestation. In early Greek thought it becomes the principle (ἀρχή) of the world. Plato sees in the highest form, the Good, that absence of all presuppositions (ἀν-ὑπόθετον) and the total selfhood (αὐτὸ καθ᾽ αὐτό) which constitute the absolute. This view affects neo-Platonism and is combined with the Jewish-Christian revelation in the age of the Church Fathers (cf., for instance, Gregory of Nazianzus: ἄν-αρχος). Later Meister Eckhart, Jacob Böhme and Franz Baader speak of the "groundless ground" or even of the "non-ground". In Aristotle, the absolute being of the eternal, unmoved first cause is distinguished from all the constituents of the sensible world by its "separateness" (κεχωρισμένη).

Scholasticism orientates the absolute towards the fuller concept of the (absolutely) necessary: it is that which is "of itself" (St. Anselm), "the first cause of being, which does not receive its being from another" (St. Thomas), *ens a se* "that which is by reason of itself" (Suarez). In St. Bonaventure, dependent beings are contrasted with the *ens absolutum,* which is the purest, most real and most perfect being: knowledge of it is the condition of possibility of knowledge in deficient, imperfect beings; it is at the base of all knowledge of truth. Later, Nicholas of Cusa affirms expressly: "God alone is absolute", to the exclusion of all relationships and restrictions (*De Docta Ignorantia,* II, 9; cf. I, 2). The philosophical systems of rationalism, especially German idealism, are philosophies of the absolute: it is not the infinite absolute, it is the finite relative which is not self-explanatory. For Fichte, Schelling and especially Hegel, the universal spirit-principle expounds itself self-creatively as the world — in an "ab-soluteness" which is transposed, by way of dialectical self-communication, into the relative, in identity in differentiation. In the nineteenth and twentieth centuries, "the absolute", which had become part of modern language since Hegel, was mostly interpreted as the irrational. Value philosophies and existentialism mostly reduce it to the unconditioned nature of matters of the spirit in general, especially to personal human attitudes. The self-understanding which is predominant today is more and more influenced by the empiricist orientation of modern thinking which, like the sophists of ancient times, tends to deny or rather to be sceptical about the absolute.

4. For the modern mind, the obviousness of the necessary existence of the absolute has been obscured, chiefly through the influence of Kant. Its obviousness comes from the step taken by thought in which the relative or conditioned is recognized as such, and hence comprised as a whole and transcended by the orientation to the absolute or unconditioned. According to Kant, however, this is not possible for human knowledge, by which we can only really know an object in so far as it is presented to us under the conditions of space or at least of time. The relative and conditioned can be known only as dependent on something else, which is in its turn likewise relative and conditioned by a third object of the same type, and so on. The endless passage from phenomenon to phenomenon, within the horizon of possible (spatial and) temporal experience, is the paradigm of knowledge as depicted by Kant in his *Critique of Pure Reason.* Kant thus took the methodology of modern science, whose task is on principle an endless research within the region of phenomena called the "world", and applied it as a formula to the classic theory of knowledge. Under the influence of the natural sciences, where this view, with or without knowledge of its philosophical origin, has a perfectly legitimate place, a fundamental attitude of more or less pronouncedly relativist positivism began to prevail, and reacted illegitimately on philosophy's view of the world. At present, psychological and sociological data are seen as giving empirical and scientific confirmation to this transformation of philosophical thought into purely relativist categories. Goethe voiced this mentality as a keen sense of life and of joyful acceptance of the world: "To make the infinite your goal, you need only aim at the finite from all directions."

5. But the effort to make the fundamental obviousness of the absolute reality comprehensible once more can be guided by Kant, once tradition is borne in mind, especially the thought of St. Augustine and St. Bonaventure.

In Kant's paradigm of knowledge, the idea of the unconditioned has the function of a "regulative principle"; it mirrors the theoretically unattainable goal which inspires perpetually all enquiry and research. It is only in another field that Kant, in his *Critique of Practical Reason,* finds the way open which leads him to the "constitutive" reality of the unconditioned: in the experience of moral obligation, in the categorical, that is, unconditional imperative of conscience. It is not the theoretical experience of the necessity of the laws of nature, but the practical moral will, whose immediate presupposition is the freedom of man, that presupposes the necessary existence of the absolute, which may be called God, as the basic postulate of its claims — claims which for Kant are just and meaningful, beyond all possible doubt. God is the guarantor of the moral order of the world, of the social life of men.

However, the experience of the unconditioned may be had by us not merely in the region of moral freedom but in every act of true knowledge. Whenever anything is known as "true", that is, as it is, this knowledge claims unconditional validity. It demands recognition of the structure of its affirmation from every subject endowed with reason, under all circumstances. The content of the act of knowledge may be even totally conditioned and limited by time and space; it may perhaps be concerned merely with the "here and now" of one of my passing feelings. But the claim to validity which the truth of the affirmation about it possesses, completely transcends the temporal and spatial. Even the most haphazard and transitory phenomenon is grasped in true knowledge *in its being, in so far as it is*. And thereby the unconditioned region of that which is as such, of being simply and solely, is disclosed. After all, this very mode of knowledge was the presupposition of all knowledge of the relative or conditioned *as such,* and hence of its essential and indisputable reference to the absolute and unconditioned. Thus the way is open to pass from the logically absolute mode in which true knowledge exists within the indeterminately infinite horizon of beings, to the ontological *actus purus,* to the definitely infinite absolute principle of truth and reality.

To observe not merely the phenomena of *what* takes place, a functional connection for instance of scientific data, but to see also the ontological reality, *that* it takes place (i.e., *that* it really *is* so) — this calls for a break-through beyond and "behind" the methodologically limited perspectives of the individual sciences, whose enquiries are confined to the phenomena as they appear; one must strive to attain the mental attitude of philosophy, which is orientated to reality as it is in itself. The actual accomplishment of this break-through is the work of freedom, which springs from man's being alerted as a totality. The preparation of the intellect for the reality of the absolute, in the field of theoretical knowledge where Kant and to a great extent modern thought believe it to be impossible, is only of limited value. It must be accompanied by the genuine realization of the true freedom of the human being, to which Kant appealed. But now the appeal to moral freedom can also be justified theoretically.

There is another way by which the obviousness of the absolute can be brought to light. It is the demonstration that the unconditioned nature of personal love can only exist and attain its fulfilment on the basis of the real existence of the personally absolute.

Of itself, the concept of the absolute, as the totally unconditioned, does not tell us whether the basic structure of the universe is theistic or pantheistic. The more existentially convincing experiences which we have briefly indicated point to the absolute as a reality of which we know more than the concept, and do in fact suggest that it must be interpreted theistically and personally. It should be seen as the only sufficient reason which can provide the truth and freedom, in which the personal selfhood of man is realized, with its existence and its goal. The character of double negation which is inevitable to all human knowledge of the absolute and unconditioned (conditioned implying of course limit, finiteness and negation) proclaims from the very start the permanently mysterious nature of the absolute.

II. The Contingent

1. The concept of the contingent in philosophy is that of the accidental, that which does not exist by virtue of its essence. Hence, from the purely logical point of view, its actual existing has to its essence the relation of an accident (from *accidere, ad-cadere*), which "falls to" the lot of the essence "from outside". In the broader sense of the term, the contingent stands for that "which can not be". Thus it is the contradictory of the absolute and necessary, which cannot but be, since it is by virtue of its essence. In the stricter sense of the term, it excludes the absolutely impossible and designates only "that which can and can not be". In any case, contingency implies that the ontological constitution of a being is characterized by a deficiency in what it has or is: it indicates the type of being which is not its own actual reality of and through itself.

What has been said about the absolute holds good in all essentials for the relationship of the contingent to the necessary, with regard to its place in the history of thought, the difficulties now experienced in the recognition of the contingent, and the efforts being made to gain a new understanding of the matter by staying closer to experience.

The *application* of the concept of contingency brings up a new element of the problem. It seems that man has normally no direct, propositional and objectivated knowledge of his own contingency, since such knowledge would undoubtedly imply an *articulate* experience of the absolute principle of his existence. But how then is contingency to be recognized? By its being caused by something else? But then the concept would be useless in metaphysics: it would not help to attain the knowledge sought from the contingent, that of the necessary as its cause. By the fact that the contingent comes or ceases to be? But then it would be impossible to demonstrate philosophically the contingency of the universe as a whole. And Greek philosophy, which argued from the coming to be and passing away of the things of the world, did not in fact penetrate to the notion of the contingent and so to that of the creation of the matter which was conceived to be the basic substance of the world. Hence it could not escape a type of dualism. A universally applicable criterion of contingency is to be found, however, in the changeability of man and the world.

2. *Man* experiences himself as subject to change in the most diverse ways: he grows up and grows old, he learns and he forgets ... Each man realizes possibilities which he possesses, one after another, in order to be himself more and more. But this successive actuation of himself is also and inevitably a selective actuation: to take one possibility always excludes another which is likewise real and desirable. This basic law of human destiny is undoubtedly most keenly perceptible in the choice of a particular vocation, because it eliminates the possibility of other types of culture and creation which, being human possibilities, were also more or less *mine*. The situations in which man is pushed to his limits, when the blows of contingency make their sharpest and most direct psychic impact (the loss of his dear ones, the oppressiveness of guilt, failure in his life's work) — these too are woven into the "formal structure" of change. Since this prevents all our possibilities being realized fully and without exception, and even prevents their ever being present and permanent in the here and now of a single, unified totality, of a compact, concentrated collection, without being resolved into a succession, it is therefore an indication that man does not exist by virtue of his own essence, by reason of the sovereignty of his own self. For had he such authority, all his possibilities would be full realities at once. In a word, change shows that man is contingent.

3. To prove the contingency of the *world* as a whole, it is not necessary to examine it piecemeal for its changeability — the perpetual and universal interchange and change of state of the elementary particles of which the world as a whole is composed is taken for granted in modern physics, as also for instance in "dialectic materialism". We mean by "world" the totality of what is accessible to our direct experience. But then, with this "operational" notion of the world, from which all philosophical thinking of the world must no doubt start, the changeability of the world as a whole and in its parts is already settled. For the immediate object of our changing experience must correspond, in fundamental changeability, with the experience which takes it in and becomes one with it. Nor can an ultimate principle, corresponding for instance to the matter of the Greeks, be excluded from the changeability and hence from the contingency of the world. For if something changes, then all its parts are changed, even those which seem the least affected: in so far as anything is the subject of change, it is also modified accordingly. When the contingency of man and the world is thus recognized, they form together the basis from which to ascend to knowledge of the necessary.

See also *Pre-Socratics, Platonism, Aristotelianism, Scholasticism, Idealism, Value, Existence* II, III, *Kantianism, God* I, III.

BIBLIOGRAPHY. J. Maréchal, *Le point de départ de la métaphysique*, 5 vols. (1922–47); M. C. Chill, *The Absolute and the Relative in Modern Philosophy* (1939); K. Rahner, *Hörer des Wortes* (1941; 2nd ed., 1963); F. Grégoire, "Condition, conditionné, inconditionné", *Revue Philosophique de Louvain* 46 (1948), pp. 5–41; J. Möller, *Der Geist und das Absolute* (1951); G. Huber, *Das Sein und das Absolute* (1955); B. F. J. Lonergan, *Insight. A Study of Human Understanding* (1957); A. Farrer, *Finite and Infinite* (1959); W. Cramer, *Das Absolute und das Kontingente* (1959); J. B. Lotz, *Ontologia* (1963), with biblio.; E. Coreth, *Metaphysik*, I (2nd ed., 1964).

Walter Kern

ABSOLUTISM

A. Notions and Forms

Absolutism means the rule of one individual legitimated solely by descent (hereditary monarchy), his power being essentially indivisible, allowing of no relatively autonomous intermediate authorities, and limited as to competence only by his own judgment. Forms of absolute sovereignty first appeared in the advanced civilizations of antiquity. The main basis of authority was the ruler's connection with a god: he might be the representative of the god, or his son, or even the realization of his presence. Christianity first encountered absolutism in the age of persecution when it was summoned to worship the Roman emperor, and then in the idea of sacred majesty which Constantine and his successors had. These emperors had a special religious place in the Christian liturgy and exercised important rights in Church government. The situation altered as the Church's hierarchy acquired more independence, especially in the west of the empire. Here the new barbarian States introduced the Germanic kingship and a political world where the inviolability of the king certainly played an important part; but kings were for long elected by their fellow-noblemen. These too were protected by their lineage and in feudalism they created a highly articulated system of government. Sacred kingship was secularized within the Church by the Gregorian reform, without losing any of its religious significance in the political world. But the growth of the Church's freedom in the West, the self-assertiveness of regional bishoprics and — from Gregory VII to Innocent III — the ascendancy of the papacy brought about a diarchy of the two powers, spiritual and temporal, which thwarted absolutism as effectively as did the relations between crown and nobles.

Contemplating this medieval social structure, we must call the establishment of princely absolutism the first revolutionary step — the revolution from above which brought in its train the bourgeois revolution of the 19th century.

The opponents against whom absolutism had to struggle were the feudal nobility with their own rights at public law, who became a nobility by patent, robbed of their political privileges and dependent on the crown; and the independent ecclesiastical hierarchy, whose ambivalent attitude to the State was to be abolished by turning it into a national Church — a policy which did not oblige Catholic States to tamper with the papal primacy so long as the exercise of papal power did not run counter to the interests of the State.

The means by which the absolutist system was constructed were a highly centralized administration, a standing army commanded by the king alone, and State patronage of production and trade, the taxes from which were to pay for the bureaucracy and army (mercantilism).

What absolutism meant to achieve was an unlimited power that reached into every department of the subject's life, kept all the economic resources, all the production, all the manpower of the State mobilized to the utmost, in the hands of the sovereign, secured without by an army instantly available and a system of alliances encircling the potential enemy, changing as circumstances demanded. Just as the all-pervading State was to grow without ceasing at home, so it was to expand beyond its frontiers, above all by inheritance, subject to considerations of political prudence and in some degree to the principle of legitimacy, the general validity of which was acknowledged within the "family" that the dynasties formed.

Power, it seemed, could be supreme only in a perfect union with the society that was identical with the State — "un roi, une loi, une foi" —, organized according to logical bureaucratic principles which were as likely to sacrifice the historical achievements of the older society as to make use of them. Where the institutions of feudal society were spared, it was not in deference to ancient rights, but only because they seemed useful in the rational pattern of the all-embracing State, which alone was supposed capable of guaranteeing the greatest good for everyone. This guarantee was embodied in the absolute ruler whom God had set over men as his "lieutenant" (Louis XIV). Or (in the so-called "enlightened despotism") the king was steward of the supreme reason which is incarnate in the State. Being the "first servant" of the State ("premier domestique", said Frederick the Great) was essentially a variant — one that well summed up the intellectual movement of the Enlightenment — of the exclusive charism which made the absolute sovereign sole ruler and lawgiver, supreme commander and supreme judge. In all countries the age of absolutism ushered in modern times, which have opened such vast new vistas to man. It was the classical age of culture for all European peoples, and laid the foundations — through the Enlightenment — of modern education and culture.

The theoretical basis of absolutism was the notion of sovereignty as worked out since the end of the Middle Ages with the help of juridical ideas borrowed from late antiquity, especially by the legists in France (Pierre d'Ailly, d. 1420; Jean Gerson, d. 1429), culminating in the political theory of Jean Bodin (d. 1596). He calls sovereignty "supreme power over citizens and subjects, unrestricted by laws". Princely *majestas* acts on its own discretion, independent of any higher power, any law, any historical circumstance, responsible directly to God and to him alone. Here we have suggestions of pre-Christian absolutism, though of course Christian belief in the dignity of the individual and the equality of all men before God could not be extinguished. In the process of secularization the ruler's power found itself limited by reason (see below), and normally the subject had a right to be treated in accordance with law (rule of law), though that did not make arbitrary treatment impossible in practice. Arbitrary government, however, as conflicting with the rational interests of the State, is not of the essence of princely absolutism.

B. History of Absolutism in Europe

The history of absolutism opens with the end of the 15th century or the beginning of the 16th. Isolated earlier examples like the autocratic State which the Emperor Frederick II (d. 1250) ruled through his civil service in Southern Italy, or the centralized constitution which Philip the Fair (d. 1324) gave France with the help of experts in Roman law such as Nogaret, were still combined with really old-fashioned traits (Frederick II's imperial policy, Philip's projected crusade). And Ranke's "strong breeze from modern times" comes to no more than a puff of wind here and there, by no means characteristic of the situation as a whole. Since the existence of a spiritual power independent of the temporal was the most serious obstacle, along with the nobility, to the growth of absolutism, and since the spiritual power owed its influence to the universal acceptance of the standards it taught, the vital step for absolutism was to create a national Church. Moves in this direction were made even before the Reformation: for example, the concordats made to ward off conciliarism gave princes the right to name bishops and administer Church funds and land. In England the religious and ecclesiastical Reformation was preceded by Henry VIII's political move of setting up a Church under strict State control, the foundation on which the absolutism of the House of Tudor (1485–1603) squarely rested and the bone of contention between the absolutism of the House of Stuart (1603–1688) and the Puritan opposition. But the limitations imposed on English royal power since the thirteenth century were too firmly entrenched for absolutism to maintain itself in England, in spite of its control of the Established Anglican Church; though in England, as in all European States, absolutism ushered in modern times. In the German Empire the ecclesiastical powers which accrued to the territorial princes at the Reformation strengthened the new national Churches, and even the States which remained Catholic were similarly affected: the maxim of the Peace of Augsburg (1555), "Cuius regio, eius et religio", practically left it to the omnipotent prince to decide what religion his subjects should profess. Though absolutism set the style of government in all the princely States of Germany, even in the ecclesiastical territories, only in the Hapsburg dominions (against some competition from Bavarian absolutism) and in Prussia did it find conditions out of which absolutist great powers could grow. When the Thirty Years War had shattered the attempt of the Emperor Ferdinand II (d. 1637), father of absolutism in Austria, to restore an empire that was historically possible only as a counterpart of the Roman Catholic Church, when Lutheranism in the hereditary Hapsburg lands had been reduced to the merest remnant, and the Emperor Leopold I had established Austria as a great power among European States, Maria Theresa (1740–1780) was able to develop the special Austrian form of professedly Catholic absolutism in the Monarchia Austriaca. There were conservative elements in it, but it chiefly armed the central authorities against family and territorial interests of the nobility. Conscious of ruling by the grace of God, Maria Theresa considered her ministers as the mere handymen of her rule, which she was wise enough to base both on a strict financial policy and on the primary school system which she set up. A contemporary of Frederick the Great of Prussia, who was odious to her, Maria Theresa outlived the form of absolutism which was firmly established by Philip II of Spain (d. 1598) and had grown into a consummate system. With all due regard for their right to protection, the Empress too looked on the Protestants of her realm as pernicious enemies of the order willed by God; but she prudently distinguished between the ancestral lands and Hungary.

The Spanish Hapsburg had exerted all his power to preserve the unity of holy faith throughout his dominions, making use of the Inquisition to that end, with whose help — this is characteristic of "religious" absolutism — he also crushed the opposition of the Estates of Aragon. To regard religious belief as an ideological superstructure added to princely rule would be to misinterpret absolutism; but on the other hand princely sovereignty was as inviolate as Catholic faith. And so we can understand Philip II's political reservations in accepting the decrees of the Council of Trent — a typical example of the relations between Catholic absolutism and the Church. In the evolution of French absolutism also, which was especially marked by the link between religious struggles and the opposition of the nobility — not Huguenot alone but Catholic as well—, the principle "une foi" ist not a mere function of the principle "un roi". Political considerations moved Richelieu to destroy, when La Rochelle was conquered (1628), the separate Huguenot State that had been set up by the Edict of Nantes (1598); and similar considerations caused him not to withdraw the Edict itself, despite the advice of Father Joseph, his Capuchin confidant — as typical a figure of French absolutism as is Richelieu. A religious man with a mystical bent, he fought fanatically to preserve the unity of the faith; and yet for the sake of French political power he unconditionally supported Richelieu's policy, including the alliance with Sweden (1634), and the declaration of war against Spain (1635), which meant the decisive weakening of the Catholic party in the Thirty Years War. When Louis XIV finally did revoke the Edict of Nantes in 1685, this was an act of political absolutism. Nevertheless the "courtly" absolutism of the *roi soleil,* with all its pagan exaltation of the king and its extravagant mode of life, would have been impossible without the historical presuppositions created by professedly Catholic absolutism.

After the Treaty of Westphalia (1648), however, the religious uniformity of the absolutist States gradually began to break up — a circumstance which favoured the spread of the Enlightenment, full of the disruptive elements which were to destroy royal absolutism and yet welcomed at first by the absolute monarchs, especially Frederick II of Prussia (1740–1786). That king's religious tolerance, really the scepticism of the Enlightenment, paved the way for a unification of the State for its own sake. Joseph II (1765–1790), the Hapsburg, followed Frederick's example — on the one hand proclaiming toleration and on the other hand extending absolutist centralization to the Austrian Netherlands and Hungary, which his mother had not been prepared to do. While the episcopalism invented by Hontheim (Febronius), Auxiliary Bishop of Trier, which was to emancipate the bishops from the Roman Curia by integrating them into the absolutist established Church, remained mere theory for Germany as a whole and was practised in various ways in particular territories, Joseph II systematically drew the Catholic Church into the service of the absolutist State and its educational programme, on account of which he thought it better to build presbyteries than monasteries. He suppressed a great many of the latter. While Josephinism cannot be called plain anti-Catholicism, neither can the Enlightenment be said to have done nothing but harm to Church life. In the territories of the prince-bishops especially, whose rule was popular (the most celebrated was the nepotist dynasty of the Schönborns) because it was limited by cathedral chapters of noblemen and because civil society benefited from the fact that there was little military expenditure the Enlightenment called forth a cultural, religious, and especially a pastoral revival.

But ultimately the Enlightenment bore within itself the ruin of absolutism. It did not merely undermine the charismatic position of the absolute ruler, but developed a political theory which argued in the name of natural law against the concentration of power and for the division of powers, and with its postulate of the rights of man started the revolution against the absolutist revolution. From John Locke (d. 1704) to Montesquieu (d. 1755) criticism of absolutist monarchy led first to demands for its limitation and then to its violent overthrow. Even if the rationality of the physiocratic *ordre naturel* of Quesnay (d. 1774) seemed compatible with the rationality of Enlightenment despotism, it led in the end to the principles of liberalism. In the Catholic Church individual representatives of Baroque Scholasticism worked out a political critique of absolutism, discussing especially the right to revolt and the principles of international law — against expansionist tendencies. But criticism was mainly directed against the notion of national Churches, to which, however, in the perspectives of the Counter-Reformation Catholicism managed to adapt itself. The real religious opposition to secularist absolutism came from the fringes of orthodoxy or outside it — from Jansenism in the Catholic Church and Pietism in the Reformation Churches. It was outside and against the Church that men carried on the successful struggle against the absolutist State and for the separation of Church and State as necessary to modern liberty. The Church itself clung to the union between throne and altar till well into the nineteenth century. How far criticism of the Church's past is in order we can gather by comparing the criticism which should have been made of absolutism (without prejudice to its historical importance) on the basis of Christian social doctrine, but which was only undertaken by a few individuals, with the unbridled criticism that was then directed against liberal and democratic society until the situation changed under Leo XIII.

See also *Constantinian Era, Enlightenment.*

BIBLIOGRAPHY. J. Hitier, *La doctrine de l'absolutisme* (1903); A. Dempf, *Sacrum Imperium. Geschichts- und Staatsphilosophie des Mittelalters und der politischen Renaissance* (1929); E. Chudzinski, *Absolutismus und Aufklärung, 1648–1789* (1930); G. Pagès, *La monarchie d'Ancien régime de France* (4th ed., 1946); F. Valsecchi, *Dispotismo illuminato* (1951); J. Lecler, *Histoire de la tolérance au siècle de la réforme*, 2 vols. (1955); M. Belloff, *The Age of Absolutism, 1660–1815* (1956); F. Meinecke, *Machiavellism,* trans. by D. Scott (1957); R. Koselleck, *Kritik und Krise. Ein Beitrag zur Pathogenese der bürgerlichen Welt* (1959); C. Petrie, *Philip II of Spain* (1963); H. M. Gwalkin and others, eds., *The Cambridge Modern History* (1964 ff.); G. Möbus, *Die politischen Theorien im Zeitalter der absoluten Monarchie bis zur Französischen Revolution* (2nd ed., 1966).
Oskar Köhler

ACT AND POTENCY

1. In the Aristotelian and Thomist tradition act and potency are the constitutive principles of finite beings. The doctrine, which has been called the "essence of Thomism" (Manser), is used in Scholasticism as a basic instrument of thought. To show that act and potency are the basic structure of all the beings we meet with, that is, of all finite beings, we must investigate them in our primordial experience of reality.

a) None of the beings we encounter presents itself to us in the simple fullness of its being. It is never wholly "there". When we are confronted with the reality of something, that is, when it is "there" in its being, it evades us at the same time, it is not "there". For every confrontation with reality is an affair of the moment, a brief instant only of success, which as such bears within itself the sign of transitoriness. If we are struck, it must be by the pang of the moment; even if the presence of a being makes itself increasingly felt, the instantaneousness must be always there, if the encounter is to go on. But if the beings that confront us concentrate the "thereness" of their being into the sharp point of the moment, they surrender essentially by the same token to the transitoriness of the moment. The "thereness" of being which we encounter is always, as such, imperilled by its own non-being. We meet it as essentially impaired by a nothingness which is intrinsic to it.

This primordial experience cannot be merely a subjective mode of our experience, thought or utterance. For when something confronts us, it displays itself in its own independent reality (see below, 1 e). But if non-being is part of this encounter with us, it enters into the reality in question as a mode of its being. It cannot, therefore, be a purely subjective expression of our reaction. It must be a real principle intrinsic to the "thereness" of the beings that confront us. It cannot, on the other hand, be anything of and in itself, for then it would have to be pure nothingness and hence not there, that is, with no reality whatsoever. Hence it always remains something of and in the "thereness" of being: not pure nothingness, but a possibility in relation to this "thereness". It is "potency", and not just the conceivable *(potentia objectiva)* but real potentiality intrinsic to all beings in their being *(potentia subjectiva)*.

b) Since non-being of and in itself is nothing, the "thereness" of the being we meet with must be something positive and as such intelligible *in itself*. It must have *within itself* a sufficient reason for its own reality. On the other hand, being something permanently permeated by non-being, it cannot be purely positive. Thus it abides as such in an ultimate ambiguity, which cannot be intelligible *of itself*. It cannot *be* the sufficient reason of its own reality. Since something is only intelligible when it has within itself a sufficient reason which is intelligible of itself, and since the "thereness" of its being itself, impaired as it is by non-being, cannot be this sufficient reason, this "thereness" must be grounded in an absolutely self-sufficient reason — which is not, of course, the "thereness" itself but which enters into it and so makes it "come to itself". Hence this "thereness", by virtue of what it is, points to something which it is not, but from which it has being. This relationship means on the one hand that the "thereness" of being which is permeated by non-being "participates" in the utterly self-sufficient and hence absolute principle, and on the other hand, since it is permeated by non-being, that it is essentially distinct and different from this principle, though in accord with it by virtue of "participation".

Since the only way that anything can display itself fully is by excluding all non-being, the absolute principle must be the pure "thereness" of being, the "thereness" which in its pure fullness is itself identical with being which excludes all non-being. This pure "thereness" which is being itself is called pure act *(actus purus)* by the scholastics. And this pure act, which, as being itself, can have nothing outside it which brings it to its "thereness" or "takes it up", must also be "non-received" act *(actus irreceptus)*. Where, however, the "thereness" of being is permeated by non-being, it is act "mixed" with potency *(actus mixtus)*. And this mixed act, which, not coinciding with being, needs something outside itself, potency, to be brought to its "thereness", must

always be act "received" in potency *(actus receptus)*.

c) Act mixed with potency, that is, the finite act, points by its reality to pure act. But since non-being is in and of itself nothing, this reference — insofar as it is not a merely negative determination of the difference between finite act and its principle, but a positive pointer to this principle — is based on the finite act's being act. But if it is based on the act as such, the reference cannot be merely something in the mind, it must imply a real dynamism orientated to the pure act. But since this dynamism is that of the finite act which is impaired in its being by non-being, it can never of itself attain its goal and hence is a *dynamism of the infinite* in a two-fold sense. It is itself an endless process, and it moves towards the infinite.

While this dynamism of the infinite is intrinsic to all finite act by reason of its being act, there is a further dynamism to be noted within the finite act. In so far as non-being permeates the "thereness" of being, it tends away from itself into the inanity of otherness. This distraction can be such as to exclude totally the presence of the act to itself or it can permit a certain presence — though it remains in the inanity of otherness. But because the act follows the trend of its being, it contains an inner dynamism which tends to bring it back to itself out of the inanity of otherness. Since, however, it is permeated by non-being, that is, since it remains finite, this return to self can never be pure presence to itself, in no way abandoned to the inanity of otherness. Concretely, this means that the act is spirit by virtue of its being act, and the non-spiritual, infra-human act is orientated towards "hominisation" by virtue of its being act.

The same truth can be elucidated by means of a differentiation of potency. The dynamism of the finite act with regard to its fullness is active potency, since it is tensed for this fullness. But since this tension can never attain this fullness directly of itself — otherwise it would at once be this fullness — it always remains at a distance from its fulfilment. The full act to which the act is open is contrasted with it as passive potency. Thus the dynamism of the finite act may also be considered as the simultaneity of active and passive potency.

Furthermore, because the finite act is always in arrears with regard to the fullness which is assigned to it as its own, it can go beyond itself to realize itself further, without becoming something else. These further realizations are called the second act by the scholastics, in contrast to the first act which is their vehicle and which realizes itself in them. They are also called the accidental act, in contrast to the substantial.

d) This gives us the ontological basis of an evolution, whatever be its precise description empirically. The infra-human act, by virtue of its being act, is a striving towards the act which is man. Hence the finite act is not merely orientated in general to self-transcendence (which is ultimately rooted in its dynamism of the infinite), but, where it is infra-human act, it is also necessarily orientated to transcending its own nature. But since the finite act is act only through the pure act, and transcendence is by virtue of act, the actual transcendence of the finite act is due to the pure act. If transcendence is thus founded by the pure act, this can only mean (according to 1 b) that the transcendence is something achieved by the power bestowed on the finite act itself. Hence the foundation is never ascertainable in the realm of empirical research, even though it alone makes possible all empirical causal connections. This is the sense in which we are to understand the principle which at first sight seems so alien to the modern understanding of evolution: "omne quod movetur, in quantum movetur, ab alio movetur". Everything that moves towards a fuller "thereness" of its being, is moved, in so far as it moves, by *the* Other, by the pure act — in the sense that its power to move itself comes from the pure act.

e) The act's presence to itself, hitherto (in 1 c) defined only in contrast to the inanity of otherness, must be further defined by its relationship to a positive mode of otherness. We have, in fact, already encountered this in the "thereness" of being (see 1 a) but without making it explicit. When in any being the "thereness" of its being dawns on us, something confronts us. But we can only be confronted by something which implies a positive content. But anything positive is only so because of its participation in the infinite fullness (see 1 b). This participation displays itself in the fact that in every positive content something comes forward that is simply self-disclosing, absolutely effective (see 1 b) and as such cannot be

reduced to my own finite subjectivity, but means positive otherness. Act, therefore, in itself and from itself always indicates positive otherness, because it implies something positive, a content, and displays therein a fullness which surpasses the finite subject.

Since we are confronted by the positive content of the act, we are also and above all enriched by the fullness which pervades the act. But such an enrichment can only be truly experienced in the encounter between persons. We may say, therefore, that the deepest meaning of act is love, which bestows itself in the visibility of truth — though strictly speaking, because it is love and therefore free, it could also have refused to give itself. It is only in the perspective of this peculiar character of personal encounter that it is also possible to experience beings on a level lower than man in the "thereness" of their being. If, then, act tends to be present to itself, this self-possession must never be misinterpreted as being closed in on oneself. It must always be seen as the free bestowal of self in love and truth.

2. In the philosophy of the West, it was Aristotle who worked out the doctrine of act and potency, in order to explain movement as becoming. But since the tension between the "thereness" and "not-thereness" of being in the various beings is the origin of time and movement, this starting-point already presupposes the experience of the intrinsic defect in the "thereness" of being. Though the experience of the non-being in the "thereness" of being can only be had in the context of the experience of movement, which is a radical form of it, still, the tension in question is objectively prior to movement. Aristotle himself includes this experience of the primordial tension in the "thereness" of being when he considers movement, as is shown by his definition of it: ἡ τοῦ δυνάμει ὄντος ἐντελέχεια, ᾗ τοιοῦτον (*Physics,* III, 1, 201a, 10f.) — "the actuality of a being still in potency, in so far as it is still in potency". Here he does not see movement merely as local displacement but as the simultaneity of "there" and "not yet there" in the being of the beings that are moved.

In Aristotelianism, the relationship of act and potency as the basic structure pervading all being was expressed in the two principles of duality, form and matter (hylemorphism), substance and accident. The doctrine was taken further by Thomas Aquinas, when he merged the dualism of form and matter, which still persisted in Aristotelianism, into the distinction between essence and existence (being and being-there). In German idealism, the doctrine of act and potency is faced above all by dialectic, as another way of grasping the tension within finite being and hence movement. While the object of the doctrine of act and potency is the dynamism of being — brought home to it in the tense effort of its own direct experience — in dialectic philosophy the dynamism of being is communicated by thought. Here the dynamism of being is no longer the object, but the subjective process of thought itself as it passes from thesis via antithesis to synthesis. The effort of dialectic is to reconstruct in this way the dynamism of being, and hence make thought itself fully transparent to itself — an effort which, contrary to the opinion of Hegel, can never be fully successful, unless being is to disappear wholly into thought. Hence dialectic thinking, if it is not to be an absolute idealism, must always be orientated and relativized by the direct objective gaze at the dynamism of being, as is done in the doctrine of act and potency. But this in turn must be fully thought out by means of dialectic, if it is not to degenerate into a naive and banal realism.

See also *Aristotelianism, Thomism, Idealism, Dialectics.*

BIBLIOGRAPHY. Aristotle, *Metaphysics,* ed. by W. D. Ross (1924); K. Rahner, *Geist in Welt* (1939; 2nd ed., 1957); L. Lavelle, *De l'acte* (1946); C. Giacon, *Atto e potenza* (1947); N. Hartmann, *Möglichkeit und Wirklichkeit* (2nd ed., 1949); G. Manser, *Das Wesen des Thomismus* (3rd ed., 1949); W. D. Ross, *Aristotle* (5th ed., 1949); J. Owens, *The Doctrine of Being* (2nd ed., 1957); G. Siewerth, *Der Thomismus als Identitätssystem* (2nd ed., 1961); M. F. Sciacca, *Akt und Sein* (1964); E. Coreth, *Metaphysik,* I (2nd ed., 1964); K. Rahner, *Hominisation. The Evolutionary Origin of Man as a Theological Problem,* Quaestiones Disputatae 13 (1965).

Oswald Schwemmer

AEONS

"Aeon" is a transcription of the Greek word αἰών which corresponds to the Hebrew ʿōlam. These terms can be adequately rendered in translation only by a number of different expressions. Thus, for a full understanding of the term we must examine the history of the related concepts.

A. USAGE

In the older books of the OT ʿōlam signifies a distant, hidden period, one whose beginning and end is lost in darkness; hence it can mean "antiquity" as well as "the future". Amos in the 8th century speaks of the time of David as the "days of old" (Am 9:11 LXX: αἱ ἡμέραι τοῦ αἰῶνος). ʿōlam is, therefore, in general a long though definitely limited period of time. In some contexts ʿōlam can mean a period of time which is experienced as an "eternity", though in reality it may be only the length of human life (e. g., Dt 15:17; Ps 37:12). The duration of the ʿōlam corresponds to the Hebrew understanding of time, and hence is considered in terms of the speaker or the agent, that is, in terms of man's experience of finite time. The Greek concept of eternity (eternal = infinite, temporal = finite) is still foreign to the OT. It is only in the later writings — since Deutero-Isaiah at the earliest — that ʿōlam took on the meaning of "an infinitely long time", "eternity", as in Is 40:28, "The Lord is the everlasting God". As ʿōlam was a genuinely temporal term, the Greek translation of the OT could bring out the full force of αἰών, which was becoming colourless, a) by doubling the singular (e. g., in Ps 44:7, εἰς τὸν αἰῶνα τοῦ αἰῶνος); b) by using the plural *(passim)*; c) less often, by the combination of both, as in the phrase εἰς τοὺς αἰῶνας τῶν αἰώνων (Ps 83:5; Tob 14:15).

The NT took over the OT usage. Hence one must learn from the context whether the phrase refers to "a long period of time" or "eternity": "from of old" (Lk 1:70; Acts 3:21), "for ever" (Jude 13; Jn 4:14; 6:51; etc.). The phrase which occurs often in the LXX, εἰς τοὺς αἰῶνας, is frequently used in doxological formulas. Thus according to Rom 1:25 the creator is "blessed for ever". In Paul and Rev especially the most emphatic phrase of all is preferred: εἰς τοὺς αἰῶνας τῶν αἰώνων, of which the meaning is also "for ever", or perhaps "for all eternity". Though the phrase, when used of the future, stresses the superiority of God and the ἔσχατα (in the strict sense), with regard to time, it indicates that the concept of "eternity" in the NT also retains its relation to time (in the world). Hence, biblical thought does not know of a timeless eternity in the Platonic sense.

B. THE AEON OF GOD

Analogous to the change in meaning from "dim primeval time" to "eternity", is the changed view of the aeon of God. The "ancient God" (Gen 21:33) is acknowledged as the "everlasting God" (Is 40:28; 2 Macc 1:25). This attribute of God is clearly expressed in the NT (Rom 1:20; 16:26), in the later writings of which the expression is used of the risen Lord (Heb 13:8; Rev 1:18, et al.). As has already been pointed out, biblical thought measures the aeon, the "eternity" of God according to the time of the world. God was before the creation of the world: "Before the mountains were brought forth, or ever thou hadst formed the earth and the world, from everlasting to everlasting thou art God" (Ps 90:2; cf. 102:25–29; Gen 1:1; Jn 17:24; Eph 1:4). God also exists after the end of this world (Ps 102:27; Rev 21:1 ff.). The aeon of God outlasts therefore the aeon of the world and is also qualitatively superior to it. Especially instructive in this regard is the doxology of 1 Tim 1:17: "To the king of ages, immortal, invisible, the only God, be honour and glory for ever and ever. Amen." Behind the expression of "king of ages" is the old reference to God as "eternal king" (Jer 10:10). As soon as "aeon" took on a spatial sense ("world", cf. especially Heb 1:2; 11:3), or could be understood in both a temporal and a spatial sense (Mt 13:39 f.; 24:3; 28:20; cf. 1 Cor 10:11; Heb 9:26), the meaning changed with reference to God. Hence, in 1 Tim 1:17 the translation "the king of ages" is preferable to the expression "eternal king". God is the "king of ages" who in grace and judgment makes age succeed to age. The aeon of God thus does not only last longer than that of the world; God is before and above the world's aeon as its Lord. Correspondingly, "eternity" in the NT is also "a propriety of the true world of salvation, of eschatological bliss and eschatological damnation" (Darlap, p. 365).

C. THE TEACHING ON THE TWO AEONS

1. *Late Judaism*. The difference between the aeon of God and the aeon of the world leads us to the teaching on the two aeons which was developed in the century before Christ by Jewish apocalyptic and which was current also among the rabbis. According to the older prophetical expectation the world is moving towards judgment, the "day of Jahweh", and "a new heaven and a new earth" is expected (Is 65:17; 66:2). Insofar as the worldly kingdoms which follow one another, according to Dan 7, are one in their hostility to Yahweh and are contrasted with the everlasting kingdom of God which replaces them, the transition to a sharply dualistic view of the future is already made in principle in this classical piece of apocalyptic (cf. Dan 2).

Only two aeons are now distinguished, "this aeon" (ha-ʿōlām ha-zeh = ὁ αἰὼν οὗτος) and "the coming aeon" (ha-ʿōlām ha-bāʾ = ὁ αἰὼν μέλλων). These two aeons are sharply defined as to content, and represent — under the influence of Iranian dualism which at least intensified their meanings — opposite senses. "This aeon" is an aeon of injustice and sin, of pain, tribulation and mortality. As the time of the present world, it is ultimately under the influence of Satan or Belial. In contrast "the coming aeon" is wholly and entirely the aeon of God; so much so that "the day of the (Davidic kingly) Messiah" usually forms in this two-aeon scheme only a transitional four hundred or thousand year period of blessing attached to the earthly aeon. Not even the Messiah and his kingdom belong to "the coming aeon". That aeon is essentially good, filled with life and happiness; some writings seem to place it in heaven rather than on the "new earth". As a new age and a new world instituted by God himself, this coming aeon is necessarily the absolute eschaton, the final end, after which there is nothing more to expect. The opposition between the two aeons is especially pronounced in the Qumran writings. The members of this community consider themselves to be the "sons of light" who struggle in this aeon with the "sons of darkness", the rule of iniquity. Through their strict observance of the commands of God and a life of priestly purity, they place themselves on the side of God whose saving intervention they eagerly await. After this struggle "comes the time of salvation for the people of God and the time of domination for all the men of his lot, but everlasting destruction for the whole horde of Belial" (*1 QM*, 1, 5).

2. *In the New Testament.* Jesus certainly did not make the pair of concepts "this aeon" — "the coming aeon" a central feature of his teaching. It is even questionable if he ever made use of it himself. Nevertheless, some sayings of Jesus in the synoptics correctly speak of "this aeon" (Mt 12:32; Lk 16:8; 20:34) and of "that aeon" (Lk 20:35), the "coming aeon" (Mk 10:30; Lk 18:30), or the "future aeon" (Mt 12:32). For Jesus' preaching of the kingdom of God clearly presupposes the distinction between two essentially different aeons. Since Jesus speaks of "entering into the kingdom of heaven" (or "of God"), i.e., "entering into life", "eating and drinking in the kingdom of heaven", etc., his hearers must have connected "kingdom of heaven" ("kingdom of God") with the "coming aeon", with the perfect world of God still in the future. Nevertheless, it was doubtless with good reason that Jesus used the abstract concept "kingdom of God" to sum up the preaching and realization of eschatological salvation. In this way he not only stressed the fact that the coming world is wholly and entirely brought about by the will and deed of God, but also that the last state "does not primarily mean the outward transformation of the world" but the full realization of the kingship of God against the power of evil (Schierse, col. 681). Above all, the notion of the kingship of God made it possible for Jesus to introduce his own modification and indeed disruption of the two-aeon scheme. While for his contemporaries the coming aeon, the final victory of God, was either still purely in the future or already simply present, Jesus in fact made the unheard-of claim that the coming kingdom already reached into this aeon, since in his person and in his words and actions as a whole the will of God was experienced as the definitive grace and call. The eschatological reign of God had in a true sense already begun.

The preaching of the early Church often speaks of "this aeon". Synonymous expressions are "this world", "the present time" (καιρός) and the phrase found only in the Pastoral Letters, "the present aeon". This aeon is in opposition to the divine will (Rom 12:2), its wisdom is foolishness before God (1 Cor 1:20; 3:18), its "god" is a hindrance to faith (2 Cor 4:4). The "rulers of this age" (1 Cor 2:6–8) are superhuman, anti-God forces, angelic powers to whom the old world is subjected, like the personified "prince of the power of the air" who is active in the "sons of disobedience" (Eph 1:2). John speaks of "this cosmos", "this world" (8:23 etc.), in keeping with the approximation of the meaning of aeon and world. This aeon was therefore understood in the preaching of the early Church as a demonic power doomed to destruction, which dominates the unredeemed and unbelieving world, and tries to drag down mankind with it to destruction. The notion of this aeon ruled by satanic powers and hastening to the end amid terrible visitations was fully developed in Christian apocalyptic, in order to explain the dire persecutions of the communities in Asia Minor and to depict vividly the final victory of God and his Christ.

It is striking that the NT speaks very seldom of the "future aeon" (Eph 1:21; cf. 2:7), although the faithful were conscious of being saved from "the present evil age" (Gal 1:4) and of already experiencing, according to Heb 6:5, the powers of "the coming aeon". Paul himself never uses the expression. What he really opposes to "this aeon" are assertions about God, Christ, the Spirit and the eschatological blessings. This represents a decisive departure from the Jewish teaching on the aeon, including the abandonment of its notion of happiness to be achieved on this earth.

See also *Messiah, Qumran, Reign of God, Millenarianism, Eschatology.*

BIBLIOGRAPHY. P. Billerbeck, *Kommentar zum Neuen Testament aus Talmud und Midrasch,* IV/2 (1928), pp. 799–976; H. Sasse, "αἰών", *TWNT,* I (1933; E. T., 1964), pp. 197–209; F. J. Schierse, "Äon", *LTK,* I (1957), cols. 680–3; O. Cullmann, *Christ and Time. The Primitive Christian Conception of Time and History,* trans. by F. V. Filson (1951; rev. ed., 1962); A. Darlap, "Ewigkeit" in H. Fries, ed., *Handbuch der theologischen Grundbegriffe,* I (1962), pp. 363–8; J. Barr, *Biblical Words for Time* (1962), esp. pp. 47–81; R. Schnackenburg, *God's Rule and Kingdom* (1963), pp. 114–77; A. Vögtle, "Zeit und Zeitüberlegenheit in biblischer Sicht" in J. B. Metz, ed., *Weltverständnis im Glauben* (1965), pp. 224–53.

Anton Vögtle

AFTERLIFE

Belief in survival after death seems to go very far back into prehistory. Funeral rites of the late paleolithic age (deposits of arms and food, red ochre) leave little doubt as to the existence of a conception of the "living corpse", such as is to be found amongst many primitive peoples, as well as in the popular mind in advanced cultures possessing a more elaborate form of eschatology. The special value attached to the cranium implies perhaps the localization in the head of the faculties essential to life and their being related to the heavenly vault. The discovery of decorated rhombs in a Magdalenian stratum suggests that the complex of ideas about initiation and the cult of ancestors connected with it for many primitives have a very distant prehistoric origin. The tomb as a dwelling place, where the dead man pursued a life similar in every point to that of the living, seems vouched for as far back as the megalithic age and in any case at Uruk I (Mesopotamia). Generally speaking, the notions of the primitives about the afterlife are connected on the one hand with their notions of action at a distance between living beings (animism, presence of the absent, haunting) and on the other with belief in the fundamental unity of all the members of the same consanguineous group. The primitives usually distinguish a number of "souls", for example, a soul which is distinct and detachable from the immanent vital principle. Their ideas about survival depend on this. The deceased excited both fear and affection, which again augments the complexity of these ideas. The positive aspect of the survival of ancestors is often bound up with a cult of fertility, the exchange between the realms of life and death being conceived on the model of the seasonal changes in nature.

Certain figures with a special relationship to the collective life of the group (chieftains, warriors, women in childbirth), who remain present to the memory as especially mourned or feared, survive as individuals. The "eponymous hero" is the object of a funeral cult in which the clan is awakened to a consciousness of values which guarantee its own survival. There is perhaps some analogy between the making of a hero or the apotheosis of a "cultural hero" and the "rites of passage", with which the funeral rites present obvious similarities. In certain cases the trials that the soul is thought to undergo on the way to its place of rest have the character of initiation ordeals. The purpose of the sacraments conferred in some Gnostic sects is to furnish the soul with the passport to be used in the course of its heavenly journey. The special destiny reserved to the "cultural heroes", like Osiris, was sometimes extended to many others. "Ozirization", for instance, was first the privilege of the Pharaoh alone. In Egypt, the archaic ideas about the multiplicity of souls and survival in the tomb attracted other conceptions belonging to higher cultures (as, for instance, immortality through solidarity with the cosmo-biological cycle, the "paradise of Osiris", "solar" immortality), but without any real fusion taking place. Belief in a sanction after death appears as far back as the fifth dynasty and was later expressed in the "negative confession" (denial of guilt) and the "weighing of the heart", employed as magic in the Book of the Dead.

At the heart of the mystery religions are to be found rites which have as their purpose the integration of the believer into the life-giving rhythm of the cosmos. As the formulas were secret, it is difficult to get a clear idea of the eschatological ideas they embodied, but there is no doubt that dating from a certain period the initiate of Eleusis hoped for a privileged destiny in the life to come. The nature of this survival did not in ancient times depend on moral dispositions. But Orphism and Pythagoreanism made the purity of the soul an essential condition for its beatitude, and in this came close to the Indian ideas on the transmigrating soul. An anthropology of dualist tendencies often implies the undergoing in the beyond of cathartic trials which are recommended to the living under the form of ascetic precepts. As there is never a great distance between dualism and monism, the universal cosmic movement was seen as destined in the end to restore all things, and souls in particular, to the unity of their beginning. After a period of rest the journey of the souls is continued in another cosmic period. Into the systematic structure which such speculations all contribute to build up are harmoniously integrated all the archaic concepts of the "living corpse", the places of delights or punishments (Orphic Katabases taken over by Christian writers, the hell and storeyed paradises of Buddhism) and the ethereal body which the soul assumes. The journey of the soul in the beyond generally corresponds very closely to the ascetical itinerary proposed by the salvation religions to the believer eager to attain to perfect freedom — for example, *jivan-mukta,* the higher heavens of Buddhism corresponding to the four higher meditations and the "stations" of the soul in Origen and in Gnosticism — according to the internal logic of a cathartic vision of salvation.

Theosophy and spiritualism integrate all the traditional views of the afterlife into a vast and comprehensive system. The framework of the system is usually provided by an anthropology and cosmology of neo-Platonic or Gnostic type. Despite the wholesale integration of exotic elements, the essentials are ear-marked by Western preoccupations, in particular the concern to give an experimental basis and scientific appearance to ideas detached from their original religious context and now dangled as a bait to satisfy a real religious need debased into idle curiosity.

See also *Last Things, Eternity, Order* IV, *Dualism, Monism, Gnosticism, Resurrection* II, *Spiritualism.*

BIBLIOGRAPHY. E. Rohde, *Psyche. The Cult of Souls and Belief in Immortality among the Greeks,* trans. from the 8th ed. (1925); M. Granet, *Chinese Civilization* (1930); J. Frazer, *The Fear of the Dead in Primitive Religion* (1933–36); W. Guthrie, *Orpheus and the Greek Religion* (1935); R. Eklund, *Life between Death and Resurrection according to Islam* (1941); F. Cumont, *Lux Perpetua* (1949); M. Nilsson, *History of Greek Religion* (2nd ed., 1949); E. Dodds, *The Greek and the Irrational* (1951); R. Onians, *The Origins of European Thought* (1951); G. Pfannmüller, *Tod, Jenseits und Unsterblichkeit in der Religion, Literatur und Philosophie der Griechen und Römer* (1953); A. Festugière, *La Révélation d'Hermès Trismégiste,* III (1953); J. Poortman, *Ochêma* (1954); M. Eliade, *The Myth of the Eternal Return* (1955); C. Bleeker, ed., *Anthropologie religieuse* (1955); C. Hintze, *Tod, Auferstehung, Weltordnung* (1955); L. Gardet, "Les fins dernières selon la théologie musulmane", *Revue Thomiste* (1956); D. Smith, "Chinese Concepts of the Soul", *Numen* (1958); U. Schleuther, *Brandbestattung und Seelenglauben* (1960); J. Maringer, *The Gods of Prehistoric Man* (1960); A. van Gennep, *The Rites of Passage* (1960); H. Cornélis, *La Résurrection de la Chair* (1962); S. Thrupp, *Millennial Dreams in Action* (1962); S. Brandon, *Man and His Destiny in the Great Religions* (1962).

Humbert Cornélis

AGNOSTICISM

While general scepticism doubts on principle the possibility of true knowledge, agnosticism is a particular form of scepticism which declares that there can be no knowledge of anything beyond the reach of the senses and hence denies the existence of metaphysics as a science, and in particular the knowability of God. The word was introduced by T. H. Huxley (1825–1895) to distinguish his position from metaphysics (that of the "Gnostics").

In the strict sense, the representatives of all forms of positivism, pragmatism and materialism are agnostics. Against these, the great traditional philosophies maintain that there is certain knowledge of truth beyond the empirical, and this is also maintained by the general conviction of the Christian faith, the teaching of Scripture (Wis 13; Rom 1:20) and the magisterium of the Catholic Church, which declare that God can be known by man's natural reason (*DS* 2853, 3004, 3026, 3475, 3538, 3892). This position is supported by philosophical reasons which demand and justify a rejection of agnosticism. It is also supported by faith's knowledge of the nature and powers of man, with its sense of responsibility to the claim of revelation. This claim is seen as binding on all men and hence as something which can be urged on them, even on unbelievers, who must therefore have a preliminary understanding of it, without which the claim could not be perceived at all and men could not be placed before the decision of accepting or rejecting it.

To uphold the dignity of this decision (and thereby the dignity of him from whom the decision is demanded), Catholic theology also rejects the more nuanced forms of agnosticism which do not deny all knowledge beyond the empirical, but still refuse to concede a rational knowledge of God which is objectively valid, can be theoretically articulated and justified and so is (in principle) communicable to all. This is the position of Kant's critical idealism, and also of the metaphysics of N. Hartmann in its concept of the "trans-intelligible". The influence of Kant has been decisive on many modern philosophies of religion, which understand the act of religious knowledge one-sidedly as a "decision" and a "leap", so unheralded that no justification of it can be given, nor can it be explained in any rational way. The element of knowledge in the religious act is referred to a special faculty not reducible to any other, a "feeling" and experience which are described in various ways, but which do not include intellect, argument and justification but are expressly opposed to them. This is the position generally held in modern Protestant philosophy and theology of religion, which mostly starts from a critical *a priori* in philosophy, as does modernism. In dialectical theology, however, the main motive for agnosticism is a supernaturalist understanding of man and of the claim of revelation, which is not to be falsified and "emptied" by human achievement. But this effort to go beyond the visible to procure a place for faith is a destructive stunting of the person as much as absolute agnosticism. For to restrict knowledge in this way is to eliminate the possibility of responsible decision. And when natural reason's quest for meaning is answered in the negative, it is hindered from reaching that openness into which alone revelation can give an audible answer.

The ultimate questions about being and meaning can also be given an affirmative answer which is as effective as the negative in stopping up the openness of the finite spirit for the historical word of the divine self-communication. It finds expression in the various forms of rationalism, and above all in an absolute idealism, which refuses on principle to admit that any thing is unknowable, because in the last resort it does not acknowledge any reality which transcends consciousness. In face of such pretentions, as indeed against the modern idea of knowledge in general, which sees it as a rule as technical efficiency and a conquest of power, the claims of agnosticism appear to be relatively just. Just as the possibility of natural knowledge of God is indispensable for the Christian faith, so too the religious character of this knowledge is essential to it. God is only known as God when he is known as the incomprehensible and is acknowledged in his incomprehensibility (Rom 11:33; 1 Tim 6:16; D 254, 428, 1782). This incomprehensibility is not merely *de facto* and provisional, as if man only did not yet know God but could grasp him by progressive efforts. It is essential and permanent. And as such, it does not stem so to speak from man, from individual, social and historical limitations, which would forbid him all correct knowledge, but from the nature of God himself who is the absolute mystery. Mystery is not the remainder of knowledge yet to be acquired, but the

unfathomable principle of all knowledge and intelligibility: tradition speaks of the light that makes things visible but which can itself be "seen" only as the invisible and must not be confused with what is illuminated. Hence according to Christian teaching even the vision of God is not somethings perspicuous, but the disclosure and sight of the very mystery which is adored. If this holds good of the highest form of knowledge, then insight is gained into the structure of metaphysical and personal knowledge in general in contrast to scientific understanding. The Catholic defence of rational knowledge of God is misunderstood when it is taken to this sort of understanding, for instance if analogy is seen as a process of technical "extrapolation". On the contrary, it exists only to serve the mystery, which can only bestow itself as itself, and can only shine in its incomprehensibility when all that is comprehensible — yet still uncomprehended — is removed from it, and when it is itself known *as* the impenetrable and overwhelming: overwhelming not as sense-sapping chaos — the senseless is not a mystery — but as meaning embraced in its incomprehensibility.

See also *Scepticism, God* II, *Kantianism, Rationalism, Dialectical Theology, Analogy of Being, Mystery.*

BIBLIOGRAPHY. J. Ward, *Naturalism and Agnosticism,* Gifford Lectures for 1896–98 (1899); G. Michelet, *Dieu et l'agnosticisme contemporain* (4th ed., 1920); F. von Hügel, *Religion and Agnosticism* and *The Reality of God,* ed. by E. Gardner (1931); M. B. Foster, *Mystery and Philosophy* (1957); J. Pieper, *Happiness and Contemplation* (1958); J. Collins, *God in Modern Philosophy* (1960); A. Konrad, *Der erkenntnistheoretische Subjektivismus,* I (1962); J. Pieper, *Belief and Faith* (1963); F. B. Dilley, *Metaphysics and Religious Language* (1964).

Jörg Splett

ALEXANDRIAN SCHOOL OF THEOLOGY

At the end of the 2nd century the capital of Egypt, Alexandria, with its scientific traditions, proved to be the most favourable situation for the development of Christian theology. The first Ptolemies, by installing famous libraries, had already created the conditions which made possible the intellectual ferment which was to affect all branches of science in the Hellenistic era. Classical scholarship and philosophy of neo-Platonist tinge were particularly stimulating for Christian thinkers. It was in this encounter that Christianity, which in Egypt as elsewhere had first been accepted principally by Jews, took on its full Greek dress.

Origins. The origins of the school are obscure. The indications given by Eusebius, *Ecclesiastical History,* IV, are unsatisfactory. But the school must have started with the growing number of conversions of cultured pagans or Jews, who were anxious to compare the "new philosophy" with other philosophies and religious trends, to display the Christian doctrine as the only true one. A mentality accustomed to rational investigation felt it necessary to compare the truths of revelation with natural reason, and produce a sort of synthesis. Paul on the Areopagus (Acts 17) had already tried to accommodate his thought to that of his philosophically-trained hearers. The apologists such as Justin in Rome, *c.* 150, likewise sougt for common ground on which Christianity and worldly wisdom could meet. Hence too in Alexandria, along with the catechetical schools which provided simple instruction for candidates for baptism, private undertakings were soon established of an academic type, which started with philosophy in order to lead all who were interested to the heights of theology in exegesis of the Bible. The first known Christian teacher to have given instruction in such a διδασκαλεῖον was the Stoic Pantaenus. His pupil Clement of Alexandria may have begun about the same time, *c.* 180, to impart the "Christian Gnosis". Tributary to both, Origen began his teaching as a young man, with the authorization of the Church. He first gave instruction to catechumens, but then left these to his friend Heraclas, to devote himself, with the consent of his bishop, to advanced students. This is the first establishment which can really be called a theological school. It continued to flourish at Alexandria till the end of the fourth century, always drawing on the spiritual heritage of its great founder, whose voluminous writings were constantly being attacked, defended and expounded throughout the exciting history of the school.

Clement of Alexandria. Pantaenus is little more than a name, but Clement has left enough works to show the special developments of Alexandrian theology. His effort to unite the gospel and Greek culture in his teaching had already been anticipated in a way by the Jews of Alexandria, in particular Philo, when they combined the Old Testament with the heritage of paganism. In writing his *Protrepticus* or "initial exhortation", Clement follows the example of pagan writers, but this time to interest the pagan public in the new doctrine which he has to propose. By stressing above all the unity of the divine Logos, teacher of the prophets as well as of the philosophers, he succeeds in reducing all truth to the same origin and hence can offer Greeks and non-Greeks the one true philosophy, in the incarnate Logos, the great teacher Jesus Christ. Those who undertake to follow him then surrender themselves to the formative force of the *Paidagogos,* in which guise the same Christ helps men to live the Christian life. Thus Clement's second main work, the "Paidagogos", aims at displaying the commandments of the divine educator in the holy scriptures. In following them the Christian acts "according to reason" in all things, that is, according to the Logos. It is only in the *Stromata* that the life of Christian perfection is introduced. The ideal of the "true Gnostic" is now the goal of Christian striving. This, the longest work of Clement, a variegated "weaving" of philosophical and theological thoughts, also provides, in the "method chapters" of the eighth book, directives for the development of Alexandrian theology. Philosophy, which Clement uses in the service of exegesis of scripture, enables one to pass from a naive acquaintance to a scientific knowledge (ἐπιστήμη). A theological investigation (ζήτησις) consists of relating the basic truths of faith to the assertions of scripture, in the same way as conclusions are drawn by comparing the first principles of thought with the data of philosophy. This procedure enables one to pass from mere faith to certainty (γνῶσις), by providing scientific proof (ἀπόδειξις). The typological and allegorical exegesis of Clement also became the predominant rule of Alexandrian theology. Hellenism had developed a type of scholarship which gave the mythologies of Homer and Hesiod a symbolical interpretation. It allowed one to recognize the forces of nature, the faculties of the soul or the mysteries of metaphysics behind the stories of the gods. Philo had applied this method to the text of the Pentateuch, to eliminate the scandal of an antiquated legislation or other repugnant features. Clement studied Philo, and probably Jewish and Christian Gnosis as well, and developed a typological interpretation. The principle was that since the one Logos taught pagans and Jews, and finally assumed flesh in Jesus Christ, David and Orpheus could be compared as harpists, Minos and Moses as lawgivers. But all in their own way are types of Christ, who can appear like Orpheus as the good shepherd, or with the traits of Hercules.

Origen. Origen adopts the procedure of Philo and Clement in his moralizing exegesis of scripture, which is also based, however, on thorough-going linguistic and historical studies, as may be seen above all in the amazing analysis of the Septuagint in the *Hexapla.* He sees the text of scripture as full of mysteries, which are often only disclosed when one traces the deeper, divine meaning behind the letter. Though Origen often interprets scripture according to its literal sense, and believes in the historicity of events to which he may also give an allegorical explanation, his narrow view of inspiration leads him to disregard the literal ("somatic") sense of difficult texts which he finds absurd, and give them a merely moral ("psychic") or mystical ("pneumatic") interpretation. In contrast to Clement, Origen undertakes a comprehensive presentation of Christian doctrine, though without arriving at a system strictly speaking. His *De Principiis,* which has often been termed the "first manual of dogmatic theology", seems to be a record of his lectures, and takes as its basis a metaphysics borrowed from Middle Platonism. The introduction explains the principles of his method: Scripture and tradition are the sources of the exposition; all the words of the Old and New Testaments are the words of Christ, since they are inspired and the same Logos speaks in all of them. Origen feels himself bound by the authority of the Church more strongly than Clement. It guarantees the genuineness of the Bible and is also its authentic interpreter. Origen always wished to be "a man of the Church", and his speculations brought about important progress in theology on all the questions he envisaged. The special views put forward in *De Principiis* were hotly

debated later. But the charge of heresy was largely based on a one-sided interpretation of some daring and ambiguous expressions. Origen must be judged by his work as a whole, since what he put forward as speculative opinion is hard at times to distinguish from what he made his own as doctrine. He also upholds conflicting opinions in various parts of his work. Tributary to the tradition of the second century, his thought is subordinationist in theology. This subordination of the Son must be understood as taking place in the history of salvation. It is part of the redemptive process and appears only in the created world. Hence it is not the subordinationism of the post-Arian period. Origen affirms that the Son is eternal and ὁμοούσιος (consubstantial). Nonetheless, the concepts are being worked out which were later to be used in the dogma of Nicaea. In Christology, he finds for Christ the designation of God-man (θεάνθρωπος). Origen's way of linking the two natures in Christ leads him to the communication of idioms, which was later taken up by Gregory of Nyssa in particular and bore fruit finally at the Council of Chalcedon. The title of θεοτόκος for Mary already points on to Ephesus. In his doctrine of creation the influence of Plato is particularly noticeable. Origen teaches the pre-existence of the human soul, which belonged to a purely spiritual creation preceding our world. Matter only came into being through the "Fall" and must be overcome by the process of purification brought about by divine grace, which is given in a measure corresponding to the magnitude of the sin committed before the world existed. The process of purification can last for many aeons, and ends in the restoration (ἀποκατάστασις) of all things, beyond which, however, lies the possibility of a new fall. In other texts the apocatastasis ist not universal, and a new "fall" seems to be excluded. The corollary of the non-eternity of hell, widely attributed to Origen, is also contradicted in some places.

This spiritualizing tendency can be seen once more in the basic traits of the mysticism of Origen which influenced monasticism in the Eastern Church and then, chiefly through Ambrose, in the Latin West. The ascent of the soul to mystical union with the Logos takes place by degrees. It demands a severe asceticism which combats through fasting, vigils and practices of humility the passions to which matter gives rise. The Logos-Christ is the bridegroom of the soul, and the surest way to him is the following of Jesus, a path which the daily reading of scripture teaches us how to tread. The bridal mysticism of Origen, chiefly inspired by the Canticle of Canticles (Song of Solomon) was perhaps the strongest and most lasting of his influences on the life of the Church, and is still reflected in the Christocentric spirituality of the Middle Ages, as in Bernard of Clairvaux.

The subsequent era. After Origen, Alexandrian theology became "a furnace in which the gold" of the great founder was purified. His disciple Denis, later bishop, defended Origen's orthodoxy in the trinitarian debate, against Denis of Rome. He thus furthered a reaction against Sabellianism, which was of service to Athanasius. On the other hand, a generation later Theognostus (d. about 280) was propounding in his *Hypotyposes* a doctrine of the Logos which was apt to serve the purposes of Arius. Athanasius also used the writings of Origen, and his allegorical and spiritual exegesis in particular shows what he owed to the Alexandrian school. When he became archbishop, he installed Didymus the Blind as its head. Didymus was in line with Nicaea on the Trinity, but as regards the pre-existence of the soul and the "apocatastasis" he followed the errors of Origen. During his fifteen years' teaching he had Rufinus and Jerome among his pupils. We owe the preservation of much of Origen's work to their translations. When the first great Origenist controversy broke out at the end of the fourth century, Rufinus remained loyal to the greatest of the Alexandrians. A comparison of their numerous commentaries shows how Jerome moved further and further away from Origen in his exegetical work.

Caesarea. When, after his quarrel with his bishop, Demetrius (230), Origen went to Caesarea in Palestine to continue teaching, the traditions of the Alexandrian school also took root there. Through the presbyter Pamphilus, who collected the works of Origen, a line can be traced to the historian, Bishop Eusebius of Caesarea. Eusebius maintained a moderate subordinationism of an Origenist type. His *Confession of Faith* was used as the theological basis at the Council of Nicaea. Another line goes through Gregory Thaumaturgus (d. 270) to Cappadocia, where Basil

was the first to take up the Alexandrian tradition, whose influence can then be seen in particular in Gregory of Nyssa's predilection for the teaching of Origen. Through Maximus the Confessor, the spiritual heritage of Alexandria was adopted by the Byzantine Church. In the West, Ambrose in particular was influenced by Alexandrian theology, as may be seen from his dogmatic writings, but above all from his exegesis. In Alexandria itself in the fifth century, Cyril understood himself as the trustee of Alexandrian theological tradition in the Christological controversies.

See also *Hellenism and Christianity, Platonism, Gnosticism, Apocatastasis, Biblical Exegesis* III, *Antiochene School of Theology.*

BIBLIOGRAPHY. W. R. Inge, "Alexandrian Theology", *HERE,* I (1908); C. Bigg, *The Christian Platonists of Alexandria* (1913); W. Bousset, *Jüdisch-christlicher Schulbetrieb in Alexandrien und Rom* (1915); J. Munck, *Untersuchungen über Klemens von Alexandrien* (1933), pp. 180–5, 224–9; R. Cadiou, *La jeunesse d'Origène* (1936); G. Bardy, "Aux origines de l'Ecole d'Alexandrie", *RSR* 27 (1937), pp. 65–90; E. Molland, *The Conception of the Gospel in the Alexandrian Theology* (1938); R. V. Sellers, *Two Ancient Christologies* (1940); H. de Lubac, "Typologie et allégorisme", *RSR* 34 (1947), pp. 180–226; J. Guillet, "Les exégèses d'Alexandrie et d'Antioche", *RSR* 34 (1947), pp. 247–302; J. Daniélou, *Origène* (1948), pp. 24–34; W. Jentsch, *Urchristliches Erziehungsdenken* (1951); J. Quasten, *Patrology,* II (1953); R. Hanson, *Allegory and Event. A Study of the Sources and Significance of Origen's Interpretation of Scripture* (1958); W. Jaeger, *Das Urchristentum und die griechische Bildung* (1963); W. Marcus, *Der Subordinatianismus* (1963).

Friedrich Normann

AMERICANISM

Americanism in the context of theology and Church history has two senses, akin but not identical: one dogmatic and one historical.

1. In the *dogmatic* sense, Americanism is a theoretical system that was outlined and condemned by Pope Leo XIII in his letter *Testem Benevolentiae,* addressed to James Cardinal Gibbons, Archbishop of Baltimore (U. S. A.), on 22 January 1899 (*Acta Sanctae Sedis* 31 [1898–99], cols. 470–9; cf. *D* 1967–1976). Americanism is a doctrine on the relations between Catholicism and its cultural environment. Briefly, the Apostolic Letter

summarizes it as follows: Not only should Catholic life be adapted to the requirements of the age we live in, we must also create harmony between the Church and the outside world by not stressing unpopular doctrines and, without denying them, by not adverting to defined dogmas. Churchmen, moreover, should make a point of using their authority with restraint, so as to allow American Catholics the freedom of thought and action that is appropriate to their national character. Too much emphasis on authority proves a hindrance to the faithful in their efforts to achieve apostolic perfection, whereas the Holy Ghost is more active now than formerly within individual souls, each of whom should lead a spiritual life in accordance with his particular cast of mind. The natural virtues, since they call for concrete activity, are more important than the supernatural virtues. Passive virtues, such as were cultivated in the older religious orders, were appropriate to former ages, but the active virtues better answer the present needs of Catholicism. The religious life, based on the traditional vows, is out of date, for vows destroy the freedom that is indispensable for a modern Christian. Consequently the older religious orders contribute little or nothing to contemporary Catholic life. Finally, the methods of the past will no longer do in our apostolate among non-Catholics; we must try to approach them in new ways. Such is the doctrine of Americanism, as described by the papal document and condemned as dogmatically false and historically unsound.

2. Americanism as a concrete *historical* phenomenon was a factor in a 19th-century controversy among Catholics that culminated in the papal letter we have mentioned. This letter refers to Isaac Hecker (1819–1888), who had founded the "Congregatio Sancti Pauli" or Paulist Fathers (1858) in order to win over American Protestants to the Catholic Church by means of an apostolate that would be as up-to-date as possible. Shortly after he died one of his followers, Walter Eliot CSP, published a biography entitled *The Life of Father Hecker* (1891). The Church in America faced a formidable problem apart from that envisaged by Hecker. The vast majority of Catholics there were immigrants from Europe, of whom a great many, especially among the Irish, wished to adapt themselves completely to

their new country and become Americans. Three prelates vigorously supported them in this attitude: James Cardinal Gibbons (1834–1921), Archbishop John Ireland (1838–1918), and Archbishop John Keane (1839–1918). Among the Germans, on the other hand, there was a persistent effort to keep Catholic immigrants inside enclaves of their own race. The conflict ended in the present century with the triumph of the assimilative party.

In France there was a struggle of a different sort. Catholic royalists maintained that the traditional polity and culture of the country should be restored, whilst Catholic republicans advocated coming to terms with the new situation. Both the Americanizers in the United States and the republicans in France looked on Hecker as the symbol of their cause. His biography, translated into French in 1897 by Louise de Guérines, was published with a laudatory preface by the Abbé Félix Klein, professor at the Institut Catholique in Paris. This publication led the royalists to call the concrete aims of their opponents "Americanism", and by dint of some exaggeration to represent the latter as a theological theory. Bitter controversy raged; Rome was asked to intervene, and her response was the letter to Cardinal Gibbons. The introduction and conclusion are the work of Pope Leo himself, but the body of the letter was written by Camillo Cardinal Mazella and Francesco Cardinal Satolli. In America the document caused painful confusion. Cardinal Gibbons wrote to the Pope: "This doctrine, which I advisedly call extravagant and absurd, this 'Americanism', as it has been styled, has nothing in common with the view, the hopes, the doctrine, and the attitude of Americans. I do not believe that in this country a single bishop or priest, or even layman, with any knowledge of his religion can be found who has ever uttered such monstrosities. No, this is not — has never been and never will be — our Americanism" (Ellis, II, p. 71). Historically, Americanism was what the Abbé Klein afterwards called a "phantom heresy". But it has an abiding practical importance as a warning against the "spirit of the world".

BIBLIOGRAPHY. F. Deshayes, "Américanisme", *DTC*, I, cols. 1043–9; G. de Pierrefeu, "Américanisme", *DSAM*, I, cols. 475–88; T. T. McAvoy, "Americanism and Frontier Catholicism", *Review of Politics* 5 (1943), pp. 275–301;

id., "Americanism, Fact and Fiction", *The Catholic Historical Review* 31 (1945), pp. 154–70; F. Klein, *Une hérésie fantôme, l'Américanisme; Souvenirs,* IV (1949); J. T. Ellis, *The Life of Cardinal Gibbons,* II (1952); R. N. Beck, *The Meaning of Americanism. An Essay on the Religious and Philosophic Basis of the American Mind* (1956).

Gustave Weigel

ANALOGY OF BEING

A. Introduction

In the exercise of its freedom and knowledge, the human spirit stands in the light of what is unconditional, yet attains the plenitude of this latter only in and through the finite. By its very nature, therefore, it is subject to the law of analogy. Hence analogy is decisively located in the ontological relation between God and finite being and in the cognitive relation between the finite mind and each of these.

In all this, analogy must not be regarded from the start as a derivative compromise and half-way house between univocity and equivocity. It must be regarded as the original and radical form of the relation between God and the finite, which is directly experienced in cognition and freedom in their self-transcending orientation towards the illimitable mystery.

This is clear from the statement of the Fourth Lateran Council (1215): "inter creatorem et creaturam non potest tanta similitudo notari, quin inter eos maior sit dissimilitudo notanda" (*D* 432). E. Przywara in particular vindicated the central importance of this formula for philosophy and theology. According to it, analogy does not ultimately rise above God and creature and comprise both in a superior unity. On the contrary, the truth and intelligibility of man and reality, the permanent, natural and supernatural knowability of God are traced back, precisely for the sake of their truth, to the mystery of this God who is "semper maior" (Augustine) — always the greater.

B. Origins

1. The word "analogy" is generally understood nowadays to mean the characteristic feature of a term which, when applied to different entities or domains of reality, undergoes an essential change of meaning but without thereby losing the unity of its content. In an analogical term, therefore, the factors of common character and difference, similarity and dissimilarity in the things referred to, combine in the logical unity of a signification. *Analogia entis* (literally, "analogy of that which is", though the expression is usually rendered in English as "analogy of being") means that all that is shares in being, but in a different way in each instance. Our knowledge of what is, is therefore expressed by an is-statement, which in each instance is different.

2. By its Greek origin, analogy literally means "proportion", "correspondence", and in this sense was already used by Plato who calls it "the most beautiful of all bonds" (δεσμῶν κάλλιστος, *Timaeus,* 31c). In addition to univocal (συνώνυμα) and equivocal (ὁμώνυμα) terms, Aristotle accepts the possibility and existence of analogical terms (κατ' ἀναλογίαν), which are founded on the similarity of a ratio ("analogy of proportionality"). Aristotle, however, also analyses another relationship which he never designates as "analogy" but which later, in scholasticism, was classified as another, and in fact the chief, kind of analogy: πρὸς ἕν, the "relation to one (first term)". This is "analogy of attribution". Such unity of relation to a first term is mentioned in connection with the "First Philosophy" viewed as the science of beings as beings, and here Aristotle wrote the famous statement which has been decisive for all later reflection on the analogy of being: τὸ ὂν λέγεται πολλαχῶς, "being (literally, the existent) is predicated in many ways" (*Metaphysics,* 1003b, 5f.). Aristotle adds: ἀλλ' ἅπαν πρὸς μίαν ἀρχήν, "but in relation to a first". He sees this first term as the οὐσία (essence; Latin *essentia, substantia*), of which alone "being", the "is", is predicated in the proper sense (absolutely). It is only said of anything else to the extent that it stands in relation to *ousia (ibid.)*.

3. Both kinds of unity (the unity of a relation of similarity and the unity of reference to a first term) are later called "analogy", for instance by Thomas Aquinas, probably under the influence of Boethius. It was always a much disputed question in Scholasticism which of the two (analogy of proportionality or analogy of attribution) was regarded by Aquinas as the genuine or primary analogy. This should now in prin-

ciple be settled because more precise knowledge is now available regarding the process
of assimilation of the fundamental concepts
of Aristotle by Aquinas and regarding the
"Thomist tradition" which on decisive points
wrongly claimed to be following him.
Thomas was not a pure Aristotelian and this
is particularly apparent in his doctrine of
analogy. Two ideas are essential to this, the
idea of a unity of order in relation to a first
term, which derives from Aristotle, and the
idea of participation which is Platonic in
origin. In order systematically to develop
his doctrine of analogy, Thomas used the
"predicamental analogy" discovered by Aristotle but not so named by him, i. e., analogy
regarded as a unity of order in relation to a
first term within the domain of *ousia* and the
other categories, but applied it to the relation
between God and world conceived on the
participation model, i. e., to what in the
scholastic sense is called "transcendental
analogy".

This transcendental analogy involves the
following. The multiplicity of finite beings
is referred to a first *(esse subsistens)*, so
that between the *esse subsistens* and the
beings deriving from it in accordance
with the idea of participation there exists a
unity of connection; on this connection the
analogical content or notion *(ratio analoga)*
is based, and this content is then predicated
of *esse subsistens* "per essentiam", "per prius",
"secundum magis", etc., and of other beings
"per participationem", "per posterius",
"secundum minus" etc. This connection of
unity or participation, which makes analogical predication possible, is regarded by
Aquinas as a causal relation. It occurs in two
forms, exemplar and efficient causality. It is
to be noted that in his earlier works Aquinas
refers almost exclusively to exemplar causality, i. e., God's operation is regarded as
the communication of a "form", so that
participation or analogy is conceived as the
relational unity of a "form" between God
and finite beings. In his later works (especially from the *Summa contra Gentiles* onwards), he places in the foreground efficient
causality as the communication of the act of
being, and participation or analogy is thought
of on the basis of "esse" *(actus essendi, per-
fectio essendi)*.

The doctrine of analogy based on these
metaphysical foundations is presented by
Aquinas in different ways in his various

works, and this is the reason for the inter-
minable disputes among scholastics all
claiming to follow Thomas. However, as we
have already noted, as regards Thomas himself the question should now in principle
have been cleared up (cf. B. Montagnes). The
following is the real point at issue. In the
famous passage q. 2 a. 11 of *De Veritate,*
Aquinas puts forward a conception of
analogy which is in contradiction both to
his earlier works *(Commentary on the Sentences)* and to his later works (especially
*Summa contra Gentiles, De Potentia, Summa
Theologica,* I). In this passage Thomas assumes
in regard to the relation between God and
world only the analogy of proportionality
("convenientia proportionalitatis") and rejects the analogy of attribution (called in this
passage "convenientia proportionis"). As
the reason for this he says that analogy of
attribution implies a *determinata distantia* or
habitudo, and this cannot be maintained of
the relation between God and the world. He
soon abandoned this view once more in
favour of the analogy of attribution *(analogia
unius ad alterum)* to which in the meantime
he had given a deeper meaning.

It is relatively easy to explain Thomas's
differing views or development in regard to
the doctrine of analogy, because we can make
detailed comparison between his various answers to the same difficulties *(obiectiones)* in
the above-mentioned passage of *De Veritate*
and in his later works. Thus, for example, he
writes in *Summa contra Gentiles* (III, 54): "nihil
prohibet esse proportionem creaturae ad
Deum ... secundum habitudinem effectus
ad causam." The doctrine of analogy was
further elaborated by Thomas, particularly
under the heading *De Nominibus Dei.* A short
summary of this teaching is found in *De
Potentia* q. 7 a. 5 ad 2 with the example of the
term "wise". "According to the teaching of
Dionysius ['the Areopagite'] these [names]
are predicated of God in three ways. Firstly,
affirmatively *(affirmative),* when we say, God
is wise; this must be said of him because in
him there is the likeness of the wisdom which
flows from him; secondly negatively, when
we say, God is not wise, because in God
wisdom is not found as we conceive and
name it. Thirdly, it must be said in an intensive sense *(supereminentius)* that God is more
than wise, for wisdom is not denied of God
because he is lacking in wisdom but because
he possesses it in a way which transcends our

power of expression and understanding." This threefold way which we follow in our statements about God, is based on the distinction between the semantic content of an expression *(res significata)* and the actual mode of expressing it *(modus significandi)* *(ibid.)*.

This more detailed account of the doctrine of analogy in Aquinas was necessary because only in this way are the disputes which have gone on for centuries among scholastics to some degree explained. In later times analogy was increasingly torn from its metaphysical context and regarded in isolation as a predominantly logical theory. While Cajetan accepted only analogy of proportionality as intrinsic analogy, and rejected analogy of attribution as purely extrinsic, *analogia entis* was interpreted by the Suarezian school as analogy of attribution, though on a different metaphysical basis. Scotus and his school occupy a special position, defending the univocity of being, which, however, does not apply to concrete being but only to the *concept* of being.

4. In modern philosophy, especially since Kant raised the question in terms of a transcendental philosophy, the problem of analogy has entered on a new phase. Kant completely eliminated analogy when he included being among, and subordinated it to, the categories and declared these to be pure concepts of the understanding (Categories of modality: existence and non-existence: 4th section of the table of categories, *Critique of Pure Reason,* B 106), and denied any possibility of cognition beyond the domain of phenomena. For Hegel, Kant's position represented "illogicality", "contradiction", for "something is only known as a limit or lack ... if one is at the same time *beyond* it". There can therefore be knowledge of a limit only if the unlimited is *on this side* in consciousness (Hegel's *Encyclopädie der philosophischen Wissenschaften,* 3rd ed., 1830, § 60). The removal of such illogicality means for Hegel, however, that knowledge of the Absolute is only possible as "absolute knowledge", i.e., as the self-knowledge of the Absolute through its own self-mediation by finite spirit. Analogy is here totally superseded by being raised into the "speculative proposition" (which is another name for "absolute knowledge"). Hegel's position is of the greatest importance for the problem of anal-

ogy, for it represents the boldest and most brilliant attempt speculatively to penetrate beyond the plane of analogy. Hence the numerous discussions there have been on "analogy and (Hegelian) dialectic". Also of great importance at the present time for the problem of analogy is the thought of M. Heidegger with his inquiry into the meaning of being. The reproach of "forgetfulness of being" which he brings against all Western metaphysics, and his concern with the problem of language (another name for the problem of analogy) have prompted and contributed decisively to a new consideration of analogy and of the whole philosophy of being. We must also mention the philosophy of linguistic analysis (principally in English-speaking countries) and the philosophical discussions of the foundations of the sciences.

It must finally be noted that since the severe rejection of *analogia entis* by Karl Barth, it has once again become an important theme of theological controversy. Barth, who met with opposition within Protestant theology itself, maintained an analogy founded purely on faith, but moderated his view considerably since the second edition of his *Church Dogmatics*.

Present-day discussion of analogy is characterized on the one hand by a more accurate exposition of tradition, particularly of Aquinas, which has led to a loosening of the rigidly opposed fronts of the traditional scholastic schools, and on the other hand by intensive contact with non-scholastic philosophy, especially with Kant, Hegel and Heidegger.

C. DEVELOPMENT

In general any attempt to define analogy by its double contrast to univocal and to equivocal terms (so, for example, Aquinas, *Summa Theologica*, I, q. 13, a. 5 c: "iste modus communitatis medius est inter puram aequivocationem et simplicem univocationem") might give the impression that analogy is a logical "mean", derivative and secondary. This would miss from the start the fundamental basis of analogy and its primordial situation in human thought. A simple analysis shows the fundamental point of analogy. Our univocal general concepts are always abstract, i.e., they comprise a definite, circumscribable content which is common to a multiplicity of individuals but which nevertheless disregards the further features which distinguish the individuals, for these of course do not enter into the content of the univocal term. Now if our knowledge in principle or primarily were to move on the plane of such univocal concepts, we should have to assume an unlimited multiplicity of different univocal concepts. In that case, however, it would not be clear how it is that our thought primarily and in principle reduces or refers back everything to unity. For no comprehensive unity springs from a pure multiplicity of univocal concepts. Univocal concepts simply present us with a plurality of different, distinctly delimited contents. The prior unity always implied in knowledge cannot therefore itself be univocal but is of such a structure that it comprises both the common character and the difference of the things to which it refers. Consequently the predication which expresses this unity is analogical. It is an is-saying, a predication of be-ing, whereby everything which is, is referred back to the unity of being and is conceived on the basis of the unity of being. And so by its very basis analogical knowledge is not something derivative but is a condition of the possibility of any univocal knowledge.

This analogical knowledge of being is not, however, a self-contained knowledge. In the analogical is-statement the absolute Being, God, is always co-signified and co-affirmed. The really fundamental problem of analogy lies in the interpretation of this relation between God and the finite which is always posited and involved in is-statements. How can the verb "is" be used of God? How in general is it possible to talk "about" God? The radical difference between God and the finite ist threatened or even annulled if the relation between God and the world is interpreted by means of an "is" which comprises within its superior scope both God and the world. And that is so whether the latter is understood in the sense of an antecedent (univocal) preconception which comprises both, or as a concept of being which though derivative is applicable to both. For in each case the difference between God and the finite is made a subsequent specification of the element common to both. This means that the predication of being in respect of God can only take place if this predication itself in its structure as cognition or logos is brought under the dominion of the God–world relation. The predication of being is

only truly analogical if it not only predicates or affirms an "objective" relation of analogy between God and the finite, but if the analogous relation prevails as an *a priori* constitutive factor in the predication itself or, to put it even more radically, as an intrinsic *a priori* law of its own articulation. In other words, the objective relation between God and world and the affirmation of this relation in cognition are not two states of affairs or factors which can be separated or interpreted separately. On the contrary, they radically constitute the fundamental structure or texture of what analogy in the ultimate resort is. Consequently, the analogy between God and the finite regarded in this way as a fundamental feature of being and cognition, is not a particular instance of a generic concept of analogy, but is a primary, original structure: the radical, irreducible reference (in both being and predication) of the conditioned to the absolute. This is not merely one characteristic among others, but permeates all other determinations of being and cognition and is their basis.

Reflection on this fundamental structure constitutes the chief problem of analogy. In this light it is possible to see why the "traditional" scholastic teaching on analogy is insufficient (which does not mean it is false), and why it must be deepened and thought out anew in contact with modern philosophy. This may be briefly shown as follows. The traditional doctrine of analogy moves within the fundamental structure of analogy which it takes for granted; it does not reflect on the fundamental structure itself. Hence the unproblematic way in which statements are made about being and God. The attempt is made to elucidate the "objective" relation between God and the finite, without explicit reflection on the language or predication which is employed (thus, for example, the characteristic talk of the "ratio analoga" which belongs in different ways to the "analogata"). It was not a matter of thinking the God-world relation on the basis of a concept of being to which both were subordinated. It must rather be said that that philosophy did not reflect on the problems involved in its own formulas. A distinction was rightly drawn between content of statement *(res significata)* and manner of statement *(modus significandi)*, and this might be regarded as a first step towards the required reflection. As such, however, this distinction still remains within the duality of the factors of analogy which had not yet been considered in their unity or in their fundamental structure. The state of the question today (prompted chiefly by Heidegger) aims precisely at considering analogy in its total structure as such. The rejection of "reifying thought" and the attempt to overcome the "philosophy of subjectivity" are clear signs of this. Such reflection on the fundamental structure of analogy means that "being" and "logos" (as the utterance of being) are considered more radically, i.e., not in and as the duality of subject and object, cognition and object, concept and reality, "anima" and "ens", but in that correspondence or identity from which the duality in the very first place derives. This "being" understood in identity with "logos" is not a self-sufficient reality. On further consideration it shows itself as the event of the absolute *identity-in-difference* of finite and infinite, conditioned and unconditioned, world and God. The attempt to interpret metaphysically this event of absolute identity-in-difference, leads to the idea of participation, a conception which derives from Plato and is central to the thought of Aquinas, but which in the perspective referred to here is repeated on a more fundamental plane. The event of being as the event of the absolute identity-in-difference is interpreted as the event of the communication of being or of participation. All that is finite, because and inasmuch as it is the event of the participation of being, is one in difference with the infinite. The language or utterance of this event is analogy, the nature of which is therefore only manifested if its fundamental structure is thought out to the end in this way. All statement "about" the infinite God has its ultimate and proper place in this event of participation in being and its essential structure is dominated by the absolute identity-in-difference. Human utterance cannot go beyond the absolute identity-in-difference into a more comprehensive unity, nor can it escape its domination over the depth of the human mind. Analogy is at once the highest capacity of language and at the same time its profoundest indigence. An ever deeper experience of this fundamental structure of analogy, and reflection on it, may be regarded as the secret law and hidden stimulus of the development of Christian thought. It is only logical that in this process discourse about God changes and must change.

See also *God* II, *Analogy of Faith, Being* I, *Aristotelianism, Scholasticism, Idealism, Unity*.

BIBLIOGRAPHY. E. Przywara, *Analogia entis* (1932; rev. ed., 1962); E. Brunner and K. Barth, *Natural Theology. "Nature and Grace" by Emil Brunner and the Reply "No!" by Karl Barth* (1946); E. Mascall, *Existence and Analogy* (1949); H. U. von Balthasar, *Karl Barth. Darstellung und Deutung seiner Theologie* (1951; 2nd ed., 1962); H. Lyttkens, *The Analogy between God and the World. An Investigation of Its Background and Interpretation of Its Use by Thomas of Aquino* (1952), with biblio.; N. C. Nielsen, *E. Przywara's Analogia entis,* Rice-Institute Pamphlet (1953); E. W. Platzech, *Von der Analogie zum Syllogismus* (1954); K. Barth, *Church Dogmatics,* III: *The Doctrine of Creation,* parts 1 and 3 (1958–61); Ch. de Moré-Pontgibaud, *Du fini à l'infini* (1958); E. Heintel, *Hegel und die Analogia entis* (1958); C. Fabro, *Participation et causalité selon S. Thomas d'Aquin* (1961); B. Montagnes, *La doctrine de l'analogie de l'être d'après S. Thomas* (1963); B. Mondin, *The Principle of Analogy in Protestant and Catholic Theology* (1963); G. Siewerth, *Die Analogie des Seienden* (1965); J. F. Anderson, *Reflections on the Analogy of Being* (1967).

Jörg Splett and *Lourencino Bruno Puntel*

1. The expression *analogia fidei* is taken from the Bible, where it occurs only once, Rom 12:6, meaning "what is in proportion to (a man's) faith" (ἀναλογία τῆς πίστεως). It is the equivalent of the "measure of faith" mentioned just before in Rom 12:3 (μέτρον πίστεως). The notion is introduced to warn charismatics, especially those endowed with the gift of prophecy, not to indulge their charism too exuberantly and to avoid heady enthusiasms. Since prophecy in particular must be tested for its genuineness, according to Paul (1 Cor 12:10; 14:29), the demand that it should be in accord with the faith is highly relevant. Faith here, however, does not mean a set of doctrinal norms, but the active faith given to each charismatic with his gift, the inward power of his faith on which the prophet must soberly reflect. The analogy of faith as understood here must be described as religious and existential.

2. Since this biblical notion involves the element of the normative, it was capable of further development in dogmatic thought, where, departing somewhat from its original meaning, it came to mean the ecclesiastical

25

norm or rule of faith. Jerome translated the Greek term by *mensura,* Augustine by *regula,* with the Apostles' Creed in mind. The Fathers often apply implicitly the analogy of faith to the relationship between the Old and New Testament, which faith sees as that of promise and fulfilment, type (prefiguration) and perfect achievement. Here the analogy of faith is silently used as a unifying or integrating principle, as which it also functions in the development of dogma and the declarations of the magisterium, to obviate the tensions and possible onesidedness which the mysterious character of faith gives rise to. It works in the same way in dogma, preserving the openness to faith as a whole, in contrast to settled theological opinion as well as to heresy.

In scholastic theology of an Augustinian type, the analogy of faith also took on the character of a methodological criterion by which the unity of revelation and natural knowledge, of faith and reason, of the orders of creation and redemption was to be attained. Thus Anselm of Canterbury (in the *Proslogium*) starts from the correspondence between divine and human knowledge given in the experience of faith, to attain the unity of divine truth and natural created knowledge, in accordance with the principle *credo ut intelligam.* A characteristic application is found in the doctrine of the *vestigia Trinitatis* in creation, which is less concerned with explaining the Trinity from creation than creation by means of the Trinity. The most decided application of the principle is found in Bonaventure, "the classic theologian of the *analogia fidei*" (Söhngen), whose exemplarism saw the divine nature reflected in the profoundly trinitarian structure of beings. Here the analogy of faith became a heuristic principle which led to the discovery of new insights, even into the natural constitution of things. This is also the role it has in the important declaration of Vatican I on the nature and function of theology (*D* 1796), which says that reason enlightened by faith can gain a most fruitful understanding of the mysteries "by reason of their connection with one another and with the ultimate end of man". Here, however, the attainment of deeper insight through the analogy of faith is restricted to the domain of faith itself, on which light is also said to be thrown by the natural analogy "with the truths which reason knows by natural means". Here too,

therefore, the unity of the *analogia fidei* and the analogy of being is also affirmed. Church doctrine in recent years has once more emphasized the normative element in the concept; it appears in close connection with the living tradition and the ecclesiastical magisterium as the rule for the study and interpretation of Scripture (*D* 1943, 2146, 2315).

3. In all these cases the notion of "corresponding to the faith" comprises the formal elements of the philosophical concept of analogy. Thus the analogy of faith, when used as a rule of faith, presupposes a proportional relationship between the individuals and the whole, and the dependence of the derivative elements from the main term of the analogy, in the line of intrinsic attribution. Unity with the *analogia entis* is thus also preserved, as may be seen in particular from Vatican I (*D* 1796). The situation is changed, however, when the analogy of faith is opposed to the *analogia entis,* as was done in recent Protestant theology, which used the term polemically, though older Protestant theology had recognized only its hermeneutic value. This is chiefly due to K. Barth's reaction to the Catholic notion of the *analogia entis,* which he stigmatized as neo-Platonic ontology and natural theology and even as "an invention of Antichrist" (*Church Dogmatics,* I, part 1). Barth made the "analogy of faith" an architectonic principle for Protestant theology, by which all ideas of the natural knowledge of God, man's likeness to God, the "point of insertion" for the word of God in man, natural theology and the whole relationship between the world and God should be judged. This was based on an erroneous idea of the Catholic *analogia entis,* which was supposed to range God under the genus of being and hence lead to a coordination of man and God — though Thomas Aquinas had long ago described God as "extra omne genus et principium omnium generum". The result was a series of negations, excluding synergism, the mediating role of the Church in salvation, "Pan-Marianism" etc., and the decided re-affirmation of the "material principle" of the Reformation, justification by faith alone. The analogy between the creature and God was asserted on p. inciple, but the correspondence was said to be rooted exclusively in revelation, given only by grace and brought by

Christ himself, so that it could never be understood as part of creation and of the heritage within man's control. The crucial point, that Christ alone is the man who corresponds to God, shows clearly that Barth's analogy of faith or grace is the result of an exaggerated Christocentricism, which has sometimes been criticized as a Christocentric monism. If man's correspondence to God comes only from Christ and his word, all prior ontological ordination of man to God must be excluded and knowledge of God and truth reduced to a pure actualism. The analogy of faith — again in strict opposition to the analogy of being — is a mere analogy of activity.

4. Barth's analogy of faith, determined as it was by a pan-actualist notion of being, and strongly developed as a polemical formula, was subjected to much criticism from the Protestant side. Attention was called not merely to the inadequacy of its philosophical presuppositions, but to the lack of sufficient biblical foundation for this total opposition between the analogy of being and the analogy of faith.

5. From the standpoint of the Catholic faith, a correspondence between man and God brought about by grace and faith can be whole-heartedly accepted. It has, in fact, always been part of Catholic thinking, as when for instance Augustine ascribes *deificatio* (likeness to God) to the believer or when Thomas Aquinas makes faith confer on man "quaedam divinae sapientiae similitudo". But this recognition of man's correspondence by virtue of grace does not exlude the existence of an ontological analogy between man as creature and God, which, on the contrary, it presupposes. If there were no creaturely correspondence between man and God, man could not respond and correspond *as man* to the action of God's grace. God would really encounter only his own act and his own self when he acted on man in grace, and the divine movement towards man would remain immanent to God himself. If man has no analogy with God in the order of creation, his (relatively) independent reality in face of God disappears and the whole notion of creation is threatened by the evaporation of the subsistence of the cosmos. An analogy of grace based strictly on opposition to natural anal-

ogy thus becomes an antilogy or contradictory relationship, and a dualism is set up between God and the world which is repugnant to the unity of the order of creation and the order of redemption. In the light of this unity, the analogy of faith (understood as a principle of being and of knowledge) is the correspondence bestowed by grace from on high which embraces and brings to full clarity the analogy of being. And this in turn has an openness for the analogy of faith. It is the likeness to God in man which is not lost even by sin and makes him capable of being approached by God and of perceiving him. This does not mean that God is comprised under a neutral concept of being, and no synergism is implied in the strict sense, since God is still viewed as in vital contrast to man. Since the third volume of his dogmatics, Barth has become less polemical against the analogy of being and has conceded the existence of a created *analogia relationis* (resemblance to God forming the relationship by which man is contrasted with man). Thus here too the relationship between the analogy of faith and the analogy of being is no longer conceived as purely antagonistic, though the interpretation of this development of analogy in Barth remains controversial.

See also *Natural Theology, God* II, *Dialectical Theology.*

BIBLIOGRAPHY. E. Przywara, *Analogia entis* (1932; rev. ed., 1962); P. Grenet, *Les origines de l'analogie philosophique dans les dialogues de Platon* (1948), with biblio.; K. Barth, *Church Dogmatics,* I: *The Doctrine of the Word of God,* part 1 (1949); H. U. von Balthasar, *Karl Barth. Darstellung und Deutung seiner Theologie* (1951; 2nd ed., 1962); H. Lyttkens, *The Analogy between God and the World. An Investigation of Its Background and Interpretation of Its Use by Thomas of Aquino* (1952), with biblio.; H. Bouillard, *Karl Barth,* I: *Genèse et évolution de la théologie dialectique,* II: *Parole de Dieu et existence humaine* (1957); C. Fabro, *Participation et causalité selon S. Thomas d'Aquin* (1961); B. Mondin, *The Principle of Analogy in Protestant and Catholic Theology* (1963); H. G. Pöhlmann, *Analogia entis oder analogia fidei? Die Frage der Analogie bei Karl Barth* (1965), with bibliography.

Leo Scheffczyk

ANGEL

I. Problem and History of Angelology: A. Problem of Angelology. B. History of Angelology. II. Doctrine of Angels: A. Introduction. B. The Teaching of Scripture. C. Systematic Theology.

I. Problem and History of Angelology

A. Problem of Angelology

The doctrine of the angels, even where it inalienably belongs (when placed in its correct context) to the content of the Christian message, meets with special difficulties at the present time. People nowadays in fact, though without justification, do not like to be told to look beyond the range of elementary immediate experience. Furthermore, even in their knowledge of what concerns salvation, they see no reason to be interested in the possible existence of angels, with whom even pious but rational people of today have, after all, nothing to do. Finally, as a matter of religious history, the angels appear relatively late in the Old Testament as a sort of incursion from outside, while in the New Testament, if one omits marginal religious phenomena which need very careful handling, the angels (demons) rather appear when worship of them is rejected or when the Christian is reminded of his superiority to all cosmic "principalities and powers". Now both these points would retain a concrete religious meaning even if no good or bad individual beings called angels existed. Even from these simple remarks a few hermeneutical principles of angelology can be drawn and these have their kerygmatic importance.

1. Despite the character of the numerous good or evil angels as personal substances (*D* 2318), we cannot and do not need to think of them anthropomorphically, as spatiotemporal forms — a collection of immaterial sprites which like the "spirits" at spiritualist séances are active in the material, human world at will, or else solely as a consequence of special divine commissions, but without any really intrinsic permanent and essential relation to the world. But the angels can be regarded as incorporeal (which is not the same thing as lacking any relation to the one material cosmos), yet as "principalities and powers" essentially belonging to the world, i. e., the totality of the evolutionary spiritual and material creation; in other words as conscious (and therefore free and personal), created, finite principles of the structure of various parts of the cosmic order. As such they are at least in principle *not* inaccessible to natural empirical knowledge (which latter is not identical with scientific,

quantitative experiment), and so they are not in themselves directly and necessarily a matter of revelation. Wherever in nature and history instances of order, structure and meaningful patterns emerge which — at least conjecturally and when envisaged without preconceptions — do not appear to be purely mechanical, material compositions "from below" nor to be planned and produced freely by men, and when such meaningful patterns in nature and history exhibit even for us at least traces of non-human intelligence and dynamism, it is meaningful to regard these as grounded on and guided by such "principles". For it is methodologically false always immediately to regard such complex, large-scale configurations in nature (cf. Rev 16:5 etc.) and history ("angels of the nations": Dan 10:13,20f.) as direct expressions of the divine mind, particularly since the antagonism of such large-scale units at least *in history* indubitably points in the first place rather to antagonistic cosmic "principalities and powers".

Such a conception presupposes that the activity of angels in nature and history as principles in this sense is not perceived only at particular moments of the individual history of salvation and perdition of men, but that their operation is thought of in principle as naturally antecedent to their and our free decision, even though the latter has a part in shaping their operation. This does not exclude a function of the angels as guardian angels. For every spiritual being (and consequently the angels too) has a supernatural vocation and therefore each in its own way has or had a history of salvation or perdition, and so even through its natural function itself, each spiritual being is of importance for every other. But we need not use this line of thought to develop and systematize further the doctrine of the angel guardians. This view of the angels also makes it clear why they cannot be an object of scientific, quantitative experimental knowledge, for the latter always has to move *within* such structures both objectively and subjectively. And if the angels' natural relation to and operation in the world has its ground in principle in their essence and not in any personal decision of theirs, it is also clear that through them as principles of partial structures of cosmic order the certainty and exactitude of the natural sciences is not called in question. Conversely, however, every other kind of experience of the angels (see above) is not thereby excluded either. Anthropomorphic representations, dubious systematizations, inappropriate applications, particular forms assumed in the history of religions and open to doubt, and purely symbolic use, are not peremptory objections against the validity of the fundamental experience of such principalities and powers in nature and history, and in the history of salvation and perdition. At the present time when people are only too ready to think it reasonable to suppose that because of the tremendous size of the cosmos there must be intelligent living beings outside the earth, men should not reject angels outright as unthinkable, provided that they are not regarded as mythological furnishings of a religious heaven, but primarily as "principalities and powers" of the cosmos.

2. If this is presupposed, it is clear on what basis and to what degree an angelology has a place in a religious doctrine of revelation. Revelation does not really introduce into the realm of human existence a reality (the angels) which otherwise would not be there, but interprets a reality in relation to God and his saving action in man, because that reality is already there. This is what happens with all other realities of man's range of experience which require elucidation in the light of faith and whose relation to man (and of man to them) have to be "redeemed". Consequently the angelology of revelation has the same function as revelation has for the rest of the created world of man's environment. It confirms his experience, preserves him from idolatry and from mistaking the numinous character of the world for God himself. At the point where, and because, the world is spiritual and personal revelation divides it (progressively) into two radically opposed realms and incorporates them into the one event with which everything in human existence is concerned, the coming of God in Christ into his creation. In this way angelology appears for the theology of man as a doctrine about the non-human world-setting, whether personal or material, of redemptive history which is a factor in theological anthropology. That is so whatever the context in which from a didactic or technical point of view it may be appropriate to deal with it. It makes man recognize a section of the world of persons of which he is a member for the decision of faith and

prevents him from diminishing its dimensions — he realizes that he stands in a more comprehensive community of salvation and perdition than that of mankind alone.

From this position in theological anthropology angelology receives its importance, its measure and an intrinsic *a priori* principle which may be used for our enquiry here and to systematize the meagre data of Scripture. On this basis, for example, the nature of the angels, without detriment to their difference as incorporeal spirits from man, could most radically be determined; it could be shown that they belong to the world by the very ground of their being, that they stand in a natural unity of reality and history with man, have a supernatural history of salvation with him which has its first design and ultimate goal (comprising the angels too) in Christ. As, however, theological anthropology and Christology are intrinsically connected, the nature of angelology is also determined by this more comprehensive context. If the possibility of the creation (although it could have been realized alone) and the actual creation as it in fact is, are grounded in the possible or actual free decision of God to express himself absolutely in the self-emptying of his Word, who by his self-utterance becomes man, then angelology too can only ultimately be understood as an inner element of Christology. The angels by nature form the society of persons surrounding the Word of the Father uttered and self-emptied, a Word uttered and heard in person. Their difference from man would have to be conceived as a variant (even if a "specific" one) of the one (generic) nature common to angels and man, and which attains its highest grace-given fulfilment in the Word of God. This would provide the basis for the treatment of such traditional themes as "the grace of angels as grace from Christ", "Christ as the head of the angels", "the radical unity of the world and of redemptive history with angels and men in their reciprocal relations of subordination and superiority", "the change which occurred in the role of the angels in sacred history". Angelology draws its ultimate measure and basis from Christology.

B. HISTORY OF ANGELOLOGY

1. Christian angelology has a prehistory; this fact is of fundamental importance for under-

standing its nature. It may be the case that even in the oldest strata of the Old Testament belief in angels is to be found. But it is scanty and is only developed in later books (Job, Zechariah, Daniel, Tobit). It nowhere appears as the result of an event in the historical revelation of God's Word, in the same way, for example, as the Covenant. The angels are taken for granted; they are simply there, as in all the religions of the world surrounding the Bible, and are simply known to exist. In this way, their relation to God, created character, clear division into good and bad, etc., could be calmly taken as a matter for subsequent theological reflection in Scripture. That would be inexplicable if their existence and nature were themselves the direct object of a revelation by God's Word. Resource has been had to the contention that doctrine about the angels belongs to the data of "primitive revelation". But even if this were conceded, we should have to ask how such a primitive revelation endured so long in the way it did, continuing to develop in a way that was essentially similar both outside and inside the history of revelation proper. A real answer to such a question would probably show that a tradition of this kind always has been and continues to be handed down because it can always originate anew. Why in fact should there be no experience (of a kind that does not intrinsically involve divine revelation) of non-human personal powers which are not God himself?

The prehistory of the treatise on the angels shows that the original source of the actual content of angelology was not divine revelation as such. Consequently angelology must bear this constantly in mind. Where revelation proper, especially in the NT, does occur in regard to the angels through reference to the word of the prophets and other primary bearers of revelation, or to inspired Scripture, it nevertheless has an essential function of selection and guarantee. "Archaic" angelology of alien origin prior to revelation was purified or kept free of elements incompatible with the real content of revelation (the unicity and truly absolute character of the God of the Covenant and of Christ as a person and mediator of salvation). The residue was confirmed as human experience legitimately handed down, preserving such knowledge for men as an important factor in their religious life which might otherwise be lost. That is shown by various features: lack of systematization, intermittent appearance of angels, general mention as an expression of other more comprehensive and religiously important truths (God's universal dominion, precariousness of the human situation, etc.), lack of interest in the precise number and hierarchy of the angels, in their sex or names, use of certain traditional non-revealed ideas without precise reflection on their meaning (angels as psychopompoi, their white garments, their dwelling-places), and in general the carefree spontaneity with which angels are introduced (e. g., appearance with the four animals of the Apocalypse, etc.).

2. The later history of the doctrine need not be gone into here (see below under II). We need only bring out what is important for the theoretical inquiry. The official doctrine of the Church codifies the actual content of what Scripture teaches about the angels, exercising reserve and restricting it to what is really religiously important "for us and our salvation", leaving all speculative questions for theological treatment. All that is taught as really a matter of dogma is the existence of a spiritual creation consisting of angels (Lateran IV: *D* 428; Vatican I: *D* 1783); this is meant to express the belief that apart from the unique Creator there exist only his creatures, so that in this way the angels too belong to a freely chosen, supernatural history of salvation and perdition (*D* 1001–5). In opposition to Jewish apocalyptic and Hellenistic ideas about angels, the Fathers of the Church insist from the first on the creatureliness of the angels, who are not to be thought of as sharing in the creation of the world, as in various Gnostic systems. A systematic treatise on the angels comes into existence: Pseudo-Dionysius wrote the first systematic treatise about 500 and in the West Gregory the Great, following Augustine, devoted considerable attention to the angels; both were of fundamental importance for medieval angelology.

The treatise on the angels was constructed by exploiting scriptural texts in probably too uniform a way without precise regard for their exact literary character, the *Sitz im Leben* or social setting in which they were composed and the actual intention of what they say (e. g., a number of individual names became a corresponding number of different choirs of angels). At the same time data of importance for the theology of salvation were to some extent neglected. The natural unity of the earthly and angelic world was not made really clear and explicit, although it is presupposed by the unity of redemptive history. Moreover, the treatise sometimes employed for its construction debatable ideas drawn from philosophical systems without sufficient express verification of their source and their right to a place in a theology of salvation. The pure "spirituality" of the angels was taught in the 6th century and was then made the absolute starting point of angelology in such a way that theologically the unity of angels and men in the one saving history of the *incarnate* Word and the natural conditions of that unity remained relatively obscure (the question whether all angels can be "sent"; when the angels were created, etc.). Consequently, the subordination of angelology to Christology (an explicit theme with Paul) does not receive its due theological weight. Even today there are textbooks of dogmatics — Schmaus is an exception — in which angelology is conceived quite non-Christologically. It was not, however, completely lacking when (as with Suarez in contrast to Aquinas and Scotus) the grace of the angels was viewed as the grace of Christ.

In the Middle Ages the angel became to a large extent the locus for metaphysical elaboration of the idea of a finite non-material intellectual being, a *forma subsistens, substantia separata* (in the wake of Arab philosophy). Such speculation, however useful and theologically stimulating it may have been, led to often quite considerable conceptual difficulties; *formae separatae* of this kind become almost like the monads of Leibniz and do not easily fit the theological data. Similarly the problem of the nature of the angels as "higher" than that of man was affirmed in a way that took for granted too readily and indiscriminately neo-Platonic conceptions of scales and degrees. For it must not be overlooked that the intellectual nature of man cannot so easily be characterized as inferior to that of the angels. That nature possesses absolute transcendence which in the beatific vision is brought to (unmerited) fulfilment and (at least, for example, in Christ) to an even more perfect fulfilment than in the angels. Why should it be an index of inferiority in every respect if

a nature reaches further down into greater material depths, if it possesses the possibility of rising equally high? If reference is made to Ps 8:6 and Heb 2:7, then we must not overlook 1 Cor 6:8 and the Pauline teaching about the superiority of the incarnate Christ to the angels and that of Christians to the Law which was mediated by angels (cf. also Eph 3:10; 1 Tim 3:16; 1 Pet 1:12). Naturally the authentic Christian element always returned to the charge, and the hierarchical stages leading up to the transcendent God (regarded neo-Platonically as supreme and aloof instead of as truly transcendent and therefore immediately close to all) were constantly ignored. Much in systematic angelology is merely transposition (justified on the whole, but sometimes carried out too simply) of the data of theological anthropology to the angels on the ground that they too are intellectual beings and called to the same goal of the vision of God.

A theological anthropology is in a certain sense for us the whole of theology, because it is self-possession through self-knowledge by the personal subject who asks the theological questions, and also because of the incarnation and grace. Yet without regard for this special position, the treatise on the angels is simply made the first section of the treatise on the creation, following the discussion of creation in general, and is usually placed before a section on man (cf., for example, Peter Lombard, *Sententiarum libri quatuor,* II, d. 1–11; Aquinas, *Summa Theologica,* I, qq. 50–64, and qq. 106–14, etc.). This purely accumulative structure does not make very clear the function of angelology in a human doctrine of salvation. Though in the post-Tridentine period the history of dogma began (with Petau) to include angelology, there has been hardly any explicit reflection on angelology from the point of view of disciplined theological investigation.

II. Doctrine of Angels

A. INTRODUCTION

The great danger at the present time is that affirmations about angels in the teaching of the Christian faith will be rejected as a mythology which is no longer credible, and so succumb to demythologization. In all particular statements about the angels it must, therefore, be kept clear that such assertions are meant as elements of a theological anthropology and Christology. In other words, it is the insertion of the angels into such a context which is actually affirmed while the "angels in themselves" remain a presupposition. Man's situation as a created being in regard to salvation and perdition, even prior to his own decision, has a dimension in depth which extends beyond his scientific and empirical experience. This is already partly qualified as good and evil by created freedom in history. But even in regard to the situation in which his life is placed when it is understood in this way, man is enabled and redeemed by the grace of God, so that he is free for a direct relation to God. He received his lot from God, not in the last resort through the cosmic "principalities and powers" of the purely created order. That is ultimately what Christian teaching regarding the angels reveals to man.

It might therefore be said, paradoxically, that this doctrine would have something to teach men even if no angels existed. However great, manifold and powerful man may think the created framework of his existence and destiny, however much he may think that this is already partly determined by higher freedom and guilt, he nevertheless remains in direct relation with God. God himself acts in him; his action is not wholly through intermediaries. Ultimately in grace by self-communication God is man's destiny and definitive life. On that basis it is also possible to make intelligible the hermeneutical situation regarding the biblical statements about angels (and demons). The existence of angels cannot be disputed in view of the conciliar declarations (*D* 428, 1783). Consequently it will be firmly maintained that the existence of angels and demons is *affirmed* in Scripture and not merely assumed as a hypothesis which we could drop today. This will be maintained without detriment to a more precise interpretation of particular statements in Scripture about angels and demons which make use of mythological, historically conditioned representational material which must not simply be included in the content of the statements. But even for Scripture, the really anthropological and Christian point of all these statements must always be carefully noted (cf., e.g., Jn 12:31; 16:11; Rom 8:38; 1 Cor 2:8; 8:5f.; 15:24; Eph 2:2; 6:12; Col 2:8–23). Existing as they do, the good angels are simply fellow servants of God with us (cf. Rev 22:9), and from the dominion of the evil angels we are set free.

The following must also be noted. If we consider on the one hand that the world as a whole and consequently the mutual relations of its components have a real history, are dynamic and not static, and on the other hand that the angels (good and bad) by their very nature, which means, in free personal activity, are integral parts of this world, then it must be reckoned with from the start that man's relation to the good and evil angelic powers will have a real history (within the history of salvation and perdition). It is, therefore, not always the same and so, for example, the angels may have had a greater role as mediators for good or ill before Christ than they have now (cf. Gal 3:19). Some loss of interest in them need not, therefore, be without justification. Even if all dimensions of human reality always remain important for salvation and consequently also the principalities and powers assigned to these dimensions as their entelechy, as it were, so that in fact many "lords" and "elements" remain in the world (cf. Gal 4:1–6; 1 Cor 8:5f.; 15:24; Eph; Col), we ourselves in a historical process of salvation become gradually more and more "grown up" (cf. Gal 4:1–4) in relation to them, and this can be regarded as being the case in regard to the good angelic powers. — As regards the "time" when the angels were created, revelation teaches nothing (not even by the *simul* of *D* 428, 1783). Yet in view of the cosmic function of the angels, it is quite meaningful to think with scholastic tradition of a simultaneous creation of the angels and the material world.

The angels are represented in Scripture as very numerous (cf., e.g., Mt 26:53; Heb 12:22; Rev 5:11). It is difficult to decide how far that is an affirmation or only a metaphor for their power. Consequently, what follows is to be read on these suppositions and in this context.

B. The Teaching of Scripture

Old Testament. The Old Testament belief is rooted, as far as the history of religions is concerned, in vestiges of the ancient Canaanite popular belief, in alien gods who have faded into servants of Jahweh, in Babylonian and late Iranian ideas.

The most important and thoroughly attested angelic figure is the Angel of Yahweh *mal'ak IHWH* sent by God with a mission. Particularly in popular belief in earlier times, he was regarded as a helpful, benevolent messenger (2 Sam 14; 2 Kg 19:35; Exod 14:19, etc.), and in Israelite theology as the organ of Yahweh's special relation by grace with Israel. In Gen 16:7; 21:17 ff., etc., he is even identified with Yahweh himself, and it is clear that the angel was inserted by a later editor in order to safeguard Yahweh's transcendence.

There were also other heavenly beings, regarded in ancient Israel as belonging to the heavenly court. These were what Jacob saw on the heavenly ladder. They are called *b⁾nē ha-'elohīm*, "sons of God" or divine beings; they appear in warlike guise but play only a secondary role in belief and worship.

The post-exilic belief in angels is elaborated into a real angelology (Job, Daniel). The angels receive names, become the guardians of countries, the heavenly court becomes immeasurably vast, they rank as explanatory mediators (*angelus interpres* in Zechariah and Ezekiel). The priestly code avoids (with polemic intent?) any statement about angels. In Job, mention is made of the limits of their holiness; before God they are not without blemish (4:18; 5:15 ff.). In the strict belief in creation, Yahweh was absolute Lord of history, and this left relatively little room for belief in angels and demons. After Daniel, Hellenistic rationalism was influential and was represented chiefly by the Sadducees (cf. Philo, Josephus), among whom belief in angels was regarded as a specifically Essene matter, and angelic appearances were termed by them φαντάσματα. On the other hand, ideas about angels had wide scope in apocalyptic and in Jewish popular piety. The Essenes, Qumran and the rabbis took them over, to some extent with dualist interpretations, in contrast to the growing rationalism, but with a strict regard for the transcendence of God. Men were assisted by special angels as guardians, companions and intercessors.

New Testament. The OT view of angels was taken over by the NT in a rather more matter of fact way. As an expression of the dawn of the reign of God, they accompany Jesus in the Temptation, in Gethsemani, at the Resurrection, etc. At the Annunciation and the birth of Jesus, the Angel of Yahweh appears. A large share in the eschatological judgment is attributed to the angels (Lk 12:8; 2 Thess 1:7, etc.; cf. Rev). A specifically angelological interest is not found; in fact Christ's superiority to the angels is emphasized, particularly at Mk 13:32; Gal 1:8; 3:19; Heb 1:4; 2:2, etc. Colossians (1:16; 2:18) seems to be directed against Gnostic doctrines about the angels.

As well as the idea of guardian angels taken over from Judaism, mention is frequently found of "powers", "authorities", "thrones", "dominions", "rulers", but it is not possible to establish precise differences between them. Some angels have demonic attributes and are in league with Satan (1 Cor 15:24; Eph 2:2). Actual angels of the devil (e.g., Mt 25:41 etc.) or fallen angels (Jude 6; 2 Pet 2:4) are also mentioned. Most copious mention of angels — comparable with Jewish speculation — is made in Revelation. They convey God's judgments and commands, and even plagues, to the world, and surround the heavenly throne of almighty God. On occasion they are viewed as cosmic powers. Those of the demonic kind have been overcome by Christ in his death and resurrection. But they are still an active threat to the faithful, and will be still more so at the end of time.

C. Systematic Theology

1. As regards their essence, the angels are to be thought of as spiritual, personal "principalities and powers" (*creaturae personales:* "Humani generis", D 2318). This is what is always implied in the official doctrinal pronouncements of the Church; cf., e.g., D 228a, 248; DS 991, D 428; 530; 1673; 1783; and also all the statements of the magisterium about the devil (e.g., D 427, 428) and his influence on sinners (D 711 ff.; 788; 793; 894). If at the same time it is presupposed that the angels are "incorporeal" in contrast to man (cf. D 428; 1783), this does not decide the more precise question of their relation to the material world. The Thomistic speculation regarding the metaphysical essence of angels (DS 3607; 3611) is an opinion which one is free to hold or not. At all events their relation to the world, which is both material and spiritual, must be thought of in such a way that they are really understood to be "principalities and powers" of the cosmos in virtue of their very nature

and do not merely intervene in the world by arbitrary decision contrary to their real nature, and in certain cases out of sheer malice.

Further speculation in scholastic theology about their spiritual nature was based on neo-Platonic philosophical theories about non-material pure spirit and is not theologically binding. The same probably applies (despite Ps 8:6) to the natural superiority of the angelic nature to man. All such theses, when they claim theological validity, go beyond the basis of all dogmatic angelology and the limits it sets to our knowledge of the angels. Similarly the classification of the angels, which like everything created are rightly to be thought of as different in nature from one another, into definite "choirs" and "hierarchies" is arbitrary and has no real foundation in Scripture.

2. Angels exist, but are merely creatures. The profession of faith of Lateran IV and the teaching on creation of Vatican I affirm the creation of spiritual beings, angels, in addition to men (D 430; 1783; cf. also D 2318, and statements of the creeds about *invisibilia* created by the one God). It cannot be said that the conciliar statements only mean that if there are such personal spiritual principalities and powers, they like everything else are creatures of the one, absolute God, though this, the ultimate import of the affirmation, is what is finally decisive. At all events the affirmation of their created character places from the start all spiritual, personal cosmic powers, and therefore their power and even their wickedness, within the circle of realities which are absolutely subject to a good and holy God and which are good by their origin. They must never be over-estimated as quasi-divine contrary principles on a level with God and against him (cf. DS 286; 325; D 237; 428; 574a, etc.). This used to happen only too often in popular preaching, tacitly and unconsciously, of course. There is little likelihood today that corporeality, marriage, carnal pleasures, etc. will be described as the work of the devil.

But what was meant by that and is rejected by the Church (cf. D 237–244, etc.) is in another guise still a temptation for man even today. He attributes an absolute character, as something purely and simply evil, to the occasions and aspects of his own guilt (e.g., technology, society, etc.), in order morally to exonerate himself in this way.

3. The angels, like man, have a supernatural goal of grace in the direct beatific vision of God (D 1001; 1003–5; 1009; DS 2800; D 2290). This conception follows from the uniformity of the divine treatment of the spiritual creation. By this, if God grants in grace his self-communication to any, then it is to all such spiritual, personal creatures. It also follows from the idea of Scripture and tradition that the good angels with God in heaven are his "court" (D 228a; DS 991; D 530). They therefore also enjoy the beatific vision. They have decided freely for or against this goal (cf. DS 286; 325; D 211; 427; 428 f.). No declaration is contained in the official teaching of the Church regarding the chronological moment of this decision. We must not attribute to it that kind of extended temporality which belongs to man in his history in time. We have to think of it as single and total and as one which from the beginning contributed to determining man's situation in the history of salvation and is manifested in the latter.

4. This final decision of the angels for God as their goal or away from him does not involve any definitive pre-determination of man's history of salvation or perdition (D 428; 907), but it is a factor in the situation in which men freely work out their salvation or freely fail to attain it. This also applies to the good angels, so that in regard to them (just as in regard to the saints, who have attained beatitude), a certain veneration *(cultus)* is possible and permitted (DS 3320; 3325; D 302; Vatican II, Dogmatic Constitution on the Church, ch. VII, art. 50). The liturgy and pious tradition consequently acknowledge guardian angels (Mt 18:10; *Catechismus Romanus*, IV, 9, 4), i.e., give concrete expression to the connection between men and angels in the one history of salvation of the one world by linking particular angels with particular human beings. No objection can be raised to this, provided it is not pictured too anthropomorphically or even childishly.

5. From the kerygmatic point of view there is no necessity at the present time to place truths concerning the angels particularly in the foreground of preaching and instruction. Yet there are occasions on which the preacher cannot avoid this theme. In the first place he must provide readers of the

Bible with guidance for understanding biblical statements about the angels, so that they can read with faith (without false demythologization) and yet critically, i. e., with due regard for the historically conditioned perspectives and the literary genre of such statements. Secondly, he has to answer questions about demons and the devil, and for this a correct grasp of angelology is required. Angelology makes it clear that the evil "principalities and powers" are a condition of the supra-human and relatively universal character of evil in the world and must not be trivialized into abstract ideas, but at the same time that these supra-human and relatively personal principles of wickedness must not be exaggerated in a Gnostic or Manichean way (as often happens in unenlightened popular piety) into powers opposed to the good God who are almost his equals in might. They are not God's rivals, but his creatures. And as with man, even evil freely chosen in a definitive state is the purely relative corruption of a natural, permanent being who has a positive function in the world; for something absolutely evil would be self-contradictory.

See also *Dualism, Neo-Platonism.*

BIBLIOGRAPHY. SCRIPTURE: W. Grundmann, G. von Rad, and G. Kittel, "ἄγγελος", *TWNT,* I (1933), pp. 72–87; L. Jung, *Fallen Angels in Jewish, Christian and Mohammedan Literature* (1926); E. Peterson, *Das Buch von den Engeln* (1935), French trans.: *Le livre des anges* (1935); E. Langton, *The Ministries of the Angelic Powers according to the Old Testament and Later Jewish Literature* (1937); H. B. Kuhn, "The Angelology of the Non-Canonical Jewish Apocalypses", *JBL* 67 (1948), pp. 217–32; G. Heidt, *Angelology of the Old Testament* (1949); G. B. Caird, *Principalities and Powers* (1956); H. Schlier, *Principalities and Powers in the New Testament,* Quaestiones Disputatae 3 (1961); id., "The Angels according to the New Testament", *The Relevance of the New Testament* (1967), ch. x. THEOLOGY: Thomas Aquinas, *Summa Theologica,* pars prima, q. 50–64, 106–14; F. Suárez, *De Angelis, Opera omnia,* II (1856); J. Daniélou, *Les anges et leur mission d'après les pères de l'Église* (2nd ed., 1953); J. Daniélou, "Trinité et angélologie dans la théologie judéo-chrétienne", *RSR* 45 (1957), pp. 5–41; P. Glorieux, *Autour de la spiritualité des anges. Dossier scripturaire et patristique* (1959); C. Journet, J. Maritain and P. de la Trinité, *Le péché de l'ange. Peccabilité, nature et surnature* (1961); K. Barth, *Church Dogmatics,* III: *The Doctrine of Creation,* part 3, para. 51 (1961); M. Schmaus, *Katholische Dogmatik,* II/1 (6th ed., 1963), pp. 260–323; E. Bertholet, *Mystère et ministère des anges* (1963).

Karl Rahner

ANGLICAN COMMUNION

"The Anglican Communion is a fellowship of those duly constituted Dioceses, Provinces or Regional Churches in communion with the See of Canterbury, which have the following characteristics in common:

"a. They uphold and propagate the Catholic and Apostolic faith and order as they are generally set forth in the Book of Common Prayer as authorized in their several Churches.

"b. they are particular or national Churches, and, as such, promote within each of their territories a national expression of Christian faith, life and worship.

"c. They are bound together not by a central legislative and executive authority, but by mutual loyalty sustained through the common counsel of the Bishops in conference." (Resolution 49 of the Lambeth Conference of 1930.)

These Churches number nineteen and are found in England, Scotland, Ireland, Wales, the United States, India-Pakistan-Burma-and-Ceylon, Australia, Canada, South Africa, New Zealand, the West Indies, East Africa, Central Africa, West Africa, Uganda-Burundi-Bwanda, Japan, China, Brazil and the Near East. In addition, certain dioceses are under the metropolitan jurisdiction of the Archbishop of Canterbury — Bermuda, Gibraltar, Hong Kong, Korea, Kuching, Singapore, Mauritius and Iran.

Of the member-Churches of the Anglican Communion, only the Church of England is established, that is, has a relationship with the State fixed by the laws of the land. All the other eighteen member-Churches are completely autonomous, having their own constitutions, choosing their own bishops, modifying their own liturgies and disciplines, and being subject neither to the State, nor to the Church of England, nor to the Anglican Communion as a whole.

The Anglican Communion is not a "confessional" body in the usual sense, the Thirty-nine Articles having no authority at all in a number of Anglican Churches and Provinces. In reunion proposals, the Articles are regarded as merely historical documents. To a considerable extent the Communion shares the "comprehensiveness" of the Church of England, "catholic", "evangelical" and "liberal" being inescapable words to describe tendencies or even groups or Provinces. At the Anglican Congress in Toronto in 1963, the Rev. Howard A. Johnson said: "In my Grand Tour of Anglicanism I was once in an allegedly Anglican church where I was obliged to take part in devotions to our Lady of Fatima and was denied the chalice. In another allegedly Anglican church it was impossible to make one's Christmas Communion because Christmas that year did not fall on Sunday." (E. R. Fairweather, ed., *Report,* London, 1963.) It is true that some Churches of the Communion tend to be Anglo-Catholic and others Evangelical; at the same time Anglicanism ought not to be judged by its extremes and the old party conflicts within Anglicanism "as we have known them in the past are dead, even if some are still lingering over the funeral ceremonies" (A. M. Allchin in D. M. Paton, ed., *Essays in Anglican Self-Criticism,* 1958, p. 177).

A "conservative evangelical" of the Church of England judges that "nearly all recent writing, from whatever denomination, represents the same school of thought, and maintains a high sacramental realism, often combined with a high doctrine of the eucharistic sacrifice. The progress made by such teaching since the rise of the Oxford movement, something over a century ago, has been phenomenal. It pours today from Anglican presses and pulpits and commands a large majority in Convocation; it has penetrated to all parts of the Anglican Communion, bringing about in many provinces a revision of traditional formularies; and, largely as a result of the Ecumenical Movement, which has reinforced it from Lutheran and Eastern sources, it is now spreading to many of the other denominations as well, both at home and abroad." (R. T. Beckwith, *Priesthood and Sacrifice. A Study in the Anglican-Methodist Report,* 1964, p. 8.) The "evangelicals" feel that they must oppose these tendencies, and, though a minority within the Anglican Communion, they show nevertheless strong convictions and very considerable zeal.

Although not a "federation" in the usual sense of the word, the Anglican Communion has a very real unity. This is founded first upon historical association, since the member-Churches sprang directly or indirectly from the Church of England, and the ecclesiastical bonds survived political severance, as, for instance, that of the American war of independence, 1775–1785, and that of the American civil war, during which Presbyterians,

Methodists and Baptists split over the issue of slavery. In general, though with notable exceptions, the Anglican Communion spread where the English language and British and American influence spread: India and Africa south of the Sahara, the Caribbean area, Alaska, the Hawaian Islands and the Philippine Islands.

Then, the liturgies of the member-Churches derive from the Book of Common Prayer of the Church of England, though various modifications have been introduced in different member-Churches. Some derive from the version of 1549, but the majority from the version of 1552 as changed in 1662. The Lambeth Conference (a ten-yearly meeting of the bishops) proposed some general principles which might govern all revisions of the Prayer Book in the member-Churches of the Communion, and particularly in the Church of England. These changes may have far-reaching effects in regard to relations of the Anglican Communion with the Eastern Orthodox and the Roman Catholic Churches.

Next, there has always been among Anglicans a sense of the continuity of the Church, and a considerable devotion to patristic studies. For this reason the Decree on Ecumenism of the Second Vatican Council said: "Among those Communions in which Catholic traditions and institutions in part continue to exist, the Anglican Communion has a special place." (Art. 13.)

There is, too, an Anglican "ethos", hard to define but perhaps best summed up in the Preface to the Prayer Book, of keeping a mean "between two extremes, of too much stiffness in refusing and of too much easiness in admitting any variation". Anglican worship is restrained and dignified; its preaching appeals rather to good sense than to emotions, and its writing rather to balance and substance than to exhaustive scholarship. To all this, of course, there are many exceptions.

In reunion plans, Anglicans hold to "the Lambeth Quadrilateral", that is, the Scriptures, the Creeds (sometimes understood as including tradition), the two dominical sacraments (sometimes conjoined with recognition of "the other five"), and "the historic episcopate". In 1958 the Lambeth Conference declared, with reference to relations with Presbyterians, that "it must be recognized as a fact that Anglicans conscientiously hold that the celebrant of the Eucharist should have been ordained by a bishop standing in the historic succession and generally believe it to be their duty to bear witness to this principle by receiving Holy Communion only from those who have thus been ordained" (*Report,* 2, London, 1958, p. 44).

Some Anglicans disagree with this Lambeth statement and hold that episcopacy is a suitable but not necessary means of Church government and of ordination; others hold the same doctrine about "apostolic succession" as do the Orthodox and Catholics. But the Anglicans in conversations with Methodists declared that this liberty of interpretation "is only possible within the strictest invariability of episcopal ordination. For, while it is possible to hold a 'low' view of episcopacy within a strict invariability of practice, it becomes impossible to hold a 'high' view where this invariability is broken" (*Report of Conversations between Anglicans and Methodists,* London, 1963, p. 45).

The Lambeth Conference, a ten-yearly meeting of bishops, is another bond of unity, and the advice given to Anglicans is weighty on matters such as reunions of Churches and intercommunion. Since 1897 there has been a Consultative Body of the Lambeth Conferences, and in 1948 an Advisory Council on Missionary Strategy was set up. In 1952 St. Augustine's at Canterbury became a kind of post-graduate college for priests. In 1959 an "executive officer" of the Anglican Communion was appointed; and at the Anglican Congress at Toronto in 1963, it was agreed to appoint nine regional officers for planning, communications and consultations.

The Anglican Communion is in full intercommunion with the Old Catholic Churches and is in dialogue about schemes of reunion with almost every Church. From 1921 to 1925 unofficial conversations took place between the Anglican and Roman Catholic Churches at Malines; official theological conversations between the two Churches began in January 1967.

In general Anglicans look forward to the ultimate disappearance of their Communion when all Churches unite; meantime, however, they account that they can best serve the cause of unity by holding to their fundamental principles and extending and consolidating their missionary outreach.

See also *Ecumenism* I, II, VI, *Apostolic Succession.*

BIBLIOGRAPHY. W. R. Stephens and W. Hunt, *History of the English Church,* 9 vols. (1899–1910); E. J. Bicknell, *A Theological Introduction to the Thirty-nine Articles* (1919; 3rd ed., 1955); C. C. Webb, *A Study of Religious Thought in England from 1850* (1933); P. E. More and F. Cross, *Anglicanism* (1935); id., *Doctrine in the Church of England* (1938); G. K. A. Bell, *The English Church* (1942); C. Garbett, *The Claims of the Church of England* (1947); J. W. C. Wand, *The Anglican Communion. A Survey* (1948); G. A. K. Bell, *Christian Unity: The Anglican Position* (1948); C. Garbett, *Church and State in England* (1950); *Lambeth Conferences, 1867–1948,* the reports of the 1920, 1930 and 1948 conferences with selected resolutions from the conferences of 1867–1878, 1888, 1897 and 1908 (1950); P. Hughes, *The Reformation in England,* 3 vols. (1950–54); C. Garbett, *The Church of England* (1954); M.-J. Y. Congar, "Brève histoire des idées religieuses dans l'Anglicanisme", *Istina* 4 (1957), pp. 133–64; G. F. S. Gray, *The Anglican Communion* (1958); *Lambeth 1958, Reports* (1958); S. Neill, *Anglicanism* (1958), with biblio.; P. Hinchliff, *The Anglican Church in South Africa* (1963); R. W. Albright, *A History of the Protestant Episcopal Church* (1964); id., *The Anglican-Presbyterian Conversations* (1966). YEARBOOKS AND PERIODICALS: *The Chronicle of Convocation; The Journal of Convocation; The Official Year-Book of the Church of England.*

Bernard Leeming

ANOINTING OF THE SICK

The sacramental anointing of the sick today holds little pastoral appeal. Sick people send for the doctor, not for the priest. Only when medical science and skill fail, do they ask for the sacrament of the sick. This sacrament is considered as the herald of coming death, and people keep away from it as long as possible. Even when presented as the sacrament of the sick, if not of healing, rather than as the sacrament of the dying, people find it hard to appreciate its precise role in the Christian life, the encounter with Christ proper to this sacrament. The difficulty may well be due not only to the modern outlook on life more intent on this world and inclined to ignore the next, but also to a defective pastoral presentation.

The anointing of the sick, in the mind of Christ and of the Church, is the sacrament of spiritual comfort for the gravely sick whose illness entails danger of death (*CIC,* 940, § 1). It is so from its very nature and institution, not only by Church law.

ANOINTING OF THE SICK

A. Historical Development

1. *Holy Scripture.* The two NT texts referring to the anointing of the sick (Mk 6:13 and Jas 5:14 ff.) of which, Trent says, the first "suggests" the sacrament and the second attests its promulgation (*D* 1695), must be set in the context of Christ's messianic mission. Christ came to fulfil the OT expectation of a messianic kingdom, not however in a temporal but in a spiritual sense. His kingdom is not of this world (Jn 18:36), yet it begins in this world. He came to put an end to the reign of Satan and of sin and to inaugurate the kingdom of God on earth. Sickness and death being, in the biblical perspective, signs and consequences of sin, the ministry of healing the sick, both Christ's own (Mt 9:35) and that of the apostles (Mt 10:1; Lk 9:1; Mk 6:7, 13), is one of the signs of the messianic times (cf. Mt 10:4 f., referring to Is 35:5 f. and 61:1). In Christ's messianic mission that ministry is directed towards a spiritual effect, forgiveness of sin and grace. This is suggested in Mk 6:13 which speaks of the charism of healing set in a spiritual perspective; it is clear from Jas 5:14 ff. where the forgiveness of sin is mentioned (15) and the terms used (σώσει, ἐγερεῖ; *salvabit, alleviabit*) designate both a bodily and a spiritual effect. In the mind of the apostle the bodily effect may well be intended first, but the spiritual effect is also included. The text hints that the sick person is gravely ill by the terms used (ἀσθενεῖ, κάμνοντα) and by the context (unable to go to the priests he sends for them). At a time when medical science was not what it is today, grave illness entailed danger of death. Here then is the biblical foundation for the doctrine of the sacramental anointing of the sick distinct from the charism of healing.

2. *Early Christianity.* St. James's directive was followed in practice from early Christian times. A recent discovery of a first century silver tablet with a 17-line Aramaic text attests the practice (*Ami du clergé* 73 [1963], pp. 490 f.). There is further evidence, for the first five centuries, of a twofold anointing of the sick (*D* 216), a private one done with blessed oil by the sick person himself or his relatives, and a liturgical anointing performed by the priest or bishop. Both of them refer to St. James's text. The first obviously supposes less grave illness and is meant for bodily cure (it pertains to the charism of healing). The second is for the case of grave illness and seeks spiritual help from the priest or bishop; it is the sacramental anointing. The difference between the two could not be clear at a time when sacramental doctrine was still undeveloped.

3. *Carolingian Reform.* From the 9th century on the "anointing with sacred oil" appears to be one of the Church's last rites for the dying (the other two being the reconciliation and the viaticum; Palmer, p. 322). The implications of this legitimate development are mainly two: the anointing is meant for the sick in danger of death; and it intends (not a bodily cure which in the circumstances is no longer hoped for but) a spiritual effect. Thus its sacramental nature becomes manifest, and so does its proper grace: spiritual help for the sick in danger of death. The name of Extreme Unction, the last anointing or, when misunderstood, the anointing for the last moments, was introduced at this time.

4. *Scholasticism.* When in the 13th and 14th centuries the doctrine of the seven sacraments reaches its full development, the anointing of the sick is counted as one of them. It is the sacrament of spiritual help for the time of grave illness when approaching death disables a sick person no less spiritually than physically. Its first effect is spiritual: sacramental grace as a spiritual remedy against sickness. Bodily health may eventually follow as a subordinate and conditional effect. The danger of death, a necessary condition for its reception, was generally overstressed. People waited for the point of death to receive the "sacrament of the departing" — *sacramentum exeuntium* —, an abuse originating in some fanciful concepts about the effects of the anointing for those who recovered and were considered as bound to a sort of penitential life (Kilker, pp. 151 ff., Palmer, p. 330), or in a misunderstood theology of the anointing of the sick as complement of the sacrament of penance as though it entailed, of its nature, immediate entrance into heaven.

5. *Council of Trent.* The Council of Trent defined the anointing of the sick as one of the seven sacraments (*D* 1716); it determined its effects, harmoniously blending the spiritual ones that come first and the corporal that are subordinate to and conditioned by the first (*D* 1696). By the provi-

dential substitution of "especially" *(prae-sertim)* for "only" *(dumtaxat)* in its text on the recipient of the sacrament (*D* 1698) it ushered in the distinction between danger of death and point of death, and thus struck at the root of the abuse of unduly delaying the anointing of the sick — which, however, persists even today.

B. Systematic Doctrine

This sacrament is the sacramental anointing of the sick in danger of death, meant primarily for a spiritual purpose and secondarily for a bodily effect.

1. The proper grace of the anointing of the sick is a spiritual remedy against sickness, intended for the religious and supernatural victory over illness, or for spiritual healing. As illness of its nature is ambiguous and ends either in recovery or in death, the sacramental grace of the anointing of the sick is also ambivalent, preparing either for a recovery or for a Christian death. It does not do away with the inherent ambiguity of sickness; in certain cases only it helps recovery, but it always is to lead to a supernatural victory over sickness. This victory consists in overcoming the spiritual disability and the hindrance to living the life of grace which illness entails. The sacramental grace of the anointing of the sick adds spiritual strength to the sick person's spiritual life, it increases his trust and fortitude (*D* 1696), the fruits of the encounter with Christ the Healer. This spiritual effect is a first reason for not delaying the sacrament. No sooner is a sick person capable of receiving this grace, i.e., in danger of death, than the sacrament can, may and should be given.

2. The anointing of the sick is not the sacrament of the dying: it is not meant only for the sick at the point of death — *in exitu* —, but also for those in danger of death. It is the sacrament of the seriously ill, even when the illness ends in death and when the sacramental grace of final perseverance ensures the paschal victory of a Christian death — a definitive victory, immediate for the departing soul (after eventual cleansing) and delayed for the body till the glorious resurrection. Its grace for the struggle with illness was operative all the time, as a spiritual remedy against the spiritual debility involved in illness. But Christian death itself, as a sharing in Christ's paschal mystery is one way of overcoming illness spiritually. In pastoral practice one should not hide from the sick this more exalted victory over sickness.

3. The anointing of the sick may lead to the restoration of bodily health. But it does not replace medical care, nor produce health after the manner of the charism of healing. It operates for bodily healing in its own sacramental way. Because of the inter-dependence between body and soul in the psychosomatic unity of man, the spiritual comfort of the soul resulting from the sacramental grace reacts on the body and so may influence its cure. No one can say when and on what conditions it does so, if for no other reason than that in God's providential design some illness must be the last. This secondary and conditional effect, however, is no sufficient reason to call the anointing of the sick the sacrament of healing; the name is a misnomer liable to give false hopes, and it suggests an impoverished idea of the sacrament by leaving out its spiritual effects.

4. When anointing of the sick is followed by a Christian death, it should not be presented as a pledge of immediate entrance upon the glory. Some such idea was proposed by St. Thomas and Suárez, and more recently by H. Kern. Yet, when it is dissociated from certain misconceptions, such as that it is meant specifically for remission of venial sins or for avoiding purgatory, and when it is considered as "consummating penance" (St. Thomas, *Summa contra Gentiles,* 4, 73; Trent, *D* 1694), then one must say: Anointing of the sick prepares for immediate entrance into heaven as far as possible according to the dispositions of the recipient. The spiritual healing may be complete and then it amounts to preparedness for immediate glory. But it would be unwarranted to suggest an easy escape from purgatory through the anointing of the sick.

5. Because anointing of the sick is a complement to the sacrament of penance, it remits mortal sin; not merely as does any other sacrament of the living when its recipient is in good faith and habitually repentant, but as a specific effect of the sacrament, viz. because of the spiritual healing which it is intended to produce. This

important spiritual effect of anointing of the sick also commends its early reception.

Conclusion

A pastoral presentation of the anointing of the sick apt to restore its spiritual appeal must be true to the mind of the Church. It should not lose sight of the twofold alternative to which its grace may lead: either to a temporary victory over illness in restored bodily health, or to a definitive victory in a Christian death. In either case it means an encounter with Christ who continues his spiritual ministry of healing.

See also *Reign of God, New Testament Books* V, *Sacraments* I.

BIBLIOGRAPHY. G. Kilker, *Extreme Unction* (1926); P. De Letter, "The Meaning of Extreme Unction", *Bijdragen* 16 (1955), pp. 257–70; P. F. Palmer, "The Purpose of Anointing the Sick. A Reappraisal", *TS* 19 (1958), pp. 301–44; id., *Sacraments and Forgiveness* (1959), pp. 273–320; id., *Doctrine on Penitence* and *Extreme Unction*, Sources of Christian Theology, II (1959); J. C. Didier, *The Last Rites* (1961); C. G. Renati, *The Recipient of Extreme Unction* (1961); B. Poschmann, *Penance and the Anointing of the Sick,* The Herder History of Dogma (1963).

Prudent De Letter

ANTHROPOMORPHISM

I. Philosophical

To think of God with human form and qualities (anthropomorphism) appears at first sight merely as an instance of the general structure of knowledge, which is to assimilate the thing known to the knower ("quidquid recipitur ad modum recipientis recipitur"), with all the attendant risks and benefits. The advantage is that man draws closer to God, whom he knows not just as a vague and unattainable being or perhaps as the silence or demonic strangeness of theriomorphism, but as one who speaks and can be spoken to, who cares about man and gives sense to his life. The danger is this closeness itself, which may lose sight of the majesty and inaccessibility of the holiness of God. But Xenophanes' criticism of the Homeric pantheon, that oxen would have gods in the form of oxen, misses the real point. From the philosophical point of view, it must be pointed

out that while man, and man alone, cannot shake himself loose from imagery even in his knowledge of God, since he is a bodily spirit, still, as a spiritual body, he is conscious of this limitation and thus transcends it without being able to abolish it. In a fully developed theological anthropology, however, man appears as *the* manifestation and revelation of God — as that which God becomes when he expresses himself in a medium other than himself. "God — in what is other than himself" constitutes the dialectical relationship within which anthropomorphism, properly understood, has its validity and must be examined for its limitations. In this sense anthropomorphism reflects the theomorphic nature of man. It does not try to explain God in the light of man, as L. Feuerbach tried to do when transforming theology into anthropology, but rather reduces man to the mystery of God — which thereby appears all the more clearly in its own proper character, since it is not merely apprehended as the negative contrast to man. The mystery of the incarnation is the supreme justification of anthropomorphism.

BIBLIOGRAPHY. E. Ehnmark, *Anthropomorphism and Miracle* (1939); G. van der Leeuw, *Religion in Essence and Manifestation. A Study in the Phenomenology of Religion,* 2 vols. (1963).

Jörg Splett

II. Biblical

Human attributes are often ascribed to Yahweh in the OT. He has hands, feet, eyes, lips, mouth, tongue, face, head, heart and inward parts, and is represented as a man (Exod 15:3; 22:19; Is 30:27; Ezek 1:26); he retains human traits even in prophetic visions (Is 6:1; Dan 7:9). This way of thinking of God is also characterized by the frequency with which human reactions are attributed to God: he laughs (Ps 2:4), is angry and whistles (Is 5:25f.), sleeps (Ps 44:25), awakes (Ps 78:65), walks about (Gen 3:8) and has regrets (Gen 6:6). Even the incomprehensibility of God is given anthropomorphic expression, in so far as God's decisions are presented as purely arbitrary (Gen 12:13; 20:2; 27:33, etc.) — a process which reveals, however, as for instance in the book of Job, the intrinsic limitations of anthropomorphism. Thus Yahweh is never clearly and completely portrayed; there are only partial descriptions of him. Along with these anthropomorphisms, we find a portrayal of God as the inaccessible and transcendent (Gen 18:27; Exod 3:5; Deut 3:24; Is 28:29, etc.). Its climax is the prohibition of images in the decalogue (Exod 20:4; 20:22; Deut 4:12, 15–18), which is a radical restriction of all attempts to give material expression to knowledge of God, except in word and name, a restriction necessary in view of the constant pressure towards materialization from the nature gods of the surrounding nations. The prophets have no misgivings about anthropomorphisms (Is 30:27 ff.), which they use to express the immediacy of their experience of God, but they are as emphatic about the infinite transcendence of God as are the early accounts of meeting God in the Pentateuch (Is 31:3; Hos 11:7). In the priestly writings, a type of thought constrained by taboos appears: God is accessible only in worship and by means of angels. In post-exilic times, the notion of God begins to be more abstract. The LXX in particular renders concrete images by means of abstract terms (Is 4:24; Exod 15:3; Ps 8:6, etc.). This is compensated for by a parallel growth of avidity for miracles in popular piety, with a highly imaginative belief in angels and spirits.

Anthropomorphic representations of God also survive in the NT (Rom 1:18 ff.; 5:12; 1 Cor 1:17, 25; Heb 3:15; 6:17; 10:31). We are also told, however, that we do not see God like a man, but as though in a mirror (1 Cor 13:2), that he does not dwell in temples built by man (Acts 17:24) but in inaccessible light (1 Tim 6:16), and that God is spirit (Jn 4:24). The full vision of God is granted only at the end (1 Cor 13:9; 2 Thess 1:7). But the portrayal of God is still possible, on an entirely new basis: Jesus Christ is the image of God (2 Cor 4:4), the likeness of the invisible God, who took on the form of man (Phil 2:7). The once distant God has come close to us (Eph 2:18). Anthropomorphisms in the OT were justified by man's being made in the image of God, in the NT by the revelation of God in Jesus Christ. But along with anthropomorphisms, we find that the supreme transcendence of God is emphasized, and in many cases this is to be taken as a deliberate reaction against anthropomorphisms. This tendency gradually prevailed and the notion of God became more abstract, which, somewhat like the abandonment of mythological assertions, prepared the way for dogmatic propositions in post-biblical times. From the point of view of hermeneutics, anthropomorphism may be interpreted as an expression of the inadequacy of human language when speaking of God, but also as an expression of a lively faith in a personal God.

See also *God* II, *God, Attributes of,* *Man* III, *Revelation* I, *Spirit.*

BIBLIOGRAPHY. T. Boman, *Hebrew Thought Compared with Greek* (1960); W. Eichrodt, *Theology of the Old Testament,* I (1961); G. von Rad, *Old Testament Theology,* I (1962).
Werner Post

ANTICHRIST

No single and consistent portrayal of the eschatological figure of "Antichrist" is to be found in Scripture and tradition. It varies alike in the manner in which it is presented and in the characteristics ascribed to it and in the significance attached to it. In the course of the Church's history the idea has been so much bandied about in ecclesiastical controversies both between hostile sects and between warring factions within the Church itself; under the impulse of hatred or fear it has so often been identified with the ideas, systems or personages of particular epochs that as a result ". . . today the concept of Antichrist is no longer real and effective" (Tüchle, col. 637). However welcome this conclusion may be from the aspect of rising above the level of heresy hunting, the question must still be put whether the idea of Antichrist in its eschatological and parenetic aspect does not still possess a vital and urgent relevance.

In contemporary theology this question is answered in the affirmative: "This teaching gives Christians a permanent right not merely to wage war upon anti-Christian powers and ideas in the abstract, but to recognize and to flee from men and powers in the concrete as its representatives" (Rahner, col. 636). "Among the traditions concerning the last days, the doctrine of Antichrist has a special pastoral function to fulfil. It serves to arm the believing community to do battle with the compact forces of darkness, in the form in which they encounter them in their own age" (Frör, p. 371).

Is is necessary, however, to beware of presenting the idea of Antichrist as a "doctrine". Such a presentation could hardly be made without bringing the scriptural references into a forced harmony by suppressing the variations and straining the meanings of the more obscure statements. Such a procedure would rather obscure than bring to light the idea of a coming Antichrist in its enduring value for the Christian community. When we consider the reasons for the obscurity of the Antichrist idea, we realize that these lie in the constant necessity for readjusting the eschatological understanding of the present and the future. For this there is no "blueprint" but only the general guidance given by faith. We must not attempt to achieve a composite picture of Antichrist from the various forms in which the idea appears in the Bible, and then look eagerly for it in the world about us. Each element of biblical tradition has its own distinctive mode of expression, and it is the intention underlying each of these that must rather be explored. Thus we may hope to depict an Antichrist which will indicate how Christian life today may be orientated.

New Testament. The expression "Antichrist" appears in the Bible only in 1 and 2 Jn. The advent of an opponent of Christ is presupposed as part of the eschatological expectation of the early Christian community (this idea probably developed under the influence of Old Testament and late Jewish conceptions, as well as of the preaching of Jesus). But the author regards Antichrist, or alternatively the Antichrists in the plural, as already come in the teachers of heresy of his own time. Hence he concludes that it is "the final hour" (1 Jn 2:28). He gives no Antichrist doctrine, but applies the traditional expectation of Antichrist (which was clearly open to such an interpretation) to the situation of his Church, threatened as it is by heretical teachers. The traditional expectation is interpreted in such a way that it serves the interests of exhortation, the eschatological equipment of the community (cf. 2 Jn 8).

The early Church's expectation of Antichrist as attested in 1 and 2 Jn is elsewhere discernible only in 2 Thess 2:3ff.; Rev 13:1ff.; 19:19ff., and in these passages it appears in a markedly different form. (Mk 13:14 par.; Jn 5:43; 2 Cor 6:15 are not instances of it.) a) In 2 Thess the belief in the coming of Antichrist, filled out with pre-existing apocalyptic material, is used to curb the fever of eschatological excitement in the Thessalonians ("The day of the Lord has come", 2:2). The "man of lawlessness ... the son of perdition" (2:3) must first come. He who is now still being restrained must appear openly (2:6f.) but then be annihilated by the Christ of the parousia "with the breath of his mouth" (2:8). The constant state of preparedness in which the community stands (cf. 1 Thess 5:2) must not be weakened by the expectation of Antichrist (about which they have already been told, cf. 2 Thess 2:5), but misguided enthusiasm must be guarded against. The expectation of Antichrist is here invoked as an argument against this, and in a parenetic sense which runs counter to the manner in which it is used in 1 and 2 Jn. b) In Revelation characteristic traits both of the Anti-Messiah and of the Pseudo-Messiah are combined in the image of the "beast from the sea" (13:1ff.). The description of the first beast points to an idolatrous power *(Imperium Romanum?)* which persecutes Christians (13:7). It is declared that the representative of this (emperor worship?) will be destroyed in the "lake of fire" (19:21). In the framework of Revelation the parenetic application of the ancient motifs (above all those found in Daniel) is already verifiable in the long introduction consisting of the letters to the seven churches (Rev 2–3). Here again no "blueprint" is given for the final age. Ever since the coming of Christ into history the "Antichrist alert" has been constantly in force, and ever since then the combined strength of the powers hostile to God as already depicted in the Old Testament and later Judaism (cf. Ezek 38f.; Dan 2:20–45; 7:7f.; Ps 2; *4 Esdr* 11f.; *Apoc Bar (Syr)* 36; 39, 5–8, etc.) have been, as they continue to be, directed against *him* (Rev 12:1ff.) and *his* community (Rev 12:17), in a form which is expected to grow in intensity as the end draws near.

BIBLIOGRAPHY. W. Bousset, *The Antichrist Legend* (1896); B. Rigaux, *L'Antéchrist* (1932); R. Schnackenburg, K. Rahner and H. Tüchle, "Antichrist", *LTK*, I (1957), cols. 634–8; R. H. Charles, *Eschatology, Doctrine of Future Life* (1963); H. H. Rowley, *The Relevance of Apocalyptic* (3rd ed., 1963); K. Frör, *Biblische Hermeneutik* (2nd ed., 1964).

Rudolf Pesch

ANTIOCHENE
SCHOOL OF THEOLOGY

As the third city of the Roman Empire, Antioch offered the development of a Christian theology a cultural basis comparable to that of the capital of Egypt. Antioch stood more in the philosophical tradition of Aristotle whereas Alexandria inclined to Plato; and these philosophical differences were soon revealed in the theologizing of the schools of both cities. The methods of rabbinic Judaism dominated scholarship at Antioch; in Alexandria the scientific approach of Hellenistic Judaism was preferred. Antiochene theology was less bound to a teaching institute than Alexandrian. It developed under the influence of individual teachers whose methods and goals were similar and who personally attracted groups of followers.

1. The origins of the school are obscure, though tradition has named Lucian of Antioch (d. 312) as the founder. Paul of Samosata (Bishop of Antioch till 268) had to defend himself against the accusation of Dynamic Monarchianism. We find no detailed teaching on the Logos in his works; in his teaching on God it is certain that he made use of the concept ὁμοούσιος which seemed to lend itself to the blurring of the distinction between the persons of the Father and the Son. The condemnation of Paul may partly explain the later reluctance of the Eastern bishops to adopt this term at the Council of Nicaea. The argumentative method of his opponent Malchion, a presbyter who was also the head of a school of rhetoric, suggests a thorough knowledge of the dialectics of Aristotle. Paul's one-sided stress on the full humanity of Christ led to the reproach that he denied the divine sonship. But the opposing thesis of the Antiochene synods was probably based on the so-called "Logos-Sarx schema". If so, the bishop was probably in the right to a great extent, while his opponents may have prepared the way for the heresy of Apollinaris of Laodicea, which was later propounded at Antioch.

Whether the younger contemporary of Paul and Malchion, Lucian of Antioch, was a follower of the bishop is now disputed. At any rate his teachings brought him into temporary conflict with the official Church.

His careful biblical criticism (revision of the LXX and the NT — or at least of the gospels) is the first example of the methodical exegesis which was to characterize the Antiochene school. According to Eusebius, Dorotheus of Antioch was teaching at the same time as Lucian, being equally learned and possessing complete mastery of the Hebrew language. At this time a regular school of theology began to form and the fact that the students called themselves "followers of Lucian" witnesses to the formative influence and authority of Lucian. It also indicates that Arius, Eusebius of Nicomedia and others thought themselves to be promoting the teaching of their master in their dogmatic theses.

Lucian's teaching on the Trinity remains for the most part unknown; but the Subordinationism of his pupil Arius reveals an approach different from that commonly found among the disciples of Origen.

Whereas in the tradition of the Great Church even before Nicaea, among the Apologists as well as the Alexandrians, a change in the status of the Logos (e. g., from ἐνδιάθετος to προφορικός) was only considered to be real on the side of creation and not on the side of God, Arius made out of this relational difference a real distinction. The Alexandrians above all made use of the Platonic concept of unity in the description of the divine nature. According to this interpretation the unifying "idea" possesses the true reality, in which individual things have only a share. But Arius's conception of the two *logoi* and his rigid monotheism were based upon the negative concept of unity used by Aristotle, according to which it is the individual being which is real and which is negated in the abstracted unity. The theological efforts of Arianism were aimed at protecting the absolute oneness of the Father as the one true God. This stress led them to give to the Logos too low a place, as he was "not eternal as the Father was, not ἀγέννητος as he was" (cf. Athanasius, *Ep. de Synodis,* 16). Apart from a few letters, Arius and Eusebius of Nicomedia, his influential "fellow-Lucianist" and protector, wrote little.

2. Eustatius of Antioch, who represented the opposite approach to these questions, is also theologically indebted to the Antiochene

tradition. He attacks impartially Arius and his followers as well as the Alexandrian master, Origen. Because of his precise and orthodox Christological statements it does not seem proper to consider him as a follower of Paul of Samosata or as a forerunner of Nestorius. In the disputes following upon Nicaea, Aetius of Antioch and his pupil Eunomius appeared as the chief opponents of the conciliar decrees. With the help of the Aristotelian categories and Sophistic dialectics, they carried the errors of Arius to their ultimate conclusion and denied even the resemblance of the Son to the divine Father.

3. The school of Diodore of Tarsus (d. 394) represented a new phase in the tradition; it can only be thought of as a part of the Antiochene tradition because of its similarity of method and theological approach. Its most famous pupils were John Chrysostom and Theodore of Mopsuestia, in whose generation the Antiochene school reached the full flower of its development. Although Diodore developed his exegesis in his numerous commentaries in conscious opposition to the allegorical and mystical interpretation of the Alexandrians, he achieves more than a mere consideration of the "bare letter" with his historical and grammatical analysis. This is evident especially in his distinction between ἀλληγορία and θεωρία, by which he attempted to resolve an important problem in biblical hermeneutics. The "spiritual" consideration of a text *(theoria)* makes it possible to link the historical understanding of the Old Testament with an interpretation pointing on to Christ and his kingdom. Thus he takes a middle position between Philo's allegorical whimsy and the slavery to the letter in rabbinical Judaism. Diodore was also the first to formulate what was later called the "Antiochene Christology". Just as he firmly defended the full divinity of Christ against Arius, he also stressed against Apollinarius that the Logos in the incarnation assumed the full nature of a man. Thus Antiochene thought came to distinguish sharply between Christ as Son of God and Christ as Son of Mary and so Son of David. To preserve the unity Diodore asserted, "but there are not two Sons" *(Adversus Synousiastas,* frag. 30 f.), though he was unable to give a satisfactory account of this unity.

4. John Chrysostom, a native of Antioch who was also schooled under the famous pagan rhetorician Libanius, succeeded in applying the exegesis of the theological school to pastoral needs, especially preaching. The sermon was his natural element, and it was as homilies that he wrote his numerous scholarly commentaries. The first object of the sermon being to demonstrate the literal sense, he frequently prefaced his exegesis with a historical explanation and discussed grammatical problems. He expressly rejected the allegorical method of the Alexandrians but he frequently brought out the typological sense of the events of the OT, e.g., the Church was prefigured by the ark, and Christ by Noah. He displayed a skill of his own in linking scholarship and life in his exhortations. His contribution to the development of dogma was slight, but he is a good example of the state of Greek theology around the end of the 4th century, mostly avoiding delicate Christological problems. One must attribute it to his typical Antiochene sobriety that he did not sing the praises of Mary along with the other Fathers, neither calling her θεοτόχος or ἀνθρωποτόχος.

5. But Theodore of Mopsuestia has a place in doctrinal development, in as much as he drew certain consequences from the dangerous principles of his teacher, Diodore. Like Chrysostom a pupil of the rhetorician Libanius, Theodore became the greatest exegete of the Antiochene school through his commentaries on practically the whole of the Bible. The accusation that in his concern for the literal sense he was merely following the rabbinic tradition (Leontius of Byzantium, *Adv. Nestorium et Eutychem,* 3, 15, ἰουδαϊκῶς) does not really do him justice, as may be seen from his Christological interpretation of at least four Psalms (2, 8, 44, 109). Nevertheless, an exaggerated critical approach brought him to deny several books of both Testaments canonical rank because of his too exclusive application of the literal sense, as in Job or the Song of Solomon. In the Christological question he succeeded in working out clearly for the first time against the Apollinarians the teaching on the two natures in Christ, defined in 451 (Christ is both Logos and man, not merely Logos and flesh). But his assertion that the human person was neces-

sary for the perfection of the human nature was bound to cause offence later. This would lead to the assertion of two persons. But as the Logos "dwells" in the man Jesus (ἐνοικεῖ), in view of this union (συνάφεια), he speaks of one person (*De Incarnatione*, I, 8). In his lifetime, his theology remained unchallenged. When Cyril of Alexandria wrote against him, and the Second Council of Constantinople condemned his writings along with the "Three Chapters" in 553, it seems to have been due more to his inadequate terminology, leading to misunderstandings, than to any professed intention of his teaching.

6. Similarly, Theodore's pupil Nestorius, because of whose teaching the tension between the followers of the Antiochene and the Alexandrian school turned into open strife, was probably orthodox in his intentions. By his Antiochene training he was compelled to oppose the formula that was accepted by Cyrill in Alexandria (μία φύσις τοῦ θεοῦ λόγου σεσαρκωμένου) which was ascribed to Athanasius, though it derives actually from Apollinarius. It is valid if φύσις is taken concretely as a being with its own proper activity. But then we should translate it not as "nature" but as "unity of being". But if — as at Antioch — φύσις is understood as nature in the abstract sense, the formula can only be rejected as monophysite. To avoid the error of mingling (κρᾶσις) the godhead and the humanity of the Logos into one nature, Nestorius always emphasized the integrity of the two natures in Christ, though he tried hard to avoid the notion of "two Sons". However, he did not succeed in showing clearly how the distinct natures (φύσεις) could be combined in a personal unity. His doctrine of the "one πρόσωπον" in Christ, in which the two "nature-πρόσωπα" of the humanity and godhead are united κατ' εὐδοκίαν, does not exclude a merely moral union of the natures. The main occasion for the flaring up of the conflict was his proposal to replace the title of θεοτόκος for Mary with χριστοτόκος, to make clear that Mary did not give birth to the divinity but only the man inseparably joined to the divinity. To describe the full reality of the human nature Nestorius spoke expressly of Jesus "learning obedience" and becoming perfect, whence the accusation that he was "Adoptianist" in holding that the Son became Son by divine approval. Here the Antiochene theology also touched upon the problems involved in Pelagianism, since to say that the human will can merit divine approval is to overestimate the capacities of human nature. It must also be remembered that along with theological reasons there were also rivalries in Church politics between the Patriarchates of Alexandria and Constantinople where Nestorius had become bishop. Both contributed to Nestorius's condemnation.

7. Nestorius was most ably defended by Theodoret of Cyrrhus, who, though he is difficult to place in the ranks of the Antiochene tradition, was surely stamped by it. Without ever fully accepting the teaching of Nestorius (which allowed him to disown his affinity with Nestorius at Chalcedon and thus to take part in the Council as an "orthodox teacher"), he nevertheless opposed Cyril's condemnation of Nestorius. It is probably through his efforts that in 433 a compromise formula was accepted by both parties. He appealed with success to Pope Leo I on the occasion of his deposition by the "Robber Synod" (449). Theodoret sums up in his extensive exegetical works the achievements of the Antiochene school in a way which characterizes him as the last representative of a venerable tradition. After him began the work of the compilers and the composers of *catenae,* a clear sign of the end of a creative period. Traces of the great school of Diodore are visible as late as the end of the 5th century in Edessa in Northern Mesopotamia.

See also *Alexandrian School of Theology, Arianism, Aristotelianism, Jesus Christ* III, *Judaism* I, *Nestorianism, Modalism.*

BIBLIOGRAPHY. F. Loofs, *Nestorius and His Place in the History of the Christian Doctrine* (1914); F. Loofs, *Paulus von Samosata* (1924); V. Schultze, *Antiocheia* (1930); G. Bardy, *Recherches sur Lucien d'Antioche* (1936); R. V. Sellers, *Two Ancient Christologies* (1940); J. Guillet, "Les exégèses d'Alexandrie et d'Antioche", *RSR* 34 (1947), pp. 257–302; E. R. Hardy and C. C. Richardson, *Christology of the Later Fathers* (1954); A. Grillmeier and H. Bacht, eds., *Das Konzil von Chalkedon. Geschichte und Gegenwart,* I–II (1951–4); J. Quasten, *Patrology,* II (1953), pp. 121 ff.; F. A. Sullivan, *The Christology of Theodore of Mopsuestia* (1956); H. Diepen, *Douze dialogues de Christologie ancienne* (1960).

Friedrich Normann

ANTISEMITISM

A. CONCEPT

Antisemitism is a very wide term, popularized by Wilhelm Marr in Germany since 1879 and then passing into other languages. It means in fact being anti-Jewish. The term is inexact since it does not refer to all Semites, which would include the Arabs, but only designates opposition to Jews, for religious, national or racial reasons. Antisemitism takes the form of 1) hostile popular sentiment and demonstrations, 2) discriminatory legislation, 3) expulsion and 4) extermination. Different forms of antisemitism are often combined.

B. HISTORY

1. *Pre-Christian antiquity.* As an unfriendly attitude towards Jews, Antisemitism is as old as the Jewish people, since any ethnic group with an outstanding individuality which embarrasses others, and any community that claims distinctive values, will be disliked, especially the Jews, who claimed to be God's chosen people and insisted on their own religious law. In the stricter sense, antisemitism did not appear until the Jewish dispersal (diaspora, *galūt*). The first typical representative of anti-Jewish prejudice was the Persian Haman who complained of the Jews as "a people scattered abroad and dispersed, whose laws are different from those of the rest of the world and who do not keep the king's laws" (Est 3:8). The first instance of anti-Jewish religious persecution in the diaspora was the destruction of the temple of the Jewish military colony on the Egyptian island of Elephantine in the Nile in 410 B.C. A religious war broke out when Antiochus Epiphanes (175–164 B.C.) tried to force the Jews to worship heathen gods. The revolt of the Maccabees saved Judaism and allowed the Jewish State to develop according to its religious laws. A pogrom against the Jewish community in Alexandria was engineered by the governor Avilius Flaccus in A.D. 38 when the Jews refused to set up statues of the emperor in their synagogues. Antisemitism in antiquity was grounded in a) *natural jealousy,* inasmuch as Greeks considered Hellenistic settlements Greek territory and thought of the Jews as intruders, and b) *religious differences,* occasioned by the Jewish claim of exclusivity.

Despite the fundamental incompatibility of Judaism with heathen religions, the Roman State recognized it as a *religio licita* because, unlike Christianity, it was a national religion. With the fall of Jerusalem in A.D. 70, Judaism lost not only its political support but also its religious centre. With the conversion of the temple tax into the *fiscus iudaicus* for Jupiter Capitolinus the first tax on Judaism was introduced. The Roman emperors, especially Hadrian, sought to hinder Jewish missions by legislation which forbade circumcision and the conversion of slaves to Judaism.

2. *Christian antiquity.* Even the New Testament reflects the religious conflict between the followers of Christ and other movements within Judaism. Until the Jewish war of A.D. 67–70, Christians understood themselves as the "true Israel" but stressed their continuity with Judaism. After the destruction of the temple and the expulsion of the Christian community from the synagogue the early Church saw itself as the "new Israel" and the continuity between Judaism and Christianity was broken. As time passed since the coming of Jesus, antipathy between the early Christian community and the Jews increased, so that John could depict them as the representatives of the godless world. True, the apostle Paul with his promise that all Israel would be saved (Rom 11:25–32) helped to foster toleration of Jews in the early Church and in the Middle Ages, but on the other hand his terminology with regard to the law and his theological depreciation of Judaism served again and again as an arsenal for anti-Jewish polemics. The anti-Jewish statements of the New Testament — to be understood as a quarrel between brothers — were all the more readily interpreted in a strictly hostile sense as Jewish Christianity, as early as the second century, shrank into numerical insignificance in comparison with gentile Christianity. In the Constantinian age Christianity took on the role of a State religion, on whose behalf older anti-Jewish laws were revived and enlarged, under Constantine, Theodosius II and Justinian. The Jews were reduced to second-class citizens and every attempt to propagate the Jewish religion was penalized. This development was aided by the anti-Jewish polemic in patristic writings.

3. *From the Middle Ages till Emancipation.* The Middle Ages were characterized by repeated efforts to identify Church and State. In such a view of society, heretics, Jews and pagans had no place. Heretics were considered culpable deserters — Thomas Aquinas compared them with counterfeiters — and were therefore severely persecuted, especially by the Inquisition. Pagans were outside the Christian world and so did not fall under the Inquisition. As regards the Jews, their common grounds with Christianity as given in the Scriptures were emphasized. In so far as Jews had never been Christians, heresy laws did not apply to them. But, according to the Dominican Inquisitor Bernard Gui (d. 1331), they came under the competence of the inquisitorial court when they were apostates from the Christian faith or had attempted to convert Christians to Judaism. The Dominican Inquisitor Nicholas Eymerich (d. 1399) wanted them to be tried by the Inquisition if they denied truths of faith enunciated in the Old Testament. Because of Paul's promise of salvation for all Israel, the Jews were tolerated in the Middle Ages, but had to accept many restrictive measures. With the growing influence of ecclesiastical on civil law in the late Middle Ages, the position of the Jews worsened: a) legally (tax for imperial protection, exclusion from civil office), b) economically (exclusion from the guilds, laws against usury), c) socially (the wearing of a badge — Fourth Lateran Council; restriction to ghettos since the Council of Basle). The legal restrictions were accompanied by demonstrations on the part of the Christian populace, provoked by religious fanaticism which broke out in connection with the crusades (first great pogrom, 1096), and then by legends of Jewish desecration of the Eucharist and of ritual murder, which multiplied from the thirteenth century on, by legends of the poisoning of wells after the outbreak of the Black Death in 1348, as also by anti-Jewish sermons. Although the Popes repeatedly spoke out against the accusation of ritual murder (e.g., Innocent IV, 1247, and later Gregory X, Paul III), they were powerless to stem the rumours. The forced conversion of Jews in Spain, introduced by the crown, made the converts, sometimes contemptuously called Marranos, suspect to Christians. Towards the end of the 15th century the antipathy to the Marranos

was so strong that religious orders began to enact laws to exclude neophytes. The Reformed Churches did not ease in any way the disabilities of the Jews.

4. *From Emancipation to the present.* The leaders of the Enlightenment thought the legal position of the Jews unfitting and made efforts to integrate them into their environment. After the French Revolution the ghettos were abolished but were partially reinstated after restoration of the monarchy; the last ghetto in Europe was the one in Rome, which lasted until 1870, the dissolution of the Papal States. The Enlightenment was not concerned to preserve Jewish identity: this would have hindered integration. Legal equality of Jews with non-Jews came into effect only by degrees, especially where the movement contrary to the Enlightenment, Romanticism, propagated the notion of the "Christian" State, which led to unwillingness to admit Jews to civil posts. They were therefore restricted mostly to the liberal professions, and that gave anti-Jewish elements a pretext for polemics against the confiscation of this sector of the economy. The release from the isolated world of the ghetto led to a crisis within Judaism. Until then religion and nationality had been identical to the Jew. In the 19th century, however, Judaism was often understood exclusively as a religious confession and the average Jew sought full identity with the world around him. The rejection of the attempt led other Jews to take more radical views. Religion ceased to be their natural homeland. Then the radical criticism of traditional faith also made the Jews suspect to non-Jews and aroused the prejudice that Jews exercised deleterious influence on the life of the spirit. Christians of all confessions subscribed to this prejudice. With the decline of the influence of Christian faith on public thought, anti-Jewish sentiment actually gained new strength. It appealed to a) *nationalistic motives,* especially where a Jewish minority was strong enough to lead a national life, as in eastern Europe, and b) *racial motives* supported by pseudo-scientific investigations and allegations, especially by the *Essai sur l'inégalité des races humaines* of the French writer, Arthur de Gobineau (d. 1882), with its philosophy of history and racial theories. His view of the superiority of the Aryan

race exercised great influence, especially in Germany, in association with "social" Darwinism. National Socialism deduced the consequences which led to the systematic extermination of six million Jews. For the first time the extermination of Jews appeared as a policy of State.

C. ECCLESIASTICAL CONDEMNATION

In 1894 the papal secretary of state, Cardinal Rampolla, warned Viennese Christian Socialists to avoid Antisemitism even in a watered-down form. It was expressly condemned by Rome on 25 March 1928 (cf. *AAS* 20 [1928], p. 104). More important than other episcopal and papal statements, however, is Vatican II's "Declaration on the Relationship of the Church to Non-Christian Religions", in which Antisemitism is expressly condemned. The World Council of Churches in New Delhi, 1961, likewise condemned Antisemitism as incompatible with the teaching of Christ.

See also *Judaism, Old Testament History, Constantinian Era, Inquisition I, Enlightenment.*

BIBLIOGRAPHY. *Encyclopaedia Judaica,* II, cols. 956–1104; *Jüdisches Lexikon,* I, cols. 331–371; H. Coudenhove-Kalergi, *Das Wesen des Antisemitismus* (1901; 5th ed., 1935); J. Parkes, *Antisemitism* (1964); M. Simon, *Verus Israel,* Bibliothèque des Écoles françaises d'Athènes et de Rome 166 (1948); J. Isaac, *Genèse de L'Antisémitisme* (1956); H. Arendt, *Origins of Totalitarianism* (2nd ed., 1958); P. Massing, *Vorgeschichte des politischen Antisemitismus,* Frankfurter Beiträge zur Soziologie (1959); P. Pulzer, *The Rise of Political Antisemitism in Germany and Austria* (1964); J. Oesterreicher, *Racisme—Antisémitisme—Antichristianisme* (1943); L. Poliakow, *The History of Antisemitism* (1965); E. H. Flannery, *The Anguish of the Jews* (1965).

Willehad Paul Eckert

APOCALYPTIC

A. GENERAL NOTIONS

In the Greek of the Septuagint and of the New Testament the verb ἀποκαλύπτω (Hebrew *gālāh,* Aramaic *gᵉlā'*) means "to reveal", and the noun ἀποκάλυψις means "revelation". Apocalyptic is the form taken by the literature of revelation in Judaism from the 2nd century B.C. on. By its very success, it had a marked influence on the literary expression of revelation in the NT, and it retained a considerable place in early Christianity, while it suffered a decline in rabbinical Judaism.

The revelation furnished by this literature bears on all the mysteries which are inaccessible to man's natural knowledge (to "flesh and blood", Mt 16:17): God alone can give knowledge of them through his Spirit and his Wisdom (Dan 2:19, 28; 5:11–14; 1 Cor 2:10–11). Several regions may be distinguished. a) The mysteries of God, of the heavenly world where he resides, of the angelic hosts who surround him, of the armies of demons who fight against him. From this point of view, apocalyptic provides a literary expression for mysticism, Jewish and Christian (cf. 2 Cor 12:1–4; *Ascension of Isaiah,* 8–11; *Apocalypse of Abraham,* 15–20), and for angelology and demonology, which in apocalyptic is closely linked with the history of salvation (*Ethiopian Enoch,* 1–6; Rev 12). b) The mysteries of the origins of the world and of the government of creation by the Wisdom of God. This theme gives rise to the cosmological passages in certain books, which describe the world of earth and the infernal abysses (*Eth. Enoch,* 17–19; 22–26) or the functioning of the stars on which the calendar is based (*Eth. Enoch,* 72–82). c) The mysteries of the divine plan which governs the course of history: here apocalyptic takes over from both the theological reflection of the ancient writers of sacred history and the eschatology of the prophets. d) The mystery of the destiny of the individual (Wis 2:22): here the texts reflect both collective eschatology (c) and the descriptions of heaven (a) and hell (b). Apocalyptic covers therefore a very wide field. This is why, apart from the works which are directly concerned with it, it also influenced works in other fields as soon as they took up matters with which apocalyptic was concerned.

B. ORIGIN AND DEVELOPMENT OF THE LITERARY FORM

The evolution of prophetic literature. After 586 B.C. prophetic literature undergoes notable changes. a) It had always contained an element of mysticism: symbolic visions describing the supernatural world (1 Kg 22:12–22; Amos 9:1–4; Is 6). In Ezekiel this literary form is given pride of place

(Ezek 1), to depict the judgment of God on Jerusalem (Ezek 9–10) as well as the final resurrection of Israel (Ezek 37:1–14) and the glory of the new Jerusalem (Ezek 40–48). The message of Zechariah is presented systematically as a series of visions in which an angel acts as interpreter. This type of structure is to some extent conventional, and the convention became a constant element in apocalyptic writing. b) The horizon of the prophetic message was always a "latter time" (Is 9:1 [8:23]), the "latter days" (Is 2.2) which was to include the judgment of all sinners and the salvation of the remnant of the just. The judgment evoked spontaneously the thought of a cosmic cataclysm (Jer 4:23–26), and salvation that of the garden of paradise (Hos 2:20–24; Is 11:6–9). History thus came to a close in a final act which was still part of it and brought it to its fulfilment. But after the exile, the portrayal of the close of history came to stand more and more on its own, in a series of anonymous texts which sought to sustain Jewish hopes by "eschatological" promises (Is 4:4–5; 24–27; 30:19–26; 34–35; 59:15–20; 63:1–6; 65:1–25; 66:5–16; Ezek 38–39; Joel 3–4; Zech 12:1 – 13:6; 14). It is an abuse of terminology to call these texts apocalypses. But it is true that a number of essentially apocalyptic themes are accentuated strongly: the final judgment executed by God himself, the opposition of the Two Cities (Is 24 ff.); the inauguration of the reign of God in which the Davidic Messiah seems to play no part; the entrance of the just into a world transformed, the "new heavens and the new earth" (Is 65:17).

The psychological climate. It is quite easy to discern the psychological situation in which this literary evolution took place. It is the feverish expectation which characterizes the times of crisis which the post-exilic community lived through. The disappointment which follows the return of the first exiles, between 515 and 440, the political upheavals of the 4th century with their inevitable repercussions on Judaism, arouse feelings of eschatological anguish (cf. Ps 44; 74; 79), which are brought to a climax by the bloody conflict with the totalitarian pagan empire of Antiochus Epiphanes (170–164 B.C.). Neither the legalism bequeathed by Ezra to the Jewish theocracy nor the reflective wisdom of the rising schools of sages

are enough to satisfy this passionate expectation. And "there is no longer any prophet" to sustain the people's courage (Ps 74:9; 1 Macc 4:46), for prophecy as practised of old is now decried (Zech 13:2–6). But the Scriptures are searched in the hope of learning when and how "the end" will come (Dan 9:1–2). This is the climate in which the eschatological message is given a new form of expression, that of a supernatural wisdom coming from meditation of the Scriptures and revealing the divine secrets to the sorely tried believers. At the height of the Maccabean crisis, apocalyptic produces its first masterpieces, with Daniel (especially Dan 2; 4 – 5; 7 – 12) and the most ancient portions of Enoch (*The Book of Dreams,* 83–90; *The Apocalypse of Weeks,* 93; 91:12–17).

Foreign influences. At every stage of history, the sacred writings succeeded in assimilating elements borrowed from neighbouring cultures to propound its own message. Ezekiel clearly has recourse to Mesopotamian symbolism (Ezek 1). The angelology and demonology of Tobit makes use of Iranian elements (Tob 3:8; 12:14). And apocalyptic was born in an environment where an Iranian and Babylonian syncretism encountered Hellenistic civilization. Judaism found itself at the meeting-place of many cultures and turned them to its advantage. This is clearly proved by the undeniable contacts of the Enoch legend with Mesopotamian traditions and by the references in Daniel to the Babylonian techniques of interpreting dreams (Dan 2; 4; 7) and presages (Dan 5). The oriental diaspora must have played an important part here. But the Judaism of Palestine itself was certainly open to influences from surrounding Hellenism, even while it was struggling to save its religious originality. In apocalyptic, the influence of Iranian eschatology is a possibility which must be reckoned with; the influence of Hellenism is restricted to marginal elements. Whatever their contribution, apocalyptic was born of the effort to oppose the authentic revelation contained in the Scriptures, bestowed on Israel by the prophets, to the pagan literature of revelation which was powerless to know the divine secrets (Dan 2:28; 5:7–17). To forge for itself means of expression, it drew without scruple on a set of widely used symbols which stemmed from the ancient mythologies of

Greece and the Orient. Thus traces of the mythical combat between Marduk and Tiamat can still be seen in Dan 7 and Apoc 12.

C. The Standard Features of Apocalyptic Writing

In spite of the wide variety of forms, which correspond to the diversity of the subjects treated, certain general characteristics recur, in varying degrees, nearly everywhere.

Pseudonymity. The classical prophets related their own personal visions. The complements added to their books after the exile were guarded by the veil of anonymity. But the writers of apocalypse had recourse to borrowed names, chosen from among the heroes of ancient times: Enoch, Abraham, Isaiah or some other prophet, Baruch, Ezra, Daniel and so on. So too non-canonical Christian writings were to invoke the authority of Peter, Paul, John and so on. The conventional spokesmen chosen by the authors always appear as the typical prophet — who becomes the typical apostle in the NT — whom God charges to transmit his message to men. The message envisages of course the contemporaries of the author, but it is given an esoteric appearance, not because it is reserved for a small circle of initiates, but because it is presented as something reserved for future times. In the NT, however, prophecy passes over directly to the apocalyptic style without having recourse to pseudonymity (so Mk 13 and par.; 1 Thess 4:15–17; 1 Cor 15:24–28, 52–53; Revelation of St. John).

The prophetic view of history. The apocalyptic writers were mainly concerned with the working out of God's plan in history in the perspective of the last judgment and a trans-historical eschatology. By letting an ancient seer speak for them, they take their stand in the distant past, thus gaining a vantage point from which they can survey at a glance considerable periods of history (e.g., Dan 7–8; 10–12). When their view of human history is compared to the theology of the prophets and the writers of sacred history, some notable differences emerge.

a) It underlines further, in a one-sided manner, the divine causality which is the sovereign master of events. These take place inevitably, as the realization of the divine plan inscribed on the "heavenly tablets". The existence of a divine judgment proves indeed that men are really free, but their liberty is exercised within the limits assigned to it by God. As a result past history appears to be a merely mechanical process, which guarantees in its own way the certainty of its eschatological consummation. This climax is always felt psychologically as imminent: once history has reached the crest formed by events contemporary to the author, divine judgment and the salvation of the just follow at once (Dan 7:23–27; 11:21 – 12:3).

b) Even more than in the classical prophets, history is a battle-field where God, his angels and his people are opposed to all the demonic forces of whom sinners and the pagan nations are the tools on this earth. This spiritual dualism results in two worlds being opposed to one another: the present world, which is delivered over to the power of evil and so is doomed to the wrath of God and the final catastrophe; the world to come, in which a transfigured universe will rejoin the heavenly realities and the just receive the reward for their sufferings. Thus the eschatology of the prophets undergoes a radical transformation, and the problem of individual retribution is solved on a new plane (Dan 12:1–3; Wis 4:20 – 5:23).

c) The symbolic language. The literary expression of the message is a tissue of symbols. The ancient Scriptures are exploited systematically and the images they use are often combined in unexpected ways. The Revelation of St. John offers good examples of this. The conventional presentation of doctrine in the form of dreams and visions often involves symbolic descriptions of the supernatural world, and even earthly realities are hidden behind masks: in Dan 7 as in Rev, the pagan empires appear as beasts. To create this world of imagery which they conjure up, the writers draw freely on the odds and ends of oriental literature. Landscapes, plants, animals, precious stones, and stars are endowed with peculiar meanings which allow the author's thought to be rendered in code-language. The symbolism of numbers is not omitted. These enigmatic pictures may have been clear for his contemporaries, but it is sometimes difficult for us to find the key. On the whole, nothing is more artificial than the apocalyptic style when it is employed without due measure, but its intriguing symbols lend it an undeniable poetic force.

D. The Extent of Apocalyptic

Old Testament and Judaism. This form of literature, which was evolved among the Hassideans during the Maccabean crisis, enjoyed great popularity about the beginning of the Christian era. The Essenes employed the style, and the caves of Qumran have yielded manuscripts of Enoch and Jubilees, and of other works hitherto unknown. It does not seem that the Pharisees objected to it at first: the Syrian Baruch and 4 Esdras seem to derive from Pharisee circles. Later on, many apocalyptic works of Essene or other origin were proscribed, though texts dealing with Jewish mysticism were spared *(Hebrew Enoch)*. The surviving apocalypses were preserved by Christian scribes, translated into various languages.

The New Testament and ancient Christianity. In the New Testament the eschatological perspective has been perceptibly modified. The new world has been already inaugurated in Jesus Christ and in the Church. The Son of Man has appeared in history and awaits the moment of the Parousia to return again. The kingdom of God has begun and the new Jerusalem is present in the Church. It is not surprising therefore that the Christian revelation should be essentially an apocalypse (Mt 16:17; Gal 1:16; Rev). But a last revelation was still hoped for, in which the heavenly realities would descend upon earth (1 Jn 3:3; Col 3:4; Rev, etc.). The apocryphal NT contains several apocalypses which describe this event. The literary form is still found in the *Pastor of Hermas,* and it is perpetuated by the writings of visionaries in all ages, as well as in such works as the *Divine Comedy.*

See also *Revelation, Mysticism, Judaism, Old Testament Books* V, *Apocrypha, Eschatologism, Dualism, Reign of God.*

BIBLIOGRAPHY. M.-J. Lagrange, *Le messianisme chez les Juifs* (1909), pp. 37–135; L. Ginzberg, "Some Observations on the Attitude of the Synagogue towards the Apocalyptic Eschatological Writings", *JBL* 41 (1922), pp. 115–36; G. F. Moore, *Judaism in the First Centuries of the Christian Era,* I (1927), pp. 125–216, and II (1930), pp. 40–60; M.-J. Lagrange, *Le Judaïsme avant Jésus Christ* (1931); P. Volz, *Die Eschatologie der jüdischen Gemeinde* (1934); H. H. Rowley, *The Relevance of Apocalyptic. A Study of Jewish and Christian Apocalypses from Daniel to the Revelation* (1944; 3rd ed., 1963); S. B. Frost, *Old Testament Apocalyptic. Its Origin and Growth* (1952); J. Bloch, *On the Apocalyptic in Judaism* (1952); S. Mowinckel, *He That Cometh. The Messianic Hope in the Old Testament and in the Time of Jesus,* trans. by S. W. Anderson (1956); F. M. Cross, *The Ancient Library of Qumran and Modern Studies* (1958), pp. 147–51; B. Vawter, "Apocalyptic. Its Relation to Prophecy", *CBQ* 22 (1960), pp. 33–46; D. S. Russell, *Method and Message of Jewish Apocalyptic* (1964).

Pierre Grelot

APOCATASTASIS

The Greek term apocatastasis, like the corresponding verb, is used to express the cure of a disease, the return of goods taken, of a hostage or of an exile, the restoration of a State, or the return of the stars to their previous positions. The restoration need not be a necessary process, it may be the fulfilment of a free promise. The astronomical sense forms part of the philosophical doctrine of the "great year" or of the "eternal return": the return of the stars to their former positions marks the beginning of a new cycle in the history of the world which reproduces the one that went before.

The NT uses the word in various senses. It denotes the spiritual renewal, expected from Elias and effected by John the Baptist, in preparation for the coming of the Messiah. The key text is to be found in the discourse of Peter which follows the cure of the lame man at the Beautiful Gate of the temple. The glorious return of Christ will take place in "the time for establishing *(apocatastasis)* all that God spoke by the mouth of his holy prophets from of old" (Acts 3:20). Does it refer to a return (a spiritualized restoration) of Israel, or to the realization of the prophecies foretelling the eschatological glory of Jerusalem (Is 60)? The doctrine is also found in other texts: Rom 5:18, 11:32; 1 Cor 15:22–28; Eph 1:10; Col 1:20; Jn 17:21–23. Christ brings about the final unity of humanity and so transmits it to his Father.

The term was employed by the Valentinian Gnostics, and then given the following interpretation by Origen. At the end of time humanity will regain the unity in Christ it had at the beginning, following the hypothesis of the pre-existence of souls. There are three aspects which could be considered heretical here: the final dissolution of the glorious body which makes pure spirits of the saved; the return to grace of the demons and the damned; a pantheistic conception of union with God. In fact, though certain texts of Origen contain the seeds of these three conceptions, there are others which imply the contrary, and taking into account the hypothetical character of his doctrine of pre-existence, it is difficult to accuse him of having clearly upheld a definitely unorthodox doctrine of apocatastasis; it is also difficult to measure the degree of assent he gives to it, for it is scarcely reconcilable with other points of his doctrine. The doctrine of apocatastasis of Gregory of Nyssa can be similarly explained. A clearly heretical form of apocatastasis is only to be found among the later Origenists, such as Evagrius of Pontus and Stephen bar Sudaili.

The problem is not entirely foreign to contemporary theology. The exegesis of the consequences of the betrayal of Judas which Barth gives in his *Dogmatik* seems to imply some form of universal salvation: Barth affirms that if we assert the necessity of apocatastasis, we are not respecting the freedom of divine grace, but that by denying it we do it still less justice. In another passage about the goodness of God, he asks if Col 1:19 does not suggest that the divine plan is actually to save all men. Many Protestant theologians, as, for example, W. Michaelis, have tried to prove that apocatastasis is demanded by the Bible.

According to certain passages in the Pauline letters, the will of God is to save all men and to reconcile the world in his Son. The vision of Teilhard de Chardin allows the thought of the apostle to be developed in the modern context of the evolution of man on all levels. But there is a second factor which Barth, as a disciple of Calvin, does not take into account: the freedom of man has to respond to the freedom of God by accepting his salvific will. Refusal on the part of man constitutes sin. As to whether human refusal can be so total and conscious as to incur the definitive loss of salvation, the NT does not allow us to rule out the possibility. But does this ever really happen? The Church, which invokes its infallibility in the canonization of the saints, has never done so with regard to the damned. We cannot know with certainty if even one human soul does in fact go to hell.

Man's free will holds such a place in Origen's thought as a result of his polemic with the Gnostics that one cannot consider his doctrine of apocatastasis as anything else than a magnificent theology of hope. The goodness of God will in the end triumph over man's evil will by converting his free will. To treat his thought on this point as a dogmatic affirmation, as did his opponents, would be to make him contradict other equally essential points of his theology.

See also *Origenism, Stoicism, Gnosticism, Pantheism.*

BIBLIOGRAPHY. A. Oepke, "ἀποκατάστασις", *TWNT,* I (1933; E. T., 1964), pp. 386–92; J. Jeremias, "Ἠλ(ε)ίας", *TWNT,* II (1935; E. T., 1967), pp. 930–43; J. Dey, Παλιγγενεσία (1937); J. Daniélou, "L'apocatastase chez S. Grégoire de Nysse", *RSR* 30 (1940), pp. 328–47; E. R. Redepenning, *Origenes,* II (1946), esp. pp. 379–454; W. Michaelis, *Die Versöhnung des Alls* (1950); H. Gross, *Die Idee des ewigen und allgemeinen Weltfriedens im alten Orient und im Alten Testament* (1956); S. Mowinckel, *He That Cometh* (1956), pp. 125–54, 311–21; H. Cornélis, "Les fondements cosmologiques de l'eschatologie d'Origène", *RSPT* 43 (1959), pp. 38–51, 201–48; H. Schumacher, *Das biblische Zeugnis von der Versöhnung des Alls* (1959); E. Staehlin, *Die Wiederbringung aller Dinge* (1960).

Henri Crouzel

APOCRYPHA

I. Introduction. II. Old Testament Apocrypha: A. Narrative Works. B. "Testaments". C. Chants and Prayers. D. Apocalypses. III. New Testament Apocrypha: A. Gospels. B. Acts of Apostles. C. Letters. D. Apocalypses. IV. The Significance of the Apocrypha.

I. Introduction

The "apocrypha" were understood by the ancient Church as secret "hidden" (= ἀπόκρυφος) books, in contrast to those which were publicly acknowledged and used by the Church (cf. Origen, *in Mt,* X, 18, on Mt 13:57, *GCS,* XL, p. 24). Their claim to stem from prophets or apostles being implausible, they were, with a few exceptions, excluded from public worship and theological debate (cf. Origen, *Comment. ser. 28 in Mt,* 23:37, *GCS,* XXXVIII, p. 51). The absence of tradition about their prophetic or apostolic origin and the presence of fables in them made them suspect (Augustine, *De civitate Dei*, XV, 23). Further, those of Christian origin often came from heretical circles, which also explains their rejection by the Church (Hegesippus in Eusebius, *Hist. eccles.*, IV, 22, 9; Irenaeus, *Adv. haer.*, I, 20, 1). Hence the present Catholic usage is to designate as apocryphal any book whose religious content and supposed author might suggest that it was part of Scripture, when in fact it has been excluded from the canon by the tradition of the Church. This tradition presents a peculiar theological problem, because it was based to some extent on the uncertainty surrounding their prophetic or apostolic origin. But the same uncertainty prevails about many of the books received into the canon, now that historical and literary criticism has examined their supposedly prophetic or apostolic authorship. That the distinction made by the ancient Church between canonical and apocryphal books is still maintained is because Catholics are convinced that the verdict of the Church was not the result of purely human and fallible considerations, much less of mere chance, but a decision taken under the guidance of the Holy Spirit.

Though the line of demarcation between biblical and apocryphal books is clear by virtue of the Church's determination of the canon, it is not so easy to distinguish between apocryphal and other ancient books of the same type. It seems best at the moment not to extend the notion too widely and we shall discuss here only the well-known apocrypha which throw most light on Judaism at the beginning of the Christian era and on early Christianity. Hence we also omit the writings from Qumran, which include in fact apocryphal books, some of which have been known for a long time. But the most frequently quoted and the most instructive texts like the *Rule of the Community*, the *War Scroll*, the *Hymns* and the *Damascus Documents* are not of the apocryphal type. For similar reasons the Sibylline books are also omitted.

OT apocrypha are distinguished from NT apocrypha according to whether in form (prophetic book, gospel, acts of apostles) and content (Jewish or Christian) they approximate to the Old or New Testament. Many "Old Testament" apocrypha have been revised by Christians and have reached us only in the revised form, or are in fact of Christian origin, though Jewish material is used. And a distinction between Protestant

and Catholic usage must be noted with regard to the OT. The books which Catholics call deutero-canonical (Tob, Jud, Ecclus, Wis, etc.) are termed apocrypha by Protestants, while the apocrypha of the OT strictly speaking are called pseudepigrapha; the term apocrypha is used by both Protestants and Catholics for 3 and 4 Esdr, 3 and 4 Macc.

II. Old Testament Apocrypha

A. Narrative Works

1. *The Book of Jubilees*, or "Little Genesis", called in the *Damascus Document* (16:3) the "Book of the Divisions of the Times according to their Jubilees and their Weeks", gives the history of the world from its creation till the law of Sinai (Gen 1 – Exod 12), in "Jubilees", that is, in seven times seven weeks of years (periods of 49 years), whence the name of the book. It tells how an angel, at God's command, read out to Moses on Sinai the events recorded on the heavenly tablets, while Moses wrote them down. The narrative follows the Bible, but is Haggadic in type, with additions and alterations from the unknown Jewish author. It inculcates observance of the law, which is supposed to have been in force from the beginning along with Jewish feasts and customs. The fact that the book is based on a solar calendar, the effort to separate Israel from all that is impure and the antiquity attributed to the Law all point to affinity with the community of Qumran. The original Hebrew probably dates from the second half of the 2nd century B.C., but survives only in some fragments found at Qumran. The book as a whole exists only in an Ethiopian version which in turn is based on a lost Greek translation. There are Greek and Syriac quotations and a large portion in a Latin version.

2. *The Third Book of Esdras* (RSV, 1 Esdr) is found in the Septuagint as Esdras A, the canonical Esdras (Ezra) and Nehemiah being combined as Esdras B. The name "3 Esdras" comes from the Vulgate, which counts the canonical Esdras and Nehemiah as 1 and 2 Esdras. It is a short book which gives part of the history of the temple of Jerusalem, its destruction and gradual re-building, with the return and work of Esdras. It appears to be a compilation mainly based on 2 Chr 35f., the whole of Esdras and Neh 7:72 –

8:13, but adds a large section of its own (3:1–5:3), describing a competition between the three bodyguards of Darius, one of whom was Zerubabel, who produced the prize essay and was then allowed to return to Jerusalem and re-build the temple. The book, which was probably in Greek from the start, may be dated to the second half of the 2nd century B.C. Many theologians of the ancient Church, like Cyprian, Basil and Augustine, treated it as a canonical book and appealed to it in quotations. But others like Origen, Athanasius, Cyril of Jerusalem, Epiphanius and Jerome did not consider it as authoritative. On account of its high standing in earlier times, the official Vulgate still prints it, though only in an appendix.

3. *3 Maccabees* is incorrectly so called, because it does not speak of the Maccabees, but describes how the king of Egypt, Ptolemy IV Philopator (221–204 B.C.) tried to enter the temple of Jerusalem after his victory over Antiochus III of Syria at Raphia, 217 B.C. He is prevented by God, and then starts to persecute the Jews of Alexandria, who are, however, saved miraculously. He is so impressed by the divine intervention that he becomes a protector of the Jews. The short book, written in Greek, is probably from Alexandria, at the end of the 1st century B.C.

4. *4 Maccabees* is a philosophical discourse on the mastery of passion by reason. The thesis is proved first philosophically, and then by examples from the history of Israel, special use being made of the famous martyrdom of Eleazar (2 Macc 6:18–31) and the seven brothers with their mother (2 Macc 7), at the hands of the Syrians. The Jewish author draws on popular Stoic philosophy to urge his people to obedience to God and his law. The book, written in Greek, possibly at Alexandria or Antioch, may come from the end of the 1st or the beginning of the 2nd century A.D.

5. A group of books are concerned with *Adam,* giving legends, sometimes quite poetical, of our first parents, their fall, repentance and death.

a) *The Life of Adam and Eve,* preserved in a Latin version of a Greek original.

b) A Greek book with the unsuitable title *The Apocalypse of Moses.* The two works coincide even verbally to a great extent, and probably stem from a Hebrew or Aramaic

edition of the material, presumably from the time of the Herodian temple (*c.* 20 B.C. to A.D. 70).

c) The so-called *Syriac Genizah* ("treasure chamber"), where the treasures of Paradise were preserved, is a history of the world from its beginning until Christ — a Christian work which made use of Jewish traditions.

d) A *Testament of Adam* composed of several parts, also known as the *Apocalypse of Adam,* containing a heavenly liturgy of the angels and other creatures, distributed over the hours of the day and night; also Adam's prophecies of Christ, with mention of the nine choirs of angels and their tasks.

6. *The Paralipomena of Jeremiah* (i.e., supplement to Jeremiah), also known as the *Remains of the Words of Baruch (Reliquiae verborum Baruch),* originally a Jewish work of uncertain date which was revised by a Christian editor perhaps in the first half of the 2nd century A.D. It is preserved in Greek and other languages. It recounts the activity of Jeremiah before and after the destruction of Jerusalem and also his death.

7. *Joseph and Asenath,* or the *Prayer of Asenath,* probably a purely Jewish-Hellenistic work, in Greek, without Christian revisions, may have been composed in Egypt in the last century B.C. or the 1st century A.D. Asenath (Gen 41:45), the daughter of an Egyptian priest, first refuses to marry Joseph because he is a foreigner from Canaan and the son of a shepherd. She is won by his beauty to confess the true God and accepts the marriage. The book, which is short, teaches chastity and love of enemies.

B. "TESTAMENTS"

1. *The Testaments of the Twelve Patriarchs.* Each of the sons of Jacob recounts his "testament", events from his life accompanied by moral exhortations and prophecies. The origin and date of the book, which is preserved in Greek and first mentioned by Origen (*In Jos. hom.,* XV, 6) are hotly debated. There is a certain affinity with the mentality of Qumran, though the work as a whole cannot be held to be Qumranite or Essene. Many scholars suppose a Jewish original, in Hebrew or Aramaic, composed between 200 B.C. and the fall of the temple in A.D. 70, which later underwent Christian interpolation. Others assume a Christian author

towards the end of the 2nd century who used a piece about Levi, the existence of which is certain since fragments of it were found at Qumran, as a model for the other testaments. Fragments of this *Testament of Levi,* which is not identical with that of the collection of the *Twelve Testaments,* exist in Aramaic, and there are fragments of a Hebrew Testament of Nephthali. But their relationship to the *Testaments of the Twelve Patriarchs* is uncertain.

2. *Other Testaments.*

a) A *Testament of Adam* (see above, A, 5 d).

b) A *Testament of Job,* a Jewish midrash on Job, preserved in a Greek paraphrase possibly of the 2nd or 3rd century A.D.

c) A *Testament of Abraham,* telling of his ascent to heaven, his return to earth and his death. From a Jewish original, possibly of the 1st or 2nd century A.D., it exists in a Greek Christian revision, in a longer and a shorter version.

d) A *Testament of Isaac,* telling of his journey into the other world and of his death, akin to the *Testament of Abraham.* It is known in a Christian revision in Coptic, Arabic and Ethiopian translations.

e) A *Testament of Moses* (see below, D. 2).

f) A *Testament of Solomon,* in Greek, of Jewish-Christian origin, perhaps from the 3rd or 4th century A.D.

C. Chants and Prayers

1. *Ps 151* is a short song in honour of David, in Hebrew, praising the shepherd, singer and king of Israel. It is also preserved in Greek in a very free translation, with the victory of David over Goliath added, and in Latin and Syriac versions dependent on the Greek. The poem, of which the original form was first discovered in a manuscript from the Dead Sea, possibly from the time of Herod, reflects in many ways the mentality of Qumran (cf. "the children of his covenant" at the end, a term not found in the OT but occurring in the *War Scroll,* 17, 8), but need not necessarily have originated there. It is not in the Hebrew Bible, whose limits were defined under Pharisee influence, but many Greek manuscripts and ancient versions of the canonical psalms contain it, in accordance with the Jewish view attested at Qumran. It was regarded as canonical by many Christian writers.

2. *The Psalms of Solomon* are eighteen chants, on various subjects, resembling the biblical psalms. They display at times a tense messianic expectation and are on the whole an example of Pharisee spirituality. They were composed in Hebrew in Palestine in the 1st century B.C., after the capture of Jerusalem by Pompey, 63 B.C., and are preserved in Greek and Syriac. The collection does not claim to derive from Solomon; it seems to have been ascribed to him only at a later date.

3. *The Odes of Solomon,* forty-two in number, of which Ode 2 is still missing, are preserved in Syriac; five are preserved also in Coptic, in the Gnostic work *Pistis Sophia,* and one, Ode 11, also in Greek. There is still no agreement as to their original language, Greek, Syriac (or Aramaic) or even Hebrew. The question of their place and date of origin is equally difficult. They were probably Christian-Gnostic works from the beginning, and not Christian works which were given a Gnostic revision. They date from the early 2nd century A.D. and were probably composed in Syria. Solomon is not the speaker in the Odes, which were possibly ascribed to him because they seemed to have some resemblance to the Psalms of Solomon and were grouped with them in Christian antiquity.

4. *The Prayer of Manasseh* is a noble and pious confession of sin and repentance, supposedly uttered by the once impious king Manasseh (7th century B.C.). It is an elaboration of the brief indications of 2 Chr 33:11–13, 18f. It was written in Greek, probably by a Hellenistic Jew. It is not clear when it was written. It is first mentioned in the *Syrian Didascalia* of the 3rd century A.D., but it may be from the 2nd or 1st century B.C., or from the Christian era. The *Prayer* was once highly esteemed, as is reflected in the fact that it is found in many editions of the Greek and Latin Bible, including the appendix to the official Vulgate.

D. Apocalypses

1. *The Books of Enoch* claim to be an account of visions and revelations received by the Enoch of Gen 5:21–24.

a) The *First Book of Enoch,* also called the *Ethiopian Enoch,* because preserved in its entirety only in an Ethiopian translation, was originally written in Hebrew or Aramaic. In its present form it is a collection of somewhat disparate apocalyptic matter from the last two centuries B.C. An introduction (chs. 1–5) is followed by descriptions of the angels, their fall and punishment (chs. 6–36), after which come the "Parables of Enoch", which treat of the coming Kingdom of God, the resurrection of the dead, the judgment, and the abodes of the blessed. They are interspersed with discussions of the angels, the flood, the mysteries of the starry regions and the processes of nature. As in Dan and more than in the NT, the figure of the "Son of Man" plays a certain role in these chapters (chs. 37–71). The book goes on to discuss astronomical questions, the sun and the moon, the winds and other atmospherical phenomena (chs. 72–82), then adds an outline of world history till the establishment of the messianic kingdom (chs. 83–90) and concludes with admonitions uttered by Enoch (chs. 91–105). The book has affinities with Essene thought and was obviously written in Palestine. It was held in high esteem in the early Christian Church and it is even quoted in the canonical Letter of St. Jude (Jude 14f., cf. *1 Enoch,* 1, 9). This letter also makes use of legends contained in the *First Book of Enoch,* but also found in other Jewish writings of the last centuries B.C.

b) The *Second Book of Enoch,* also known as the *Slavonic Enoch* because it is preserved only in a Slavonic translation, was probably written originally in Greek. It has affinities with *1 Enoch,* but does not depend on it. It exists in a longer and a shorter version, which recount Enoch's journey through the seven heavens and what he learned there about the angels, paradise and hell (chs. 1–21). Then come revelations which Enoch is supposed to have received about creation, the history of mankind until his own times, the flood and Noah's deliverance (chs. 22–38). Discourses of Enoch follow, containing doctrine and admonitions (chs. 39–66) and then his assumption into the highest heaven (chs. 67f.). The work seems to have been composed in the Jewish diaspora, possibly before A.D. 70, though in its present form it represents a Christian redaction.

2. *The Assumption of Moses.* The *Assumptio Mosis* is the Latin translation of a Greek testament of Moses. Here Moses prophesies the history of the Jewish people up to the time of the sons of Herod I, along with the general judgment and the coming of the Kingdom of God. This suggests that it was composed about the beginning of the 1st century A.D., probably in Palestine. It is impossible to say with certainty whether it was written originally in Greek or a Semitic language. The early Christian Church was acquainted with a book entitled the *Assumption* or the *Ascension* of Moses, of which the surviving testament is commonly supposed to be part. The question remains open. According to some early Christian theologians (Clement of Alexandria, *Adumbrationes in Epist. Judae;* Origen, *De Principiis,* III, 2, 1; Didymus, *In Epist. Judae Enarratio*), the *Assumptio Mosis* contained the legend of Michael's contest with the devil for the body of Moses, which is mentioned in the canonical Letter of St. Jude (v. 9).

3. *The Fourth Book of Esdras,* an apocalypse which enjoyed a wide circulation in antiquity, originally written in Hebrew and translated into Greek, is preserved only in (Christian) translations based on the Greek text, in Latin, Syriac, Ethiopian, Armenian and Arabic. It is a Jewish composition which has been added to in the Latin version. There are seven visions, in which Esdras receives revelations about religious matters through an angel, and then a number of allegorical images, in which a weeping woman represents Sion, an eagle Rome, a man from the sea the Messiah, concerning the miseries of Israel after the fall of Jerusalem in A.D. 70, which the Messiah is to remedy. The book, which has affinities with the *Syriac Apocalypse of Baruch,* was composed about A.D. 100 and incorporates a number of elements from an earlier date, especially from the 1st century A.D. It avoids exaggeration, shows deep religious feeling and was intended above all to console the Jews after the catastrophe of A.D. 70, which it sought to understand in the light of the coming world of justice and salvation. The book was highly esteemed in the ancient Church, and was quoted by many ecclesiastical writers. It is still printed in the appendix to the official Vulgate. Some texts from the Christian interpolations were adopted into the Roman liturgy, e.g., the introit versicle for Whit Tuesday (from 4 Esd 2:36f.), and especially the prayer for the faithful departed, "Requiem

aeternam dona eis, Domine, et lux perpetua luceat eis", which is modelled on 2:34f.

4. *The Apocalypse of Baruch.* Two apocalypses are extant under the name of Baruch, the disciple of Jeremiah (Jer 32:12–16; 43:6; 45:1–5): the *Syriac Apocalypse of Baruch,* so called because preserved only in Syriac, and a second known as the *Greek Apocalypse of Baruch,* after the language in which it is extant.

a) The *Syriac Apocalypse of Baruch* contains revelations supposedly granted to Baruch at the time of the destruction of Jerusalem by the Babylonians (6th century B.C.). The book falls into seven sections, in which Baruch is instructed about the fall of Jerusalem, the punishment which will finally overtake the pagans, the tribulations before the coming of the Messiah, the rule of the Messiah, the tribulations of the last days, the resurrection of the just, their eternal glory and the torments of the damned. Part of the instruction is given in allegorical imagery, in which black and white water represent Jewish history, lightning the Messiah. It ends with admonitions to Israel. Like *4 Esdras,* it seeks to console Israel by pointing away from the devastation of the Holy Land and Holy City by the Romans to evoke the future time of the coming of the Messiah. And it likewise tries to answer the questions raised about God's providence by the catastrophe. The book cannot have been written before A.D. 70, and possibly dates from a little after A.D. 100. The uncertainty with regard to the dating comes from the connection between the *Syriac Baruch* and *4 Esdras* and the impossibility of saying which is earlier. The Syriac is a translation from the Greek, but the work may have been written originally in a Semitic language.

b) The *Greek Apocalypse of Baruch,* which is also preserved in a shorter form in a Slavonic translation, contains revelations supposed to have been given to Baruch during his journey to the fifth heaven. He sees, for instance, the movement of the sun and moon (chs. 6–9) and the angels with baskets of flowers, which are the virtues of the just. They bring these to Michael, who is keeper of the keys of the kingdom of heaven (chs. 11f.). The book has contacts with the *Slavonic Enoch* and the *Syriac Baruch,* but in its present form is a Christian production of perhaps the 2nd century A.D. It is impossible to say whether the author drew upon a Jewish source or was simply inspired by Jewish conceptions.

III. New Testament Apocrypha

A. GOSPELS

Though many of the apocryphal gospels have been lost, a number of examples of this type of writing survive, of which the most important are mentioned here.

1. *Jewish-Christian Gospels.* Clement of Alexandria (*Stromata,* II, 45, 5; cf. V, 96, 3), Origen (*In Jo.,* II, 12 [87]) and Eusebius (*Hist. Eccles.,* III, 25, 5; 27, 4; 39, 17; IV, 22, 8) mention a *Gospel according to the Hebrews.* Eusebius also mentions (*Hist. Eccles.,* IV, 22, 8) a "Syrian" gospel, already used by Hegesippus (second half of the 2nd century) which was current "in Hebrew" among Jewish Christians (*Theophania,* IV, 12). It was probably a work in Aramaic. Finally, Epiphanius says that the Nazoreans, Jewish Christians of Syria, possessed a Hebrew gospel, which he wrongly identified with the original Aramaic Gospel of Matthew (*Haer.,* XXIX, 9, 4). He also knows of a gospel "according to the Hebrews" (*Haer.,* XXX, 3, 7) or a "Hebrew" gospel (*Haer.,* XXX, 13, 2) which he considers a falsified and truncated Gospel of Matthew (*ibid.*). Jerome (*Dial. adv. Pelag.,* III, 2; *De Viris Illustr.,* 2) also knows a gospel "according to the Hebrews" and also speaks (*De Viris Illustr.,* 3) of a gospel in Hebrew in the library of Caesarea, which was also used by the Syrian Nazoreans. For some time at least he thought it was the original text of the canonical Matthew. In both cases he has the same work in mind (cf. *Dial. adv. Pelag.,* III, 2), which was clearly an Aramaic gospel which differed notably from the canonical Matthew.

Since no Jewish-Christian gospel has been preserved in its entirety or even in considerable fragments, it is not easy to form a judgment on the works in question from the information and the fragments at our disposal. But according to the present state of research, we may probably distinguish three Jewish-Christian gospels:

a) The *Gospel of the Nazarenes,* which is attested by Hegesippus, Eusebius, Epiphanius and Jerome, was used by Jewish-

Christians of Syria, the Nazarenes or Nazoreans. It was an Aramaic gospel akin to the
canonical Matthew. The surviving fragments
show that it was mostly secondary in relationship to Matthew. It may have originated
in the first half of the 2nd century, and
certainly comes from Aramaic-speaking
circles of Jewish Christians, perhaps in
Syria.

b) The *Gospel of the Ebionites,* used according to Epiphanius by the heretical
Jewish-Christian sect of the Ebionites. From
the passages which he cites (*Haer.,* XXX,
13, 2–4. 6–8; 16, 5; 22, 4 f.) it seems to have
been a free re-working of synoptic narrative
matter, intermingled with legends and
coloured at times by Gnosticizing tendencies.
But the gospel as a whole is lost. In spite of
its Jewish-Christian character, it may have
been in Greek from the start, possibly from
the first half of the 2nd century. Its use
by the Ebionites, whose communities were
mostly east of the Jordan, could indicate
that it originated in that district. It is often
identified with the *Gospel of the Twelve*
(known only from its title), which was
known to Origen (*In Luc. Hom.,* I: *GCS,*
XXXV, 5), Ambrose (*In Luc.,* I, 2), Jerome
(*In Matth. Prol.; Dial. adv. Pelag.,* III, 2) and
others. But the question of such identification
must be left open.

c) The *Gospel of the Hebrews,* attested
chiefly by Clement of Alexandria and Origen,
is the only Jewish-Christian gospel of which
the title is known, *The Gospel according to
the Hebrews.* According to the "Sticho-
metry" of the ancient writer Nicephorus, it
was only a little shorter than the canonical
Matthew. Only a few fragments survive,
which differ notably from the NT gospels
but display traces of Gnostic syncretism and
Jewish-Christian heresy. The gospel, obviously in Greek from the start, presumably
originated in Egypt, among Greek-speaking
Jewish Christians, which would explain its
name. Like the two foregoing, it may be
from the first half of the 2nd century.

2. *The Gospel of James,* also called the *Proto-
evangelium* of James since the 16th century,
was perhaps already used by Justin (*Dial.,* 78,
5, cf. *Ev. Jac.,* 18, 1). It seems to be presupposed by Clement of Alexandria (*Stromata,*
VII, 93, 7; cf. *Ev. Jac.,* 19 f.) and is certainly
attested by Origen (*Comm. in Matth.,* X, 17,
on Mt 13:55 f., *GCS,* XL, 21) under the

title of *The Book of James.* It is the first
Marian legend of Christian literature, recount-
ing the life of the mother of Jesus up to the
massacre of the innocents. In part it is a
free adaptation of Mt and Lk, indulging in
fantasies and ignorant of Jewish conditions,
but with popular appeal and a certain
impressiveness. Joachim and Anne are Mary's
parents — their first mention. Mary is a
virgin serving in the temple at Jerusalem,
her spouse Joseph is a widower, and her
virginity is preserved inviolate even at the
miraculous birth of Jesus, which is transferred to a cave near Bethlehem. The author
calls himself James (25, 1) and claims to have
been at Jerusalem at the times of which he
speaks, meaning that he is James the
"brother of the Lord". But the gospel is
from the middle of the 2nd century and
undoubtedly from somewhere outside Palestine. It has a number of still later additions.
There are many manuscripts, the oldest from
the 3rd century, showing the original Greek
form, and also several ancient versions.
Its influence was greatest at first in the East,
the West being inhibited by the *Decree of
Gelasius.* But through such re-editions as
the Latin pseudo-Mt (6th century?) and
the Latin *Evangelium de Nativitate Mariae*
(c. 800?) which depends on the pseudo-Mt,
it finally gained influence in the West.
Directly or indirectly, it is the main source of
most Marian legends, with great influence
on Christian art and even on the liturgy,
notably the feast of the Presentation of the
Blessed Virgin Mary, 21 November, which
has no historical basis.

3. *The Story of the Childhood of the Lord,* by
Thomas the Israelite, has often been known
as the *Gospel of Thomas,* but to avoid confusion, the latter title should be reserved
for the recently-discovered Gnostic gospel
(no. 7 below). The boyhood of Jesus is
copiously related, partly in legends perhaps
Indian in origin; the stories are silly and
tasteless but throw light on the life of the
people and their children at the time, e. g.,
games and schooling. It was earlier held to
be a revision of a longer Gnostic work, but
it has nothing in common with the Gnostic
Gospel of Thomas, and was perhaps never
anything but a collection of legends as it
now is. The traditional attribution to an
Israelite named Thomas clearly means the
Apostle, who is also mentioned in the book.

Written in Greek, it survives in a shorter and longer recension and also in revisions in other languages. It was probably composed in the East as early as the end of the 2nd century.

4. *The Acts of Pilate,* or the *Gospel of Nicodemus* as it was known in the Middle Ages, survives in Greek and ancient versions. Justin already appeals to *Acts of Pilate* (*Apol.,* I, 35, 9; 48, 3; cf. Tertullian, *Apologeticum,* 21, 24; also 5, 2; 21, 19). Eusebius says that in the persecution under Maximin Daza (311–12), *Acts of Pilate* forged by pagans were read in schools to hold Christ up to derision (*Hist. Eccles.,* IX, 5, 1; cf. I, 9, 3; 11, 1). The first mention of Christian *Acts of Pilate* is in Epiphanius (*Haer.,* L, 1, 5, 8). In our *Acts,* a Christian named Ananias claims to have found an account of the trial of Jesus written in Hebrew by Nicodemus, which he translated into Greek in 425. It recounts the proceedings before Pilate, the crucifixion and burial of Jesus (1–11), the Sanhedrin's enquiries which proved the fact of the resurrection (12–16) and the testimony of two men raised from the dead about Jesus' descent into the underworld and his doings there (*Descensus Christi ad Inferos,* 17–27). All the blame for Jesus' death lies with the Jews, Pilate being completely exonerated. It is a 5th century composition, originally in Greek, into which older items have been incorporated. It was later expanded, notably by the "descent into hell", and altered. Its relationship to the *Acts* mentioned by Justin, if they ever existed, is unknown.

5. *The Gospel of Peter,* possibly used by Justin (*Apol.,* I, 35, 6 = *Ev. Petri,* 7), is mentioned *c.* 200 by Serapion of Antioch (in Eusebius, *Hist. eccles.,* VI, 12, 4, 6), then by Origen (*Comm. in Matth.,* X, 17) and Eusebius himself (*ibid.,* III, 3, 2, cf. 25, 6; VI, 12, 2–6). Serapion says that it was used by Syrian Docetists at the end of the 2nd century. The work is lost except for a larger fragment from Akhmim, Upper Egypt, containing the passion and resurrection as in the canonical gospels but embroidered with wild fantasy. Herod and the Jews have all the blame for the death of the Lord. A 2nd century work, originally in Greek, it probably originated in heretical circles in Syria and was foisted on the Apostle Peter.

6. A *Gospel of the Egyptians* is attested by Clement of Alexandria (*Stromata,* III, 63, 1; 93, 1), Hippolytus (Ref. V, 7, 9), Origen (*In Luc. Hom.,* I: *GCS,* XXXV, 5) and Epiphanius (*Haer.,* LXII, 2, 4 f.). It is described as heretical, and said to be used by Encratites, Naassenes and Sabellians who rejected marriage and were modalist in trinitarian doctrine. The work is lost, except for a dialogue between Jesus and Salome in which marriage is condemned (Clement of Alexandria, *Stromata,* III, 45, 3; 63, 2; 64, 1; 66, 2; 92, 2, cf. 97, 4; *Excerpta ex Theodoto,* 67, 2). It is uncertain whether other texts belong to this gospel, e.g., sayings of Jesus in *2 Clement* absent or differing from the canonical gospels (e. g., 4, 5; 5, 2–4; 12, 2), quotations in the *Acts of Peter* and the *Apostolic Church Order* (*c.* 300). Probably written in Greek in Egypt in the 2nd century, it may have been used by Egyptian Christians there to offset the *Gospel of the Hebrews* used by Jewish Christians (no. 1 c, above).

There is another and quite different *Gospel of the Egyptians,* completely different also from apocryphal gospels in general, among the finds of Nag Hammadi, in Coptic. It is also called *The Holy Book of the Great Invisible Spirit,* and claims to have been written by the "Great Seth", but is really by a Gnostic teacher Goggessos Eugnostos.

7. A *Gospel of Thomas* used by the Gnostic group of Naassenes is mentioned by Hippolytus (*Ref.,* V, 7, 20), who quotes a text from it; also by Origen (*In Luc. Hom.,* I: *GCS,* XXXV, 5), Eusebius (*Hist. Eccles.,* III, 25, 6) and Ambrose (*In Luc.,* I, 2). A Coptic *Gospel of Thomas,* originally no doubt in Greek, has been found at Nag Hammadi. It contains 113, or if divided otherwise, 114 sayings of Jesus, ostensibly written down by the Apostle Thomas, which recall in part the canonical gospels, especially the synoptics, and in part the apocryphal gospels and Gnostic and Manichean writings. The opening and seventeen logia are also preserved in Greek in three Egyptian papyri of the 3rd century (*Pap. Oxyrh.,* 1; 654; 655). The Coptic does not have the text quoted by Hippolytus, but it may not have been the original or only form of the gospel, which is 2nd-century.

A *Gospel of Thomas* is also mentioned by Cyril of Jerusalem (*Catech.,* IV, 36; VI, 31), as a forgery done by a pupil of Mani. We do not know whether it is the Gnostic work, which could well have been prized by the Manicheans, or a Manichean production. Cyril's note on the authorship could be an effort to exclude the Apostle Thomas from the debate.

8. A *Gospel of Philip* was in use among Egyptian Gnostics according to Epiphanius, who quotes a text from it (*Haer.*, XXVI, 13, 2 f.). There may be an allusion to it in the Gnostic *Pistis Sophia* (42, 44), where it is said that Philip wrote down relations of Jesus. A Coptic *Gospel of Philip* has been found in Nag Hammadi, but without the citation in Epiphanius. There is very little of a "gospel" about the newly discovered piece, which is a collection of 127 sayings of Gnostic origin, mostly Valentinian, few of which are attributed to Jesus. There is no particular link with Philip, who is mentioned only once and very cursorily (logion 91). Possibly the work was only ascribed to him subsequently. The gospel of which Epiphanius speaks was apparently composed in Greek, which is probably also true of the Coptic work, though some logia may have been in Coptic from the start. It cannot as yet be decided whether the two works are related. The work of which Epiphanius speaks may be of the 2nd century, perhaps from Egypt; the document underlying the Coptic work is from the same or at the latest from the next century.

9. A *Gospel of Truth,* classified as Gnostic, is stated by Irenaeus (*Adv. Haer.*, III, 11, 9) and pseudo-Tertullian (*Adv. Omnes Haereses,* 4, 6) to have been used by the Valentinians. The Coptic document from Nag Hammadi which starts with the words, "The gospel of truth", may be the work mentioned by Irenaeus. Though typically Gnostic, in many respects it is close to orthodox Christianity. The genre is not that of a gospel, but rather an edifying meditation on the fact that Jesus has brought the knowledge through which men truly know God and attain salvation. It presupposes the four canonical gospels and uses the Revelation of St. John and the Pauline letters, which is to some extent a testimony to the crystallization of the canon in the Church. It is probably from the middle of the 2nd century, and was originally in Greek.

B. ACTS OF APOSTLES

The apocryphal Acts are popular storytelling, filling in what is felt to be wanting in the NT account of the travels and activities of the apostles. Many come from heretical (Gnostic) circles, pleading the authority of an apostle to spread the doctrine of their authors. Some of these were later revised by Catholics, but even then their original intention often remains clear. The apocryphal Acts have much in common with the type of ancient literature in which the pagan heroes were celebrated, with their exploits and travels (frequently named in the original titles) and their marvels. Superstition plays a part in both literatures, and the Christian works can propound quite pagan views and tell nonsensical tales. Some historical information may be concealed among the mass of the incredible and even bizarre events, but it is hardly ever possible to sift it out.

1. The *Acts of Peter* are mentioned by Eusebius (*Hist. Eccles.*, III, 3, 2) and Jerome (*De Viris Illustr.*, 1), but have long been lost as a whole. From them there survives in Latin translation the *Actus Petri cum Simone,* also known as the *Actus Vercellenses,* after the place, Vercelli, where a manuscript of the 6th or 7th century was found. Paul has left Rome to preach the gospel in Spain, and Simon Magus leads nearly the whole of the Church in the capital into apostasy. Peter, who was still in Jerusalem, is summoned by Christ to Rome, to oppose Simon and put the Church to rights. Finally, Simon meets with a fatal accident when trying to fly up to God. Many women are led to leave their husbands by Peter's preaching, which brings him into a danger which he tries to escape by flight. He is met by Christ and induced to return to the city (the *Quo Vadis* legend, *Acts of Peter,* ch. 35 = *Martyrdom,* ch. 6). On his return he is crucified head downwards. The *Acts* show Encratite and Gnostic tendencies. The account of the martyrdom and fragments of the rest of the text are preserved in Greek, probably the original language of the whole. It is a 2nd century work, obviously earlier than the *Acts of Paul,* which seem to have been influenced by it. It may have been composed in Rome, or perhaps in Asia Minor, where the *Acts of Paul* was certainly written. The Latin Acts may be from the 3rd or 4th century.

2. The *Acts of Paul* are mentioned and rejected by Eusebius (*Hist. Eccles.*, III, 25, 4) and Jerome (*De Viris Illustr.*, 7). The work as a whole is lost, but there are considerable fragments. The following works, though known for a long time, have only recently been recognized as parts of the Acts of Paul:

a) The *Acts of Paul and Thecla*. At Iconium, the preaching of Paul, whose appearance is described (ch. 3), converts a virgin named Thecla who then abandons her fiancé. She is condemned to the stake, but escapes; and afterwards she is saved from wild beasts at Antioch. She baptizes herself, and finally dies at Seleucia.

b) An *Answer of the Corinthians* to 2 Cor, and a *Third Letter of Paul to Corinth* (see below, C, 3, a).

c) The *Martyrdom of Paul*. He ist beheaded at Rome under Nero, and milk spurts on to the clothes of the executioner.

These are extant in the original Greek as well as in ancient versions. Then there is a Coptic version of the work as a whole, preserved only in fragments (in a papyrus at Heidelberg) and large fragments of the Greek original (in a papyrus codex at Hamburg), which recount, for instance, Paul's being condemned to the beasts at Ephesus (cf. 1 Cor 15:32) and his escape, in which a baptized lion figures which can talk. Tertullian says (*De Baptismo*, 17, 5) that the work was composed by a presbyter in Asia Minor, who was deprived of office for this falsification of history. This must have been at the end of the 2nd century.

3. The *Acts of John* were known and rejected by Eusebius (*Hist. Eccles.*, III, 25, 6). They are preserved in copious fragments, which recount the Apostle's travels, his two stays at Ephesus where he worked many miracles and destroyed the temple of Artemis, his preaching about Christ and his death. Gnostic, Encratite and Docetic views constantly recur: Jesus' death is only an illusion. It was written in Greek, perhaps in Asia Minor, in the 3rd century at the latest. Some of the traditions incorporated may have been extant in the 2nd century, but this need not mean that the work was composed so early. Later writers attribute it to a certain Leucius (Innocent I, *Epist. 6 ad Exsuperium,* 7, and others).

4. The *Acts of Andrew* are first mentioned by Eusebius, who rejects them (*Hist. Eccles.,*

III, 25, 6). They circulated in heretical circles and are preserved only in fragments, being composed probably in the second half of the 2nd century. They do not seem to have been Gnostic products, though there are certain contacts with Gnosticism. But contemporary Hellenistic philosophy is featured, and many of the views expressed resemble those of Tatian. Apart from the fragments, there are later Catholic works which deal with the same matter, probably not before the 5th century, though it is uncertain how far they take it from the *Acts.* The later works include various Greek and Latin versions of the martyrdom of the Apostle, who is crucified at Patrae. This legendary story has strongly influenced the liturgy of the feast of St. Andrew.

5. The *Acts of Thomas,* read especially in Gnostic and Manichean circles, were probably written originally in Syriac, in Syria, in the first half of the 3rd century. They survive in more or less thoroughly Catholic revisions, chiefly in Syriac, Greek and Latin, though preserving much Gnostic and Manichean matter. They recount the travels of the Apostle and his Encratite type of preaching in India, his miracles and martyrdom. Many liturgical pieces are included, such as prayers and hymns. The underlying doctrine of redemption is that of Gnosis, as in the Hymn of the Soul (Song of the Pearl), which is poetically very beautiful (chs. 108–13).

C. LETTERS

There are relatively few apocryphal letters, though letters predominate in the NT on which many apocrypha are modelled. For reasons not clear to us, the apocryphal writers found the other types of writing, gospels, acts and apocalypses, more to their purpose, which was the spread of their doctrines or the satisfying of the curiosity of the Christian people. Further, few of the apocryphal letters are of much importance, though there are some items of interest.

1. The exchange of *Letters between Abgar of Edessa and Jesus* is first mentioned by Eusebius (*Hist. Eccles.,* I, 13, 2f., 6–10), who clearly thinks they are authentic. He takes them from the archives at Edessa and translates them from Syriac into Greek (*ibid.,* 15, 4). The Toparch Abgar Uchama ("the black"), who reigned at Edessa from 4 B.C. to A.D. 7

and from A.D. 13–50 is suffering from an incurable disease when he hears that Jesus works many miracles. He sends a messenger with a letter to say that he believes that Jesus is the Son of God, and asks him to come to Edessa, to heal the ruler and find protection from the Jews. Jesus' letter in reply, to be delivered to the ruler by the messenger, reads as follows: "Blessed are you, who have believed in me but have not seen me. For it is written of me that those who see me will not believe in me, and that those who have not seen me will believe and live. But as regards your requesting me to come, I must first accomplish here all that I was sent to do, and then, when it is accomplished, I must be taken up to him who sent me. But when I am taken up, I shall send you one of my disciples, to cure your sufferings and give life to you and yours."

Abgar's letter, in a slightly different version, and Jesus' answer, transmitted orally and in an expanded form, are also to be found in the Syrian *Doctrina Addai* from the beginning of the 5th century. As in Eusebius, the two letters are linked with a legend from Edessa about a missionary visit of the Apostle Thaddaeus (in Eusebius) or Addai (in the *Doctrina Addai*). The letters were probably written originally in Syriac in the region of Edessa, no doubt to provide the local Church with apostolic origin and standing. At the latest, this must have been at the end of the 3rd century.

2. The *Epistula Apostolorum,* nowhere mentioned in early Christian writings, professes to be an encyclical of the eleven apostles "to the Churches of the East and West, the North and South". Besides a brief account of the life of Jesus, it contains chiefly conversations between Jesus and his disciples during the interval between the resurrection and the ascension. Christ foretells the history of the Church, and gives instruction on the judgment and the signs of the parousia, the resurrection of the dead and the eternal recompense. Though the letter attacks Gnostic (Docetic) heresies, and names Simon and Cerinthus as teachers of false doctrine, it contains a number of notions which are known to be Gnostic, like that of Christ descending to Mary in the form of the Angel Gabriel. It was composed about the middle of the 2nd century, but it is hard to say where; scholars have suggested

Asia Minor, Egypt or Syria. It may have been originally in Greek or perhaps Syriac. It is preserved as a whole only in a revision in Ethiopian, in Coptic with lacunae and in small fragments in Latin.

3. *Apocryphal letters of Paul:* a) There is a *Third Letter to the Corinthians,* with an introductory letter of the presbyters of Corinth to Paul. Paul propounds the Christian view against heresies which reject the authority of the prophets, deny God's omnipotence and his creation of man, the coming resurrection of the body and the true incarnation of Christ in material flesh. The letter also forms part of the *Acts of Paul* (see above, B, 2), but is often found as a separate item. We do not know whether the exchange of letters was originally independent and then inserted into the *Acts,* or formed part of them and was later detached. They are from the 2nd century and are preserved in the original Greek and in translations. The esteem in which they were held may be seen from the fact that Ephraim the Syrian (4th century) considered them canonical and included them in his commentary on the Letters of Paul.

b) A *Letter to the Laodiceans,* in Latin, containing only twenty verses, is composed of phrases from the canonical Letters of Paul, especially Philippians. It is found in the West towards the end of the patristic era and was perhaps always in Latin; there are no indications of translation from a Greek original. But a *Letter to the Laodiceans* was mentioned as early as the 1st century, as in Col 4:16. It has either been lost, or has lost its title, if it is in fact the letter "to the Ephesians", as has often been surmised since Hugo Grotius (17th century). Marcion included a *Letter to the Laodiceans* in his Pauline canon. According to Tertullian (*Adv. Marc.,* V, 11, 12; 17, 1) it was the Letter to the Ephesians. The Muratorian fragment (lines 63–68) mentions a letter to the Laodiceans, ostensibly of Paul, used by the Marcionites but rejected by the Catholic Church, which is distinguished from the Letter to the Ephesians. If this information is correct, there must have been a heretical production of the 2nd century, no doubt in Greek, called a *Letter of Paul to the Laodiceans.* But the surviving letter can have had little to do with this, in spite of affirmations to the contrary, e.g., by A. von Harnack and G. Quispel, since it shows no trace of Marcionite origin. It was probably not earlier than the 4th century, the author apparently being impelled by Col 4:16 to supply the missing letter. He did it so successfully that the apocryphon found its way into many manuscripts of the Vulgate, mostly after Colossians, and was considered as a genuine letter of Paul, though not canonical, in the Middle Ages and as late as the 16th century.

c) A *Letter to the Alexandrians* is mentioned in the same terms as the *Letter to the Laodiceans* in the Muratorian fragment *(ibid.)*. No other traces survive.

d) The correspondence between Paul and Seneca, preserved in more than three hundred manuscripts, consists of eight short letters of the Roman philosopher L. Annaeus Seneca (d. 65), and six of Paul, mostly shorter. All are fictitious. They are written in Latin, and the style and thought are poor. Seneca admires the doctrine of Paul, but finds the language untutored and sends him a book entitled *De Verborum Copia* (*Epist.*, 9) to improve his Latin. Seneca also reads to Nero some of Paul's letters, which make an impression on him. But Paul asks Seneca to stop, for fear of arousing the anger of the Empress Poppaea against the Apostle. Seneca laments the burning of Rome and the martyrdom of Christians. Finally Paul charges Seneca to preach the gospel at court. The correspondence is mentioned as early as Jerome (*De Viris Illustr.*, 12) and Augustine (*Epist.*, 153, 14), and may have been composed in the second half of the 4th century, as is generally supposed.

4. The *Letter of Barnabas* is an early Christian document in Greek, ascribed in antiquity and the Middle Ages, and even by some modern scholars, to the Apostle Barnabas. This is not asserted in the letter, which is a theological treatise composed from different sources, in the form of a letter, like Hebrews. A dogmatic section (1–17) discusses the value and interpretation of the OT, which is inspired by God and committed to the Church and must be revered by Christians. The precepts about sacrifice, circumcision and foods were never meant to be taken literally. They had a higher, spiritual sense, that God wanted the interior disposition and not outward ceremonial. The Jews took it all literally, being misled by a bad angel, thus mistaking

the will of God. A shorter ethical section (18–20), akin to *Didache* 1–5, gives the well-known doctrine of the two ways, describing the way of light which man should tread, and the way of darkness which he should avoid. The author indulges freely in allegorical interpretation of Scripture, finding references to Christ in the OT which are very difficult to see. The letter shows a special aspect of the controversy between Christianity and Judaism in the early days, so partial and uncompromising that it has lost sight of reality. The predilection for allegory indicates Egypt, perhaps Alexandria in particular, as the place of origin, as may also be suggested by the high esteem in which the Alexandrian theologians Clement and Origen held the letter. It probably dates from the first half of the 2nd century. It was sometimes treated as one of the authoritative documents of the Church, and is given along with the canonical books in the famous Greek *Codex Sinaiticus*. But Eusebius (*Hist. Eccles.*, III, 25, 4; cf. VI, 13, 6) and Jerome (*De Viris Illustr.*, 6) exclude it from the canon.

D. APOCALYPSES

Apocryphal Christian apocalypses were produced in relatively large numbers from the 2nd century A.D. on. Jewish apocalypses were re-modelled and new ones were written by Catholics and by heretics, but above all by Gnostics. Their literary history is often hard to follow, because the original text was often re-edited, interpolated and transformed.

1. *The Ascension of Isaiah* (also known as the *Apocryphum Isaiae* or the *Visio Isaiae*) is a Jewish, perhaps Essene, legend from the last century B.C., concerning the martyrdom of Isaiah (1:1–2a, 6b–13a; 2:1–3, 12; 5:1b to 14), into which is inserted a prophecy about Christ and his Church, perhaps from the time of the persecution of Nero (3:13b to 4:18). The legend is followed by a "vision" of Isaiah, from some time towards the end of the 2nd century A.D. The vision, which shows Gnostic influences, describes the ascension of Isaiah through the seven heavens and the redemption which Christ is to bring (6:1–11:40). The three items may have been combined as early as the 2nd century, though a later date is also possible, in the 3rd or 4th century. The complete work, originally in Greek, is preserved only

in an Ethiopian translation, with one Greek (2:4–4:4) and three Latin fragments (2:14 to 3:13; 7:1–9; another version in 6–11). From the point of view of the history of dogma, it is noteworthy that the Holy Spirit is considered to be an angel (3:16; 4:21; 7:23; 9:35f., 39f.; 10:4; 11:4, 33), who sits at the left hand of God as does Christ on the right (11:32f.).

2. *The Apocalypse of Peter*. This is preserved in Ethiopian and in a large Greek fragment. It was originally written in Greek. While Christ is seated on Mount Olivet, the disciples come and ask him to tell them when his return and the end of the world will take place (cf. Mk 13:3f. par.). Then the Lord describes his coming, warns against seducers and expounds the parable of the fig-tree (Mk 13:28f. par.). He foretells that Enoch and Elijah will come as opponents of Antichrist, who will be a Jew. Then Jesus indicates the terrible signs which will precede the resurrection of the dead and the general judgment. He shows his disciples the places where the damned suffer various punishments corresponding to their sins and describes the joy of the elect. Finally, Christ ascends to heaven, accompanied by Moses and Elijah. The book was written in the 2nd century, perhaps before A.D. 150.

3. *The Apocalypse of Paul*. The preface claims that it was found at Tarsus, in the time of the Emperor Theodosius (379–395), in the house where St. Paul once lived. The author was a monk who lived therefore at this time or somewhat later. He may have used an older work, but this is not certain. The work is in Greek, but a better text is given in a Latin translation, the *Visio Pauli,* which is preserved in more than a dozen medieval redactions, most of which shorten it, and also in Syriac, Coptic, Ethiopian, Arabic, Old Slavonic and medieval German, French and English versions. This extensive manuscript tradition indicates that the work was once very popular. St. Paul is charged by Christ to exhort sinners to repent. He sees how the guardian angels of the peoples and of individuals inform God of the behaviour of their charges, every morning and evening. He also sees the judgment which awaits each man immediately after death, and the new Jerusalem with the patriarchs and the prophets, David and the "Holy Innocents". He sees the fiery river of

hell and the damned in their torments. At the intercession of Michael and Paul, they have a respite on Easter Sunday (ch. 44). The Latin version says that these are the revelations which St. Paul received according to 2 Cor 12:2–4. From the point of view of history of dogma, it is interesting to note that the heretics who suffer special torments are those who deny the true humanity of Jesus Christ and the real presence in the Eucharist. The respite at Easter in hell is also noteworthy. It is a development of the Jewish notion of a Sabbath rest in hell (Billerbeck, IV, pp. 1076, 1082, 1093) which in later Christian times became a Sunday rest in purgatory. The Roman liturgy, till as late as the 20th century, showed traces of this idea: Monday was dedicated to the angels, in the list of votive Masses, and on certain Mondays the prayer for the faithful departed was added to the Mass. It was the beginning of a new week of suffering for the souls in purgatory, and they were to be prayed for and commended to the protection of the angels. Dante possibly alludes to the *Apocalypse of St. Paul* in the *Divina Commedia* (*Inferno,* II, 28).

4. *The Shepherd of Hermas*. The apocalyptic colouring of this work makes it necessary to mention it here, although it differs from the other apocalypses in many ways. The subject of the apocalyptic experiences calls himself Hermas and is clearly a historical figure of the 2nd century A.D., who lived at Rome (Muratorian Fragment). Nowhere does he appeal to a man of God from earlier times, and there is no revelation about cosmic phenomena or eschatology. The work is rather a call to penance, dressed up in apocalyptic form. Christians must recognize the sinfulness which is inherent in them even after baptism, so that the spirit of penance may be aroused and Christian life renewed. These exhortations are based on divine revelations and mandates, which are first communicated to Hermas by a woman representing the Church who appears to him, and then by the angel of penance, who appears in the guise of a shepherd. The book takes its name from this visionary figure. It is divided into five visions *(visiones),* ten precepts *(mandata)* and ten parables *(similitudines)*. The name of the author may really be Hermas, as he styles himself, but it may be a fiction, like so much in the book about

the life of the author and indeed the whole stylistic apparatus of visions. The author seems to have been a Jewish Christian or at least to have been very much associated with Jewish Christianity. The *Muratorian Fragment* makes him the brother of the Bishop of Rome, Pius (144–155?). The work has been preserved, almost in its entirety, in the original Greek, and there are two old Latin translations, and one Ethiopian, of the whole book. In early Christian times it was revered in some places as a canonical work, though it was already excluded from the Muratorian canon. The work is of great importance for the history of sacramental penance in the Roman Church of the 2nd century. It offers the possibility of penance to those who have sinned after baptism. Penance consists of a change of heart and works of expiation, upon which God forgives sins. But if anyone falls again in spite of this second penance, he will "hardly gain life" (*Mand.,* 4, 3, 6). The author's thinking on the Trinity was not very precise, since he failed to make a clear enough distinction between the Son of God and the Holy Spirit.

IV. The Significance of the Apocrypha

The writings discussed above amply demonstrate the wide field covered by the designation "apocrypha". They differ notably in origin, mentality and purpose, though they are at one in being rather alien to the modern mind. Their world has vanished and much of what they say appears entirely antiquated. But it would be wrong to dismiss them as curiosities of human naivety and to leave their study to the few students of literature who have a taste for such things. The insight into the mentality and background of the ancients which they provide makes them well worth studying.

The OT apocrypha are often useful supplements to fill out our knowledge of the OT, of Hellenistic Jewish writings such as those of Philo and Josephus and of rabbinical literature. We learn of Jewish views on religion and morals about the beginning of the Christian era, which is a help to the understanding of Jesus and primitive Christianity.

In the apocalypses the highly developed angelology is important. Many of the views put forward in the apocalypses have their parallels in the spirits of nature met with in pagan religions. Phenomena which we now understand as the results of natural forces were then ascribed to the operations of angels. Such views can be met with in popular piety and especially in popular superstitions, down to modern times, and made their way in a purified form even into Scholasticism (cf. the angels of nature in St. Thomas Aquinas, *Summa Theologica,* I, 110, 1–3).

The Messianism of Jewish apocalyptic is of particular interest. In some ways it runs parallel to the NT, as, for instance, the title of "Son of Man" in *1 Enoch,* though indeed this had already been used in a special way in the canonical book of Daniel (7:13). The designation "my son", that is, son of God, for the messianic saviour in *4 Esdras* is almost certainly due to the Christian translator. But on the whole, they have very little to say about the person of the Messiah, compared to the NT. Thus these writings show us the Messianic expectations of Jewish apocalyptic circles before and after the beginning of the Christian era, but they reveal at the same time how great a distance separates them from the Christology of the primitive Church. This should prevent us from assessing too highly the contribution of the messianic hopes of Jewish apocalyptic to the Christology of the Church.

Some apocrypha show contemporary attitudes to the Jewish law, by the Halachic prescriptions which they add to the Torah. There is also much Haggadic material in the legends tacked on to OT stories or in the tendentious interpretation of these stories.

The "New Testament apocrypha" are almost useless if one looks for reliable information about Jesus and his doctrine or other persons mentioned in the NT. The apocryphal gospels are dependent to a great extent on the canonical ones, presupposing the events and words recorded there, but often altering them to suit the purposes of the writers. The Acts which recount the travels and doings of various apostles could contain here or there a historical reminiscence, though so much is clearly fictitious and incredible that it is hardly possible to sift out the grains of truth. The many legends in apocryphal gospels and acts show how the revered figures of Christianity were imagined, and also the lengths to which writers dared to go with their readers. But these writings had great influence on posterity, as may be seen from the amount that survives in

Christian legend of medieval and even modern times, and also in liturgy and art. Even dogmatic development, especially in Mariology, may have been occasioned by these writings, particularly by the "Gospel of James" and its revisions.

The so-called NT apocalypses take a great interest in the other world, and treat of it even more fully than Jewish apocalyptic had already done. Graphic descriptions are given of hell, where each sin has a special punishment. This was the authors' way of deterring people from sinning, and it may then have had a certain amount of success, though such descriptions leave us rather cold today, because we recognize the metaphorical element in them. Nonetheless, the genre greatly influenced Western literature, preaching and painting, being given its most moving expression by the master hand of Dante.

Many NT apocrypha come from Gnostic or other circles which had diverged from the Catholic form of faith. They are not only valuable sources for research on such thinking, but also show how widespread and influential such faiths were. There is food for thought in the fact that in Egypt and Eastern Syria, for instance, the first known literary products of Christianity were of a Gnostic or similar type, while Catholic literature only appears later. The Church, in fact, was already divided into various confessions in the 2nd and 3rd centuries, and there was a dire struggle before the Catholic form of Christianity could triumphantly eliminate the other orientations.

See also *Canon of Scripture, Apocalyptic, Gnosticism, Qumran.*

BIBLIOGRAPHY. OLD TESTAMENT: R. H. Charles, *The Apocrypha and Pseudepigrapha of the Old Testament in English,* 2 vols. (1913); W. O. E. Oesterley, *The Books of the Apocrypha, Their Origin, Teaching and Contents* (1914); R. T. Herford, *Talmud and Apocrypha. A Comparative Study of the Jewish Ethical Teaching in the Rabbinical and non-Rabbinical Sources in the Early Centuries* (1933); W. O. E. Oesterley, *An Introduction to the Books of the Apocrypha* (1935); E. J. Goodspeed, *The Story of the Apocrypha* (1939); R. H. Pfeiffer, *History of New Testament Times with an Introduction to the Apocrypha* (1949); B. M. Metzger, *An Introduction to the Apocrypha* (1957); O. Eissfeldt, *The Old Testament. An Introduction,* trans. by R. Ackroyd (1965). NEW TESTAMENT: M. R. James, *The Apocryphal New Testament* (1924); E. Hennecke, W. Schneemelcher and R. M. Wilson, *New Testament Apocrypha,* 2 vols. (1963–5); C. W. Barlow, *Epistolae Senecae ad Paulum et Pauli ad Senecam* (1938); A. Guillaumont and others, *The Gospel according to Thomas.* Coptic text established and translation (1959); K. Grobel, *The Gospel of Truth. A Valentinian Meditation on the Gospel* (1960); R. M. Grant and D. N. Freedman, *The Secret Sayings of Jesus according to the Gospel of Thomas* (1960); A. F. J. Klijn, *The Acts of Thomas* (1962); R. M. Wilson, *The Gospel of Philip* (1962); A. de Santos Otero, *Evangelios Apocrifos* (2nd ed., 1962).

Johannes Michl

APOLOGETICS

I. Apologetics in General: A. Theological Situation. B. Biblical Motivations. C. The Changing Forms of Modern Apologetics. II. Immanence Apologetics.

I. Apologetics in General

A. THEOLOGICAL SITUATION

Apologetics, in a general and fundamental way, is a permanent feature of all Christian theology. The effort to answer for the faith is as old as Christian theology as such and is inspired by the testimony contained in the bible itself (see B). As a result of the new cultural and political situation of the Enlightenment, where Christianity and religion in general were no longer identified, and Christianity ceased to be an interest of all society as such, apologetics was developed as an independent discipline at the beginning of the 19th century. The lead was taken among Catholics by the Tübingen school of S. Drey, among Protestants by the school of Schleiermacher. It is now more or less identified with the theological themes and enquiries which are grouped under the name of fundamental theology.

1. The readiness to give an account of the faith which is voiced in apologetics is a readiness to accept responsibility, that is, a readiness to share the questioning and problems of the world in which it lives. This readiness is not a sort of afterthought, a purely apologetical concession, when the Christian faith is fully established. It is part of its very essence (see below, B, 2).

When the believer gives an account of his faith to the world around him, he himself penetrates more deeply into the realities of faith. He is only "hearer of the word" in a theological sense when he listens at the same time to the objections and difficulties of the social and historical situation of which he himself forms part.

2. Though it may be necessary to treat apologetics as a separate subject for technical reasons, it may never be pursued in isolation so that it loses its constant reference to the basic character of all theology, which is to "give answer". The history of apologetics show that two typical dangers arise here. One is that apologetics ceases to see itself as a theological discipline, in spite of the fact that when it comes into contact with the non-theological and non-Christian mind, the full force of the Christian faith must be mobilized, its intellectual appeal, its power to form and transform the mind. The other danger is that apologetics may adopt the typical features of a purely apologetic attitude and policy, such as conclusions reached with a haste which savours of ideology, formalism in argument, loss of the sense of the permanent danger to which faith itself is exposed, insensibility to the nuances and intrinsic variations of the social and historical situation, the inclination to be on the defensive in a negative way which surrenders to the very mentality to which it is opposed, incomprehension of the historically valid elements of the opposing positions, and the temptation to treat as permanently relevant the set of questions raised by a given situation.

B. Biblical Motivations

There are two themes above all in the NT message which determine the basic task of apologetical theology.

1. There is the theme of the universal nature of the gospel and the mission. In the NT, the horizon within which faith explicitates itself is universal. The wall of partition between Jews and gentiles is broken down, the veil of the temple is torn asunder, and the synagogue becomes the Church among the nations and for the nations. The passage of the frontiers is obligatory. Such a faith necessarily entails an attitude to the universalism of Hellenistic philosophy and a conscious detachment from a setting now recognized as unduly restricted. The language of the Palestinian homeland is abandoned and the danger of sectarian isolation averted. Facing a Hellenistic system where all were on principle citizens of the world,

the "apologetic" attitude, of which there are already traces in the NT, begins to develop, not primarily to build up defensive barriers but to remove obstacles and give the missionary impulse free rein.

2. The second theme is the readiness of the faith to give an account of itself. The Christain faith is thereby distinguished from all religious ideologies which by means of intolerance and the arbitrary apotheosis of a particular viewpoint strive to impose themselves universally. The universal conquest which Christianity aims at cannot be attained by any power except that of love and truth. It must give a responsible account of the faith to all who ask to know the grounds of its hope (1 Pet 3:15). This calls for complete mental integrity and unmasks the "blind faith", which refuses to reflect and see clearly, as a lower and defective form. Christian theology must be the account (*logos*) of a faith which knows it must answer for its hope or for the universal divine promise which that hope accepts. Hence it cannot but strive to explain itself in the terms relevant to its given historical situation. Nonetheless, the intrinsic limits of this apologetical effort to communicate the Christian faith must not be blurred or disregarded. Apologetics is not adaptation or accommodation. And it is not an effort to embody the faith in a ready-made thought-form, no matter how purely formal or generalized, of any type whatever — cosmological and metaphysical, transcendental, existential or personalist. In its account of the faith, apologetics is the critic and emancipator who strives to break through all the thought-forms of this faith, by constantly fixing his gaze on the foolishness of the cross and resurrection of Jesus Christ (which Bonhoeffer calls the *Gegenlogos* — the anti-logos, the reason the other way round). It is a truth which cannot be guaranteed like a pure idea, but only in a (historical) action orientated to its eschatological promises.

C. The Changing Forms of Modern Apologetics

By the very nature of apologetics, which is a critical, responsible re-affirmation of the understanding of faith in face of a given situation, it cannot itself determine what questions it must ask. It cannot set itself its problems, in the light of its own history, or it will exhaust itself fruitlessly in the reproduction of problems of the past. Its themes and tasks change more than in any other theological discipline.

1. *The changing audience.* Apologetics first addressed itself in its defence of its hope to the pagan world of the Roman Empire, whose intellectual representatives were Hellenistic philosophy and the political principles of Rome. In the Middle Ages, Islam in particular was envisaged, as by Aquinas in his *Summa contra Gentiles.* After the Reformation, it was primarily non-Catholic Christians, and after the Enlightenment, the critics of religion who based themselves on philosophical, scientific or socio-political grounds. In any case the audience envisaged was the outsider from the point of view of Church theology, the unbeliever or the heterodox. Hence apologetics mainly took the form of an apologia *ad extra.* Today apologetics is more and more an apologia *ad intra,* the account of the believer's hope given to the believer himself. The menaces to which faith is exposed by its very nature are being expressed more and more in terms which go beyond the situation of the individual to take in the world: the separation of religion and society; the isolation of believers as in a diaspora; the untoward intellectual and spiritual demands made of believers by the inevitably pluralistic milieu in which the experience of faith has to prove its worth. The days of simple faith, when at least society and its traditions posed no question, are drawing to a close. The faith of the individual is challenged by his milieu as well as by his own sinful failings and no level of life in the Church is exempt. Hence the clear and responsible account of the possibility of faith is not just a secondary development, a sort of theoretical superstructure for the educated faithful or an arsenal of arguments in ideological controversy with non-believers. It is becoming more and more an intrinsic element of the individual believer's situation and a condition of possibility for his own belief. Hence the apologia *ad intra* must also be envisaged in preaching, which must not reserve discussion of difficulties against the faith to the encounter with "outsiders". The sermon which envisages unbelievers is by no means out of place in the Church itself.

2. *The changing method.* We confine ourselves here to the most important changes in method which have ensued since apologetics became an independent discipline. It has taken the form, above all in the 19th century, of a rational and historical enquiry which sought to "defend" the Christian faith or demonstrate the grounds of its credibility by philosophical and historical arguments. Prescinding for the moment (but see below, 2 c) from the basic question which was little discussed in classical apologetics, as to how the use of philosophy and history is based on the notion of faith itself, that is, how apologetics can be a legitimate *theological* discipline, we shall illustrate the changing methods of apologetics from its three classical elements — the philosophical, the historical and the strictly apologetical.

a) *The philosophical element.* A change has come about in the presuppositions of the rational argument, which considered philosophy as the "purely rational" and unprejudiced theory of reality and hence the ideal basis for a demonstration of the credibility of faith. Since the Enlightenment, the relationship of theory and practice, of truth and social reality has been re-considered, and since Kant "the end of metaphysics" is at least an unavoidable subject of discussion. Philosophy, which in apologetics was practically identical with the medieval Aristotelian tradition of the West, has ceased to be homogeneous and has become a pluralism which the individual thinker cannot bring fully into focus in his search for *the* one philosophy. Philosophy itself threatens to become a sort of irrationalism, not the result of lack of reflection, but of lack of conclusiveness in all reflection. At any rate, there is now no such thing as a standard philosophy to which apologetics can appeal without more ado. Apologetics must provide its own philosophy. And this it understands more and more not as a pre-existing system which it can simply "apply", but as the hermeneutic, maieutic and critical reflection which is demanded by each new situation of apologetics. On the hermeneutic element, see further 2 b below. As regards the maieutic and critical elements, it may be said that philosophy functions not as a material but as a "formal" system. It is the relentless questioning of all assumptions, a fertile negativity which robs the conventionally "obvious" of its self-assurance. It is a struggle

against the surreptitious efforts of all particular thought-forms or sciences to erect
themselves into absolutes and trespass beyond the categories, and a protest against
the anonymous dictatorship of the purely
factual. It is a perpetual summons to a
critical aloofness which can understand itself
— to use a phrase of Hegel's — as "its own
times summed up as a question". It is partial
only to what offers ever greater scope to
human existence, which can never be reduced
to the merely factual. And thus it manifests,
if only negatively, that concrete "openness"
of human thought and action in its historical
changes which faith must constantly create,
if it is to proclaim its hope responsibly.

b) *The historical element.* To the problems
posed since the Enlightenment by the historical criticism of the foundations of the
Christian faith theology sought an answer
in historical apologetics, which appealed in
turn to historical science to establish the
historicity of the events attested in the bible.
But meanwhile the starting-point of historical
apologetics has changed. First, the self-
understanding of faith embraces more and
more clearly its own immanent historicity.
This makes inevitable the discussion of the
basic hermeneutical question of the relationship between faith and history, as adumbrated
by Lessing, Hegel and Kierkegaard. Then,
the notion of historical science itself has
been modified by the hermeneutical question
as to the nature and conditions of historical
understanding in general, and by allowance
being made for the various forms in which
historical reality may appear and be expressed. This was discussed in the theological
sphere since Schleiermacher, in that of the
history of thought by such writers as P. Yorck
von Wartenburg, W. Dilthey and M. Heidegger (see Gadamer, *Wahrheit und Methode*).
Further, the most recent research on the
Bible (such as form-criticism and history of
redaction) has shown the special nature of
the biblical assertions and the many levels
on which they are made. They can appear
for instance as attestations of the faith which
are orientated to the kerygma and moulded
by theological reflection. Hermeneutical reflection on the form of historical understanding appropriate in this case is obviously
necessary. Finally, against the background of
the technological reasoning dominant today,
knowledge of a reality which happened only
once and cannot be reproduced is in danger

of becoming less and less decisive and more
and more a matter of taste. The upshot of it
all is that historical apologetics must be more
subtle and critical in its approach. Two tasks
are particularly urgent. One is the development of the category "future" for the understanding of history, in contrast to a too
one-sided attention to history as something
in the past. This will enable historical apologetics to escape certain dilemmas of the
hermeneutical question, and also to display
a dimension of history to which a technical
civilization seems particularly responsive.
The other task is the examination of the
relevance and validity of the hermeneutical
reflection on time, which threatens to turn
a faith conscious of its historical foundations
into a new type of irrationalism. Here the
relationship between theological reflection
and religious institution appears in a new,
"post-critical" form.

c) *The apologetical element as such.* Here the
change is characterized by the fact that the
process of apologetics is no longer a marginal
effort which takes place in the non-theological
approach to faith. It is a basic effort of theological responsibility in which the "spirit",
the full intelligibility of Christian faith itself,
and its immanent power to form and transform the mind are mobilized for the task.
The theological answer has the following
fundamental traits. First, it excludes all
ideological features. It may and need make
no pretensions to a knowledge and an answer
of which it is not itself in possession. It may
and need not expose itself to the charge of
being a modern mythology by claiming to
have too many answers and too few questions. While it need not fall into the other
extreme, the barren cult of questioning
everything, the theological answer cannot
consist of a discussion which will dispose of
all challenges and problems, as if man could
become fully perspicuous to himself with
the help of a well-formulated religion, and
thus be spared the questionableness of his
existence and the hazards of the future. The
theological answer must be determined by
the permanent menace which is indissolubly
linked to the faith itself. It must be guided
by the conviction that the question of unbelief
is first and foremost a question put by the
believer to himself. Then, apologetics must
be built up on a critical sense of solidarity
with the menaced values of man. This does
not mean that the theological answer is

abandoned and reduced to purely humanist terms. This could well be branded as the typical danger to which an aging religion is exposed. It tries surreptitiously to attain, by purely humanistic thinking, the universality and validity which is denied it in terms of its historical mission. But solidarity with all that is human is vital to the intelligibility and persuasiveness of a theological answer which confronts the radical threat to the humanity of man with the proclamation of a universal salvation, a salvation implying brotherly responsibility "for the least of these", a salvation in the light of which all is false which only appears true to the individual in isolation. It is especially important today that the theological answer should have this orientation, because unbelief does not now take primarily the form of a vision of life and the world which is planned contrary to God, but of the offer of a positive possibility of existence, of a humanity fully achieved without God. An articulate and militant atheism is not the focus of this unbelief, but its presupposition. We are in an age which is to some extent "post-atheist" and strives to understand itself as "humanistic", without intermediate stages.

It follows further that the theological answer must now expound above all the social implications of the Christian faith and promise. Modern criticism of religion, which has been there in germ since the Enlightenment, appears above all as criticism of ideologies. It tries to expose Christianity as a function or the champion of a given system of social and political rule. And then, the claim of the Christian message must not be reduced to the private interests of the individual or restricted to ideals. Here it is important to explain the purifying force of Christian hope in the evolution of society. Finally, the theological account of the faith in apologetics is becoming more and more of a "dialogue". This does not mean uncritical adaptation, cursory compromise and the levelling down of the Christian message to a symbolical paraphrase of the spirit of the times. It is an effort to stimulate the fruitful conflict which goes on within our pluralistic society and its common strivings. And one motive of this effort is the recognition of "how weighty are the questions which atheism raises" (Vatican II, Pastoral Constitution on the Church in the Modern World, article 21).

See also *Apologists, Atheism, Enlightenment, Hermeneutics, History* I, *Islam, Fundamental Theology, Theological Methodology, Theology* I, *Pluralism, Tübingen School.*

BIBLIOGRAPHY. K. Aland, *Die Apologie der Apologetik* (1948); H. U. von Balthasar, *Die Gottesfrage des heutigen Menschen* (1956); R. Aubert, *Le problème de l'acte de foi* (3rd ed., 1958); H. G. Gadamer, *Wahrheit und Methode* (1960; 2nd ed., 1965); B. Ramm, *Varieties of Christian Apologetics* (1961); J.-B. Metz, "Unbelief as a Theological Problem", *Concilium* 1 (1965), pp. 32–42; id., ed., "Christian Faith and Modern Atheism", *Concilium* 2 (1966); id., "Kirche für die Ungläubigen?", in T. Filthaut, ed., *Umkehr und Erneuerung* (1966), pp. 312–29; id., "Theologie", *LTK*, X (1965), cols. 62–67; H. Bouillard, *The Logic of the Faith* (1967).

Johannes-Baptist Metz

II. Immanence Apologetics

Immanence apologetics is the name given to certain considerations, developed in particular by M. Blondel and L. Laberthonnière, on the philosophical preparation for faith. It is an effort to bring about the subjective dispositions for the assent of faith by showing the value and relevance of the Christian revelation as the fulfilment of a fundamental "natural desire" of man. So far from being a particular historical form of apologetics in general, the method of immanence is, therefore, a) by the very nature of apologetics, and b) by reason of the trend of modern thought, an integral element demanded in all apologetics.

1. In apologetics as a whole, the method of immanence forms part of the *demonstratio religiosa,* with a fundamental task in the preparation of the *assent* to revelation similar to that of natural theology for the *understanding* of revelation. The truths of revelation only have a meaning for the hearer because they proclaim a message about the God of whom he has some "previous" knowledge, independent of the truths of revelation (cf. Acts 17:23). In the same way, the fact of revelation is only "interesting", and worth the trouble and self-denial of listening to closely, in so far as it can be shown to have some real relevance to man. This relevance and value of revelation is the first thing that must be demonstrated in leading men to faith; for even "blind submission to the authority of God's testimony

to himself" presupposes the knowledge that such submission is rational and hence justifiable or even imperative as the act of a responsible person. Revelation must, therefore, be displayed as a value for man, as the answer to a sensible question which he may or must pose. And since revelation lays claim to the whole man, it must be displayed as the answer to the absolutely basic question about the meaning of life itself, about the whole potentiality of man. For the Jews, this "point of insertion" for the Christian message was already theologically present in the work of salvation which they knew God had begun in them and had promised to fulfil. But the approach to the "heathens" must now be philosophical, through the analysis of human existence and the expectations which cannot be naturally fulfilled but remain insistent — the *existential* or significant and determinant hopes, not just the *existentiel* or unintegrated shocks and surges (cf. Acts 14:15f.; 17:23–30; Rom 1:20, 32; 2:14–16).

2. The specific method of immanence, with its stress on the subjective preparation of the assent of faith, is imposed by the development of modern philosophy, of which Descartes was the forerunner, and which, since Kant, is essentially a philosophy of the subject or the ego — and necessarily so, if it is to meet the demands of a stringent argumentation. The older apologetics was "objective", like the philosophy of its times, which treated all that confronted it in terms of the object or as things. Thus the apologist had a number of objective facts in view (words of revelation, accredited by miracles) which spoke to him of God's action of self-disclosure. God appeared as the specific, i.e., super-natural objective cause behind this whole particular field of objective realities — just as his general causality in creating and conserving all things was never seriously questioned. Today the thinking mind must first be induced to envisage objective realities (the necessary vehicle of revelation) as the possible means of self-communication of an absolute, personal "thou" — by virtue of which the realm of objects can also lay claim to absolute truth. For this, reflection on the subject and on the "immanent" conditions which self-realization postulates in the concrete is needed. Then certain implications are disclosed. First, the I is always primarily directed to "another", a "thou", and indeed is fundamentally constituted by this orientation. Then, the subject must try to grasp the realm of things as the mediation of an absolute "thou". Finally, the subject must strive for explicit communication with this "thou", by means of a function of sign which the divine "thou" has specially conferred on the realm of things — by means, therefore, of a "revelation". In this process, the method of immanence discloses a "natural desire" for a historical and incarnational revelation, thereby anticipating the *demonstratio Christiana* and *catholica*. It provides a sort of framework into which the specific historical factors of the *demonstratio* can be fitted — prophecies, miracles, words and person of Jesus, the faith and the phenomenon of the Church. But they are no longer treated as proofs of the action of a supernatural cause. They are regarded as signs of the presence of the divine "thou".

3. The practical application of the method of immanence is determined by the two levels on which the question as to the meaning of life (and every other question) is posed. Firstly, it implies ignorance and hence openness for every possible answer. But then, and more profoundly, by the very fact that the question is posed, it already contains in the state of a tendency an anticipation of the definitive answer which it expects. Thus the first thing to demonstrate is man's capacity to hear the word of God — his *potentia oboedientialis* for revelation. This can be done by analysing (with K. Rahner) the transcendence of the finite spirit even in its sensible perception and displaying it as "hearer of the word". Or it can be done more concretely (with M. Blondel) by the dialectical demonstration that all evasions of the question of the meaning of life pose the question anew, and that all egocentric (immanentist) satisfactions with which one may try to give meaning to life leave the urge which has led to their installation hopelessly unsatisfied and hence intrinsically contradict one another. This done, the conditions are created for undertaking the second and more difficult task. The tendencies which remain unfulfilled must be confronted with the structure of the ever-changing goals which are constantly being sought after. This should result in the adumbration of a possible perfect fulfilment as the outline of a supernaturally-bestowed

grace in general ("idée d'un surnaturel in-déterminé": H. Bouillard). Thus the method of immanence does not rely on a psychologically verifiable "need" of the supernatural — which would fail to provide a universally valid proof. And it is not — as H. Duméry explains it — simply a description of essential phenomena in an effort to deduce the concept of the supernatural on the notional level, while omitting all reference to the reality of the gift of grace. But by confronting what is necessarily foreshadowed in man as he *de facto* finds himself, with what is actually achieved, it reveals a real orientation towards a supernatural reality which can only be vaguely indicated, because it stems from the initiative of God's grace.

4. Theologically, the method of immanence thus understood presupposes in man a quest for meaning which points on towards revelation, and hence that the call to the supernatural does not do violence to man's structure as a creature but ordains it to a connatural fulfilment by an ontologically effective intervention. Historically, both the method of immanence in the stricter sense, and the present discussion of the relationship between nature and grace go back to Blondel's *L'Action* (1893) and its application to fundamental theology in the *Lettre sur l'apologétique*. The authors whom Blondel cites explicitly as his predecessors, St. Augustine, St. Thomas Aquinas in the *Summa contra Gentiles,* Pascal and Deschamps (with his doctrine of the "fait interne"), had stressed above all the link between nature and grace. But here, of course, one must always be careful to avoid the misleading idea that this link is set up by nature, which would mean that it was ontologically prior to the *de facto* call. In this view whether nature is taken in the psychological sense of Modernism (*D* 2103, 2106) as the religious yearning, or whether the nature of created spirit as such is analysed (as in the doctrines condemned in *Humani Generis* [*D* 2323]), in both cases the supernatural is reduced to a mere correlative to nature, though still unattainable. Hence the method of immanence would be an immanentist estimate of the perfectibility of nature in order to reduce nature to a closed system. But in fact its effort is that human nature should be *open* to receive a completely incalculable revelation of God which is not merely transcendent but gratuitous.

See also *Immanentism, Revelation, Potentia Oboedientialis, Order* III, *Natural Theology, Nature* III, *Modernism.*

BIBLIOGRAPHY. V.-A. Deschamps, *Entretiens sur la démonstration catholique de la religion chrétienne* (1856); M. Blondel, *l'Action* (1893; 2nd ed., 1950); L. Laberthonnière, *Essais de philosophie religieuse* (1903); B. Pascal, *Pensées,* trans. by W. F. Trotter, introduction by T. S. Eliot (1908; reprint 1943); M. Blondel, *Le problème de la philosophie catholique* (1932); H. Duméry, *Blondel et la religion* (1954); R. Aubert, *Le problème de l'acte de foi* (3rd ed., 1958), pp. 265–392; M. Blondel and L. Laberthonnière, *Correspondance philosophique* (1961); H. Bouillard, *Blondel et le christianisme* (1961); H. Duméry, *Raison et religion dans la philosophie de l'action* (1963); M. Blondel, *The Letter on Apologetics and History and Dogma.* Texts presented and translated by A. Dru and I. Trethowan (1965); H. Bouillard, *The Logic of the Faith* (1967).

Peter Henrici

APOLOGISTS

Position in Church history. The era of the Apologists in the 2nd century is marked by two movements which led to a new understanding of the faith and of the Church. Pagans with an educated grasp of their religion, culture and philosophy received Christian baptism. Christianity responded to changing conditions by abandoning the mentality of the self-contained group to enter the public life of the non-Christian world, which for its part did not remain indifferent to Christianity.

Definition. The term Apologists is used for the 2nd century writers who were the first to debate Christianity methodically and on a large scale against the non-Christian world. In Greek, the most important are Quadratus, Aristides, Aristo of Pella, Justin, Tatian, Miltiades, Apollinaris of Hierapolis, Athenagoras, Pseudo-Justin, Theophilus of Antioch, Melito of Sardes, Hermias and the Letter to Diognetus; in Latin, there are Minucius Felix and Tertullian. Later authors of apologetic writings are not included among the Apologists in the strict sense. Apologetics was carried on in the 2nd century chiefly by writers who were attacking their own past in their opponents, while using its thought-forms and literary procedures. They employed chiefly the literary form of the discourse *(apologia),* the dialogue and the petition, with the clear intention of showing that Christianity, even when on the defensive, could withstand competition, and when its contents were proclaimed could gain the mastery. Facing attitudes which wavered between toleration and persecution, they varied between declarations of loyalty, informative propaganda, defensive explanations and denunciations. The preaching of the faith was no longer within the communities and a simple missionary effort. It had become a public debate on the literary level with neighbours of various types. The literature of Jewish propaganda and popular philosophy were models which could be availed of in many instances.

Literary resources. Christianity was using the instrument of literature for the first time to make its voice heard, and the public which it envisaged was more or less universal, though it started from concrete situations and addressed itself to specific personalities. The Apologists used the terms of their environment to explain, defend and present Christianity in a favourable light to adversaries like Crescens, Lucian, Fronto and Celsus, who saw in it the sum of all that was irrational, perverse and crude. They did not always succeed at once in their efforts. Inadequate literary equipment produced defective exposition and terminology. The Apologists were, in fact, often not well enough equipped for their task. Even their arguments were at times fragile, and their matter not well enough mastered intellectually, though their apologetics grew more and more skilful and relevant as time went on. These early efforts were therefore on very different levels, but they also drew on very different types of argument, as they sought to define and articulate the Christian message. In their various ways they aimed at the same goal: to expound the real nature and the supreme excellence of Christianity under the eyes of the hostile or the ignorant. And they resolutely made use of the intellectual and rhetorical instruments of their heathen environment. This in itself was a new departure in the history of Christianity. In the sub-apostolic age the transmission of the preaching had used purely religious genres, such as the written sermon, in its literary efforts. Now a type of writing with a wider appeal is used, calculated to obtain a hearing from the cultured and critical public. The creation of a Christian literature is no longer just an adjunct to preaching but an achievement valid in itself.

Outline of thought. The acceptability of Christianity was not the only main interest of the Apologists. They also took the absoluteness of Christianity as their theme. All earlier knowledge and worship of God, among Greeks, Jews or Orientals, was erroneous or at least inadequate, as were also their moral doctrines. This approach sometimes took the form of a total rejection of all earlier values, which meant that Christianity had to be presented as the sole truth in complete contrast and isolation. Following methods developed by Jewish apologists, the Christian writers used biblical chronology to prove that all pagan wisdom was a disjointed effort of recent date and full of borrowings from the OT. Another approach was to try to enlist sympathy by a more friendly and conciliatory tone. Christian truth is in harmony with the best in pagan thought and life. All that is true in paganism finds its perfection and its real home in Christianity. A far-reaching agreement between Christianity and philosophy is acknowledged with remarkable frequency. In the context of this discussion of similarities, Christianity is seen as the new philosophy which alone is true. Here the Logos doctrine was fruitful in explaining convergence and contrast (Justin). The Logos of the philosophers is none other than Christ. In all ages and in all places truth had been his gift, so that the best of the pagans were frankly called Christians, since the Logos spoke through them. But they were lonely voices because the demons were at work from the start to distort the known truth and to make a caricature of religion. The definitive manifestation of the Logos brought with it in Christianity true knowledge of God and enlightenment with regard to man's proper conduct in the world. Proof of the identity of Christ and the Logos is drawn from the OT, as a conclusive argument from prophecy and history. In the logic of this thinking, the truth and authority of the words of Jesus Christ then become imperative for all philosophers, while all that is "rational" (i.e., belonging to the ratio or Logos) can be claimed for Christianity. This interpretation of Christianity uses to some extent the vocabulary of contemporary philosophy and ethics, but of course this philosophy was theological to the core. A Christianity understood predominantly as a doctrine thus claims to be fully valid and universally intelligible. The two approaches, contrasting and linking Christianity with pagan philosophy, aim at establishing the superiority of Christianity. Its novelty ceases to be an obstacle, because it is presented as the ancient truth which was always sought for and of which glimpses were had at times, but which remained shrouded in error till at last it could be grasped in its entirety in the Logos.

Thus the Apologists do not aim at putting the deepest possible gulf between Christianity and the pagan world around them. They try, on the contrary, to point to bridges. When interpreting philosophy in this way and claiming it for Christianity, they have no intention of making a synthesis of the two. Their goal is rather to point out, in the service of the defence and propagation of the faith, that it is not a far cry from Platonism (the main philosophy of the times) to the Christian faith, which is therefore not the danger and aberration which it was supposed to be. This task is carried out in various ways, and the details are highly complicated. We must always take into consideration the special characteristics of the author in each case, since their personal history of conversion has coloured their interpretation of the Christian faith. We must also consider how uncritically the works of the thinkers were read in those days. Contacts in terminology were seized upon, but less attention was paid to the whole mental framework of the system from which individual themes were singled out. Terms and concepts were taken from philosophy to help to interpret Christianity. It was a novel and courageous enterprise, in which the Apologists always remained aware of the contrasts involved, though the new method brought with it certain shifts of emphasis which must not be overlooked.

The eschatology which had been the dominant factor in primitive Christianity was reduced by this approach to an afterthought, which could only be attached very loosely to the system, where it appeared in the form of a discursive treatment of judgment, rewards and punishment, immortality and fullness of knowledge. The Apologists were primarily interested in expounding the philosophical concept of monotheism and in multiplying arguments against pagan polytheism. In contrast to the widespread moral confusion, they could point to the effectiveness and superiority of the Christian teaching:

the commandments of Jesus were kept and men were assured of eternal life. The Logos Christology is centred on the history of the cosmos rather than the history of salvation, which is again understandable in view of the background of the writers and the public which they aimed at.

The same factors explain why the Christian literature of this period is notably restricted and selective in its subject-matter. Nonetheless, apologetics in philosophical guise still leaves room for propounding the Church tradition (on the Trinity, redemption, the sacraments and the liturgy) as well as the biblical. The OT is regarded as the one reliable and sufficient source, because God, the Logos and the Spirit speak in it. The individual sayings are to be judged in the light of this truth, and nothing certain can be said about God except on the basis of these Scriptures. The NT canon only began to take definite shape in the second half of the century. A circumstance fraught with consequences for Christian theology is that a decisive phase of its formulation took place in the context of Hellenistic thought. The weapons with which the theologians of the day sought to master the new situation were the spiritual superiority and the demonstrability of Christianity. To denounce their thinking as "early Catholicism" in a pejorative sense, and as the Hellenization of Christianity in the sense of its being overwhelmed and alienated by pagan philosophy, is to use very rigid categories. They are little use in tracing the thought-forms and problems of an earlier time, and can give the history of ideas and history itself only very superficially. In the present case they are also to a great extent inexact. In view of the fact that the NT itself contains apologetical items of very different types, especially in the presentation of the Acts, a more reserved judgment seems desirable. This early epoch should not be viewed at first in the light of dogma, but as a stage on a way, an orientation taken in a situation never to be repeated and scarcely to be paralleled, when early Christianity, impelled to understand itself and make itself understood, struck out spiritedly in the direction then open to it.

See also *Hellenism and Christianity, Platonism, Neo-Platonism.*

BIBLIOGRAPHY. TEXT: Justin, *The Apologies,* Greek text with English notes, ed. by A. W. F.

Blunt (1911); E. J. Goodspeed, *Die ältesten Apologeten*, texts with German introductions (1914); Athenagoras, *Embassy for the Christians; The Resurrection of the Dead*, ACW 23 (1956). LITERATURE: A. Puech, *Les apologistes grecs du second siècle de notre ère* (1912); M. Pellegrino, *Studi sull'antica apologetica* (1947); J. Quasten, *Patrology*, I (1950), pp. 186–253; B. Altaner, *Patrology* (1961), pp. 114–37; K. Baus, *From the Apostolic Community to Constantine*, vol. I of H. Jedin and J. Dolan, ed., *Handbook of Church History* (1965), pp. 171–80.

Norbert Brox

APOSTASY

Development of the concept. The word in classical Greek means either simply to "stand apart", to "depart", or to "abandon an alliance", to "revolt". In the Jewish tradition it was then used to signify "abandonment of belief", "infidelity to Yahweh"; so Jos 22:22; Jer 2:19; 2 Chr 29:19; see also Acts 21:21 and 2 Thess 2:3, where Paul is reproached with having rejected the Torah. It was then the obvious word to use to speak of abandonment of the Christian faith. Tertullian (*De Pudicitia*, 8: *PL*, II, 1047) calls the Jews "apostatae filii"; cf. "dabis apostatae veniam" (*De Pudicitia*, 6: *PL*, II, 1042), "omne apostatarum genus" (*De Pudicitia*, 9: *PL*, II, 1050). The word has the same meaning in Cyprian: "Eos qui vel apostataverunt et ad saeculum cui renuntiaverunt reversi gentiliter vivunt" (*Ep.*, 57, 3, 1: *CSEL*, III, 652). The usage became general, possibly under the influence of the case of Julian "the Apostate" (see Augustine, *De civitate Dei*, V, 21: *PL*, XLI, 168; *Ep.*, 105, 2, 10: *PL*, XXXIII, 400).

Later the word was used to take in also abandonment of the religious life or of holy orders; see Thomas Aquinas (*Summa Theologica*, II, II, q. 12, a. 1): "Apostasy means falling away from God, which takes place in various ways, corresponding to the various ways in which man is united to God: by faith, by the duly submissive readiness of the will to obey his commandments, and by works of supererogation, such as the religious life, the clerical state or holy orders."

Meaning. Here we take apostasy in the sense of the baptized believer abandoning his faith totally or by rejection of an essential truth of faith, e.g., the godhead of Christ. It does not necessarily imply the adoption of another faith or ideology, though this may under certain circumstances be an aggravating factor. But those who simply give up all practices of the Christian life are not, strictly speaking, apostates. We prescind from "apostates" from the religious life or holy orders.

Apostasy has always been regarded as one of the most serious sins (the "lapsi"), incurring very grave penalties. As early as the Councils of Ancyra (314) and Nicaea (325) the case-law of apostasy was highly developed. Under Justinian, civil penalties were also imposed, such as confiscation of goods and loss of the right to make a will (cf. *Codex Justiniani*, I, 7, "De Apostatis"). The civil penalties were later abolished, but the ecclesiastical ones remained, though gradually modified. The most important documents are: the bull *In Coena Domini* of Clement VII (1724), which reserved the annexed excommunication to the Pope; the Constitution *Apostolicae Sedis* of Pius IX (1869) and *CIC*, especially can. 2314, whereby the apostate is *ipso facto* excommunicated, and on refusal to repent after due warning loses all ecclesiastical offices, dignities and benefices; the excommunication is reserved *speciali modo* to the Holy See.

Moral responsibility. The attitude adopted for so many centuries towards apostates was dictated by the notion that they were guilty of grave sin. This was always considered unquestionable till in the 19th century a group of theologians, mostly German, raised doubts about it (e.g., G. Hermes, J. Frohschammer, A. Schmid). In their view, a distinction was to be made between the objective and the subjective aspect. Objectively, no Catholic could have a reason for abandoning his faith; but subjectively he could — even though erroneously — if he was sincerely convinced that his faith was not well-founded and hence not only might but even should be abandoned. Other theologians, such as A. Bauer, M. J. Scheeben and J. Kleutgen, still maintained the opinion that a Catholic could not have even a subjectively just cause for abandoning his faith, since if he fulfilled his obligations and hence remained in the state of grace, God would preserve him from such errors. Vatican I intervened in this controversy with the declaration: "Hence those who have once accepted the Catholic truth through the gift of faith are not in the same position as those who have been misled by human opinions to confess a false religion. For those who have once accepted the faith under the magisterium of the Church can never have a just cause *(justa causa)* for changing this faith or calling it in doubt." (*D* 1794.) Hence the solemn definition of the Council: "If anyone says that the faithful are in the same position as those who have not yet attained to the one true faith, and hence that Catholics may have a just cause for withdrawing their assent and calling in doubt the faith which they have received under the magisterium of the Church, until they have arrived at a scientific proof of the credibility and truth of their faith, let him be excluded." (*D* 1815.)

The historical background of this declaration was the demand of G. Hermes that the faithful, especially the cultured, should submit their faith to methodical doubt, till they could recognize that it was scientifically certain. This process of methodical doubt was supposed to be the same in the case of Catholics and non-Catholics. But the statement of the Council did not silence the debate. Controversy broke out anew on the question of the meaning of the phrase *justa causa*.

In this later debate, three periods can be clearly distinguished. In the first, which began after the close of Vatican I, authors in general maintained the subjective interpretation. They held that the statement of the Council meant that no Catholic could have even a subjectively just cause for abandoning his faith. He could not fall away from the faith unless he had lost grace. In the second period, in which the protagonists were T. Granderath and A. Vacant, the general inclination was to hold that the words of the Council were to be understood only in an objective sense. The Council had not pronounced on the subjective responsibility of Catholics who lost their faith. The third period began after the First World War, inspired above all by the writings of S. Harent. The subjective interpretation again came to the fore.

The present position appears to be that the subjective interpretation is generally accepted, though not without opposition here and there. Discussion continues. One trend (R. Aubert) is to take the words of the Council as applying only to normal cases. The possibility of exceptional cases, in which even a Catholic may abandon his faith, without loss of grace, is held to be open. According to A. Stolz, however, the words of the Council are to be considered as a universally and absolutely valid assertion. No case can be conceived in which a Catholic could fall away from the faith and still remain in the state of grace. It should, however, be noted that discussion has been concerned with the precise meaning of the Council's words, and not with the concrete case itself. Hence even if one concludes that the Council did not pronounce on subjective guilt, it does not follow that there need not be subjective guilt in apostasy. It is one thing to say that the Council has not defined that a Catholic can never have even a subjective reason for abandoning the faith, and another thing to say that in reality a Catholic may have a just cause, at least subjectively, to abandon his faith, so that in doing so he would not commit sin.

Apostasy and religious liberty. Religious liberty is a question which cannot be avoided in the treatment of apostasy. The affirmation of religious liberty does not imply that one is morally free to preserve or abandon one's faith. The religious liberty affirmed by Vatican II clearly envisaged the civil and political level and ultimately one's relationships to other men. It affirmed that no one should be compelled to give up or practise a given religion — a matter of "tolerance". Accordingly, the Constitution on the Church affirmed (art. 14): "Whosoever, therefore, knowing that the Catholic Church was made necessary by God through Jesus Christ, would refuse to enter her or to remain in her could not be saved." It must, however, be emphasized that the phrase of Vatican I, "those who have once accepted the faith under the magisterium", certainly does not apply to all who belong to the Church sociologically. Hence no certain moral judgment may be passed on any concrete individual who leaves the Church.

See also *Atheism, Heresy, Tolerance.*

BIBLIOGRAPHY. A. Beugnet, "Apostasie", *DTC*, I (1931), cols. 1602–12; H. Lennerz, *De obligatione catholicorum perseverandi in fide. Documenta Concilii Vaticani* (1932); G. B. Guzzetti, *La perdita della fede nel cattolico* (1940), pp. 1–214; id., "Necessità e perdita della fede", *Problemi e orientamenti di teologia dogmatica*, II (1957), pp. 709–49; R. Aubert, *Le problème de l'acte de foi* (3rd ed., 1958); id., *Vatican I* (1964); id., *Essais sur la liberté religieuse* (1965).

G. B. Guzzetti

APOSTLE

Methodological note. The apostolic office will be considered here not only in its origin but also in regard to its permanent presence in the course of the Church's development. The historical consideration must proceed from an attempt to understand the original nature of the apostolic office, and must take into account the intentions of Jesus in instituting the office, as well as the significance which it has for the constitution of the Church. One can trace with some certainty the constitutive significance which the apostolic office had for the early Church both from the exercise of the office as recorded in the NT, which is the founding document of the early Church, as well as from the place which that office assumed in the course of the history of the Church. But the intention which Jesus had with regard to the apostles can only be deduced from a comparison of the parallel texts forming the record of the words and deeds of Jesus. In trying to determine the exact meaning of the concept "apostle" in the NT it is difficult to decide when the actions of the apostles are to be ascribed to their office or to their purely personal capacity. The office is not limited to the institutional and its function is therefore difficult to fix. Besides this, the different stages through which the concept of the apostle and the apostolic office evolved are all dove-tailed and overlapped in the various writings of the NT.

New Testament. 1. The NT term ἀπόστολος derives from the *šālîaḥ* of late Judaism. The idea embodied by the Hebrew word is already attested by the time of Jesus (Jn 13:16), though the term itself is only verified in the 2nd century A.D. It is related to the Semitic law of delegation and means the authoritative representation of an individual or a group in juridical or religious matters. The dignity and respect shown to a representative depend entirely upon the authority of the sender. The LXX translates *šālîaḥ* by ἀπόστολος (1 Kg 14:6 — the prophet as a messenger of God).

2. The concept of apostle in the older Pauline letters, as the earliest NT record of the title, is especially significant because it precedes all controversy about the nature of the apostolic office. In 1 Thess 2:7 Paul refers to himself together with Silvanus and Timothy as apostles of Christ. This clearly shows that the office of apostle did not necessarily depend upon the fact of one's having seen the Lord. The apostolic charge did not have to be a charge imposed directly by the risen Lord; it could also be delegated indirectly. The encounter with the risen Lord was important for Paul because he thereby became a direct witness of the resurrection of Jesus (1 Cor 15:8). Similarly, we may deduce from 1 Cor 15:6 (the appearance of the risen Lord to the five hundred brethren) that according to the earliest Pauline letters, a meeting with the risen Lord is not the sole requisite for the office of apostle. Later, however, the early Church came more and more to consider the witness of the resurrection next to the call to apostleship as a criterion for the title of apostle.

What is essential for the concept of apostle in the older letters of Paul is that the apostle proclaims the gospel as one so delegated by Christ. The apostles are responsible to God alone. Since God speaks through them, the Spirit of Christ is present in the community. The salvation or damnation of men depends upon their acceptance or rejection of the apostolic message (2 Cor 2:15f.). The charge of proclamation as imposed by Christ (cf. Gal 2:7ff.) is the basis of the apostolic office of the original apostles who remained in Jerusalem, as well as of the travelling missionaries, Paul and his companions.

3. The synthesis of the Pauline conception with that of the evangelists (to be treated later in another connection) is to be found in the description of the apostolic office in the Acts. According to Acts 1:2f. and 1:21, three things characterize the apostle. a) The apostle must have been a disciple of Jesus. b) Only a reliable witness of the ministry, passion and resurrection of Jesus can be an apostle and his testimony must rest upon the actual fact of having "seen" the risen Lord and of having received the Holy Spirit. (Acts 14:14 appears to be evidence of an older tradition, since along with Barnabas·Paul is also called an apostle, though he was not a witness of the public ministry of Jesus.) c) But the decisive criterion for apostleship is the fact of having been sent by Christ to proclaim the gospel (Acts 1:8; 10:42). This criterion is indispensable, universal, and final. According to

Acts, therefore, only the Twelve and Paul can be called apostles in the strict sense of the word.

4. How does the intention of Jesus in sending forth his apostles correspond to the concept of Acts which was decisive for the further interpretation of the apostolic office? That Jesus called men to follow after him (Mk 1:16–20), and the Twelve in a special way (Mk 3:14: "and he appointed twelve"), cannot be open to doubt. The word ἀπόστολος, however, seems to have been transposed by the synoptics back into the time of the public ministry of Jesus. Nevertheless it is certain that Jesus at least occasionally charged his disciples to proclaim the kingdom of God in word and signs (1 Cor 9:14; cf. Mt 10:10; Lk 10:7; Lk 9:1f.). This mission which was only temporary during the public ministry of Jesus became, after the resurrection of Christ, an office through the gift of the Spirit (Mt 28:18ff.). The apostles share in the power of Jesus to bring salvation and doom, according to Lk 10:16, "He who hears you hears me, and he who rejects you rejects me, and he who rejects me rejects him who sent me" — words which already have a Johannine ring.

Theology. Even at the time of the apostles, the Church saw in the apostolic office one of her essential marks (Eph 2:20; Rev 21:14), though the self-designation of the Church as apostolic in the Creed dates from the 4th century (*D* 14, 11). That the Church is apostolic guarantees its truth as opposed to all the other Christian communities. The apostolicity of the Church not only involves claims with respect to the authenticity and extent of revelation, treated of in fundamental theology (*D* 783, 1836, 2021), but it also has ecclesiological consequences with respect to the unity and the visible nature of the Church. The Church's understanding of the juridical and institutional character of the apostolic office cannot, it is true, be substantiated by Jn 21:15–18 alone — the thrice repeated mandate given to Peter before witnesses. Its character as office is rather witnessed to by tradition and is seen to be a necessary consequence of the basic incarnational structure of the Church. The author of the fourth gospel had the clearest insight into a theology of the apostolate which follows from the very mystery of the Incarnation, and gave it the fullest develop-

ment (although in Jn the term ἀπόστολος appears but once, in 13:16).

The Incarnation embodies a comprehensive revelation which is addressed to all men. With the incarnation of the Word, the pre-existent Logos subjected himself to the conditions of human life. But to comply with the universality of his mission, Jesus had to make use of human emissaries. As the Incarnation meant God's rendering himself visible on the fixed categories of the spatial and the temporal, the Twelve together with Paul were made mediators and witnesses of revelation in a concrete and as it were hierarchical order after Christ. They share in the authority of Christ (Jn 20:21; cf. 17:18), which in turn derives from the authority of the Father (Jn 12:44). For John, the essential elements of the apostolate are the following.

a) Unity with Jesus assures for the disciples the intimate love of the Father (Jn 1:12f.; 16:27). b) Union with Christ is guaranteed through the gift of the Spirit. The Spirit enlightens the disciples so that their teaching is true (Jn 14:16f.; 16:14). c) Election passes into mission: Christ made his disciples his representatives, his ἀπόστολοι. In their hands he places the fullness of authority which he received from the Father (Jn 14:27; 15:15; 17:2. 14. 18. 22. 26), the mission which has its source in the Father. It is therefore understandable that the world treats the envoys in the same manner as it treated the Son (Jn 15:19f.).

Through the inseparable unity with Christ, there is in his Church a) the message of the apostles which is the word of Christ, which is in turn the fathomless wisdom of the Father (Jn 21:15); b) the apostles are trustworthy witnesses of Christ — revelation is indeed an act of the grace of God which can only be responded to with faith; c) the apostles are representatives of Christ whose messianic powers as shepherd, priest and teacher are bestowed upon them. (Similarly, the number twelve which was stressed by the synoptics is an indication that Jesus claims for his apostles the position of emissaries of the Messiah.) This transmission of power was a real one so that the saving activity of Christ should have a visible continuation, and at the same time it represents a vicarious exercise of authority so that the unity of the mission might not be endangered, the mission which was reserved solely to the one mediator between God and man. Thus, because the transmission of the office was a real one, the office of apostle represents the invisible presence of Christ in his Church. The bond between the Church founded upon the apostles and the ἐκκλησία is so close that the Scriptures sometimes ascribe the founding of the Church to Christ (1 Cor 10:4) and sometimes to the apostles (Mt 16:18; Eph 2:20). The apostolic founding of the Church continues for all time, inasmuch as the apostolic preaching remains active in the Church through the Scriptures. This lasting confrontation of the Church with the apostles as those empowered with the authority of Christ does not only occur over and over again with each new confrontation with the Scriptures, but it is also guaranteed in an abiding way through the episcopate as the institution which derives from the apostolic office — as the ultimate logic of the Incarnation. Thus, along with the handing on of the word, the transmission of the sacraments is assured. And so 1 Clem expands the Johannine conception in the following manner: "The Father sent his Son, the Son lives on in his apostles, and the apostles bestowed the teaching office upon their successors the bishops."

See also *Judaism* I, *New Testament Theology* II, III.

BIBLIOGRAPHY. A. Médebielle, "Apostolat", *DBS* I (1928), cols. 533–88; K. H. Rengstorff, "ἀποστέλλω, ἀπόστολος", *TWNT,* I (1933), pp. 397–448, E. T. (1964), pp. 398–447; H. von Campenhausen, "Der urchristliche Apostelbegriff", *Studia Theologica* 1 (1947), pp. 96–130; H. Mosbech, "Apostolos in the New Testament", *Studia Theologica* 2 (1948), pp. 166–200; J. Munck, "Paul, the Apostles, and the Twelve", *Studia Theologica* 3 (1949), pp. 96–110; H. von Campenhausen, *Kirchliches Amt und geistliche Vollmacht in den ersten drei Jahrhunderten* (1953; 2nd ed., 1963); J. Colson, *Les fonctions ecclésiales aux deux premiers siècles* (1956); K. E. Kirk, ed., *The Apostolic Ministry* (2nd ed., 1957); B. Rigaux, "Die 'Zwölf' in Geschichte und Kerygma", in H. Ristow and K. Matthiae, eds., *Der historische Jesus und der kerygmatische Christus* (1960), pp. 468–86; G. Klein, *Die Zwölf* (1961); K. Rahner und J. Ratzinger, *The Episcopate and the Primacy,* Quaestiones Disputatae 4 (1962); J. Knox, "Romans 15:14–23 and Paul's Conception of His Apostolic Mission", *JBL* 83 (1964), pp. 1–12; W. Schmithals, *Paul and James* (1965); K. H. Schelkle, *Discipleship and Priesthood* (1965).

Antonio Javierre

APOSTOLIC CHURCH

I. Primitive Community. II. Apostolic Church.

I. Primitive Community

Concept and date. The terms "Apostolic Church", "Primitive Community" and "Primitive Christianity" designate, not very precisely, the Palestinian Christianity of the first decades of the Church. The notion is based on the existence of the NT canon, seen as a mirror of the primitive community, on the important role which the apostles played for a definitely limited period in NT revelation, and also on romantic notions of the ideal and normative character of the first Christian community — drawing on the presentation given in Acts. The *terminus a quo* depends on how one answers the question of when and how Jesus founded a Church. Thus R. Bultmann and H. Braun make the beginnings of the primitive community coincide with the dawn of faith in the resurrection, while H. Schürmann stresses the objective and personal continuity with the pre-Easter group of disciples, especially Peter. As regards the *terminus ad quem,* A. Vögtle suggests the end of the apostolic generation, the growing sense of the delay of the parousia, the cessation of charisms and religious enthusiasm, and the appearance of heresies and persecutions. Protestant writers like W. G. Kümmel suggest the time when the Church became an institution within which salvation was to be sought, while H. Conzelmann thinks of the time when the Church began to be conscious of having a past which could be designated as "apostolic" — this period then being obviously "post-apostolic". This would have brought with it a temporal dimension of the Church and a changed notion of tradition.

But since the concept of "apostle" varies widely in the NT (in John it is only used by Jesus), the notion of "apostolic" is also somewhat artificial. Since according to Conzelmann the transition from primitive Christianity had already been made when the Church started to reflect on its past, only a few writings of the NT would belong to primitive Christianity. Kümmel too finds that the transition has been made where the parousia is no longer seen as imminent, as in the Pastoral Letters and 2 Peter. On the question of the significance of the primitive period, Kümmel affirms that it is "a historical norm, to be traced by critical reflection". But the whole notion of norm becomes questionable if one remembers how restricted was the field of unity in Church life and theology, and that the contrasts have already appeared which were to remain operative in the Church of later times. It is only the systematic presentation of Lk which imparts the notion of a norm, as an interpretation of the first days of the community. Hence when the question of "primitive Christianity" is analysed, the answers depend partly on the previous decision with regard to the notion of the Church in general, and partly on the assumption that there were in fact such historical entities as a single primitive community and Christianity.

Historical treatment. An approach may be made to determine the period in which the primitive community flourished by using the NT to see what theological aspects were prior to others. Thus the Pastoral Letters presuppose Paul, as does 1 Peter. But this way of determining what is primitive Christianity leads only to the definition of basic types of theology (synoptic, Johannine, Pauline, Letter to the Hebrews), none of which can be deduced from the others; a uniform basic kerygma can be provided for them only by a process of abstraction, as the contrast between Paul and John in particular shows. And one must agree with Wilckens, against Geiselmann, that such a kerygma cannot be deduced from the missionary discourses of Acts, since these are Lucan compositions. Hence from the point of view of the history of theology, primitive Christianity should be defined as the sum total of a number of different theological principles, all equally primordial, used to interpret the coming of Jesus. Another approach to primitive Christianity may be made through the historical events and early Christian forms of fellowship which can be deduced from the NT. According to Galatians, 1 Corinthians and Acts, the decisive elements were the conflicts between Jews, Jewish Christians and gentile Christians, and also the beginnings of the mission to the gentiles.

The beginnings of the primitive community. The origin of the primitive community presupposes the pre-Easter calling of the disciples, the call of Peter, John and James being beyond all critical doubt. According to the ancient tradition of 1 Corinthians 15, which

also appears in John and Luke, Peter was also granted the first and decisive apparition of the risen Lord. The apparition to the Twelve is presented as a parallel to this. It must be maintained, against Bultmann, that visions as such cannot have been generative of the community. It is also certain that there was now a fact of decisive importance for salvation, which, once it was formulated as a confession of faith, needed to be embodied in tradition. Hence its acceptance in faith was also a factor in the constitution of the community. Phenomenologically, the common recourse to the fact of the resurrection of Jesus was the initial factor in the formation of a post-Easter community. And here the affirmation that it was Jesus who rose again presupposes that there were men who already knew who Jesus was and could also recognize that the resurrection was the fulfilment and confirmation of his eschatological claim. In a fellowship with a structure of this nature, the witnesses of an apparition of the Lord were necessarily the first and chief members. Hence later writings also presuppose (Jn, Heb) that the leaders of the community were those who had seen the risen Lord. (The five hundred brethren of 1 Cor 15 form an exception.) The apparition to Peter remained throughout the norm. The first believers in the resurrection were undoubtedly centred on Jerusalem — in spite of the indication of Galilee in Mk 16 and the general tendency of transposing the apparitions to Jerusalem. In addition, "pneumatic" events were clearly very numerous after Easter, and gave a special stamp to the primitive community. Luke sums up these events in the sending of the Spirit on the Twelve together. No doubt, after Pentecost, the regular channel for the reception of the Spirit by Christians was the imposition of the hands of the apostles, which followed baptism, but the descent of the Spirit could also be direct (Acts 10:44). According to Luke, the preaching of the Twelve also began after Pentecost. It seems that the Twelve went in pairs to preach to the Jews, using a style which may have resembled that of the Baptist and Jesus (Mark). Luke's placing the Twelve permanently in Jerusalem need not be taken too literally, since Paul did not meet them when he visited Jerusalem and according to Luke's own presentation, in Acts, there is another group, the Elders, who have charge of the community (see

Bishop I). According to Gal 1 and 2, Cephas and James represented Jerusalem, and he met no other apostles. Fourteen years later James, Cephas and John are the "pillars" of the Church in Jerusalem. The order of the names may indicate some change of function, but it is certainly clear from Acts 21:18 that in later times James "the brother of the Lord" was the sole head of the Jewish-Christian community at Jerusalem. (He was put to death in A.D. 62 according to Josephus, *Antiquities,* XX, 200.) He was probably the head of the group of Elders mentioned by Luke. Acts as far as 2:41 practically confines its attention to the Twelve, but Acts 2:42–47 gives a brief sketch of the life of the community. The community of goods (2:44) is described in terms of the Hellenistic ideal of friendship, adding lustre to the sunny beginnings of the Church as depicted by Luke.

It is no doubt historically accurate that the eschatology preached by Jesus and the faith in the resurrection of Christ which characterized the community caused no breach with Judaism. Nor did the titles of "the holy one, the elect, the just", which were probably applied to Jesus very early. These titles, like the institution of the Twelve, show that the community applied to itself the notion of the "Remnant". Nonetheless, the rites of baptism and the Eucharist were already paving the way for a breach with Judaism. There is a clearer picture of conditions in Acts 6, according to which there were two relatively independent groups at an early stage, the Hellenists (Jews speaking only Greek) and the Hebrews (Palestinian Jewish Christians). The conflict signalled by Luke apropos of the relief of widows explains only their function of "deacons". But they must also have been independent missionaries ("evangelists"). Wilckens suggests that for linguistic reasons they could have had no access to the pre-Easter traditions about Jesus — a view not confirmed by the third volume of the *Discoveries in the Judaean Desert* which depicts Palestine as largely bi-lingual, if not tri-lingual (Aramaic, Greek and Latin). The question at issue between the two groups was probably the one which brought about Stephen's death at the hands of the Jews: the relation of the Hellenists to the temple and the law. In their concept of the law, these Hellenists may have been essentially at one with the liberal circles of the Jews of the diaspora. And as regards the temple, their attitude was probably determined not only by Hellenistic criticism of external religion but also by the saying which played so important a role in the trial of Jesus — the prophecy of the destruction and re-building of the temple in three days (Mt 26:62; 27:40; cited only here by Luke, Acts 6:14). This was interpreted as an attack on the temple, and therefore provoked sharp nationalistic reactions. The stoning of Stephen made the Hellenists still more critical of Jewish tradition. They fled (Acts 8:4) and founded the community of Antioch (11:19 ff.). Obviously, these were the events which occasioned the actual breach with Judaism on the part of the community. They also opened up the way for a mission to the gentiles without the preaching of circumcision.

The gentile mission, the law and circumcision. The breach with Judaism could not have merely been the consequence of the conviction that the resurrection of the crucified Jesus was the beginning of the end of the world. There must also have been differences in actual religious practice. The mission to the gentiles, with no obligation of circumcision, began at Antioch, before Paul came on the scene. No definite answer can be given to the question of how these Jewish-Christian Hellenists arrived at the notion of a gentile mission. It may be taken as certain that Jesus himself saw his mission as a task confined to Israel. And the Jewish notion of an eschatological pilgrimage of the nations (Mt 8:11 f. par.) is specifically distinct from that of an active mission to the gentiles. The notion of a gentile mission without circumcision probably presupposes the following principles: a) The coming judgment is universal, affecting all men. b) The omission of circumcision signifies that under this judgment Jews and gentiles are on the same plane. Possibly the importance of baptism as the rite of initiation had made circumcision meaningless. c) The omission of circumcision means that the division of mankind into just and unjust, common in late Judaism, was regarded as in principle independent of Israel — since it depended only on moral factors. d) Omission of circumcision presupposes the definitive breach between this group and Judaism. And in fact it was also in Antioch, according to Acts 11:26, that the new name of Χριστιανοί was given to the group. Henceforward the fellowship between the baptized is stronger than the link with Judaism. e) The tendency already present in Hellenistic Judaism to eliminate national idiosyncrasies, was thus combined with the eschatology of Jesus (so too the attitude to the temple combined elements from Hellenism and from the preaching of Jesus); the missionary impulse itself was inspired by the example of Jesus.

But the new type of mission underlined the contrast with the Jewish Christians of Jerusalem. F. C. Baur regarded the ensuing opposition between a Pauline freedom from the law and a Petrine adherence to the traditions of Judaism as constitutive for Christianity. E. Reuss, however, rightly distinguished between Jewish Christians of the strict and of the moderate observance. But apart from the law and "doctrine", there were also differences in the type of communities which developed. The "Council of Jerusalem" was to clear up the question of the Law. In Acts it appears as an answer given to Paul and Barnabas by the Twelve and the Elders, while Paul presents it as an agreement between Paul and Barnabas on the one hand, and James, Peter and John on the other. But in both versions the gentiles are granted freedom from the law. Nonetheless, the link with Jerusalem, and the bond between the Church and Israel, are considered so essential by Paul (see Romans) that he lays an increasing stress on the collections there agreed upon for the community in Jerusalem (Gal 2:10; 2 Cor 8; 9; Rom 15:20f.). Thus the collection gives expression to the fact that the link with the historical existence of Jesus among the Jewish people was maintained.

The "apostolic decree" (Acts 15:20, 29; 21:15), which Paul makes no mention of, can hardly have been an immediate fruit of the Council. It is much more likely to have been the result of the conflict at Antioch (Conzelmann). For it is, in fact, a decree envisaging cases left unsolved by the Council of Jerusalem, the very type of case which was the occasion of the conflict at Antioch — the question of Jewish and gentile Christians eating together. The agreement reached at the Council, permitting gentile missions without circumcision, could only be applied directly in purely Jewish-Christian or purely gentile Christian communities. It raised problems in mixed communities, since the Jewish Christians always went in fear of incurring ritual impurity. The decree imposed on gentile Christians the minimum of ritual purity, just enough to enable meals to be taken together. But the decision in favour of a gentile mission without circumcision was not universally accepted among the Jewish Christians of Jerusalem. There was an uncompromising minority which reacted first by trying to introduce circumcision for gentile Christians (which occasioned the disturbances in the Pauline mission of which Galatians gives some idea), and then by schism (possibly the kernel of the later Ebionites). At the beginning of the revolt against the Romans, the Jewish Christians left Jerusalem for Pella (Eusebius, *Hist. eccles.*, III, 5, 2). But the influence of Jewish traditions remained particularly strong in the Syrian missions, which was important for Matthew. A few decades later, the Great Church was composed almost exclusively of gentile Christians. Thus before the end of the 1st century, the basic theology and ecclesiology of the Hellenistic group in the disciples of Jesus at Jerusalem had prevailed, being enriched and differentiated in many ways during the process.

BIBLIOGRAPHY. F. C. Baur, "Die Christuspartei in der Korinthischen Gemeinde", *Tübinger Zeitschrift für Theologie* 4 (1831), pp. 61ff.; E. Reuss, *Geschichte der heiligen Schriften des Neuen Testaments* (6th ed., 1887); J. Parkes, *The Conflict of the Church and the Synagogue* (1934); J. Weiss, *The History of Primitive Christianity*, 2 vols. (1937); J. Klausner, *From Jesus to Paul* (1944); G. B. Caird, *The Apostolic Age* (1955); R. Bultmann, *Primitive Christianity in its Contemporary Setting*, trans. by R. H. Fuller (1956); M. Simon, *St. Stepen and the Hellenists in the Primitive Church* (1958); H. Conzelmann, "Heidenchristentum", *RGG*, III (1959), cols. 128–41; W. G. Kümmel, "Urchristentum", *RGG*, VI (1962), cols. 1187–93; M. Goguel, *The Primitive Church*, trans. by H. C. Snape (1964); A. Vögtle, "Urgemeinde", *LTK*, X (1965), cols. 551–5.

Klaus Berger

II. Apostolic Church

1. Apostolic Church means the Church of apostolic times and thus covers the period up to about A.D. 70. The apostolic Church is known to us above all through the writings of the NT which either, like the gospels, present its tradition about Jesus Christ, or, like Acts and the epistles, describe its way

of life. But a number of ancient non-canonical texts, such as the *Didache,* the *Epistles* of Clement and Barnabas contain liturgical, exegetical and disciplinary elements which date back to early Christianity. The NT gives us the picture of official Christianity, but, as Baur has shown (in *Rechtgläubigkeit und Ketzerei*), early Christianity included various marginal currents of thought. We must add that geographically the NT describes only the expansion of the Church in the Graeco-Roman world of the Mediterranean. But there was also an Aramean mission in Transjordania, Syria and Osroenes of which only traves have come down to us through traditions which were difficult to check, such as those concerning Thomas's mission to Edessa.

This early period presents a number of definite characteristics. The first is the pre-eminent place occupied by the apostles. They were witnesses to the faith and founders of the community. But we see that they also chose others to collaborate with them in their twofold function, such as James at Jerusalem and Titus and Timothy in Asia Minor and Crete. Another characteristic of early Christianity was the place occupied in it by charismatic gifts, of which Pauline letters in particular have much to say. Though the simultaneous existence of ecclesiastical office and of charisms is certain, it is often difficult to decide to which category certain figures, described variously as teachers, prophets and apostles, belonged. A further characteristic was the normative role of the oral tradition passed on by the apostles. The writings of the NT were only just beginning to be compiled during this period. Scripture meant the OT and the instruction given by the "teachers" was for the most part a Christological exegesis of the OT in the manner of the Jewish Rabbis (Gerhardsson, *Memory and Manuscript*). Many examples of this type of exegesis have been preserved in the *Testimonia.* Finally, the whole period was dominated by the conflict between Jewish and Gentile Christians, as appears from the Acts of the Apostles and the letters of St. Paul. Such a conflict implies great differences between the communities.

2. The primitive community has always appeared in Christian history as a point of reference with regard to a certain number of problems. But in most cases the idealistic image of the community is a creation of theology bearing little relations to reality. Here we can distinguish a number of questions.

a) The primitive community was very soon put forward as a model of charity and poverty, the embodiment of evangelical perfection. This is the picture portrayed in the Acts of the Apostles. Luke describes the union of hearts and the sharing of possessions in a way which is possibly inspired by the Essene ideal with perhaps a suggestion of Platonist influence (Cerfaux). This nostalgia for the primitive state inspired many spiritual renewals in the Church. This was so in the case of St. Basil, St. Francis of Assisi, the evangelism of the Reformers and also the apostolic vision of St. Ignatius. But it seems that the early community was split by serious divisions which first came to the surface in the controversy over the widows and then when the problem of the observance of the Mosaic law had to be faced.

b) A certain number of writers (Harnack, Loisy) contrast early Christianity with what they call *Frühkatholizismus,* early Catholicism. For them early Christianity had the following characteristics. It was essentially charismatic, guided by the Holy Spirit and completely free. The existence of a hierarchical authority was a secondary phenomenon due to the requirements of organization. Early Christianity was dominated by the expection of the imminent return of Christ and it was only secondarily that the Church sought an anchorage on this earth, which entailed a compromise with the world. This version of early Christianity is accurate in certain respects, but completely disregards the primitive character of the hierarchical structure established by Christ during his life on earth and also the existence of different currents of thought in early Christianity.

c) The importance of the primitive community is also exaggerated in the *formgeschichtliche Schule.* For Dibelius und Bultmann, the writings of the NT are the expression of the faith of the primitive community. They tell us very little of the historical Christ. For Oscar Cullmann the apostolic times have a privileged character which is normative in relation to post-apostolic Christianity. Here again the early community appears as highly idealized. Studies of 1st century Rabbinism (Gerhardsson, Le Déaut) have shown that the tradition of Christ's own teaching was of great importance in the NT and that the part played by the community was less than has been suggested. Moreover, the writings of the NT are not so much the expression of the faith of the community as of the faith of the apostoles and their successors. The creative genius of the communities found its expression rather in an abundant apocryphal literature. Hence it is not the primitive which is the criterion, but the apostolic. And the criterion of apostolicity is continued in the apostolic succession. As such primitive Christianity has no privileged character. It simply represents a form of expression of Christianity which is characterized by its Semitic structure.

See also *Apostolic Church* I, *Apostle, Early Church, Church History*.

BIBLIOGRAPHY. A. von Harnack, *The Expansion of Christianity in the First Three Centuries,* trans. by J. Moffat, 2 vols. (1904–5); W. Bauer, *Rechtgläubigkeit und Ketzerei im ältesten Christentum* (1934); M. Dibelius, *From Tradition to Gospel,* trans. by B. L. Woolf (1935); A. Loisy, *The Birth of the Christian Religion,* trans. by L. P. Jacks (1948); L. Cerfaux, "La première communauté chrétienne à Jérusalem", *Recueil L. Cerfaux,* II (1954), pp. 125–57; O. Cullmann, *The Early Church* (1956); B. Gerhardsson, *Memory and Manuscript* (1961); W. D. Davies, *Christian Origins and Judaism* (1962); R. Bultmann, *History of the Synoptic Tradition,* trans. by J. Marsh (1963); J. Daniélou, *The Theology of Jewish Christianity* (1964); K. Baus, *From the Apostolic Community to Constantine,* vol. I of H. Jedin and J. Dolan, ed., *Handbook of Church History* (1965), pp. 59–85.

Jean Daniélou

APOSTOLIC FATHERS

Definition. By Apostolic Fathers is meant a group of post-canonical (and non-canonical) early Christian authors, whose number has been differently determined according to inconsistent criteria, and which has recently been reduced with a view to "saving and clarifying the concept" (J. A. Fischer). The decisive feature is direct contact with the apostles, or just an evident nearness to them according to the time and content of their preaching. The reason for the fluidity of the concept of "Apostolic Fathers" lies in the difficulty of applying this principle. In any case the distinctive point is that they were men of the apostolic age, whose writings were disregarded when the canon of the NT was being formed, even though

some of them achieved, occasionally and regionally, canonical prestige. Their delimitation in contrast to the Apocrypha of the same time and to related literature is based on their nearness to the apostolic preaching as attested by the NT.

Writings. Under these conditions the following writings, among those which are normally designated as Apostolic Fathers, are to be included in any case under this name: the (first) letter of *Clement* of Rome, the seven letters of *Ignatius* of Antioch, as well as the letter (or the two letters) of *Polycarp* of Smyrna to the Philippians. Whether the apologetical fragment of *Quadratus* is added (Fischer) or not, makes little difference to the corpus of the Apostolic Fathers. If one applies a strict historical standard, then we have only these writings to deal with. In the case of other documents, which are also commonly reckoned among the Apostolic Fathers, the following points are to be considered: the *Didache* is too uncertain in age and authorship to be accounted as belonging to early times. The *Letter of Barnabas* as well as the *Second Letter of Clement* must be considered as pseudonymous; in their content they do not display any particularly close connection to apostolic times. The early form of the traditions of presbyters from Asia Minor, used by Irenaeus, is too uncertain to justify an early dating in apostolic times. According to Eusebius (*Hist. Eccl.,* III, 39, 2), Papias does not reckon himself to the first generation. The anonymous *Letter to Diognetus* is to be dated most likely about A.D. 200 (H. I. Marrou) and, in line with its intention and content, must be reckoned among the Apologists. For the *Shepherd of Hermas* one must reckon with more than one author (St. Giet); its content shows a considerable departure from the original apostolic kerygma. And finally, the *Martyrdoms of Ignatius and Polycarp* were reckoned among the Apostolic Fathers merely because of the heroes whom they celebrated; objectively and chronologically, however, they do not belong to them.

But even with the group which then remains *(1 Clement, Ignatius, Polycarp, Quadratus Fragment)* the idea of the Apostolic Fathers, seen purely historically, is not entirely without problems; it encompasses an inconsistent body of writings and these writings show, in terms of their contents, various degrees of approximity to the apostolic preaching. It may well be that for these authors the designation as Apostolic Fathers is valid in a historical sense, since the fact that they go back to the apostles cannot be reasonably doubted; but none of these writings is ultimately a repetition of the apostolic New Testament message.

Apart from the literary uniformity of the short list (the form of a letter) they have the following characteristics in common. The concept and collective name Apostolic Fathers is not, particularly if it is to be taken in the larger sense, useful as a *genus literarium* or chronological classification, but as a grouping in the history of theology. It encompasses — over and beyond all differences — the written documents of the post-apostolic era "between" the NT and the Apologists, i.e., of a stage in Christian self-understanding which stands on the threshold of the transition from the first generation to the later age of the Church. We have, of course, to reckon with the fact that part of the Apostolic Fathers is not later than some canonical writings of the NT. And there are traces in later NT writings of the same transition to an age in which one is conscious of being at one remove from the source. On the other hand, some writings, which do not belong to the apostolic age, testify to a situation in the history of faith which is basically the same. The grouping of these writings can, therefore, be separated from strict questions of form, authorship and dating, so that there would be no objection to a more comprehensive concept of the Apostolic Fathers. Thereby the consequence would merely be drawn from the fact that it concerns a category in the history of theology. The content of the writings of the limited group, as well as their comparison with documents of a few decades later, which are now generally distinguished from them, places the value of this narrow grouping in doubt as far as an "epochal" classification is concerned. One cannot speak of their more obvious apostolicity in all points, and so deduce a characteristic which might bind them closer to one another than to writings of a slightly later date. Here the possible association of some authors with the apostles carries less weight. The specific connection with the apostolic age, which is what one wants to

emphasize by the concept of Apostolic Fathers, is not dependent upon the decade in which a work was composed. Here too, thought which is of the one temper and impact cannot be exactly delimited chronologically. Early Christian pseudepigraphy is instructive on this point.

This concept of Apostolic Fathers might comprise the diverse testimony of this early age, which is no longer the age of origin, but not yet the age of the Apologists — in a distant and formal analogy to the NT canon with its rich diversity. Writings such as the *Didache, Barnabas,* or the *Shepherd of Hermas* could well find a place under this concept because it would stand for the post-canonical and non-canonical early Church literature *in toto*.

Characteristics and thought. The few surviving writings from this epoch of the early Church are the remains of a much more copious literature. No independent form of expression was aimed at in this early stage "between the time of revelation and the time of tradition" (Quasten). The authors rather sought to demonstrate their continuity with the apostolic writings by using the epistolary form. This is so clear that possible influences of secular literature may be disregarded. They are for use in the Church, in the form of a written sermon and, beyond this simple role, can claim no literary value. The interests of this age are concentrated on the fixation, proclamation and handing-on of the preaching as attested by the apostolic age. The method of direct address and disregard of art-forms and erudition is continued. An exclusively Christian circle of readers is addressed. This explains the fluidity of the boundary between the primordial and later tradition, between immediate interests and permanent claims. The development of a special Christian language, despite many borrowings, takes on clearer contours. An explicit confrontation with the surrounding world is prepared for by the struggle with heresies and the rejection of all syncretisms with the paganism which has been discarded. The keynote is the consciousness of the redemption which has occurred and which is attainable, as well as the anxiety about final loss of salvation through apostasy. The questions of the permanent and institutional raise their claims.

The contrasts with the age of origin are

unmistakable, and characterize the Apostolic Fathers as representatives of a period of transition in the early Church. It faced an extended period of time, which was to be mastered in the light of the origin. A wholesale characterization is only possible with reserves, because it necessarily distorts the diversity of the testimony and cannot be just to the individuality of the writings. Some more general elements may, however, be mentioned as common characteristics.

Of fundamental importance is the vivid expectation of the parousia; however, it is not the eschatological understanding of time and history as found in the original apostolical kerygma, but becomes more and more the other-worldly and futuristic eschatology of the Church existing permanently in the world. Christian behaviour is considered in view of detailed prescriptions, sometimes based on non-Christian models. Next to a hope in the future, the Christian faith, understanding itself biblically, gains in importance in its retrospective, preservative element as knowledge of the truth, being confronted with heresies and lacking a circumscribed tradition. In a varied Christology a repetition of biblical terminology goes hand in hand with the rudiments of an independent set of notions. Redemption is attained in the future sacramentally (or through martyrdom) and above all by reason of moral effort. In consequence of an imprecise concept of the Spirit trinitarian ideas are correspondingly fluid. The constitution of the Church and its structure of ministries are delineated with increasing clarity. The explosive spread of the Christian message in these decades clearly goes hand in hand with a swift consolidation of the structural forms of the Church and its liturgy. The process is by no means uniform and leaves many directions open for the following age.

In comparison with the first generation it is characteristic of the Christian situation of this epoch that the separation of the Church from Judaism is completed and the question of the law as posed in the NT no longer presents a relevant problem. The Bible of the early Church was, as it had always been, the OT. Christ speaks in it and through it, the Gospel is its fulfilment. Despite the use of some of the writings of the later canon of the NT by the Apostolic Fathers, one can only say that they had collections of various extent. There is no question of the existence of a NT biblical canon. After the oral message of Christ comes the OT (in a thoroughgoing christological interpretation) as the only norm; it is "Scripture".

In numerous elements of their theological as well as practical and pastoral remarks the Apostolic Fathers share the intensity of earnest faith, of joy and hope, to which the NT testifies for the apostolic age; in others, however, they express themselves differently. Their relationship to the apostolic preaching cannot aptly be described as simply an unfolding development, or as decadence. The Apostolic Fathers represent the age immediately after the beginning, which still participates in the origin, does not, however, know properly a Christian past, and yet already has to endure the circumstances of the later generation and feel all its difficulties. It is the epoch of orientation within the Church in the changed situation of a relaxing tension and an incalculable duration. The understanding of faith, as testified to in these documents, remains the practically orientated theology of the ecclesiastical communities, along with the projects and systems of the theologians, as in the subsequent generations.

See also *Apostle, Apostolic Church, Early Church*.

BIBLIOGRAPHY. texts: J. B. Lightfoot, *The Apostolic Fathers*, revised texts with introductions, notes, dissertations and translations, 5 vols. (2nd ed., 1889–90); K. Lake, *The Apostolic Fathers*, Greek text with an English translation, Loeb Classical Library, 2 vols. (1912–13); E. J. Goodspeed, *The Apostolic Fathers*, an American translation (1950); R. M. Grant, ed., *The Apostolic Fathers*, 5 vols. (1964–7). literature: L. Choppin, *La Trinité chez les Pères Apostoliques* (1925); G. Bardy, *La Théologie de l'Église de St. Clément à St. Irénée* (1945); J. Klevinghaus, *Die theologische Stellung der apostolischen Väter zur alttestamentlichen Offenbarung* (1948); J. Quasten, *Patrology*, I (1950), pp. 40 ff.; H.-I. Marrou, *A Diognète*, Sources Chrétiennes 33 (1951–65); B. Altaner, *Patrology*, trans. by H. C. Graef (1961), pp. 97–113; S. Giet, *Hermas et les Pasteurs* (1963).

Norbert Brox

APOSTOLIC SUCCESSION

1. *The present issue*. The notion of Apostolic Succession presents the office of the Church (hierarchical ministry) as the authority which succeeds the office of the apostles. It is constituted through sacramental admission into ecclesiastical office by means of the

visible sign of the laying on of hands. According to the prevalent view, the sacramental laying on of hands is the primary prerequisite for the legitimacy of the office-holder as administrator of (most of) the sacraments. In the era of the undisputed Catholic understanding of the office, the conviction of this connection between the administration of sacraments and a sacramentally ordained office-holder was rather taken for granted than demonstrated. It was all the more evident because even the OT and the antique religions obviously had priests. The Protestant questioning of such a chain of succession as bearer of the most important priestly functions in the Church, or the express denial of it, was felt to be an attack on the hierarchical structure of the Church. Hence the emphasis on the demonstration that the authority of Christ himself had willed this office, and that the apostles had obediently handed it over to the Church in order to preserve for all times this hierarchical structure willed by Christ. If this train of thought appears altogether too simple to the Christian of today, it is not because the authority of Christ does not suffice for him. Rather, he has recognized the Church as an institution of Christ in the sense that Christ's directives essentially concerned the mode in which he himself, as the real content of the life of the Church, could and should be "handed on" in word, sacrament and pastoral guidance. In other words, the question involved here is that of demonstrating, in the office with its succession, the structure which manifests its ministry as a *traditio Christi* in accordance with the nature of the Church. That is, the succession in office must be examined as to how and why it is the organ of the *traditio Christi* in his Church.

2. *Apostolic Succession and preaching.* The significance of the transmission of the office is seen in the Pastoral Letters, especially in connection with the ministry of preaching. If we view the emphasis on the commission to teach as the most important characteristic appertaining to "the bishop" (1 Tim 3:2; Tit 1:9), according to the basic intention of the Pastoral Letters (as expressed, for example, in connection with the office, 2 Tim 1:6, 13f.; 2:2), it follows that it is the function of the bishop to preserve the congregation on the foundation on which it was built. The foundation is the apostolic preaching of Christ. Even though Christ is the only content of this preaching, the apostolic form of its mediation also plays a role, according to the manifold witness of the NT. The apostles had fellowship with, and received their commission from, the risen Jesus whom "God has made . . . Lord and Christ" (Acts 2:36). It is from this authority that their mission derives. It also bestows authority on the envoys, but for a very specific "ministry": namely, to mediate further fellowship with the living *Kyrios* and thus open the Church for all times to all men. In this way the conviction that Christ is the only foundation (1 Cor 3:11) is inextricably linked with the other, that the Church is built on the foundation of the apostles (Eph 2:20; Acts 21:14; cf. also Mt 16:18). The apostles do not replace the only foundation, but their *communio* with Christ, the foundation, is itself in turn fundamental for the Church.

3. *Constitutive function in the Church.* If the meaning of the apostolate is in harmony from the start with a theology of the Church which sees it as the house of God founded on the *mysterium paschale* (the Jesus made Christ and *Kyrios*), then the scanty theology of the ecclesiastical office in the NT fits into this picture of the Church founded by Christ: the office has a function of building up the Church, and this function is a gift of the Lord who imparts the *Pneuma* (Eph 4:11f.). Acts 6:1–4 explains the first transmission of the office by the necessity of easing the burden of the apostles. The transmission of the office authorizes the execution of functions hitherto performed by the apostles. The burdens of the apostles are eased, however, in order to enable them to fulfil their pastoral function all the more clearly. The organization of missions, as reported in the Acts of the Apostles, takes for granted the establishment of official ministries of leadership (Acts 20:17, 28). This is also affirmed by direct testimonies from the sphere of the Pauline mission (1 Cor 12:28; Phil 1:1; 1 Thess 5:12; Eph 4:11). Paul knows that this constitution may also be taken for granted in the Church of Rome (Rom 12:7). Though we know practically nothing about the concrete manner of the exercise of this ministry, some of the Pauline letters show how much Paul himself remained the responsible leader of his churches. Accordingly, in addition to the original motive behind the

transmission of office (easing the apostles' burdens), the motive behind succession becomes evident only with the departure of the apostles (Acts 20:28). It is in this perspective that the above-mentioned Pastoral Letters should be viewed. The successors in office do not, however, simply assume the function of apostolic ministry. Nor can they do so, if the fellowship of eye-witnesses with the risen Lord is its foundation. But the office has the active function of preserving the Church on this decisive apostolic foundation. In its turn, it is so indispensable because it alone leads to communion with the living Lord.

4. "To preserve on the apostolic foundation" is a thoroughly conservative activity. Nonetheless it requires the creative principle of the Church, which manifests itself at every point in history: the *Pneuma* (1 Tim 5:14; 2 Tim 1:6). The preaching of the conservative office-holder is not a mechanical repetition of apostolic formulae — which would require no charism —, but, in response to each given situation, a proclamation of the Lord whom the apostles preached (2 Tim 2:1ff.; 4:1ff.), communicating himself by means of the faith preached and accepted by the Church, and so re-presenting his primary mystery. The preaching office preserves the Church on its paschal foundation, by constantly re-interpreting the gospel. In this sense the office-bearer is the successor of the apostles. The situation of "succession" distinguishes him from those who have been apostles, but also supplies the cohesion, because it is precisely the apostolic foundation which the succession presents. Within the living house of God the foundation is also preserved through a dynamic and active force. The dynamic pneumatic gift of the office always hands on to the Church the one and the same Christ. "Thus it is seen that 'apostolic tradition' and 'apostolic succession' mutually define each other. The succession is the form of tradition, and tradition is the content of succession." (Joseph Ratzinger.)

5. This truth was recognized in all its significance in the 2nd century confrontation with Gnosticism. It was this which first led to a conscious and articulate understanding of what had already been practised in the Church as *Successio Apostolica* and which could be used as a proof in the opposition to Gnosticism. The secret traditions which the Gnostics alleged could be confronted by the authentic apostolic tradition of the Churches, whose list of bishops could be traced back with certainty to an apostolic founder. As early as Papias, the ascertainable line of the bearers of tradition acts as a criterion for the authenticity of the preaching. During his journey from the East to Rome, Hegesippus was interested in the tradition of the Churches which, on the basis of their bishops' lists, could be verified as apostolic. In Irenaeus we find the fully developed principle of Apostolic Succession (*Adversus omnes Haereses*, 3, 3, 1, and *passim*). Similar ideas are to be found in the African Church in Tertullian, who employs the expression *Ordo Episcoporum* for the line of succession (*Adversus Marcionem*, 4, 5, 2).

In the anti-Gnostic argument the main role is played not by the tradition of an apostolic community as an individual witness, but by the common tradition of the apostolic Churches. Underlying this was the conviction which we also find in the NT itself: the Church is not a sum total of individual Churches, but, transcending them all, it is the fellowship by which all Churches are formed into one Church. Hence that we can speak of *the* Church as a concrete reality with one faith and one fellowship of life and prayer, is also due to the functions of the office. The structure of the office is in keeping with this truth: it is itself constituted collegially. The practice and theological statements of the primitive Church show that this truth was taken for granted as an obvious presupposition; hence it was not formulated directly. (Cf. the procedure of Irenaeus and others when determining the tradition.) It is in the Second Vatican Council's Constitution on the Church (art. 21) that we first find an express statement. But the statement of the Constitution is based on the ancient facts: the office, in its very inception in the college of the Twelve, was founded as τάξις (*1 Clem*), as *ordo*, as brotherhood of a plurality of office-holders. The special position of Peter (Mt 16:18ff.) does not weaken the collegiate character of the office. It is only the other aspect of the institution of the office, namely that in the Church the office exists only as indivisible unity. And precisely this aspect is based on the fact that Peter is one of the Twelve to begin with. The collegial office does not proceed from him; rather, he amalgamates it into an effective unity. The indivisible unity is, of course, also a characteristic of the entire Church itself; yet the office does not impose itself as a super-Church over the community, but rather stands in the service of this one indivisible *communio* of the Church with its Lord. It thus becomes a ministry for the building up and edifying of the Church.

6. In ancient times this fact was mirrored most clearly in the rite of episcopal consecration, as depicted in the Egyptian Church Order. This type of rite was already in use in most parts of the Church and was definitively prescribed by the Council of Nicaea (with the stipulation that there must be at least three consecrators). In accordance with its sacramental character, the succession admits the recipient to the one common office. It is because the bishop is admitted to the college, the *Ordo Episcoporum,* that he can be bishop, pillar, of his local Church.

7. The priests, who help the bishop, *participate* in his ministry; they themselves are incorporated, collegially around the bishop, into the one office, and, in turn, themselves stand in the line of the ministries attested by the NT, which aided the apostles.

8. The firm incorporation of the office-holder into the one common office does not jeopardize his position in the individual community, but rather establishes it. What he represents in the Church, the link of the individual Church with the Church, he also effects, by bringing into his local Church the life of the whole Church — Christ as he is really present in the preaching and the sacraments. The individual Church is Church insofar as it participates in the whole Christ, in *the* Church. This — and not the general adoption of a conception of priesthood in terms of the history of religion — also explains the position of each consecrated minister in the sacramental life of the community which he presides over and administers. In this function he is not reduced to the impersonality of a sacred sign. He brings into his *ordo* his entire human individuality as a building stone. But he does so not only by virtue of his ancestral line of predecessors taken individually; rather, he can do so only "una cum famulo tuo, Papa nostro . . . et omnibus orthodoxis" (= bishops).

It is in this fact that the familiar theological distinction between *successio materialis* and *successio formalis* is rooted.

Although ordination makes the office-holder a member of the one office fraternally administered *(successio materialis),* the ordained, as a servant who builds, stands in the succession only insofar as he is member of the Church, insofar as in him the *communio* with all bishops united with the Pope (and thus with all Churches in the one Church) is realized *(successio formalis).* This is the same as saying that the college of bishops is a body which succeeds the college of apostles (Constitution on the Church, ch. iii) and that the individual bishop is a successor of the apostles insofar as he belongs to the college. Hence the affiliation of the schismatic bishop to the college would be analogous to the affiliation of the schismatic Christian to the Church.

At the same time it becomes clear that the jurisdiction of the individual bishop ensues from his membership of the college, and that it must also be subject, according to circumstances, to certain limitations imposed by his membership, because he can never build up his Church alone on his own behalf. But it also becomes clear that in a theology of succession conceived in terms of the college, both the spheres of Church office — priestly worship, and authoritative preaching as pastor — spring from a Church office which is one in its source.

9. Thus, in the correct understanding of succession, two theological lines converge, which are attested very early. *1 Clem* places the ministry of ecclesiastical office in the context of the commission: the Father sends Jesus, Jesus sends the apostles, the apostles pass on the commission further (ch. 44). Ignatius, on the contrary, sees the bishop in a sacramental-representative way as steward of God or Christ. Both lines disclose their meaning only when one takes into account the fraternal institution of the office: the line of commission shows the authorship of salvation from above. But the ecclesiastical envoy is not, at any time, the authoritative representative of God, as he might seem in a paternalistic conception of society. He is himself a brotherly participant in the office, and so represents and brings into his Church the brotherly fellowship which builds up the whole Church. Even the apostles first had

fellowship with Christ; it was only then that they were sent. However, their commission concerned only this fellowship with Christ, which they were to pass on in such a way that the Church's fellowship with Christ was not to be less than that of the envoys. And it is only by experiencing fellowship with Christ in the reception of Christ's envoys that the Church can ever have fellowship with Christ.

See also *Apostle, Bishop, Hierarchy, Tradition, Gnosticism.*

BIBLIOGRAPHY. H. von Campenhausen, *Kirchliches Amt und geistliche Vollmacht in den ersten drei Jahrhunderten* (1953); Y. Congar, *Le St. Esprit et le corps apostolique* (1953); A. Ehrhard, *The Apostolic Succession in the First Two Centuries of the Church* (1953); J. Guyot, ed., *Études sur le sacrement de L'ordre* (1957); G. Dix, "The Ministry in the Early Church", in K. E. Kirk, ed., *The Apostolic Ministry* (2nd ed., 1957), pp. 183–303; M. Schmaus, *Katholische Dogmatik*, III (1957), pp. 141–45, 186–98, 515ff., 623–30; A. Ehrhard, *The Apostolic Ministry* (1958); W. Telfer, *The Office of a Bishop* (1962); K. Rahner and J. Ratzinger, *The Episcopate and the Primacy,* Quaestiones Disputatae 4 (1962); Y. Congar and B.-D. Dupuy, eds., *L'Épiscopat et l'Église Universelle* (1962); G. G. Blum, *Tradition und Sukzession* (1963); J. Colson, *L'épiscopat catholique* (1963); H. Küng, *Structures of the Church* (1965); F. A. Sullivan, "De Ecclesia I", *Quaestiones Theologiae Fundamentalis* (1965), pp. 143–253.

Wilhelm Brenning

ARCHAEOLOGY

I. Biblical. II. Early Christian: A. Concept, Sources, Method, Tasks. B. History of Research and Some Urgent Problems.

I. Biblical

As late as the 19th century the Bible was almost the sole source of our knowledge of the ancient Near East. The records of secular historians preserved in medieval Latin manuscripts were scarcely able to add anything to the historical picture of the period prior to the 1st millennium B.C. provided by the OT. This position was radically altered by archaeological excavations.

In accordance with the aims set before the Pontifical Biblical Institute in 1909 by Pius X, the Jesuit Fathers, under the leadership of A. Mallon, commenced excavating at Teleilat-el-Ghassul at the north-eastern corner of the Dead Sea in 1929. Their intention was to excavate the five cities mentioned in Gen 14:2. Although they failed to find Sodom and Gomorrah, they did discover a culture which flourished about 2000 years before Abraham entered Palestine, that is, at the precise period in which, according to biblical chronology, Adam was created. Today biblical archaeology no longer confines its aims to proving the statements in the Bible to be correct by means of excavations. The purpose of biblical archaeology is not to show that the Bible "is right after all", but simply to bring to light the truth of history. In the long run such an unbiased quest for historical truth will provide the only reliable "confirmation" of the biblical record.

In biblical as well as non-biblical archaeology the proper subject of investigation is the pottery and buildings of earlier cultures. Paleontology is concerned with the earliest human epoch, from which only bones or stone tools have been preserved, for example, the recent discoveries at Ubeidiya at the south-western corner of the Lake of Gennesaret, which date from the period 800,000 to 600,000 B.C. Historical science is concerned with written records of past events, although it is not infrequent for archaeology to supply it with fresh material in the form of cuneiform tablets, inscribed potsherds (ostraca), leather scrolls or papyri.

Unlike secular archaeology biblical archaeology confines itself solely to those excavations in biblical lands which bear some relationship to the biblical account of the history of salvation. Thus, for instance, the excavations of Homeric Troy by H. Schliemann cannot be reckoned as belonging to biblical archaeology, while on the other hand the excavations at nearby Alexandria Troas, the flourishing sea-port on the north-western coast of Asia Minor, which was visited several times by the Apostle Paul, certainly do fall under it. The methods of biblical and secular archaeology are however identical, and in this respect this branch of biblical science possesses an asset of apologetic value which should not be underestimated.

Among these methods two are particularly important. Since 1894 the Petrie-Bliss method, so called after the Englishman F. Petrie and the American F. J. Bliss, has been employed. This method is based upon the hypothesis that each stratum has potsherds which are characteristic of it. Since pottery is virtually indestructible, and since, in addition, jugs, dishes and pots constantly change according to the fashions of different centuries in form and ornamentation, in the technique of their manufacture and in the way in which they are painted, the Petrie-Bliss method has established itself as pre-eminent for all excavations. In addition to this, the possibilities opened up by modern techniques of photography and reproduction make it easy to compare the pottery of one archaeological site with that of another. The discovery of identical pottery in the strata of different archaeological fields entitles one to conclude that these strata are of the same date.

Only a relative chronology, however, can be deduced from this method of dating, one which cannot of itself be expressed in terms of definite dates in history. Since 1950 this deficiency has been to some extent supplied by the radio-active carbon method of dating. It can be ascertained from organic material (wood, grains, leather) when it was felled, harvested or stripped from the dead animal. For the isotope carbon 14 deteriorates at a very constant rate. Admittedly the method is not reliable for the period before 70,000 B.C., and even for periods subsequent to this date it always has a margin of error of $\pm 10\%$. Thus if an age of 2000 years is deduced for a fragment of leather such as those found in caves of Khirbet Qumran on the shore of the Dead Sea, this leather may be dated anywhere in the period between 200 B.C. to A.D. 200. Only the discovery of coins, characteristic pottery or inscribed material can then lead to a more precise dating and so supply the answer to the question which in this case is vital, namely whether the piece of leather derives from the period before or after Christ.

Archaeological periods vary widely in different regions of the world. The most important of the Palestinian periods are: The early, middle, and late Stone Age (Paleolithic, Mesolithic and Neolithic) from 100,000 B.C. at the earliest to 4000 B.C. In 4000 B.C. pottery begins in Palestine, and with it, from 4000–3000 B.C. the Chalcolithic Age. The ensuing Bronze Age (3000–1200 B.C.), which is important for the history of the patriarchs, is subdivided into the early (up to 2100 B.C.), middle (up to 1550 B.C.), and late Bronze Age (up to 1200 B.C.). Israel's conquest of Palestine falls in the period of transition from the Bronze to the Iron Age (c. 1200 B.C.).

A few examples must now be adduced, in order to show the manner in which biblical archaeology can be of assistance in attaining a deeper understanding of biblical texts, without actually setting out to "prove" them. a) Discoveries in Mesopotamia bear witness to a flourishing culture towards the end of the third millennium B.C. Against this background it becomes clearer that when God chose Abraham he was not choosing one of the powerful or wise of this earth (cf. 1 Cor 1:26f.), but a nomad who, with his solitary life of the steppes, was more suitable for God's salvific purpose than those who belonged to the more highly cultured societies of that period. b) In the light of the discovery of the stele of Hammurabi the ethical commandments of the Decalogue no longer appear as absolutely unprecedented in the ancient Near East. It does appear, however, that no parallels for Israel's monotheism or for the name "Yaweh" and its interpretation are to be found among the gods of this early period. c) The exegesis of the OT by the method of literary criticism postulated a relatively late date for the crystallization in writing of the account of Israel's sojourn in Egypt. However, archaeologists have been able to establish how appropriate several of the features depicted in these accounts are to the circumstances which prevailed in Egypt during the period of the 19th dynasty (13th century B.C.). d) It must be admitted that after the excavations of J. Garstang at Jericho, 1930–36, archaeologists actually believed that the walls which crumbled when Joshua had the trumpets sounded (Jos 6) had been discovered. However, the more accurate excavations conducted by Kathleen M. Kenyon have shown that from c. 1650 to 650 B.C. the city was not occupied to any significant extent. Exegesis will be able to do justice to these conclusions only when it reappraises the question of whether the book of Joshua claims to present in any sense whatsoever an account which is historically exact in the modern sense. e) The excavations on the south-eastern hill of Jerusalem conducted since 1961 by R. de Vaux and K. M. Kenyon make a far more exact picture of the "city of David" of the monarchical period available to us today. f) The excavations of the Herodian forts, the Herodion and Massada, have established the accuracy of the information supplied by the Jewish historian Flavius Josephus. Hence his works acquire greater weight as a historical source.

The nearer we approach to NT times, the more important it becomes to keep in mind both the monuments excavated by the archaeologists and the records which have come down to us in ancient manuscripts. The ideal case is one in which "the voices of the documents and the voices of the monuments are in harmony" (E. Josi). This is to a large extent the case with the most significant discoveries of biblical archaeology, namely the finds at Qumran. Since 1947 the remains of several hundred written scrolls have been found in eleven caves situated at the north-western end of the Dead Sea. On the grounds that the pottery in the caves and in the nearby ruin of Khirbet Qumran is the same, a connection can be established between the deposits in the caves and the ruins. The ruins have turned out to be the remains of a pre-Christian Jewish "monastic" settlement. From 135 B.C. to A.D. 68 it was inhabited by "monks". They lived according to a community rule, several copies of which have been found in the caves.

The discoveries of Qumran throw new light on the Gospel of John, though the discourse sections of this gospel are stamped with the distinctive Johannine theology. But the chronological and topographical references of the fourth evangelist are shown more and more by biblical archaeology to provide extremely exact information. Above all, the excavations of the pool of Bethesda at Jerusalem (cf. Jn 5:2, "it *is* in Jerusalem", not "it *was* in Jerusalem") have shown that John worked on traditions which must have derived from the Palestine of the period before 70 B.C.

There are places in the Holy Land such as the pool of Bethesda, where archaeologists have simply laid bare the stones, the "witnesses" of Jesus' public acts, for the modern traveller to see. At such places he will find it easier to make personal contact with the history of salvation than at the pilgrimage sites of Golgotha or Bethlehem, with their overlay of velvet and marble. Therein lies the pastoral value of biblical archaeology. In addition to this there are a number of instances in which it enables one to achieve a better and deeper understanding of biblical history and its significance. In such cases it also acquires the significance of a theological discipline, a branch of modern biblical science with which it will henceforward be unthinkable to dispense.

Nonetheless, NT scholars are still to be found — especially in non-Catholic circles — who for practical purposes confine themselves to philological and philosophical approaches to the texts of the evangelists and the Pauline letters, and fail to give due value to the results of biblical archaeology. If such scholars gave serious consideration to the result of biblical archaeology, they might perhaps be led back in spirit to the earthly arena, with its concrete limitations of space and time, in which Christ really lived and suffered, and upon which, after his resurrection, he founded his Church. Biblical archaeology leads us on to the mystery of the Son of God "coming in the flesh" (2 Jn 7). On the other hand, biblical archaeology cannot be the ultimate norm. To the decisive questions of biblical interpretation, for example the question of what happened on Easter Sunday morning, biblical archaeology can only contribute indications. This is equally true of textual and literary criticism. In the last analysis the answer must be given on the basis of an exegesis that is theologically schooled, and grounded in the faith of the Church of Christ. It is, therefore, necessary to place exegesis, the interpretation of the *text,* first, before biblical archaeology, even after the recent sensational discoveries in this field of research.

See also *Bible* I, *Biblical History, Old Testament History, Qumran.*

BIBLIOGRAPHY. J. B. Pritchard, ed., *The Ancient Near East in Pictures Relating to the Old Testament* (1954); id., ed., *Ancient Near Eastern Texts Relating to the Old Testament* (2nd ed., 1955); W. F. Albright, *Recent Discoveries in Bible Lands* (2nd ed., 1955); J. B. Pritchard, *Archaeology and the Old Testament* (1958); W. F. Albright, *The Archaeology of Palestine* (4th ed., 1960); G. E. Wright, *Biblical Archaeology* (1962); H. J. Franken and C. A. Franken-Battershill, *A Primer of Old Testament Archaeology* (1963); K. M. Kenyon, *Archaeology in the Holy Land* (2nd ed., 1965).

Benedikt Schwank

II. Early Christian

A. CONCEPT, SOURCES, METHOD, TASKS

Early Christian archaeology is a historical science and as such part of Christian antiquities. But the latter is a wider concept, embracing patristics, hagiography, liturgy and Church order in so far as they throw light on the life of the Church in the Graeco-Roman culture up to the death of Gregory the Great (604). Christian archaeology is a subsidiary discipline which confines itself to the investigation of the monuments surviving from the early Church. Critical research here involves the establishment of their authenticiy, place of origin, age and significance, all of which are of decisive importance. The literary tradition is not its primary concern, though as a sort of secondary process it must be used as an indirect source for the precise theological interpretation of the actual monuments. Among these indirect sources may be mentioned the Bible, the *Didache,* the *Traditio Apostolica,* the Apostolic Fathers, the Greek apologists and the anti-heretical writings of the 2nd century, Christian writers of the 3rd to 6th century, apocrypha, acts and passions of martyrs, calendars, martyrologies, synaxarions, menologies, sacramentaries, lists of Popes and bishops, itineraries and topographical catalogues (cf. Testini, pp. 3–36).

These two sets of sources must be used to complete each other if Christian archaeology is to do its task properly and supply useful information for the history of the Church and of dogma, for comparative religion and for the history of art and of law. This methodical research into the monuments does not make it primarily a theology of the monuments or an archaeology of art and L. Voelkl is right in saying that "Christian archaeology is a branch of the study of antiquities, which draws primarily on monumental sources but maintains its independence both as regards the archaeology of art and the theology of the monuments" (*LTK,* II, col. 1134). The monuments must be examined, but once this is done, the question of their theological statement is posed at once. This assures its independence, but it must then provide the matter for a theology of the monuments and also throw light on early Christian life. Hence Pius XI could note in the motu proprio setting up the Pontifical Institute of Christian Archaeology (11 December 1925): "The monuments of Christian antiquity are venerable and authentiç witnesses to the faith and religious life of early days, and are primary sources for the study of Christian institutions and culture as early

as the sub-apostolic age" (*AAS* 17 [1925], p. 619). For this reason, Christian archaeology was ranged among the *disciplinae principales* in theological studies ("Ordinationes adn. Const. Apost. *Deus Scientiarum Dominus* de Univ. et Facult. stud. eccles. rite exsequendam", *AAS* 23 [1931], p. 271).

While the archaeology of art is concerned with artistic monuments, Christian archaeology is interested in all monumental testimony, whether artistic productions or handiwork, and hence may not be simply identified with "early Christian art". It must, however, be noted that the monuments of artistic value are of special importance. And thus, secondarily, Christian archaeology can become to a considerable extent a science of early Christian art, contrasting, for instance, its formal elements of style with those of Hellenistic Roman art. The primary monumental sources may be divided into the following five groups, according to C. M. Kaufmann:

1. Architecture. a) Funeral monuments: catacombs, open-air cemeteries (graves in the earth, sarcophagus graves, mausoleums, cemetery churches). b) Sacred buildings: basilicas, baptistries, coenobia, xenodochia, presbyteries (episcopal), guesthouses (pandochia), hospitals. c) Private houses.

2. Painting: frescoes, mosaics, paintings in books.

3. Sculpture: statuary, reliefs, ornamentation, sarcophagi.

4. Popular and minor art *(Kleinkunst):* figurines and finer plastic art, wood, ivory and metal carvings, textiles, liturgical vessels, devotional objects such as cruets, gilded glass, ornaments, coins.

5. Epigraphy: inscriptions on tombs, graffitti, the Damasus and post-Damasus inscriptions, encomiums of martyrs and mottoes on buildings from the Roman catacombs, mottoes on basilicas.

B. HISTORY OF RESEARCH AND SOME URGENT PROBLEMS

In the 15th century pilgrims were visiting the catacombs and leaving their scribblings on the walls. No scientific interest was as yet being taken in the catacombs. This is also true of the cursory visits to the catacombs by members of the Accademia Romana (Pomponius Laetus), who were looking for pagan monuments and paid no attention to those of early Christianity. Nonetheless, they prepared the way for those who from the 16th century on began to search these underground passages out of a real interest in the life of the early Church. Epigraphical studies also helped. P. Sabino made a collection of 235 Christian inscriptions about 1494. Philip Neri, who visited the catacombs under S. Sebastian's and Charles Borromeo were among the pioneers of this interest in early Christian life, which was first exploited scientifically by A. Fulvio and O. Panvinio, the latter being the real precursor of C. Baronius and A. Bosio. The *Annales Ecclesiastici* of Baronius was the first work to make full use of the Roman inscriptions. From 1593 on, Bosio made himself the first systematic explorer of the Roman catacombs, allowing himself also to be influenced by patristic and hagiographical literature. Only Book I of Part II of his *Roma Sotteranea* (1634) was published. The labours of Bosio were given publicity by G. Severano and P. Aringhi, R. Fabretti (d. 1700) promoted archaeology by his studies of inscriptions, and the Strasbourg professor, B. Bebel, made a first attempt to present Christian archaeology systematically (1679).

But there were also trends, especially about the beginning of the 18th century, which restricted archaeological progress. One, set in motion in high places, was to ransack the catacombs uncritically for the bodies of martyrs. Another, inspired by controversy with the Reformers, tried to use the finds for theological and apologetic purposes, in the fanciful hope of reconstructing from the catacombs a catechism or dogmatic text-book of the early Church. In spite of these drawbacks, the explorers of the 17th and 18th centuries have the undoubted merit of having collected an immense amount of valuable material. Unfortunately their zeal led them at times not merely to make drawings of their finds, but to haul them away, which was particularly unfortunate in the case of inscriptions, as these can only properly be read *in situ,* or at least when their original setting is fully recorded.

An important contribution was made by the study of the literary sources as pursued by G. Mabillon, B. de Montfaucon, L. A. Muratori and the Bollandists. After a period of individual efforts, a new wave of scientific investigation started with G. Marchi and was continued with G. B. Rossi (d. 1894) in the modern sense of Christian archaeology. Study

of itineraries, inscriptions, calendars and martyrologies enabled de Rossi to make discoveries in the catacombs, such as the grave of Pope Cornelius and the tombs of the Popes of the 3rd century, which were important for the early history of the Popes and Christian attitudes to final salvation. De Rossi also laid down the lines along which the reconstruction of the topography of the Christian cemeteries of ancient Rome was to proceed.

His immediate successors were O. Marucchi, M. Armellini and R. Guarrucci. Guarrucci's *Storia dell'arte cristiana,* drawing on biblical and patristic studies, did much to help the theological interpretation of the finds, and hence furthered the work of J. Wilpert (d. 1944) on the iconography of the catacombs. Wilpert's work was exemplary exact scientific research of the monuments (catacombs, sarcophagi and mosaics) being accompanied by an effort to reach their theological statement. In contrast to the archaeologist P. Styger, he did not restrict the simple pictures taken from the Old and New Testament to their historical bearings, but tried always to find their symbolical meaning as expressions of faith. No doubt he often went too far, but his two-fold approach enabled him to preserve the independence of Christian archaeology while restoring it to its place as part of the study of antiquities and using the monuments to throw light on the creed of the early Church. The trend was continued, more circumspectly perhaps at times, by F. Benoît, A. Ferrua, E. Josi, E. Kirschbaum and U. Fasola. Continued study of biblical scenes, and representations of Christ and the saints from the catacombs and the other monuments enabled such researchers as J. Kollwitz, T. Klauser, F. van der Meer, A. Graber, A. Stuiber, E. Stommel, F. J. Dölger, L. de Bruyne, A. Weis, C. Ihm and F. Gerke to sketch a theology of Christ, redemption and the Church in early Christianity, with important bearings on its spirituality.

Of particular interest in this connection is the work of G. A. Wellen on representations of the Mother of God in the monuments. As from the other images, there is more to be learned than what the artist stated as spokesman of the life of the faithful. They can also stimulate modern art and the faith of the present day. The place, say, of Mary in the monuments provides food for thought and possibly for re-thinking. Architecture is also eloquent. The basilica appears, in the light of the literature of the day, as symbol of Christ and of the Church in which he reigns. It is an image of the community and the tabernacle where God dwells, the relationship between community and Christ being strikingly expressed in the structure, which soon becomes a single throne-room for Christ. More light is thus thrown on the concepts of the day, with possible pointers once more to rethinking (cf. Sauser).

An important problem throughout such research is that of the relationship of the work to pagan art-forms, that is, the question of the independence of early Christian art or its partial adoption of pagan forms, in the plastic arts as well as in architecture. In the latter field the great authority is L. Voelkl, in iconography T. Klauser with his series of studies on the origins of Christian art in the *Jahrbuch für Antike und Christentum*. In recent research, the excavations under St. Peter's have been important for the question of Peter's burial in Rome. The claim that his bones have been found has been of particular interest (see Guarducci and Kirschbaum). Excavations in Milan (S. Tecla, S. Simpliciano) have been important for the history of the Church in Milan under Ambrose. Pavement mosaics at Aquileia and Verona, and the basilicas and sarcophagi of Julia Concordia have offered interesting material for iconography and Church history. Notable finds have also been made at Barcelona (the basilica) and Santiago de Compostela, and the catacombs discovered in Rome on the Via Latina are interesting from the point of view of iconography, since the paintings combine Christian and pagan motifs. Very important finds were also made in Rhaetia (Imst, Pfaffenhofen, Martinsbühel) and Noricum (Lorch bei Enns, Agunt, Laubendorf, Teurnia).

See also *Early Church, Apostolic Fathers, Apologists*.

BIBLIOGRAPHY. R. Guarrucci, *Storia dell'arte cristiana nei primi otto secoli della chiesa,* 6 vols. (1837–81); W. Smith and S. Cheetham, eds., *Dictionary of Christian Antiquities,* 2 vols. (1876–80); F. X. Kraus, *Real-Encyclopedie der christlichen Altertümer,* 2 vols. (1882–86); C. M. Kaufmann, *Handbuch der christlichen Archäologie* (3rd ed., 1922); F. Cabrol and H. Leclercq, eds., *Dictionnaire d'archéologie chrétienne et de liturgie* (1924 ff.); F. J. Dölger, *Antike und Christentum,* vols. I–V (1929–36), VI (1960); D. Marucchi and H. Vecchierello, *Christian Archaeology* (1936); T. Klauser, ed., *Reallexikon für Antike und Christentum* (1941 ff.); P. Testini, *Archeologia Cristiana* (1958); L. Voelkl, "Christliche Archäologie", *LTK,* II (1958), cols. 1133–6; G. A. Wellen, *Theotokos* (1961); K. Wessel and M. Restle, eds., *Reallexikon zur byzantinischen Kunst* (1963 ff.); E. Kirschbaum, "Zu den neuesten Entdeckungen unter der Peterskirche in Rom", *Archiv. Hist. Pont.* 3 (1965), pp. 309–16; M. Guarducci, *Le reliquie di Pietro sotto la confessione della Basilica Vaticana* (1965); E. Sauser, *Frühchristliche Kunst: Sinnbild und Glaubensaussage* (1966). PERIODICALS: *Römische Quartalschrift für christliche Altertumskunde und für Kirchengeschichte* (1887 ff.); *Rivista di archeologia cristiana* (1924 ff.); *Cahiers archéologiques. Fin de l'Antiquité et Moyen-âge* (1945 ff.). CONGRESS REPORTS: *Atti del III. Congresso internazionale di archeologia cristiana* (1934); *Atti del IV. Congresso internazionale di archeologia cristiana,* 2 (1940–48); *Actes du Ve Congrès international d'archéologie chrétienne* (1957); *Atti del IV. Congresso internazionale di Archeologia Cristiana* (1965).

Ekkart Sauser

ARIANISM

Arianism is the name given to a complex development in the 4th century in ecclesiastical, intellectual and political history. The founder of this movement, Arius (d. 336), was an Alexandrian presbyter, formerly of the Antiochene circle of the Syllucianists. His intellectual forebears were the Antiochene Adoptionists, Paul of Samosata and Lucian. Aetius of Antioch and Eunomius of Cyzicus gave an extreme form to the theology of Arius.

Arianism, together with its Athanasian and early Nicaean counterparts, marked the end of an epoch in Christian thought which centred on a Christology dominated by the concept of the Logos in the history of salvation. It signalled the beginning of an epoch of *Theologia* in which contemporary metaphysics and especially formal dialectic were used to the full to put the question of God, his unoriginatedness and his Logos. Arianism sprang from a scholarly concern within theology and grew to be one of the great moving powers of its age, both because it organized its own Church and because in the political sphere it was a central issue for two generations.

Theological and philosophical aspects. Arius operated on the basis of the Aristotelian concept of unity, according to which unity is ultimately the negation of division. Such a concept of unity, in contrast to the positive

Platonic or neo-Platonic concept, did not admit of a divine being which was active in its unity in more than one person. Arius, in general, connected the unity and the being of God so much with the unoriginatedness and the unchangeability of the Father that Logos-Son could only be thought of as created by the will of God. But as biblical texts and ecclesiastical tradition referred to a Logos co-eternal with the Father, Arius asserted the existence of a "double Logos". This meant a break with the subordinationist tradition of the 2nd and 3rd centuries in which the identity of the Logos ἐνδιάθετος, προφορικός and ἐνσαρκός (immanent, *ad extra* and incarnate) was maintained, and linked up with the concept of the ἀειγεννεσία (eternal birth) of the Logos ἐνδιάθετος. For Arius, the "Logos always with God" was a propriety of God himself. This Logos is not active in the actual process of creation, though the "created Logos" is. The latter is a work and a creation of the Father, who alone is uncreated: ποίημα καὶ κτίσμα τοῦ πατρός. The Son is created out of nothing (ἐξ οὐκ ὄντων ἐστίν) as God's one "work" in view of the creation of the world. There was a time when the Son was not: ἦν ποτε, ὅτε οὐκ ἦν. After the creation of the Logos-Son, who then, as the first and highest among creatures, created all else, God remained at the infinite distance from the world and from man which belongs to his being. The created and creating Logos stands entirely on the side of the world. For this reason, Jesus had no additional need of a human soul of his own; his moral life, as well as his life as a whole, must be interpreted as the life of the Logos. The world is relatively independent and contains within it the possibility of knowledge and virtue; these are the foundations of Arian "Deism" and "ethics". In stressing the creaturely beginning of the Logos, Arius sought to avoid any idea of physical generation or emanation. The Arian position was consciously opposed to emanationist theories and their confused conception of the relation between God and the cosmos.

The Athanasian accusation against the Arians, "What you cannot conceive of, you consider to be inexistent", is certainly not true with regard to Arius himself. For him, the being of the "unoriginated" was incomprehensible. Nevertheless, there is evidence to support the assertion that Arianism was opposed to the concepts of mystery and analogy, in the radical application of the rationalistic and formalistic dialectics of Aëtius. His *Technologia* consisted, apparently, of 300 logico-theological inferences. It is here clear that the biblicism of the Arians is not so much the foundation of their system as the special pleading used to further their theological aims.

Significance in Church history. The "great and holy Synod of the 318 Fathers" of Nicaea signalled the beginning rather than the end of the ecumenical attempts to resolve the Arian problem. The large centre group of Origenists at the Synod, who were caught unprepared by the procedure of the Emperor, rallied themselves behind Eusebius of Nicomedia, the first of the important "imperial" bishops. At the Synods of Antioch, Tyre, and Constantinople (330 and 335) they were successful in outmanoeuvering the leaders of the Nicaean party (Eustathius of Antioch, Athanasius and Marcellus of Ancyra). The strength of the followers of Eusebius lay in the support they derived from the theology of Origen, their conciliatory intentions, the partial justification they had for charging their opponents with Sabellianism (Marcellus of Ancyra), and the ecclesiastical policy of Constantius. The events surrounding the four formulas of Antioch (341) and of Sirmium (351–359) show how Arianism was making progress and how it finally divided into moderate and radical groups. The attempt of the Imperial Synod of Sardica (342/43) to settle the difficulties miscarried. It marked, in the mutual anathemas of the Western (Nicaean) and the Eastern (Eusebian) groups, the first formal division between the Churches of the Eastern and Western Empire. The second attempt of an imperial synod led to the dramatic and unseemly events of Ariminium and Seleucia (359/60), in which first the policies of the radical Anomoean bishops Valens, Ursacius and Gennadius, then those of the Homoeans under the leadership of Acacios of Caesarea (originally an Anomoean) gained the upper hand.

The development between the death of Constantius and the Second Ecumenical Council of Constantinople in 381 was characterized by a gradual *rapprochement* between the positions of the progressive late-Nicaean theologians (the Cappadocians) and the followers of the moderate Eusebianist-Homoiousian group. Both the radical Eunomians and the cruder interpreters of the early Nicaean position were pushed to the background. The Council of Constantinople is an excellent example of the process of Christian self-interpretation in the history of dogma. The debated word *homoousios* was retained, but it was so explained in relation to *ousia* and *hypostasis* that it could no longer be taken in the sense of *one* hypostasis.

Not the least important among the by-products of the Second Ecumenical Council was the establishment of the patriarchate structure, which was treated of in view of the fact that the Latin adherents of Nicaea at Sardica in 343 had attempted in canons 3–5 to have Rome recognized as the supreme court of appeal in the entire Church. The Arian conflict revealed the forces at work within the Church and threw into sharper relief the religious capitals of the Empire, Rome, Alexandria, Antioch, and Constantinople with their own unmistakable theological, legal, and charismatic structures.

Political aspects. The epoch in which the Arian conflict occurred witnessed the rapid development of the Christian religion into a State Church. Diocletian had already attempted to achieve a unity in heathen belief by a persecution of Christians. Constantine, with his edict of toleration, began by renouncing a policy of religious uniformity: only for the heathens did he remain the *Pontifex Maximus*. But shortly after, at Nicaea, he emerged from his role as arbitrator; his intervention for the *homoousios* was prompted by his conviction that this formula was a useful and necessary instrument for imperial religious policy. The equality in nature between the Father and the Logos would be the prototype of the unity of the Empire. When he became convinced after 332 that the Arian and Eusebian formulas could also be of use in solidifying the Empire and that he could bring about unity in the Christian faith more easily with the Eusebian formula, he re-orientated his policy.

After him, Constantius clearly intended to restore, on Arian principles, the ancient union, in one person, of *Imperator, Legislator* and *Pontifex Maximus* which Christians also were to recognize: his "Caesaro-Papist tendencies" were unmistakable. For Theodosius, the Church and the Empire were *utriusque legis:* the laws of the Empire and the laws of the Church were binding on each other. He made Church law imperial law and left to the five patriarchs and the bishops all decisions about faith and order in the Church. It was for the bishops, with the advice of the leading theologians, to determine who was heretical. Imperial law treated condemned heretics as rebels. All Eunomian churches were to be given over to the bishops who were in the Catholic communion. Semi-Arians were not allowed to celebrate divine service within the cities. These developments brought on the definitive decline of Arianism within the Empire; it was only among the East-Germanic tribes that an Arian Church continued to exist until into the 7th century.

See also *Antiochene School of Theology, Jesus Christ* III, IV, *Modalism, Constantinian Era.*

BIBLIOGRAPHY. Athanasius, *Select Treatises in Controversy with the Arians,* freely trans. with an appendix by J. H. Newman, 2 vols. (1842–44; reprint, 1900); N. Baynes, "Constantine and the Christian Church", *Proceedings of the British Academy* 15 (1929), pp. 341–442; G. Bardy, *Recherches sur Lucien d'Antioche et son école,* Études de Théologie historique (1936); W. Telfer, "When did the Arian Controversy Begin?", *JTS* 47 (1946), pp. 129–42; A. Fliche and V. Martin, ed., *Histoire de l'Église depuis les origines jusqu'à nos jours,* III (1950), IV (1948); J. N. D. Kelly, *Early Christian Creeds* (1950); A. Grillmeier, ed., *Chalkedon* I (1951); V. C. de Clercq, *Ossius of Cordova* (1954); P. Worrall, "St. Thomas and Arianism", *Recherches de Théologie ancienne et médiévale* 23 (1956), pp. 208–59; W. Marcus, *Der Subordinationismus* (1963).

Wolfgang Marcus

ARISTOTELIANISM

I. The Philosophy of Aristotle: A. Aristotle's Place in Philosophy. B. The Structure of Aristotle's Philosophy. II. Historical Influence.

I. The Philosophy of Aristotle

A. Aristotle's Place in Philosophy

The life and work of Aristotle are usually distinguished into three periods: the first or Athenian, when Aristotle was still entirely under the influence of Plato; the intermediate period in Asia Minor; and the second Athenian period, when Aristotle opposed Platonism by his own "Peripatetic" philosophy. The decisive impulse to the study of Aristotle's development was given by Werner Jaeger's famous *Aristoteles*. The significance of Aristotle in the history of philosophy is generally ascribed to two achievements:

1. The transformation of the speculative idealism of Plato into a speculative realism. Like his teacher Plato, Aristotle holds that the supra-individual, universal and spiritual which transcends particulars of time and space is on a higher plane of being and value than the sensible, which is characterized by spatio-temporal material individuality. But in spite of this superiority of being and value, the spiritual is only real when it has entered beings as a principle and is sustained by beings which along with this spiritual principle have another non-spiritual constitutive principle; or when it is living spirit which is its own principle of being as an immaterial entity; so God who is the object of his own thought is actual pure spirit as pure thought (νόησις νοήσεως). The spiritual is not *eo ipso* real as being, form, exemplary form and structure, norm and value as in Plato. All these are only real either in beings which contain them or in a life which actuates them or as life really as such.

2. The second decisive characteristic is generally taken to be the transition from the oneness of philosophy to a multiplicity of philosophical disciplines. Aristotle gave separate treatment to movement in general (physics), vital movement on the human and infra-human level (psychology and philosophy of biological life), pure thought (the Organon, logic), art (the Poetica) and social life (politics and ethics). The factor common to all these "second" philosophies is that they combine Aristotle's empirical observations — an enormous collection for his day — with speculative principles of order on a comprehensive scale: act and potency, substance and accident and the various modes of causality: formal cause, material cause, efficient cause and final cause, and also the basic modes of movement itself, etc. Prior to all these comes a type of knowledge sought and striven after by Aristotle (ἐπιστήμη ζητουμένη) which calls for a new justification, the "first philosophy" (πρώτη φιλοσοφία). It implies that the question of beings in so far as they "are", in so far as they

are considered simply as being (the question of ὂν ᾗ ὄν, later to be known as ontology) is one with the question of the supreme and divine, the one self-sufficient being (θεῖον, from which the word theology derives). Here ontology is intrinsically linked with theology in as much as it is only the relationship to the divine (as the οὐσία, strictly speaking) which determines the degree and value of being in all other beings. Hence it is only through theology that the ontological question can be pursued to its close. This combination of the ontological and theological question was given the title of "metaphysics" soon after Aristotle. Thus Aristotle may be termed the founder of metaphysics as the primary, fundamental and supreme discipline.

B. The Structure of Aristotle's Philosophy

It is through the question of movement that the first philosophy is linked with the second philosophies (later to be known as the philosophical disciplines, but in Aristotle still identical with the various branches of science, which had not yet been fully distinguished from philosophy). Aristotle's empirical starting-point is always change, movement, the imperfect which moves towards fulfilment (or at any rate to another state of being) — processes not self-explanatory for which the explanation must be sought. Hence the intention of Aristotle is to go from beings as they are met with in the state of movements to the permanent principles and elements (ἀρχαί) underlying the restless movement which is not its own sufficient reason. This effort of speculative thought seeks to refer all becoming to an intelligible being which is the only possible beginning and end because of its being self-contained. This being which is the beginning and end of all movement is ultimately the divine movement of which circular motion is the image. The divine self-contemplation is the absolute mover of all things, since it is the one mode of being which reposes and is rounded off in itself, does not need to go out of itself and pass over into anything else, and is striven after in all movement (ὡς ἐρωμένον, "as that which is striven after"). This self-sufficiency and self-containment is also the true prototype of all that can be understood as "fulfilment" or "happiness".

Thus Aristotle's philosophy does not allow for a God who is really superior or transcendent to the world; hence there is in it no creator of the world. The world is eternal, and in its perpetual movement tends towards the centre of its movement which as such is the divine, blessed and self-sufficient life and movement of the spirit. This spirit (νοῦς) is also co-active in the vital movement of man (ψυχή). But while my soul is my own, proper only to me as the determinative principle ("form") of my movement as far as it is self-engendered, the spirit remains, even in me, the one, divine, supra-individual mind which is no one's own but is owner of all things. It is the loftiest thing in man, and hence supreme happiness and supreme fulfilment are to be found in "theoria", the spirit's own vision, the contemplation of the philosopher, in which all particularity is merged and disappears and the individual life becoms unimportant in the supra-individual life of the philosopher. It is a type of life at which few can succeed. If it is to be successful, it needs the basis of a well-ordered society within which contemplation can be pursued without the distractions and hindrances of material cares. Hence the notion of happiness as the "theoria" or contemplation of the spirit which does not belong to us but to which we belong must be completed by the doctrine of the accessible happiness of individual life and self-realization. Hand in hand with metaphysics go ethics and politics, along with contemplation there is the practical and productive life (*praxis* and *poiesis*). The practical life is individual life orientated to the actualization of all its innate potentialities.

Thus, besides the distinction between first and second philosophies, and the distinctions taken over from Plato between logic, physics and ethics, theories of thought, nature and life, there came a further division into contemplation, practical life and productive life. The practical life is involved with the individual material things in time and space and in this situation uses the powers of the soul as it investigates, weighs, takes counsel and decision, to attain in manifold wise to what the spiritual vision achieves directly as a unity: the vital movement of a life which is completely self-sufficient. But if *praxis* is to be a successful realization of life, it must produce the objects of common endeavour which together make this life possible and protect

and further it. This productive work and the heritage of intelligence exercised on it are called *poiesis,* its scientific synthesis "poetics", as the doctrine of the art and skill (τέχνη) which are at the service of the practical life as the realization of the individual existence of man.

Having thus described the characteristic structures of Aristotle's philosophy, we can do no more here than enumerate briefly the chief headings of its contents. Aristotle bases formal logic on the doctrine of the proposition and inference, and sets forth basic concepts and rules of the syllogism which have undergone no essential development except in our own day. Their validity is founded on the indissoluble intrinsic relationship between thought and being, so that the categories, for instance, are both formal basic modes of thought (the concept in its basic forms) and basic structures of being (the fundamental types under which beings are classified).

We have already spoken of the principles of metaphysics, which deals with beings as beings and hence also is concerned with that which supremely is. Movement is understood as act and potency and hence points to the unmoved source from which it originates, in the light of which the gradation of beings in the analogy of being is to be understood. This order, as the totality of movement in space and time beneath the incorruptible substances of the heavenly world is chiefly considered in *Physics*. In ascending degrees, it goes from lifeless things to living things, in which the soul produces substantial unity as the "first act" and unique essential form, vegetative in plants, sensible in animals — and so on to man in whom the supreme element is the immortal spirit. The spirit enters as it were from without (θύραθεν), as an event which happens to the soul, and alone enables it to exercise the properly human activities of generalized knowledge and free decision in its permanent relationship of acceptance ("passivity") by which it is bound to the world.

In keeping with this complex nature of man, ethics provides the frame of reference for his values, the virtues being the mean between faulty extremes. Politics likewise describes the right order in the State as the well-calculated mean (monarchy, aristocracy and democracy as opposed to tyranny, oligarchy and ochlocracy). There is no transcendent norm in the ethics of Aristotle, its place being taken by the insight of the prudent man and by the judgment built up by tradition in the healthy community. Man, after all, as λόγον ἔχων, that is, having not only reason but the faculty of discourse, is essentially a social being (ζῶον πολιτικόν). Hence a social phenomenon also takes place when man and nature are interpreted in the process of *poiesis* (τέχνη) of which the theory is given in *Rhetoric* and in the fragmentary *Poetics*. Even the life of contemplation, lived apart from the community, has a social task: to keep man open to the all-encompassing good which is the supreme end of man.

See also *Pre-Socratics, Platonism, Neo-Platonism, Metaphysics, Ontology, Act and Potency, Dialectics, Entelechy*.

BIBLIOGRAPHY. E. Zeller, *Aristotle and the Earlier Peripatetics,* 2 vols., trans. by S. F. Alleyne and A. Goodwin (1897); W. D. Ross, ed., *The Works of Aristotle,* 12 vols. (1908–31); id., *Aristotle* (1923; 5th rev. ed., 1949); W. Jaeger, *Aristotle. Fundamentals of the History of His Development,* trans. with the author's corrections and additions by R. Robinson (1934); F. C. Copleston, *A History of Philosophy,* I: *Greece and Rome* (1948), pp. 266–378; D. J. Allan, *The Philosophy of Aristotle* (1952); C. J. de Vogel, *Greek Philosophy,* II: *Aristotle, the Early Peripatetic School and the Early Academy* (2nd ed., 1960).

Max Müller

II. Historical Influence

In antiquity. In the philosophy of antiquity the differences between Plato and Aristotle made themselves felt in the formation of opposing schools. But the general attitude was so eclectic that it is hard to define exactly the influence of Aristotle. His logic was very generally adopted and developed, particularly by the Stoa, with regard to the logic of propositions. The real successor to Aristotle was the Peripatetic school, which continued to exist down to the 3rd century A.D. Its last great figure was Themistius, at Constantinople. In contrast to the mysticism and other-worldliness of Platonism, the school was strongly marked by the spirit of empirical research, beginning with Theophrastus, the first leader of the school, and continuing with the great scientists of the following centuries (Aristarchus of Samos, Ptolemy, Galen). A decisive

factor in the spread of Aristotelianism was the publication of the works of Aristotle by Andronicus of Rhodes (about 50 B.C.), who was also the first commentator of Aristotle. The work of commenting reached its most intense level with Alexander of Aphrodisias in A.D. 200. Then, with neo-Platonism, the differences between the schools became almost completely blurred; but study of Aristotle continued. The neo-Platonist Porphyrius is the author of one of the most important text-books of early Scholasticism, the Εἰσαγωγή to Aristotle's treatment of the categories.

In the Middle Ages. Though in the patristic age the influence of Aristotle was less felt than that of neo-Platonism and the Stoa, it gained greater importance in later times. Boethius, basing himself on various forerunners, especially Marius Victorinus, transmitted the logic of Aristotle to the Middle Ages, as the instrument (ὄργανον) of philosophy and theology — which at the start were mostly not treated as distinct subjects. The only philosophical discipline generally taught was logic, as one of the seven liberal arts. Through it the influence of Aristotle came to be of increasing importance, as may be seen from the abandonment of (Platonic) realism in favour of a more moderate view (Abelard). The *Organon,* however, as then known, contained only the Περὶ ἑρμηνείας and the *Categories* with the introduction by Porphyrius. Boethius's other translations had been lost. But then in the 12th century the two *Analytics,* the *Topics* and the *Sophistics* were re-discovered and became the *logica nova,* in contrast to the *logica vetus.*

At the same time, translations of the *Metaphysics* and the works on natural philosophy appeared. With this Aristotle begins to influence the philosophy and theology of Scholasticism to a greater extent. His indirect influence had been felt hitherto through Syria and the Jewish-Arab philosophers. After the conquest of Syria, the Abbassides had set Syrian scholars to work on translating Greek treatises on medicine, mathematics and philosophy into Arabic. The result was the combination of neo-Platonic and Aristotelian thought which is characteristic of the doctrines of Alfarabi and Avicenna (Ibn Sina). The most professedly Aristotelian is Averroes (Ibn Rashid), whom St. Thomas calls "the Commentator" as he calls Aristotle "the Philosopher". This Arab philosophy is responsible for the essential traits of the Jewish philosophy of Avicebron or Avencebrol (Solomon ibn Gebirol) and Moses Maimonides (Maimuni). The homeland of this philosophy, like that of Averroes, was Spain, and here, especially at Toledo, a translating centre was set up which, along with Arab and Jewish writings, translated the works of Aristotle himself from Arabic into Latin, partly via Spanish. The translators include Raymond of Toledo, Dominic Gundissalinus, John the Spaniard, Gerard of Cremona, Michael Scotus, Hermann the German.

Inspired by the work at Toledo, scholars at Oxford like Robert Grosseteste took over the task. Robert went back to the original Greek text, especially for his first translation of the *Nicomachean Ethics*. The third centre of translation was Italy, including Sicily, where it was done on the original texts, the work beginning in the middle of the 12th century with Henricus Aristippus and Eugene of Palermo, and being completed in the 13th. Among others (like Bartholomew of Messina) William of Moerbeke is of particular importance, who worked above all for St. Thomas Aquinas, improving previous translations and producing some of his own.

However, the adoption of the Aristotelian philosophy did not come about without friction and opposition. This was less marked with regard to his writings on logic, to which Tertullian, St. Gregory of Nyssa and St. Jerome, and later St. Peter Damian and Walter of St. Victor had raised objections. It was his writings on metaphysics and natural philosophy above all which were obscure enough in part to seem to contradict the Christian faith. Thus in 1210 the provincial council of Paris forbade under pain of excommunication the public use and the private reading of Aristotle's writings on natural philosophy and the commentaries on them. Warnings against his philosophy were issued to the University of Paris by Pope Gregory IX, and to Dominican theologians by the constitutions of their order. In 1231 the same Pope extended the prohibition of Aristotle to Toulouse, but declared that he was prepared to have the works on metaphysics and natural philosophy submitted to investigation. We do not know the result of this step: the commission

heard, among others, William of Auxerre and Simon de Alteis. At any rate, the universities paid little heed to the prohibition (at Paris, Roger Bacon, of the school of Grosseteste, was one of the first to ignore it), and it resulted in the faculty of arts' attaining a higher status than that of a preparatory course.

One of the upholders of Aristotelianism, Siger of Brabant, became the centre of the Averroist controversy, since Averroes, where Siger claimed to find the true doctrine of Aristotle, maintained the necessity and eternity of the world and denied the existence of free will and personal immortality (the *intellectus agens,* the immortal active intellect, being supposed to be a single entity in all men). In 1270 and 1277 Archbishop Tempier condemned philosophical and theological theses which were upheld by St. Thomas in his moderate form of Aristotelianism as well as by Siger. The condemnation affected St. Thomas chiefly in so far as he divided theology from philosophy, contrary to the Augustinian view, and defined metaphysics as an independent science (based on *ens qua ens,* on *esse*). Even the Dominican Archbishop of Canterbury, Robert Kilwardby, officially rejected several propositions of Aquinas. But the prohibition fell into oblivion; in the same 13th century, St. Thomas was declared Doctor ordinis by a general chapter of the Dominicans, and the study of all the works of Aristotle was demanded by the papal legates for the licence in the faculty of arts.

Though the Aristotelians — including no doubt even Siger — did not teach the doctrine of the double truth, still, the debates between the various schools (Thomists, Scotists, Gandavists [Henry of Ghent], Augustinians [Aegidius of Rome], etc.) led to theology being so sharply divided from philosophy that the controversy proved baneful for both subjects. Philosophers turned from metaphysics to logic and mathematics and natural philosophy, while theology lost its ontological basis. Its metaphysical roots were replaced by "positive" determinations (of God's will in Scotus and especially in Occam) and by the dialectical method, which, while developing more and more along the lines of natural philosophy, was thought to provide the links between propositions of theology. There was a similar development — inspired above all by the debate with Platonism and the Alexandrist Aristotelianism (the school of Alexander of Aphrodisias) — in the doctrine of creation and of the *intellectus agens* of Averroistic Aristotelianism. Its protagonist P. Pomponazzi was condemned in 1513 at the Fifth Lateran Council (*D* 1440; cf. 738). Its doctrine of the State was notably affected by the development (cf. the *Defensor Pacis* of Marsiglio of Padua).

In modern times. After the anti-dialectical movement about 1400, which aimed at a true and reverent theology (especially John Gerson), and the basically anti-Scholastic propaganda of the humanists came the Reformation with its hostile attitude to all philosophy. The response was the revival of Scholasticism in Spain and Italy in the 16th century (Francis de Vitoria, Melchior Cano, Thomas Cajetan, Francis Silvestris de Ferrara). The influence of Suárez affected even the philosophy of the schools in Protestantism. In the 17th century Aristotelianism loses its force: the Enlightenment, Kant and German idealism hardly know Aristotle at all. Hegel pays some attention to him, but what divides them is greater than what unites them. The neo-Scholasticism of the 19th and 20th centuries took up the threads again, both in historical studies (H. Denifle, C. Baeumker, F. Ehrle, M. Grabmann) and in philosophical systems (the Louvain school, Cardinal Mercier). See also the works of E. Gilson, A. D. Sertillanges, F. van Steenberghen, A. C. Pegis, A. Marc, M.-D. Chenu, C. Fabro. The magisterium of the Church, from *Aeterni Patris* (Leo XIII, 1879) to *Humani Generis* (Pius XII, 1950) emphasized the value of Aristotelian-Scholastic philosophy. J. Maréchal brought it into the dialogue with German idealism; his intention was followed out by P. Rousselot and others, and in Germany — in relationship above all to M. Heidegger — by M. Müller, K. Rahner, G. Siewerth, B. Welte and others. But the Thomism represented here is not simply an Aristotelianism, which is indeed also true of the Aristotelianism of the Middle Ages, which can now be seen to have been essentially much more differentiated than it was thought to be, before the finds and researches of recent years. Even where Aristotle is principally followed, in contrast to other traditions of thought, the Aristotelian philosophy has been essentially marked and moulded by neo-Platonic, Arab and Jewish thought, and not least by Christian thought and experience. One result of modern research is precisely a clearer insight into the difference between Aristotle and Aristotelianism.

See also *Scholasticism, Thomism, Suarezianism.*

BIBLIOGRAPHY. F. Ehrle, *Die Scholastik und ihre Aufgaben in unserer Zeit* (2nd ed., 1933); M. Grabmann, *Methoden und Hilfsmittel des Aristotelesstudiums im Mittelalter* (1939); F. van Steenberghen, *Aristotle in the West. The Origins of Latin Aristotelianism* (1955); id., *The Philosophical Movement in the 13th Century* (1955); F. Coplestone, *Medieval Philosophy* (1952); E. Gilson, *History of Christian Philosophy* (1955); M. Grabmann, *Die Geschichte der scholastischen Methode* (1909–11); id., *Die Geschichte der katholischen Theologie seit dem Ausgang der Väterzeit* (1933); M.-D. Chenu, *Towards Understanding St. Thomas,* trans. by A.-M. Landsy and D. Hughes (1964).

Jörg Splett

ART

I. Concept and Meaning of Art: A. The Word and the History of the Concept. B. Art and the Beautiful. C. The Historical and Social Character of Art. D. Tradition and the Age. II. Theories of Aesthetics.

I. Concept and Meaning of Art

A. THE WORD AND THE HISTORY OF THE CONCEPT

Art, like craft, in the widest sense of the term, means "cunning" ("know-how"), "skill" — man's mastery of what he can do. From the Latin "ars", which is a translation of the Greek τέχνη, it indicates primarily the realm of ποίησις, productive work, one of the three basic means whereby man installs himself in the world, the others being θεωρία, scientific knowledge for the sake of its truth, and πρᾶξις, moral action for the sake of the good. As the Greeks understood it, "making" is a primordial unity which includes both craftsmanship in general and strictly "artistic" production. This is because the free and "artistic" production of man is here seen in its original unity with what is done necessarily and "naturally", man himself being seen as the product of a "divine" nature which allots him directly the limited field of his free work. This direct reduction to the gift of nature explains the Platonic view of art as imitation of the imperfect natural form, through which its perfect "idea" becomes transparent. It also explains the Aristotelian view of art, as the perfecting of what remains imperfect in nature, and hence also the imitation of nature's original formative powers.

The unity of technical handiwork and strictly artistic production is still maintained in the late antique and medieval concept of *ars* and in the general and personal view of the *artifex* himself. But the word took on a wider meaning and embraced skill in practical action (e.g., politics) and mastery of theoretical knowledge (the pure sciences). Thus the various modes of human behaviour were all considered as developments of an original *ars humana,* the art of continued existence in the world. But then the contrast between man and the world, art in the widest sense and nature, became radical and fundamental in the Christian experience of faith. Because here man receives his freedom not from the natural orders that encompass it but from the transcendent and absolute creator God. As his *creatio ex nihilo,* the world itself displays a technical and artistic structure, and the *ars humana* participates in his *ars divina.*

Man is thus free as distinct from the world and as regards the world. But the absolute character of this freedom remains latent as long as theological transcendence restricts the relationship of man to the world to the *uti* of what is there and open to him and reserves the *frui* to the fulfilment in the other world (H. Blumenberg). But when, as in modern times, the fundamental link with theological transcendence ceases to be obvious and compelling, the distinction between use and enjoyment disappears, and man's relationship to the world must now become fundamental and "creative". The absolute character of human freedom in its radical distinction from the world and as regards the world is now factual and decisive. This explains a) the possibility and necessity of treating the world not as a datum already manifest, but as something to be ordered and moulded and above all, disclosed — a task always ahead; b) the autonomy of this fundamental process in its various "cultural" forms; c) the violence, reckless of all but its own powers, which is inherent in these "creative achievements", as they open up the world and construct society, through technology, politics, science, art in the strict sense, etc. ("Art is there in nature; it belongs to those who can prize it out." — Albrecht Dürer.) This immanent violence is quite compatible with a sort of passionate devotion to the world, and actually includes a reposeful enjoyment in the contemplation of work accomplished.

This changed understanding of God, world and self is the key to many modern developments. It explains the "hiving off" of the various forms of culture, though in fact one or all can influence the others, in spite of the supposed autonomy of each form. It also explains the difference now visible between activities carried out within the bounds of a certain unified world-order, and a creative activity which shapes the world and sets up new orders of things, as when the handiwork of the artisan is contrasted with art in the strict sense. In the latter, each work at once displays and reproduces the total mental horizon or "world" of each age, though at the same time art increasingly makes use of technical aids, not only in production and distribution but in the discovery of basically new art-forms such as photography, films, television and electronic music. It explains further the fundamental "liberation" of art from its previous bondage to "religion", though it cannot be denied that when art is now seen as the "fulfilment and intensification of existence" or as the "redemption of things for their true and definite nature", it may be revealing essential traits which were originally rooted in religious experience. Finally, this explains why the artist is now extolled as an ideal for human existence and even as a genius, in the sense of the perfect embodiment of humanity — the sovereign spirit, visionary and revealer at once, whose fertile and world-shaping vision makes the world itself a work of art, a dramatic festival (E. Brunner).

Where the mere contemplation which finds full satisfaction in sensible and spiritual self-expression is taken as a pre-eminent and basic feature of art, art is made the subject of aesthetics (see below). "Contemplation" here means the primordial and optimum mode of encounter with things as mediated by the senses in time and space. According to the temporal or spatial aspect which predominates, we may distinguish the temporal arts which are primarily addressed to the hearing (poetry as the art of words, music as the art of sounds), the spatial arts which are primarily addressed to the sense of sight

103

(architecture, sculpture and painting) and those which present themselves in spatio-temporal movement (the dance, the theatre).

B. Art and the Beautiful

Aesthetics works out the principles of pure contemplation which remains in the medium of the sensible, and its object, the sensible apparition purely as such. This aesthetic contemplation and its object are treated under the heading of "the beautiful" and the distinction between the work of art as artistically beautiful in this sense, and the naturally beautiful is ignored. The "aesthetic object" is not considered as the real resistant everyday thing which points away from itself as part of the realm of theoretical and practical means and ends. It is not, for instance, an essentially replaceable subject by which theoretically conceptual laws can be traced, nor the essentially replaceable means in a process of attaining a practical goal. The concrete datum, the perceptible reality, has, on the contrary, no other end but to "appear" — disinterested, transparent, its own sufficient reason, aiming at no other realization. This sensible appearance, unique, irreplaceable, self-contained and significant in itself, exhausts its function. And in this selfhood it is strange and distant, aloof as a "lovely vision" (not an illusion, psychologically speaking) from everyday reality. These are the essential traits which characterize both the artistically and the naturally beautiful. Hence in face of both, in "aesthetic contemplation" man finds that he is freed from the disintegrating influence of the multiplicity of daily tasks. He finds himself and hence repose in the act of self-sufficient, disinterested contemplation which takes the place of a listening and looking which is usually directed to goals extraneous to itself.

When the question of what art is is directly determined by the concept of the beautiful, it is inadequate to the subject as long as it does not start from the fact that the work of art is a work, that is, a work of man. But then the decisive question is how man is understood. Is he to be understood in terms of a biological and psychological anthropology, still often used as the basis of social and cultural theories? He would then be a being equipped *inter alia* with certain aesthetic faculties, urges and needs, formally unalterable throughout history, which gave rise indifferently to pre-historic wall-painting, the ornamental weaving of North American Indian totems, Japanese temple-dances, Greek sculpture, Gothic cathedrals, romantic lyrics, etc. And so too, from the same aesthetic point of view, all these human testimonies could be "enjoyed" in the same way aesthetically, with no reference to the fact that this aesthetic point of view itself is historically conditioned and with no questions raised about its adequacy and validity with regard to these testimonies. Or is man not rather to be regarded as a being who as an individual and a society is constantly surpassing himself (imperfectly and hence in ever new ways) and surpassing the individual realities of his personal and community life? He would then be free for that greater whole which transcends man himself, society and all particulars — for the constantly changing historical meaning of the whole, which sustains and determines each individual item.

From this point of view, art does not appear primarily as a human achievement, constructed of individual and collective elements, which would "have" a history as the personal expression of relationships within society. It would rather be a basic mode in which history itself is realized. It would be a way in which in each individual human work the totality of beings is plastically revealed, that is to say, the truth, or the world as the ever changing, ever new fundamental and structural order of all that is historically. And again it would be a way in which the man of a given age would be brought by this work to face the truth of his world and hence to be alerted to his own nature and the nature of his society.

C. The Historical and Social Character of Art

Because art involves the truth of the whole and hence transcends the realm of ordinary experience and its partial verities, it can never be fully planned or coerced. In spite of the personal and social effort which it entails, it remains in the end a happy accident, effortless, liberated and liberating. Times of "cultural crisis", when the compelling force of the older order is collapsing and the new world of the individual or society is not yet born, demonstrate most clearly that art is not always possible for man or fundamentally independent of history. It is not merely the product of individual and collective effort, but, like history itself, the irruption of the indissoluble unity of the favour of history and human will, of what is given and what is taken, of blessing and merit.

In this totality of the artistic event, various elements are integrated, which may be singled out methodically and legitimately, for the scientific study of particulars, as long as its limitations are remembered and it does not claim to give a total grasp of art as history and of the history of art. For instance, the medium of art is, no doubt, contemplation, the sensible synthesis in which a multiplicity becomes an articulated unity and the sensible representation of this one thing. But neither the manner (the "style") of this synthesis nor the qualitative character of the representation remain unchangeably the same throughout history — as is presupposed by aesthetics and to a great extent by theories of art. And the recognition of historical change does not explain this change in the nature of contemplation as an independent process governed by its own laws (as, for instance, H. Wölfflin tried to do in his history of style as a history of "seeing"). Contemplation is linked to the work, to the formal and material technical possibilities of its making.

But materials and tools and their development (G. Semper) do not alone constitute the essence of art and are not the sole determinants of its history. The work is a testimony of man, of the individual in society, of the relationships within society, of the social standing of the artist, of the significance of art in the life of a community, of the receptivity of the community and its influence on artistic work. But art and its productions cannot be reduced to one social function among others, to be investigated above all in the relationships between artist (producer), work of art (artistic experience) and public (consumer) — and their historical changes (the sociology and social history of art). As testimony of man in the form of a work, art is rather the visible sign of his dedication to the world, and of the free appropriation and moulding of the world and of man himself, as individual and society. It is a sign, therefore, of man's response to a claim which can and must become concrete to some extent in the challenges and tasks which a society imposes on its members. But it is not simply identical with such expectations and charges, because the claim does

not originate from society and is not its instrument. It is made on the individual and on society itself and concerns them both.

Art can only be "expression", "communication" and "experience" — as it ought to be — by virtue of the social character of individual men and their shared responsive dedication to and appropriation of the world. Communication can take place only within and by virtue of a common mental horizon embracing at a given time the meaning and order of the world and of men's existence in common. It is indeed possible that the art of an epoch could be historically so "advanced" in its formal presentation or in its content and intention that it remains in fact "unintelligible" in the times to which it can be historically dated, and is only "understood" when its own truth of the future has become today's commonplace. But where art renounces on principle the effort to be "understood", or deliberately restricts itself to a limited circle of the "initiated" and "elect"; where, therefore, it bases itself on the immediate experience of an absolutely individual or esoteric "truth" (which is self-contradictory), and not on the claim of the truth of a common call essentially binding on all: there art fails to be itself. In so far as it becomes something private, the esoteric possession of a restricted coterie, the passionate artistic impulse takes on more and more the traits of pathological monologue and withdrawal, which comes to grief not only in face of the community, but in face of the work itself.

On the other hand, art may also cease to be understood for the opposite reason. It is, in fact, the symbolic embodiment of an immediate experience of the claim which dominates individual and society — that of truth in history summoning man to mould the world and find himself. But this claim may be wholly identified with the expectations and tasks of society, and truth regarded as the resulting accord. Then art ist reduced to a phenomenon which takes place exclusively on the human level, and becomes something to be interpreted in function of its character as "communication". Sociologized totally and methodically in this way, art is abused as a means of propagating theories and of realizing practical ends, as in the totalitarian State. Here art may no longer be a testimony of transcendence, of a comprehensive historical meaning and of the experience of an absolute claim, in face of which testimony the freedom of one's own decision remains. Here art must rather become the instrument of a policy, of a partial truth erected into an absolute and of a political end — an instrument by which the freedom of the individual is violated, reduced to a uniform tendency and made a mere function of a policy.

Another type of decadence in art is when the energy and the effort are lacking, to discover the true form of artistic production which will be in keeping with the original experience and truth of a given time, and when deliberate imitation of past styles is substituted. Such art remains inauthentic even if the formal mastery of the style of a past epoch seems to attain real virtuosity. The absence of the effort to find the artistic forms proper to the age also indicates that society lacks the strength and unity to shape its common world and its common life responsibly.

D. Tradition and the Age

The proper attitude towards the greatness of an earlier art cannot consist of the unthinking imitation of a style. It can only stem from loyalty to one's own origins, obedience to the experience of the basic, historically given truth of the age and courage to carry out one's own irreplaceable task. That the great art of a past age is an example is not merely due to the formal perfection of its works, as though it were an "eternal" canon for all times. It is due rather to the happy accord between the ourtward form and the inner law to which that and only that age was subject. We can see from such successful, classic accord that the men of the time accepted their historical task and sought and found in it their true nature. Thus in every great epoch of art we encounter a different historical way of being man. But it is only through such encounters that personal and communal creation is possible today, when culture is so highly differentiated, with so many influences from a living tradition and so many contacts with alien cultures. Hence the proper attitude to the art of the distant past cannot be a piety only anxious to restore and preserve ancient works like museum-pieces. And it cannot be merely a diligent and well-informed pilgrimage to collections, concert halls, theatres and monuments. It must rather be a serious effort of discovery and interpretation, not making the works of a past age the object of an aesthetic contemplation where historical peculiarities and differences fade, but replacing them in their world, even (and especially) if they then seem to lose their familiarity and independence and take on an alien air.

The sense of estrangement will and must grow when we return to earlier epochs of our own cultural tradition, but above all when we make the transition to foreign cultures of the past. In such researches we encounter not only differences of form and style and new readings of the world, but together with these a profound change in the qualitative character of sensible representation in the contemplation itself. For instance, the art of the early "primitive" cultures is a magico-mythical "realization", a real presence of the uncanny, the holy, the demonic, the divine — the dancer, the masked figure as God; the hunting "magic" of the palaeolithic representations of animals, etc. This art is so closely identified with religion and its cultic acts that it is questionable whether we can still — or as yet — speak of "art" and "works of art" in a true sense. This unity still reigns, in the higher cultures, in a way in keeping with their form of religion (the Egyptian statue as incarnational representation of the god, the king, of man; the Japanese temple-dance as actualizing presentation and reproduction of the rhythm of the cosmos, of God's rule and sway; contemplation of images as a religious ceremony in China; Greek drama in its origin in the sacrificial cult of Dionysus, etc.).

Art remains as sacred representation well into the history of Christian antiquity and the Middle Ages (the Byzantine icons; the medieval images as sources of grace and objects of devotion; the religious significance of the place of worship as "church", etc.). Here, however, the Christian faith, in its experience of the absolute transcendence of the All-holy, and at the same time, of his unique historical incarnation, opened up the way for the radical disjunction of art and religion. This disjunction could allow to art only the power of a spiritual and symbolic representation, though this at first was entirely in the service of religious life. With the Renaissance came the decisive breakthrough and art became "independent", that is, its proper nature was revealed, and with it, its essential limitations. Since then art can no doubt continue to depict religious "themes" and perform religious "tasks". But the cultic and religious element is no longer a necessary constituent of art. This art is henceforth no longer merely "profane" in its essence, on the perimeter outside the sacred and hence looking to it because conscious of its exclusion and contrast. Art is now essentially "secular"; its essential theme is the "world" as the task imposed on man.

With the disjunction of art from religion and worship the arts themselves diversify and expand, having previously been to a great extent combined in a purposeful unity, which opened up possibilities but also imposed limitations (as when sculpture, painting and decoration were combined in medieval church architecture). And the emancipation from religion also made a completely new relationship to the religious element possible. Even in the free adoption of religious themes, art remains detached in its view of the world and man and hence can discover new and primordial sources of religious experience, above all the inevitable interlocking of splendour and riches with meanness and poverty in the world and in man, which demonstrates the need for redemption. Or art can put forward its own claim to announce and fulfil the religious promise, through the aesthetic transfiguration of the world, through the "sacerdotal" exaltation of the artist and the formation of a "church" from his followers. But there are more profound and oppressive problems which are set by the inexorable growth of economic, social and political organization in all departments of life, in this modern world of planned economies. They come from the classification of the artist among the "liberal professions" as modern society registers its effectives; from his being reduced to an employee increasingly involved in the institutions of the modern "business of culture"; from the change of character in the work of art which is making it more and more a product to be marketed; and from the still unforeseeable impact of the modern mass audience on artistic production and on art in general.

See also *Man* I, *World, Symbol, Natural Philosophy, Culture, History* I, *Society* I, II.

BIBLIOGRAPHY. H. Wölfflin, *Principles of Art History* (1915); W. Hausenstein, *Die Kunst und die Gesellschaft* (1917); id., *Bild und Gemeinschaft. Entwurf einer Soziologie der Kunst* (1922); H. Read, *Art and Society* (1937; 3rd ed., 1956); A. Malraux, *La psychologie de l'art,* 3 vols. (1947–50); M. Heidegger, "Der Ursprung des Kunstwerkes", *Holzwege* (1950; 4th ed., 1963); N. Hartmann, *Ästhetik* (1953); *The Artist in Modern Society,* ed. by UNESCO (1954); A. Sedlmayer, *Die Revolution der modernen Kunst* (1955); J.-P. Weber, *La psychologie de l'art* (1958); A. Hauser, *Philosophy of Art History* (1959); F. Kaufman, *Das Reich des Schönen* (1960); C. Greenberg, *Art and Culture* (1961); H. E. Bahr, *Poiesis. Theologische Untersuchungen der Kunst* (1961); H. U. von Balthasar, *Herrlichkeit. Eine theologische Ästhetik,* 4 vols. (1961–64); A. Hauser, *Social History of Art,* 4 vols. (new ed., 1963); H. Read, *To Hell with Culture and Other Essays on Art and Society* (1963); P. Régamey, *Religious Art in the Twentieth Century* (1963); A. Halder, *Kunst und Kult* (1964); H.-G. Gadamer, *Wahrheit und Methode* (2nd ed., 1965); É. Gilson, *The Arts of the Beautiful* (1965).

Alois Halder

II. Theories of Aesthetics

Aesthetics is the science which is concerned with the beautiful and with art. Since art and beauty are on the plane of the sensible, the question arises as to whether they can have transcendental dimensions and what their relations may be to the transcendent. This difficulty was felt very early, quite apart from Christian thought. In his *Republic* Plato judged art as fatally linked to the sensible. Nonetheless, condemnation of art was followed by praise of beauty, which was given its most significant interpretation in the *Symposium,* the beautiful in question being the physical and natural, from which man rises by degrees to the beauty of the spiritual order and to the supreme value of the forms. The beautiful has, therefore, a purificatory function in its metaphysical dimension, through which it transcends the merely sensible. The justification for this view is found in Pythagoras, who held an essentially metaphysical view of the beautiful. The beautiful is the real, in so far as it is sustained by the (mathematical) laws of (musical) harmony. This type of metaphysics found little echo in the naturalism of Aristotle, but passed into medieval Christian speculation through Plotinus. But some Christian thinkers returned to the sensible value of the beautiful which had been underestimated by Plato but paid its due honour by Aristotle. Aristotle accorded the sensible qualities of art the power of expressing the form, and hence too the power of developing a "purgative" function (*Poetics,* ch. xiv). Augustine took up a position which was not without its dramatic qualities. He felt himself greatly drawn by the beauty of the sensible in its finest forms, especially music. But as though to evade a source of possible distraction, he took refuge in the supreme religious values, which transcend the sensible (*Confessions,* ch. xxxiii).

Medieval Christian thought continued to be interested in the sensible beauty expressed in art, but this appears in technical dissertations on the individual arts rather than in philosophy. Philosophy, on the other hand, stressed the metaphysical rank of the beautiful as a transcendental. This idea is most fully and clearly expressed in the *Summa* ascribed to Alexander of Hales and in the *De Pulchro et Bono* of Albertus Magnus (1243). In his *De Veritate* Thomas had not mentioned the beautiful among the transcendentals (1256–59), but in the *Summa* (I, q. 9, a. 5 ad 1) (1266–71) he used the formula "Pulchra sunt quae visa placent" and proposed a new interpretation of the beautiful which gave it a metaphysical character in the epistemological order. The importance of disclosing a metaphysical dimension in sensible beauty and above all in art is that aesthetics is thus given an objectivity which frees it from pseudo-psychological interpretations and includes its field in a transcendental explanation of the world.

It must of course be remembered that all modern aesthetics (since the Renaissance) rejects the great Christian synthesis of medieval thought and holds itself more and more aloof from all metaphysical interpretations of the beautiful. Interest was transferred from the ontological structure of the beautiful to the contribution of subjectivity, especially in the objectifying of the beautiful in works of art. The contribution in question is either an element of imagination or of knowledge. G. B. Vico opted for the former. In his *Scienza Nuova* (1725 and 1730) he anticipated theories which were later propounded by J. G. Haman and by J. G. Herder. The aesthetics of Kant and the idealists stressed the function of art in knowledge, F. Schelling, for instance, maintaining that art was an instrument of philosophy itself. The beautiful loses metaphysical significance and is absorbed in a special kind of knowledge. So too Hegel, who brings art into the realm of the absolute spirit. It is in dialectical opposition to religion and has a definite function in knowledge through its crystallization of the concept, whereby it transforms the idea into reality by giving it sensible form. In terms of classical metaphysics, the theories of Vico, Kant and the idealists are dangerously close to total subjectivism, all the more so because the dimension of knowledge is never completely separated from the imaginative components, on account of the creative character of thought. The danger is not so great, however, because the I, its creative activity and the work of the imagination have their own transcendental quality and a supra-individual "objectivity" on the basis of intersubjectivity. Further, the metaphysical dimension and its relationship to the Absolute does not wholly disappear by the restriction of aesthetics to the realm of knowledge, since according to the idealists knowledge ultimately takes in all reality and represents the Absolute totally, precisely because knowledge is creative.

A much more serious threat to traditional metaphysical theories seems to come from another type of aesthetics which started with the inductive methods of G. T. Fechner, was fully developed by the positivists and is still represented today. It excludes aesthetics entirely from philosophy and claims it as a science or, as M. Dessoir did well to prove, a whole complex of sciences. The dangers of restricting aesthetics to the purely sensible and to what is "scientifically" verifiable are illustrated by the latest developments in Anglo-American aesthetics. Here art loses all intrinsic content and is reduced simply to the character of sign. But even this view is not without value, since it can help to correct the tendency latent in aesthetic theories based on metaphysics, to abandon too quickly the sensible, with the risk of substituting empty abstractions for universals. Hence the schools which now recur to the older metaphysical notions of aesthetics no longer try to avoid discussing the concrete sensible dimension. The great figure here is J. Maritain who called for the unreserved acceptance of the medieval theories of the beautiful as a transcendental, while basing it on the data of sense-perception. This was not an isolated phenomenon.

Other schools with similar metaphysical claims based their research more and more on the sensible realm, as, for instance,

L. Stefanini and L. Pareyson. H. U. von Balthasar sees the sensible, in so far as it is the terminus of the crystallization of the beautiful, as a way by which God manifests himself to man. The recognition of the independent value of the sensible makes a relationship between aesthetics and metaphysics possible in a new way, and hence indirectly with theology. This is, however, *a posteriori,* not *a priori,* as if the sensible could in the concrete be deduced from a metaphysical sketch-plan. The metaphysically universal, the absolute, the transcendental and the transcendent are to be grasped in the sensible itself, which must be seen in its own proper nature, and rank, in its referential character and its limitations.

See also *Platonism, Aristotelianism* I, *Scholasticism, Transcendentals, Idealism, Kantianism.*

BIBLIOGRAPHY. E. Müller, *Geschichte der Theorie der Kunst bei den Alten* (1831–7); B. Croce, *Aesthetics as Science of Expression and General Linguistic* (1902; rev. ed., 1922); G. Simmel, *Zur Philosophie der Kunst* (1922); M. de Munnynck, *L'esthétique de Saint Thomas* (1923); E. de Bruyne, *Esquisse d'une philosophie de l'art* (1930); E. F. Carritt, ed., *Philosophies of Beauty from Socrates to Robert Bridges* (1931); E. de Bruyne, *Études d'esthétique médiévale* (1946); K. E. Gilbert and H. Kuhn, *A History of Aesthetics* (3rd ed., 1956); G. Morpurgo Tagliabue, *L'esthétique contemporaine* (1960); H. Kuhn, *Wesen und Wirken des Kunstwerkes* (1960); W. Perpeet, *Antike Ästhetik* (1961); J. Maritain, *Art and Scholasticism and the Frontiers of Poetry* (1962); E. F. Carritt, *Theory of Beauty* (1962); F. E. Sparshott, *Structure of Aesthetics* (1963).

Elisa Oberti

ASCENSION OF CHRIST

The account of the ascension of Christ (Acts 1:1–14) constitutes part of the Lucan kerygma of the exaltation of the Lord. For this reason it must be viewed in the context of the NT theology of exaltation as a whole. In Matthew and Paul resurrection and exaltation constitute a unity. The raising of Jesus from the dead by the Father is at the same time his installation in regal authority as the Lord to whom all power is given in heaven and on earth (Mt 28:18). The Johannine theology depicts the Crucifixion as already an exaltation (3:14; 8:28; 12:32f.). Thereby it reveals a mysterious two-fold significance in the cross, in that it is not only the cross but the royal throne of Christ as well, from which he exercises his cosmic power and draws

mankind to himself. The contradiction between the essential hiddenness inherent in all these presentations of Christ's exaltation on the one hand, and the Lucan description of it as a visible ascension into heaven on the other is apparent rather than real. For in Matthew, Paul and John too the exaltation is depicted as an event which took place before witnesses in the apparitions of the risen Christ.

Thus it is not wholly confined to the realm of the "other-worldly" and the suprahistorical. On the contrary, it also has a solid basis in history, even though in its inward reality it exceeds the limits of that history and so must remain hidden from the unbeliever. For this exaltation takes place in the dimension of a concrete encounter with the Lord after he has passed through death. It is this aspect of verifiability by witnesses that is brought out in the Lucan account of the Ascension. It is based upon the greater length of time ("forty days") during which encounters with the risen Christ took place. The whole context in which this account is embedded is pervaded by the idea of witness, and it is in the light of this idea that it is to be understood (G. Lohfink).

It also follows that it would be a misunderstanding of the Ascension if some sort of temporary absence of Christ from the world were to be inferred from it. The "sitting on the right hand of the Father" of which Scripture speaks (e.g., Acts 2:33; 5:31; 7:55; Rom 8:34; Eph 1:20; Col 3:1, etc.) signifies rather the human Jesus' participation in the kingly power of God, and so precisely his authoritative presence in the world and among those whom he has made his own (cf. Mt 28:20). On this basis the Johannine theology finds it possible to combine the Resurrection with the return of Christ (e.g., 14:18ff.). With the resurrection of the Lord, in virtue of which he is henceforward and forever in the midst of his own, the parousia has already begun. Hence we must understand that the Lucan account of the Ascension is directed against a fever of false eschatological excitement, and — without denying the reality of eschatology (Acts 1:11) — lays the emphasis on the "present tense" of the time of the Church with its two factors: the gift of the Holy Spirit, through whom the Lord is already present here and now, and the task of bearing witness which the Christian takes up in response to his experience of the Spirit, placing himself at the service of the kingship of Christ.

It could also be said that although the reality of the exaltation of the Lord remains hidden in the age of history through which the world is passing, it still makes itself felt in history by the witness of the faithful who spread his message (Jn 15:26f.: ". . . he will bear witness to me; and you also are witnesses . . ."). This implies that exaltation and mission are closely connected. The mission is the form in which the world-embracing kingship of Christ expresses itself in the intermediate period during which he exercises his lordship through the humble medium of the word.

The idea of witness, then, is used to express the fact that the exaltation of Jesus is already beginning to be revealed, while at the same time including the further idea that this exaltation must of its nature be veiled from the eyes of the world. This Luke expresses by the image of the cloud (Acts 1:9) familiar from the OT theology of the temple, while John includes it in his presentation by the device of fusing the theology of the cross with that of the exaltation both in their existential significance and in their significance for the theology of history. The Christological hymn of Phil 2:5–11 has the same tendency. Here Christ is presented in the "emptying" of himself on the cross as the counterpart of that divinization of self which was the hybris of the first Adam. Moreover, by opposing the exaltation of the humble Christ to the downfall of hybris this hymn makes it clear to man that the way to "divinization" lies not through the self-sufficiency of hybris, but through participation in the humiliation of Christ's cross. Thereby this cross becomes paradoxically a sign of the exaltation of the Lord in this world. Hence the apostle boasts precisely of his weakness, for in this he experiences most of all the victory of God's strength (2 Cor 12:9f.).

From what has been said it will also be clear that the message of the Ascension as presented in the NT is, so far as its central statements of it are concerned, completely independent of the so-called "three-storeyed mythical" picture of the world, and hence cannot be "dismissed" along with it (against Bultmann). On the contrary, it opens up a new and positive understanding of the reality called "heaven", which is totally independent of any theories concerning the structure of the world. What the "Ascension" tells us about heaven is that it is the dimension of divine and human fellowship which is based upon the resurrection and exaltation of Jesus. Henceforth it designates the "place" (in the strictly ontological sense) in which man can live eternal life. Thus the Christian is aware that even in the present time his true life is hidden in "heaven" (Col 3:3) because, by believing in Christ, he has entered into the dimension of God and so, already in the here and now, into his own future.

See also *Biblical Exegesis* II, *New Testament Books* I, *Demythologization, Kerygma, New Testament Theology* II, III, *Parousia, Resurrection* I.

BIBLIOGRAPHY. V. Larrañana, *L'Ascension de Notre Seigneur dans le Nouveau Testament* (1938); P. Benoît, "L'ascension", *Revue Biblique* 56 (1949), pp. 161–203; A. M. Ramsey, "Ascension", *Theological Word Book of the Bible* (1950), pp. 22–23; E. Schweizer, *Erniedrigung und Erhöhung bei Jesus und seinen Nachfolgern* (1955); J. G. Davies, *He Ascended into Heaven* (1958); P. A. van Stempvoort, "The Interpretation of the Ascension in Luke and Acts", *NTS* 5 (1958–59), pp. 30–42; K. Rahner, *On the Theology of Death,* Quaestiones Disputatae 2 (2nd rev. ed., 1965), pp. 63–66; J. Dupont, *Études sur les Actes des Apôtres* (1967), pp. 81 ff.

Joseph Ratzinger

ASCETICISM

A. The Traditional Teaching

The word asceticism was taken into Christian usage from the Greek by Clement of Alexandria and Origenes, since ἄσκησις and ἀσκέω had never passed into Latin; since the word became common in the theological language of the 17th century and was contrasted with mysticism in the 18th, it has generally meant in Catholic writings the deliberate and persevering endeavour of the Christian to attain Christian perfection. As in practice there are a great many obstacles to such an endeavour — the conflict between body and spirit, disintegration of inner forces and effort, concupiscence, the sinful influence of the world around, demonic powers — it necessarily means a painful struggle, self-denial and renunciation. Hence the word ascetics, which really means exercise (ἀσκέω = exercise, practice), has, in the Catholic sense, acquired a special meaning of exertion, struggle and abstinence.

The immediate reason and purpose of ascetic acts is divided in Catholic writings into two kinds, moral and mystical. The negative aspect of moral asceticism concerns μετάνοια, man's conversion, the turning away from evil, from sinful inclination and desires and overcoming the threefold lust; positively it implies a loving turning towards God and one's neighbour, the practice of moral principles and virtues, restoration of the sin-disturbed inner order, the dominance of the personal spirit and selfless love. Mystical asceticism (which aims at a growing experience of God and of unity with him) involves a cleansing of the heart, inward recollection and composure, abandonment of one's own self and all one calls one's own, a patient waiting in darkness and dryness, the practice of hopeful expectation of God's visitation. Moral and mystical asceticism cannot be separated; they merely stress different aspects of the same search for Christian perfection; they merge and interlock. Nevertheless it is right to distinguish between them. All asceticism, or for that matter any human effort towards salvation, must be preceded and accompanied by the grace of God, which is obvious to the Catholic theologian. It is also agreed (although other voices can repeatedly be heard within the Church) that Christian asceticism is only of value if accompanied by a positive acceptance and regard for the created order, a sense of responsibility for the world and fidelity to temporal tasks.

Along with moral and mystical asceticism, there is also a Church tradition of cultic asceticism, which is concerned with abstinence and other acts, preparatory to participation in the mysteries of divine service, and aims at the cleansing of sinful man before the meeting with God. It plays a great role in some non-Christian religions where it is often attributed magical properties. It can also be found in the OT, particularly in connection with the great feasts and sacrificial worship — fasting and vigils, sexual abstinence, ablutions. From there it passed into Church practice; fasting, vigils, eucharistic fast. However, the OT prophets already gave warnings against excessive emphasis on this kind of asceticism and stressed the inner meaning. It plays no great part in the modern Church. But there is also a cultic asceticism in a wider sense, when some self-denial or other excercises are undertaken to make reparation and penance, or express one's dedication to God and therefore have the character of a sacrifice. There will always be this type of asceticism; its deepest sense lies in the recognition that God is absolute and holy and supreme Lord of man and all creation, in imploring his forgiveness and in making a concrete act of dedication to him and his service. But this must be done by virtue of the one and only valid sacrifice, that of Christ and must not be taken (subconsciously) as one's own meritorious religious achievement; otherwise it is without value and to be rejected.

The traditional Catholic view places the main emphasis on moral asceticism, as a glance at modern ascetic literature will show. The anthropology which underlies this view is often very defective. It is not quite free of an unconscious dualism and hence pays insufficient attention to the task posed by the union of body and soul which requires the integration in the whole person of all forces, including those of the body and the senses, such as sexuality, instinct, imagination, etc. In the *Enciclopedia Cattolica* asceticism is still defined as "methodical effort to suppress the lower impulses of human nature by gradually realizing spiritual perfection". Such oversimplifications, sometimes pernicious, have been countered in recent decades by a call for a psychology of asceticism (cf., e.g., J. Lindworsky, H. E. Hengstenberg, R. Egenter). There is no doubt that an essential problem is being tackled here which is of the highest significance for the Christian way of life. The results of modern psychology, psychology of character and anthropology are indispensable for an asceticism that is suitable for the person and the situation. This then is the general traditional teaching on asceticism as put forward in moral theology and spiritual books.

But does this really cover everything that can be said about asceticism in the Christian sense? Efforts are increasingly being made towards a theological and spiritual deepening of asceticism. The sharp distinction between asceticism and mysticism is deplored, on the grounds that such an approach connects asceticism too onesidedly with moral perfection. And as this distinction was made at a time when the former close ties between theology and spirituality had been greatly loosened and theology itself was not entirely free of rationalism, Stoic and Pelagian undercurrents are said to have entered into the notion of asceticism, and to have encouraged an individualistic attitude towards salvation; it is time, therefore, the argument goes on, to look upon asceticism and mysticism as one unit, to give the religious element precedence before the moral element and to place asceticism on a deeper theological basis.

B. THEOLOGICAL DIMENSION

The truly fundamental Christian asceticism or "exercise" is undoubtedly faith, which is of course primarily a gift of God's grace. But God who makes himself known in his revelation and in man's heart, must be answered, not once, but every day. This "exercise", this acceptance of the grace of faith, this yes to the God who is revealing himself, does not only give fulfilment and enlightenment to man, opening up a new, all-comprehensive horizon, but it is essentially also a renunciation, an act of self-denial. In faith man accepts the mystery of God which for him is unfathomable and impenetrable (cf. 1 Tim 6:16), he gives himself trustingly to God without seeing what he has been promised (cf. Heb 11:1). He thus renounces any isolated attempt of his own to find the meaning of his own existence, of the world in general and its history. He trusts him who has promised eternal life, without having any other guarantee than God himself who cannot be called to account before any court (Job). Through his faith the believer transcends the world and its immanent sensible character, he orientates it and himself toward God, and no longer holds fast to the things which alone, according to his natural judgment, would seem to provide fulfilment of his being. In fact, he no longer builds his life on himself and his own powers, but on God. All this, if done in earnest and in full awareness of the decision involved, is extremely difficult for man, for he has the ineradicable inclination to understand himself in terms of himself, to plan for himself and for his future, to lay hold of life and to make it secure. This was the original temptation of man who walked with God in his grace, before sin was known (cf. Gen 3:1–7). If he gave way to this basic temptation, the threat is still graver for fallen man who is thrown back upon himself and is beset by his lusts (concupiscence).

Guided by his faith, he must constantly fight against himself, transcend himself, let go of himself. This is the very basis of his asceticism. One might call it the asceticism of faith, the exercise of self-surrender to almighty God whom one cannot see, whose "judgments are unsearchable" and whose "ways are inscrutable" (Rom 11:33). Such asceticism will be all the more existential, i.e., touching man's basis of existence, the more his actual experience of life seems to contradict a faith in a God of love who has created man and has promised a fulfilment to transcend everything temporal. It is necessary to accept one's self, one's painful unsurmountable limitations, weaknesses and inadequacies, the sorrows, disappointments and frustrations of life, and in the end, death, the ultimate absurdity of human existence, to cling firmly to God's promise and thus to quell insistent doubt and revolt, to take life upon oneself willingly and to follow its call. The more radically the believer does this, the more clearly will he realize, while drawing only on the ordinary occurrences of life, what God wants of him and of him only. He must be attentive to God's will, he must submit to it and allow himself to be guided by it. This requires a new initiative, which once again means the practice of asceticism and renunciation. Its aim is an Ignatian indifference, a permanent readiness to be called anywhere. It is at this point that asceticism of faith becomes a true obedience in faith, as exemplified by Abraham in a way that cannot be surpassed and is valid for all times. Only where such an obedience of faith is practised do the various forms of asceticism – moral and mystical – make sense. They must be based on the obedience of faith, integrated with it, pervaded by it; otherwise there will always be the danger that it will aim rather at man for his own sake than at God.

But all this is still insufficient for a Christian asceticism, founded in the grace of faith. It only becomes Christian in the strict sense within the explicit context of sin, the divine judgment on sin, and redemption through the cross of Christ. Man did not only lose through sin his original fellowship with God, he has become God's debtor and he is constantly reminded of his debt by the sufferings of this life, the harbingers of the distress and terror of death. As a Christian he will therefore connect with sin the suffering and death, which is the fate of man and the world, and will accept it willingly in the consciousness of his guilt. His asceticism of faith takes into account the sentence of punishment which God has imposed on sinful humanity (cf. Gen 3:16 to 19; 6:5ff.). But he knows that he can never extinguish his debt on his own. He will always look to God imploringly and trustingly and hope for forgiveness. This fact alone shows that the perfection aimed at in moral asceticism can never be the primary and certainly not the only aim of the Christian. Asceticism must remain grounded in the consciousness of the indebtedness and of the impotence of the sinner, for otherwise it would be constantly in danger of striving after personal achievement in spite of the knowledge that the help of God's grace is indispensable.

Against the background of this redemptive situation — indebtedness and impotence — the Christian must see Christ who is not only the Word of the Father's forgiving love, but in "the form of a servant" (Phil 2:7), the real ἀσκητής, who has taken our own lot, death, upon himself and has carried it through to the bitter end. Unprotected, dispossessing himself of all divine power, he exposed himself to the sins of men, to self-seeking, inconstancy, ruthlessness, enmity, hatred, unbelief; he carried the guilt of all mankind on to the cross (cf. 1 Pet 2:24) and in his body suffered the sentence of condemnation imposed on man (cf. Rom 8:3). In obedience to the Father which he learned through what he suffered (Heb 5:8), he endured the cross, despising the shame, and thus became "the pioneer and perfecter of our faith" (Heb 12:2). What we were incapable of doing, he has done for us all: not only did he place himself utterly at God's disposal who, although he was his Father, seemed far away often enough and threatened to vanish in the night of the senses and the spirit, but through his voluntary death, he "cancelled the bond which stood against us with its legal demands; this he set aside, nailing it to the cross" (Col 2:14), thus re-establishing once more our fellowship with God.

Therefore all Christian asceticism must be, at its deepest level, participation in Christ's asceticism, that is, an asceticism of the cross. Only then will it be meaningful and salutary. In baptism the fundamental grace of participation in Christ's redemptive death is given, and the Christian must constantly take Christ's death upon himself and die with him each day. Obedience in faith thus becomes the imitation of Christ: "If any man would come after me, let him deny himself and take up his cross and follow me" (Mk 8:34). This imitation of Christ is not only the basis of moral asceticism, but of a far more radical asceticism: an active approach towards death, taking up the cross through free renunciation of things important to life. The spirit of the beatitudes and of the evangelical counsels is realized in such an asceticism. It does not rest with the (pious) man and (zealous) Christian, but it is always launched anew by the call of the spirit of Christ, of his crucified love, the spirit of obedient, loving readiness to serve, expressed in the renunciation of one's own life. It is the Spirit who is its norm. Asceticism of the cross is penance, atonement and witness all in one; it tears down the barriers to make way for an out-flowing love.

One other aspect of Christian asceticism must be mentioned, the eschatological. It is of course implicit in the asceticism of faith and of the cross, for both look to the promised final glory beyond this world; nevertheless it must be brought to the fore and specially emphasized, for it requires a special ascetic attitude on the part of the Christian. The Christian is a pilgrim, part of the pilgrim Church, on his way to the holy city which God has built for his people (cf. Heb 11:10). He is going through the last stage of his wanderings, the time between the "already" of God's irrevocable bestowal of salvation in his Son, and the "not yet" of the manifest glory of the new heavens and the new earth, always a stranger in this world, an exile and stateless (cf. 1 Pet 2:11 alluding to Lev 25:23; Ps 39:13, etc.), yet already fellow-citizen with the saints and member of the household of God (Eph 2:19). Although already "in Christ", he will die, "not having received what was promised", he will only be able to behold and salute it from afar (cf. Heb 11:13). In this redemptive situation three things are demanded of the Christian: waiting in patience (the ὑπομονή of the apostles' letters), preparedness and constant vigilance for the coming of the Lord. This practice could be called eschatological asceticism. In the midst of the labours and disappointments of our time, which increase with age, the Christian will have to defend himself repeatedly against a dangerous weariness of faith, against a disgust of religion and the defeatism of accidie. Often he will want to take the easy way out and shut his eyes to the inexorable decision of faith. He must then resist his weak nature by looking to the example of our Lord and accepting in the depth of his heart the grace of patience and the strength of perseverance. Furthermore, the *status viatoris,* the life of the pilgrim, demands of the Christian that he should always remain open to the future, constantly receptive to God's voice. He must not, therefore, become attached to opinions, plans, etc., or else he would be in danger of taking them to be God's will. He must each day break loose from himself and his world, lay himself open to the "ever greater God" whose ways are impenetrable and unaccountable. This is always true, not least in the ecclesiastical sphere.

How much stubbornness, narrowness, pharisaism, excess of authority, legalism, self-righteousness, all of which are strains on faith, could be avoided if all members of the Church, of whatever rank and station, clerics as well as laymen, would always bear in mind that the Church is still on its way and must therefore remain open to change, constantly seeking the fullness of truth, responsible for proclaiming God's word anew in every age. Lastly, an eschatological attitude in the narrow sense, that is, readiness for the last days, preparing for our Lord's coming in judgment and glory, requires a constant asceticism, affecting thoughts and actions at the deepest level. Hence our Lord's many exhortations to be vigilant (Mk 13:33 ff.; Mt 24:37 ff. par.; Lk 21:34 ff.). The concrete application of this asceticism is expressed in St. Paul's classic formulation (in Cor 7:29–31) which requires the Christian to remain detached from the world in its present form and direct his eyes towards the other, final world. There is also a special place here for what we have called mystic asceticism.

Only when Christian asceticism is looked upon and lived in its theological dimension, will it be free of the onesided anthropocentric narrowness of which it is sometimes accused — not always without cause — and it will become clear that asceticism and mysticism are simply two aspects of the Christian life which cannot be separated (cf. J. de Guibert). But in order to exclude any possible misunderstanding to which both are frequently exposed, they should not only be aids to personal perfection, but should be seen to be part of the mystery of the Church. This would show that ultimately they could not be anything but "service" within the Church and within the mystery of the Church, the Body of Christ and God's people (cf. Przywara, *Deus semper maior,* pp. 300 f., note 1). No one becomes perfect for himself, but only in the service of the all-embracing *Mysterium Christi* which proclaims God's love and radiates his glory.

C. The Problem of Asceticism

If asceticism and mysticism merge into one another and are basically inseparable, it is doubtful if asceticism can be regarded as a subject to be studied on its own, as has been done in the past, though only since the 17th century. This inherent difficulty is clearly demonstrated by the fact that there is not, and has never been, a uniform definition of asceticism. Sometimes it is said to be the way of purification and illumination *(via purgativa et illuminativa),* while the way to union *(via unitiva)* is reserved to mysticism, sometimes it is confined to those moral religious acts which are chiefly aimed at practising virtues with the help of ordinary grace, while mysticism needs extraordinary graces and special gifts; then again it is said to include the whole spiritual life and all stages of perfection with the exception of infused contemplation. This explains why, although the teaching about the spiritual life and perfection has been split into asceticism and mysticism, both have generally been treated together and regarded as *one* theological subject. The method of teaching asceticism and mysticism as separate theological disciplines was adopted officially for the first time in 1919 (cf. *AAS* 12 [1920], pp. 29 ff.); in 1931 it was adopted for the official curriculum through the constitution *Deus scientiarum Dominus* (*AAS* 23 [1931], pp. 271, 281). But as asceticism and mysticism are so intimately related, the tendency now is to speak of "spiritual theology", which cannot, however, be clearly separated from the other basic theological disciplines (especially the exegesis of dogma and morals) in so far as they themselves become *spritual* theology, i.e., when they go beyond the level of a one-sided philological exegesis and a rationalistic school of theology. If one is to speak of asceticism in the narrow sense at all, it can only be within the context of a more comprehensive order, in fact spiritual theology.

The fundamentals of such an asceticism should be determined primarily by the theological dimension of Christian asceticism, that is, by the basic Christian exercises as outlined above, asceticism of faith, asceticism of the cross and eschatological asceticism. Christian moral (and mystic) asceticism must be placed within the context of these "exercises" and be subordinate to them; otherwise there would always be the danger of aiming at a pious achievement for its own sake and of making *man,* his own personal perfection, his individual loving communion with God, the centre of religious effort. From the point of view of the doctrine on virtue, asceticism must be so constructed that the theological virtues provide the core, inspiration and direction for the moral virtues, the immediate concrete direction being towards the mystery of the Church and service within it. Only within and through the Church can the Christian give himself completely to God and his fellow-men; only the Church which is the "sign of intimate union with God, and of the unity of all mankind" (Vatican II, Dogmatic Constitution on the Church, art. 1), can say "Amen" to God's offer of love, as manifested in Christ (cf. 2 Cor 1:19 f.).

Christian asceticism must also include an anthropology which avoids all one-sidedness, suspicion, and curtailment, such as one can meet at times in the traditional Christian attitude towards the body, sex, marriage and worldly matters in general; it must see man as a unit of body and soul in all his aspects (spirit, soul, body; individual, one with mankind, living in the world), for the grace of God speaks to the whole man in all his aspects. God, by allowing man to share his life through Christ's redemption, opens possibilities of a deeper and fuller human development. In man's concrete redemptive situation this can only be done through participation in the cross and death, but this does not prevent all aspects of human existence from being included in God's call of grace. Thus all anthropological disciplines have a place in Christian asceticism: physiology, psychology, sociology, etc., as well as the various ways of being man and developing as a human person: individual and social aspects, especially the polarity and meeting of the sexes, marriage and celibacy; property and poverty, work, vocation, ("political") action; age, the course of life, etc. All these are necessary in order to arrive at an asceticism, suitably adapted to the individual's sex, psychology and character, age, stage of maturity, status, environment and task, and to prevent any false kind of asceticism. But it would be wrong to lay one-sided stress on the *"suitability"* of asceticism (as tends to happen nowadays), just as it would be wrong to see the theological side only. Both aspects belong together like the realities they are based on: the world and the supernatural world, the reality of creation and the reality of salvation, nature and grace. Hence the variability of Christian asceticism, from the sober mood of a world-based existence to the intoxication of the imitation of Christ in death and resurrection, according to the demands of one's Christian vocation and the concrete situation.

No systematic exposition of the kind of asceticism due from a Christian can ignore the realities of temptation and sin, which are so significant for the religious life; to overcome these is not the least object of Christian asceticism. They must, therefore, be not merely included in ascetics, but must be expressly and thematically treated. But here too — as with the exposition of asceticism itself — it is necessary to differentiate in accordance with their existential depth. Particular attention must be paid to the Christian's basic temptation or sin: ever since original sin (Gen 3), man, bent back upon himself *(homo incurvatus),* has had the ineradicable temptation to ignore his transcendental destiny and to close his inner world to the call of God's grace. This inclination, rooted in original sin, is, according to St. Augustine, in some way connected with all sins, particularly those that come within the sphere of the theological aspects of asceticism, asceticism of faith, asceticism of the cross and eschatological asceticism. This is also the place for some classification of man's temptation: actual and potential, open and secret and, what is more than ever necessary today, to differentiate or to point the way to differentiation (helped by depth-psychology and based on the discernment of spirits) between real moral religious guilt and psychological, sociological and other factors in a given situation.

One further point must not be lacking in any asceticism: the idea of the Christian life as a way or, more precisely, a way of various stages, an ascent towards the perfection of loving God and one's neighbour, towards sanctity. The act of making an effort, of renunciation, in fact asceticism, plays a decisive role in the progress and growth of *moral* sanctity; this applies particularly to the traditional understanding of the three well-known stages of beginning, progress and perfection which have become classical since St. Thomas Aquinas (*Summa Theologica*, II, II, q. 24, a. 9; q. 183, a. 4); the idea of three stages, purification, illumination and union, which found its way into Christian tradition through Plato and Plotinus via Pseudo-Dionysius, and which aims at the mystical experience of God, has been understood in modern times more in the sense of moral perfection. Now there can be no doubt that according to the NT as well as unanimous Christian tradition, there can be growth in perfection. But apart from the fact that all statements to this effect in the NT and in tradition are of a general and sometimes purely formal nature and therefore say little about the "how" of such growth, we have become very sceptical nowadays about any success of moral asceticism (the necessity of which is not in question) in "attaining perfection", because we have become increasingly aware of our own incapability. We do not even trust our most sacred emotions; our daily life, as well as what we have learnt from depth-psychology, has taught us that we can say little about the existential genuineness and depth of our Christian acts of virtue and our attitudes. This scepticism is supported by theological arguments. Modern theology on grace lays greater stress than before on the personal character of Christian sanctity (including sanctifying grace); we therefore cannot imagine its growth in a concrete way, as used to be possible within the traditional concept of grace and the theological notion of the *habitus;* sanctity, to us, is not something one can "possess", but something that is dependent on personal union with God, having the character of a gift and including human co-operation, even though existential

(and therefore permanent, though terminable) sanctity ranks higher than moral sanctity. The problem which thus arises of the stages on the way to perfection must be faced in modern ascetics. It will then become clear that, for the modern Christian, the way to sanctity must first be seen to belong to the theological aspect of asceticism. Any growth in sanctity will show itself in the extent to which he allows himself to be guided by the loving God in all the happenings and calls of his daily life.

See also *Spirit, Spirituality, Body, Metanoia, Dualism, Psychology, Stoicism, Pelagianism, Concupiscence, Discernment of Spirits.*

BIBLIOGRAPHY. P. Pourrat, *Christian Spirituality,* 3 vols. (1922–24); E. Przywara, *Wandlung* (1925); id., *Majestas divina* (1925); H. Windisch, "ἀσκέω", *TWNT,* I (1933; E. T., 1964), pp. 494–6; J. Lindworsky, *Psychologie der Aszese* (1935); H. E. Hengstenberg, *Christliche Aszese* (1936); J. de Guibert and others, "Ascèse", *DSAM,* I (1937), cols, 936–1010; R. Egenter, *Die Aszese in der Welt* (1957); E. Peterson, "Eine Beobachtung zu den Anfängen der christlichen Aszese", *Frühkirche, Judentum und Gnosis* (1959), pp. 209–20; H. U. von Balthasar, "Theologie und Heiligkeit", *Verbum Caro, Skizzen zur Theologie,* I (1960), pp. 195–225; id., "Spiritualität", *Verbum Caro. Skizzen zur Theologie,* I (1960), pp. 245–59; id., "Aktion und Kontemplation", *Verbum Caro. Skizzen zur Theologie,* I (1960), pp. 245–59.

Friedrich Wulf

ATHEISM

A. In Philosophy

1. *Concept and incidence.* Philosophically speaking, atheism means denial of the existence of God or of any (and not merely of a rational) possibility of knowing God (theoretical atheism). In those who hold this theoretical atheism, it may be tolerant (and even deeply concerned), if it has no missionary aims; it is "militant" when it regards itself as a doctrine to be propagated for the happiness of mankind and combats every religion as a harmful aberration. We speak of the practical atheism (indifferentism) of a mode of life in which theoretical recognition of God's existence has no perceptible consequences. To decide precisely what constitutes atheism, depends on just what conception of God is assumed. All systems of materialism and materialistic monism are

certainly atheistic (early Greek atomists, post-Socratic Cynics, Epicureanism, certain philosophers of the Renaissance such as Campanella; the naturalism of the Enlightenment in France: Voltaire, Holbach, Lamettrie; German positivism and monism of the 19th century: Vogt, Büchner, Moleschott, Haeckel; left-wing Hegelianism: Feuerbach, Marx; popular 19th century socialism; dialectical materialism and bolshevism; the State-encouraged militant atheism of the godless movement in the Communist States); unqualified positivism, sensualism and pragmatism; all forms of philosophy for which atheism is a postulate, that is to say, theories such as those (deriving from Nietzsche) of A. Camus or the existentialism of J.-P. Sartre, or the ethics of N. Hartmann, which seek positively to prove that God cannot or ought not exist. Whether every form of pantheism (especially in German idealism) is to be classified as atheism, depends on how far it succeeds in not simply identifying man and the world with the absolute.

Polytheism will have to be characterized as atheism to the extent to which it makes the act of genuine religion directed to the absolute ground of the world difficult or, in an extreme case, impossible. (Conversely, the polytheism of antiquity persecuted as atheist the monotheism of some philosophers and of Christianity because it rejected the gods of the State; and again the Fathers of the Church sought to detect a hidden atheism behind heresies.) In the perspective of the history of ideas, atheism as a philosophical system has always appeared at moments of crisis and transition from one intellectual, cultural and social epoch to another. That shows that it is a crisis phenomenon, the projection of a question disguised as an answer, not the answer of an age that has attained assured certainty. In every transition to a new epoch of man's experience of himself, some particular experience of his own limitation appears to be overcome; this obscures man's recognition of his radically finite character and produces the impression that there is no place for a genuinely infinite and absolute reality. Further, the new grasp of the problems posed by modes of representation and terms once thought adequate to express the knowledge of God, now suggests that to speak about God would be to apply such concepts to a non-existing "object". Or at least the impression is given that no meaningful assertions may be made about it.

2. *Its possibility.* That theoretical atheism is possible is shown by actual experience in the history of religion and philosophy. How this fact is to be theologically interpreted will be considered later. Even from the purely philosophical point of view, atheism is not simply one of the many differences of opinion between men about the existence or demonstrability of some particular being. For if atheism really understands itself and comprehends what is meant by God, it denies that the whole question of being, and of the personal subject as such who is propounding that question, can or may be raised at all. But such a question arises anew as a condition of its very denial. To the extent, therefore, that atheism understands its own nature, it suppresses itself. Nevertheless it is possible, because man is a being who by misconceiving his own nature and through his own real fault, can be in contradiction with himself.

3. A *philosophical criticism of atheism* will first have to show, by a transcendental method, that, epistemologically (critically) and metaphysically, absolute scepticism or a positivist, pragmatist or "criticist" restriction of human knowledge to the realm of immediate experience is self-destructive, and that therefore the very possibility of metaphysics is always affirmed by its implicit existence in man's necessary knowledge. Then on that basis, in a rightly conceived proof of God's existence, God's existence and nature would both have to be made explicit together. The absolutely unique character of this knowledge (as a knowledge by analogy of the mystery of God's incomprehensibility) would have to be brought out, and on that basis the possibility of atheism, and its limits, explained. Such a critique of atheism would have to be completed by an interpretation in sociological and cultural terms of the milieu in which atheism appears as a mass phenomenon, by an explanation in terms of depth psychology of the "defence mechanism" which lies at the root of doubt and the "impossibility" of accepting the transcendent (atheism as a "flight" from God). A philosophical critique of atheism would also have to include a critique of theism whether popular or philo-

sophical as it exists in fact. For atheism essentially lives on the misconceived ideas of God from which theism in its actual historical forms inevitably suffers. The criticism of atheism would finally have to be linked to a sort of maieutic of the religious act because in the long run theoretical knowledge of God only lives when it is taken up into the yes of consent to God given by the whole person, and a whole life.

B. In Theology

1. *The teaching of the Church.* Materialist atheism is characterized as shameful (*D* 1802). Atheism as a denial of the one true God, Creator and Lord of all things visible and invisible (*D* 1801), and as pantheism in various forms (*D* 1803–5; cf. 31, 1701), is anathematized. The anathema is necessarily only a recent one. That God can be known with certainty by the natural light of reason is actually defined (*D* 1785, 1806; on the demonstrability of God's existence: *D* 2145, 2317, 2320). At the same time, however, it is emphasized that he is inexpressibly raised above everything that exists apart from him or that thought can conceive (*D* 428, 432, 1782). The teaching of modernist agnosticism is described as "atheism" in the encyclical *Pascendi* (*D* 2073, 2109). The doctrine that theism is the product of social conditions or only affirmed on the basis of social conviction is, objectively speaking, also rejected by the Church's condemnation of Traditionalism (*D* 1649–52, 1622, 1627). That does not of course deny the essential importance of tradition and society for the individual's knowledge of God.

The Church first dealt really seriously with atheism as a new, world-wide mas-phenomenon at the Second Vatican Council. It was considered rather incidentally in the Dogmatic Constitution on the Church, art. 16, in the following terms: "Nor does divine Providence deny the help necessary for salvation to those who, without blame on their part, have not yet arrived at an explicit knowledge of God, but who strive to live a good life, thanks to his grace." "Inculpable" atheism (in the domain of clearly articulated knowledge, *expressa agnitio*) is obviously considered as a real possibility, which does not exclude salvation. Two questions remain unanswered here. One is whether in the existential, spontaneous act

of existence there can be an inculpable no to the theism which is necessarily implied in this act. The other is whether such explicit atheism can remain inculpable in an individual, on the level of conscious reflection, throughout his whole life. The answer to the first question must be in the negative. As regards the second, in view of our present-day experience of atheism, we must be more cautious in saying either yes or no than most theologians have been hitherto when they denied the possibility of inculpable theoretical atheism being maintained for a long period.

But the most important text (a pastoral rather than a doctrinal one) is in art. 19–21 of ch. 1 of the Constitution on the Church in the Modern World. It first gives the various forms and causes of atheism, then the modern forms of theoretical atheism, and concludes with the attitude of the Church to atheism. The urgency of the present-day problem is recognized. Then come a number of concessions. Atheism is at times merely the rejection of a god who does not really exist. It is often the reaction to the atrophy of a genuine religious experience, or to the theodicy problem — the evil of the world. Its causes can be social. It is often a wrong interpretation of a legitimate sense of freedom and autonomy in modern man, or of his will to emancipate himself from economic and social bonds in order to mould his life "creatively". Or it may be the erection of human values into absolutes. The possibility of atheism as sin is recognized, but with great reserve, briefly, and without going deeply into this particular problem. Christians are said to share the guilt of atheism in so far as it is a critical reaction against defective forms of theism in theory and in life. The Council stresses the fact that theism is not a self-alienation of man but the answer to a question which in the long run and at decisive moments man cannot evade. The task of moulding the future by action within the world loses none of its meaning through theism and the Christian eschatological hope, which are, on the contrary, the real source of its nobility and dynamism. Here the Council speaks of an *intima ac vitalis coniunctio* between man and God, of an *inquietudo religiosa,* and of the *quaestio insoluta subobscure percepta* which is none other than man himself. The perspective is that of a more existential and comprehensive relation to God which is already there when man poses the question of God in intellectual reflection. But these initiatives of Vatican II remain at the stage of preliminary efforts.

2. *Scripture.* In general in Scripture (as in the whole Semitic world) God's existence is assumed or affirmed as a matter of course. The folly of the man who says there is no God (Ps 10:4; 14:1; 53:2) refers to the denial of his government of the world as providence and judge. Interest, development, conflict and confession of faith in the Old and New Testaments all in this respect concerned monotheism, so that the most fundamental article of faith proclaimed the activity of the living God of the Covenant, and the Father of Jesus, experienced in the history of salvation (Dt 4:35; 6:4; Mk 12:29, 32; Jn 17:3; Rom 3:30, etc.). In this connection the doctrine of creation is important, as is the doctrine of the angels, and the interpretation of the gods as really demons. Both these show that men knew of profound realms of existence lying beyond experience, but that even in comparison with these God is totally different and incomparable (1 Cor 8:5). That testifies to awareness of God's radical transcendence. This should be taken into account when the scriptural doctrine of the possibility of knowing God by natural reason (Wis 13; Rom 1:20) is to be more precisely expounded. The doctrine of the creation of the whole reality of the universe and the principle, already clearly perceptible in Aquinas, that the world is to be explained as far as possible by "second causes", anticipate, fundamentally, the modern conception of the universe as in itself susceptible of investigation and control. But that is how there arises the temptation of modern times, to contrive to "explain" the world without God. The biblical removal of "magic" from the world, by the doctrine of creation (leaving in it, however, created "numinous" aspects, which was, however, often overlooked) is necessary for true, reverent theism. But it involves as its inevitable counterpart the danger of atheism to a degree unknown in antiquity.

At all events in Scripture man does not simply have God "also" as one of his possible objects of thought. Men, as "God's offspring" are created expressly that "they should seek God" (Acts 17:27 ff.). Consequently the atheists (cf. Eph 2:12) are not to be excused, for their refusal to know and give recognition to God is the profound folly, which takes itself for wisdom, of really knowing God and yet not acknowledging him, and of exchanging the known God for something else (Rom 1:21 ff., 25, 28) in a culpable "suppressing" of the truth (Rom 1:18). Scripture therefore knows no atheism of a purely neutral kind, which would be merely incidental (or at least does not reflect on any such atheism). It only recognizes an atheism which lies somewhere (impossible to locate in the individual case) between pious inarticulate veneration of the "unknown God" (Acts 17:22 in the light of Eph 2:12) and the guilty ignorance of the God whom in actual fact one knows in the "suppressed" accomplishment of one's own human nature (Rom 1).

3. *Traditional theology* chiefly deals with the question of the possibility of atheism. The basic view of the Fathers of the Church was that the knowledge of God is easy, almost inescapable and in that sense "innate". In view of the (relatively easy: Wis 13:9) possibility of knowing God and the "inexcusable" character of "foolish" atheism (Wis; Rom 1), Catholic theologians generally hold the doctrine that an atheism which is inculpable and negative (i.e., reaching no judgment on the question of God) is in itself (i.e., in normal human conditions) not possible over a certain length of time for the individual human being. Positive atheism (i.e., which positively asserts God's non-existence or unknowableness) is conceded to be a possible fact and also a lasting condition (and is lamented as a militant mass-phenomenon which has only appeared very recently: Pius XI in *AAS* 24 [1932], pp. 180 ff., 29 [1937], p. 76), but is declared to be culpable. But this teaching admits of many shades and in fact has been given them. L. Billot stressed the social and cultural dependence of individuals on their milieu and consequently considered it conceivable that many "grown-ups" do not reach the adult stage in regard to the question of God. Conversely, M. Blondel and H. de Lubac put so much stress on the radical orientation towards God as the essence of man, that at bottom there cannot be any atheists, but only those who simply think they do not believe in God. In view of the mass-phenomenon of modern atheism and the teaching

of Vatican II, the latter view will probably be more widely adopted in future, with the necessary developments and modifications.

As against the first of these opinions, it will have to be stressed that in view of God's universal salvific will it is not theologically possible to assume that so many human beings will remain inculpably, and despite their having lived their lives, excluded from their vocation. As against the second opinion, it has to be said that empirical atheism cannot after all, according to Scripture, be an ultimately harmless misinterpretation of a hidden theism. Alexander VIII condemned (*D* 1290) as a theological error the proposition that there could be a sin which was only an offence against human nature and not against God. We may then say that a fundamental moral decision, even when not recognized as an attitude towards God, nonetheless involves such an attitude, at least implicitly. On the one hand we must hold fast to this connection between theism and ethics. On the other hand we see more clearly today (in agreement once again with Aquinas) that the dependence of the individual (beyond his free and personally responsible decision) on the opinion of the society of which he is a member, is greater than was previously realized. The right to distinguish between men as a whole and in general and a particular individual, in regard to the knowledge of God, is certainly guaranteed by Vatican I. (See *Collectio Lacensis*, VII, 236, 150, 520.)

4. *Systematic treatment.* a) Generally speaking theology will have to refer in the first place to man's absolute transcendence. (This is to be understood from the start as his openness to the "living" God freely acting, so that "natural" knowledge of God does not draw up a closed theological system which would represent an *a priori* law imposed on the revealed word of God.) This transcendence which, as the condition of the very possibility of all intellectual knowledge and free action, implicitly refers to God and tacitly but truly makes that reference in every act of cognition and of freedom, can be present as obediently accepted or as denied; or it may be present as merely implicit and not thought about, or it may be taken as the theme of reflection and consequently it may name God as the term to

which it tends, and which does in fact correspond to it.

From this it follows (by way of systematic elucidation of the data of Scripture and tradition) that there cannot be a serene atheism which is in harmony with itself, for even atheism draws life from an implicit theism; there can be a nominal theism which despite its conceptual talk about God either does not yet genuinely accomplish in personal freedom the true nature of the transcendent orientation towards God or else fundamentally denies it atheistically, i.e., godlessly; there can be an atheism which merely thinks it is one, because in a tacit way transcendence is obediently accepted but there is no success in making it expressly and explicitly clear enough to the person concerned; there can be a total (but as a consequence, necessarily culpable) atheism in which transcendence is denied in a proud closing of the self, and precisely this is consciously made into atheism expressly and deliberately. Which of these possible forms of atheism is present in the individual and in what combination they are present in any age, is ultimately the secret of God who alone can judge. As, however, by the nature of man and the nature of Christianity (in which the Absolute himself in an "incarnational" way has entered the empirical world and its categories) transcendence is only fully realized and accepted when it finds explicit expression in "religious acts" addressed to God named and invoked, an atheism which explicitly doubts or denies (whatever its basis) is the most terrible thing in the world, a revelation of the folly and guilt of mankind and a sign of the growing eschatological distinction of men's lot because of God.

b) In particular the impossibility of a serene atheism can be shown in the domain of moral experience. Whenever an absolute moral obligation is affirmed, an implicit affirmation of God is present, even when the individual concerned does not succeed in giving it objective expression in a conceptually explicit theism. For absolute affirmation here and now in the concrete of an absolute obligation and consequently of the existence of an objective foundation for it, is an affirmation of God, even if not an explicit one. And when the moral law is not seen and willed as an absolute obligation, either explicitly or in the concrete accomplishment of moral action, there can be no question of complete presence of morality as such (even if this is contradistinguished from its foundation in God as law-giver); conduct would remain on the plane of the instinctive, conventional, utilitarian, etc. There can of course be an atheist ethics, to the extent that there are values, and the norms that derive from them, which are distinct from God (the personal nature of man and all that corresponds to it) and which can be perceived and affirmed without explicit knowledge of God. To that extent ethics and its norms constitute a natural domain of reality which like other domains of created reality possesses its relative independence and is directly accessible to cognition, so that agreement can be reached about it, at least in principle, even with atheists. But the absolute validity of all these values (their obligatory character because absolute) has its foundation in man's transcendence. It is only grasped as absolute to the extent that man grasps it and implicitly affirms it in affirming the absolute being and value which is implied in the open acceptance of his own transcendence. (It can be left entirely an open question whether that affirmation is explicit or only implicit.)

To the extent, therefore, that morality includes this absolute affirmation in its very concept, it is not merely one domain of reality among others, on which human *a posteriori* knowledge and behaviour are intent. It possesses in the absolute claim of moral duty an incomparable dignity which other domains do not. And this special dignity cannot simply be thought of as only indirectly grounded in God in the same way as all other realities have their "ultimate" ground in God. In the absolute obligation there is found precisely in the moral domain an active transcendent relation to God, so that in this respect an atheistic ethics complete in itself, even subjectively, and as a consequence atheism, are not possible. Certainly someone can think he is an atheist whereas in truth he affirms God by the absoluteness with which he bows to the claim of morality, provided he is really doing so, which does not follow from the mere fact that in civil life he is a "respectable man". He also knows it in the depth of his conscience, even though in the actual conceptual apparatus of the ideas he consciously holds he wrongly interprets what in actual fact he is doing.

c) In the effort to overcome atheism, Christians must realize — in the present and future situation of mankind — that they will meet all the factors which dogmatic theology sees in sin in general. Its roots are permanent. There is a sense in which it is potent even in the justified. It is not merely ineradicable in the world but its power will be eschatologically intensified as history proceeds. There is a difference between objective and merely subjective sin. Man cannot finally judge whether a given phenomenon involves subjective guilt or not. All this must now be applied to the theology of atheism, because it is the form of sin which marks the present age most clearly and powerfully, and which will no doubt continue to make itself felt in history. Just as the Church has faced and still faces serenely the phenomenon of sin — which is at least objective, but often *merely* objective — and believes throughout this inescapable experience that grace will triumph in the individual and in mankind, it must learn to maintain the same attitude in face of atheism.

Rational proofs of the existence of God remain valid and important, but they can now only be effective if they are combined with an apt initiation into the religious experience of the transcendence which is intrinsic to the concrete moral life in general, to the acceptance of active responsibility for the future, and above all to a really personal and genuine love of others. As we address ourselves to the atheist, culpable or inculpable (a distinction whose concrete application always escapes us), we must try to show him where he encounters God in his actual existence — even though he does not call this ultimate end and source of his moral freedom and love "God", shrinks from "objectivating" it, and often (wrongly) feels that intellectual and institutional religion is in contradiction with this inexpressible mystery of his existence. We can now no longer suppose that "God" means what it should mean to everyone, and that the only question is whether this God really exists. We must be extremely careful that all religious discourse makes the incomprehensibility of God, his holy mystery, definitely real and vital. Otherwise "God", as we call him, will not remain the true God, and the God whom we profess may be rejected by an atheism which considers itself purer and more "pious" than everyday theism.

The "struggle" against the mass-phenomenon of atheism must begin by taking it seriously, learning to know it, giving their due weight to its causes and values, and must not shrink from admitting publicly that theism was often misused as "opium for the people". There must be genuine dialogue with atheists, with all that true dialogue presupposes and entails. And hence we must be ready to co-operate with atheists in shaping our common world. The "struggle" cannot be confined to the doctrinal level. It is carried on above all in the testimony of life, in the individual Christian and in the whole Church, by means of constant self-criticism, self-purgation and reform, by means of a religious life demonstrably free from superstition and false security. Christians must let their light shine in true justice, love and unity, and by being a living testimony that one can accept the darkness of existence in faith and hope, as the dawn of the infinite meaning of existence, which is none other than the absolute God who communicates himself (cf. Vatican II, Pastoral Constitution on the Church in the Modern World, art. 21).

See also *God* I, II, *Devil* I, *Transcendence* I–III, *Religious Act, Materialism.*

BIBLIOGRAPHY. F. Mauthner, *Der Atheismus und seine Geschichte im Abendland,* 4 vols. (1920–23); F. A. Lange, *History of Materialism and Criticism of Its Present Importance,* with an introduction by B. Russell (3rd ed., 1925); H. Beylard, "Peccatum philosophicum", *NRT* 62 (1935), pp. 591–616, 672–98; M. Rossi, *Alle fonti del deismo e del materialismo moderno* (1942); M. Carrouges, *La mystique du surhomme* (1948); W. Kamlah, *Die Wurzeln der neuzeitlichen Wissenschaft und Profanität* (1948); H. de Lubac, *The Drama of Atheist Humanism* (1949); G. A. Wetter, *Der dialektische Materialismus* (1952); E. Rideau, *Paganisme ou Christianisme. Études sur l'athéisme moderne* (1953); A. Camus, *Rebel* (1954); H. U. von Balthasar, *Die Gottesfragen des heutigen Menschen* (1956); R. Garaudy, *Dieu est mort. Étude sur Hegel* (1962).

Karl Rahner

AUGUSTINIANISM

A. The Augustinian Tradition

Aurelius Augustinus (354–430) is one of the most remarkable figures in the history of the Western Church and in the development of Christian thought. He is one of those personalities whose influence upon antiquity, the Middle Ages, and modern times has been equally great and constant. It is to Augustine that men have gone again and again for insight into the question of their own self-understanding, so much so that in the course of the centuries an "Augustinian" dialogue has developed within which varying interpretations of the master and his work have been proposed, to which corresponded a varying interpretation of each period of history. It is this changing dialogue which may be referred to as a whole under the name "Augustinianism". The works of Augustine are, with those of Thomas Aquinas, the basis and determining influence in the acceptance and application of classical metaphysics within the Judaeo-Christian tradition. This application, nevertheless, was accomplished in different ways at the hands of both men, and thus ever since the 13th century Augustine's influence had largely been determined by its relation to Thomism. Augustinianism refers in a narrower sense to certain philosophical and theological theses which are based upon actual or purported works of Augustine.

B. Life and Work of Augustine

Along with some biographical data, we shall give here in outline the main aspects of Augustine's thought, which may help to provide a consistent explanation of his historical influence. The course of his great spiritual Odyssey, so uniquely chronicled in the famous *Confessions,* led him from the Christian faith in which his mother Monica had reared him through a period of aimless passions brought on by the reading of Cicero's *Hortensius* (now lost), to the religion of Mani (Manicheism). Though he remained a Manichean for eleven years, he finally abandoned Manicheism in his disillusioned search for truth, to lapse then into a phase of fundamental scepticism. Through the study of neo-Platonism and his acquaintance with Ambrose of Milan he drew ever closer to Christianity, until finally, at the climax of a long and intense inward crisis, he decided — under the influence of his reading of the Letter to the Romans — to accept the Christian faith and to lead a monastic life. Being baptized at the hands of Ambrose, he then retired from his position as teacher of rhetoric and returned to Africa, settling in Hippo. Most of his works were composed in Hippo, of which he was elected bishop in 396. His *Confessions* inform us in detail of the development of his way of life, and an accurate list of his own works is to be found in his *Retractions*. Other works of his which should be mentioned are the *Soliloquia, De Libero Arbitrio, De Vera Religione, De Trinitate, Enarrationes in Psalm I–XXXII* (the title was given by Erasmus), and the *De Civitate Dei*.

Augustine never received a systematic scholarly education but was essentially a self-taught man; and it is this which gives to his thought a genuinely independent cast and to his language a spontaneous vitality. His works were produced not out of scholarly interest alone but as a result of his involvement in the discussions and disputes of his day. In the question of grace, for example, he develops his theses with reference to Pelagianism, and in the teaching upon the sacraments it was the Donatist dispute which stimulated and determined his writings on that subject. His philosophical and theological principles were conceived in the course of his encounter with the neo-Platonists. As his thought was thus constantly pursued in the course of his varied dialogue with travelling companions, friends, and opponents, and also under the influence of his progressive dialogue with his God, Augustine never produced a self-contained system. His thought and writing were determined by and correspond to the concerns of a given situation. Nevertheless, the history of his dialogues is the history of his truly fundamental search for truth. It is this constant questioning, ever stimulated by his original experience of truth, of God, which is the source of his life and thought. It is from such experience that he derived the insight that man need not fly to that which is without, but only to return to that which is within: "in you yourself does the truth dwell". It is more intimate than one is to oneself. In the consciousness of this most intimate relation of the understanding of the self and of truth he is led to say (addressing God): "When I recognize myself, I recognize You!"

Point of departure for Augustine's thought. Such experiences of God, of truth in his sense, led Augustine to develop his ideas on illumination. Here he proposes that that which makes man what he is, is primarily his relation to truth; in all knowledge "truth" is also known as the indispensable light of consciousness; and in every activity its goodness is willed, as the necessary life of all freedom. Truth, in the form of illumination and the source of vitality, is not something which is possessed by man, like a fixed attribute or condition of reason. For Augustine it is rather an event — the confrontation of man with God. Truth is thus in one way the constant illumination of man by God, to which man, however, does not always actually respond in his free decisions (because of his original sinfulness); and in another way it is those individual instances of illumination in which the glory of God, both judging and forgiving, is experienced as salvation. God is present to a man as the *mysterium tremendum ac fascinosum,* and is experienced in both the dread and the happiness of man's heart, the *acies mentis*. Man experiences himself as one addressed in an I-Thou dialogue with his divine partner. In Aristotelian metaphysics the absolute ground, the being of beings, is part of the universe, immanent to the spirit or to the world, where it is the permanent principle of order: the κόσμος νοητός is not "otherworldly" in relation to the κόσμος αἰσθητός. In Platonism there is at least a presentiment of a living God who is the "wholly other" but who nonetheless draws nigh to man as person to person. But Augustine clearly recognized that man is constituted as such by the call of God. Illumination is a dialogue in which the transcendence and the historicity of man are realized at the same moment. The history of transcendence and of freedom are the two dimensions which Augustine had to add to Greek thought, while making their immanence radical. Such a penetrating grasp of the relationship between transcendence and history, conceived of as dialogue and event, seems not to have been attained even by Thomas Aquinas. For Augustine the relationship was perfected in God's becoming man while man became man.

Having thus briefly sketched the permanent principle and framework of the life and thought of Augustine, we may at least catalogue the specific teaching and positions which Augustine adopted in the course of his work. These positions cannot here be presented as they proceeded from the original context of Augustine's thought, but will simply be treated in the terminology by which they were developed and handed down in the course of dogmatic theology even though such language does not always correspond fully to the original purposes of Augustine.

Main teachings. a) Augustine applied his speculative abilities most intensively to the teaching on the Trinity. He developed the conception of the divine persons as subsistent relations, proceeding from a consideration of the nature *(essentia)* of God, and not from the Father as origin — in contrast to the approach of the Greek Fathers. Augustine explains the generation of the Son and the procession of the Holy Spirit from the Father and from the Son as being analogous to processes of mental life, such as the act of speaking and that which is spoken. The possibility of a self-revelation of God *ad extra* is attributed to the three divine persons in the *same* way, which is to propound, according to sense if not in actual words, the appropriation-theory.

b) In his works on grace and predestination, composed before his consecration as bishop, Augustine interpreted the relationship set up by revelation between the free personal God and man as one to which man's activity made an essential contribution. Later he was to restrict all salutary value to the activity of grace alone, asserting that the will of man is itself totally impotent unless assisted by God. Goodness and badness, belief and unbelief, salvation or reprobation — all is made to depend so much on the divine will that those who are saved by a sovereign and inscrutable act of God attain to blessedness independently of meritorious deeds; while the rest, because of the "passivity" of God, are eternally lost. There is no wrong done to them as no one has any claim upon salvation after the Fall and original sin. Thus, Augustine recognizes a predestination to blessedness according to which God grants to the elect even the gift of perseverance, and also a predestination — not *ad peccatum* — but *ad sempiternum interitum* (*Tract. in Jo.,* 48, 46). He thereby limited the salvific will of God. According to Augustine, the absolute justice of God must be upheld even when it is impossible to explain how it is that he is just.

c) In Christology Augustine anticipates the teaching of Ephesus (431) and Chalcedon

(451), according to which there are two natures *(substantiae)* in Christ. He is God and man but only one person — the Logos, the second divine person. Augustine's soteriology, which is not consistent, is determined by his conviction that through the sin of Adam the devil obtained the right to tempt man to his undoing. But this right was then abolished through the death of Christ. The devil was caught in the "trap" of the cross. Attacking Christ as though he had a claim upon him, which in fact he did not have, he forfeited his right and thus man can be delivered from the snares of the devil.

d) In his ecclesiology Augustine sees those who have received Christ's grace and redemption as forming the *one* community of the Church. He accepts the principle *salus extra ecclesiam non est;* and the Church is to be recognized through its unity, holiness, and apostolicity. In its totality it forms the body of Christ. In this sense there is an invisible Church as well as the visible one. Hence, outward membership is no guarantee of salvation, and conversely, those who are not members of the visible Church through no fault of their own, may in fact be among its invisible members.

e) In antiquity, history was sometimes conceived of after the pattern of physics, where nature eternally repeated its cycles. But Augustine saw man and his history as constituted by the confrontation with and the relation to the God who is transcendent to history. Human history begins with the "illumination" and is to end with the perfect revelation of God. The meaning of history is the revelation of God and union with him. Human history is thus the story of the acceptance or the rejection of God in Jesus Christ, the history of salvation or damnation. Only those events are meaningful by which God enters into the affairs of the world; the history of iniquity will remain impenetrable and will only be revealed in its full meaning at the end of time. The majority of men belong to the *civitas terrena,* the *civitas diaboli.* The *civitas Dei* is the community of the elect and the redeemed. But no concrete community or institution in history can be identified with either of these titles. The Church and the State, for example, are *civitates permixtae,* and the Church itself is only the prefiguration of the *civitas Dei* to be fully revealed at the end of time.

C. Augustine's Influence

The general approach and the main tenets of Augustine's thought reveal the themes which inspired "Augustinianism": the relation between habitual and actual illumination, the contrast between nature and grace, metaphysical order and salvific events, empirical knowledge of the world and experience of God in dialogue, and finally the relation between reason and revelation, philosophy and theology in general. But those who took over his rich and comprehensive thought had not the same penetrating insight, and soon after his death many themes were taken out of their context and treated in isolation. The darker side of Augustine also remained influential: the dualism of his esteem and scorn for the body, his love for man and also a certain contempt for him — a dualism which was finally projected upon God (as the notion of predestination shows). These gloomier aspects are to be understood in the light of his whole development, and have only a relative value in the light of his personality as a whole. But their effects may be seen in many of the ascetical, pastoral and even philosophical and theological trends which invoke Augustine most zealously.

Patristic period and the Middle Ages. Even within the lifetime of Augustine disputes arose with regard to his teaching on grace, between Semi-Pelagians and "Predestinarians". The Pelagianizers advocated synergistic ideas, while the latter stressed Augustine's view of the depravity of human nature and the essential role of grace in the freedom to do good. The Augustinian notion of the absolute efficacy of grace *(gratia irresistibilis)* was reinforced, and joined to the doctrine of the non-universal salvific will of God. The image of the God working in the background given by the champions of predestination who invoked Augustine, seemed sinister to their contemporaries. Such a "terrifying concept of God" (Altaner) was bound to lead to dispute and demanded clarification. At the Council of Orange in 529 the official decision was in favour of a "moderate Augustinianism". Against the Semi-Pelagians the Council defended the necessity of grace for the initial movement towards salvation, that is, for the first conversion of the will towards God and the *initium fidei* and hence the necessity of grace for the healing of human nature as such (*D* 176 f.; 186). The conception of the limited saving will of God was abandoned, though the predestination tendency was again to appear three centuries later in the teaching of Gottschalk of Orbais (d. *c.* 867) in a very pronounced form. In the name of Augustine, whom he called *maximus post apostolos Ecclesiarum instructor* and upon whose Anti-Pelagian positions he especially based himself, Gottschalk proposed with great vigour and stubbornness the thesis of total predestination: to blessedness as well as to damnation. At the two Synods of Quiercy (849 and 853), convened to deal with this problem, Gottschalk and his teaching were severely condemned. Finally, at the Synods of Savonnier (859) and Toncy (860), the moderate Augustinianism was again reaffirmed and was to remain the basic tendency in Scholasticism and in theology in general.

Early Scholasticism. Similarly, in the debates of early Scholasticism, the opposing parties based themselves upon Augustine: from Anselm of Canterbury (d. 1109) to Abelard (d. 1142), from Peter Damian (d. 1072) to Bernard of Clairvaux (d. 1153). For Anselm, Hugo of St. Victor (d. 1141), and Peter Lombard (d. 1160), Augustine was the authority most frequently quoted. Through the *Sentences* of Peter Lombard, which was the basis for many commentaries in succeeding periods and which finally came to be used as a general textbook, many quotations from Augustine became a classical heritage. Through this tradition Augustine's teaching on the Trinity and his stress on the primacy of love over knowledge (the *bonum* before the *verum*) were especially influential and together created an attitude in which the life of faith could give rise to a theocentric union of theology and philosophy.

Classical period of Scholasticism. This period was ushered in by the discovery of the work of Aristotle, as handed down by the Arabian philosophers and their Latin translators. In a remarkably short period this teaching was so widely adopted that from that time on, along with the hitherto undisputed authority of Augustine, there was a new master finally quoted by Aquinas simply as "the Philosopher". Aristotelian philosophy had the effect of disjoining philosophy from revelation, at least in principle, and of creating a separate discipline. It thus stimulated the development of a logically conceptualist method within theology. It was inevitable that this revolution should lead to conflicts. And for the first time the followers of Augustine, faced with the adoption of Aristotle by the Thomists, had to consider themselves simply as "Augustinians". They sought to protect theology from being appropriated by merely natural knowledge. The Aristotelian analysis of abstraction which Thomas took up and further developed in the sense of the transcendence of the human spirit for infinite being, seemed to the Augustinianists to lose sight completely of the old concept of illumination. They felt in general that the value of the world for theology was too strongly stressed. A climax in the dispute of Augustinianism with Aristotelianism, in the form of the Averroism of Siger of Brabant (d. 1282) and also in the adaptations of Albertus Magnus (d. 1280) and Thomas Aquinas (d. 1274), was the condemnation of several Aristotelian-Thomistic theses by the Bishop of Paris, Stephan Tempier, in 1277. This restricted the influence of the new school (which, however, by no means excluded Augustinian thought, Augustine being one of the authorities most frequently quoted by Thomas), and Augustinianism had scored a victory. But a profound re-thinking of it could not be long delayed. The Augustinianists tried gradually to combine the theory of illumination and of abstraction, the latter being allowed validity with regard to the understanding of wordly experience. Augustine's doctrine of the "seminal forms" (rationes seminales) which God implanted within matter as intrinsic principles at the beginning of time, was the starting-point of the discussion, together with the concept of the "plurality of forms" whereby the spiritual soul was considered to be the last but not the only essential form of the human body. These are the classical doctrines, as it were, of Augustinianism, in opposition to the Thomistic doctrine of abstraction. Its main proponents at this time were Bonaventure (d. 1274), John Peckham (d. 1294) and William de la Mare (d. 1298).

Late Scholasticism. In this period it was the Augustinian Hermits who preserved the legacy of their master. Giles of Rome (Aegidius Romanus, d. 1316) founded the school of the "Early Augustinians". He achieved a far-reaching reconciliation between the Augustinian and Thomistic positions, though in the process many important

interests of Augustinianism were lost sight of. Nevertheless, it was these monks, standing apart from the disputes between the schools of Thomas and Scotus, who occupied themselves with the works of Augustine and who together with the tradition of the Dominican and Franciscan Orders formed the link between Augustine and modern times.

There was a growing interest in the Middle Ages in thoughts developed in the *De Civitate Dei* with regard to the relations between Church and State. But the *civitas caelestis* (which Augustine had understood eschatologically) came to be more and more identified with the institution of the Church, as was the *civitas terrena* with the temporal State. According to this interpretation, the Church was to represent the *civitas caelestis* in political matters and also to be the last judge of the secular state. This "political Augustinianism" was of great historical importance. It gave rise, after the collapse of the Roman Empire, to the notion of an empire universal enough to absorb all individual kingdoms. Through the theocratic ideas of Charlemagne, this finally issued in the medieval notion of the Holy Roman Empire, which was regarded as the manifestation of the *corpus Christi*. The unique authority of Augustine was used in the ideological opposition between papacy and empire. In the course of this struggle between crown and tiara for the *plenitudo potestatis,* the Decretalists of the 13th and 14th centuries, who regarded the Augustinian writings as a source for canonic papal law, used Augustine just as much as did William of Occam when championing the national State and opposing absolute curial power. So too later, when the reform of the papacy was being urged on all sides, both parties appealed to Augustine, the Conciliarists as well as those who claimed that reform was a matter for the central authorities of the Curia. Although Augustine's thought was treated in this debate in a distorted ideological way, the constant invocation of his authority assured him of great influence in the development of social and political theory.

Modern times. Augustine was of great importance to the Reformers (which started a new Augustinian tradition, that of Protestantism), and the Council of Trent was strongly influenced by the medieval Augustinian tradition. The controversy about the Augustinian doctrine of grace broke out once more in France with Baianism, Jansenism and Quesnel, extreme positions being defended both as regards the goodness and the depravity of human nature. Henry Noris formed a school of Later Augustinianism, in opposition to the Jansenists. The interpretation of Augustine's teaching on grace put forward by this group was finally held to be as valid as that of Thomas and Molina, which gives freedom greater play. The dispute concerning grace which had already arisen in the life-time of Augustine, and which was always resolved in favour of a moderate form of Augustinianism, was thus cleared up as regards the extreme positions, though the question itself has remained basically undecided and open to the present day. It was at this time that the first scholarly editions of the works of Augustine were published and thus for the first time the question of the "real" Augustine arose. This is the main question in the present discussion of Augustine and it is channelling studies into a critical analysis of the history of Augustinian tradition.

The basic Augustinian positions were taken up as the fundamental philosophical questions by German idealism, and considered in terms of its revolutionary transcendental approach. Great speculative energy was applied, for instance, to the great themes of the relationship between (or the primacy of) the theoretical and/or practical reason, faith and knowledge, life and concepts. The great insights of Augustine into the relation between self-understanding and the understanding of revelation, between transcendence and history, are here both confirmed to a great extent and more thoroughly systematized and enunciated. Similarly, in the life-philosophy and in existentialism Augustinian insights are found, e.g., with regard to the significance of concrete life as opposed to all merely abstract conceptuality, and the "historical" understanding of self and of being, as opposed to merely static and generalized concepts of essences and orders. The analysis of existence employed in this type of thought, oriented primarily upon phenomena, has heightened the sense of personal decision and responsibility and also brought more to the fore the misery and perils of personal existence as such. Present-day theology, influenced as it has been by German idealism and by existentialism, has a new regard for Augustine, as it evaluates its transcendental and existential elements in its pursuit of its dialogue with God.

See also *Baianism, Jansenism, Idealism, Life-Philosophy.*

BIBLIOGRAPHY. *Sancti Aurelii opera omnia, studio monachorum ordinis S. Benedicti,* 11 vols. (1679–70); reprinted in J. P. Migne, *Patrologia Latina,* vols. 32–47; E. Portalié, "St. Augustin", *DTC* I (1903), cols. 2268–472, with biblio.; A. Harnack, *Lehrbuch der Dogmengeschichte,* III (1910); M. Grabmann and J. Mausbach, *Aurelius Augustinus. Festschrift der Görres-Gesellschaft* (1930); H.-I. Marrou, *S. Augustin et la fin de la culture antique* (2nd ed., 1949); M. Blondel, *Exigences philosophiques du christianisme* (1950); S. J. Grabowski, *The All-Present God. A Study in St. Augustine* (1954); J. O'Meara, *The Young Augustine. Growth of St. Augustine's Mind up to His Conversion* (1954); R. Battenhouse, *A Companion to the Study of St. Augustine* (1955); A. Forest, F. van Steenberghen and M. de Candillac, *Le mouvement doctrinal du XIe au XIVe siècle,* in A. Fliche and V. Martin, ed., *Histoire de l'Église,* XIII (1956); S. J. Grabowski, *The Church. An Introduction to the Theology of St. Augustine* (1957); H. I. Marrou, *St. Augustine and His Influence* (1957); E. Portalié, *A Guide to the Thought of St. Augustine* (1960); É. Gilson, *Introduction to St. Augustine* (1961); C. Andresen, *Zum Augustin-Gespräch der Gegenwart* (1962), pp. 465–574, with extensive biblio.; H. de Lubac, *Augustinisme et Théologie moderne* (1963).

Eberhard Simons

AUGUSTINIAN SCHOOL OF THEOLOGY

This school of thought in the Order of Hermits of St. Augustine goes back to Giles (Aegidius) of Rome (d. 1316). It includes numerous independent thinkers from the 13th to the 18th century who, despite differences in detail, clearly reveal a single Augustinian line of thought. Its chief representatives are Gregory of Rimini (d. 1358), the Cardinal Legate at the Council of Trent, Girolamo Seripando (d. 1563), the poet and theologian Luis de León (d. 1591), as well as Cardinal Henry Noris (d. 1704) and Lorenzo Berti (d. 1766), who as opposed to the distortions of Baianism and Jansenism, endeavoured to give a genuine interpretation of the Augustinian doctrine of grace.

These thinkers exhibit a fundamentally more dynamic conception of theology by answering in the sense of the Augustinian primacy of love, those questions, decisive for a theologian's mental attitude, that concern the relative rank of the faculties of the human soul and of the different tasks of human life. They defend the precedence of good over truth, of will over understanding. They point to charity as the highest aim of all theological inquiry and as a consequence they characterize theology as an affective science of the heart which leads man to adhere to the highest truth in love. For them the object of theology is God the *glorificator,* the giver of heavenly glory, and they conceive the nature of eternal bliss to consist more in an act of the will than of the intellect. Like Augustine, they regard the operation of divine grace in man not as a physical influence, but as a moral one, *per amorem alliciendo.*

Another typically Augustinian concern of the school was expressly to emphasize the sovereignty of God (primacy of grace). They regarded the predestination of the elect as absolutely a matter of grace, which occurs without regard for human works *(ante praevisa merita).* They taught the complete impossibility of meriting the first justification and considered the assistance of actual grace *(auxilium Dei speciale)* as necessary to every truly good work. They opposed as a Pelagian error anything in Occamism or Molinism that seemed to them to obscure the operation of God's grace. Finally, with Augustine, they described human merits as God's gifts.

Like Augustine, these theologians had that concrete and historical mode of thought which always envisages and evaluates man and his action in the perspective of the supernatural goal which in fact God wills for him. A state of pure nature seemed to them to be not indeed impossible, but not very appropriate to the divine wisdom and goodness. They denied to purely natural virtues any authentic value in the eyes of God. This attitude of mind also explains the considerable criticisms and reserve with which medieval Augustinian theologians — quite after Augustine's pattern, cf. *De Civitate Dei,* XII, 17 — confronted pagan philosophy. Giles of Rome himself attempted to promote a critical approach to pagan philosophy by his treatise *De Erroribus Philosophorum.* Fundamental objections to theology's employing the "harlot" philosophy were made by Simon of Cascia (d. 1348). With Gregory of Rimini and especially Hugolin of Orvieto (d. 1373), we find a moderate scepticism regarding natural knowledge generally, but without indulgence in fideism or agnosticism.

Furthermore, even in the Middle Ages, the Augustinian theologians showed high esteem for the primary sources of theology. Hermann of Schildesche (d. 1357), for example, assigned what was for that age a remarkably large role to scriptural proofs. Gottschalk Hollen (d. 1481) of Osnabrück, and the Erfurt professors John von Dorsten (d. 1481) and John von Paltz (d. 1511) criticized the small esteem for, and inadequate acquaintance with, the Bible even in cultivated circles, and recommended very warmly the reading of this "ars mineralis caelestis" (Paltz), and defended German translations of the Scriptures. Seripando and Luis de León are well-known for their insistence on the original texts of the Bible. Medieval acquaintance with the Fathers was promoted by the ambitiously planned florilegia of Bartholomew of Urbino (d. 1350), the *Milleloquium S. Augustini* and the *Milleloquium S. Ambrosii.* An epoch-making advance in the technique of citing sources was made by the Augustinian theologians of the 14th century, John of Basle (d. 1392) in particular.

Not the least among the consequences of their concrete Augustinian mode of thought was the special interest taken by many theologians of this school in questions regarding justification. A profound experience of the duality of the human heart and psychological insight into the slow preparation of man's pardon and conversion give their doctrine an eminently existential stamp. They strongly emphasize the weakness of the fallen human will and the strength of concupiscence. As a consequence — before the appearance of the Tridentine decrees — the freedom of the will and the value of human works were not denied but nevertheless markedly restricted. The reward of eternal glory was held to lie outside the domain of strict merit, and man's righteousness was considered to be necessarily imperfect all through life owing to concupiscence and to require completion by Christ's righteousness. A characteristic of the pre-Tridentine theologians was the important function which they attributed to faith *(fides per cari-*

tatem operans) in the process of justification.

In all this the school was always grounded on Catholic dogma. The assertion that Simon of Cascia, Gregory of Rimini, Hugolin of Orvieto, Augustine Favaroni (d. 1443) and James Pérez (d. 1490) anticipated important doctrines of Luther, has been shown to be false. The accusation of Jansenism brought against Noris and his pupils was rejected by the Holy See itself. Nor does the teaching on grace of these later Augustinian theologians contradict the encyclical *Humani Generis* of Pius XII, for it adequately brings out the totally gratuitous character of the gift of grace to man.

See also *Concupiscence.*

BIBLIOGRAPHY. M. Grabmann, *Die Geschichte der katholischen Theologie seit dem Ausgang der Väterzeit* (1933), pp. 105–8, 197–8; H. Jedin, *Girolamo Seripando,* II (1937), pp. 250–9, 268; D. Trapp, "Augustinian Theology of the 14th Century", *Augustiniana* 6 (1956), pp. 146–274; A. Zumkeller, "Die Augustinerschule des Mittelalters", *Analecta Augustiniana* 27 (1964), pp. 167–260; H. de Lubac, *Augustinisme et théologie moderne* (1965).

Adolar Zumkeller

AUTHORITY

A. Modern Man and Authority

Men are ambivalent towards authority today. They are credulous when experts speak and avid for commanding personalities who they hope have the secret of prosperity. They are buoyed up by the past achievements of specialists and recognize that a process of collectivization is at work which needs first-class guidance. They are sometimes ready to accord disproportionate value to the pronouncements of specialists even outside their own spheres. But men are also distrustful of authority, feeling there a vague threat to their personal life. They know of the abuses of authority and are uncomfortable under its totalitarian trends.

Nonetheless, the continual extension of authority is inevitable in this age of technology, with its new powers of control and need of co-ordinated effort. The sciences, from biology to sociology, make it so easy to manipulate public and private life that at times the exercise of freedom is drastically curtailed. Even the Churches can mould opinion massively, right down to the realm of conscience. The growing complexity of modern culture and the greater interdependence of its members also demand greater efforts at co-ordination. It is becoming more and more difficult for the individual to survey the whole of society and its structures and hence he is more and more dependent on the authority which mediates to him the achievements of the age — and also suffers more from the incompetence of authority. Men also feel that the authorities themselves are unsure of the future. The profound "crisis of authority" is therefore understandable.

An antidote is sought in the conferring of greater responsibility on the individual and a general "democratization". In the Church, it is emphasized that the layman has "come of age". In education, the relationship of teacher and student is being revised in terms of partnership, and the role of authority is being reconsidered. This is the general background to the problem of authority today.

B. Definition

1. The word authority is from the Latin *auctoritas,* from *auctor* (cause, sponsor, promoter, surety), from *augere* (to increase [transitive and intransitive], to enrich). It is hardly accidental that the term comes from Roman culture, with its sober rule of law. *Auctoritas* was the legal term for a surety in a transaction, responsibility for a minor, the weight of an opinion. It then came to mean the respect, dignity and importance of the person concerned. Later, the Senate had an institutional "authority", which had to be heard — though this authority did not exercise the power of governing. Nowadays "authority" is attributed to persons with special abilities and prestige or with an official function in society. The former may be called subjective or personal, the latter objective or official.

2. Personal authority comes from the recognition of someone's superiority in a given sphere. It exists in so far as it is respected. For this a personal moral decision is needed.

3. Official authority is the authority which a person has, not by reason of his personal superiority, but by reason of a function conferred on him or at least respected by society. It is desirable that the wielder of such authority should also have personal authority, but

since it is based essentially on its role in the good of society, its range and nature must be determined by its function, and not by the bearer's qualities. An office sanctioned by society and hence legitimate, can impose obligations and so be "authoritative" even when the office-holder is inadequate and unworthy. But the exercise of such authority is confined to his function in society — within which he can claim recognition.

4. It is only in a derivative sense (going back to personal or official authority) that we can speak of "something", like a book, an institution, a code of laws or a symbol, having authority. Their claims are founded on the "subject's" personal relationship to the authorities which they embody in some way. If such "authorities" are honoured, it is the persons behind them that are honoured. At times, as for instance in American culture, the symbols are more respected than the wielders of authority. This is probably due to a fear of an exaggerated cult of personalities.

C. The Nature of Authority

Authority is therefore the subjective or objective superiority of certain persons, by which they are entitled to make demands on others. It is formally an exigent superiority. It appears as valuable in itself for the authority's fellow-men. It is ontologically valuable in so far as it shares in the fullness of God's being and can thus impart its own fullness to those under it, and so help them to greater fulfilment. Authority comes from God and has a right to exist only in so far as it possesses and mediates perfection which it does by its transparency to the divine demand on man, that he should be perfect as our heavenly Father is perfect.

Authority can only exist with respect to intellectual beings. Man's freedom and reason are addressed by authority. It appeals to the free assent of the person. For its task is to further the fulfilment of man by demanding personal involvement from him. Hence authority must be fully integrated into the freedom of the subject's decision.

Thus authority must be distinguished from power and coercion. Power is the ability to exercise one's own freedom without the previous consent of the other and so alter the conditions of his decisions. Coercion or force further implies that one's will is imposed on another contrary to his will. Knowledge, for instance, confers authority where one can reckon on a hearing by reason of one's knowledge. Knowledge confers power in so far as it makes it possible to intervene in another's situation without his consent and create a mentality which prevents him from treating a problem in the usual way or in the way he originally intended. Hence authority begins where it is freely recognized and ends where it becomes power. And it is obviously typical of authority that it addresses itself to freedom. Authority is exercised on children only in so far as they are free, reasoning agents, and cannot be exercised over beasts or the insane. And real authority does not compel, but persuades. It appeals to the moral element of man, and can be exercised only in so far as subjects are capable of moral actions. But since imperfect man is only capable to a limited extent of moral actions, it may at times be right and necessary to influence others by power and coercion. But this is precisely not an authoritative procedure. To have authority is not just the same as to rule, lead, educate or exercise power. There is a certain polarity here. Rule should strive to become ruling authority and so on. But on this sinful earth this identification will never be total, and all the elements must be continually employed to complete each other.

Hence official authority, with its rights, privileges and power, does not summon the individual directly to free action. What it demands first is the recognition of the justification or necessity of the group in question, and then the recognition of the authority serving this organization. For the immediate foundation of official authority is the priority of society over its individual members. It follows that authority is a function of society and not vice versa, that it is limited by the needs of society which define its claims. To belong freely to a certain organization or necessarily to a society means that one freely acknowledges authority or at least necessarily respects it. But real authority exists for the subjects only in so far as they accept willingly the necessary social order. The anarchist rejects all official authority because he rejects social directives for his freedom. It remains true that official authority summons man to freedom, in its own ways.

It follows that authority is always in the service of others and their freedom. Its object is always to help men to attain their personal values and their full manhood. It embodies the claim of an end to which it and its subjects are ordained. This end is human, and therefore personal fulfilment. And it is this which gives authority its dignity and validity. The authority of reason, for instance, represents the claims of truth, which we strive after for its own sake. It serves truth by trying to establish and explain it. Parental authority represents the claims of human maturity — of the adult who is of himself adequate to his various tasks. This is the end and object of education, and parental authority serves it by helping the child to free itself from the slavery of instinct, ignorance and helplessness in order to reach mature independence.

Human nature calls for such authority because man is not only a person but a free creature of undefined possibilities who must become a "personality" in his historical development. Basically both a social being and an individual, he is further ordained to find his fulfilment in dependence on others — through mutually complementary functions of rule and obedience in society. Here it is well to remember that authority can sin and make mistakes. It does not always lead automatically to fulfilment, as is too readily assumed in classical interpretations of authority.

Like everything human, the measure of excellence in authority is its ordination to God, and its success in ordaining its subjects to God. Because of the relative autonomy of the earthly, this orientation to God must conform to the intrinsic laws of the various limited fields where authority is exercised. To exaggerate the transcendence of authority would lead to a pseudo-consecration of it and impede its proper functioning in the world. But neglect of the relationship to God would lead to a total absolutism and the arbitrary manipulation of subjects, since earthly authorities would proudly treat contingent values as absolutes. How in the concrete authority is to be ordained to God cannot be determined *a priori,* since we can only see *a posteriori* how it contributes to man's fulfilment and hence represents the will of God. This is because its tasks change as potentialities change. And the constant change of potentiality is determined by the history and historicity of freely developing man.

Two functions of authority may be deduced from its role in helping man to his fulfilment.

1. Authority functions as a substitute (improperly) in a tutelary role. This is exercised when it helps those who are non-adult in any respect to reach their goal — a goal of which they would have been frustrated through lack of the autonomy which would have made the intervention of authority superfluous. As long as children, for instance, cannot be responsible for their own destiny, their parents must guide it — to educate them to independence and thus prevent disaster. Or again, where men cannot assure their basic rights to health, work or education, the State may enforce fitting laws, e.g., compulsory schooling, social security for the sick and aged, prevention of alcoholism, etc. Otherwise those under authority could themselves make their autonomous development impossible. Such authority seeks to persuade, though it can take compulsory powers in the interests of those entrusted to it.

It should be the effort of such "vicarious" authority to make itself superfluous, since only thus can it attain its real goal. Hence educators, the State, and all other authorities must grant as much freedom as possible and develop the spirit of independence, while using compulsion where necessary, but even here leaving as much scope as possible to freedom. We call vicarious authority in this sense "improper", since its task is to eliminate itself and it works by methods of compulsion — though force is used only to make force avoidable. But in many cases the imperfection of man and the necessity of the goal in view will mean that coercive authority can never fully eliminate itself. In one respect or another we all need care of a paternal or maternal kind, and hence of an authoritative nature.

2. But authority also has a permanent function which must be considered its essential task. It always has the task of regulating and organizing, when its goal demands the co-ordination of the persons affected by it. This is perhaps clearest in the State's task with regard to "objective culture", which we understand as the totality of the citizens' individual contributions, as co-ordinated by the State for the common good. The diversity of individual functions must not be a source of division. They must

be distributed and directed towards the necessary ends. A unity of action must be realized, and the objective culture must further the subjective culture of the individuals. Hence order is the formal element of society, that is, the many are properly directed to the one end. Society is a unity of order, and, as Aquinas says, the chief task of authority in society is the preservation of order.

The need for authoritative order grows with the diversity of elements of which a society is composed. A highly cultured society is less homogeneous than a primitive one. To regulate and order all its elements to one end demands a much more complex organization. All progress makes the preservation of order more difficult, and demands a more complicated structure of the measures and institutions which we call society. Hence the essential task of social authority is not based on the inadequacies of its members, but corresponds to social progress.

Hence the members of society whose initiatives and self-fulfilment promote objective culture are not in opposition to social life, but rather enrich it. If personal initiatives are suppressed rather than favoured by the State, diversification, that is, the source of a rich and fruitful life, is also suppressed (L. Janssens).

The greater the evolution of a society, the more necessary authority becomes. The maturer an objective culture is, the more freely can the individual develop. And the more fully personal initiative is given play, the stronger the objective culture will be. Hence freedom and authority, when rightly used, are not opposed but complementary. They involve one another, because both serve man by reverencing the person and personal values, and hence ultimately God.

D. Conclusions

Each personal value must be served by authority in the appropriate way. Hence the one formal concept of authority has various analogous applications. Parental authority, which is concerned with the family unit and the education of children has another scope than that of the teacher, who takes on tasks which the parents cannot execute. State authority is different from that of the Church, the former aiming at the temporal good of all, the latter serving a supernatural end. The task of any particular authority can only be determined when general notion and concrete end are compared. The more concretely the goal can be envisaged (*a posteriori*), the more exact the authoritative measures can be. Hence the tasks of Church or State should properly be discussed in connection with the doctrine on the Church and so on.

The analogous character of the various forms of authority can hardly be stressed strongly enough. It results in very varied forms of the exercise of authority, in keeping with the varied ends. If this had been borne in mind throughout Church history, the Church could not have borrowed so many of its outward forms and so much of its self-understanding from the State (cf. Y. Congar). The application of the notion of *societas perfecta* to the Church and to the State should also be considered in this connection. Discussion of the specific tasks of the various forms of authority is proceeding, but not with the same speed in each case.

A second point to note is that authority must not only respect freedom, it must promote it, avoiding authoritarian measures which would degrade it to mere power or coercion. Power does not promote freedom, and coercion ends it. Authoritarian procedures generally reflect pride and arrogance, or an inferiority complex. True authority is aware of its limitations and tries the method of persuasion, respecting the personal dignity and the fundamental equality of those it addresses. It therefore also seeks to temper the social inequalities which may arise in the various order of those under authority.

The service which authority gives to men consists in the exercise of authority, as it fulfils its task of educating, sanctifying, organizing and so on. The danger is always that the authority will not be exercised. For it must contribute to the individual's personal development inwardly and essentially as well as outwardly and accidentally. The *laissez faire* policy of classical liberalism, and the naturalism of the Enlightenment, with nature doing everything well, overlooked the real freedom of man — which has to integrate the laws of nature into his personality, by autonomous decisions which are not always basically correct. Authority comes in here, with its pressures and its appeal to reason and freedom. Not to give due authoritative directives would be to hinder or waste the potentialities of the subjects. Since authority is equally responsible to the values it represents and to the men it seeks to persuade, the golden rule is *fortiter in re et suaviter in modo*. Success depends on the degree of synthesis between these values and these subjects. The reason for neglect of authoritative functions is generally a selfish disregard of others' needs or a feeling of inadequacy in the wielder of authority. Moral theology has put a great deal of emphasis on the proper obedience of subordinates. But the ethics of authority and command have been to a great extent neglected (cf. A. Müller). A full study should include the findings of modern management experts (cf. H. Hartmann). The way authority is exercised as a service depends, of course, on the service to be done, since the love which serves takes many forms. The function of authority as service is stressed particularly in the NT. Lk 22:24–27, for instance, tells the master to be like a servant, and Jn 13:1–17 makes the washing of the feet by the Lord an example for the disciples.

The authority which comes from God and is ordained to God will always try to preserve equilibrium among its contrasting elements by making its relationship to God as clear as possible, thus putting its pre-eminence and dignity in the proper light. It will therefore strive ultimately not for loyalty towards itself, but towards our absolute origin and end. In a democracy, for instance, the absolute supremacy of the will of the people would in certain cases be the supremacy of the wilfulness of the people. The people can determine who are to wield political authority, but the authority of the leaders does not come from the people but from God ("designation theory"), to whom the official rulers are therefore ultimately responsible. It is in this sense that the Syllabus of Pius IX opposed certain positivistic views and condemned the proposition that "authority is nothing but the sum-total of numbers and of material forces" (*D* 1760). This is also true of other forms of authority, *mutatis mutandis*. An earthly authority which does not point beyond itself becomes demonic and will show itself as arbitrary naked power.

The response to authority will be faith, obedience, reverence and so on, corresponding to the type of authority in question. But the ambivalence of earthly authority and its intrinsic connection with historical change makes it always necessary for authority to rely on dialogue with those entrusted to it. Otherwise it will miss its goal, which is to serve men and the absolute authority of God — which last it can never represent except in an analogous way.

See also *Obedience, Culture, Education* II, III.

BIBLIOGRAPHY. A. de Tocqueville, *Democracy in America*, 2 vols. trans. by P. Bradley (1944); G. Fessard, *Autorité et bien commun*, Théologie 5 (1944); B. Russell, *Authority and the Individual* (1949); T. W. Adorno and others, *The Authoritarian Personality* (1950); C. Sullivan, *The Concept of Authority in Contemporary Educational Theory* (1952); L. Janssens, *Droits personnels et autorité* (1954); M. T. A. Foley, *Authority and Personality, Development According to St. Thomas Aquinas* (1956); M. Marsal, *L'autorité* (1961); J. M. Todd, ed., *Problems of Authority* (1962); H. Hartmann, *Funktionelle Autorität. Systematische Abhandlung zu einem soziologischen Begriff* (1964); S. Müller, *Das Problem von Befehl und Gehorsam im Leben der Kirche* (1964); R. Guardini, *Power and Responsibility. A Course of Action for the New Age,* trans. by E. C. Briefs (1961); Y. Simon, *Authority* (1962); Y. Congar, *Power and Poverty in the Church* (1964); K. Rahner, "The Theology of Power", *Theological Investigations,* IV (1966), pp. 391–409.

Waldemar Molinski

AVIGNON EXILE

Avignon, a small university town and bishopric, under the Counts of Provence, became the residence of the Popes in 1309, which it was to remain for nearly seventy years. The change was not very startling. Two general councils had recently been held at Lyons, and four of the Popes had been French. The change, inspired by the hope of reconciling France and England for a crusade, by the over-attachment of Pope and Cardinals to their own country, and by the chaos in the Papal States, was not at first meant to be permanent. The building of the palace of the Popes by Benedict XII and the purchase of the town from Jeanne of Anjou marked a really new policy. The term "Babylonian Captivity" is inexact, though many felt that the Pope was in effect a vassal of France.

In 1305 Bertrand de Got, Archbishop of Bordeaux, was elected Pope, taking the name of Clement V. He was crowned at Lyons in the presence of Philippe le Bel, and after staying in various French cities, settled at Avignon in 1309. The annates (first collected in England, 1306) and other taxes went in great part to enrich his relatives, of whom five were cardinals. At the Council of Vienne (1311–12), convoked at the desire of the king, the Knights Templar were suppressed (*D* 471–483 gives the dogmatic decrees; the king's plan of impeaching the late Boniface VIII was dropped). The cry for reform of the Church "in head and members" was to persist in vain for two centuries.

The next Pope, John XXII (1316–34), was elected only after a conclave of over two years which almost brought about a schism. A sound administrator, he consolidated the Papal States in Italy, but came into conflict with the Emperor (Louis of Bavaria) who declared the Pope deposed for heresy in 1328, and nominated a Franciscan friar as "Nicholas V". The antipope found little support, and abjured two years later. John then had difficulties with the Spiritual Franciscans (the "Fraticelli"), finally having to anathematize those who held that Christ and the apostles owned no property even collectively (cf. *D* 484–90). The Curia's fiscal machinery was developed on an enormous scale. Of John's twenty-eight new cardinals, twenty-three were French, and nine from his home-town, Cahors.

Benedict XII (1334–42), an austere Cistercian, carried out many reforms, but continued the quarrel with the Empire, throwing in his lot with France. For his dogmatic decree on the beatific vision, see *D* 530–31.

Under Clement VI, a Benedictine (1349 to 1352), Avignon reached its greatest worldly splendour, but little was done for the Church. Papal absolutism was manifested in the claiming of all benefices for the Pope (letter to Edward III of England, 1344) and the continued quarrel with the Emperor. A solution was reached only with the death of Louis and the election of the devout Emperor Charles IV.

Innocent VI (1352–62) returned to the reforming spirit of Benedict XII, fostering, for instance, the restoration of poverty in the Dominican Order. He sent the able Cardinal de Albornoz to pacify the Papal States, but died before he could accomplish his projected return to Rome.

Urban V (1362–70) actually returned in 1367, but left again for Avignon three years later, in the illusory hope of reconciling France and England. Gregory XI, nephew of Clement VI (1370–78), who condemned Wycliff (1377) and strengthened the Inquisition, yielded to the entreaties of St. Bridget of Sweden and St. Catherine, and returned to Rome in 1377 — possibly ultimately to safeguard the Papal States. He died a year later, with schism threatening.

The Avignon Popes, who came under the lash of Dante and Petrarch, have been accused of over-servility to the king of France, over-development of the fiscal system of the Curia and of bringing on the Western Schism. But except for Clement V, servility cannot be proved, though the undue leanings to the French caused bitterness in Italy, England and Germany. The apparatus of taxation (*servilia communia, annatae, expectativae, jus spolii, vacantes, decimae,* etc.) lent a sad image to the Church — but might just as well have developed in Rome. The Western Schism was the result of Italian and French nationalism — though embittered, no doubt, during the Avignon period. The sojourn at Avignon certainly encouraged schism, since it allowed an antipope to exploit the prestige of the See of Rome.

BIBLIOGRAPHY. S. Baluze and G. Mollat, *Vitae paparum Avenionensium,* 4 vols. (1916–28); G. Lizerand, *Clément V et Philippe le Bel* (1910); G. Mollat, *La collation des bénéfices ecclésiastiques sous les papes d'Avignon* (1921); G. Monticelli, *Chiesa e Italia durante il Pontificato Avignonese* (1937); E. Dupré-Theseider, *I papi di Avignone e la questione Romana* (1939); G. Mollat, *Popes at Avignon, 1305–78* (1963); M. Wilks, *The Problem of Sovereignty in the Later Middle Ages. The Papal Monarchy with Augustinus Triumphus and the Publicists* (1963); J. Glénisson and G. Mollat, *L'administration des états de l'église au XIVe siècle. Correspondance des légats et vicaires généraux Gil Albornoz et Androin de la Roche* (1964).

Ricardo García Villoslada

B

BAIANISM

The doctrine. The wish for a more vital theology sent the Louvain professors M. Baius (1513–89) and J. Hessels (1522–66) back to the sources, especially to Augustine. Baius's chief interests were the corruption of man and the necessity of grace. Taking the former as his theme, he started with the nature of man, which he saw as primarily ordained to adhering to God through the observance of the commandments, *pietas* and the other charisms of the Spirit. Another element of nature is the subordination of sensual desires to the Spirit. It is also part of the natural order that the keeping of the commandments are rewarded with eternal life. For man before the Fall, as for the angels, the gifts of paradise and even of heaven are not strictly supernatural or a grace. This does not mean that these gifts derive necessarily from the constitutive principles of the creature. But since without them it is unhappy, God cannot refuse them. Nature is what God gave man in the beginning. Original sin is the perversion of this natural righteousness: blindness for the things of God, love of the world which is contempt of God, the revolt of the passions, above all the sexual ones. Hence without grace fallen man sins in every act. He can overcome a passion by the opposite or by love of virtue, but even a virtue exercised for its own sake is sin. For there are only two possible orientations of action, love of God or sinful love of the world. To maintain that there could be a sort of natural morality would be Pelagian. The rest is the consequences deduced from this main doctrine or the refutation of objections. Since the sincere catechumen or penitent seeks God and keeps the commandments, he has love. But his sins are not yet remitted. His acts merit heaven, but the unforgiven guilt makes its attainment impossible. Hence justification has two elements: the change of heart and will, which can be brought about only by God, and the pardon of sin through the sacrament. How is this inevitability of sinning to be reconciled with the freedom of the will? Baius's answer is that true Christian freedom is not freedom of choice, but spontaneous submission to God. He does not deny freedom of choice, but restricts it in the sinner to morally indifferent values. The principle that God does not command the impossible is true in the state of original justice; but to apply it to fallen man would be Pelagian. Hence concupiscence, though indeliberate, is also sin. Even in the justified it is a real transgression of the commandments, though not sin, because the punishment due to it is remitted and because the will does not allow itself to be dominated by it. Righteousness on earth is less a state than a progress.

Its condemnation. The bull of Pius V (1567; *D* 1001–1079) contains 76 (or 79) propositions, all taken from the Spanish censures of Alcalá and Salamanca universities and, with a few exceptions, from the writings of Baius — some of them, more or less skilfully, only giving the sense, not the words. It concludes: "Though some (of these opinions) could be defended in a certain sense . . . we condemn them as heretical, erroneous, suspect, temerarious, scandalous and offensive to pious ears." The loss of the acts of the Roman commission makes it impossible to determine the exact qualification given to the individual propositions, but the Spanish censures, which add a note to each proposition, provide some indication. The commission may have been milder than the Spanish theologians, but followed their verdict to a great extent. Hence most of the propositions were condemned as contradictory to the faith or a danger to it, some as erroneous, but none merely as a blow to scholastic theology. Were the propositions condemned in the sense in which Baius understood them? In the conclusion of the bull, between the two clauses cited above, the "comma Pianum" says: "in the strict and proper sense of the terms as intended by the authors". According to whether these words are attached to the foregoing or the following, they mean that some of the propositions are defensible in the sense intended by Baius or that this is the precise sense in which they are to be condemned. The latter interpretation became predominant from the 17th century on, but in the first decades after the bull the former was also allowed by the Church authorities. Possibly the ambiguity was intentional, because in the Spanish censures each proposition was given a distinct qualification. The aim of the bull was to reject the propositions and put an end to the discussion, without deciding whether some of the propositions had an orthodox meaning in the mind of Baius.

Assessment. Baius put a number of real problems very acutely, but did not solve them properly. His cult of the letter of Augustine's writings and his distaste for Scholasticism, which led him to underestimate the Council of Trent (whose doctrine he did not deny, though he paid no attention to it in his treatment of original sin, justification, merit, etc.) barred the way to a solution. But as long as the problems raised by Baianism have not been fully and satisfactorily solved, it remains a temptation or a spur to Catholic theology. The university of Louvain, by adopting an explicitly anti-Baianist line, kept the discussion alive. Jansen was formed in this milieu, as were the clergy who prepared the minds of

people in the Netherlands for the advent of Jansenism.

See also *Augustinianism, Jansenism, Original Sin, Concupiscence, Nature, Necessity.*

BIBLIOGRAPHY. M. Baii, *Opera*, ed. by G. Gerberon (1696); F. X. Jansen, *Baius et le Baianisme* (1927); X. le Bachelet, "Baius", *DTC,* II (1932), cols. 38–111; F. Litt, *La question des rapports entre la nature et la grâce de Baius au Synode de Pistoie* (1934); N. Abercrombie, *The Origins of Jansenism* (1936); E. van Eyl, "L'interprétation de la Bulle de Pie V portant condamnation à Baius", *RHE* 50 (1955), pp. 499–542; G. Fourure, *Les châtiments divins. A Study of the Problem of Evil in Baius and Jansenius* (1959); E. Boissard, "Note sur le sens propre et rigoureux de certaines propositions de Baius", *RSR* 36 (1962), pp. 140–53; J. Oreibal, "De Baius à Jansenius, le Comma Pianum", *RSR* 36 (1962), pp. 115–39; A. Kaiser, *Natur und Gnade. Die Kontroverse zwischen Bajus und Ripalda,* Münchner Theologische Studien, II 30 (1965); H. de Lubac, *Augustinisme et Théologie moderne: le Mystère du Surnaturel* (1965).

Pieter Smulders

BAPTISM

I. Sacrament of Baptism: A. New Testament and Liturgy. B. Baptism in Theological Thought. C. Modern Theology. D. The Foundation of All Christian Life. II. Baptism of Desire.

I. Sacrament of Baptism

It is difficult for us today to feel the resonant joy in the opening words of Tertullian's *De Baptismo:* "Felix sacramentum aquae nostrae" — the bliss of the oath of allegiance taken in the sacramental water. For the early Christians baptism was the conscious and blessed beginning of the Christian life, a new birth and a re-birth in the image of Christ, accomplished by bathing in water while a few words were uttered. With all the simplicity of a divine act, in contrast to pomp of the initiation rites in pagan religions, "the washing of water with the word" (Eph 5:26) brought about something incredibly magnificent, the life of eternity (cf. Tertullian, *op. cit.,* 1–2).

Nonetheless, the content of our belief is the same. For the Christian of today baptism is still the entrance to all the sacraments, the gate to Christian life and hence to the eternal life which is its ultimate, eschatological consequence. Baptism blots out original sin and all personal sins, makes the Christian sharer of the divine nature through sanctifying grace, gives the adoption of sons, calls him and entitles him to the reception of the other sacraments and to share actively in the priestly adoration of the Church. These are abstract formulae which contain vital truths. We must try to penetrate their riches once more, in the light of the original sources of revelation.

A. NEW TESTAMENT AND LITURGY

How the apostolic preaching interpreted "washing of water with the word (of life)" is plain to see in the NT.

Words of the Lord. It is intimately bound up with the injunction of the risen Christ: "Go therefore and make disciples of all nations, baptizing them in the name of the Father and of the Son and of the Holy Spirit, teaching them to observe all that I have commanded you" (Mt 28:19f.). These words certainly record the will of the glorified Christ to institute the sacrament of baptism, though the trinitarian formula may be an echo of apostolic practice. The inner meaning of baptism is intimated by the mysterious images our Lord uses in his conversation with Nicodemus (Jn 3:1–10). These, of course, are fully intelligible only to one who has experienced Christian baptism. At any rate the reception of baptism is regarded from the beginning as the foundation of all discipleship and Christian life (Acts 2:37–41 and *passim*). After the descent of the Holy Spirit at the first Pentecost, the apostles looked upon baptism as a rite already hallowed by tradition and administered it as such. Attempts to show that baptism was borrowed from the religions of the Hellenistic world have been fruitless, but the practice is certainly foreshadowed in the OT.

Earlier analogies. The OT frequently mentions practices analogous to baptism (which took the form of washings; among other texts see Exod 40:12; Lev 8:6; 13:6; 14:4–9; 16:4,24; Ezek 36:25). In the time of Christ such "baptisms", that is, washings, were much in use (Mk 7:2–4); Jewish sects like the Essenes made much of them (Josephus, *Jewish War*, 2, 117–61) and they were a special feature of Qumran (*1 QS,* 6, 16f.; 3, 4–9). It is easier to understand the "baptism of John" against this background, though he contributed important new features: as an emissary of God he baptized *others* to call them to repentance, in preparation for a nobler baptism to come. Jesus' disciples baptized during his lifetime in an obviously similar manner (Jn 4:1–3).

Apostolic practice. But after the glorification of the Lord the apostles administered the traditional rite in a new way and with a new import; they now baptized in the name of Jesus, that is, in accordance with the gospel in the name of Jesus, assigning men to him, invoking his name over the candidate. Finally (a further development), they baptized in the name of the Father, Son, and Holy Spirit. (The continuity of usage emerges in Acts 18:25–26 and 19:2–6, where the transition to the new form is indicated.) The washing with water and the word is the climax of a whole process: penance and faith are perfected in baptism. With this procedure, because it intimately unites one with Christ, come salvation, the remission of sins, and the gifts of the Holy Spirit. Christ is the light which shines in baptism; he is the life that it bestows, the truth that the baptized person confesses and to which he pledges his loyalty, the source whence flow the rivers of living water, the water and the blood from the open wound in his side. They wash away all the guilt of a man's sins.

Deeper insights. These relatively sparse data from the synoptics, from Acts, and not least from the fourth gospel — when full justice is done to the intentions underlying its composition — are admirably expounded in other books of the NT especially in St. Paul, 1 John, and 1 Peter. These books work out a theology of the washing of water with the word, as a unique personal and sacramental act that confers "being-in-Christ", which is the sum of Christian existence. For "you were buried with him in baptism, in which you were also raised with him through faith in the working of God, who raised him from the dead" (Col 2:12). Fruitful controversy in recent years has again brought these results to the fore. Passing over minor obscurities and differences of interpretation, this article will simply be concerned with what was arrived at in common as part of the faith. The essential thing, then, is that by baptism, when we were dead through our trespasses and sins, God who is rich in mercy, out of the great love with which he loved us, made us alive together with Christ, and raised us up with him, and made us sit with him in the heavenly places in Christ Jesus (Eph 2:1, 4–6). For all its noble simplicity, the rite of initiation through the washing of water with the word — so that we may gain salvation by the forgiveness of sins and the gift of the Holy Spirit — conveys several truths. First of all, baptism is the culmination of a man's personal encounter with God in Christ, of his personal response to the appeal of God's word. "So those who received his word were baptized" (Acts 2:41). In order to be baptized one must obey the word, listen to it: "Repent" (Acts 2:38), and respond to the good news Jesus brings: "Yes, I believe that Jesus Christ is the Son of God." (Acts 8:37, the Western reading.) Baptism bodies forth the faith which is the fundamental way of our living in Christ; without faith it would be a lifeless outward show. But it is more than a "symbolic" expression of active faith; the washing by water in the word is real access to Christ and his redemption; it is "being baptized into his death", it is dying with him and rising with him, truly sharing his sufferings, so that becoming like him in his death we may attain the resurrection from the dead (see Phil 3:10f.).

Another important aspect of baptism is that of purification. Washing of water with the word cleanses the Church (Eph 5:26); as this pure water sprinkles the body it cleanses our hearts from an evil conscience (see Heb 10:22). Sharing in Christ's death, being purified in the sacred waters that flow forth from him, brings about fellowship with the living Christ, a new life; one is a new creation, born again, enjoying even now a share in his resurrection that will be perfected in the eschatological future when the Lord returns. All this is reality, but the Christian's faith must apprehend and affirm its fullness in advance, ponder the consequences and accept them in the serious constancy of a truly Christian life. "So (after all that has been said about this reality) you also must consider yourselves dead to sin and alive to God in Christ Jesus." (Rom 6:11.) Baptism, then, must produce the whole breadth and depth of a life rooted and grounded in Christ (Eph 3:16–19). In Rom 6:12–14 the apostle forcefully points out the practical ethical consequences of baptism. What is demanded of the baptized is nothing less than a thoroughgoing conversion. Baptism has given them a completely new being and they must walk — shape their lives — accordingly. The ancient Church took this passage from the "indicative" to the "imperative" in baptism very seriously: "it is impossible to restore again to repentance those who have once been enlightened (in baptism), who have tasted the heavenly gift, and have become partakers of the Holy Spirit, and have tasted the goodness of the word of God and the powers of the age to come, if they then commit apostasy" (Heb 6:4–6). We cannot here examine the problem of penance after baptism; but Heb 6:4–6 shows what weight was then attached to the obligations imposed by baptism.

The baptismal liturgy. The evolution of the baptismal liturgy now reveals the riches of that simple but mighty action. We are able to trace it thanks to Justin's *Apology* (I, 61), Tertullian's treatise on baptism, and in particular Hippolytus's *Apostolic Tradition* (*c*. A.D. 200). First comes a lengthy catechetical preparation of the candidates; next an immediate preparation of fasting, prayer, and solemn promises; then the solemnity of baptism itself. Baptism proper is an actual bath in flowing water. The candidate is thrice immersed, and each time one of the divine names is pronounced *(epiclesis)*. Finally come the anointings and the imposition of hands. The new Christian is now admitted to the common worship of the faithful, to the kiss of peace, and to the Eucharist.

These basic lines were kept unchanged subsequently. The ritual added a confession of faith, the renunciation of Satan and the baptismal promises. The central act of baptizing and the ceremonies that follow were re-moulded. The catechumenate included a series of scrutinies. After a certain amount of fluctuation this liturgy then settled into the form we now have in the Roman Ritual.

The basic structure. The basic structure of baptism remains quite visible even when its liturgy has fully evolved: faith and penance as personal acts of the adult candidate; the sacramental power of ablution in the name of God; immersion, that is, insertion into the death of Christ so that our sins being forgiven, we may live a new life in Christ, the earnest and the beginning of eternal life, symbolized by the white garment, the burning candle, the admonition, "Preserve thy baptism". These things remind us that when the Lord returns we must go to meet him with our lamps alight.

All this imagery is fraught with meaning for the adult candidate. The baptism of adults is presupposed throughout the NT and the early Christian period.

Infant baptism. As yet we find no references to the baptism of young children. But this is no proof, of course, that the practice was unknown. Infant baptism developed naturally out of the entirely different circumstances in which Christianity found itself when society had become Christian. It was thought fitting to receive children into the fellowship of Christ and the Church. But no special rite of infant baptism was ever devised. In the early days the baptism of children was something almost "incidental", a sort of appendage to the baptism of adults, which was always the main concern; the catechumenate did not include children. But child baptism became the normal practice from about the 4th or 5th century onwards. The existing rite was slightly modified for the purpose, the various stages coalescing in a continuous ceremony. But basically nothing changed, so that even today through the intermediary of their godparents infants are treated at their baptism as if they were adults: they renounce Satan, confess the faith, and state that they wish to be baptized.

Present practice. Though its outward form may not be altogether appropriate, the present baptismal liturgy of the Latin Church proclaims clearly enough what baptism has been ever since its origin in the NT, namely a sacred action, a washing of water (though now confined to pouring water over the head) with the word, a sharing in the death, burial, and resurrection of Christ, purification by water hallowed in the power of God's name, the remission of all sin, the communication of life, a new birth, adoption as a child of God — but all this ratified by the personal faith, resolution, and obedience of the candidate who undertakes to embody these things in his own life.

In baptism, then, the Church possesses something that is alive and operative. We depend on it; it is the beginning of everything, the source of all our obligations; by uniting us with Christ's death and resurrection it enables us to hope for the great eschatological fulfilment in the future.

B. BAPTISM IN THEOLOGICAL THOUGHT

The early period. It is the riches bestowed in baptism that first engages attention. Descent into the water washes away our old mortality (sin), ascent from the water is the passage from death to life (*Pseudo-Barnabas; Shepherd of Hermas*). Thus baptism is a bath that washes away sin, the free remission of the penalties of sin and illumination on the way of salvation. It perfects and seals us, transports us over the frontier of death into the life of Christ (St. Clement).

Origen. As occasion arises, Origen fits these truths into his own profound view of the history of salvation, which was to be so widely influential. Baptism sums up all the OT types and prefigurations which are fulfilled in Christ. As usual Origen upholds the primacy of the interior spiritual order over the outward and visible. Thus ecclesiastical baptism has its true place between the OT (with John the Baptist), and the new heaven and new earth of the end of time. The OT merely hinted at things to come; it will culminate in eschatological baptism "with the Holy Spirit and with fire" (Mt 3:11). The link between the two is the Church's baptism, the fulfilment of the antecedent sign, yet itself a sign of the consummation that is to come, drawing all its force from Christ. Origen does not lose sight of the meaning or absolute necessity of baptism. He simply wishes to insist that the outward form of baptism derives its meaning from the spiritual realities, that Christian baptism fulfils the ancient types, gives us the grace of Christ, and thus bears us onward to the final stage of baptism, the final resurrection from the dead. Origen further stresses that the person being baptized must seek practical understanding of what baptism signifies. Baptism is renunciation, conversion, penance. It completes sacramentally the ascetical death of the catechumen; but "if anyone comes to the washing of water (continuing) in sin, then his sins are not remitted" (21st homily on Luke).

Controversy on heretical baptism. These thoughts, however, remain fragmentary. Practical necessities drew attention to the truth that baptism cannot be repeated. Controversy arose about baptism conferred by schismatics and especially heretics. When a member of such a sect was reconciled, the African and some Eastern Churches rebaptized, whereas the Churches of Rome and Alexandria recognized his "heretical baptism" as valid and merely received him into communion with a solemn laying on of hands. This difference in practice led to open conflict between Cyprian and Pope Stephen I. Both agreed that baptism could not be repeated; the question was whether heretics had validly baptized. Eventually the Roman view prevailed. By defending a primacy of the official and sacramental element, independent of the personal holiness of the minister, even if he belongs to a body that is not the true Church, Rome vindicated the primacy of God's power, which is decisively exercised in baptism regardless of human limitations.

St. Augustine. This principle underlies the theology of baptism which St. Augustine worked out against the heretics of his own time. Augustine reaffirms that since Christ, the author and possessor of baptism, is its real minister, the sacrament is valid even when administered by a heretic; he too confers the Church's baptism, the baptism of Christ, "which is always holy of its own nature and therefore does not belong to those who separate themselves but to that (communion) from which they separate" (*De baptismo,* I, 12, 19). Later, notably during his struggle with the Pelagians and his preoccupation with the problems of infant baptism, he laid even more stress on the objective aspect of the sacrament. Unless a man be in sacramental communication with Christ's redemptive act (fundamentally through baptism, and then through the Eucharist), "he cannot reach the kingdom of God, nor gain salvation and eternal life" (*De peccatorum meritis et remissione et de baptismo parvulorum,* I, 24, 34). On the other hand — and this is the real heritage that comes down to us from the Donatist controversy — Augustine never ceased to inveigh against a mechanical conception of the sacraments. Without faith there can be no sacrament at all. Every sacrament embodies a personal act of faith, at least on the part of the Church: it is a sacrament of this faith, a holy sign of belief in Christ and his salvation; furthermore, though valid of itself, without love it remains barren. Such considerations finally brought it home to Christians that baptism, conferred in the proper form, in the power of Christ who is its real minister, is and remains valid (not, of course, because of any "magic" power in the rite but because of the sustaining faith which gives access to Christ), but that its fruitfulness depends on the dispositions of the recipient, his faith and love. Here are the foundations for the later doctrine, familiar to us today, that baptism imprints an indelible character on the soul.

The mature doctrine. The theology of baptism reached maturity in the 4th and 5th centuries, the classical patristic age. The various strands of NT and early patristic theology are harmoniously interwoven, and an impressive summary of the great mystery of baptism is now found in the baptismal catechesis of the bishops: baptism is that sacred action whereby Christ's redemption, his death, and his resurrection are given to us here and now, initiating us into Christian life by a concrete, tangible, symbolic confession of the faith, so that we may be made conformable to the crucified and risen Lord. What once happened to Christ now happens to us in baptism, so that we may be reborn to a new life; and the Holy Spirit, sent by the risen Lord who sits at the right hand of the Father, fills and consecrates the water, so that this sensible element may wash us immaculate and clothe us in splendour.

The Fathers from Tertullian on call this "washing of water with the word" a *sacramentum* or *mysterium* (μυστήριον), a term they also use for other sacred acts. By the 3rd or 4th century at the latest the word had permanently acquired this technical sense. Baptism is sacrament, an initiation that involves swearing fidelity in the service of Christ (like the oath of allegiance, the sacramentum of the Roman soldier). But since *sacramentum* also took on the fuller force of μυστήριον, it was a sacred act which communicated symbolically what it represented, and moulded the believer to its likeness. As image of the death and resurrection of Christ, the mystery made the believer participate in the Passover of Christ from death to life.

Parallel to this very Pauline theology of baptism into the death of Christ, another conception looms even larger — the impregnation of the baptismal water with the sanctifying power of Christ's spirit. Baptism produces its wonderful effects by the might of the crucified and risen Lord. Invoked during this solemn ceremony — which becomes more and more elaborate as time goes on — he fills the water with the power of his Holy Spirit and fructifies it, so that it may beget new life in the Church: ". . . may a heavenly offspring, conceived in holiness and re-born into a new creation, come forth from the stainless womb of this divine font" (Roman Missal: rite for the blessing of baptismal water on Holy Saturday).

Scholastic synthesis. This patristic doctrine was then preserved and made more systematic. Thus the schoolmen saw baptism as a holy sign — *sacramentum fidei,* a sacrament of faith which acknowledges and lays hold on Christ and the whole work of our redemption — a sign composed of an element (matter) and certain words (form), which represents our sanctification in a threefold manner: in its cause (which belongs to the historical past but is still efficacious today), the passion of Christ; in the formal being of its grace (which exists in the present but has its archetype in Christ); and in its eschatological fulfilment (which is yet to come and will perfectly conform us to the image of Christ). But at the same time, in the hands of the real author of all salvation, Christ himself, this sign is the instrumental cause of the sanctification it signifies. Christ remains master of his gifts and chooses on occasion to save a soul without the intermediary of the sacraments — as when an unbaptized martyr turns to him in death, or a catechumen dies in the faith but is baptized only in desire.

This analysis of the nature of baptism is followed by an exhaustive treatment of all that relates to the administration, the minister, the recipient, and the effects of the sacrament; its place in the general structure of the seven sacraments of the NT is described.

Much attention is paid to the indelible character which baptism imprints on the soul. It is thought to be because of this character that baptism cannot be repeated.

Baptism administered with the right intention is always valid, even when it remains fruitless for want of the proper dispositions in the (adult) baptized. (Such a case does, of course, presuppose a minimum of faith and goodwill, without which no salvation at all can be bestowed.) Validity without fruitfulness is explained by the sacramental character, a mysterious, impersonal, objective gift of grace, a mark of dignity and distinction which foreshadows greater things to come and occupies a middle ground between the outward, merely symbolic sacramental act (the *sacramentum*) and the ultimate inner being of the life of grace (the *res*), as a kind of basic conformation to Christ. St. Thomas ingeniously and suggestively argues — though not all theologians today accept his view — that the character is "a certain power in respect of hierarchical (cultic) acts, that is, dispensing and receiving the sacraments and other things proper to the faithful" (*In Sent.,* IV, d. 4, 1.1 sol.).

The Reformers and Trent. Exaggerating as they did the importance of the word and of fiducial faith, the 16th century Reformers theoretically repudiated the Catholic idea of the sacraments, but in fact shrank from fully implementing the revolutionary logic of their own principle. At any rate (with the exception of the Baptists) they were content to continue baptism, especially infant baptism, as a means of grace in the strict sense of the word. The Council of Trent defended the traditional doctrine as it had developed in the course of the history of dogma: efficacious Christian baptism takes precedence over that of John the Baptist; the washing of water (with the word) must be something physical; rightly administered in accordance with the intention of the Church, baptism is always valid; it is not a mere sign of faith but takes effect *ex opere operato,* that is, by the power of God that is at work in the sacrament (not by the will or sanctity of men); infant baptism too is valid by the same operation of God's power; any repetition of baptism is void; the stress here laid on the power of the sacrament in no way diminishes the necessity for the adult candidate for baptism to approach it in the proper frame of mind; baptism is necessary for salvation; baptismal grace may be lost through serious sin (Sess. 7, Canons on the Sacrament of Baptism, 1–14, *D* 857–70).

C. Modern Theology

These Tridentine decrees are merely designed to set down and secure the traditional faith concerning baptism. Within their framework all of us must try to grasp the positive truth in full measure; it will not do simply to repeat anathemas. Such, however, was the tendency of theologians in the ensuing age; understandably enough, the remarkable achievements of Trent had the effect in practice of narrowing a little their field of vision. But today the situation is quite different. Not only the exigencies of ecumenical dialogue but, even more important, the new vitality that is stirring thanks to liturgical reform and deeper study of God's word, impel us to recast our theology of baptism in an ampler mould, taking full account of Scripture, liturgical experience, and the storehouse of patristic and scholastic theology.

Liturgical renewal. The renewal of the liturgy has given us a keener sense of baptism. We have a deeper understanding of the sacrament itself, a sacred action full of inner meaning that should be plainly expressed in a becoming ceremony. A certain sacramental minimalism, therefore, which paid too little attention to the concrete symbolism of baptism, is now in retreat. We realize that the solemn administration of baptism is essentially linked with the celebration of Easter Eve: baptism is a paschal sacrament, the sacrament of a person's "passover" — *transitus paschalis* — from death to life, from sin and the old man to the resurrection and the new man in Christ. Precisely because we have this new awareness of the reality of the sacrament, we long for a clear and convincing expression of this reality.

Desire for reform. The suggested reforms which have also been discussed at the Second Vatican Council mainly concern the ritual for infant baptism, which in practice means the majority of all baptisms. To pretend that the infant is a responsible partner is forcing matters. Our keener sense of authenticity demands that the child be treated as such, and regarded as a "partner" only within his limitations. We must state what really happens: here is a human being on whom God is pleased to bestow salvation in Christ through the intermediary of the Church, giving the Church, the parents, and the sponsors the duty of bringing him to the point where he can freely affirm the saving grace he has been vouchsafed and thenceforward preserve it for himself. Otherwise no changes of any importance would need to be made in the rite of infant baptism.

A more urgent matter is the reform of the ritual for adult baptism, no rarity nowadays even outside missionary countries. We seem to be faced with the following choice: in order to give the adult convert a genuine and active part in his own baptism, we must either prune the present unbalanced set of ceremonies (much of them a mere anachronism preserved by force of habit, since they are a condensation of the catechumenate which ceased to exist long ago) by discarding all that is antiquated, or else revive the catechumenate in a form adapted to modern conditions. There is much to be said for the latter idea, which would mean that a certain interval would once more elapse between the preparation and the baptism. What is now done all at once might be allotted to three separate occasions, at intervals to be decided in each case. The first stage, *ad catechumenum faciendum* (opening of the catechumenate), would set forth the partnership between the candidate and the Church; the second would be mainly "exorcist" in character; the third stage would be the actual sacrament: abjuration (with anointing) — confession of faith — the act of baptism — concluding ceremonies.

Problems of infant baptism. Important as adult baptism is at the present time, we must not forget that infant baptism exists in its own right and has its own claims to our appreciation. The problems it raises have much exercised Protestant theologians in the past few years. For anyone who takes seriously the original Protestant principles that we have mentioned, infant baptism presents all but insuperable difficulties. But the fact that all Churches, including the Reformed, accept infant baptism in practice shows that they take a realistic view of baptism and see it as something objective.

Sacramental realism. It is precisely Protestant exegetes, Church historians, and experts in comparative religion, who now acknowledge the realism of the ancient Christian sacramental idea. At first, to be sure, they felt that this realist conception smacked of magic; and even today the fear that a sacrament may be confused with magical signs (when there is in fact no such confusion) sometimes makes it difficult for these theologians to form a balanced judgment. But they often emphasize "that St. Paul ascribes an 'action réelle mystique' to baptism, which makes of the sinner a man freed from sin, who is bound in a mysterious way with the death and resurrection of Christ" (Neunheuser, p. 229, following M.-J. Lagrange).

Such an insight opens the door to a new defence of infant baptism, but has, of course, a much broader significance — it allows of a new approach to the traditional doctrine, in terms of the immediate action of God's word. Catholic theologians must now stress the following points:

a) The event of baptism is a sacred mystery; it is a sacrament that communicates grace, but it is no less a highly personal act on the part of the adult convert. As a mystery, baptism is an act of initiation — an introduction to truly Christian life — whereby the redemptive death of Christ which happened but once in history is cultically made present in the shape of a visible rite (in this case the symbolic immersion which remains recognizable even in its present abbreviated form, and the invocation of the Blessed Trinity). The person baptized can die with and like Christ, and rise again with him to the new life that is being-in-Christ-Jesus, in the hope of one day attaining the full glory of the resurrection.

b) But if we consider the outward sign as an ablution — the dominant aspect at present — then baptism is seen to be the cleansing of sinful man in the precious blood of the Lamb of God, by the water that flowed from the open side of the Crucified. The baptismal water is the instrument Christ uses to effect this redemptive purification: filled with the power of the Holy Ghost, on the invocation of God's name, it purges of all sin and awakens one to the new life of those "born again of water and the Holy Spirit" (Jn 3:5). The door to the kingdom of God is opened in baptism. As fellowship with Christ in his crucifixion, death, and risen life, or as instrument in the hands of the Redeemer to cleanse and give grace and life, baptism remains a sovereign act of God's omnipotence, applying Christ's redemption to the sinner out of mercy and prevenient love,

without any merit on our part, and demanding thenceforward a life of obedience to God.

c) Nothing at all in this sacramental action savours of magic. Magic, indeed, is fatal to all true religion. If the action which proceeds from faith and is achieved in baptism is unfailingly efficacious, that is simply evidence of the power of God, who of his own free grace has willed this way of salvation appropriate to the basic event which is the incarnation of the Logos, appropriate as well, therefore, to the double structure of man. Baptism proclaims the utter sufficiency of the redemption which Christ wrought once for all in history and which takes effect now in the sacrament.

The obligations of baptism. Baptism imposes obligations in keeping with the spiritual nature of man. It gives the child all it can bear: to be a child of God, freed from the burden of original sin, of the wrath of God. But by this very fact he has the duty when he reaches the estate of a responsible person, of freely confessing the reality of his baptism by faith and love and shaping his life accordingly, in the hope of preserving that grace till he can enjoy its consummation in eternity. Otherwise baptism would fail to achieve its real and ultimate effect. But baptism addresses the adult convert directly. Unless he approaches the sacrament in the dispositions that become a responsible person, yields the assent of his faith, resolutely turns his back on sin, and freely commits himself to Christ crucified and risen, the baptism remains barren, even though it be correctly administered and even though it truly gives the convert that first contact with Christ which marks him forever as Christ's possession, so that whatever his present deficiences he can at any time turn repentant to the Lord and giver of true life. Baptism is living fellowship with Christ, the inauguration of that New Testament life which is inwardness, spontaneous obedience to God in the power of Christ's Holy Spirit, the mature freedom of the sons of God (e.g., Heb 8:8–13 and 10:15–17 in the light of Jer 31:31–34).

Baptism may be conferred only when a person believes with all his heart (Acts 8:37), freely desires this sacrament, is ready to be "baptized into Christ's death" (Rom 6), ready to preserve his baptism, to remain a true disciple by obeying the commandments, so that when the Lord comes to the wedding feast of the Lamb at the end of time he may hasten forth to meet him, lamp still alight, with all the saints, entering by grace into the kingdom of heaven.

As the primal sacrament, then, baptism is in a special sense both the sacrament of faith in Christ and the embodiment of that faith. This is why, should circumstances make baptism impossible, faith alone can impart fellowship with Christ and redemption, through what is called baptism of desire. Baptism does not thereby become superfluous. One who truly believes in the Lord is prepared to do his bidding without reserve, and therefore wishes, so far as in him lies, to receive baptism. He is not saved without the desire (at least the implicit desire) of baptism; and once justified in this way, he must still receive the sacrament, for it aggregates him to the Church's visible communion, thus entitling him to take part in all its sacramental and liturgical life in Christ.

D. THE FOUNDATION OF ALL CHRISTIAN LIFE

When we reflect on this plenitude we perceive that baptism is indeed "the blessed sacrament of our washing in water", the foundation of a high-minded life, life in Christ Jesus; for "our commonwealth (even now) is in heaven, and from it we await a Saviour, the Lord Jesus Christ, who will change our lowly body to be like his glorious body" (Phil 3:20–21). For the "little while" remaining until then, baptism demands that being dead to sin, we live in Christ our Lord. Moreover, it requires of us a life of active worship befitting the man of the New Testament and the dignity of that royal priesthood whose character we received in baptism. We must be prepared to join in celebrating the eucharistic mystery, calling to mind what the Lord did, giving thanks to God the Father through Christ, offering the Father that adoration in spirit and in truth which he expects (Jn 4:23–24).

But this is by no means all. We must abide in the love to which and in which Christ has called us, bear one another's burdens and so fulfil the law of Christ. Strong in the fellowship with Christ that baptism gives us, we can and must discharge what is known today as "the responsibility of Christians to the world": by playing our proper part on earth we shall also bear witness to Christ in the midst of the world, hoping for the final revelation of his glory till God is everything to every one (1 Cor 15:28).

See also *Sacraments, Sin, Original Sin, Baptism II, Martyrdom.*

BIBLIOGRAPHY. A. Oepke, "βάπτω, βαπτίζω, βαπτισμός, βάπτισμα, βαπτιστής", *TWNT,* I (1932), pp. 527–44; K. Prümm, "Mysterium von Paulus bis Origenes, *ZKT* 61 (1937), pp. 391–425; H. G. Marsh, *The Origin and Significance of the New Testament Baptism* (1941); W. F. Flemington, *The NT Doctrine of Baptism* (1948); J. G. Crehan, *Early Christian Baptism and the Creed* (1950); G. W. H. Lampe, *The Seal of the Spirit. A Study of the Doctrine of Baptism and Confirmation in the NT and the Fathers* (1951); W. M. Bedard, *The Symbolism of the Baptismal Font in Early Christian Thought* (1951); W. A. Van Roo, "Infants Dying without Baptism", *Gregorianum* 35 (1954), pp. 406–73; V. Warnach, "Taufe und Christusgeschehen nach Römerbrief 6", *Archiv für Liturgiewissenschaft* 3 (1954), pp. 284–366; J. H. Crehan, "Ten Years' Work on Baptism and Confirmation, 1945–1955", *Theological Studies* 17 (1956), pp. 494–515; A. Stenzel, *Die Taufe. Eine genetische Erklärung der Taufliturgie,* I (1958); J. Jeremias, *Infant Baptism in the First Four Centuries* (1960); E. C. Whitaker, *Documents of the Baptismal Liturgy* (1960); G. R. Beasley-Murray, *Baptism in the New Testament* (1962); B. Neunheuser, *Baptism and Confirmation.* Herder History of Dogma (1964); R. Schnackenburg, *Baptism in the Thought of St. Paul* (1964).

Burkhard Neunheuser

II. Baptism of Desire

Historical sketch. The Fathers of the Church, interpreting the message of the Scriptures, taught that there was no salvation outside the baptism and faith of the Church. During the Middle Ages theologians began to reflect systematically on the ways in which grace is accessible to men outside of the visible boundaries of the Church. It was generally taught that while the sacraments are the normal means of grace, the perfect disposition to receive them, created by faith and charity, would already communicate justification. Since such a disposition was ordained towards the sacrament by a *desiderium sacramenti,* the justification prior to the reception of the sacrament was regarded as a kind of anticipation of sacramental grace. In regard to baptism this doctrine was commonly taught. It was adopted by the Council of Trent (*D* 797).

The medieval theologians reflected on the kind of disposition necessary to receive the effects of baptism. A widely held position, taught by St. Thomas, was that prior to the coming of Christ it was sufficient to believe in God and his merciful providence in regard to men. Such a belief was regarded as implicit faith in the Christ who was to come. However, according to St. Thomas, after the coming of Christ the explicit acknowledgment of the Christian message is required. This, at least, was his view when discussing the general plan of God's redemptive action.

It was generally assumed in the Middle Ages that the world as a whole had been evangelized; the infidels were regarded as living in comparatively small numbers on the edges of civilization. After the discoveries of America and the Far East, however, the question of human salvation was asked with a new urgency. Many theologians taught that the peoples across the seas who had never heard the message of Jesus were in the same state as men before the coming of Christ in the flesh: their faith in a God who regarded the universe with mercy and justice was an implicit acknowledgment of the Christian gospel and therefore counted for them as the baptism of desire. Speculating on how God acted in men beyond the reach of the gospel, these theologians were convinced of two things: that Christ was the one and unique mediator of salvation and that the grace of Christ touched the heart of every single man in an invitation to which he must respond.

This general understanding of baptism of desire received its most formal ecclesiastical expression in the Boston Letter, sent by the Holy See to Cardinal Cushing in 1949, explaining the meaning of the dogmatic statement "No salvation outside the Church". According to this letter, it is Catholic doctrine that under certain circumstances, which are specified, an implicit desire to belong to the Church is sufficient for salvation, as long as this desire is inspired by a supernatural faith and alive with the love of God, in other words as long as this desire is the work of God himself in the heart of man.

Vatican II speaks of the universal salvific will of God in connection with membership of the Church: "Finally, those who have not yet received the gospel are related in various ways to the People of God. In the first place there is the people to whom the covenants and the promises were given and from whom Christ was born according to the flesh (cf. Rom 9:4–5) . . . But the plan of salvation also includes those who acknowledge the Creator. In the first place among these are the Moslems, who, professing to hold the faith of Abraham, along with us adore the one and merciful God, who on the last day will judge mankind. Nor is God himself far distant from those who in shadows and images seek the unknown God, for it is he who gives to all men life and breath and every other gift (cf. Acts 17:25–28), and who as Saviour wills that all men be saved (cf. 1 Tim 2:4). For those also can attain to everlasting salvation who through no fault of their own do not know the gospel of Christ or his Church, yet sincerely seek God and, moved by grace, strive by their deeds to do his will as it is known to them through the dictates of conscience." (Dogmatic Constitution on the Church, art. 16; see also art. 9.) For those, however, who have recognized the necessity of the Church for salvation, baptism is indispensable as the "door" to the Church and hence to salvation (*ibid.*, art. 14; Decree on the Church's Missionary Activity, art. 7).

Theology. In our own day when we realize more than ever before that the biblical people of the Old and New Testaments is a small minority in the totality of the human family, the need to reflect on the destiny of the majority of mankind is still more urgent than in the age of the great discoveries. Does the gratuitous election of God's own people imply that his saving action outside of this people is rare or exceptional? May we not suppose that the God who has revealed his universal will to save in Christ, is working for the salvation of men within the Church where his action is acknowledged, as well as outside the Church where his action is not as such acknowledged? Many contemporary Catholic theologians believe that God's irrevocable election of mankind in the Incarnation, the once-for-allness of Christ's sacrifice and the completeness of his victory imply that, with Jesus, mankind as a whole has entered a new situation, that is, has acquired an objective orientation, based not on its own nature but on the free divine choice, to be reconciled with God.

Under the notion of "baptism of desire", then, we may include the vast action of God to save and sanctify men outside the visible boundaries of the Church. While this baptism, as distinct from the baptism of water, does not introduce men into a believing community in which they are fed by an intimate communion with their God (and hence remains a weak initiation into a reality which is fully present only in the Church), one may seriously wonder whether baptism of desire is not the way of salvation for the great majority of men in this world, chosen to be saved.

If baptism of desire is the way of salvation for the vast majority of men chosen by God, we must attempt to describe the necessary predisposition of the mind for this with some psychological plausibility. What happens in the hearts of men beyond the reach of the gospel who submit to God's saving action? Since Christ is the only mediator, we believe that the mystery of salvation in non-Christians must be in basic continuity with the salvation of Christians through faith, hope and charity.

We believe that holiness is always the work of Christ. Because we are by nature divided, torn between two opposing tendencies in us, the decision making the selfless triumph over the selfish tendency in us is God's merciful doing in us. Wherever a man finds in himself the freedom to renounce his self-centredness and give way to a selfless concern for another, what happens to him may be described as a dying unto himself and a rising to a new life, liberated — at least on one level — from the connatural ambiguity of his own striving. Since such a victory is the work of grace, we may justly describe what happens to such a person as a share in the death and resurrection of Jesus, in other words as a kind of baptism. In some way, however tentative and faint, the image of Jesus has been imprinted on that person.

Yet the victory over the death of self-centredness is not in any way experienced as a moral achievement of which one may be proud. It is not a work on account of which such a person feels justified before God (if he believes in him) or entitled to the gratitude of men. On the contrary, the person capable of being engaged in selfless action regards himself as the recipient of gifts, of gifts which do not really belong to him, which transcend him, which he wants to share with others, and for which he wants no credit or reward. This person has accepted himself, *in an act of faith,* as one who has been enriched, undeservedly endowed with seeing and loving, as one who no longer belongs to himself but is turned to others in a gesture of sharing. It is from such an act of faith and not from an ambitious will to be virtuous that selfless action proceeds. In this faith the person finds the freedom to forget himself, to abandon the fear of others, and to transcend the insecurity of his lone existence.

Such a person — and who will say that he has never met one? — knows that this consciousness of being undeservedly rich will only last if he is willing to turn away again and again from the self-centredness still existing in him and its symptoms of which he becomes ever more sensitive. At the same time he will experience himself as one who is loved: forgiven, secure, ready for action. He will feel at one and the same time unworthy and reconciled. If you ask him how this transformation has come to him, he will say, "I did not do it myself."

If this is a valid description of baptism and faith as they are available to men to whom the gospel is either inaccessible or meaningless, then it must also express an experiential dimension of the Christian faith as lived in the Church. This is the theological context of studies, such as the controversial *Honest to God* by the Anglican bishop Robinson, which try to express the Good News of salvation in terms taken from contemporary thought and experience. It is a great mystery that the divine truth revealed to the Church, which is altogether unique, shows itself to the Christian reflecting on it in faith as truly universal.

See also *Baptism* I, *Justification, Salvation* I, III, *Faith, Grace.*

BIBLIOGRAPHY. Y. Congar, *Wide World, My Parish* (1961); V. Valeske, *Votum Ecclesiae* (1962); H. E. Schillebeeckx, *Christ, the Sacrament of Encounter with God* (1963); O. Semmelroth, *Church and Sacrament* (1965); H. R. Schlette, *Towards a Theology of Religions,* Quaestiones Disputatae 14 (1966).

Gregory Baum

BAPTISTS

The Baptists, with 26 million members, form one of the world's largest Protestant bodies but constitute more a religious movement than a well-defined Church or sect.

1. *Origins and history*. In the 16th century, printed translations of the Bible into the vernacular, humanism and the Reformation attracted the attention of laymen to primitive Christianity and thus to the problem of the baptism of believers. Both Luther and Calvin taught that baptism was a confession of faith and that faith was necessary to obtain divine forgiveness. From these teachings and from private studies of Scripture in this and the following centuries, several groups in Europe and America came to the conclusion that only those who had personally experienced rebirth in Jesus Christ should be baptized.

About 1609, John Smyth, a former Anglican clergyman who had joined the Separatist movement and fled to Amsterdam, established with 36 adherents a new Church on the principle of baptizing believers only. In 1611 T. Helwys led the group back to England, where they came to be known as the General Baptists for their Arminian teachings on general or universal atonement. In 1644 a Calvinist group known as the Particular Baptists published a "confession of faith" defining baptism as immersion and advocating liberty of conscience for all. The General Baptists soon adopted the practice of immersion and with the waning of differences over predestination united with the Particular Baptists in 1891.

Both groups enjoyed freedom of worship under Cromwell, but endured much persecution after his death until the Toleration Act of 1688. Thereafter they enjoyed a revival, began missionary work through W. Carey (1792), supported the Sunday-school movement and produced several great preachers of the last century, such as H. Spurgeon. In 1708 A. Mack founded the "Dunkers" or German Baptists, who practised triune immersion and preached strict adherence to the letter of the Bible. About 1800 G. Oncken in Germany came to Baptist views from independent studies of Scripture, was later immersed by an American church member, and spread the movement throughout Europe. A historical connection between these movements and the Anabaptists is controversial.

In the United States, Roger Williams, an English Puritan and champion of religious liberty, founded the colony of Rhode Island for religious refugees and in March, 1639, formed a church of 12 members who concluded from Scripture that the baptism of infants was unwarranted. Similar groups formed at Newport, in the Massachusetts colony and around Philadelphia; but until the Great Awakening in 1740 there were few churches in New England. Self-made preachers effected great gains with the settlement of the West. About 1810 L. Rice successfully interested American Baptists in the world missionary enterprise. Although differences over the questions of predestination and the formation of societies and institutions, as well as in minor practices, had from the beginning caused disunity among the various denominations, the slavery dispute divided the Baptists into two major groups. In May 1845 the Southerners broke from the General Missionary Convention and formed the Southern Baptist Convention, which today has over 10 million members. The Northern Baptist Convention was formed in 1907 and in 1950 became the American Baptist Convention. After the civil war, Baptist preachers Christianized the Negroes, two-fifths of whom now belong to the National Baptist Convention, U.S.A., Inc. (1895) and the National Baptist Convention of America (1915). Today in the United States alone there are 27 Baptist bodies with nearly 24 million members, supervising several mission societies and over 100 colleges, universities and hospitals. The Baptist population of the rest of the world is about 2 million, with large groups in Russia and England and members on all continents.

2. *Teachings*. Apart from general Protestant teachings on *sola scriptura* and justification by faith alone, Baptists commonly believe that a) membership in the Church through baptism is a matter of free, personal decision and follows the conscious experience of rebirth by faith in Jesus Christ; b) Christ commanded and the apostles practised a baptism of immersion; c) the Church is a spiritual democracy independent of external authority in its own affairs. True to this last tenet, Baptists have been strong advocates of the separation of Church and State. Baptists reject all binding creeds and dogmas as well as any sort of Church mediation between God and the individual soul. Only the formal Word of God in the Bible is authoritative. Baptists generally recognize the Trinity, original sin and the need of redemption, the divinity of Christ and

salvation through him. The sacraments, principally baptism and the Lord's Supper, represent the proclamation of the personal experience of salvation. The ministry is of great importance, but the governing power of the Church lies in the people. In all ecclesiastical matters, local Church authority is final. All Churches are doctrinally independent and their power cannot be delegated.

There is no central organization ruling the Baptist communion. Thus differences among the sects are common. Some denominations such as the Brethren or German Baptists reject oaths, are opposed to war, and teach the apocatastasis.

The Free-Will Baptists uphold the Arminian position against predestination, and practise "open" communion and the washing of feet; the Primitive Baptists support Calvinist teachings and hold that all Church institutions are human inventions. The American Baptist Association is basically Fundamentalist and teaches a form of millenarianism. In general, Northern Baptists are more liberal and ecumenically minded than the Southern churches in the United States.

See also *Reformation, Calvinism, Protestantism, Millenarianism, Apocatastasis, Ecumenism* VI.

BIBLIOGRAPHY. T. Crosby, *The History of the English Baptists from the Reformation to the Beginning of the Reign of King George I* (4 vols., 1738–40); A. H. Newman, *A History of the Baptist Churches in the United States* (1894); J. M. Rushbrooke, *The Baptists on the Continent of Europe* (1923); H. W. Robinson, *The Life and Faith of the Baptists* (1946); R. G. Torbet, *History of the Baptists* (1950); J. D. Franks, *European Baptists Today* (1950); E. T. Hiscose, *The New Directory for Baptist Churches* (1954); H. C. Vedder, *A Short History of the Baptists* (1957).

John Charles Maraldo

BAROQUE

I. Historical Survey. II. Baroque Scholasticism.

I. Historical Survey

The word "baroque" was originally derogatively used to indicate a style of art that was thought to be exaggerated and peculiar. In the scholarly world, however, it refers to the style which developed in the 16th century out of the Italian Renaissance and spread throughout Europe and its colonies, terminating with the end of the 18th century. The date of its beginning and end in each country varies: the baroque culture north of the Alps, for instance, could only fully develop after 1650 with the end, or at least the localization, of the Great Wars, and more especially after the decisive victory over the Turks in 1683. In the beginning the expression "baroque" was reserved more for the art of the Romanic and Catholic peoples. While the Baroque found its richest development in Catholic countries, it also became characteristic of the epoch for the Protestant world. Today we understand by the Baroque the whole of Western culture of the 17th and 18th centuries. The Baroque is the last of the great cultures to come from the common culture of Western Christianity. It received a decisive impetus from the Counter-Reformation, which expressed the renewed self-consciousness of the Catholic Church. In the midst of the crisis brought on by the Protestant Reformation, the Church produced a potent instrument of religious renewal and resurgence in the Council of Trent (through re-affirmation of the most important dogmatic teaching and through necessary reform decrees). Wherever the ancient Church experienced this renewal, from the end of the 16th century onwards, it clothed itself in festive baroque finery, varying according to national and regional taste. Politically and sociologically the culture of the Baroque was based on the assumption of the absolutistic society: strictly defined classes, control by the aristocratic court, culminating in the absolute ruler "by God's grace". The culture was also, however, deeply rooted in the people. Its end came with the breaking through of the Enlightenment, already in the shadows of the French Revolution.

The most palpable expression of this new temper and style is to be found in the realm of art. Its characteristic is a new experience of God, of his infinity and freedom, but also of his overwhelming goodness and redemptive love towards men. After the weary and often outright doubting mood of the late Middle Ages and after the excitement of the period of the Reformation, man found again trust in God and in himself. A new, gripping and triumphant dynamism surged forward. In the baroque renovation of Rome, the pontificates of Sixtus V (1585–1590) and Urban VIII (1623–1644) represented the grandiose highpoint. Quite early the Jesuits, the most important Order of the period, became the heralds of the new style and the new forms of religious life. The impulse spread out from Rome towards the North and the West. After Rome, the most important centres of art were Paris (under the Roi Soleil, Louis XIV, at Versailles) and Vienna (after the victory over the Turks in 1683). Not only were gigantic palaces, of a conception often bordering on the utopian, built for the secular and religious nobility, but also imposing monastic complexes and innumerable churches — with a joy that often amounted to a passion. Architecture held the first place, with painting and the plastic arts marshalled into its service as never before. The conceptions of the Renaissance form, reasoned and well balanced, were no longer satisfying. Even less so was its effort to find harmonious repose in the visible, tangible and clearly defined. Individual features of the Renaissance were retained, but now transformed, with almost unbridled sensibility, into the colossal and the dramatic *(Theatrum Sacrum)* and the picturesque. Music also flourished. In the baroque period, strictly speaking, the Protestant world was preeminent (Johann Sebastian Bach, Georg Friedrich Händel). The final stage was dominated by Viennese Classicism (Mozart, Haydn, Beethoven). The interiors of the baroque church gave men, suffering yet fundamentally redeemed (with all creation), a reflection of the heavenly. The deep piety of an age given over as much to princely demonstrations as to the majesty of death, reveals itself to the thoughtful observer throughout all the power and splendour of the Church. The Catholic churches of the Baroque and the wonderfully spiritualized ecclesiastical rococo (native only to Southern Germany) are, as it were, expressions of the glory of redeemed mankind in the language of art. The whole history of salvation from creation and fall to final judgment and glory, through the redemption, and, above all, the great "communion of saints", are presented to sensible experience.

As in its art, the baroque age attempted in every sphere visualization and representation. It lavished its energies upon pageantry and feasts. The theatre of religious moralism was cultivated, above all, in the numerous Jesuit schools. Elaborate processions with many tableaux vivants and other figures,

pilgrimages and confraternities (often attached to the various classes), all reached a new highpoint which in part continued the forms of piety of the late Middle Ages, and often far surpassed them in exuberance. Feasts of saints and churches were celebrated with the greatest munificence. In the enormously profuse and diversified forms of baroque piety — both in the liturgical sphere as well as in that of popular piety — a vigorous religious vitality was revealed. Its fundamentally Christocentric nature was manifested above all in an ardent eucharistic piety, in the growing devotion to the Sacred Heart, in mystical piety, in the numerous wayside calvaries, and in the Stations of the Cross, a devotion which was now practised inside the churches. Preaching was diligently cultivated but was often content with vivid examples and moral exhortations without really penetrating to the spirit of the Scriptures.

In religious instruction, and in liturgical and non-liturgical piety, the central truths were frequently obscured by a profusion of pious and sometimes even superstitious embellishments. Here the Catholic Enlightenment intervened with its necessary but sometimes misguided efforts at simplification. The deep sensibility of the age was constantly threatened by false exuberance, by over-indulgence in sentiment and by over-sensual imagery which could lead to an exteriorization of religion.

Important achievements in theology testify to the new surge of vitality in the Church. Scholasticism too had its baroque period. Biblical science revived. Great collective works and critical editions were published in all disciplines. The questions of grace, freedom and election which had been debated since the Reformation flared up again and again, in such long and painful controversies as *De auxiliis,* on probabilism etc., in morals, and on Jansenism. Jansenism, along with Gallicanism and similar national movements, caused great difficulties in all countries.

It was a period of great expansion for Catholic missions, which now became worldwide, under the direction of the Roman Congregation of Propaganda (after 1622) and with the support of the great religious orders. But rivalry between the orders, the long disputes about adaptation and ("Chinese") rites, and finally the suppression of the Jesuits caused major set-backs in the second half of the 18th century.

The shadows upon the great achievements of this period should not be overlooked. The Church suffered not only from those internal tensions and disputes already mentioned. The ever-accumulating results of the empirical sciences were not taken seriously enough and could no longer be creatively mastered. The ability to achieve a genuine and convincing synthesis, as classical Scholasticism had attained for its own time, was enfeebled. Modern secularization and the ebbing of Christian influence generally, proceeded slowly at first, but gained momentum in the 18th century. This process reached a first climax in the Enlightenment. The gulf between faith and reason widened relentlessly and appeared at first to be unbridgeable. The Church often took no notice of the widespread social needs of the lower classes, especially in southern Europe and in Latin America, although great voices were raised in warning.

With the advance of the Enlightenment after 1700, the general attitude towards the world and towards life altered imperceptibly. Instead of the illusion of immensities, men sought rather for well-defined orders; instead of emotional rapture, rational clarity and sobriety; instead of heavenly pageantry on earth, what was practicable and helpful in the daily life of man. On the men of the Enlightenment the festal garments of the Baroque hung too heavy and in too many folds. Hence the Enlightenment was one of the great emancipatory movements in the intellectual history of the West. To lighten a ballast of history which had become too massive and heavy, the Enlightenment sought to reach back to the primordial: man himself as a rational being. The mystical and celestial light of the Baroque was replaced in the "Age of Criticism" (Kant) with the light of nature and of reason.

BIBLIOGRAPHY. H. Brémond, *A Literary History of Religious Thought in France,* 3 vols. (1928–36); G. Schnürer, *Katholische Kirche und Kultur in der Barockzeit* (1937); C. J. Friedrich, *The Age of Baroque, 1610–1660* (1952); E. Preclin, "Les luttes doctrinales et politiques au XVIIᵉ siècle", in A. Fliche and V. Martin, eds., *Histoire de l'Église,* XIX, parts 1 and 2 (1955); L. E. Halkin and L. Willaert, "La restauration catholique, 1563–1648", in A. Fliche and V. Martin, eds., *Histoire de l'Église,* XVIII, part 1 (1960); J. Bourke, *Baroque Churches of Central Europe* (2nd ed., 1961); H. Wölfflin, *Renaissance and Baroque* (1964).

Georg Schwaiger

II. Baroque Scholasticism

The expression "baroque" is applied to Scholasticism on the analogy of the architectural and literary style of the baroque age, of which it was the contemporary. It may be said to have begun in Catholic circles with the founder of the school of Salamanca, Francisco de Vitoria, and on the Protestant side with Melanchthon, called the father of Protestant orthodoxy. Among Protestants the end of this period coincided with the end of ecclesiastical Scholasticism (which had often taken in Catholic elements) and the emergence of pietism; among Catholics there was no definite corresponding termination.

Baroque Scholasticism is distinguished from the earlier forms of Scholasticism in a literary way by its more elegant Latin, and in its methodology by a systematic historical treatment. Neither characteristic was accidental: the former was due to the cultural expansion in the period, the other to the prevailing understanding of tradition. The Reformation necessitated renewed reflection upon tradition; Catholics understood themselves to be the guardians of continuity, while Protestants rejected this claim and then proceeded to "canonize" the Reformers and their theology. Both conceptions demanded constant reflection upon the authoritative sources and on their authenticity, transmission, and interpretation. From this point of view Baroque Scholasticism is the direct descendant of humanism. Both sides sought legitimacy in tradition: a thesis is only valid if it can be shown to correspond with the Scriptures and the authorities in each case. Hence Baroque Scholasticism is traditionalist insofar as it is the product of groups who looked to tradition for the legitimation of their views. But it is not traditionalist in regard to the views themselves. Here it is progressive and is always ready to take up the latest idea as long as it can be somehow supported by authorities. Well-known examples of this are the early adoption of the Copernican theory in Salamanca and that of Tycho Brahe in Coimbra. Progress goes as fast as the art of interpretation which supplied its proof of validity. Interpretative methods thus became an all-important factor. Hence the most diverse systems of theology were put forward as interpretations of the same authorities and cognizance was taken of this in the methodology of these systems.

Philosophy too, which included all the natural sciences, based its legitimacy upon past authorities and especially upon Aristotle. On this point there was complete unanimity among the confessions.

The conflicts between Baroque Scholasticism and modern science probably did not derive from the contents of the new teaching, but rather from the refusal of the innovators to practise the art of interpretation and to support their theses with the weight of authority. This was not just to disregard the peripheral. It was fundamentally an attack on the "Establishment". Whoever does not cite authorities rejects the normative function of tradition and concentrates his effort on bringing the facts to light on his own responsibility as a rational agent. This attack upon the Establishment provoked a persecution of the new systems, which was finally to be the ruin of Baroque Scholasticism. The break was less abrupt on the Protestant side than it was on the Catholic for many reasons. This was partly due to the tense ecclesiastical situation in the Netherlands which made possible a Reformed version of Cartesian Scholasticism, and partly because Protestants, unlike Catholics, could point to the authority of Leibniz who was fully abreast of modern science and nevertheless professed to be an interpreter of tradition. This change in the relation to tradition was due not only to the new concept of person but also to practical considerations of a social nature. From the 16th century onwards social problems could no longer be dealt with by the traditional means of hospitals and charitable works. They required the development of modern medicine and new techniques, along with the sciences on which they were based. The new sciences could advance all the more quickly, the more easily they could be learned, and they could only be learned with ease when they did away with the copius historical apparatus employed by Baroque Scholasticism.

The relation of Baroque Scholasticism to tradition, though it eventually proved harmful, also constituted its greatness, its sense of the historical. The impressive systematic handbooks produced in this age, which are thoroughly modern in breaking with the traditional form of the commentary, are not only examples of a fruitful confrontation and co-existence of opposing systems, but also remain even today inexhaustible mines of information for the history of ideas. The great editions and commentaries on Scripture brought about permanent advances in method. The fine editions of the Fathers and other authorities were standard works for centuries and the monumental literary and ecclesiastical histories deserve admiration. The application of Baroque Scholasticism to contemporary problems proved fruitful in questions of the philosophy of law and of politics, as well as in the ethics of economics and colonialism.

BIBLIOGRAPHY. K. Werner, *Geschichte der katholischen Theologie seit dem Trienter Konzil bis zur Gegenwart* (2nd ed., 1889); H. Hurter, *Nomenclator literarius theologicae catholicae,* III (1907), IV (1910); M. Wundt, *Die deutsche Schulphilosophie im Zeitalter der Aufklärung* (1945); M. Grabmann, *Die Geschichte der katholischen Theologie seit dem Ausgang der Väterzeit* (1933; repr. 1966).

Rainer Specht

BEATIFIC VISION

1. In theological language "beatific vision" usually means perfect salvation in its entirety, though verbally it particularly stresses the intellectual component in the single whole which constitutes salvation. This is the full and definitive experience of the direct self-communication of God himself to the individual human being when by free grace God's will has become absolute and attained its full realization. Since this absolute will (efficacious grace of perfect salvation in predestination) attains the individual precisely as a member of redeemed humanity in Christ and because of Christ, the term also implies in the concrete, if not formally, the unity of the redeemed and perfected in the perfect Kingdom of God, "heaven", as the communion of the blessed with the glorified Lord and his humanity, and with one another — the perfect accomplishment of the "communion of saints". As the definitive, irrevocable completion of God's action on man and on human freedom (which freely wills what is final), the beatific vision is "eternal life". The difference of "time" (to the extent that it can and has to be conceived) between the perfect fulfilment of the one human being in his spiritual and personal dimension and his perfect accomplishment in his corporeal dimension, is ultimately of little account. Scripture in fact always refers

to the total fulfilment of man and simply envisages it from different aspects. This is why Scripture sometimes speaks of the "resurrection of the flesh" (1 Cor 15), which means total fulfilment, another time of "being with Christ" (Phil 2:23) and seeing God "face to face" (1 Cor 13:12). Consequently the perfect fulfilment of man's bodily nature must quite simply be included in the actual concept of the "beatific vision". Theologically in fact it is an open question whether the vision of God does not actually receive an increment through man's bodily transfiguration, i.e., is in fact partly constituted by the latter. All this in no way calls in doubt the truth that with Benedict XIV (*D* 530) we must firmly hold that the direct vision of God ensues "at once" (*D* 530; 693; 696) in those who are free from sin and the consequences of sin (temporal punishment for sin).

2. The beatific vision is totally gratuitous (*D* 475), because it is God's free personal self-communication and the culmination of supernatural grace, i.e., grace which is not owed to any spiritual creature even prior to its eventual sinfulness and unworthiness. It is the miracle of God's love which on the part of those to whom it is addressed can never constitute a claim in justice or equity, or a mere consequence of their nature which the Creator of that nature could not reasonably refuse to it as its exercise and fulfilment (cf. also 1 Tim 6:16; Jn 1:16; 6:41; Mt 11:27; 1 Cor 2:11, none of which could be true if the beatific vision were the natural fulfilment of the human mind). The beatific vision is indeed the most perfect conceivable actuation of a spiritual creature inasmuch as the latter is open absolutely without limits to being, truth and value. But this unlimited transcendent capacity of man still has meaning and purpose even if it is not fulfilled by God's self-communication. For it serves to constitute meaningful, spiritual, interpersonal life in a freedom and history oriented towards a definitive possession of such life, none of which is possible without such transcendence. Consequently God's perfect self-communication even to a spiritual creature as such (as "nature") is free grace, yet can be the perfect and ultimately the only absolute fulfilment of the spiritual creature. To say that the beatific vision is purely gratuitous is not to deny that in the *de facto*

order of reality the spiritual creature is freely willed by God *because* God willed to communicate himself freely. Hence nature is, because grace was to be. In every creature endowed with freedom there is, therefore, an indelible orientation towards the beatific vision of God (a "supernatural existential") by which the highest "claim" of the spiritual creature and the ultimate meaning and the goal of the drama of its history is precisely the beatific vision.

3. a) As regards the ultimate essence of the beatific vision in the strictest sense, we must start from the position that the specific nature of created mind is spiritual knowledge and love which determine one another in radical unity, just as the transcendentals *verum* and *bonum* are inseparable though not identical attributes of being and of beings as such, and just as there are two and neither more nor less than two necessary "processions" in God, the Word of truth and the power of love. And this knowledge and love exist in intercommunication between persons. It must also be noted that "salvation" in its definitive sense means the perfect fulfilment of the spiritual person as such and as a whole, and therefore principally concerns his specific essence which distinguishes him from beings below the level of spirit. We must also consider that if this perfect fulfilment of man consists of God's gracious *self-*communication, then from the start the very concept of such a fulfilment cannot leave out of account the fact that this God is necessarily the Trinitarian God, that the Trinity of the economy of redemption is the immanent Trinity, that this is confirmed by the whole christological and pneumatological structure of redemptive history, the perfect fulfilment of which is the beatific vision. The doctrine of the beatific vision must, therefore, from the start make its Trinitarian aspect clear. When reference is made to a "sharing in the divine nature", it must not be overlooked that this participation is necessarily triune and is given for there to be a direct relation between God and the spiritual person of the creature. It is, therefore, implied that there is a direct relation of the creature to God precisely as Father, Son and Spirit.

b) However, it is of course true that by the nature of things the beatific vision can best be described on its intellectual side. For the knowledge of the personal spirit when put into words most easily describes spirit in terms of knowledge itself. Consequently it is described in Scripture as knowledge of God as he is, face to face, without mirror or image, as vision in contrast to hope (1 Jn 3:2; 1 Cor 13:12; cf. Mt 5:8; 18:10; 2 Cor 5:7). The parallel drawn between this knowledge and being known by God (1 Cor 13:12) emphasizes the personal character of the mutual loving reception and self-communication as compared with purely objectivating cognition. Benedict XII (*D* 530) accordingly describes the beatific vision as *visio intuitiva et facialis* of God's essence. The specific feature of this is that no object other than God conveys this knowledge. The divine essence itself shows itself directly, clearly and openly (*D* 530; cf. also *D* 693), in contradistinction to analogous knowledge of God which is mediated by the knowledge of finite beings different from God. To this, theological speculation rightly adds that what specifies really and ontologically the cognitive power of the creature and by which this must be actuated for direct knowledge of God, must be God himself as he is. God himself fulfils in a quasi-formal way the necessary function of a *species impressa* for cognition. If in addition a *created* real, ontological specification of the mind is required (the *lumen gloriae* as perfecting the *habitus* of faith — *D* 475), the relation of this to God's quasi-formal self-communication for the beatific vision must be described in a similar way to the relation between "created" and "uncreated" grace. The beatific vision does not of course annul God's incomprehensibility (*D* 428; 1782). It is rather the direct experience and loving affirmation of God as incomprehensible. His mystery is not merely the limit of finite cognition, but its ultimate positive ground and final goal, the beatitude of which consists in the ecstatic raising and merging of cognition, without suppressing it, into the bliss of love. In God, as the origin and goal of all reality that is not God, all other reality is known and loved, in the manner and measure in which it concerns us (cf. Aquinas, *Summa Theologica*, III, q. 10, a. 2).

See also *Revelation, Grace, Nature* I, *Mystery, Transcendence, Existence* III B.

BIBLIOGRAPHY. J. V. Walshe, *The Vision Beatific* (1926); A. Michel, "Vision intuitive", *DTC,* VII (1927), cols. 2351–94; R. Garrigou-Lagrange, "La possibilité de la vision béatifique peut-elle se démontrer?", *Revue Thomiste* 16 (1933), pp. 669–88; id., *L'altra vita* (1947); P. Bastable, *Desire for God* (1948); L. S. Roy, *Desir naturel de voir Dieu* (1948); K. Forster, *Die Verteidigung der Lehre des hl. Thomas von der Gottesschau durch Johannes Capreolus* (1955); P. Althaus, *Die letzten Dinge* (8th ed., 1961); V. Lossny, *Vision de Dieu* (1962); H. de Lubac, *Le mystère du surnaturel* (1965); K. Rahner, "The Eternal Significance of the Humanity of Jesus for Our Relationship with God", *Theological Investigations,* III (1967), pp. 35–46.

Karl Rahner

BEING

I. Being and Beings. II. Nothingness.

I. Being and Beings

1. *The state of the question.* Philosophy has revolved about the notion of being since the beginning. And here a fundamental distinction stands out, that between beings and being. Every thing and every man is a being, as that which is; but being is the ground by which all beings are or a being is. For this distinction Heidegger chose the term of the "onto-logical difference", since it distinguishes being from each being (ὄν), as its ground (λόγος). In infra-human beings, this difference remains latent. It is only known as such in man, where being displays itself as different from beings. This gives man, in contrast to the non-intelligent infra-human, understanding both of beings and of being. He understands beings by referring them to being; but he understands being by understanding beings with reference to being and in the light of being. Thus being provides man first with understanding of the being which he himself is, and then of all other beings. The understanding thus circumscribed characterizes the whole life and action of man, all of whose activities are illuminated by being. When such understanding becomes fully conscious and methodical, man enters upon philosophy. More precisely, philosophy is implicitly present in the experience of the ontological difference; philosophy begins explicitly with the express recognition of this difference, which is therefore its foundation and its whole life, and finds in philosophy its full development.

Here various emphases are possible, by reason of the connection between beings and being. There is a consideration of beings by virtue of being where being itself and the difference between it and beings only come into play as the obscure and unarticulated background. Nonetheless, reflection based on beings can also be brought to bear explicitly on being and on its difference from beings. According to Heidegger, the philosophy of the West has persistently taken up the former and thus bogged down in "oblivion of being", while it was only the thinking that began with him that came to formulate explicitly the oblivion of being and hence began to take being itself into its perspective. Gilson comes to a similar conclusion, though making an important exception for Thomas Aquinas, who already investigated being explicitly. The problems here outlined throw some light on the main stages in which being disclosed itself to the thought of the West.

2. *History of the philosophy of being*. In Heraclitus, being at once displays and conceals itself in the Logos, in which, as the conflicting harmony of opposites all things are based and unified (frs. 50 and 51). Though men have a constant and most intimate perception of the Logos or being, they turn away from it, and hence though present they are absent and all beings are alien to them (frs. 1, 34, 72). For Parmenides, being appears in sharpest contrast to non-being. Only the way of being is passable, while that of non-being cannot be divined (fr. 2). Being alone is, while beings in their becoming and their multiplicity cannot be truly said to be (frs. 7, 8). Hence being is imperishable and unchangeable; as the one all it is at once all things (*ibid.*). As regards man, his thinking is most intimately identical with being (fr. 3).

According to Plato, the multiplicity of things which is subject to becoming have indeed being, but not in the full sense. They participate in the forms, which alone are truly beings (*Phaedrus,* 247 c), eternal, imperishable, unchangeable, and fully what they are (*Symposium,* 210e – 211 d). The supreme form is the Good, which alone is being in its absolute perfection, and is even perhaps beyond being (*Republic,* 509 b). Man is most intimately akin to being in the guise of the forms, and above all to the form of the Good. He attains the forms by anamnesis or dialectics (*Republic,* 510 b–511 d). Aristotle

also regards earthly things as real beings, through which he penetrates to the "first philosophy", in which beings are considered as beings (*Metaphysics,* IV, 1; 1003 a, 21–26). It is also the task of this science to investigate the divine as the highest type of all beings. It is the eternal, unmoved or unchangeable, and separated from all that is visible, to some extent therefore transcendent (*Metaphysics,* VI, 1; 1026 a, 10–30). Nonetheless, Aristotle does not designate God as being itself, because he understands being as substance and hence attaches it too closely to earthly beings (*Metaphysics,* VII, 1; 1028 b, 2–4). In neo-Platonism, as represented by Proclus, the first emanation from the ultimate ground is being, which mediates between the ultimate and the multiplicity of things. The ultimate ground, as the One, is above being, since this is at once one and many, finite and infinite.

In the Middle Ages, Thomas Aquinas was inspired by ancient philosophy and the revealed mystery of creation to consider being more explicitly than had ever been done previously. Though he does not make being so expressly central in his work as Heidegger, he penetrated further into its ultimate depths. According to Aquinas, being is not merely the opposite of nothing-(ness), or the actual. It is the infinite fullness of all perfection or of all that exists and can exist (*Summa Theologica,* I, q. 4, a. 1 ad 3; q. 4, a. 2). The real things which we encounter are beings since they have being or have share in being according to the measure of their nature (*ibid.,* I, q. 3, a. 4; q. 75, a. 5 ad 4). By the fact that they merely have share ("part-take") in being, finite beings point on to infinite subsisting being, where the philosophical approach to God is opened up (*ibid.,* I, q. 4, a. 2). God is being itself, or being according to its inmost self, which is therefore identical with the ultimate ground (*ibid.,* I, q. 3, a. 4; q. 75, a. 5 ad 4). Thus the question of being and the question of God are intrinsically connected and belong to the same science (*In Metaphysica,* Prooem.), which can be investigated by man because his spirit is intrinsically orientated to being (*Summa Theologica,* I, q. 5, a. 3; *De Ver.,* q. 1, a. 1).

Thinking did not succeed in remaining on this level. In Cajetan and John of St. Thomas, for instance, the place of being is taken by existence, which is actuality as contrasted with possibility. This perspective continued to be dominant as time went on, through the influence of Suárez, though he himself at times reflects Aquinas's view of being. Thus he speaks of the whole fullness of being which God contains as subsisting being and in which finite beings participate (*Disp. Metaph.*, XXIX, sect. 3, n. 19; XXX, sect. 4, n. 3). The development here initiated gradually transferred the primacy of being to essence, with a corresponding mode of thinking, while the essence was more and more at the mercy of subjectivity. This gave rise to modern rationalism, and to empiricism as its opposite pole. Oblivion of being grew more and more widespread.

The situation did not change fundamentally with the great synthesis of Kant, of which the influence is still at work today. The theoretical reason at any rate did not attain to being, in as much as the thing in itself remained inaccessible to it. It is restricted to the essences under the guise of the categories, among which being was ranged by a total misunderstanding of it. The categories are *a priori* forms of consciousness, which knows objects as phenomena by means of the categories (*Critique of Pure Reason*, B 166). The practical reason opens up that which is-in-itself, but only in faith, and this means that we come to the three realities or beings corresponding to the postulates, without passing through being. Among the German idealists we may mention Hegel, who undoubtedly returns to the thing in itself and so to being, but reduces being to spirit and considers it as posited by spirit. The spirit is ultimately the absolute spirit, in which the human spirit is absorbed as a dialectical moment of it. The spirit comes to (full consciousness of) itself, just as being does, namely in becoming. Hence being is only fully itself as becoming, which combines with nothingness to build it up. Since becoming also falls under the categories in its development, being disappears not only in becoming but in the essences (cf. especially Hegel's *Logic*). Just as here being is sacrificed to becoming on the plane of the infinite, so too in Nietzsche on the plane of the finite. Nietzsche sees "the supreme achievement of thought" in "stamping the character of being upon becoming" (*The Will to Power*, no. 617). This comes from the eternal return of the Same, a process in

which "the closest possible approximation of a world of becoming with that of being" takes place *(ibid.)*. In the "cycle of absolutely identical series" (*ibid.*, no. 1066) the will to power develops, which is "the innermost essence of being" (*ibid.*, no. 693). Thus being is submerged in becoming as the will to power, whereby it is also put on a lower plane than value, for every thing is in so far as it has value, that is, contains the necessary "conditions for sustaining and intensifying" (*ibid.*, no. 715) the "growth in power" (*ibid.*, no. 14).

At the same time the return to being became more and more definite. Schelling in his later works sought to go beyond Hegel, and completed reason by freedom and essence by existence or being. Kierkegaard's struggle for "a fully human existence" took him in the same direction, though on different principles. The all-important thing was "to find himself", which inevitably meant that he was "implanted in the divine". The free act of man's will raises him to realized existence and hence to his authentic being, through which he at once adheres to God or is founded on absolute being. Here the way to being is opened up once more, though the quest for being remains involved in the quest for (Christian) man. This is also more or less true of Jaspers and Marcel.

Heidegger's is the supreme effort to place being at the centre of thought, since he unreservedly gives being precedence over man. For existing ontology or metaphysics, which considered beings in the light of being, he substitutes fundamental ontology, which considers being itself as the foundation of beings and the difference between it and beings. Thought is claimed by being and for being (*Humanismus*, p. 5); hence man is not there as a subject for himself, but as "there-ness" or existence is the historical "there" of being, and as "ek-sistence" is both a standing out into being and a standing within being (*ibid.*, pp. 20 f., 25, 35 f.). Man and being, though distinct, are indissolubly one, "since human nature itself contains the relationship" to being (*Seinsfrage*, p. 27), while "being is released into the act of attention" (*ibid.*, p. 30). By reason of this correlativity, thought stops at the historical communications of being, though openness for the supra-historical being of God is not excluded (*Humanismus*, pp. 35 ff.).

At the same time, oblivion of being continues. Neo-Kantianism with its theory of sciences does not escape it. Husserl's phenomenology, developed as a description of essence, also excludes the question of being; furthermore, the essences are constituted by the transcendental subject. A universal ontology only appears marginally and late. So too N. Hartmann surmounted idealism, but only to reach beings, while being strictly speaking remains outside his vision. "Analytical philosophy" — logical positivism or linguistic analysis — misses being entirely by its positivist logic which retains of being only the copula, as a function of thought. All philosophical content is, of course, rejected, since to ignore being is to lose the kernel of philosophy and consequently philosophy itself.

3. *Systematic view*. The historical survey has brought us to the situation in which thought finds itself today with regard to being; it must also be the starting-point for an explicitation of the content of being which will do justice to the points of view put forward above.

a) *The claim of being*. Being is disclosed to us in the action of man, who never ceases to understand being in his contacts with beings in the world. In contrast to the beasts, he has beings as such before him, instead of merely feeling their impact dully and stupidly; but this involves, as condition of its possibility, that being discloses itself to him. This, therefore, is the intellectual horizon which reveals beings according to the being proper to them; and there also being discloses itself as the ground of beings. Thus man is not merely referred to beings. He is, above all, claimed by being, and thus distinguished from all mere things. Nonetheless, he can lose himself in the beings which occupy the foreground of his world. If so, being, which at first forms only the background, eludes his grasp, by being dissolved very often into mere appearances. But the more man gives himself to being, the more imperiously does he experience the unconditional precedence of being over all beings. In the same proportion, being dawns on him in the limitless fullness and significance from which his destiny most profoundly depends. Thus the communication of being bestows on man freedom in face of being; he is called to make the decision through which alone he can truly find being. He wins or loses himself accordingly, having to preserve himself in his history and historicity by taking the risks which they never cease to impose upon him.

b) *Being and world*. More precisely, man finds himself confronted by two types of beings in the world, things and persons, which are distinguished by their different relationship to being. Things participate in being according to their essence, and strive towards the fullness of being accordingly. But they cannot distinguish being from its crystallization in essence, and hence their actuation does not break through to being itself and ultimately explicitate the essence. Hence things remain blanks for themselves and for other things. Consequently, they are of themselves silent partners for man, who can only make them speak in so far as he makes them participate in his own openness to being. In persons, man encounters beings like himself, that is, other men; through their essence they participate in being in such a way that in their actuation they at once distinguish being from essence and so attain to being itself. In other words, the person is capable of complete reflection on himself *(reditio completa)*, by virtue of which he can reduce the outermost externals of things to the most intimate inwardness of being itself. Hence the person, in the course of explicitating his essence, strives not merely implicitly but explicitly to the limitless fullness of being. At the same time, he is disclosed to himself, a process expressed in the self-consciousness in which he says "I" and in his free disposal of himself. And since all beings are rooted in being, the person is likewise opened up to all others. Consequently, with regard to other persons, he is a partner who responds, bringing about thereby the "I-You" encounter dialogue.

Clearly, there is an essential connection between person and being. In things, being is alienated from itself, while in the person it is at home or has possession of itself. Consequently, things appear as diminished beings, over which persons tower as full beings. Being is most intrinsically personal; that is why it appears in its own self only as person. Heidegger's switch from beings to being is completed by the switch from things to persons, which by all appearances is now being made and will be decisive for the future of philosophy.

c) *Being and reflection.* Being, as the non-explicitated background, is attained by the reflection which goes hand in hand with our encounter with beings. Reflection, in its experience of objects, experiences being as that which transcends objects. Then reflection looking back on our action places this being in the foreground and explicitates it according to its kind. Here the supra-conceptual being revealed in the beings grasped in concepts must be provided with an adequate set of conceptual expressions. The instrument is the analogous concept, in which agreement and difference are indissolubly mingled, and which can therefore grasp being in the light of beings, without the distortion which would place it among beings.

How then does being appear in this process of explicitation? Heidegger's explanations revolve around the historical communications of being, and hence its finite and historical, that is, its relative form. Its further depths are not indeed ignored, but they are not included in the investigation. Nonetheless, it is precisely these depths which are the enabling grounds for our human action and the transcendental explanation of these grounds leads to absolute and hence infinite and supra-historical being. This may be demonstrated with regard to three fundamental types of action, the contemplative, practical and artistic *(theoria, praxis, poiesis),* that is, the absolute validity of knowledge, the absolute obligation of the moral imperative and the absolute radiance of the beautiful form.

d) *Being and the judgment.* Let us take the claim of the judgment to absolute validity. The characteristic element of the judgment is the affirmation of identity, in which the "is" usually links a predicate with a subject and hence appears as the copula. This logical element of the copula is as far as logical positivism or linguistic analysis goes; such analytical philosophy gives all its attention to the affirmation of beings and has no room for the different language of being. But in fact the logical function of the copula already signals its onto-logical significance; for the judgment is essentially an affirmation that beings are or that being is characteristic of beings, the predicate marking the way in which being belongs to beings. But every "is" that is uttered tends towards absolute validity, and this pre-supposes that we know what absolute validity means and can distinguish it from non-absolute or relative validity. But whereas relative validity holds good only for certain aspects or limited regions, validity conceived as absolute leaves all such restrictions behind, since it is simply there and hence is true for all minds. Consequently, the "is-so" which is the expression of absolute validity has the same extension, and so the being contained in it is all-comprehensive or displays itself as absolute. Beings are therefore revealed in the judgment according to their grounds in absolute being and their participation in it. In other words, finite historical beings are seen to be made possible by infinite supra-historical being. It is only through the dawning of this being that man's action is possible and hence man himself.

e) *Being and divine being.* We encounter absolute being as it meets us in its historical communications, but it is always distinct from these. Thus subsistent or self-sufficient being, infinitely transcendent and immanent with regard to all beings, announces itself as profoundest mystery and thus lays open the philosophical way to God. Absolute being, as found by man in himself and in all beings, is at first indeterminate; but its progressive determination elaborates its intrinsic relationship to subsistent being and hence leads on to subsistent being itself.

BIBLIOGRAPHY. É. Gilson, *The Philosophy of St. Thomas Aquinas,* trans. from the 3rd rev. ed. by E. Bullough (1924); N. Balthasar, *Mon moi dans l'être* (1946); L. de Raeymaeher, *Philosophie de l'être* (2nd ed., 1947); M. Heidegger, *Über den Humanismus* (1949); G. Maurer, *Das Wesen des Thomismus* (3rd ed., 1949); G. Marcel, *Le mystère de l'être,* 2 vols. (1951); É. Gilson, *Being and Some Philosophers* (2nd ed., 1952); L. B. Geiger, *La participation dans la philosophie de S. Thomas d'Aquin* (2nd ed., 1953); J. B. Lotz, *Das Urteil und das Sein* (1957); K. Rahner, *Geist in Welt* (1939; 2nd ed., 1957); J. Owens, *The Doctrine of Being* (2nd ed., 1957); A. Hayen, *La communication de l'être d'après S. Thomas d'Aquin,* 2 vols. (1957–59); G. Siewerth, *Das Schicksal der Metaphysik von Thomas zu Heidegger* (1959); M. Heidegger, *The Question of Being* (1959); J. B. Lotz, *Metaphysica operationis humanae* (2nd ed., 1961); id., *Ontologia* (1963); E. Coreth, *Metaphysik,* I (2nd ed., 1964); J. de Finance, *La connaissance de l'être* (1966).

Johannes Lotz

II. Nothingness

1. *The state of the question.* There are several important theological reasons for the con-

sideration of non-being or nothingness. a) The Christian faith considers that the world was created out of nothing. The Christian understanding of fall, redemption and fulfilment of the world is determined throughout by this irretrievable commencement. What does "nothing" mean here? b) All statements about God affirm rather what he is not than what he is. This is true even of the revelation in which God expresses himself, since it is uttered in human words. All statements about the ineffable mystery only point to what they say in so far as they point away from what they say. The mind's supreme approach to God ends in silence, in the utterance of a negation and the negation of all that is thought. Why is this so, and what is the content of this No? c) In contrast to this satisfactory enunciation of nothing before the overwhelming power of the mystery bestowed in faith, there is the nothingness of despair: existence is nothing, there is nothing at all. But the contrast of faith and despair does not exhaust the many meanings of nothing in the thought and experience of the past and the present. How does the Christian faith understand such thought and experience, and, living in the midst of them, how does it understand itself? There are no quick solutions to these problems. One must try instead to find an approach to the one thing with which the various interpretations of nothing are concerned.

2. *The approach of thought.* a) As long as man applies his mind directly to what confronts him, the thought of "nothing" does not arise. He may notice afterwards that he has thought of nothing, but at the moment of thinking of nothing he does not notice what he is doing. It is only when something occurs to re-mind him that he thinks of "nothing" as the content of his act. The other basic attitude by which the thought of "nothing" is attained is expectation. The questing look or the listening ear which waits in vain for something, notices — nothing. Nothingness then has the guise of something that is in default, something cancelled out. It has to be measured by something if it is to be remarked: it cannot be seized directly in the repose of the present, but only in the memory of the past and the expectation of the future.

b) Nothingness is not conceivable in it-

self, but only in relation to something. And so too anything that is met with is always a nothing that has been cancelled out. "It is this and not something else" — something that is defined by the contrast with the other endless possibilities which it is not. And it is only when one realizes that it and everything else might not exist at all that anything emerges from the nonchalance of the obvious and takes on the consistency and decisiveness of its true presence. Presence as such is the exclusion and hence precisely the realization of nothingness. In the absence of this nothingness, what is present is not present to itself.

c) Nothingness is only indirectly present in what is present. Of itself, it makes its presence felt in self-recollection and in anxiety *(Angst)*. Neither of these things are connected with anything, but with that other contrary of nothing, the all. I recollect myself means that I abandon everything and try to think of "nothing", but simply to be there open and empty. "All" is never attained by the human act, as something positive, complete and assured; each gain leaves the question open: is that really all? Only in the total detachment of self-recollection is all demonstrably there — demonstrably, by virtue of the comprehensiveness of nothing. If I have shed everything and let everything go, all is present in the resulting nothingness and I too find myself for the first time. What is accomplished by me in recollection, comes of itself in anxiety. All is swept away from its foothold, and I from mine. And the solvent is not this or that, but really and truly: nothing. Neither my thought nor my will nor any other thing can resist the force of nothingness. But it cannot be escaped by precipitate flight, and to allow oneself to be swept away in precipitate surrender is equally pointless. I am assailed by the nothingness into which all things crumble, and in the assault I hear the call to quiet and to patience. If I obey, I realize that the being that I have to be is the being that I may rightfully be, I know not why, and this shields me from the mortal dread of nothing.

d) In recollection and anxiety, it is not only I that am liberated from all that is about me: "nothing" too stands out, takes on contours for me, and the vague nonentity becomes the true nothingness, which is missed if one just tries to think it out, apart from the serious challenge of recollection and anxiety. Otherwise nothingness is objectivated, whereas by right it is not in the nature of an object, being other than anything or all.

3. *How nothing appears.* This approach discloses three negative and three positive traits of nothingness. Negatively: it is other than anything; other than all; other than "to be" itself, it is non-being, of which it cannot be affirmed that it is. Hence positively: a) Nothingness is comprehensive; if I notice something, my mind concentrates on something limited; if I notice nothing, this means nothing at all, the elimination of everything. Nothing has an unlimited extension, wider than any possible being. b) Nothingness is primary; when my thought strips beings of all they have, or when I strip myself in self-recollection, there is nothing left, nothing more to be taken away or shed. Any being is, and is what it is, only because it is bounded by the exclusion of nothingness: nothing is posited as the pre-condition along with the being of all things. c) Nothing is not merely the opposite of being, it is the same as being. If I try to think, not of something, not of some being, but of being, the same result ensues as when I try to think of nothing. Being appears as the comprehensive and constitutive contrary of something, all and "to be". If I think of being with regard to beings as their actual being, it is of course the opposite of the nothingness which is excluded by such entities. But if I think of being as such, I think of nothing in terms of thinking of any particular thing. Once more self-recollection and anxiety withstood in patience perceive the quiet power of being in the purity of nothingness. When the mind looks out beyond all beings, the opposition between nothing and being fades away into the pure receptivity of thought.

4. *Distinctions to be made with regard to nothingness.* a) *Nothing that is naught.* The questing mind that looks for the being of beings does not find at first that nothing is the same as being. It sees it as something other than being, as nothing that is naught. Before, after and apart from their being, beings of themselves are just nothing, and this nothingness may not be dissolved away, either into the beings themselves or the

unconditioned commencement, if nothing is to remain the limit which preserves beings in their finiteness and independence. The fact that it originates from its own nothingness shows us on the one hand that the being of beings is fragile, since it is neither self-supporting nor self-explanatory, and on the other hand that it is wonderful — for why should there be anything at all and not just nothing? b) *Being as nothing.* If when faced with the origin of beings from nothing the mind escapes the nihilism which says, "There is nothing to it", and the preoccupation with the finite which says, "There is nothing *more* to it", it will be in a position to re-live this nothing; it can be "as it was when it was not". This poverty which brings about in itself the nothingness of its own being and of the being of beings reaches back behind the opposition between nothing (that of beings in themselves) and being (that of beings which of themselves are not). True, there is "nothing" in the mind, but this nothing is the silent presence of inchoate being. c) *Holy origin as nothing.* Thought does not stop at the nothingness in the guise of which being dawns on it. It asks why beings are; what is the reason why being itself is present to the mind? The answer is — nothing: there is no reason. It can only be from the liberality of self-bestowing graciousness. The mystery of this favour eludes all that thought and question and answer can define and recedes into the holy nothing of the unimaginable origin. And it is not because our thought has reached it, but because it so wills, that this origin wells up into this nothing as the God who is truly God.

See also *Existence* II, *Dialectics, Transcendental Philosophy, Aristotelianism, Thomism.*

BIBLIOGRAPHY. M. O'Brien, *The Antecedents of Being. An Analysis of the Concept* (1939); M. Heidegger, *Was ist Metaphysik?* (1949); E. Paci. *Il nulla e il problema dell'nomo* (1950); H. Kuhn, *Begegnung mit dem Nichtsein* (1950); M. Heidegger, *Holzwege* (1950); J.-P. Sartre, *Being and Nothingness. An Essay on Phenomenological Ontology,* trans. with introduction by H. E. Barnes (1957); E. Fink, *Alles und Nichts* (1959); G. Siewerth, *Das Schicksal der Metaphysik von Thomas zu Heidegger* (1959); M. Heidegger, *Discourse on Thinking* (1966); K. Hartmann, *Sartre's Ontology. A Study of Being and Nothingness in the Light of Hegel's Logic,* trans. from the German (1967).

Klaus Hemmerle

BIBLE

I. Introduction: A. Exegesis. 1. Old Testament.
2. New Testament. B. Theology. II. Versions:
A. General. B. English Versions. III. Biblical
Hermeneutics. IV. Scripture Reading.

I. Introduction

A. EXEGESIS

1. *Old Testament*

a) *Name and contents of the Old Testament.* The
collection of books which Jesus, the primitive community and the sub-apostolic generation regarded as sacred Scripture is known
to Christians as the Old Testament, in the
form later determined by the fixing of the
canon. The term "Old Testament", by which
it is distinguished from the New and
honoured as the attestation of the first divine
plan of salvation, ordained by God in earlier
times (cf. Heb 9:15), occurs first in St. Paul.
He speaks in 2 Cor 3:14 of the "reading"
of the documents of "the Old Testament".
The old Latin translation of the text gave
currency to the word testament which
stresses the gratuitous nature of the covenant
established by God, even more than the
term διαθήκη. With the "New Testament"
as its counterpart, it became the general term
for the writings which after 1 Macc 12:9
(τὰ βίβλια) were known as "the Bible".

According to the Jewish view, the OT
comprises three groups of writings, designated as the law *(Torah)*, that is, the Pentateuch ascribed to Moses, the prophets
(Nebiim), divided into the earlier (Jos, Jdg,
1 and 2 Sam, 1 and 2 Kg) and later prophets
(Is, Jer, Ezek, the twelve [minor] prophets),
and the writings *(Ketubim)*, Pss, Job, Prov,
Song of Solomon, Eccles, Lam, Est, Ruth,
Dan, Ezra, Neh, 1 and 2 Chr. The placing of
the so-called historical books, Jos – 2 Kg,
among the prophetic writings is justifiable,
since they recount the deeds and sayings of
such prophets as Samuel, Nathan, Gad,
Ahijah of Siloh, Elijah and Elisha, and are
not mere annals, but history interpreted by
the word of God and seen in faith. The
Church took over with the books of the
Hebrew Bible also the additions of the Greek
version, the Septuagint, in keeping with the
broader view of the canon prevalent in
Alexandria. These are the deuterocanonical
writings: Tob, Jud, 1 and 2 Macc, Wis,
Ecclus and Baruch. By calling it the Old
Testament, the Church put it beside the New

and accepted it along with it as the word of
God. The term Old Testament can only be
used by those who accept this theological evaluation and relationship. The term
Old Testament is necessarily a Christian
one.

b) *The origin of the Old Testament.* The OT
contains the writings of the people of Israel,
which knew itself called to hear the word of
God and to observe his commands. The whole
literature of the people of Yahweh has not
been preserved, and not all its documents
have been incorporated into the OT. It is the
record of what was recognized as the word
and self-attestation of Yahweh, and as human
response — all, in fact, that appeared essential
and important for faith in the sight of God.
This alone tells us that the growth of the
collection had a long history, that it included
uncertainties as regards the inclusion of
certain parts such as the Song of Solomon,
and that it did not come to an end before
NT times. Israel was convinced that the
impulse and command to write down events
(Exod 17:14), divine directives (Exod 34:27)
and words (Is 30:8; Jer 30:2; 36) came from
Yahweh. What was written down was to be
a living and inspiring "witness for the time
to come" (Is 30:8). It was to be the Lord's
way of addressing those for whom it was
written (Jer 36:2).

The commandments of the law may have
been the first writings produced among the
people of Yahweh, as seems to be indicated
by the texts which say that Moses caused the
law to be written down (Exod 24:4; Deut
31:24). The covenant by which the tribes
were linked together and to Yahweh needed
to be expressed in fixed terms. But the
Decalogue (Exod 20; Deut 5), the Book of
the Covenant (Exod 20:22 – 23:33), the
Law of Deuteronomy (Deut 12–26) and the
Law of Holiness (Lev 17–26), in their
present form, which contains many changes
and additions, is from a later time, about
the 9th to the 6th century B.C. The great
deeds of Yahweh, as experienced by the
tribes of Israel, were recounted at the great
liturgical feasts. At Gilgal the conquest of
the land was given special mention (Jos 4–6),
at Shechem, the covenant (Jos 24), on Tabor
the victory of Taanach (Jg 5), and at Siloh
probably all the ancient traditions of the
covenant. At sanctuaries like Bethel and
Hebron the traditions about the patriarchs

and the divine promises to them were kept alive.

Under Solomon, however, interest began to grow in writing down the past of the people of Yahweh. The story of the succession to the throne of David recounted how the God of Israel had granted the great king a worthy successor (2 Sam 9 – 1 Kg 2). This work inspired the Yahwist to write the first account of the history of salvation, in which he used the story of human origins and of the patriarchs as a prelude to the traditions of the exodus, the desert wanderings, Sinai and the entry into Canaan, which had perhaps already been combined into a basic narrative.

Then the second half of the 8th century was of importance for the writing down of traditional material. Not long after the work of the Elohist, the prophets Amos, Hosea and Isaiah, and especially their disciples, began to commit prophetic words to writing. When the northern kingdom was conquered and reduced to an Assyrian province, its corpus of tradition was transferred to Judah, where King Hezekiah had paid attention to the collection of traditional material. It was probably there that the Yahwish and Elohist were combined into what has been called the Jehovist work. This possibly took the historical presentation down to the fall of the northern kingdom or the end of the 8th century, which would mean that the basic elements of Jos – 2 Kg 17 were then committed to writing. Other matter, including in particular laws, went to make up the book of Deuteronomy, which also contained material pertaining to Jerusalem. In its basic form, it was found in the temple in 621.

The exile was a fruitful period from the literary point of view. Shortly before the destruction of Jerusalem (587), Jeremiah dictated to Baruch the scroll which was to be the basis of the book of Jeremiah. Ezekiel, at Babylon, wrote down his visions and sayings in a sort of diary. The message of Deutero-Isaiah (Is 40–55) was written down by his disciples before the end of the exile. The Deuteronomic writings (Deut – 2 Kg), which had been worked over at various stages, were perhaps brought to a conclusion in Palestine about 550. But above all, it was the age of the collection, redaction, elaboration and re-working of the prophetic writings. This activity was continued after the exile, by the Levitical priests who had been deprived of their office when the "high

places", the sanctuaries outside Jerusalem, were abolished in the reform of Josiah, and also no doubt by the non-Zadokite priests of Jerusalem. These former priests became "doctors of the law". In the 5th century, the "Priestly Writings" were still being composed and elaborated in Babylon, on the basis of older material. But Ezra, returning to Jerusalem from the Persian diaspora, could already bring with him the Pentateuch as the whole law. In the lands of exile, as in the homeland (Lam), psalms were collected and composed.

After the restoration (539–22) there was much literary activity in the religious community of Jerusalem. Work on the prophetic books continued. The collection of sayings known as Trito-Isaiah (Is 56–66) was formed. The writings of Zechariah were drafted (Zech 1–6), added to (7–8) and completed by two short prophetic books (9–11; 12–14). Malachi and Joel were written, and Haggai edited. Sayings of older prophets were expanded into books (Obad, Mic, Nah, Hab, Zeph) into which cultic chants were inserted (e.g., Is 33f.; Hab 3). About 350, the Jerusalem community used Sam and Kg, old traditions and documents, the memoirs of Ezra and of Nehemiah to compose the "Chronicler's" historical work (1 and 2 Chr; Ezr; Neh). The authors of Job and Eccles posed their critical questions. Edifying stories were written, some in the diaspora, at times in the style of the novel (Tob, Ruth, Est, Judith, Bar, Jon). The prophetic vision of the future developed in the direction of apocalyptic (Zech, Joel, Ezek 38f., apocalypse of Isaiah, Is 24–27).

A new impulse to literary activity was given in the time of the Maccabees. As early as 190, the tension between Judaism and Hellenism had given rise to Ecclesiasticus, of which the motto was that the law was the true wisdom. Later, at Alexandria, about 100 B.C., the author of the Book of Wisdom sought a solution in a different direction: the faith and traditions of Israel also merit the title of "Wisdom". The apocalyptic vision was in full flower at the beginning of the religious persecution (Dan 7–12). Sufferings, struggles and victories are portrayed, with edifying embroidery, in 1 and 2 Macc. The other works of the Chasidim and the groups which stemmed from them remained outside the canon (the "apocrypha"). The formation of the canon, with the rejection of many books, was the end of the development of the OT.

c) *Spiritual trends and theological principles.* The growth of the OT was not as consistent in all its manifold developments as the final redaction would suggest. The tribes and clans which migrated across the Jordan into central Palestine brought with them the experience of a special salvific intervention of Yahweh at the exodus and on the way to the land of Canaan. From the beginning they found themselves sharply opposed to the peoples of Canaan and their gods, and therefore formulated the theological statements of the separate and unique position of the people of Yahweh, of the covenant and of God's promises, claims and saving guidance. This theological trend is clear in the Elohist. It appears in Hosea along with the exodus tradition and the proclamation of God's love of his people. In Deuteronomy it takes the form of emphasis on the election of Israel, on the graciousness of the covenant and the obligations of the covenant. Jeremiah, influenced by Hosea and the language and mentality of Deuteronomy, is also tributary to this northern Israelite theology, since he is preoccupied by Israel's relationship to God in the desert period and by the thought of a new covenant. The verdict of Deuteronomy on the causes of the great catastrophe is formed by the fundamental notions of this theology.

The fundamental assertions of Israel's faith had been also cherished by Jerusalem and Judah. They came to them from the same covenant of the tribes, but were given a different emphasis. The southerners, installed in the great kingdom of David, which offered them and their neighbours spacious living-room in the land of Canaan, God's gift to his people, envisaged salvation for all the nations. Influences from the spiritual currents at work in their environment were adopted and exploited. Their religious perspective included Yahweh's work of creation, his kingship, and the place of his presence. This mentality inspired the narratives of the coming of David to power and of the succession to his throne, and also of the adventures of the ark (1 Sam 4–6; 2 Sam 6), which with 2 Sam 24 forms the foundation story of the sanctuary at Jerusalem. The Yahwist's presentation of the ancient traditions was guided by the thought of the salvation of the nations, the blessed gift of the land and the divine guidance mirrored in the story of David. The theology of creation was the occasion of his story of the origins. Isaiah, the prophet from Jerusalem, was chiefly interested in the Sion theology — which was carried on by Deutero-Isaiah and Trito-Isaiah — and in the Anointed of Yahweh. Deutero-Isaiah constructed his theology in the light of the notion of creation. Ezekiel planned for the New Jerusalem (40–48).

These two basic trends are not unconnected. Isaiah remembers the events of the exodus (the framework of the promises in Deutero-Isaiah) and the laws of the covenant (Is 5), as does Micah (2f.). Jeremiah does not pass over in silence the hope of an anointed of the Lord who will rule in justice (23:1–6), while Ezekiel takes up the theme of the new covenant (36:26ff.). In both prophets the theme of the land given by Yahweh, announced long before by the Yahwist in the story of the patriarchs, plays a great part. The law of the central sanctuary, which confines sacrifices to the one place chosen by Yahweh (Deut 12 in particular), shows the interest of Deuteronomy in Jerusalem, in its final redaction.

After the fall of the northern kingdom, the northern Israelite theology was incorporated into that of Jerusalem and Judah. From then on, and especially after the exile, the latter theology was predominant, as may be seen from the Chronicler's work, which is centred on the temple and its founders, David and Solomon, and which excludes northern Israel from sacred history after the beginning of the divided monarchy. The books of the OT were given their final form in Jerusalem, so that only some typical features of the theology of northern Israel can be distinguished. It is hardly possible now to say how far such theology was under sapiential and priestly influences.

A tradition of sapiential teaching was built up in Jerusalem under Solomon. It absorbed the practical wisdom and nature-lore of the neighbouring countries, especially Egypt and Canaan, in its effort to shape daily life successfully in dealings with men and things and to develop personal qualities. First directed to the formation of state officials, and then made available to all, the study of wisdom covered a field which was regulated neither by cultic encounters nor by the express command of Yahweh. Wisdom was concerned with mastering the world and life. Precepts for social life were developed from its rules of personal conduct. Even the perspectives, content and formulation of the doctrine of creation were determined by the study of wisdom. It also influenced the other sets of concepts and traditions.

In particular, the mentality of the priestly school and its theology had close contacts with the sapiential, as may be seen from its statements on the order of creation and the nature of man (Gen 1; Ps 8; 104). But the priest's task included knowledge, enforcement and explanation of the divine commands as well as the charge of public worship and the temple. The wise man had to give counsel, the prophet had to announce the word of God, but the priest had to give Torah, that is, directives. He was entrusted with care of the ritual precepts and also, especially after the fall of the kingdom of Judah, with the law. The holiness of God, of the place of worship and of divine service performed in ritual purity were his main interests, the expiation of sins and the assuring of salvation his great work.

These characteristic ideas and efforts coloured the traditions which arose or were preserved in the holy place. They are fully voiced in the "Priestly Writings", which proclaimed in their history of salvation and "Law of Holiness" that Yahweh would restore to a pure and holy people the land which he had promised the fathers in his eternal covenant. Circumcision and the sabbath, observance of the law and the true worship of God were the preconditions of God's dwelling with his people and of the salvation promised in the covenant. The unalterable order of creation was to be a motive for confidence in the equally steadfast promises of God.

The priestly theology was strong at Jerusalem. Since the building of the temple its influence was great, and after the exile it was all-powerful. Drawing on Canaanite tradition, which had revered here at his immovably fixed site a supreme God as creator and hence as Lord of heaven and earth, it developed a theology of the holy place which was moulded by faith in Yahweh: Sion was chosen by Yahweh as the place of his presence, the dwelling-place of his name, where the people of God and the kingship of God would have a focus.

This perspective dominates the work of the Deuteronomists and the Chronicler. But the royal ideology worked out in Judah was also subordinated to this theology of Sion. The descendant of David is the anointed of Yahweh, chosen and installed by Yahweh as steward and mediator of blessings at the site of God's kingship. Ritual and courtly language were no doubt borrowed from Egypt, partly through pre-Israelite Jerusalem, but subordinated to faith in Yahweh (Ps 2; 110). The king is the adoptive son of Yahweh and receives his coronation titles from him (cf. Is 9:5); Yahweh proclaims him as king, makes him sit at his right hand and bestows on him the sceptre. He is placed by God in the special realm of sanctity established by the covenant with David. To establish the claims of the house of David and its special position in the eyes of Yahweh, use was made of the promise uttered by Nathan (2 Sam 7), which was the prophetic deduction from David's triumph. It became the source of all messianic expectations, such as were intoned by Isaiah, grew stronger at the end of the monarchy (Ezek 34) and then applied texts from the royal ideology, especially from the psalms, to the ruler and saviour of the future.

The two fundamental perspectives, the sapiential and the priestly thought, the theology of the holy city and palace were all enriched by views from levitical and prophetic circles. Mutual influences were not lacking. This is evident throughout the whole of the OT writings. The reader can only have access to their essential statements and purposes if he bears in mind the important theological trends in Israel.

d) *Old Testament theology*. The theology of the Pentateuch is to be found in the thought of the four sources, the Yahwist, Elohist, Deuteronomist and Priestly Writings. The combination of these documents resulted in a work which is practically all narrative matter as far as Exod 19 and then mainly laws and precepts, so that the covenant on Sinai is the turning-point, the climax and the centre of all, even on the most mechanical reckoning. The narrative comprises the time between creation and the conquest of Palestine, all of which is seen in the light of God's will and action as history of salvation, which, however, through human sin and refusal often becomes a history of calamity. Nonetheless, Yahweh's will to save prevails. It is presented in five themes which make up Israel's experience of salvation — the patriarchs, the exodus, the desert wanderings, the covenant, the conquest of Palestine — which are summed up in a sort of confession of faith, Deut 26:5–9. The history of salvation also comprises the story of the first men, which is prefixed to the other five themes. In the covenant Yahweh promises salvation and manifests his will, hence Israel is given the law. It is a gift of God which is the key to the covenant relationship and hence to God's presence (Deut 4:7f.) and to life (Deut 30:15–19), the sign of election (Deut 7). Hence the events of the desert and the voice of "Moses" summon Israel to observe this law faithfully. Only by doing so can it have life and continue to be the people of God, gaining the salvation of the call anew each day.

The prophets who wrote down their preaching understood themselves as mediators of the word of Yahweh, which they proclaimed in his name as messengers — "Thus says the Lord". This word is of irresistible force (Jer 23:29) and accomplishes what it signifies. It is the instrument of the Lord by which he achieves what he has decreed (Is 55:11). The prophet speaks by Yahweh's command, and indeed as his mouth (Jer 15:19). He pronounces menaces which bring down God's judgment on men's actions. This message of judgment is addressed to the people of the Lord and its rulers. Israel is thereby warned that the word of judgment will bring punishment with it, if Israel continues to reject the will of Yahweh. The message of salvation is also conditional. No doubt the Lord does not make his gifts dependent on human achievement. But their continuance and their growth to a new plenitude are linked to the demonstration of the will to serve Yahweh. When speaking of salvation the prophets concentrate in particular on the great promises: the call as God's people, the land, the anointed of Yahweh and the covenant. Since Yahweh is Lord of the whole earth, the other nations also come under his judgment. This can be salvation for Israel. Its enemies having become adversaries of Yahweh, their punishment means deliverance for the people of Yahweh. But the nations are not excluded from the promise of salvation. The words of the prophets are a message addressed to men in their historical situation at a given time,

not an abstract timeless doctrine. Immediate and actual, it comes warning, judging, punishing, guiding and restoring those to whom the envoy of God is sent. The events of the day are interpreted as a summons of Yahweh to his people.

The prophets describe the attitude which God demands by means of these events and point to the elements of guilt and punishment in them. Amos, for instance, sees in droughts and failures of crops Yahweh's answer to the fertility cult offered to Baal, and a new effort to bring the people to acknowledge Yahweh as the giver of all that brings life (4:6–9). According to Isaiah, the Syro-Ephraimite war is a test of faith (7:9) and Sennacherib's attack a warning to trust only in Yahweh (30:15). The triumphant advance of Nebuchadnezzar shows Jeremiah that God has made him master of the world and hence that Israel must submit to him (Jer 27). Ezekiel affirms that Jerusalem must be destroyed, and explains why. The conquering march of Cyrus allows Deutero-Isaiah to see in him the anointed of the Lord (Is 45:1). The topical element in the prophets' words does not diminish their valid and permanent truth, but brings it out in the form of examples: just as Yahweh acts here and now in judgment and salvation, so too he will always act. He is always Lord of history, his will always prevails and events are shaped by him to form a summons to men.

The prophets were not innovators in the sense of trying to place Israel's life and faith on a new basis. They were concerned with enforcing the ancient law of God, especially the social demands of the covenant: "He has showed you, O man, what is good; and what does the Lord require of you but to do justice, and to love kindness, and to walk humbly with your God?" (Mic 6:8) They were sharp in their condemnation of a worship which sought to assure salvation through outward observances and even through magic. They demanded a worship of God which would be the expression of inward obedience (Amos 5:21ff.; Is 1:11–17; Jer 7; Hos 6:6). They argued from Israel's past to denounce a false faith in election (Amos 3:1f.; 9:7) and to restore Israel to the purity of its origins (Hos 2; Jer 2–4).

But the prophets did not confine themselves to the here and now. Their faith and their perspectives were wide open to the future, since they knew that they were sent to announce what Yahweh would do in the light of his faithfulness to the covenant and the conduct of his people. The words of the prophets, condemning or promising good, are necessarily related to the future: and "the Lord God does nothing, without revealing his secret to his servants the prophets" (Amos 3:7). They look into the future and include it in their words. They proclaim the coming of God to judgment (and salvation), whose Day will be darkness and disaster for all his enemies (Amos 5:20). Their view of the future leads them to expect God's intervention. The present is to be judged in the light of that future, and the shape of the future is determined by the present.

But each prophet has his own theological perspective. Hosea thinks chiefly of Yahweh's love for Israel, Amos of his action on the nations, Isaiah of the sovereign rule of the holy One of Israel, exercised from Sion. Jeremiah thinks of Yahweh's care for the misguided and apostate people of the covenant, Ezekiel of his care for the individual exposed to tribulation in the divine judgment of the exile. For Deutero-Isaiah, the creator God, the Lord of history is the one God and redeemer. Habakkuk thinks of his justice, Trito-Isaiah and Malachi of his proper worship, while Haggai and Zechariah concentrate on the establishment of his kingdom. What they all have at heart is that man should have a true and genuine relationship to God. Amos demands that Israel should seek Yahweh, Hosea calls for knowledge and love of God, Isaiah for faith and confidence, Jeremiah for whole-hearted conversion, Ezekiel for responsible obedience to the will of God. All proclaim the almighty, transcendent, personal, morally exigent and freely gracious God, whom Israel had encountered at each stage of its history.

The verdict of the Deuteronomical writers on the history of Israel is based on the main ideas of Deuteronomy, with which they began. But they then also see it in the light of the exile. Israel is the people of Yahweh, through the covenant which he has bestowed on them: they must serve him alone and keep the law. Obedience brings blessing and life, disobedience malediction and ruin. The misery of the exile was their own fault. It had to come, because in spite of frequent warnings and punishments the people (espe-cially its kings) had not been obedient, that is, had fallen away from Yahweh, worshipped other gods, failed to abolish the "high places" or persisted in the sin of Jeroboam (the image of Yahweh as a bull at Bethel). Nonetheless, as the favours bestowed on Jehoiachin show (2 Kg 25:27ff.), he can begin anew with Israel if he wills. But true conversion to God must be presupposed (1 Kg 8:47f.).

The writings of the Chronicler treat the post-exilic community of Jerusalem, which has to serve God in holiness and in ritual purity at and around the temple, as the realization of God's kingship on earth and the goal of history. The psalms were really chanted, it was thought, as David had desired, as hymns of praise, extolling God's help, the grace of his covenant and his gifts of salvation.

The older parts of the Wisdom literature (Prov 10:1–22:16; 25–29) give rules for living based on experience, which presuppose an order of creation according to which the action determines the result. The words of exhortation include religious and ethical motivation, which later becomes predominant. The innocent sufferer Job criticizes the schema of cause and effect. Yahweh, the cause of all, is completely free, bound to no world-order, incalculable in his actions but still true to his justice and kindness. Hence Job flies to Yahweh, his seeming enemy, as to his saviour. The Ecclesiast, himself a Wisdom teacher, flatly denies the Wisdom principle, that a law can be recognized in events and exploited for the successful shaping of life. There is nothing to be done but to be modest and temperate, to fear God and take his good gifts gratefully. But when Wisdom was identified with the faith and law of Israel, Yahweh spoke through it. It became teacher of men (Prov 1–9), mediator of revelation (Ecclus 24), moulder of history (Ecclus 44–50; Wis 10) and agent of creation (Prov 8; 3:19; Wis 7:22).

Various theological interests made use of the edifying tale, partly coloured by sapiential teaching. Jonah proclaimed God's salvific will for the pagans, Ruth his providence at work among David's ancestors, choosing its beneficiaries in response to human loyalty. Esther praises the divine retribution meted out to the enemies of God's people, Judith his mighty intervention through the hands of a weak woman. Tobit holds up the example of a God-fearing life in a pagan country (cf. Dan 1–6).

Towards the end of the OT era, the ever-widening prophetic view of the future (eschatology in the broad sense) became apocalyptic (Dan 7–12). Apocalyptic puts a radical break between this evil world dominated by forces hostile to God and the future blessed world to be brought about by God as his kingdom. The goal is a new heaven and a new earth (Is 66:22), after the universal judgment and the resurrection of the dead.

e) *The unity of the OT.* This survey of the growth and contents of the OT has shown that its theological trends and statements are very diverse. The various statements, at times seemingly opposed to one another, are linked by the profession of faith: Yahweh is our God, we are his people. For all the writers and all the books, Yahweh is the God who has turned to man, willing to save and about to judge. His people remain the one same Israel. The future belongs to God's kingship. The OT is open to this fulfilment. Here the NT begins. It sees and esteems the whole of the OT as the promise of the lordship of God, fulfilled and to be fulfilled in Jesus Christ.

f) *History of interpretation.* The use of the OT in the NT, every translation, all application of it in instruction and liturgy is interpretation. Interpretation began in the OT itself with the redaction of the prophetical books and continued in Jewish circles in the *Targums,* the *Midrashim* and the *Mishnah.* In patristic as in medieval times allegorical and typological interpretation was predominant, mainly under the influence of the NT, to the detriment of the literal sense. Four senses of Scripture were distinguished in the Middle Ages (on which see *Biblical Exegesis,* I, III). A new approach was opened up by historical criticism, which began effectively with R. Simon and his work on the Pentateuch. Literary criticism, which reached its high-point with J. Wellhausen, was followed by form-criticism, comparative religion (Gunkel, H. Gressmann), and then the history of traditions and of redactions (M. Noth, G. von Rad). The aim is to find the real statement of each book and each section. More recently, stylistic criteria have been developed with a view to grasping the literary production as a whole in its true import.

g) *Present-day methods.* Modern exegesis is based on historical criticism in its various branches as mentioned above, with of course the textual criticism which has always been basic. The latter strives to reach the original text as far as possible and produces critical editions of the text. Literary criticism strives to decipher the possibly multiple stages in the composition of a work, to determine their origins, authors and sources, and to assign them their various dates. This makes it possible to hear the voices of the individuals through whom God announced the biblical message and to distinguish their words. Form-criticism takes seriously the affirmation that "God spoke of old in many and various ways to our fathers" (Heb 1:1). It enquires into the literary genres employed (proverb, song, psalm, prophetic oracle, treaty, charter, list, letter, law, tale, midrash, etc.), their *Sitz im Leben* or site in real life and their mode of assertion. It thus traces the content and the message aimed at in the individual items. It recognizes that genres were adopted which, from the point of view of form-criticism, must be designated as saga and legend. Israel was able to make use of them to depict the origins of humanity and pre-history in the light of its faith, and to express the holiness and divine power attached to certain persons or places.

The history of redaction aims at showing the motives at work in the juxtaposition of the individual items, while the history of traditions investigates the principles at work in the combination of pre-existing matter. Cultic history investigates the forces and tendencies which sprang from the religious life and worship of the people of Yahweh. The history of religions is invoked for comparison with the religions of the surrounding nations, in order to demarcate what is special to the OT. All these methods are used in harmony by Christian exegesis in the theological exposition which strives to make the OT message, in and by virtue of the whole divine message of both Testaments, audible to the people of God of today.

See also *Apocrypha, Apocalyptic, Form Criticism, Old Testament Books.*

BIBLIOGRAPHY. S. R. Driver, *An Introduction to the Literature of the Old Testament* (9th ed., 1913); G. E. Wright, *God Who Acts* (1952); J. L. McKenzie, *The Two-Edged Sword* (1956); H. J. Kraus, *Geschichte der historisch-kritischen Erforschung des Alten Testaments* (1956); E. Würthwein, *The Text of the Old Testament. An Introduction to Kittel-Kahle's Biblia Hebraica* (1957); T. C. Vriezen, *An Outline of Old Testament Theology* (1958); J. Bright, *A History of Israel* (1959); M. Noth, *The History of Israel* (2nd ed., 1960); R. de Vaux, *Ancient Israel. Its Life and Institutions* (1961); A. Weiser, *Introduction to the Old Testament* (1961); W. Eichrodt, *Theology of the Old Testament,* 2 vols. (1961–67); G. von Rad, *Old Testament Theology,* 2 vols. (1962–66); L. Hartmann, ed., *Encyclopaedic Dictionary of the Bible* (1963); O. Eissfeldt, *The Old Testament. An Introduction* (1965); M. Noth, *The Old Testament World* (1966).

Josef Schreiner

2. New Testament

a) *The name.* The expression "New Testament" is used to designate a group of twenty-seven canonical writings, the products of the Christian communities of the 1st and 2nd centuries, which were brought together to form a collection in two parts (gospels and letters). The expression "New Testament" was first used in Jer 31:31 (which is quoted in Heb 8:8; cf. Dam) and is to be found in the NT in the Pauline-Lucan tradition of the Last Supper, in Jesus' words over the cup (1 Cor 11:35; Lk 22:20), and in 2 Cor 3:6; Heb 9:15; 12:24. The complementary expression παλαιὰ διαθήκη is first found in Paul (2 Cor 3:14). In every case the καινὴ διαθήκη stands for the order of redemption inaugurated by the death of Jesus in contrast to the order deriving from Moses. Thus διαθήκη in the NT is used much in the same sense as the Hebrew *bᵉrīt* (in the theological sense: the covenant established by God). While διαθήκη in Hellenism was only occasionally used in the sense of "arrangement" (Aristophanes, Dinarchus) and mostly meant "testament", in the LXX and NT it acquired the broader meaning of *bᵉrīt* (except in Gal 3:15, 17), that is , "order of salvation". The rendering "new testament" (first used by Tertullian) narrows the meaning of διαθήκη once more to "final disposition" (which is also the meaning of the word in the title of apocryphal writings such as the *Test. XII* and the *Testament of Our Lord Jesus Christ.* The expression "New Testament", as the title of a book, is really a shortened form of the genitive — meaning the writings "of the New Testament". Thus, *c.* 180 Melito of

Sardes drew up a list of books τῆς παλαιᾶς διαθήκης; *c.* 192 we find the expression ὁ τῆς τοῦ εὐαγγελίου καινῆς διαθήκης λόγος, while Tertullian speaks of "totum instrumentum utriusque testamenti". The way was thus open to call the books themselves the "New Testament". But Eusebius (*Hist. Eccl.,* V, 16, 3) still speaks of the "gospel of the new covenant". It was therefore customary at that time to speak of the writings of the New Covenant when one contrasted them with those of the OT and claimed for them at least an equal standing.

Jesus and the authors of the NT understood by the expression ἡ γραφή only the OT. The NT writings, however, are not primarily an interpretative canon of the OT but the transmission of the eschatological message of salvation, which could not have been derived from the OT but was made known only in the messianic age which began with Jesus. Jesus and the post-resurrection community already felt themselves outside the OT, the imperfect product of a past age of salvation, which the new stage of the history of salvation had left behind. The OT only became a problem when the now "unfaithful" Jews appealed to their scriptures against the Church. Thus began the struggle for the secondary legitimation of the message of Christ before the Jews, which made it necessary for Christians to interpret the whole of the OT in a positive and consistently Christian way. It began with the assertion that the suffering and resurrection of Jesus were "according to the Scriptures". From this positive assertion there soon followed the negative one, that the Jews did not understand the Scriptures, an accusation which then proceeded to a discussion of individual passages. As early as the reflective citations of Mt, the prophetic and Deuteronomic schema of "promise-fulfilment" was applied, and in Mt 5:17 it was invoked for Jesus' interpretation of the Law. Whereas the life and teaching of Jesus were originally considered against the horizon of the apocalyptic tradition, as the fulfilment of the sacred history of the Jewish people, they then became more and more the exegetical principle for the interpretation of the OT. But the promise-fulfilment schema was soon largely abandoned for the allegorical method (*Letter of Barnabas*). The proof from Scripture basically had only a secondary and anti-Jewish function, whereas the NT writings primarily

167

derived their validity from the eschatological authority of the Lord or the "apostles". In 2 Clem we have the first instance of a NT citation referred to as "scripture".

b) *The different types of writings*. The different literary genres in the NT depend to a certain extent on the theological purposes of the writings in question. The genre "gospel" was created by Mark, for a collection of traditions concerning the earthly life of Jesus which were viewed in the light of a post-resurrection theology. With the help of biographical data, the whole of the theological outlook of a community was moulded into a description of Jesus' preaching. With the addition of the infancy narratives this draft was considerably expanded by Mt and Lk and became an early sort of "Life of our Lord". Whereas Mk grafts his whole theological conception on to the period before Easter, Mt distinguishes between the time of Jesus in Israel before his death and the sending out of the Twelve to the gentiles after Easter (Mt 28). With this the gospel-form was decisively changed; it now contained post-Easter meetings with Jesus and his words on those occasions. This trend is carried still further by Lk. The history of Jesus is followed by the history of the gospel among Jews and gentiles in Acts. The two volumes of Lk's work are an expression of the theological notion of the time of Jesus as the "middle of time". In Jn, as in Mk, the post-Easter period has been fully incorporated into the pre-Easter, the theological work appearing much more clearly, however, than in Mk. The addition of the "prologue" was a decided innovation in the gospel genre.

While each of the gospels preserves the form of historical narration, the theology expressed in the second part of the NT, the letters, is largely independent in content of such historical reports. Because of the different nature of this theology it seems highly unlikely that Paul could have written a gospel, or even that he would have wanted to. Paul's theology, entirely and exclusively centred upon the risen Lord, is expressed in community-letters (e.g., Gal), didactic epistles (Rom), open letters (Col), and private letters (Phm). These distinctions can be applied to other NT letters: Heb can be considered as an epistle; Eph, 1 and 2 Pet and Jude are "open letters"; 1 Jn etc. are like

sermons; and the pastoral letters are similar in form to the community-letters. A special genre from late Judaism is found in the Book of Revelation. The degree of literary independence in the writers varies. In the four gospels one must presume the existence of written sources (Mk for Mt and Lk; Q for Mt and Lk; the so-called *semeia-source* for Jn). In Rev and the Pastoral Letters the material from other sources is much more extensive (liturgical hymns in 1 Tim 3:16; Rev 12) than in the letters of Paul (1 Cor 15:3f.; 11:23ff.). The problem of pseudepigraphy must be dealt with on its merits for each individual work. One must always reckon with the possibility that writings were handed on under the names of apostles which merely came from where the traditional influence of the apostle in question was at work (cf. the non-canonical gospels of Peter, James and Thomas).

c) *Methods of research*. These begin with textual criticism, which has the task of comparing manuscripts and establishing the main families in the tradition of a text (an "original text" can hardly be hoped for). It must determine the value of various readings and possibly offer conjectural emendations. Literary criticism examines a text (or a whole book) for its literary unity. Negative criteria include grammatical, stylistic or conceptual harshness, unnecessary repetitions (e.g., in Mk 2:27 "and he said to them" which is repeated after v. 25, although Jesus had not been interrupted) and doublets. Thus the text is broken down into the basic elements of its literary composition and its technique laid bare. After literary criticism there follows the establishment of the "smallest unities", i.e., certain phrases which can be shown to be fixed formulas by comparison with other texts (a concordance is used for this). The next step is to determine the various literary forms (e.g., controversies, didactic passages, hymns, etc.).

Form criticism is the comparison of a form as it appears in various texts. The *Sitz im Leben* or actual setting of a form varies according to where it is used. Thus the original setting of the controversy was Jesus' opposition to the Pharisees, but its later context was the general anti-Jewish polemic of the early community. Not enough attention is paid as a rule to the distinction between the literary form or unit and the literary genre, the latter being difficult to define. The history of the genre should be noted as well as the history of the form. The genre contains as a rule more than one literary form, and has a more definite sociological function. Hence its content is also easier to determine. The gospel is a genre linked to a biographical type of presentation and is not confined by its nature to doctrinal exposition. Its *Sitz im Leben* is the communal liturgy. An examination of Lk on the basis of the history of genres shows that it approximates to biographies of the profane type. Forms foreign to the literature in question must not be adduced. Saga and legend, for instance, occur in completely different cultural milieux and are unsuitable as classifications of biblical forms. And form-criticism is not concerned with the historicity of the material, but only with literary techniques. To throw light on the material, the history of concepts and motifs may be used, along with comparative religion and history of traditions. History of traditions must be applied to the text itself, to bring to light, with the help of the history of redaction, the various stages in the development of a text and their theologies. History of redaction tries to see how a tradition is affected by the theological "system" of the author. Hence the object of historical criticism is to determine the theology of the individual author.

d) *The problem of theological unity.* The various theologies of the NT can be divided into three basic types: the Pauline (between *c.* A.D. 35 and 60), the synoptic (70–90), and the Johannine (*c.* 100). The Letter to the Hebrews represents a theology of its own. The starting-point in each system is the death and resurrection of Jesus. While Mk uses the life of Jesus to reflect his interpretation of the death and resurrection — a procedure developed most unmistakably in Jn — the epistles and Rev do not. Paul appeals to sayings of Jesus only in three places, and in Jas 5:12 what appears as a saying of Jesus in Mt 5:33ff. appears as a precept of the author. Paul teaches by the authority of his apostolate (for which of course he can also invoke the risen Lord), while the synoptics feel bound to attribute all teaching to Jesus himself. What is common above all to these three theologies is the conviction that the community of salvation possesses the Spirit. It is this which is decisively and demonstrably

new in the condition in which the post-Easter community finds itself. It is the link between the receding past (Jesus' life, death, and resurrection) and the still unseen future. This conception of the Spirit, however, as salvation, is combined with different viewpoints regarding the manner of the presence or the futurity of the imminent kingdom of God. Whereas in Jesus' preaching of the coming kingdom the central salvific event is in the future, after the resurrection salvation was considered as already definitively granted in the person of Jesus. Jesus, indeed, already saw in his own possession of the Spirit the beginning of the kingdom, and this is also the pre-Easter origin of Christology. The danger threatening post-Easter theology was to lose sight of the eschatological perspective by making the resurrection of Jesus too exclusively the centre of history. The Gnostics succumbed to this danger.

Against such groups Paul stresses that salvation is linked both to the historical existence and death of Jesus, and to the judgment which is yet to come. Mk solves the problem by depicting the Spirit as already poured out upon Jesus and manifest in the activity of the Twelve, but not to be given to all until the end. The justification of such a long intermediary period preceding the end became one of the more pressing problems facing post-Marcan theology, the problem of what is called the delay of the parousia. In Lk and Jn the time of the Church is presented in a positive way as a planned and necessary time of salvation. According to Jn this is the time of the Paraclete through whom alone the full revelation of Jesus is uttered. But even in Paul the presence of the Spirit in the community was not distinct from the presence of the risen Lord. Thus the problem of the intermediary period and of the function of the community was solved independently of the kingdom of God: with respect to the kingdom of God the community is characterized not only by the fact that its universality is as yet unfulfilled, but also by the fact that in it the return of the Lord has already occurred in the possession of the Spirit. The varieties of theologies in the NT are based not only on different views of the coming end, but also on the different views of the person of Jesus and consequently of the role of the community.

These Christologies are expressed in a series of titles, each of which comprises only one aspect and which are hard to define on account of the obscurity of their origins. The pre-Easter titles are: rabbi, teacher, prophet, son of David, king of the Jews; the title "Son of man" is found on the lips of Jesus himself (only in the third person). The title most important subsequently was "Son of God". Other names are: servant of God, Messias, Kyrios, Christos, redeemer, the holy and just one, lamb of God, and high-priest. The titles which the community applied to itself either indicated its pre-Easter relationship to Jesus as teacher, such as μαθηταί (disciples), or placed the community on the level of the Israel of the OT, e.g., "the saints" (Paul, Acts), the "little ones", also the poor, the elect, the called, χριστιανοί, *ecclesia,* brethren, people of God, household and friends of God, strangers, Nazareans and Galileans. It is striking that the plural titles with a personal character (saints, etc.) predominate over the singular collective titles (*ecclesia,* people). The death of Jesus in particular is given different interpretations. The Synoptics are hardly aware of the significance of Jesus' death for the salvation of Christians; only the formula "for many" in Mk 10:45; 14:24 seems to indicate the vicarious function of his death. The predominant interpretation is that of the suffering just man. In Jn terms descriptive of suffering are avoided, and the death of Jesus is presented only as exaltation and the departure requisite for the sending of the Spirit. It was Paul above all who saw the death of Jesus as the decisive condition of possibility of salvation: through his death Jesus took upon himself the burden of sin which man had borne since Adam and the malediction which fell upon all. Here too the death itself has a merely negative function, the removal of malediction and sin; the positive gift of salvation is seen by Paul also as the possession of the Spirit through the presence of the risen Lord. In this view the sphere of the *sarx* is eliminated only by that of the *pneuma.*

In contrast to the Pauline theology, the basic idea of Hebrews is that Jesus' death on the cross was a high-priestly act, through which he could win the blood with which he could purify the heavenly sanctuary. Rev also considers the blood of Jesus to be the most important element of the death, for through it Christians were cleansed and their accuser conquered; it also saw the exaltation as a victory. Next to these dogmatic differ-

ences of the authors there is also another aspect which should be considered. The NT writings are witnesses of the history of early Christianity as a whole as well as theological products of the individual authors. The development therefore is not only dogmatic but concerns the constitution, liturgy and ethics of the communities. These differences in the NT interpretation of the salvation brought by Jesus need not be a difficulty for dogmatic theologians, who will see there the temporal variations of a revelation in Jesus Christ which must necessarily remain many-sided until the final revelation in glory. Accordingly, ecclesiastical tradition has the task of unifying these theologies to some extent, to prepare in a way for the unity of the final revelation. This procedure of tradition does indeed run counter to the direction of exegesis, since the latter by determining the peculiarities of each of the theologies shows that the unity in question, though valid, is only provisional, in relation to the *eschaton.* But the two efforts are complementary, since the Church must constantly look back to its beginnings as it longs for the end.

e) *History of interpretation.* To use any piece of writing is at once to give it an interpretation; the NT writings were first used in the liturgy, which interpreted them chiefly by combining them with other texts. A similar type of interpretation is represented by the fact that they were combined to form the canon, since this meant that they were considered to be of apostolic origin, free from heresy (Gnosticism), acceptable by the Catholic Church (Muratorian Canon), and substantially uniform in content. This interpretation of the NT was then adopted by systematic theology in particular, which sometimes included even the OT in this perspective. A special type of interpretation is represented by the textual history of the NT, since the text itself was altered to introduce interpretations of varying degrees of importance. This is a wide field, as the texts include 72 papyri, 242 majuscules, 2570 minuscules, and 1909 lectionaries.

Another type of exegesis takes the form of translations, paraphrases, glosses, scholions, commentaries, postils, and catenae. A strictly scientific examination of the text, to see which the author meant and not how the reader could use it, was first introduced, for all practical purposes, by Richard Simon (1693). His lead was subsequently followed mainly by Protestants, especially J. S. Semler and J. D. Michaelis. The beginning of the 19th century was dominated by "critique of tendencies" of F. C. Baur, Tübingen, and the "mythical" explanations of D. F. Strauss. The most important Protestant exegetical trends of the 20th century are the "thorough-going *(konsequente)* eschatology" (J. Weiss, A. Schweitzer), the school of history of religions (Bousset), form-criticism (Dibelius, Bultmann) and the return to theological interpretation in the programme of demyth-ologizing put forward by R. Bultmann. The acme of Catholic exegesis was the Humanist period of the 16th century; the pioneer work of R. Simon, and other efforts in the time of the Enlightenment were not followed up.

A revival of Catholic exegesis set in at the beginning of the 20th century, chiefly stimu-lated by J.-M. Lagrange. Important achieve-ments may be signalled in textual criticism, translation and archaeology. The critical reading of the text was encouraged in particular by the encyclical "Divino afflante Spiritu" of Pius XII in 1943 and by the Constitution on Revelation of Vatican II.

See also *New Testament Theology, Apocrypha, Salvation* III C.

BIBLIOGRAPHY. M. Dibelius, *From Tradition to Gospel,* trans. from the 2nd rev. ed. by B. L. Woolf (1934); R. Bultmann, *Theology of the New Testament,* trans. by K. Grobel, 2 vols. (1952–55); W. G. Kümmel, *Das Neue Testament. Geschichte der Erforschung seiner Probleme* (1958); R. Bultmann, *History of the Synoptic Tradition,* trans. by J. Marsh (1963); R. Schnackenburg, *New Testament Theology Today,* trans. by D. Askew (1963); W. G. Kümmel, *Introduction to the New Testament,* trans. by A. J. Mattill (1966).

Klaus Berger

B. THEOLOGY

1. *The theological basis of a theology of holy Scripture.* a) It must not be forgotten in the first place that for us Christians today this fundamental basis can and must be a specif-ically Christian one. Only then can the OT be seen as a part of our sacred Scripture. For us the situation is just the opposite to what it was in NT times, when the significance for salvation of the events concerning Christ had to be demonstrated from the OT scriptures, for it was their validity which was taken for granted. This historically conditioned start-ing-point is unavoidable and should not be blurred (Vatican II, for example, in *Dei Verbum,* art. 2 [cf. art. 7] takes its starting-point for the concept of revelation the revelation in Jesus Christ and not revelation in general which it only begins to discuss in art. 3). Consequently we must first seek a theological basis for the theology of the NT. For our purpose here we must assume that the ques-tions of the relation of faith to the rational and historical demonstration of its legitimacy, and of dogmatic to fundamental theology, have already been answered. We are dealing with a strictly theological question, not really with one that belongs to fundamental the-ology.

b) The theological conception of Scripture (in regard to its inspiration, canon, inerrancy, its relation to tradition, its normative char-acter for the Church and the Church's profession of faith and theology) has its sole root in the faith under two of its aspects. On the one hand — and this becomes historically clear for the first time in the Christ-event — God mercifully communicates himself by turning in his grace to mankind throughout its whole history of salvation, of which he is the origin and goal. On the other hand, this history and God's self-communication shows itself to be victorious by attaining its irre-versible manifestation and final form in Jesus Christ crucified and risen. And the now irreversible historical manifestation of God's grace-giving will involves the abiding exist-ence of the community of those who believe in Jesus Christ. This is the Church, which in its faith and worship always remains related to the eschatological saving event itself, which is Jesus Christ, and therefore to its own history. It can only remain true to its own nature if it understands itself to be the Church of the apostolic age, however ready it has to be to accept its own changes in the course of history. For it is only through the apostolic Church and its testimony to the faith that the Church attains Jesus Christ.

c) The normative presence of the Church of the apostolic age in the later Church primarily occurs through tradition (as life and teaching), in the legitimate authoritative mission of the ministry. The preaching which produces faith by the power of the Spirit, and the formal authority conferred by the mission condition one another. But precisely this perpetual recourse, in tradition, to the first age of the Church requires the Church to be able to distinguish between its own attestation of the activity and teaching of the apostolic Church and the content of its testimony: the activity and faith of the primitive Church. For that reference has to serve as a critical standard of the Church's activity and teaching. That need is met if written testimony of a normative kind concerning the activity and belief of the primitive Church is available. The importance of authoritative tradition is not diminished by it. For the interpretation of the written testimony has to be given existentially in a way binding on faith by the living magisterium of the Church (which preserves the historical link with the primitive Church and so with Jesus Christ). And above all, this reality which serves as a critical standard has itself to be transmitted by tradition, both as regards its nature (inspiration) and extent (canon). The written testimony is therefore not something which stands quite outside tradition and its authoritative representatives (magisterium). It is an element of, and in, tradition itself. Only the abidingly victorious power of the Spirit ultimately guarantees that a unity and distinction of that kind will remain effective, in other words, that the normative function of Scripture will endure. Belief and hope that this power will prevail and preserve that unity and distinction is involved in faith in God's eschatological victory in Jesus Christ. There can therefore only be sacred Scripture in an authoritative tradition. But the latter "posits" Scripture for itself as its own criterion, i.e., as an element intrinsic to it but distinct from it, needed for tradition itself to exist.

d) We can therefore provisionally say that holy Scripture is the verbal, written objectivation of the apostolic Church in its activity and confession of faith, as an element and intrinsic norm of the tradition in which the Church of later times attests the eschatological saving event itself, which is Jesus Christ. If the "beginning" of the Church is envisaged not just as its first phase in time but as laying the permanent foundation for its continued existence, that beginning must be permanently present. It must remain present in the Church's historical dimension (though not only in this) in the explicit profession of faith (even when this faith is given conceptual formulation), in the norm of faith binding on all, in the possibility of a humanly verifiable recourse to this enduring normative begin-

ning of the Last Days. Consequently there exists a pure and therefore absolutely normative objective expression of the permanence of that beginning, a *norma non normata*. This is what we call Scripture.

2. *Inspiration of Scripture.* From what has been said it is clear that the origin of Scripture is not to be imagined as dictation from God received by the sacred writers in a purely passive way. They are truly authors (*Dei Verbum,* art. 11), each writing his own work under the "inspiration of the Holy Spirit" (*ibid.*). But while it is their own work, in each particular case it also attests the faith of the community to which the writer belongs. And that community knows that it is a valid member of the one Church. Consequently these writings in their unity and multiplicity attest the faith of the apostolic Church, which was to be the permanently valid norm of the faith of the Church in following ages. These writings are "inspired", because willed by God in formal predefinition as a permanent norm of that kind. For God in Jesus Christ willed the Church to be permanent and apostolic, the latter understood in its two aspects as norm and as normative, as apostolic Church and as later Church. The Church recognizes these writings to be in conformity with its own kerygma and is conscious that it is permanently bound to them because they are writings of the Church which is the norm. It does not thereby constitute their inspiration, but recognizes it, without needing any special and detailed revelations in order to do so. Such revelations are improbable in view of the historically merely "occasional" character of some of these writings and the late date of some in relation to the apostles themselves.

3. *The canon and its formation.* The theologically decisive statement about the canon and the Church's recognition of it has already been made. The canon as a dogmatic question, and the problem it raises in the history of dogma, hinges on the problem of how it could be recognized. How can the revelation of the canon appear historically probable? In particular, how is it compatible with the fact that the formation of the canon was long and hesitant? A revelation must in fact be involved, for the truth of the canon cannot be regarded as *fides ecclesiastica* as opposed to *fides divina*. In the first place the idea of the

apostolic Church (the Church of the first generation, of the period when revelation was still taking place, down "to the death of the last apostle") must not be taken too narrowly. Otherwise difficulties will arise over the rather late date of composition of some NT writings. But there is no need to interpret it too narrowly if we regard the first generation not on the merely biological plane but in intellectual history. A reality of that kind cannot be fixed *a priori* by a precisely ascertainable measure of years and days. On the other hand, the formation (i.e., recognition) of the canon in the post-apostolic period had a long history, although no new revelation was then possible. But if it were necessary to regard revelation concerning the canon as the direct communication of particular propositions about the various writings, then a new revelation in the post-apostolic period would have been needed, because of the slow and hesitant formation of the canon. The question therefore is whether it is possible to conceive an original revelation of the canon in the apostolic period which was so implicit that its explication took time and passed through various fluctuations (the development of dogma). Can the nature of Scripture be conceived as being essentially willed by God as an element of the primitive Church which was to be normative for all time, an element forming part of the divinely established constitution of that Church in its character as norm of the future? If so, its inspiration would be radically revealed *in* the revelation of the comprehensive reality of the normative primitive Church. This would then be the explicit element from which the later Church was able gradually to recognize the limits of the canon without a new revelation.

4. *"Sufficiency" of Scripture.* On the basis of the relation between Scripture and tradition which we have briefly outlined, it is also possible to give some answer to the question of the "sufficiency" of Scripture and so arrive at a Catholic answer to the Protestant principle of *sola scriptura*. In the first place it is obvious that the Church's kerygma of the apostolic period preceded Scripture. That authoritative Church kerygma, which was proclaimed with perpetual reference to previous preaching, did not cease when Scripture came into existence. Consequently that kerygma is "tradition"; and hence tradition

is not purely and simply a reference back to Scripture as such (*Dei Verbum*, arts. 7 and 8). This tradition also transmits Scripture as inspired, and as having such and such an extent (canon). Tradition therefore attests the character and range of Scripture and to that extent Scripture is not self-sufficient. At least to that degree too it is clear "that the Church does not derive from holy Scripture alone the certainty it possesses about all that has been revealed" (*ibid.*, art. 9). In the concrete therefore it can only be a question of whether the apostolic tradition in fact originally contained not only the attestation of the nature and extent of Scripture but some particular propositions which are not found in any way in Scripture, and which were transmitted as binding in faith by purely "oral'tradition". If that is so, revelation (over and above the testimony of tradition to Scripture) comes to us in two "streams" which in content are partly distinct and which are often misleadingly called "sources". To the question framed in these terms the Council of Trent gives no plain answer (*D* 783). At any rate the interpretation of its text is disputed to this day. Vatican II strictly avoided adopting any position on the question. In seeking an objective solution it has to be noted first that an obscure and largely unsolved problem arises about the development of dogma. How exactly are we to conceive the explication of what was implicit in the original revelation?

Only on the assumption that an answer has been found to this question is it possible to attempt to determine *a posteriori* whether or not some particular dogma at the present day which cannot be found explicitly in Scripture may nevertheless be contained there implicitly. Conversely it is possible to say that it is unlikely that something which was defined later as a dogma of the Church should have existed as an explicit proposition in the apostolic age without also being present in Scripture, and that we could prove this historically. Yet this would have to be the case if the appeal to an apostolic tradition materially different from Scripture were to have any meaning and not remain a purely dogmatic postulate. Appeal to a materially distinct apostolic tradition, therefore, solves no concrete problems of the history and development of dogma. In that direction at least, nothing stands in the way of an assertion of the material sufficiency of Scripture, within the limits stated. What is not explicitly or in some way contained in Scripture cannot be historically proved to have been part of the original apostolic kerygma. The definition of a proposition by the magisterium guarantees of course the fact that it is so contained (at least implicitly) but does not dispense the theologian from raising the question how this presence there is to be conceived. It is no easier to find an answer to this question by appealing to oral tradition than to the implications of Scripture.

5. *The Old Testament in the canon of the Church.* The old covenant was part of the context of the Christ-event and was willed by God precisely as such. The primitive Church understood and held fast to the old covenant as its own legitimate pre-history. Consequently the OT scriptures, as an element of that covenant, were willed by God and inspired. While this is true, it must be remembered that in the old covenant there was no authoritative, infallible court of appeal able to determine the canon. It was impossible for there to be one, for such a thing is an eschatological reality and could exist only in and after Christ. Before Christ, therefore, the holy scriptures of the OT were still in process of coming into existence as scriptures in the absolute NT sense (in contradistinction to the vague sense of sacred writings such as is used in comparative religion). This will be clear if we realize that the setting up of Scripture as a definitive *norma normans* plainly marked off from other writings necessarily demands the setting up of a subject who recognizes it for what it is. The OT is only Scripture in the *full* sense to the extent that the new covenant is already present in a hidden way in the old — already there but still hidden (*Dei Verbum,* art. 16). Consequently the writings of the old covenant only "*acquire* and display their full signification in the New Testament" *(ibid.).*

It is important to realize this because it is the basis of the principle of interpreting the OT in the light of Christ (cf. arts. 14–16). Of course that does not mean that the experience of the sacred history of redemption and of the relation between God and man as reflected in the OT is only important for men in the new covenant by its specifically Christological implications. The OT books not only "illuminate and interpret" the Christ-event (art. 16) but are in themselves of permanent validity, despite "much that is imperfect and ephemeral" (art. 15) in them because of the phase of sacred history to which they belong, which is no longer ours. There is an OT theology of the OT scriptures and a NT theology of these writings, just as there is a unity, a difference and a relation between the two covenants. Conversely, it must also be remembered, however, that in the new covenant Jesus Christ himself is what is revealed. Furthermore, in his eschatologically victorious Spirit he turns men's hearts to faith and causes this victory to be made manifest in the Church. Consequently, NT revelation essentially goes beyond the letter of something written. From this point of view, therefore, Scripture is more essential to the old covenant than it is to the new. The NT does not simply continue the scriptures of the old covenant in the same line.

6. *Inerrancy of Scripture.* The inerrancy of Scripture follows from its divine inspiration and authorship and its function as *norma non normata* in the Church and for its infallible magisterium. The latter is not superior to Scripture but serves it (*Dei Verbum,* art. 10). This inerrancy is a dogma of faith, as far as the authentic revealed doctrine of Scripture is concerned (*D* 706f., 1787, 1809, 1950, 2180). But this statement does not answer the more precise question that inerrancy raises. In this respect the best starting-point will be the declaration of the Dogmatic Constitution *Dei Verbum,* art. 11: "It is to be professed that the books of Scripture teach certainly, faithfully and without error the truth that God for our salvation willed to be recorded in the sacred Scriptures." (Cf. on this the references quoted by the Council, *D* 783, *Enchiridion Biblicum,* 121, 124, 126–7, 539.) That statement is certainly not positively intended to bear a restrictive sense and to teach that only truths regarding salvation, in contradistinction to secular truths, are meant. But neither is such a meaning clearly excluded, for it is not clear that the references appended are to be regarded as a binding interpretation of the text. The distinction between salutary truth and secular statements — the latter assumed to be made as absolute affirmations in Scripture — was chiefly current at the time of Modernism, and was rejected in this connection from Leo XIII to Pius XII.

In practice the distinction perhaps leads to a superfluous, unreal dilemma. If it is made, the answer (at least according to Leo XIII and Pius XII) must be that even secular statements of that kind in Scripture cannot be false. But in fact the real question is whether, if the rules of biblical hermeneutics (cf. *Dei Verbum,* arts. 12, 19; *D* 2294; *Enchiridion Biblicum,* 557–62; instruction of the Biblical Commission, "Sancta Mater Ecclesia", *AAS* 56 [1964], p. 715) are applied precisely and strictly, Scripture really contains any purely secular affirmations the correctness of which the sacred writer intends absolutely to guarantee in the sense of a modern historical (and scientific) concept of truth, and the accuracy of which creates a problem for us. If we can deny that this question arises, then the statement of *Dei Verbum,* art. 11, can be taken as affirming only the inerrancy of truths of salvation in Scripture, without thereby coming into real conflict with papal declarations from Leo XIII to Pius XII. In scriptural statements, whether theological or secular in content, we must be slow to assume that there is an error in a proposition which is really affirmed as binding. This can be avoided if note is taken of the following.

a) The *genus litterarium* (*D* 1980, 2302, 2329). What are the precise limits of what the text is intended to affirm, in other words, what is really meant and asserted by the statement? b) The unavoidable blurring of outline which characterizes all human speech and therefore even every true statement. This cannot be described as error. This is evident, e.g., in reports from two sources. c) We must carefully distinguish between mode and content of statement, between what is meant and the pattern of notions which is used but not affirmed (the perspective in which a statement is made and conceptual schemata which are assumed but not subjected to judgment), between personal statement and mere report of current opinions and mere appearances (implicit quotations: *D* 1979, 2090, 2188). d) It must be remembered that an absence of knowledge which is apparent in the mode of statement is not itself a denial of what is not known. Nor does the impossibility of harmonizing two statements on the plane of representative schemata of itself mean that it is impossible for the two statements nevertheless to agree in content. The fact that a statement is made within a certain limited perspective does not mean that it is erroneous.

The dogmatic theologian starts from Scripture's origin as the normative attestation of revelation and formulates the thesis of the inerrancy of Scripture *in globo* on that basis. The exegete starts from the individual writings, their statements and their immediate meaning. He then inquires critically into the correctness of the various statements. In this way there arises a tension, impossible to resolve in every particular case, between the postulates of the dogmatic theologian and the findings of the exegete. This is so particularly because the former determines the meaning of a particular statement on the basis of his general principle, whereas the second determines the meaning and limits of the general principle on the basis of an exegesis of the particular statement. If the dogmatic theologian is clear about his method and its limitations, he cannot forbid the exegete to qualify as inaccurate, in the light of modern demands for truth, certain sentences which are taken by themselves and do not concern any salutary truth. That does not contradict what is really meant by the Church's doctrine of the inerrancy of Scripture. There are such statements in Scripture, and a judgment of that kind cannot be avoided in exegesis, where the individual statement in itself has to be examined as regards its meaning and correctness and not only in regard to what it means in relation to the whole of Scripture and the ultimate *genera litteraria.*

7. *Theologies in the New Testament.* The Church is composed of historically unique, free persons, and their uniqueness (which cannot be reduced to being a mere instance of the universal term "man") shows itself even in their faith. In all ages the Church has been a unity of Churches differing in time, place, culture and theology. This also applies to the Church of the apostolic period. By the very nature of the Church, then, these features must also appear in the NT writings since these are an expression of the Church of that age, and they do not simply contain the simple statement of the original revelation-event. They also embody theological reflection on it. Consequently by the very nature of the Church and of Scripture there must be a variety of theologies in the NT itself. That means that it contains what in the later

history of the Church were called "schools of theology". Now the real nature of these schools does not of course reside in the points where they contradict one another and where one of them at most can be right. It consists in the difference of their general perspectives, of the concepts they employ etc., things which need not necessarily be in flat contradiction, yet which cannot simply be replaced by a higher synthesis.

It is the exegete's right and function to perceive and work out such a plurality of theologies in the NT. Before a biblical theology is possible, he must expound the biblical theologies. From the dogmatic point of view the ultimate unity of these theologies is ensured and guaranteed by the Church's awareness of its faith, which determines the canon and understands Scripture as a unity therein. But that does not mean that the biblical theologian can overlook the plurality of theologies in the NT, nor that he (or the dogmatic theologian) has the task of completely replacing that plurality by raising it into a single higher system. For various reasons, that is impossible, though such a "reduction to unity" is a goal which theology seeks to approach asymptomatically. What the exegete may not do is to assert that in canonical Scripture statements are to be found which contradict one another even when each is correctly interpreted (with due regard for the analogy of faith: *Dei Verbum,* art. 12), so that one or other must be accepted and the other rejected. It is of course possible to conceive of a "canon within the canon" (as a norm which would permit of a certain critical, i.e., more precise interpretation) in the sense in which the Decree on Ecumenism, art. 11, speaks of "basic Christian belief". But a canon of that kind cannot be set up as a norm in opposition to Scripture, to individual elements or to theologies within it, as for example against what has been termed "early Catholicism" in later writings of the NT.

8. *Scripture (biblical theology) and dogmatics.*
a) All tradition is always a unity of divine and human tradition which it is not possible absolutely to separate by reflection. Every stage of the development of dogma and of the history of theology confirms this. Any theological thought examining and appealing to one or other of these particular traditions therefore requires a criterion of what precisely in each can be regarded as *traditio divina* and what can only be held to be *traditio humana.* Especially when clarification is sought about some proposition which may perhaps be definable as a truth of faith, but which had not previously been expressly handed down as such, as well as in other previously controverted questions which are to be elucidated by the magisterium, tradition as it in fact stands does not of itself provide this discrimination. In Scripture, on the other hand, such a mixture of divine and human tradition is not found. It is, if we may use the expression, pure *traditio divina.* And so it can serve as one criterion at least for this distinction within the rest of tradition.

This does not of course mean that such a process of clarificatory discrimination does not require a long time. The application of that criterion is not a mechanical or even a purely logical operation. It is itself history. And Scripture, like all human truth, bears the stamp of history and has an intrinsically temporal character. It employs an already existing terminology which need not necessarily be simply and in every respect the best. It envisages the truth, which it attests, from various points of view and within mental perspectives which are not the only possible ones. Its statements may in many respects be historically conditioned. Scripture expresses a truth which will have a further history, the history of dogma, in fact. But, unlike any other possible or actual literature of the apostolic age, Scripture is a pure expression of divine truth in a human embodiment. In Scripture, knowledge of divine truth has indeed a starting-point which is both divine and human. But it has no starting-point from which a definite human element would have to be eliminated if we were not to miss the truth from the start. That of course can be so when we are dealing with "unpurified" tradition. Consequently, for theology, Scripture is a reality which has to be interpreted in the spirit and under the guidance and guarantee of the Church and its magisterium. Yet such interpretation is not really a criticism of Scripture but of its reader. Even the magisterium which interprets Scripture under the assistance of the Spirit, does not thereby place itself above Scripture but under it (cf. *Dei Verbum,* art. 10); it knows that Scripture brought into existence by the Spirit and read by the Church with the assistance of the Spirit conveys its true meaning. In that way

Scripture remains the *norma non normata* of theology and the Church.

b) This is the basis on which the relation of biblical to dogmatic theology should be viewed. Dogmatic theology cannot avoid engaging in biblical theology. For dogmatic theology is a systematic, deliberate attention to God's revelation in Jesus Christ. It is not merely a theology of conclusions drawn from the principles of faith assumed as premises, as medieval theology theoretically conceived itself to be, though its real practice was quite different. Consequently dogmatic theology must listen most attentively to revelation where the most direct and ultimate source of Christian revelation is to be found, namely in Scripture. Of course dogmatic theology always reads Scripture under the guidance of the magisterium, because it reads Scripture in the Church, and therefore instructed by the Church's present proclamation of the faith.

It follows that theology always reads Scripture with a knowledge which is not simply to be found in that precise form in Scripture. The theologian has always to study his theology on the basis of the Church's present awareness of its faith. And there has been a genuine development of dogma. Nevertheless theology has not simply the task of expounding the present teaching of the faith by the Church's magisterium and of showing it to be justified from Scripture by finding *dicta probantia* for it there. Its own function as dogmatic theology in regard to Scripture goes beyond this process, which is unfortunately too often almost the only one. In the first place, the existing Church itself is always reading Scripture, reading it to the faithful and ordering it to be read. It is, therefore, not the case that *only* what is taught in the Church by councils, encyclicals, catechisms, etc. belongs to the actual teaching of the Church's magisterium. Scripture itself is also what is actually officially proclaimed at all times in the Church. If then the present teaching of the Church is assigned to the dogmatic theologian as the immediate object of his reflection, by that very fact Scripture itself is assigned to him as the immediate object of his endeavours as a dogmatic theologian. Scripture is therefore not merely a *fons remotus,* i.e., the ultimate source to which the dogmatic theologian traces back the Church's teaching. It is his direct concern, because he cannot really totally separate Scripture as a distinct reality and source from the Church's present teaching.

Furthermore, theological concern with God's revelation in the actual teaching of the Church's magisterium, and in the mind of the Church of one's own time, inevitably leads back to Scripture. That is so even where that teaching is not the actual reading of Scripture in the Church of the present. The full understanding of present doctrine demands a perpetual return to the source from which, on its own admission, this doctrine is derived. There has to be a return to the doctrine which the Church's teaching itself is intended to expound and actualize here and now. In other words, there has to be recourse to Scripture (cf. on this *Optatam totius,* art. 16). Biblical theology is therefore an intrinsic element in dogmatic theology itself. And it is so not merely as one element side by side with other elements of "historical theology". It is an absolutely pre-eminent and unique part of dogmatic theology itself. This does not mean of course that biblical theology should not for various reasons establish itself as an independent branch of study within theology as a whole. That is quite appropriate, even on practical grounds. In practice it is only in the rarest cases that the dogmatic theologian himself can be a professionally qualified exegete, as he would have to be if he were to try to do his biblical theology for himself. The pre-eminent position which belongs to biblical theology within dogmatics, in comparison with its other concerns (patristic theology, medieval scholasticism, modern scholastic theology) is therefore better provided for, if biblical theology is not pursued solely as part of dogmatics. Perhaps in the course of the reform of ecclesiastical studies, a separate specialist department will be formed in which biblical theology will be pursued neither as a mere prolongation of ordinary exegesis nor as a mere element in dogmatic theology, but as a separate branch of study which will represent the correct intermediary between exegesis and dogmatic theology.

9. *Scripture, spiritual life and pastoral work.* a) As regards "holy Scripture in the life of the Church", we may simply refer here for the sake of brevity to Vatican II, *Dei Verbum,* chapter vi (arts. 21–25). To this should be added what is said in arts. 7, 24, 51, 56, 92

of the Constitution on the Liturgy, in *Optatam totius,* art. 16, in the Decree on Ecumenism, art. 21, and in *Presbyterium ordinis,* art. 13. Nothing needs to be added here to these urgent admonitions that Scripture should be read by all Christians, that they should live by it, that it should be made the living principle of theology, given its right place in the liturgy and employed as the starting-point of ecumenical theology.

b) These conciliar admonitions are now probably the most imperative prescription for the life and work of the Catholic Church, because Scripture still to a large extent does not occupy its rightful place in the Church. There is, however, also the danger of a false biblicism which also has to be avoided. The scriptural homily must be cultivated more than it usually is. But it would be a mistake to neglect sermons devoted to a particular subject. Christians have the right and need to receive instruction on many questions connected with their present situation which can only be given in very general terms, if at all, in a biblical homily. The mental world of the present time is so remote in the history of ideas from the world of the Scriptures that the average Christian of today cannot usually find his own way from Scripture to the circumstances in which his own life is set. Often the preacher himself will have to find this way. He will have to preach in a way which proclaims the gospel as it has already been actualized in the Church's present consciousness of its faith.

BIBLIOGRAPHY. O. Cullmann, *Die Tradition als exegetisches, historisches und theologisches Problem* (1954); K. Rahner, "The Development of Dogma", *Theological Investigations,* I (1961), pp. 39–77; G. Ebeling, *Word and Faith* (1963); K. Rahner, *Inspiration in the Bible,* Quaestiones Disputatae 1 (2nd rev. ed., 1964); H. Vorgrimler, ed., *Dogmatic versus Biblical Theology* (1964); L. A. Schökel, *The Inspired Word. Scripture in the Light of Language and Literature* (1965); W. Kasper, *Dogma unter dem Wort Gottes* (1965); J. R. Geiselmann, *The Meaning of Tradition,* Quaestiones Disputatae 15 (1966); W. Marxsen, *Das Neue Testament als Buch der Kirche* (1966); Y. Congar, *Tradition and Traditions,* I (1966); K. Rahner, "Considerations on the Development of Dogma", *Theological Investigations,* IV (1966), pp. 3–35; id., "Theology in the New Testament", *Theological Investigations,* V (1966), pp. 23–41; K. Rahner and J. Ratzinger, *Revelation and Tradition,* Quaestiones Disputatae 17 (1966); H. Schlier, *The Relevance of the New Testament* (1968).

Karl Rahner

II. Versions

A. GENERAL

This article will not offer a detailed survey of the main translations of the Bible, for which the reader is referred to the biblical dictionaries (see also bibliography). The aim will rather be to note the more or less theological problems to which translation has given rise in history.

1. *Historical survey.* Translation of the Bible began in the OT period, in the 3rd century B.C., when Hebrew had been replaced by Aramaic as the usual language of popular intercourse. Since the religious and national consciousness of the Jews was centred on their sacred Scriptures, it was vitally necessary to have these in the language of daily life. The first versions were the Aramaic Targums (at first only oral paraphrases), following the readings of the Hebrew in the synagogues. A more consistent effort was the Greek translation made in the diaspora for the benefit of Hellenistic Jews (the Septuagint). This was the Bible of the young Christian Church, and other Jewish translations (Aquila, Symmachus, Theodotion) were produced in reaction to the use of the Septuagint by Christians. Latin translations appeared from about A.D. 200 on, the Old Latin being a translation of the Septuagint while the Vulgate of St. Jerome was translated from the original Hebrew.

The NT was also translated at an early date, though at first the original Greek could be understood throughout almost the whole of the Roman empire. But before the end of the 2nd century, a harmony of the gospels appeared in Syriac in the *Diatessaron* of Tatian, while other Syriac translations followed (Old Syriac, 2nd or 3rd century, Peshitta, etc., 5th to 7th century). Other translations include Coptic (3rd to 6th century), Gothic (4th century), Armenian (4th or 5th century), Georgian (5th century) and Ethiopic (6th century). Thus there was no question of the NT being the reserve of the educated or the priestly class, nor was it kept behind the barriers of a purely religious or liturgical language. Nonetheless, the development of the various vernaculars always left the original translations — the received or authentic Church books — in a remote and somewhat artificial position. The Old Church Slavonic, for instance, soon became as unintelligible to the Slavs as Latin to the West.

Till the beginnings of modern times, in spite of many complete or partial translations into English, French, German and other languages, the message of the Bible was mediated to the people through the preaching of the Church. The advent of vernacular translations — which of course could only become "popular" with the invention of printing and the spread of literacy — was both a tendentious effort to eliminate the mediatory function of the Church in general as well as the positive desire to have the word of God in a language "understood of the people". The connection between vernacular translation and immediate access to the word of God was to some extent accidental, and kerygmatic and liturgical motives also played their part. Nonetheless, on the whole translation was a symptom of the trend towards individualistic emancipation which marked the coming of modern times. Thus the great watershed in Germany was marked by Martin Luther's translation — a work enhanced by the warmth, vigour and general accuracy of the language. So too the French of Jacobus Faber (Lefèvre d'Etaples) in 1528 was not wholly inspired by orthodox motives. It cannot be said, however, that the Italian of Nicola Malermi (1471), the Spanish Bible of Valencia (by Boniface Ferrer in 1478), the Dutch Bible of Delft (1477) and of Cologne (1478) were in any sense polemical. But the English versions from Tyndale and Coverdale on (1525 to 1535) were "reforming" works, copiously buttressed by tendentious notes, which had their Catholic counterparts in the Reims NT of 1582 and the Douai OT of 1609.

2. *Texts.* As the Renaissance developed a sense for textual criticism (of which earlier times were not unaware, as the 13th century *Biblia Parisiensis* and the numerous subsequent *correctoria* of the Vulgate show) and provided better tools, demands for more accurate texts and versions grew. The Protestant NT suffered for centuries from the influence of the Greek *Textus Receptus,* supposedly more "original" than the Latin Vulgate, but actually based on a few late manuscripts only, of the Byzantine or conflational type. A glance, for instance, at the version of the Lord's Prayer in Lk 11 in the Authorized Version shows that the English Catholic version, in spite of being based on the Vulgate, has here, as in many other places, a superior text from the scientific point of view (since St. Jerome had followed some of the best of the most ancient Greek manuscripts). More modern translations such as the English Revised Version of 1881–85, and the innumerable translations into other modern languages have always sought the best Hebrew and Greek texts available, with the result that no more than nuances remain as a rule between the various translations. Thus the (American) Revised Standard Version (NT 1946, OT 1952) could be published in a Catholic edition in 1966 with little difficulty and negligible textual changes. The "authenticity" of the Vulgate as decreed by the Council of Trent (*D* 1506) referred to the choice among Latin texts, and to its authority in matters of faith and morals, especially in public debates. Its authenticity was not "critical" but "juridical" (cf. the encyclical *Divino Afflante, D* 2292). Hence the closer attention in modern times to the original texts is a break not with dogmatic but at most with scholarly tradition in the Catholic Church.

3. *Problems.* In so far as Christianity is a "religion of the book", difficulties necessarily arise from the double effort required in reading the Bible. First, it must always be read in the light of the particular historical occasions or practices for the sake of which the various elements were incorporated in the course of centuries, that is, with an eye to the *Sitz im Leben* throughout. But secondly, it has to be read and translated in such a way that it can form the basis of the living faith of the Church in each day and age. This tension can perhaps be best exemplified from the original Greek of the NT itself, which was basically a rendering of a Semitic world of thought. It should be obvious that the NT writers on the whole were more intent on the first way of reading — the preservation of the original thought-forms and expressions — than in "popularizing" in the everyday language of the readers. No doubt everyone could read Greek. But the Greek of the NT, in spite of its being Koine, the common Greek of Hellenistic times, was still strongly "Semitizing", often merely transliterating, so to speak, a religious idiom (e.g., that of the Septuagint or of rabbinical Judaism) unfamiliar and enigmatic to the Greek world.

On a minor and comparatively indifferent level, we can see the contrast between the NT and the ordinary Greek by comparing the first paragraph of Luke's gospel with the remainder. The prologue is in normal literary Greek, but the gospel proper begins with an "It came to pass" which sets the key-note for a persistently Semitizing or Septuagint style. On a more challenging level, there are such phrases as the "kingdom of heaven", or even "kingdom of God", especially in the introduction to parables ("the kingdom of God is like . . .") which are simple reminders of how much translation — in the second sense of the word, mentioned above — the NT itself required of its first readers. Modern readers in general are so habituated to biblical expressions that they fail to realize how far they would have been from ordinary language. But Origen felt compelled to apologize to his Greek readers for the simple "man of iniquity", which was actually uncouth in Greek.

The language of religion and liturgy always tends to be "hieratic" and static, out of a certain sense of awe before a "sacred" text, and by reason of its intrinsically "traditional" nature — inevitable above all in Christianity, because it is a historical religion, where the "horizontal" component can never be ignored. This brings with it a certain tension between the language of religion and of life. This is not always happily resolved by stressing the "horizontal" component, as when "biblical" terms are retained to the exclusion of, say, "scholastic" terms in theology and preaching. When, for instance, certain schools try to confine language about the after-life to such terms as "being made conformable to Christ", they are taking a biblical term but stripping it of the field of reference and connotations which it had in the minds of the original writers and readers. Whatever be the hermeneutical justification of such a procedure, the problem of translation strictly speaking is hardly solved. The history of Bible translations mostly represents an effort to make a unique, remote and unrepeatable past live again in the language of different ages.

The Jewish paraphrases in the Targums were a laudable hermeneutic effort, though scientifically unsatisfactory because of the freedom with which the original text was handled, and because of the uncritical importation of the theological preoccupations of each era into the sprawling paraphrase. The Septuagint, much closer verbally to the original, reveals at once the immense difficulties of Bible translations. It deliberately adapted itself to the thought-forms of "middle-brow" Hellenistic philosophy, avoiding for instance anthropomorphisms where this could be easily done, and substituting Kyrios, as being readily understood by Greeks, for the divine name Yahweh. Thus the effort to find Greek equivalents for Hebrew thought often led to the substitution of vaguely analogous expressions. But the Targums and the Septuagint are simply basic instances of the problem of translation, which becomes more acute when it is done into Asian or African languages with their own peculiar heritages of symbolism and connotations.

Modern translations are generally based on the principle that paraphrases should be relegated to footnotes, while the text should render the original as literally as possible (within the true idiom of the language in question at a given date). E. Dhorme says in his introduction to the French OT in the *Bibliothèque de la Pléiade* that the first concern of the translator must be faithfulness not only to the thought but to the expression of the original. This principle has the advantage of a certain "objectivity", which many find desirable for the wrong reasons, such as that of "verbal inspiration". This type of translation throws much of the burden on the reader — as did, however, the NT writers themselves — and sometimes retains an aura of "sacred language" remote from ordinary life. It is sometimes criticized for reducing the Bible to the status of historical documents of the past. This objection means simply that such translations do not make the Bible "live", in the sense of addressing directly the reader of the day. On the other hand, since Christianity is a "historical" religion, the constant reminder that it is rooted in past times and places and thought-forms can only be stimulating and salutary. The objective method may encourage a certain fundamentalism or biblicism, but it can never be superseded.

It has been said that such translations as that of Luther or the Authorized Version succeeded in making the language of their day an adequate and popular vehicle of biblical thought. But this is only partly true, because Luther was to some extent crystallizing and standardizing the modern German language — almost creating as he went, though moulding popular speech. So too the Authorized Version rather imposed than reflected a language. The great competitors of the "objective" translation, such as the versions in "modern English", are of quite a different calibre. They deliberately substitute conventional modern phraseology for biblical expressions and even images, basing themselves sometimes on the mistaken principle that the NT was written in the popular speech of the day, but more fundamentally and correctly on the "kerygmatic" or directly communicative character of the NT message.

Such modernizing translations have been immensely popular, which is, however, a testimony to the wide interest in the Bible rather than to the technical achievements of the translators. This is clear from the success of the Knox version, written in a supposedly "timeless" English, which is, however, a highly questionable concept — saved only by the constant brilliance of the execution. The technical difficulty of the "living" translations is to produce a text which is suitable for liturgical, scientific and private reading. And then, above all, translators are working in a medium — modern popular speech — which is so fluid that the relevance to "life in the concrete" is speedily lost. Further, modern widely-spoken languages are so diversified in idiom that classes and professions tend to have almost specialist languages of their own. The effect of this multiplicity of idioms is that "foreign" idioms are assimilated by a process of emptying them of their distinctive content and blurring their contours. It is sometimes said that modern popular speech is "degenerate", but such judgments are often based on sophisticated "literary" standards. What is true is that popular speech tends to smooth out all awkwardness and to reduce all language to a uniform vapidity. A simple instance may be seen in the use of the word "dedicated" in the New English Bible to translate "holy" or "saints". Such is the attraction of the mass-media and handy jargon that people are now familiar with the notion of "dedicated" — but as applied to actors, writers, explorers or even jockeys. The sense intended by the translators is

buried among the modern connotations, with their tendency to level out the sublime and the trenchant — all the more so, since modern language, being the reflection of a mostly "secularized" world, has practically eliminated such concepts as "holiness" from its world of ideas.

There are no rules to be laid down for translation, since it must always be a vital struggle with language, which has a life and history of its own. Translators of the Bible can only be warned against the archaic if they tend to be "objective", against the paltry and inadequate if they seek to modernize. But translations which pretend to smooth away all difficulties and dispense from study do a disservice to the message and to the (underestimated) reader. Ancient translations like the Targums and the Septuagint performed a hermeneutical task as well. The other ancient translations left their readers with the same problems which the NT writers posed. Modernizing translations, in their search for the clear and topical, have often tended to rob language of its history — to present the Bible as if it had been written for the first time in the present day. The fault does not lie with the effort, which is laudable, but with the lack of appreciation of the "historical" character of the writings and the wish to simplify what should be a challenging and rewarding study. As an ancient Eastern book, the Bible can only be read — in literal or periphrastic translation — in the context of historical scholarship. And as the book of revelation, and therefore permanently relevant, the translation can only be "living" when to the efforts of scholarship is added the correct orientation to the historical present moment. But this is no doubt rather the task of the preaching Church, which can never wholly surrender its books even to the scholar-poet, where such masters of language are available. The simplest fundamental statement of the NT, "Jesus is Lord" (which would probably appear in an equivalent form in all cultured languages) needs a further translation, both intellectually and kerygmatically — to render the sense and convey the summons — which is ultimately the function of the authorized preachers of the gospel. Thus the permanent problem of translation can only be solved from day to day as the books are returned by scholars to the preaching Church, and the studious reader.

B. ENGLISH VERSIONS

Some general remarks on the principles of translation with regard to English versions have already had to be made in the general article (above) on Bible versions. The present article treats the history of English translation in more detail.

After the Anglo-Saxon interlinear glosses on the gospels and the psalms, and a number of metrical paraphrases of single books, the first complete translation appeared at the end of the 14th century, mostly the work of Nicholas of Hereford (d. 1420). A revision of this, known as "Purvey's Version", was published probably before 1408. Both were made from the Vulgate, to which they adhered so closely that at times they must have been almost unintelligible. Though they came from circles influenced by Wycliffe, and were often attributed to him, there is no proof that Wycliffe was a translator. Though many MSS circulated, the "Wycliffe" Bible was not printed till 1731.

W. Tyndale's NT (1526, frequently revised by the author) and Pentateuch (1530) were based on the original texts as then available. Much of it was taken over by the later "Authorized Version". M. Coverdale's Bible appeared in 1535, complete, but owing much to Tyndale and to M. Luther's version. This was revised in 1537 ("Matthew's Bible") and 1539 (the "Great Bible" — after its format — and "Taverner's Bible"). The "Geneva Bible", printed abroad in the reign of Mary, continued to use Tyndale and the Great Bible, but contained many new renderings from continental influences, and copious annotations of Calvinistic trend (1560). The "Bishops' Bible" (1568) again built on the previous works. Thus there was a general continuity in the work of the English Reformers, which was to be crowned by the Authorized Version of 1611 (known as the "King James's Version" in U.S.A.). This, though the work of a committee of fifty scholars, was in a sonorous prose of which the key-note was Tyndale's style, and has generally been regarded as one of the great monuments of English literature. The translators consulted all earlier versions, with special attention to the Catholic NT of Reims, and excluded terms which had been used tendentiously in older translations, such as "congregation" for "Church" and "washing" for "baptism". It also omitted the marginal notes which had been used for special theological purposes.

Some years earlier, in 1582, a Catholic version of the NT had been published at Reims, the main authors being G. Martin and R. Bristow. This was followed in 1610 by the OT, at Douai. The text followed was the Latin Vulgate, though the Greek was consulted for the NT. Even more than the Protestant versions, it followed very closely the structure and expressions of the text before the authors, sometimes choosing very literal and obscure renderings, such as "loaves of proposition", and making no concession to the difficulties of the language, even in the Psalms, where the text was that of Jerome's first version, based not on the Hebrew, but on the often unintelligible Old Latin which was itself based on the rather exotic Septuagint version. The Douai version was revised 1750 under Bishop Challoner, but without notable changes, so that the OT remained especially difficult to read.

The Protestant Revised Version of 1881 (NT) and 1885 (OT) was conservative in its terms of reference: "to introduce as few alterations as possible . . . consistently with faithfulness" — and "to limit, as far as possible, the expression of such alterations to the language of the Authorized and earlier English versions". It never became really popular, though it contained great improvements in the line of textual criticism, the NT *Textus Receptus* being abandoned in favour of better ancient texts. An American Revised Version was published in 1901, the "American Standard Version", which was replaced by the Revised Standard Version in 1946 (NT) and 1952 (OT). This was so clear, accurate and traditional in diction that it was taken over, with a few slight changes authorized by the Standard Bible Committee, as a Catholic version, with ecclesiastical approval, in 1966. (The only change worth mentioning in the text is that the Catholic edition retains the traditional "full of grace", Lk 1:28, instead of "O favoured one".) With this ecumenical achievement, interest in other modern Catholic efforts at "objective" translation has died down, such as the American "Confraternity Version" (NT 1945) and the English "Westminster Version" (NT 1935, OT unfinished). The version of R. Knox, however, from the Vulgate with reference to the Greek and Hebrew (NT 1945, OT 1949) continues to have a wide and well-merited appeal, even outside the Catholic Church, on account of its readable and dignified style.

Such English translations have left the Bible more or less in its "historical" form, rather close to Hebrew or NT idioms and avoiding only the archaic, but without really modernizing. Many other efforts have been made, however, to make the Bible speak more decidedly in the language of the present day. Of these the most notable have been the translations of J. Moffatt (NT 1913; OT 1924; the whole Bible, revised, 1935); J. Philips ("The NT in Modern English", 1958–61) and the "Jerusalem Bible", edited by A. Jones, a Catholic production which made use of the French Catholic *Bible de Jérusalem,* especially for the quite full notes and introductions to the various books. The translation itself, though considering throughout the French version, was made from the original texts, and attains a remarkable degree of vigour and readability. The "New English Bible", sponsored by all the Churches of the British Isles, except the Roman Catholic, published its NT in 1961; work on the OT continues.

The NT of the New English Bible in particular met with an almost startling success. It is almost in the nature of a paraphrase, which makes for clearness and readability, but then suffers from the defect that an obscurity in the original is removed by coming down on the side of one possible meaning, to the exclusion of the more probable, as at Jn 1:4, "darkness has never quenched it (the light)" (for "grasped", i.e., "accepted"). At times, as has been mentioned above (see Versions, General), Semitic ideograms have been translated, e.g., Mk 14:62, "You will see the Son of man seated at the right hand of God" (Greek: "of the Power", a Semitism); but this has not been done consistently, as the same verse shows, since it retains the at least equally enigmatic "Son of man". While offering a built-in commentary, as it were, which is helpful and attractive especially in the Pauline literature, the New English Bible does not perhaps signal well enough the intrinsic problems of the text for which the reader should go to commentaries as such. As has been already noted on the versions in general, it also suffers from the general tendency of the popularized versions to take the sting out of strange terms. Two more instances may suffice. Lk 1:27 reads:

"The angel Gabriel was sent with a message to a girl" (Greek: "virgin"); Jn 2:4, "Your concern, mother, it not mine" (Greek: "What is that to you or to me, woman?").

Translations should not conceal problems, but stimulate study. The general tendency of modernizing translations is to make reading easy. This is not necessarily the best way to communicate the message. But so far, no real effort has been made to "translate" such history-laden terms as "Lamb of God" etc., and rightly so, since the sacred books are of an age, though they are for all time.

BIBLIOGRAPHY. A. Deissmann, *Die Hellenisierung des semitischen Monotheismus.* Neues Jahrbuch für das Klassische Altertum 1 (1908); E. Hirsch, *Luthers deutsche Bibel* (1928); P. A. Sims, *The Bible in America* (1936); R. Knox, *On Englishing the Bible* (1949); H. G. May, *Our English Bible in the Making* (1952); H. Pope, *English Versions of the Bible* (1952); W. Schwarz, *Principles and Problems of Bible Translating* (1955); R. Knox, *On English Translations* (1957); F. F. Bruce, *The English Bible. A History of Translations* (1961).

Kevin Smyth

III. Biblical Hermeneutics

Hermeneutics (ἑρμηνευτική sc. τέχνη, the art of interpretation) is to be distinguished from exegesis, which is the actual process of interpretation. In the technical sense, biblical hermeneutics is the investigation and determination of the rules and principles which guide the interpretation of Scripture. It is the theory or method of scriptural interpretation.

1. *History.* The effort to work out hermeneutical principles was begun in the ancient Church by Origen.

It received new impulses from the Reformation, the rationalism of the Enlightenment and the progress of modern science and historical research. A new approach was opened up by Schleiermacher, who defined hermeneutics as the art of understanding. Then, in the present century, as existential philosophy pointed out how deeply the hermeneutical question was rooted in human life itself, R. Bultmann took it up in a much more radical way than had hitherto been attempted. Catholic hermeneutics received strong impulses from the great biblical encyclicals of Leo XIII, Benedict XV and especially Pius XII (1943: *Divino Afflante*), which opened up perspectives which were only fully exploited by the most recent exegesis. The widespread tendency to restrict the principles of interpretation given by *Divino Afflante* to the OT was countered in 1964 by the "Instruction on the Historical Truth of the Gospels" published by the Pontifical Biblical Commission, as also, in general, by the Dogmatic Constitution of Vatican II on Divine Revelation (*Dei Verbum*). Ch. 2 of the Constitution proposed a very significant re-assessment of the truth of Scripture. "The books of Scripture must be acknowledged as teaching firmly, faithfully, and without error that truth which God wanted put into the sacred writings for the sake of our salvation" (art. 11). In the next article the most important hermeneutical principles are discussed at length. The Constitution should inspire Catholics to new efforts, especially as it emphasizes that scientific research prepares and helps the Church to form its mature judgment (art. 12). This verdict on the relationship of exegesis and magisterium acknowledges implicitly that it is of fundamental importance to work out a hermeneutics which will do full justice to Scripture.

2. *Possibility and necessity of biblical hermeneutics.* The fact that Scripture can and must be interpreted implies biblical hermeneutics. According to *Dei Verbum,* God has spoken through men in Scripture in a human way, and these men, under the influence of inspiration, still functioned as real authors (*veri auctores,* art. 11; earlier official documents had merely called them — cautiously — *auctores instrumentales*). It follows that the writings in the two Testaments are products of human language in the full sense of the term. It was through human language that God said what he wished to say, and hence the meaning intended by God is that which is given in human words. Since Scripture is truly human utterance, since the words of Scripture are uttered by men undergoing the historical process, its thought and language are necessarily linked with the date, place and mentality of the authors. This quality of Scripture, that it is human words, brings with it, as for all the products of human language, the possibility of following its thought, since its expression in language is not intrinsically obscure, being aimed at communication, intelligibility. It also brings with it the task, that is, the necessity of interpretation.

3. *General hermeneutical approaches.* Among the ordinary tools of hermeneutics is the reconstruction of the original text as far as this is possible (textual criticism). Then there is the study of biblical languages and concepts, in general and with attention to linguistic and stylistic peculiarities in given periods, authors or works. Studies must also include archaeology, topography, ethnography, comparative religion and in general the developing cultures and history of the surrounding nations, with reference to the two Testaments and to the individual books. Another task is to find out all that is possible about the author of a given work, his background, state of life and culture, the situation which his work envisages.

4. *Basic hermeneutical principles.* The fundamentals are determined by the double claim of the Bible, to be word of God and word of man. Since the word of God is met with in the Bible as human speech, we must first enunciate the principles which are valid even when we prescind from the claim of Scripture to be the word of God, and then the principles which result from this claim.

a) *General principles.* "Since God speaks in sacred Scripture through men in human fashion, the interpreter of sacred Scripture, in order to see clearly what God wanted to communicate to us, should carefully investigate what meaning the sacred writer really intended, and what God wanted to manifest by means of their words." This statement of the Constitution on Revelation (art. 12) recognizes the assertion which the sacred writer intended to make as the real and literal sense (which does not necessarily coincide with the superficial meaning of the words). It lays down as the fundamental and general principle of biblical hermeneutics the precise investigation of the intention of the text in each case. To find out the intention of the assertion three main instruments are to be used. The first is the consideration of the fact that the mode of expression is determined by the thought and language of the general environment. Here, for instance, the peculiarites of Semitic, Hellenistic and Judaeo-Hellenistic thought and expression must be taken into account. Then there is the investigation of the *genus literarium*. The Council explains here that "truth is proposed and expressed in a variety of ways, depending on whether a text is history of one kind or another *(in textibus vario modo historicis)*, or whether its form is that of prophecy, poetry or some other type of speech" (art. 12). This leaves open the number of literary forms that have been or may be determined, and also notes the variability of the concept of "history". Finally, there is the investigation of the milieu in which and for which the writer composed his work. Over and above these three approaches, we must note the procedure known as the "hermeneutical circle". This means that a general picture is built up from the clearer and more easily intelligible statements, and this result is used in turn to throw light on what is uncertain and difficult. This process may be used with regard to individual writings, groups of writings and for the Bible as a whole.

b) *Theological principles.* In the light of the Church's teaching that the writings of the Old and New Testaments are the "word of God" by virtue of inspiration, the normative testimony to the divine revelation which was brought to its completion in and by Jesus, three principles of hermeneutics are ordinarily accepted. They are also mentioned expressly in the constitution *Dei Verbum*, art. 12. The first is the living tradition of the Church universal. The second is the reading of Scripture as a unified whole. The third is the analogy of faith. The validity of the living tradition of the universal Church as a rule of interpretation is at once established by the fact that all the books of the NT were produced within the Church in the service of its actual preaching. Further, the definitive fixing of the canon of the Old and New Testaments, as a *norma non normanda,* is also a function of this living Church, in which, as the NT asserts, the glorified Christ is at work through the Holy Spirit as the agent of the self-disclosure of God. However, the positive heuristic contribution of the living tradition of the Church universal is not to be overestimated or overtaxed. The "unity of Scripture" means that an individual text or work may be explained by the whole biblical context. This is primarily a matter of comparing parallel texts, especially in later books. The "analogy of faith" means that a text is explained by means of the inner harmony of the whole revelation proposed by the Church. When these two means are invoked in interpretation, care must be taken with regard to

individual texts that forced comparisons are not made, apart from the legitimate use of the proximate or remote context. To avoid mistakes in this matter, attention must also be paid to the stage of revelation to which a particular text belongs (see *Enchiridion Biblicum,* 109).

Scripture is the message of the God of the covenant, the testimony to his will to save and sanctify as revealed definitively in Christ. And understanding and decision go hand in hand in the historicity of human existence. It follows that interpretation can only reach its real goal when the greatest possible mastery of historical method is accompanied by a basically existential and personal attitude on the part of the exegete. He must be ready to be a "disciple" as well as a "historian" (L. Bakker), seeing the works and words of God attested in Scripture as having "historical" significance, as an event which impinges on himself, bringing promise and fulfilment, grace and judgment. It is only when the exegete confronts Scripture in this "connaturality" of mind that the supreme demands of biblical hermeneutics can be met.

5. *A consistent hermeneutical principle.* The debate on demythologizing has brought into the forefront of discussion the meaning of "faith" in the Bible, especially the NT, as well as the concomitant question of "precomprehension" (that is, of the philosophical framework within which the Bible is read). As is now generally recognized, there is no such thing as an absolutely unprejudiced interrogation of historical texts. Even the present-day exponent starts from a concrete historical situation and brings with him his own instinctive and acquired pre-comprehension, philosophical or theological. His subjectivity is of a certain order, and this it is which inspires his interrogation of the sources and his effort to gain a comprehensive understanding of the phenomena attested in the Bible. If by pre-comprehension (or prejudice) we mean some general or particular "sketch-plan" which the exegete brings with him, certain previously settled opinions or judgments, then he must be ready to have them called in question, tested or corrected by the texts, in so far as these provide surer or at least better justified solutions. But apart from such cases, it must be admitted, as is maintained in particular by R. Bultmann,

"that every interpretation is inspired by some pre-comprehension of the matter in question", that is, by "the previous vital relationship to the matter" treated in the text, a relationship which alone makes understanding of it possible (*Glauben und Verstehen,* II, p. 227). Bultmann is also right in saying that the pre-comprehension necessary for the understanding of Scripture is implicit in the quest for God which is the mainspring of all human life, and which can take on various forms, such as the question of happiness, of the meaning of the world and history, of deliverance from death, of security amid the vicissitudes of destiny, of the purpose and object of each individual life. Finally, he is also correct in saying that it is a legitimate hermeneutical question to ask what is the understanding of human existence and its fulfilment which is expressed in the NT's message about Christ, that is, that Scripture is to be interpreted existentially.

That men should acknowledge and lay hold of revelation as the fulfilment through grace of their deepest yearnings, would undoubtedly be in keeping with the supreme goal of Scriptural interpretation as propounded above. Misgivings only arise with the hermeneutical demand that this "mythologically" couched message about Christ can only be appropriately interrogated in terms of an understanding of reality and of self possible to modern man, whose understanding of existence is supposed to be currently determined by the natural sciences. Nevertheless, we still await the solution of the problem posed by the varying explicitations of the Christian revelation adduced in the NT, which are far from being co-ordinated into a system. Can a hermeneutical principle be found which will enable us to grasp the exact import of the various biblical assertions, conditioned as they are by the notions and modes of expression current in their times, and also by the pastoral exigencies of their situation? One of the happy results of the recent discussion has been to bring out the hermeneutical value of the exact meaning of divine revelation, action and speaking, that is, how the self-communication of God can take place and has in fact taken place.

6. *The hermeneutical problem of the Old Testament.* Two elements have contributed to enliven the discussion here. One was the general desire to evaluate the theological relevance of a historical criticism which was accepted in principle as a method of exegesis. The other was the hermeneutical postulate put forward by R. Bultmann, that the OT history of the Jews was prophecy precisely "in its inner contradiction, in its failure". The main question is the relationship of the Old and New Testament, the legitimacy of a Christian pre-comprehension in the hermeneutics of the OT. If we prescind from the extreme position which reduces both Testaments to the one level, there are two main tendencies among Protestants. One emphasizes the difference between the Testaments and hence affirms that the OT is to be read on its own terms, without any appeal to the gospel for the justification of its self-understanding. It is thus that it is a force which impinges on our existence and which must be integrated into our understanding of the gospel (so P. Baumgärtel). The other view is based on the notion of the unity of the biblical testimony. The action of the OT has a "prefigurative" significance, which allows of a "typological" explanation, applied with moderation and with many different nuances (cf. G. von Rad; W. Eichrodt; J. Barr). The hermeneutical justification varies from text to text, and sometimes the procedure is understood as not coming under strict hermeneutical rules.

Modern Catholic exegesis also seems to find the conflict between "historical" and "Christian" interpretation "the most exciting hermeneutical problem of the Old Testament" (N. Lohfink). There is general agreement that both are necessary. "We have to give a historical interpretation, because intellectual honesty demands that we investigate the original meaning. We have to give a Christian interpretation, because the Bible speaks to us as the word of God." (N. Lohfink, p. 105.) The most common attempt to reach a synthesis makes use of the *sensus plenior,* by virtue of which the literal sense also contains a fullness of meaning intended by God which goes beyond that which was recognized and willed by the sacred writer, or which was at best only vaguely guessed at by him. The full sense is defended, for instance, by D. de Ambrogi, R. E. Brown, P. Benoît, P. Grelot, and rejected by such authors as R. Bierberg, G. Courtade, J. Schmid and B. Vawter. Even where the existence of the full sense is admitted on principle, the great problem remains as to what justifiable and practical hermeneutical criteria can be used to extract the full sense from any particular text. There is also the difficulty that the ancient methods of exegesis used by the NT writers and their explanation of individual texts, sometimes as mere illustrations, sometimes as prophetical proofs of the Christian message, are often in conflict with the obvious demands of historical exegesis. And it is impossible to show that the OT quotations or scriptural proofs in the NT in general are in harmony with the literal sense of the OT texts, as established by historical scholarship. It is true that there are many quotations where "the meaning intended by the OT writer, or at least by God, is already in line with the *sensus plenior* of the words in the Christian sense" (J. Schmid, p. 173). But there are many cases where the NT writer attributes to OT texts a different meaning from that intended by the OT writers, and sometimes even the opposite meaning. In such cases there is no direct link with the literal sense. Efforts have been made to reach a synthesis of historical and Christian interpretation which will exclude arbitrary judgments. B. H. Gross, for instance, speaks of "correspondence on a higher plane as the structural principle of biblical promise and fulfilment". N. Lohfink calls for a Christian interpretation which makes use of the complete history of tradition, including the interpretation given by the NT. In any case, once it has been emphasized that the coming of revelation and the scriptural attestation are intrinsically ordained to Christ, the genuinely historical character of revelation in general and of that which began in Jesus in particular must be borne in mind. And we must avoid the untenable notion that the person, way and work of the eschatological redeemer can be seen as the simple, straightforward execution of a programme outlined in the OT, or at least to be deduced from its data or a combination of them. The question of a valid and consistent principle of interpretation for the Old and New Testaments, and for the canon as a whole, still needs further investigation.

See also *Hermeneutics, Existence* II, *Form Criticism, Analogy of Faith, Scripture and Tradition, Canon of Scripture, Demythologization.*

BIBLIOGRAPHY. E. Fuchs, *Hermeneutik* (1954; 3rd ed., 1963); G. Ebeling, "Hermeneutik", *RGG,* III (1959), cols. 242–62; J. Schmid, "Die alttestamentlichen Zitate bei Paulus und die Theorie vom *sensus plenior*", *Biblische Zeitschrift* 3 (1959), pp. 3–17; C. Westermann, ed., *Probleme alttestamentlicher Hermeneutik* (1960); J. Barr, *The Semantics of Biblical Language* (1961); R. Bultmann, *Glauben und Verstehen,* 4 vols. (1961–65); K. Frör, *Biblische Hermeneutik* (1961; 2nd ed., 1964); E. Castelli, ed., *Herméneutique et Tradition* (1963); M. Robinson and J. B. Cobb, eds., *The New Hermeneutic* (1963); R. Marlé, *Le problème théologique de l'Herméneutique* (1963); A. Fitzmeyer, "The Biblical Commission's Instruction on the Historical Truth of the Gospels", *Theological Studies* 25 (1964), pp. 386–408; H. Vorgrimler, ed., *Dogmatic versus Biblical Theology* (1964); N. Lohfink, "Die historische und die christliche Auslegung des Alten Testaments", *Stimmen der Zeit* 178 (1966), pp. 98–112; J. Barr, *Old and New in Interpretation. A Study of the Two Testaments* (1966); H. Schlier, *The Relevance of the New Testament* (1968).

Anton Vögtle

IV. Scripture Reading

In the tradition of the New Testament as of the Old, Scripture reading made an important contribution to the knowledge and vitality of faith. In the Synagogue and in the Christian community, the written word had such high esteem because the writings of the OT, the gospels, and later the letters of the apostles, were understood to be the "Word of God". Scripture reading was therefore a religious act. This is clearest when Scripture is read as part of divine worship. The theology of Scripture reading affirms that when Scripture is thus read, it is not merely retailed and relayed. The reading renders God's action actually present, so that God here and now addresses his people. God himself speaks when his representative reads from Scripture. This understanding of the liturgy was taken over from Israel by the primitive Church, where the Kyrios, powerful in the Spirit, is present when the gospels or the letters of the apostles are read out. Hence it is ancient tradition that the Church's preaching at divine service should be on themes from the liturgical Scripture readings. And in this it is less a question of the re-telling of an event than of bringing out its importance for concrete decisions here and now.

Liturgical Scripture reading is regulated

by the order of appointed passages, and the real purpose of this is to allow the kerygmatically important sections and themes of holy Scripture to be heard. The old Roman order of lessons applied this principle, despite the *lectio continua,* by having a cycle of three or four years. In a one year cycle and with only two readings in the "Liturgy of the Word" at Mass, it is impossible to do justice even to the NT. Attempts are at present being made to supplement the present one year cycle of the Roman liturgy by an additional three year scheme, so creating a four year cycle. As the Sunday reading is the only one for many of the faithful, such an enrichment of the material would be welcome from a pastoral point of view.

A derivative of the scriptural readings in the Mass are the lessons in the Divine Office. Readings from the Old and New Testaments have had a place in it, with the psalms and prayers, since the 4th century. The close connection between gospel and exposition is shown by the fact that patristic homilies now form part of the Breviary lessons. Private reading of Scripture in addition to liturgical, corresponds to the importance of the Word of God for the whole life of the Christian in the world. This private reading shares the religious character of Bible reading generally; here too the living Kyrios speaks through the words of holy Scripture. If that is understood, private Scripture reading can advance beyond acquiring information about biblical narratives to a grasp of biblical history, that is, God's action in regard to his people. To the liturgical Scripture reading there corresponds the homily, and to private there corresponds meditation. Neither mental prayer nor theological study can do without the reading of Scripture. For either to bear fruit, however, a minimum of knowledge of exegetical principles is needed, and these differ according to the literary genre of the various books of the Old and New Testaments.

BIBLIOGRAPHY. J. Pascher, *Das Stundengebet der Römischen Kirche* (1954); J. Daniélou, *Bible and Liturgy* (1961); M. Buber, *Werke,* III: *Schriften zur Bibel* (1964); P. Drijvers, *The Psalms. Their Structure and Meaning* (1964); I. Hermann, *Encounter with the New Testament* (1965).   *Ingo Hermann*

BIBLICAL CHRONOLOGY

A. RELATIVE AND ABSOLUTE CHRONOLOGY

Dates are not lacking in sacred Scripture, especially the OT, but it is difficult to put them into chronological order.

1. *Relative chronology.* Following the example of Egypt, Babylon and Assyria, dates were sometimes indicated in Israel by reference to important events (Amos 1:1, the earthquake; Is 20:1f., the conquest of Ashdod), but the usual way was to give the regnal year of the kings of Israel and Judah (Kg, Chr, pre-exilic prophets), or of Babylon or Persia (Dan, Hag, Zech, Ezra, Neh). Ezekiel dates events according to the year of the first Jewish deportation, 1 and 2 Macc according to the Seleucid era, either from autumn 312 or spring 311 B.C. In the 170th year of this era (143–142 B.C.) the Jews introduced their own system of dating, according to the regnal years of the high priest Simon (1 Macc 13:41f.). In counting regnal years the systems of ante-dating and post-dating must be distinguished. In the former, which was used in Egypt till the Persian epoch, the period between the death of a king and the beginning of the civil year was counted both as the last year of the king's reign and the first year of his successor's. In post-dating, the period between the new king's accession to the throne and the new year was known as the "beginning of the reign" and the first regnal year was counted only from the new year on. Post-dating was used in Assyria and Babylonia, and also in Judah, at least towards the end of the monarchy (cf. Jer 26:1; 49:34). It may have been used from the beginning.

2. *Synchronisms.* Light is cast on the relative chronology of the Bible when synchronisms or equivalent datings can be established with regard to the history of the ancient East and the Roman Empire. The Assyrian annals narrate that Shalmaneser III defeated the Syrian coalition, including King Ahab of Israel, at the battle of Qarqar in the 6th year of his reign, 853 B.C., and also that he received tribute from King Jehu of Israel in the 18th year of his reign, 841 B.C. King Josiah fell in the battle against Pharaoh Neco of the 26th dynasty (2 Kg 23:29; 2 Chr 35:20–24), and this battle took place,

according to the Gadd Chronicle (Babylonian), in the 17th year of Nabopolassar of Babylon, therefore 609 B.C. The Babylonian Chronicle published by Wiseman mentions the battle of Carchemish (Jer 46:2) and Nebuchadnezzar's first capture of Jerusalem (2 Kg 24:10–12). In the NT, Mt and Lk say that the birth of Jesus took place during the reign of King Herod; Lk 3:1 says that John the Baptist began his public ministry in the 15th year of the Emperor Tiberius, and Acts 18:12 tells us that Gallio was proconsul in Corinth during Paul's first stay there.

3. *Absolute chronology.* To give ancient oriental dates in terms of the Christian calendar, we can draw upon the *data of astronomy.* By means of astronomical tables, the rising of Sirius in Egypt or Venus in Babylon and eclipses of the sun and moon mentioned in ancient documents can be reckoned and fixed with reference to the Christian era. It has been calculated in this way that the eclipse of the sun which took place in the 9th year of the Assyrian King Ashurdan III fell on 15 June 763 B.C. Starting from this and other absolute dates, the relative Assyrian chronology can be transposed into dates corresponding to our computation of time, and synchronisms help us to do the same with the other oriental and biblical dates.

B. DIFFERENT PERIODS OF BIBLICAL HISTORY

1. *The time of the Patriarchs.* Their way of life and their customs as well as the archaeology of the Negeb invite us to place them in the Middle Bronze Age (*c.* 2200–1500 B.C. = the Egyptian Middle Kingdom, with the Hyksos period), and perhaps more precisely from 1800 B.C. on. The identification of King Amraphel, contemporary of Abraham (Gen 14:1), with Hammurabi of Babylon (1728–1686 B.C.) remains doubtful.

2. *The exodus from Egypt and the conquest of the promised land.* Archaeology and the political situation of the Near East suggest the 13th century B.C. (19th dynasty) rather than the 15th (18th dynasty), in spite of Jg 11:26; 1 Kg 6:1.

3. *The period of the Judges.* This was about the 12th and 11th centuries B.C. The dates given in Jg provide no sure basis for a chronology.

4. *The period of the Kings.* The beginning of the building of Solomon's temple, in the 4th year of his reign, offers some sort of starting-point for the chronology of the beginnings of the royal period. According to data provided by Josephus (*Apion.,* 1, 17; *Ant.,* 18, 3, 1), Justin (3rd century A.D.; *Epitoma Pompei Trogi,* 18, 6, 9) and the marble tablet from Paros, the building was begun in 969 or 968, though according to other indications in 959. Solomon would then have reigned from *c.* 972–932 (cf. 1 Kg 11:42) and David from *c.* 1012–972 (cf. 1 Kg 2:11). The divided monarchy must have begun about 932. Kings and Chronicles give many synchronisms between the kings of Israel and Judah, but they provide many unsolved problems. Samaria fell in 722 (and 720), and the northern kingdom was destroyed. The Assyrian King Sennacherib besieged Jerusalem in 701. On 16 March 597 the Babylonians took Jerusalem for the first time. They took it again about the middle of 586 and destroyed the city and the temple. The Babylonian exile followed.

5. *Babylonian exile: 597 and 586 to 536.*

6. *The Persian period: 539–331.* The edict of Cyrus in 538 permitted the Jews to return. The first group returned in 536. Rebuilding of the temple, 520–515; Nehemiah in Jerusalem, 445; Ezra in Jerusalem, 458 or 398.

7. *The Hellenistic period: 331–166.* The Jews were under the rule of the Ptolemies till about 200, and under the Seleucids till 166.

8. *Maccabean and Hasmonaean period: 166–63.* Judas Maccabeus, 166–161, Jonathan, 161–142, Simon, 142–135, John Hyrcan I, 135–104. Pompey conquered Jerusalem in 63.

9 *The Roman period: 63 B.C. to A.D. 70.* King Herod the Great, 40–4 B.C., Archelaus Ethnarch, 4 B.C. to A.D. 6, Pontius Pilate, Governor of Judaea, 26–36; destruction of Jerusalem by Titus in A.D. 70.

10. *Chronology of the life of Jesus.* a) *Birth:* According to Mt 2:1 and Lk 1:5, 26, Jesus was born during the reign of Herod the Great, who, however, died in the year 750 after the foundation of Rome, that is, in 4 B.C. The most probable date therefore for the birth of Christ is 7, 6 or 5 B.C.; cf. Lk 2:1f.; 3:23.

b) *The beginning of the public ministry:* According to Lk 3:1, John the Baptist began to preach in the 15th year of Tiberius, which according to the ancient historians and chronographers would be A.D. 28–29, since Augustus died on 19 August 14. But the Lucan date could suppose the oriental reckoning, in which the first year of Tiberius would correspond to the few weeks between the death of Augustus and the beginning of the next civil year, 1 Oct 14. His second year would be from 1 Oct 14 till 30 Sept 15 and then his 15th would cover the same period of the years 27–28. Thus Jesus began his public ministry in the first months — before Easter, cf. Jn 2:13 — of the year 29 or 28. The latter date appears to suit Jn 2:20 better: the building of the temple had been going on for 46 years.

c) *Length of the public ministry:* John mentions three Paschs (2:13, 23; 6:4; 11:55; 12:1; 13:1) during the public ministry of Jesus, which lasted therefore 2 years and some months. The feast mentioned in Jn 5:1 is either the same as that of 6:4 or Pentecost; 4:35 is probably a proverbial saying. It is not therefore necessary to assume a three-year ministry. The synoptics speak only of Jesus' last Pasch, but Lk 13:1–5 seems to suppose an earlier Pasch.

d) *The date of the Crucifixion:* If Jesus' public ministry began in the first months of 29, or, by the Syrian reckoning, 28, and lasted for over 2 years, he died in or around April of A.D. 31 (or 30). He died on the Friday before the Pasch (Jn 19:31). Efforts have been made by means of astronomical calculations to determine in what year the 14th or 15th Nisan fell on a Friday, and when all factors have been taken into account, it has been concluded that the date of Jesus' death was either 7 April 30 or 3 April 33. In view of what was said above about the beginning of the public ministry, the most probable date for the death of Jesus appears to be 7 April 30. It has recently been proposed to divide the passion of Jesus over 3 days, from Tuesday evening to Friday afternoon.

11. *The apostolic age.* Paul: King Herod Agrippa died in the summer of A.D. 44. The martyrdom of James the elder and the imprisonment of Peter took place therefore in this year (Acts 12:1–23). According to the "Delphic Inscription", Gallio was pro-consul of Achaea in 51–52 or 52 or 52–53, so Paul was in Corinth about the years 51–52 (cf. Acts 18:1, 11–18). Then his second missionary journey began in the autumn of 49 or 50, and the Council of Jerusalem took place in the summer or autumn of 49 or 50. Paul's conversion was between 33 and 36 (cf. Gal 1:18; 2:1; 2 Cor 11:32). Imprisonment in Jerusalem and Caesarea in A.D. 57 or 58, journey to Rome from autumn (Acts 27:9) 59 or 60 till the spring (Acts 28:11) of 60 or 61. Imprisonment in Rome till 62 or 63, second Roman imprisonment and martyrdom (along with Peter) in A.D. 66 or 67.

See also *Biblical Historiography, New Testament Books, Old Testament Books.*

BIBLIOGRAPHY. V. Concke, "Chronologie biblique", *DBS,* I (1928), cols. 1244–1304; J. Begrich, *Die Chronologie der Könige von Israel und Judea* (1929); E. R. Thiele, *The Mysterious Numbers of the Hebrew Kings* (1951); D. J. Wiseman, *Chronicles of Chaldaean Kings in the British Museum* (1956); A. Jaubert, *La date de la Cène. Calendrier biblique et liturgie chrétienne, Études Bibliques* (1957); J. Bright, *A History of Israel* (1959); P. van der Meer, *The Ancient Chronology of Western Asia and Egypt* (3rd ed., 1963); E. Ruckstuhl, *Die Chronologie des letzten Mahles und des Leidens Jesu* (1963); A. Jepsen and R. Hanhart, "Untersuchungen zur israelitisch-jüdischen Chronologie", supplement to *ZAW* 88 (1964); J. Finegan, *Handbook of Biblical Chronology* (1964); M. North, *The Old Testament World* (1965).

Balduino Kipper

BIBLICAL COMMISSION

The Biblical Commission is a permanent body of biblical scholars founded in 1902 by Leo XIII for the purpose of promoting the Catholic study of Scripture. Like other Roman Congregations it is centred on Rome and headed by a number of cardinals.

The encyclical *Providentissimus* which preceded the foundation of this Commission, the charter *Vigilantiae* by which it was established, the composition of its first board of consultors, the adoption of the advanced *Revue Biblique* as its quasi-official organ, the moderate tone of its early directives — all this indicates that the original purpose of the Commission was progressive rather than defensive, that its aim was to encourage Catholic biblical studies and bring them abreast of scholarly work outside the Church, rather than merely to act as a worried watchdog and give warning of danger. This original purpose would seem to have been diverted by force of historical circumstances. The Modernist crisis which overwhelmed the Church at the beginning of this century forced the Commission to entrench itself in an almost entirely negative position. Most of its directives have consequently been couched in the form of an artificial question expecting the answer no, and have sounded a note of extreme caution. Until 1915 fourteen replies appeared at the rate of about one a year. They dealt with the problems then current — the authenticity of the Pentateuch, Isaiah, the Psalms, the Gospels, the Acts and the Epistles, and the historical nature of the OT and the Gospels. Since that date only five further replies have been issued on a variety of topics. The four directives since 1948 have been expressed in a less artificial form, and under the influence of *Divino Afflante* have been more liberal in tone. The 1964 decree *Sancta Mater Ecclesia* in particular, while re-emphasizing the historical nature of the Gospels, acknowledges that form-criticism can throw much light on them, and asks that exegetes recognize their complex reality as professions of faith of the early Church.

It has long been understood that the(se) restrictive decrees must be interpreted strictly, that is, must not be made to restrict more than their explicit terms assert. When a question asks whether the arguments so far produced are of sufficient weight to force one to conclude that the book of Isaiah was written by several authors, and the answer given is no, it means that and nothing more. It does not mean that further investigation will not produce stronger arguments which make the plurality of authors a conclusion accepted by all scholars, as has in fact happened.

This interpretation of the decrees has been confirmed by an official statement made in 1955 by the secretary of the Biblical Commission. This explicitly admits that the decrees issued before 1915 were contingent in nature, and that their main interest

for the modern scholar is a historical one, to provide a record of the controversies with which the Church was faced at the time they were framed. Now that these controversies have been peaceably settled, there is no longer the need to maintain positions which were regarded as necessary fifty years ago, or to imagine that on critical matters which have no bearing on faith or morals these decrees forbid the Catholic exegete to pursue his investigations freely.

Less still should one imagine, as some seem to, that the decrees of the Biblical Commission are the only means by which the Church exercises its right and duty to offer guidance on the interpretation of Scripture. The Church's magisterium in this respect has always been exercised principally through the liturgy, where it continues from day to day to expound the meaning of God's Word to God's People.

See also *Modernism, Magisterium.*

BIBLIOGRAPHY. "Epistula ad Cardinalem Suhard", *AAS* 40 (1948), pp. 45–48, 2302; J. Dupont, "A propos du nouvel Enchiridion Biblicum", *Revue Biblique* 62 (1955), pp. 414–19; J. Levie, *The Bible, Word of God in Words of Men* (1962), pp. 61–76, 186–90; A. Bea, "Il carattere storico dei vangeli sinottici", *La Civiltà Cattolica* 155 (1964), pp. 417–36, 526–45.

Hubert J. Richards

BIBLICAL EXEGESIS

I. Historical Survey. II. Biblical Criticism: A. General. B. Gospel Criticism. III. Spiritual Exegesis: A. Grounds for Spiritual Exegesis. B. History of Spiritual Exegesis.

I. Historical Survey

1. *Old Testament and Judaism.* The interpretation of the Bible begins in the OT when later authors, such as the prophets and certain psalms, give a theological interpretation of the history of Israel handed down in the older writings (see Ezek 38:7; Dan 9; Ecclus 44 ff., and especially the re-moulding of the matter of the Books of Samuel by Chronicles, and the midrash on the ancient history of Israel in Wis 10 ff.). There was particular need to interpret the Torah in the post-exilic period because of its importance as the foundation of the whole religious and social

life of the community. Ezra is regarded as its first exponent (Ezra 7:10; Neh 8:8). Later the task was taken over by the Pharisee "doctors of the law" who endeavoured to draw from the Torah new laws adapted to the constantly changing conditions of life. The mention of the "school" in Ecclus 51:23 indicates that this institution goes back at least to Sirach's time. The legal interpretations of the older rabbis, the Tannaites, at first transmitted by word of mouth only, were written down towards the end of the 2nd century A.D. in systematic order in the Mishnah in the form of commentaries on Exodus — Deuteronomy in the oldest midrashim. The Amoraites for their part took as their task the interpretation of the Mishnah, and the result of their work is contained in the Talmud. We find similar interpretation of the OT to meet contemporary needs in the Qumran sect.

In the 10th century A.D., after a long period of sterility, Saadia opened the way to a new study of the OT and was a pioneer of Jewish linguistic studies. He found no followers in the East, but a new centre of intensive biblical and linguistic study sprang up in Spain. The Jewish scholars of the Middle Ages produced a large number of scriptural commentaries and grammatical and lexicographical works which also influenced Christian biblical scholarship. It was in accord with their strong attachment to tradition that Jewish scholars only hesitantly adopted the critical methods of modern Christian biblical research (Moses Mendelssohn, 1786). Interpretation of Scripture is also found in the targums, the Aramaic translations of the OT which first became necessary for liturgical use when Hebrew was replaced in common speech by Aramaic. The targums, however, are to a large extent paraphrases, free renderings of the Hebrew text.

Comparable to them is the LXX, the Greek translation of the OT made when most Jews in Egypt knew only Greek. The LXX, however, as well as a translation is also an interpretation of the original, its transposition into Greek thought. This is even truer of the exegetical writings of Philo of Alexandria, loyal in principle to the Jewish faith in the Bible, but at the same time influenced by the philosophy of Plato and the Stoa. He wanted to show that the Bible and Greek philosophy could be perfectly well harmonized and that Greek wisdom is contained in the Torah. By the allegorical method which he took over from the Greek interpretation of Homer, Philo also exercised a lasting influence on Christian exegesis from the Alexandrians onwards. The Latin Fathers of the Church then transmitted this legacy to the exegesis of the Latin Middle Ages.

2. *Primitive Christian community*. The earliest Christian community took over from Judaism the OT as holy Scripture and applied it by an eschatological and Christological interpretation to Christ's redemptive work and to the Church as the true Israel. The influence of the exegetical method of Palestinian Judaism is particularly evident in the rabbinically educated Paul.

3. *Patristic period*. The oldest Christian exegesis after the NT period is characterized by controversy with Judaism (Letter of Barnabas; Justin), and with Gnosticism. The starting-point for all later exegesis was provided by the Alexandrian school (Clement, Origen), as compared with which the earlier writer, Hippolytus of Rome, was of slight importance. The Alexandrian Origen was the most important exegete of the ancient Church, both by the range of his writings, which chiefly consist of biblical commentaries of various kinds, and by the influence of his allegorical method on the whole subsequent patristic age and at least indirectly on the Antiochene school. For him it is not the facts of sacred history which are important but the supra-historical truth which is revealed in Scripture. Side by side with the Alexandrian school, and in conscious opposition to it, was the Antiochene school founded by Lucian of Antioch (d. 312); its most important members were Diodore of Tarsus, Theodoret of Cyrrhos and especially Theodore of Mopsuestia, the "blessed exegete" of the Nestorians; with these must be numbered the great homiletic writer John Chrysostom. The great Cappadocians, in particular Gregory of Nyssa, were under Origen's influence. The Antiocheans resolutely rejected allegory and emphasized the typological meaning of Scripture, viewing biblical revelation in the perspective of the sacred history of redemption. The 6th century produced the only two commentaries on the Revelation of John, which after Dionysius of Alexandria never attained

undisputed recognition among the Greeks; they were by the Severian Oecumenius and his orthodox opponent Andrew of Caesarea. In general, however, in the 6th century the age of independent biblical exegesis in the Greek Church was at an end. Its place was taken by the catenae which, renouncing original work, assembled fragments from the standard exegetes into continuous commentaries. And after the 2nd Trullan Synod (692) declared the interpretations given by the Fathers to be binding, we find no more independent works with the exception of a commentary on Paul by the Patriarch Photius (9th century), for even the commentaries of Euthymius Zigabenus and Theophylact (11th and 12th centuries) are simply free excerpts from John Chrysostom and other ancient exegetes.

The first *Latin* exegete known to us is the commentator on the Apocalypse, Victorinus of Pettau (d. 314). In the Latin Church too the allegorical method became predominant. Ambrose, and in his earliest years Jerome, as well as Augustine, adopted it and under Augustine's influence Gregory the Great at the end of the patristic period (d. 604). Lasting influence was also exercised by Tyconius the Donatist, highly esteemed by Augustine, through his commentary on the Apocalypse, and through his *Liber Regularum,* in the spirit of which Augustine composed a handbook of hermeneutics in his *De doctrina christiana.* The Antiochene method of exegesis is represented by the important commentary on Paul by an unknown author, the so-called Ambrosiaster, and that of Pelagius and his disciple Julian of Eclanum. Isidore of Seville was only a compiler.

4. *The Latin Middle Ages.* The scriptural exegesis of the early Middle Ages was entirely designed for practical purposes, preaching and liturgy. The oldest commentaries were catena-like compilations of patristic texts, chiefly from Ambrose, Jerome, Augustine and Gregory the Great, which also means that the allegorical interpretation prevailed, as suited the practical purpose of these works. The first author of commentaries of that kind was the Venerable Bede (d. 735), whose reputation endured for centuries. With Alcuin and Theodulf of Orleans we see the first attempts to reduce the considerable textual confusion of the Vulgate manuscripts to some uniformity. Similar to Bede's commentaries were those of Rabanus Maurus, while those of Paschasius Radbertus, Christian of Stablo and especially of John Scotus Eriugena and Remigius of Auxerre (all 9th century) already attempted greater independence. In the 11th century the schools of Laon (Anselm) and Utrecht (Lambert) became centres of biblical study. In the "gloss" produced by Anselm and his collaborators the form given in preceding centuries to the exegetical tradition came to a provisional conclusion. Partly between the lines of the biblical text *(glossa interlinearis),* partly in the margin *(glossa marginalis),* short comments were added from the works of the Fathers or other ancient exegetes. For the books most frequently commented, the Psalter and Paul, Anselm's work was improved by later editors, in particular by Peter Lombard, and in this form became the standard "handbook" for all the later Middle Ages.

Of importance for the growth of medieval theology was the production of *Quaestiones,* the more detailed treatment of particularly important single texts. Robert of Melun (d. 1167) then took the decisive step of separating the *Quaestiones* from the Gloss, and so dogmatic theology freed itself from the sacred text and became a separate branch of study. But even in the golden age of Scholasticism in the 13th century, the Gloss was retained as a basis for treating biblical matters in lectures and disputations. Important theologians of the 13th century who made significant contributions to scriptural exegesis were Bonaventure, Albert the Great and especially Thomas Aquinas. In the same period also, Alcuin's and Theodulf's efforts to provide a uniform biblical text were resumed in correctories and concordances, in particular by Hugh of St. Cher. The latter was also the first to use the term "postilla" for the continuous commentary on the biblical text. The most important work of this kind is considered to be the Postilla of Nicolas of Lyra (d. 1349). With Lorenzo Valla and G. Manetti, classical scholars begin to occupy themselves with the Bible and its text, and this heralds a new period of biblical study.

5. *From Renaissance humanism to the present day.* The Catholic exegesis of this epoch may be divided into three periods, the last of which is not yet closed: a) a flourishing period from 1500 to about 1650, characterized

by the great number of Catholic biblical scholars, particularly Spaniards and Italians, and the abundance of their works; b) the period from 1650 to about the end of the 19th century, in which biblical scholarship declined in comparison with other branches of study; c) recent times.

With Renaissance humanism, a new age in the intellectual history of Europe began and brought with it a shift of interest in the Bible and a change of exegetical method. There was an awakening interest in history, especially that of Greco-Roman antiquity and its literature. This involved both a turning away from the philosophical speculation of Scholasticism and the abandoning of allegorizing, though the latter only took place gradually. Interest began to be directed to questions of the kind now treated in general introductions to scriptural study, and to the auxiliary sciences (biblical geography, biblical archaeology, ancient history). It began to be recognized how important for the correct understanding of the biblical text is the study of ancient languages, which previously had been so seriously neglected. The uncertainty of the current text of the Vulgate had, of course, been recognized in the Middle Ages, without its being possible effectively to remedy the fault. Now the invention of printing created a new possibility of establishing and distributing without difficulty a uniform text of the Bible. Then came the Reformation which declared the Bible to be the sole source of faith and so attributed pre-eminent importance to it. Catholic biblical scholarship could not remain unaffected. It is true that controversy with the Protestant view of the Bible was inevitably detrimental to its Catholic interpretation; for on both sides men looked to the Bible primarily for *dicta probantia* for dogmatic theology, apologetics and polemics. In this respect the commentaries of G. Seripando are typical. Moreover, a long time was needed for the new knowledge and methods to find general recognition.

Many commentators were still as intent as ever on supplying materials for homiletics and ascetics (e.g., Salmeron, Cornelius a Lapide). The decree of the Council of Trent regarding the Bible declared the Vulgate to be the official text of the Latin Church and so gave textual criticism a powerful impetus. Though the humanists primarily cultivated the study of the Greek and Latin languages,

people now began to recognize more clearly the importance of Hebrew, especially under the influence of the Jew Elias Levita. Eminent for their knowledge of Hebrew were Lefèvre d'Étaples (Vatablus) in France, Johannes Reuchlin in Germany, Santes Pagnino and Giles of Viterbo (the pupil of Elias Levita) in Italy. At this time the Collegium Trilingue was founded at the University of Louvain. Luther separated himself from the Middle Ages by abandoning the multiple sense of Scripture; he distinguished only between the spiritual, i.e., Christological sense and the literal sense. Of theological importance was his classification of the books of the Bible according to their religious value and according to the degree to which they "concern Christ". Calvin and especially Zwingli were strongly influenced by humanism. On the Catholic side the first representatives of a new kind of biblical exegesis were Cardinal Cajetan in Italy, Erasmus of Rotterdam in Germany, and J. Lefèvre d'Étaples in France. Of these Cajetan in particular, by his astonishingly modern principles, with which he placed himself in contrast not only to Scholasticism but even to the Fathers, roused a storm of opposition. In order effectively to meet the Protestants, he held, the Bible must be expounded in its original text instead of the Vulgate and, instead of penetrating its mystical sense, we must ask what its words really say. Erasmus too wished to liberate exegesis from Scholasticism but thought that the allegorical sense must be retained, at least in the OT. As opposed to the exaggerated dogmatism of many representatives of Protestant orthodoxy, who, like M. Flaccus, regarded as inspired not only every word of the Bible, but even the vowels of the Massoretic Hebrew text, Catholics such as S. Masius, B. Pererius, J. Bonfrère and J. Morinus adopted a detached attitude to the Massoretic text. Among the numerous commentators of that age the two Spaniards J. Maldonatus and F. de Ribera and the Dutchman W. Estius stand pre-eminent.

That flourishing period was followed by an even longer period in which Catholic theology turned in the main to other fields and achieved little in biblical scholarship, especially as far as progress in method is concerned. Its closed, self-contained character, which was in sharp contrast to the multiplicity of trends and schools of Protestant exegesis at that time, was not due solely to dogma, but to a traditionalism averse to new thought. As a consequence, it had no better and more effective method to oppose to the hypotheses of English Deists, French Encyclopaedists and Protestant Rationalists of the 17th and 18th centuries. The 18th century counts a few useful achievements in the domain of biblical archaeology and textual criticism (the work on the *Vetus Latina* by the Maurist P. Sabatier). The outstanding figure of this period was the French Oratorian Richard Simon (d. 1712), who was far in advance of his time and as a consequence was opposed and persecuted from all sides, but who was the real creator of the critical historical method. The fact that his principles, universally rejected by his contemporaries, were first adopted by the rationalist J. S. Semler, definitely made them suspect and robbed them for a long time of their effect, to the detriment of Catholic biblical research.

In the meantime Protestant biblical study produced not only a large number of commentaries, among them the important works of H. Grotius and J. J. Wettstein, but also valuable philological aids (John Lightfoot, Ch. Schöttgen), as well as the gigantic collection of variants in the text of the NT by John Mill (d. 1707). With Semler (d. 1791) there began in Protestant research the emancipation of scriptural study from dogmatic theology. Since then the conflict between Rationalism and Supernaturalism has dominated Protestant research down to the present day, though in method the conservative tendency has gradually come closer and closer to the rationalist. Just as in the 19th century Pentateuchal criticism and the history of OT religion, discussion of which had been brought by J. Wellhausen to a certain provisional culmination, was to the fore, so too work on the NT was dominated by literary criticism of the synoptic gospels and in conjunction with this, research on the life of Jesus. A major influence was that of F. C. Baur, who was inspired by Hegel's philosophy of history to try to depict the NT as a reflection of the conflict between the original Jewish Christianity and Pauline gentile Christianity moving away from the Law in the direction of the Catholic Church. A lasting inheritance from the controversy for and against the "Tendency-critique of Tübingen" was the recognition that the various NT writings must be understood on the basis of their historical situations. The investigation of the history of the text of the NT was pursued almost exclusively by Protestant scholars (Tischendorf, Tregelles, Westcott and Hort), and the *textus receptus,* previously regarded as almost inviolable, was shown to be in the main the latest stage of the text.

Towards the end of the 19th century a strong influence was exercised by the students of history of religions, H. Gunkel for the OT, W. Bousset, W. Heitmüller, R. Reitzenstein and others for the NT; their programme was to provide a genetic explanation of OT religion, and that of Judaism and the NT, from their earliest roots, which they considered were to be found in the syncretism of the surrounding world. From the controversy about this school and its methods, present-day scientific Catholic exegesis has retained the principle that biblical religion cannot be understood at any stage without study of the religious currents present in the environment; but this does not necessarily reduce that religion to a syncretist formation. Interest in history of religions was superseded by form-criticism and history of traditions, methods opened up for the OT by H. Gunkel, for the NT by K. L. Schmidt, M. Dibelius, R. Bultmann and others. In the NT this chiefly concerned the synoptic gospels. This led to the conclusion that the gospels have their basis in the original Christian kerygma and are therefore testimonies to the original Christian belief in Christ; this also involves the question how far we can know the historical Jesus through this picture of Christ. This is the question which chiefly occupies NT research at the present time and not only Protestant scholarship. As contributions to NT research of special importance and world-wide influence, we must mention the commentary on the NT from the Talmud and Midrash of the Lutheran pastor P. Billerbeck, and the theological dictionary to the NT founded by G. Kittel (both in German; the latter in course of translation).

Even in the 19th century Catholic exegesis was chiefly determined by defence against Rationalism and therefore by apologetics, and was extremely tied to tradition. It was only at the end of the 19th century that an advance set in in Germany, France and Belgium which can really be called the beginning of a new age. The foundation of the École Biblique in Jerusalem by M.-J. Lagrange (1890) was epoch-making in the first place for the advance in geographical and archaeological research on the soil of Palestine itself, but above all because Lagrange resolutely declared himself in favour of the historico-critical method which, he urged, was objectively required and which alone was capable of debating seriously the results of Protestant research and of recognizing what was of value in them. The organ of the École Biblique was the *Revue Biblique* (1892 onwards), to which after 1900 were added the *Études Bibliques*. Lagrange's discourse at the international Catholic Congress in Fribourg in 1899 and his book *La méthode historique* (1903) precipitated, however, a long dispute between the *école large* and a strictly traditionalist trend (L. Méchineau, J. Brucker, A. Delattre, L. Fonck) on the compatibility of the historical-critical method with the Catholic conception of inspiration. On the same lines as Lagrange there were F. Prat in France, A. van Hoonacker in Belgium (Louvain) and in Germany the *Biblische Zeitschrift* (1903 ff.), edited by J. Goettsberger and J. Sickenberger, as well as N. Peters, K. Holzhey, A. Schulz and others. The debate was still going on when the movement suffered a set-back through the reaction against Modernism, of which the exegete A. Loisy was one of the protagonists, for the progressive trend was suspected of a Modernist attitude.

The Pontifical Biblical Commission founded in 1902 by Leo XIII issued from 1906 onwards a number of decrees on controverted questions. The Pontifical Biblical Institute founded in 1909 by Pius X was intended to ensure the formation of future professors of biblical sciences according to the mind of the Church. Of the three papal encyclicals concerning biblical research (*Providentissimus Deus* of Leo XIII, 1893, *Spiritus Paraclitus* of Benedict XV, 1920, *Divino Afflante Spiritu* of Pius XII, 1943), the last-named, the "liberation encyclical", which explicitly declared the historical-critical method to be appropriate and necessary, opened the road for modern Catholic biblical scholarship and so gave it a powerful impetus. The restrictions under which it suffered even in the first decades of the 20th century and which forced it to excessively cautious formulas or to take refuge in "safe" questions, if it did not wish to be completely silent, are now

removed, at least in principle, though attacks from the conservative side have not yet been ended. It is now possible to deal more simply with important matters like the Pentateuch, the synoptic problem, form-criticism and history of traditions. So too as regards the methods, problems and results of Protestant scholarship, its attitude has more and more "changed from critical rejection to respectful discussion" (W. Michaelis, *RGG,* I, col. 1084) and in many fields collaboration between Catholic and Protestant exegetes has been started.

If it is possible at the present time to note with good reason that Catholic biblical scholarship displays a new vitality, it is simply because it now enjoys a freedom of movement which it did not before, and can now investigate the manifold problems of the Bible and especially the revelation it contains, in their historical development, instead of merely providing *dicta probantia* for dogmatic theology. In this way and only in this way, in constant fruitful discussion with Protestant biblical scholarship, can it penetrate more and more deeply the thoughts of the Bible. Only when it is allowed to do this does it fulfil its real task as a theological science and only then will its results endure.

See also *Judaism* I, II, *Alexandrian School of Theology, Modernism, Biblical Commission.*

BIBLIOGRAPHY. G. Bardy, "Commentaires Patristiques de la Bible", *DBS,* II (1934), cols. 73–103; F. Stegmüller, *Repertorium Biblicum medii aevi,* 7 vols. (1940–61); F. M. Braun, *L'œuvre exégétique du P. Lagrange* (1943); C. Spicq, *Esquisse d'une histoire de l'exégèse latine au Moyen-Age* (1944); B. Smalley, *The Study of the Bible in the Middle Ages* (1952); H. J. Kraus, *Geschichte der historisch-kritischen Erforschung des Alten Testaments* (1956); W. G. Kümmel, *Das Neue Testament. Geschichte der Erforschung ihrer Probleme* (1958); H. de Lubac, *Exégèse Médiévale,* 4 vols. (1959–64); J. Daniélou, *From Shadows to Reality. Studies in the Biblical Typology of the Fathers* (1960).

Joseph Schmid

II. Biblical Criticism

A. GENERAL

The Bible contains God's message to mankind, but this message takes the form of a literature which, though divinely inspired, is nonetheless composed in the ordinary human way. It was written two or three thousand years ago, by and for men who lived in historical, social, political, economic, cultural and religious conditions quite different from ours. While possessing their own imaginative and intellectual resources, their own style and literary purpose, the writers were also subject to the ideas and the literary forms of their time. The society they belonged to was in continual development, deeply influenced by the culture and mentality of the various other societies it came into contact with: this becomes more and more evident as we come to know their literatures better, by archaeological and other discoveries. Moreover, the original biblical texts have long been lost and we now have nothing but copies, some of which date from only a few, others as much as twenty, centuries after the originals were written; and they have been exposed to all the hazards attached to the transmission of any other ancient document. All this must be taken into account before the divine message of the Bible, formulated and transmitted in such a human way, can be rightly understood; and this is the purpose of biblical criticism.

Textual criticism is the first step: it tries to restore the original text as far as possible. The many surviving copies contain numerous variants due to inevitable scribal errors (addition, omission, permutations of letters because of the old Hebrew and Aramaic script in use, haplography, dittography, homoioteleuton, homoioarcton) and to tendentious alterations (harmonizing parallel texts, facilitating difficult readings, correcting what seemed to be corrupt or what was not in accordance with the doctrinal or other views of the copyist, even omissions for the same reason). The various readings have to be evaluated; they have to be compared with variants in early translations, often based on older and sometimes better texts now lost, or found in quotations of ancient Jewish or early Christian writers. This is how we reach a standard critical edition of the original text of Scripture. The best complete editions now available are: for the OT, R. Kittel, *Biblia Hebraica* (1905–6; 13th ed., 1962); for the Septuagint, H. B. Swete (1887–94) and A. Rahlfs (1935); and for the NT, B. F. Westcott-F. J. A. Hort (1881; 7th ed., 1962), Eb. Nestle (1898, 25th ed., 1963), H. J. Vogels (1920, 4th ed., 1955), A. Merk (1933, 8th ed., 1957), G. D.

Kilpatrick (2nd ed., 1960), K. Aland, M. Black, B. M. Metzger, A. Wikgren (1966).

These editions need to be improved in the light of recent discoveries and research. The Dead Sea scrolls, found between 1947 and 1956, have provided a great number of Hebrew MSS, mostly very fragmentary, of all the books of the Hebrew Bible except Esther, dating from the end of the 3rd century B.C. to A.D. 68, and thus sometimes ten centuries older than the MSS hitherto known. In general they correspond to the standard Massoretic text of Kittel's edition but they show some divergent readings, agreeing with the Septuagint and/or the Samaritan Pentateuch and thus showing the value of both. The scrolls also yielded fragments of the Hebrew text of Ecclesiasticus, Hebrew and Aramaic fragments of Tobias, a fragmentary Greek text of the minor Prophets, and some other texts not yet published. The greater part of Hebrew Ecclesiasticus and other fragments of biblical MSS were discovered in the geniza of a synagogue in Cairo (1896–98): these texts have not yet all been published and properly studied.

All such material must be taken into account in the preparation of a more complete critical edition of the OT. The new (4th) edition of Kittel at present in preparation will surely incorporate it. But a perfect edition will not be possible until the Septuagint, all the other ancient versions and the works of Philo, Josephus, and the early Christian writers, have also been critically edited. Here we should refer to the two great critical editions of the Septuagint in course of publication: A. E. Brooke, N. Mc Lean, H. St. J. Tackeray (1906 ff.) and the Göttingen Academy (1926 ff.), of which the latter has a wider *apparatus criticus;* and also to the critical editions of the *Vetus Latina* (1949 ff.) and of the Vulgate (1926 ff.).

The object of *literary or higher criticism* is a correct account of the literary composition of the various books of the Bible. An attentive reading of practically any of them will reveal many discrepancies: unevenness in structure, defective connections or transitions between sentences and pericopes, differences in vocabulary, language and style, differences in religious, cultic, ethical, juridical or cultural ideas and situations, differences in history and chronology, doublets, parallel texts, even obvious contradictions.

Such books must have been compiled from various existing but previously separated texts. With the help of the vast literature of the Ancient Near East now at our disposal, scholars have attempted to disentangle the different components (whether their sources be documents or traditions) of which the various sacred books are constituted; then to define the part to be attributed to authors, editors and compilers; and thus to determine the character, purpose and period of the writers and of the different strata of the material; and finally to identify and analyse the literary forms or *genres* of the material.

As regards the OT, scholars have learned to distinguish many rudimentary and more sophisticated types of poetry, in primitive chants and in sapiential, prophetic and sacerdotal literature; several different kinds of laws; and many different kinds of narrative: myth, legend (both in special senses), epopee, saga, aetiological stories, *Novellen, midrashim,* popular tales, historical reports; for the NT, scholars distinguish the *logia:* sapiential, eschatological and apocalyptic sayings, legal and disciplinary prescriptions, sayings in the first person *(Ich-Worte),* parables, allegories and narratives, apophthegms, paradigms, miracle-stories, and so on.

The study of literary forms has made great progress since the introduction of *form-criticism.* This concentrates on identifying the nature, purpose, application and import of the basic literary units or elements, on discovering their *Sitz im Leben,* their "situation" in the life of the people, *before* they made their appearance in Scripture. First used on the formation of the OT by H. Gunkel (e.g., *Commentary on Genesis,* 1901), then by such OT scholars as H. Gressmann, J. Hempel, A. Alt, and G. von Rad, this method was soon complemented by that of the history of *tradition* (M. Noth), which aims at penetrating into the pre-literary history of those original units, to find out how they arose and what their precise meaning and object was in oral tradition. The great importance of oral tradition has also been stressed by Scandinavian scholars (I. Engnell, G. Widengren, H. Riesenfeld).

Working on the ideas of J. Weiss, Martin Dibelius introduced form-criticism into NT study *(Die Formgeschichte des Evangeliums,* 1919; E. T.: *From Tradition to Gospel,* 1934).

In 1921 Rudolf Bultmann published *Die Geschichte der synoptischen Tradition* (E. T.: *The History of the Synoptic Tradition,* 1963). Other leading form-critics include M. Albertz, K. L. Schmidt, and G. Bertram. The movement has always been primarily German and its methods and particularly its results have been treated with great reserve by the more conservative school of English exegetes (but cf. V. Taylor, *The Formation of the Gospel Tradition,* 1933, and C. F. D. Moule, *The Birth of the NT,* 1962). The method concerns primarily the *Sitz im Leben* of the various forms of preaching and liturgy in the primitive Church, to see how the words and deeds of Christ were understood and interpreted at a given stage, as well as to show how far this material may have been adapted for the purposes of composing the gospels.

It will be clear from what has been said that literary criticism, in its development into form-criticism and history of tradition, demands as its correlative *historical criticism;* for this inquires into the historical setting of the literary forms, which to a great extent can be known only from delicate analysis of those forms. But as regards the Bible, historical criticism has a much wider range: its object is to examine the precise nature, meaning, purpose and scope of biblical history as presented in the various sacred books, and to confront it with all we now know about the historical development, the religion and the culture of the ancient Near East to which the Bible belongs. Here we may mention such works as J. Pedersen, *Israel, Its Life and Culture,* 1926–40, and R. de Vaux, *Les Institutions de l'AT,* 1960, E. T.: *Ancient Israel,* 1961.

Biblical criticism has undoubtedly arrived at a great many results now commonly accepted and our understanding of what the sacred writers meant to say has been greatly deepened and enlarged. Theories and hypotheses have often had to be abandoned or at least corrected by later scholars. The Catholic exegete uses the new methods, while remembering that they are often tributary to theological and philosophical categories which the Catholic cannot share. The encyclical *Divino Afflante* (30 Sept. 1943) urged the Catholic exegete to exploit all the resources of history, archaeology, ethnology, etc., to identify the precise literary forms used in the OT. The recent instruction of the Biblical Commission on the historical truth of the gospels (*AAS* 56 [1964], pp. 712–18) not only invites exegetes to extend the method of historical criticism to the NT but also advises them "to find out what sound elements the method of form-criticism contains, so as to be able to employ them correctly for a richer understanding of the gospels".

BIBLIOGRAPHY. E. Norden, *Agnostos Theos. Untersuchungen zur Formgeschichte religiöser Rede* (1913); H. Gunkel, *Ziele und Methoden der Erklärung des Alten Testaments. Reden und Aufsätze* (1913); V. Taylor, *The Formation of Gospel Tradition* (1933); M. Dibelius, *From Tradition to Gospel* (1934); M. Noth, *Überlieferungsgeschichtliche Studien,* I (1943); P. Benoît, "Réflexions sur la 'form-geschichtliche Methode'", *Revue Biblique* 53 (1946), pp. 481–512; J. Coppens, *La critique du texte hébreu de l'Ancien Testament* (1950); H. J. Kraus, *Geschichte der historisch-kritischen Erforschung des Alten Testaments* (1956); E. Würthwein, *The Text of the Old Testament. An Introduction to Kittel-Kahle's Biblia Hebraica* (1957); A. Bentzen, *Introduction to the Old Testament* (2nd ed., 1957); R. de Vaux, *Ancient Israel. Its Life and Institutions* (1961); C. F. D. Moule, *The Birth of the New Testament* (1962); G. S. Glanzman and J. A. Fitzmyer, *An Introductory Bibliography for the Study of Scripture* (1962); B. Rigaux, *Saint Paul et ses Lettres* (1962), pp. 163–99; R. Bultmann, *The History of the Synoptic Tradition* (1963); X. Leon-Dufour, *Les évangiles et l'histoire de Jesus* (1963); "Instructio de historica Evangeliorum veritate", *AAS* 56 (1964), pp. 712–18; B. M. Metzger, *The Text of the New Testament. Its Transmission, Corruption and Restoration* (1964); O. Eissfeldt, *The Old Testament. An Introduction* (1966); A. Robert and A. Feuillet, *Introduction to the New Testament* (1966).

Petrus Gerard Duncker

B. GOSPEL CRITICISM

The respect due to books that are divinely inspired in no way deprives men of the right, even the duty, they have to subject these books to the scrutiny of textual, literary, and historical criticism.

1. *Textual criticism.* The gospels have come down to us in over 12,000 manuscript copies dating from before the invention of printing, some containing the complete text and others portions of it, either in the original language or in ancient translations. So close is the agreement among all these codices, and between them and the innumerable quotations from the gospels found in ancient Christian writers, that we may conclude that the original text has reached us in an excellent state of preservation. Textual criticism has substantially accomplished its task.

2. *Literary criticism.* The gospels are inspired books; they were born of a mysterious collaboration between certain human writers and God, the principal author, who really used the literary activity of those writers as his instrument; and therefore literary criticism is interested in knowing, for example, who the human authors were, when, where, in what language, and for whom they wrote, to what extent their books depend on each other, what literary influences they were exposed to, what genres they adopted.

It was contended at one time that the sources of the gospels must be looked for in profane literature outside the biblical world, but that view is now completely outdated. Modern scholars agree that the literary features of the gospels mainly derive from the books of the OT, or rabbinical writers, or earlier Hebrew literature apart from Scripture. These influences make themselves felt particularly in the oral catechesis that existed before the gospels were committed to writing and on which, no doubt, the authors of the synoptics heavily drew.

3. *Historical criticism.* The basic problem, however, where the gospels are concerned, is that of historical criticism. How accurate, historically speaking, is the portrait of Christ given us by the evangelists, who after all reflect the faith of the Christian community in the first century? May not the figure of the historical Jesus have been idealized by the belief of the evangelists, or of the authors of the primitive catechesis?

For Christians, of course, the inerrancy of the books God has inspired, and therefore of the gospels, is a revealed dogma. Inerrancy, however, must not be confused with historicity. Everything the Bible says is free of error but not everything it says is historical. Inerrancy admits of no degrees, but historicity does. However, the range and degree of the gospels' objective historicity depend on the purpose the authors had in mind, a purpose that is to be gathered from, and understood in the context of, the literary genre they chose to employ. What historical criticism must do is ascertain how far the authors meant the gospels they wrote to be objectively historical.

Here we must recollect that there were at least two stages in the formation of the gospels: their written composition by the evangelists, and the earlier oral catechesis which provided the evangelists with their material.

Actually the evangelists did very little, though perhaps not quite so little as students of the history of forms maintain. Most of their source material had already become stereotyped by use in oral catechesis and they respected these established forms. Suffice it to recall what Papias says about Mark: "Mark, the interpreter of Peter, carefully wrote down the things he remembered. But not in the order in which the Lord had said and done them. He had not heard the Lord, nor followed him, but later — as I have said — he was with Peter, who preached the gospel according to the needs of his hearers, not designing to relate the words and deeds of the Lord in chronological order. Mark made no mistake in recording certain things as he remembered them. His idea was to omit nothing of what he had heard, much less falsify anything." (Eusebius, *Hist. eccl.*, III, 39.) The historical purpose of the synoptics was to make an exact record of the Christian catechesis, or to some extent of the testimony "of those who from the beginning were eye-witnesses and ministers of the word" (Lk 1:2). Accordingly their accounts reveal a substratum of thoroughly Semitic language dating from the period before Christianity had spread through the Hellenistic world. Moreover, the social life, the religious customs, the cast of thought underlying the whole, are all anterior to the vast changes brought about in Palestine by the disaster of A.D. 70. Compared with the Pauline literature, the catechesis set down in the gospels is decidedly archaic; it portrays Jesus in surroundings still remote from the ecclesiastical organization and systematic doctrine that are already far advanced in the letters of the apostle. All this is proof that the evangelists soberly and conscientiously recorded the earlier oral catechesis as they knew it, and rules out the hypothesis that the figure of Jesus was over-idealized either in the gospels themselves or in the period just before their composition. Throughout, it is the archaic catechesis that dominates, not the influences of the contemporary world.

The concerns of the moment would have suggested quite a different approach.

So much can be taken as agreed. But our problem is not thereby resolved, it is only shifted a stage farther back: what historical objectivity had the original form of oral catechesis? Its authors, being much closer to the events concerned, eye-witnesses indeed, were in a position to know their subject and while they lived it was, to say the least, improbable that idealization would get out of hand.

Nevertheless we have good reason to be wary of crediting those witnesses with historical objectivity in the modern sense. Assuredly the catechesis is based on historical fact: it bears the stamp of truth. Yet what carries conviction is the substance of the facts related and not the details, much less their exact situation in space and time. Papias pointed out, in the text quoted above, that "Peter preached the gospel according to the needs of his hearers, not designing to relate the words and deeds of the Lord in chronological order"; and doubtless this was also true of the original Aramaic catechesis, of which St. Peter must have been a principal author and which must have formed the basis of his preaching at Rome. The deeds and sayings he cited in support of his doctrine were necessarily authentic; but for the practical reason mentioned, details need not have been so. It was only logical that his material should have been systematized for the purposes of preaching, with the result that the acts of Christ may on occasion have been taken out of their precise historical context.

Nor is this all. Given the Palestinian background of the primitive catechesis and its scrupulous fidelity to the Aramaic original, even after Christianity had spread through the Hellenistic world, we must conclude that those who composed or edited it expressed themselves in Semitic literary genres — deriving particularly from the books of the OT — whose historical objectivity, in the modern sense, is more than dubious. Consider, for example, the fondness of the OT for "exteriorizing", "materializing", dramatizing, interior signs or revelations from God, and one will see why modern authors who are perfectly orthodox question the *strict* objective historicity of certain passages in the gospels, like the temptation of Christ or the angelic apparitions in Luke's Gospel of the Infancy. To deny that these things ever happened at all would be jumping to conclusions. But to take the texts literally without regard to the type of writing they represent — the Midrashic influence is obvious — would be "to make the mistake of applying to them the norms of a literary genre with which they have no connection", as the Pontifical Biblical Commission said of the first eleven chapters of Genesis (Letter to Cardinal Suhard, 16 Jan. 1948).

Historical criticism, then, not only may but must be applied to the gospels, and its conclusions will be sound if the aim in view is neither to dismiss everything supernatural nor to attempt to prove the strict objective historicity of the whole text.

It has the noblest of tasks: to seek out the real historical intention of the evangelists, which is the intention God had when he inspired them; to show what truth it is those writers meant to teach whose books can contain only truth; to translate in terms of our modern conception of history the picture of the historical Christ which the gospels painted according to the literary conventions of their day.

In the course of this unavoidable duty exegetes may on occasion hazard opinions that later meet with the disapproval of the Church's magisterium. These are new and difficult matters. But fear of making a mistake must not deter them from throwing themselves whole-heartedly into this work. Pastors of souls will prudently refrain from making use, in preaching, of purely tentative opinions, but should keep abreast of these and give them due consideration so long as the magisterium has not rejected them, requiring no more of anyone than the Church requires of all.

And in any case "as to the efforts of these zealous workers in the vineyard of the Lord, let all the other sons of the Church judge them not only with all fairness but also with the utmost charity, shunning that imprudent attitude which leads people to think that anything new, simply because it is new, must be attacked or held suspect" (Pius XII, *Divino afflante Spiritu*).

See also *Bible* I B, II, *Inspiration, Form Criticism, Kerygma, Jesus Christ* II, *New Testament* IV, *Hermeneutics, Demythologization.*

BIBLIOGRAPHY. K. L. Schmid, *Der Rahmen der Geschichte Jesu* (1919); M. Dibelius, *From Tradition to Gospel* (1934); R. Bultmann, *Jesus and the Word* (1935); M. Dibelius, *Jesus* (1949); A. Schweitzer, *The Quest for the Historical Jesus* (1954); W. Marxsen, *Der Evangelist Markus* (2nd ed., 1959); J. M. Robinson, *New Quest of the Historical Jesus* (1959); G. Bornkamm, *Jesus of Nazareth* (1960); H. Conzelmann, *The Theology of St. Luke* (1960); K. Schubert, ed., *Der historische Jesus und der Christus unseres Glaubens* (1962); R. Bultmann, *The History of the Synoptic Tradition* (1963); E. Fuchs, *Studies of the Historical Jesus* (1964).

Salvador Muñoz Iglesias

III. Spiritual Exegesis

Writers of the first Christian centuries were familiar with a literal exegesis and a critical exegesis which hardly differed in aim from our present exegesis; only they did not have the benefit of our tools and improved methods. Origen, the pioneer of Christian allegory, became with his *Hexapla* the first great critical exegete and a great literal exegete whom St. Jerome often simply copied. Neither these two men nor their successors saw any such conflict between the different methods as certain moderns do. But here we shall only consider the kind of interpretation which was peculiar to the Fathers and which was used throughout the Middle Ages: spiritual exegesis.

Because of the many influences it has undergone, spiritual exegesis is a complicated subject. One can see why certain historians of our day have tried to distinguish what is properly Christian and what is the result of extraneous cultural influences more or less compatible with Christianity. Unfortunately, the distinction between "typology" and "allegory" which has been contrived to that end seems to us a dubious one. Apart from the fact that neither the ancient and medieval exegetes nor the magisterium of the Church ever betrayed the least awareness of this distinction and the value judgments that it involves, it seems to us to rest on too systematic and limited an idea of Christian time. Christian time, unlike the recurrent cycles of some Greek thinkers, has the horizontal dimension of a unilinear, progressive, irreversible evolution, marked by the event of the Incarnation and culminating in the second coming of Christ. The partisans of the distinction identify as "typological" such interpretations as fit into this scheme, considering them the only really Christian exegesis. But Christian time also has a vertical dimension, its reference to a higher, supernatural world, which the theory we are discussing uses to identify an allegory as of non-Christian origin. But the NT does not admit of such an exclusion, which moreover would ignore the sacramentality of time in the Church's eyes: the Christian already possesses supernatural, eschatological realities, "in a mirror dimly", while hoping for the full possession of them. Besides, man's attempt to know God — through his intelligence, his life and his love — always has to work on the two levels: God can only be represented anthropomorphically, even in the loftiest theological concepts and the best of our approaches; and yet one realizes that God is infinitely beyond all that. Unless one is content to pass a superfical judgment or to consider nothing more than literary genres, it is impossible to isolate a "typological" dimension and an "allegorical" dimension in a given exegesis: the two co-exist in fact, and rightly so, because they are inseparable.

A. Grounds for Spiritual Exegesis

It is the example of Scripture, more particularly the NT, which forms the main justification for spiritual exegesis. The OT paves the way by frequently using symbolic language, by attributing bodily members or human passions to God, and especially by its constant rethinking and further spiritualization, in the prophetic and sapiential books, of the great events in Israel's history, above all the exodus. In many passages of historical value in both Testaments the modern exegete discovers a didactic purpose beneath the narrative which is the sacred author's motive for writing: thus the miracles and other facts related by St. John illustrate the spiritual themes of the fourth gospel. Today this didactic purpose will be recognized as an essential part of the literal sense, which *Divino afflante Spiritu* defines as what the sacred author intended to say. But the early Fathers used different terms: for them the "corporal" or literal sense covered only the material narrative, parable, or metaphor, whereas the symbolic meaning, whether intended by the author or not, formed the spiritual sense.

The OT, however, could only prepare for Christian exegesis, which only came into being through the event of the Incarnation. Spiritual exegesis substantially identical with that of the Fathers is found in the gospels and the apostolic writings, where certain facts of the old covenant are shown to foreshadow realities of the new. In the synoptics, for example, the temple symbolizes Christ's body (Mt 26:61), the three days Jonah spent in the belly of a whale represent the time in which Jesus' body lay in the tomb (Mt 12:40), and Jonah's preaching to the Ninevites represents the preaching of the gospel to the Gentiles (Mt 12:41). In St. John's Gospel the brazen serpent prefigures Christ on the cross (Jn 3:14), and manna the Bread of Life (Jn 6:49–50). The Letter to the Hebrews considers the high priest an image of Christ's priesthood and sacrifice. Everywhere in the NT the Church is the New Israel and the Christian "the spiritual Jew" (Rom 2:29).

But the exegesis which the Fathers most often appeal to is St. Paul's, especially 1 Cor 10:1–11 and Gal 4:21–31. According to the former text the cloud and the passage through the Red Sea prefigure baptism; manna and water from the rock, the Eucharist; and the rock itself, Christ. These events are "types" for us. Indeed "these things happened to them (the men of the OT) as a warning, but they were written down for our instruction, upon whom the end of the ages has come". The second text makes the two wives of Abraham symbols of the two covenants, for "this is an allegory"; that is to say, underneath the obvious sense there lies a deeper meaning. But the symbolic interpretation does not prejudice the historicity of the account for Paul any more than it does for the Fathers.

Two other texts help the early theologians to work out the theory of their exegesis: 2 Cor 3:6–16, setting forth the antagonism between the letter, all that the Jews apprehend, and the spirit which Christ reveals; and Heb 10:1 with its distinction: "The law has but a shadow of the good things to come instead of the true form of these realities..." Origen and St. Ambrose understand this text to mean that the eschatological good things of the OT are the figure, the hope, the foretaste, but that the NT gives us their true form here below, a real though imperfect possession of them "in a mirror, dimly". Hence will emerge the doctrine of the fourfold sense.

It may be said that all this justifies a spiritual

exegesis of the Old Testament but not of the New. The NT applies to each Christian the events of Jesus' life: I must be personally identified with them if I would share in his redemption. One could cite all the NT texts which speak of imitating or "following" Christ, but the opening of the Christological hymn in Phil 2:5–11 will suffice: "Have this mind among yourselves, which you have in Christ Jesus" when he humbled himself and became obedient unto death; or Rom 6:35, which says that baptism conforms one to the death and resurrection of Christ. So there is a spiritual exegesis of the NT which draws from the facts of Christ's life the lessons they contain for each Christian — either the good things to come that we hope for or the life we are to lead through the "time of the Church" in the veiled possession of eschatological realities and the expectation of them.

Scripture, therefore, attests and supports the kind of interpretation we are examining, which reflects truths of a theological order. Revelation is not primarily a book, the Bible, but a Person, Christ: the Word, God speaking to men, becomes flesh to translate that divine word into a human person, into the gestures, deeds, and speech of men. The NT is revelation because it gives us this witness; the OT can be revelation only if it does the same. On the one hand the early Fathers consider the Second Person, as well as the Third, to be the author of all Scripture: to their mind the theophanies of the old covenant are the direct work of the Son, the only mediator, and not of the Father; again, God's word sent to the prophets is Christ, for God has no other word. Scripture and the Word are not two different words but one, for the Word speaks in Scripture. Thus the Bible is as it were an incarnation of the Word in the letter, which prepares and proclaims the one Incarnation, and the whole OT must be looked on as a prophecy of Christ. But this is possible only "when Jesus reads it to his Church" (Origen) as he did to the disciples at Emmaus, showing them that the Bible speaks of himself.

Must we then, like the exegetes of antiquity, seek this kind of meaning in every detail, at the risk of interpretations that are strained or arbitrary? The Fathers had an oversimplified idea of inspiration. They thought of it as dictation and neglected the part of the human author, who expresses himself in a human way even if the Spirit gives his writing a transcendent meaning. Thus they felt that it was beneath God's dignity to dictate an idle word: mysteries must be hidden in every jot and tittle. Nevertheless behind this exaggeration there lies a truth which must not be overlooked. Unless they have a spiritual sense, what are the ordinances and ceremonies of the Law to me, since Christ has abolished the letter of them? What are the historical narratives to me if those past events have no present meaning? The approach of the Fathers is spiritual and pastoral; they are not historians or archaeologists. All those things "were written down for our instruction, upon whom the end of the ages has come" (1 Cor 10:11a). And so those ordinances and chronicles have a meaning which Christ discloses.

For spiritual exegesis is only comprehensible against a background of prayer and contemplation. Through the Bible God speaks to the Christian, provided that his soul can grasp the Lord's interior word. Origen considers that the charism of the exegete is the same as that of the sacred author: a man will not understand Daniel unless he have within him the Spirit that spoke to Daniel. No doubt spiritual exegesis must be rooted in literal exegesis with all its research — critical, grammatical, historical, geographical, and even scientific. Origen and St. Jerome use all their learning to this end. But the voice which God makes the soul hear, even in connection with a text, is tied to no words and no objective sense of words. When a preacher fills out his sermons with the lights he has received at prayer, he is not laying down his interpretations as unquestionable truths unless he has found them in the NT. His chief aim is to provide "food for meditation", to show his hearers the Christian mystery, its implications for the life of the individual Christian, the eschatological good things in store for us which in a measure we already possess. As St. Ignatius would have the director of the *Spiritual Exercises* do, he tries to raise the hearer's mind to God and give him a start at prayer: if the soul, once in contact with God, feels him leading it, it must surrender to his leading.

Moderns as a rule think all this is arbitrary. The writer attaches his own ideas to a text of Scripture instead of setting himself to listen to God's Word. The early Fathers would have resented this charge. In most cases it is unfair, whatever the distance one sometimes finds between the literal sense and the elucidations which the exegete draws from it. These modern critics show that their understanding of the notion of tradition is not all it might be. Jesus did not dictate the writings of the NT. The apostles bore his message in themselves, delivered to them by his word and the example of his life, but they would not have been able to itemize it all in a set of propositions. They were promised the Holy Spirit, who in the course of the Church's history would gradually unfold that message fully. Now a part of considerable historical importance in this progressive explicitation of the faith was played by patristic exegesis, which is in good measure the source of theology. For if the bond between the letter and its interpretation sometimes seems arbitrary, the interpretation is linked with tradition by a bond that is not arbitrary. The exegete has drawn on the instinct of faith which is his as a member of the Church. Spiritual exegesis and its status cannot be properly appreciated without a sound idea of tradition, which antedates and in a sense embraces the writings of the NT, giving one the mind with which to understand them in Christian fashion and the OT with them.

In order to understand spiritual exegesis it is particularly necessary to distinguish its purpose from the purpose of literal exegesis. The latter tries to establish what the sacred author meant to say; the former relates his message to that of Christ.

B. History of Spiritual Exegesis

1. A variety of influences have affected Christian exegesis, complicating a relatively simply pattern. First there are the Jewish interpretations apart from the OT: rabbinical, apocalyptic and those which have come to light in the Qumran scrolls. They influenced the NT itself, notably St. Paul, the 2nd century Fathers, and through them their successors. The Greeks were also acquainted with an allegorical exegesis which discovered various philosophical meanings, according to the school concerned, in the myths of Homer and Hesiod; working on the assumption that their interpretation must be worthy of the deity (θεοπρεπές, an idea that Christian exegetes adopted), they tried to dispose of

by exegesis the many shocking passages in those poems, in reply to the criticisms voiced by Xenophanes of Colophon and by Plato. Many of their methods, like onomastics or symbolic arithmetic, were taken up by Christian writers, who also found them in the Bible and in Jewish writing. Besides the example of his philosophic myths, Plato furnished patristic exegesis with a framework for its symbolism: the two planes, that of the "forms", which alone are perfectly existent and intelligible, and that of sensible things, which have only a participated existence and intelligibility, become the plane of mystery, that is, of supernatural and eschatological values summed up in Christ, and of symbol, embracing sensible things and the letter of Scripture, the shadow and image of the supernatural. This world-view particularly influenced the Alexandrians. Then we must consider Hellenizing Judaism, the first blend of Jewish and Greek exegesis, which affected the NT in the Letter to the Hebrews. Its chief representative, after Aristobolus of Paneas and the Letter of Aristeas, was Philo, who sees the history and institutions of Israel as symbols of the wise man's interior life, under the influence of Posidonius and the Middle Stoa, an amalgam of Stoicism and Platonism. Certain Philonic exegeses, with no mention of Christ, are found in the Alexandrian school. And finally let us not forget that symbolism was a trait common to all the Eastern civilizations of which Alexandria was the meeting-place.

2. The exegesis of the 2nd-century Fathers is more restrained than that of later times, for it is much influenced by Jewish sources, including Hellenistic Judaism and the Epistle of Barnabas. We find it in Melito, St. Justin, St. Irenaeus, and in the 3rd century in Hippolytus. With his contempt for the OT Marcion rejects all interpretations of this sort, which might redeem it, and the work of the Alexandrians is partly inspired by their polemics against him. By showing figures of Christ in the history of Israel they affirm the unity of the two Testaments — the main purpose of spiritual exegesis — and the value of the Old. Though various Gnostic sects share Marcion's contempt for the old Scriptures, allegorical interpretation is nevertheless part of their method: Heracleon, the disciple of Valentinus, uses it to find the

substance of his doctrine in St. John's Gospel.

After his teacher Clement, Origen is the great theorist of spiritual exegesis, which he brings to full flower. He explains it by his theory of the three senses of Scripture — corporal (historical), psychical (moral), and spiritual (mystical), which correspond to the three elements of his anthropology, body, soul, and spirit. This trichotomy comes from St. Paul (1 Thess 5:23, among other texts), not from Plato as is often asserted. Plato's "concupiscence", "noble passion" and "intellect" play a different role. In fact, as we shall see, the theory of the three senses does not really account for Origen's method, on which the theory is imposed from without; it is not intrinsic to it.

Opponents of this type of exegesis were by no means lacking in the Great Church at the time. We are given glimpses of them through the homilies of Origen. Confused by the depth and occasional over-subtlety of his explanations, these literalists are said to adhere to "Jewish fables", that is, the literal sense of the OT stripped of all reference to Christ: they are akin to the Anthropomorphists, who take scriptural anthropomorphisms literally, to the Millenarians or Chiliasts, who understand future beatitude in a bodily sense. Though they often murmur against their preacher, they do not seem to form an organized opposition. The only name that can be mentioned, after the death of Origen, is that of the Egyptian bishop Nepos, a Millenarian who repudiated Origen's exegesis of the promise made to God's people. Against Nepos Dionysius the Great defends the interpretations of his master in his book "On the Promises".

3. In the 4th century disciples of Origen, in exegesis, abound: at Alexandria there are Didymus and St. Cyril; in Palestine Eusebius; in Cappadocia St. Gregory of Nyssa; there is also the leader of the Origenists, Evagrius of Pontus. Though St. Basil does not allegorize the first chapters of Genesis, he still takes an interest in Origen's method of exegesis (witness the *Philocalia* which he compiles together with his friend St. Gregory of Nazianzus) and sometimes follows it. Epiphanius, the first to criticize Origenism, lists allegorism among his complaints but is not above using it on occasion for his own purposes.

But opposition to the "School of Alexandria" hardened, led by the "School of Antioch". Founded in the late 3rd or early 4th century by the martyr Lucian of Antioch, teacher of Arius, it produced a series of great exegetes who forcefully attacked the Alexandrian interpretations. After Eustathius of Antioch and Diodorus of Tarsus its leading theorist was Theodore of Mopsuestia. But other representatives of the Antiochene trend — Isidore of Pelusium, St. John Chrysostom, Theodoret of Cyrrhus — baulked at Theodore's radicalism and steered a middle course between the two schools.

The friction between Alexandria and Antioch has often been called a misunderstanding rather than a conflict. If the two most characteristic theologians of each school are compared, they prove to agree on the basic issues, concern for the literal sense and belief that the OT contains a more hidden sense revealed by Christ. But the temperaments are worlds apart. Aristotle rules Antioch with his positivism, his logic, and his rationalism: it is prepared to recognize only those types of Christ which are quite plainly such. Theodore drastically cuts down their number. In prophecy what Antioch mainly sees is prediction and its miraculous character, which can be useful in apologetics. It accepts indirect prophecies couched in hyperbolic terms that are not borne out by any speedy fulfilment, but requires the prophet to be at least dimly aware of the discrepancy. Having the spiritual sense squarely based on the literal sense in this way is what the Antiochenes call θεωρία, contrasting it with Alexandrian ἀλληγορία which they hold is not so based. Alexandria continued loyal to the mystical orientation of the Platonic type. The prophet is not so much the herald of the future as the interpreter of all things in relation to God, and of biblical history in relation to Christ. Alexandrian exegesis also starts with the letter but rises above it with more ease, tending to transfigure everything in the OT, to see everything as symbolic of the eschatological blessings revealed by Christ. If the Antiochenes often give a sounder interpretation of a particular text, the Alexandrians have a profounder grasp of what Scripture means as a whole. M. Wiles has compared the commentaries of Theodore and Origen on the fourth gospel and finds that only Origen fathoms the mind of the Evangelist, while Theodore remains at the surface.

4. In the 4th century the Alexandrian exegesis of Origen's followers was adopted on behalf of the West by Ambrose and Hilary, Jerome and Rufinus. The Antiochene reaction seems hardly to have affected the Latins, except for the Pelagian, Julian of Eclanum. A new classification of the senses of Scripture, "the four senses", which the celebrated couplet of the Dominican Augustine of Dacia was to popularize in the 13th century ("Littera gesta docet, quid credas allegoria, moralis quid agas, quo tendas anagogia"), holds its ground side by side with "the three senses", throughout the Middle Ages. It first occurs, apparently, in Cassian, but it chimes in far better with Origen's practice than that of the three senses. Besides the literal it distinguishes the allegorical sense, which affirms Christ as the centre of history (note that in the present contrast seen between "typology" and "allegory" this allegorical sense belongs to the latter); the tropological or moral sense, which guides a Christian's conduct between the two comings of Christ; and the anagogical sense, which gives a foretaste of heaven. In fact tropological and anagogical meanings are mere corollaries of the allegorical. The main difference between the two formulae is that in the formula of the three senses the moral sense precedes the spiritual, thus seeming to prescind from the coming of Christ, as in the "Philonic" exegeses of the Alexandrians, whereas in the formula of the four senses the moral sense follows from the spiritual.

Most of the great Western writers of late antiquity and the early Middle Ages persevere with Alexandrian exegesis: among many others St. Augustine, St. Gregory the Great, the Venerable Bede, and St. Bernard. Until the upheaval of the 12th century, theology remained much as it was in the Fathers. It is a science in which all sciences meet, and exegesis, often spiritual exegesis, is its foundation. Or rather exegesis makes possible that progressive penetration of the data of the faith whereby tradition evolves. The lessons drawn from it are many: dogmatic and speculative theology, moral and ascetical theology, mystical theology, pastoral theology. In many of these writers, as in their predecessors, attachment to spiritual exegesis follows a careful and laborious study of history and the literal sense of Scripture. At times, like the Fathers before them, they indulge in fantasies which the moderns find distasteful.

With the advent of Scholasticism, the rise of Aristotelian dialectic, and the division of theology into various branches, spiritual exegesis gradually loses its importance. But St. Bonaventure assiduously cultivates it and St. Thomas sets forth the traditional doctrine of the four senses.

At the Renaissance Erasmus is always sympathetic towards this sort of interpretation, characterizing as it does the work of his favourite authors, the ancient Fathers. But the rationalism of modern times could hardly pass fair judgment on it. First many Protestants and then many Catholics dismissed it as an absurdity, an insult to the letter and to history, not adverting to the profound Christian vision of the world to which it gives utterance. Only very recent historians, pre-eminent among them Père de Lubac, have rehabilitated patristic exegesis.

5. A knowledge and understanding of spiritual exegesis as offered by these historians is indispensable to the historian of ancient and medieval theology and to the historian of art, for it dominates many works of the period; it is indispensable to the exegete, for the work of scientific modern exegesis would be of little use to the Christian if it did not help him find spiritual nourishment in Scripture. But is spiritual exegesis merely an element in the culture of the past, of interest to none but specialists? One must be able to read the Fathers without too much exasperation if the spiritual riches they contain (now available to the reader in modern languages) are not to be lost on one. And how, without an understanding of spiritual exegesis, is one to take a real part in the liturgy of the Church, which abounds with it? How, for example, can one read the psalms of vengeance which the Church has retained in the breviary, not as museum pieces but as food for a cleric's prayer? Without this exegesis they would clash with the gospel. To meditate on Scripture is to practise such exegesis. No doubt the bare literal sense of the OT is itself of value; but if one sees in it no foreshadowing of Christ, then one reads it as a Jew, not as a Christian. Again, how can one meditate on the life of Jesus as on events that have no meaning for us in our heart of hearts? What we say of prayer applies equally to preaching. Of course we cannot take such liberties as the ancients did and we must keep spiritual

exegesis pruned down to its essentials. But no one can preach as a Christian on the two Testaments without making use of spiritual exegesis. The dogmatic truths it evokes are of such weight for the spiritual life and even for preaching that one may wonder whether we do not often practise it unaware.

See also *Time, Redemption* II, *Anthropomorphism, Inspiration, Alexandrian School of Theology, Antiochene School of Theology, Cappadocian Fathers.*

BIBLIOGRAPHY. A. Vaccari, "La teoria nella scuola esegetica di Antiochia", *Biblica* 1 (1920), pp. 3–35; A. Oepke, *Geschichtliche und übergeschichtliche Schriftexegese* (1931); L. Puech, *L'Écriture dans S. Irénée* (1936); C. Spicq, *Esquisse d'une histoire de l'exégèse latine au Moyen-Age* (1944); J. Daniélou, *Origène* (1948); H. de Lubac, *Histoire et Esprit* (1950); H. U. von Balthasar, *Origenes, Geist und Feuer* (2nd ed., 1952), pp. 11–41; R. Hanson, *Allegory and Event* (1959); H. de Lubac, *Exégèse médiévale*, 4 vols. (1959–64); J. Daniélou, *Message évangélique et culture hellénistique* (1961); H. Crouzel, *Origène et la "connaissance mystique"* (1961); P. Grelot, *Le sens chrétien de l'Ancien Testament* (1962), pp. 407–97; J. Daniélou, *The Theology of Jewish Christianity* (1964); K. Frör, *Biblische Hermeneutik* (2nd ed., 1964); G. von Rad, *Old Testament Theology*, II (1966).
Henri Crouzel

BIBLICAL GEOGRAPHY

A. Physical Structure

1. *General survey.* Biblical Palestine lies along the Mediterranean border of the Arabian plateau. This region covers the greater part of the present State of Israel, except the southern desert, and the Kingdom of Jordan, except the eastern desert. In length about 150 miles, it falls within the parallels 31^0 to 34^0 latitude.

Moving from east to west, the relief map of the country may be divided up into four zones: a) The mountain range of Transjordan, whose height varies from 2,000 to 4,250 feet and runs in the south to the Red Sea. From base to base, this range is about 20 miles wide. b) The Jordan Valley, 5 to 20 miles wide, 685 feet below sea level at Tiberias and 1,275 feet at the Dead Sea. c) The highlands of Palestine, height from 670 to 4,000 feet, width at base about 25 to 30 miles. Running north to south, they are cut by the plains of Esdraelon and Bethshan which separate Galilee from Samaria. Then come the mountains of Samaria and Judaea which end at Beer-sheba on the edge of the desert.

d) The coastal plain, 10 to 12 miles wide, cut by the headland of Carmel.

2. *Communications.* The geography of these regions offers few major difficulties to local movement. But the great lines of communication are definitely restricted. The principal route follows the coastal plain across the Sinai peninsula to Egypt. It served to transport goods which arrived by sea. The Plain of Esdraelon is reached by the famous pass of Megiddo in the Carmel range. From Esdraelon one can join the coastal route to Lebanon or go north-east to the Upper Jordan and Syria. From Arabia, routes cross the southern deserts to reach the sea at Gaza, and the eastern deserts to reach Damascus. Thus the roads bypass rather than cut across the central mountain range of Palestine. This does not mean that the highlands were isolated. They were fertile enough to develop some trade and the monarchies of these regions played a part in the political history of the ancient East.

3. *Climate and products.* The dominant climate is Mediterranean with its usual features. It is warmer and drier than Europe. There is no rain in the summer months, and even in the mountains frost at any time is rare. The country is divided into four climatic zones:

The low-lying plain along the coast and the region of Esdraelon. In its natural state, it was often marshy or encumbered by sands, and hence unhealthy and unproductive. After much reclamation work, nearly all European products are grown there, including sugar-beet. There is intensive cattle-rearing and decisive progress has been made with cotton and bananas. Citrus fruits have long been a staple. Machinery can be used, communications are good and industries can be established. The plain is therefore open to all modern developments.

The central highlands, from 600 to 3000 feet, are generally rocky but healthy and well-watered (16 to 32 inches of rain a year). Cereals, olives, grapes and fruits are grown, as in similar regions of Europe, and the farms are similarly stocked with sheep and goats. But by modern standards, only a few valleys or plateaus can be called fertile. Communications and the use of machinery are difficult. In Europe, such levels were well-populated a century ago, but would now be empty, were it not for tourism and the neighbourhood of industrial centres. It is not surprising, therefore, if the highlands of Palestine, almost all in the Arab zone, have at times an old-fashioned air.

The level of high wooded mountains is barely represented by a few summits in Upper Galilee, Transjordan and Judaea. Elsewhere the ancient forests can only be maintained or replanted with difficulty, and economically they are of little value.

A level proper to Palestine is that of the Jordan Valley. It has practically a desert climate, but the many springs water real oases, where tropical plants such as the date-palm and the banana are cultivated. The desert region on either side of the valley rises to about 1800 feet, with a total width of about 16 miles. The rearing of sheep, asses or camels is only possible here because it is carried on by nomads. The region is a sort of outpost of central Arabia in the middle of the Mediterranean highlands.

B. The Land and the Religion

It was one of the fundamental convictions of Israel that God could be properly worshipped only in Canaan. It was only in Canaan that the patriarchs set up their altars. The temple was in Jerusalem, towards which the Jews of the synagogue turned to pray, as they still do today. While Jesus' words (Jn 4:21 ff.) warn us against legalism in revering the Holy Land, Palestine is always *the* holy land in the Old and New Testaments. It was the scene of God's great deeds, the land of the covenant and the witness to this pact between Yahweh and his people. Here the great heathen cultures clashed, and the desert close by was the setting of the prophets' call.

1. *A witness to sacred history.* More than half the sites mentioned in the OT and nearly all in the NT have been identified with reasonable accuracy. This is because the sacred writers, from the earliest times, took pains to localize the events of the history of salvation (cf. Jos 4:9; 7:26, etc.). Tradition was kept alive by Jewish and Christian communities and by the age-long practice of pilgrimages. Ecclesiastical writers like Eusebius of Caesaraea and Jerome gathered good source material containing the local traditions of the

Talmud writers. Historical research turned to Palestine in the 19th and 20th centuries. Many names and remains of ancient biblical sites were rediscovered. The most important archaeologists were the Americans Robinson and Albright, the Englishmen Conder and Warren, the Frenchmen Clermont-Ganneau and Abel, the Germans Dalman and Alt.

Present-day Palestine makes the biblical phrase, "a land flowing with milk and honey" (Exod 3:8, etc.) something of an enigma, frequent though it is, and often so eloquently dwelt on (Deut 8:7–10; 11:10–15). But history tells us that economic, cultural and social life prospered in these zones till towards the end of the 16th century A.D. The variety of agricultural products allowed the population of the Levant a healthy and balanced way of life. Poverty may now be obvious, but it is not degrading. Arable land is well exploited. Nearly all sorts of farming are carried on from all villages. Agricultural development must plan far ahead. Sociologists acquainted with the Near East have observed that the orchard owner has a far higher social standing than the cereal grower in the inland steppes. It must be assumed that this was also true in biblical times.

Israel was not a land, like Syria, open to all enterprise, and it was not extraordinarily fertile like Egypt — whose riches also contributed to the development of idolatry. Israel was a land which offered the natural conditions to the special religious position of its people.

2. *Political and religious conflicts.* But the geographical situation did not make it easy for Israel to live at peace. It was crossed by the main commercial and strategic routes between Mesopotamia and Egypt and was also easily accessible from the sea. The great heathen cultures could enter from these directions. This is attested by the Egyptian and oriental collections in our museums.

An almost endless fight was necessary to defend the political and religious independence of the nation in these circumstances. The political pretensions of Israel finally collapsed. Jerusalem was captured in 587 B.C. But the religious struggle was successful. A "remnant" remained faithful to the one God and could restore the holy people, while the false gods of Egypt, Assyria and Babylon were destroyed. This could only strengthen the chosen people in its faith. It was able to resist effectively when a new heathen culture, that of the Greeks, became influential in the East. After all the liberations which Israel itself experienced, it seems to have learned that true freedom is not a natural thing, but a gift of God's grace. The "great and gracious God" of the religions of the Mediterraneum manifested himself to Israel as the deliverer who wished man to be free (Lev 25:39–42 and *passim*).

3. *The desert as school of the prophets.* In Palestine, the hostile influences clashed with one another, while the neighbouring territory of Phoenicia assimilated them all. This has been made clear once more by the findings of archaeology. Two lands with much in common reacted very differently. Can this be explained, at least in part, by the special nature of the Holy Land?

The Bible seems to suggest so, when it notes that many of the prophets lived for considerable periods in the desert — such as Moses, Elijah, John the Baptist, Jesus and Paul of Tarsus. But the frequent assertion that the desert was the birthplace of monotheism is false. All that is known of the early inhabitants and of the Arabs before Islam proclaims the contrary (cf. Gen 31:13 to 35; 35:2ff.). No doubt life in the desert can simplify and concentrate thought, steel the body and thus help to deepen faith. Those who opted for the desert life could take no pleasure in the idol shrines "upon the high mountains and upon the hills and under every green tree" (Deut 12:2; cf. Hos 2:16; Jer 15:15–20 and *passim*). But in Scripture the desert is also a land without blessing (Gen 2:5), or accursed (Jer 4:26f.), which can become the place of temptation and was so in fact very often during the desert wanderings (Exod 14:11f.). Only in retrospect Scripture sees the desert period chiefly as the time of great grace and the fulfilment of God's promises. This evaluation also explains the bedouin type of life of the Rechabites (2 Kg 10:15f.), deliberately adopted to maintain the religion of Yahweh in its purity.

The land of the history of salvation, where free men lived in a land of beauty, though plagued by the great clashes of history; where restless city life and the hermit's solitude were not far apart — such was Palestine, and such it can still be. It is no longer the chosen land which adores the one God and follows the law of Moses. But it has a special place in the memory of Christianity.

See also *Biblical Historiography, Old Testament Books, New Testament Books.*

BIBLIOGRAPHY. F.-M. Abel, *Géographie de la Palestine,* 2 vols. (1933–38); L. H. Grollenberg, *Atlas of the Bible* (1956); G. E. Wright and F. V. Filson, *The Westminster Historical Atlas to the Bible* (2nd ed., 1956); *Atlas of Israel,* published by the Bialik Institute (1956); E. G. Kraeling, *Bible Atlas* (1957); J. Simons, *The Geographical and Topographical Texts of the Old Testament* (1957); D. Baly, *The Geography of the Bible* (1957); P. Walker, *All the Plants of the Bible* (1957); M. du Buit, *Géographie de la Terre Sainte* (1958); Y. Aharoni, *The Land of Israel in Biblical Times* (1962); H. G. May, ed., *Oxford Bible Atlas* (1962); C. Kopp, *The Holy Places of the Gospels* (1963); G. Eichholz, *Landscapes of the Bible* (1963); B. Mazar and M. Avi-Yonah, *Illustrated World of the Bible Library,* 5 vols. (1965).

Michel du Buit

BIBLICAL HISTORIOGRAPHY

The historian E. Meyer remarked that "an independent historical literature in the true sense only appeared with the Israelites and the Greeks". It is generally agreed that history, as understood in our culture, originated at two points very distant in space and time, in 5th-century Greece with Herodotus and Thucydides, and, five centuries or more earlier, with the first redactor of Genesis whose work can be identified, the anonymous author called the "Yahwist" and the other author who recounted the story of the succession from David to Solomon (2 Sam 9–20; 1 Kg 1–2). These are the first two examples of historical narratives which embrace a certain length of time and group a number of diverse events, of which they bring out the special features and show the continuity. They connect the facts by a deliberate and objective appeal to the manifold and complex factors which constitute human history: the play of natural elements, passions, characters and social customs, along with the plan and will of God who directs all from within by his creative action.

These two histories, the story of the establishment of a people on earth, the story of the establishment of a dynasty on a throne, can, on a more modest scale and a field more restricted in general, be compared favourably for firmness of design, truth of analyses and depth of insight either with the immense fresco in which Herodotus confronts the fabulous world of the Orient with the brand-new world of Greece, or with the political study in which Thucydides lays bare the causes of the Peloponnesian War and the intrinsic connections of its events.

Though the Israelite histories are clearly superior to those of their neighbours, this does not mean that the originality of Israel does not allow of natural links and analogies with the culture of the ancient East.

1. *History in the ancient East.* The effort to record and fix the memory of past events plays no little part in the culture of the ancient East. This interest in preserving a record of the past is shown in royal inscriptions in palaces and temples, in the annals registered by scribes and preserved in archives, in chronicles of reigns and chronological tables. Till about 2000 B.C., this interest is predominantly practical, concerned with administrative needs. From 2000 B.C. on the first historical syntheses appear, consecrated to re-creating the past. Their object is to legitimate existing authority by showing its continuity with that of the past. Thus lists of kings and lists of royal cities were drawn up. They are sometimes taken back beyond historical times and the deluge, to the days when the gods reigned on earth.

These syntheses show history as a series of crests and troughs: it is a vision of a succession of conquests and ruins, of advances and collapses, of periods of prosperity and of catastrophes. The explanation of these cycles is religious. They depend on the changing favours of the gods, and this in turn is generally explained by their reaction to the piety or irreligion of the sovereign.

The historical value of these documents is far from negligible. Under serious critical inspection, they furnish modern historians with a large number of solid data. It would have been impossible to write the history of Egypt without them, and so too the history of Sumer and Accad, of Assyria and the Hittites. Nonetheless, these documents never constitute the history of a reign, a people or a city. The histories of Egypt or of Babylon are the creation of modern historical science.

These historical records are in fact little more than enumerations, without real unity,

intrinsic continuity or human depth. They do not recount the march of events, they do not describe their special features. They simply list the memorable feats of kings, their great warlike deeds, their hunting exploits, their political conquests, their administrative and architectural achievements, their munificence towards the sanctuaries. At times, however, they take another tone, when trying to justify the claims of a conqueror or a usurper, and then they enumerate the series of faults and crimes which have brought down the anger of the gods.

The fact that the king appears everywhere as the sole protagonist of the action is not simply to be attributed to a sense of mission. It can also testify to authentic piety towards the gods. Triumphal inscriptions are often carved in front of gods' statues to show that they are meant to be read by the gods. Still, this way of concentrating all the action in the person of the king, of reducing all the other personages to the role of defeated adversaries or admiring witnesses, to the elimination of all human conflict, all personal attitudes, all encounter between the actors, all risk of defeat, only retains the most superficial aspect of events and leaves them without coherent links and real intelligibility. Hence they can be interchanged without difficulty: it was, for instance, the common practice of Ramses II in Egypt to efface the name of the sovereign who had had an inscription engraved and insert his own name instead. Only some Hittite inscriptions of about 1300 B.C., especially those of Mursilis II and Hattusilis III, evoke the adventures of a royal succession, the diplomatic manoeuvres and the strategic calculations of these princes in such a way as to form, in spite of their primitive style and awkward narrative, the first attempts at true history in the eastern world.

Similar principles and structures seem to have dominated the history-writing of the Persian and Seleucid empires. The constant effort is to legitimate the reigning monarch by showing that the sovereigns had never acted like conquerors or usurpers, but as the legitimate heirs, charged by the divinity to rid the earth of an unworthy master. Every change of dynasty claims to be based on the bonds of kinship, real or fictive, with the preceding dynasty. The official history of the Achaemenids sees the Persian empire as the third (and final) empire of the world, the definitive successor of the Medes and the Assyrians. After Alexander, the official view maintained by the Seleucids substitutes a system of four empires for the previous three. The apocalypse of Daniel (Dan 2:37–45) makes use of this system against the Seleucids, by announcing the coming of a fifth empire, that of the God of heaven (2:44; cf. 4:31; 7:14) which will be inaugurated by the Son of Man.

2. *The origins of history in Israel.* In contrast to these compositions, at once monumental and bloodless, the literature of Israel presents, from the 9th century onwards, typical examples of real works of history, solidly historical enough to form to the present day, even among critical historians, the framework of the history of Israel.

The soundness of these histories does not come principally from the exceptional quality of their documentation. The records were drawn up and transmitted in Israel more or less as in the courts and administrations of its neighbours. The author of the books of Samuel probably used archives, and these were necessarily affected by political currents. The redactors of Genesis collected traditions about the patriarchs coming from the distant past, which could not have escaped being coloured by intervening events. Modern historians are struck by the archaic atmosphere preserved in these memories, which is a good sign of their authenticity. Biblical inspiration, however, does not render the tradition any the less human, or any the less subject to the hazards of human transmission.

The factor that seems to have been decisive in the origins of historical writing in Israel was the following: the first compilations do not come from the courts and chancelleries, like the annals of the eastern kings, which were usually composed for the glory of the sovereign. They are based on memories which crystallized round well-known personages, and were gathered and repeated orally by storytellers. This explains the fact that in Israel the historical genre is popular in origin, anonymous and therefore ancient, existing long before the royal court and administration. It also explains why Israelite history adopts so readily and preserves so long the form of biographical narrative, a set of tales grouped round a venerable figure like a patriarch, Moses, Samuel, David,

Elijah and Elisha. It explains the lively and dramatic movement of the narrative.

But this factor alone does not explain the origins of Israelite history or the forms it took in the Bible. Its origins are religious. History is the history of the deeds of God. The originality of this history manifests the unique nature of this God.

The royal annals and chronicles outside Israel are also religious: they proclaim the power of guardian and avenging deities. But this power is exercised in a series of reactions, sometimes beneficent, sometimes fearsome, to be explained either by the natural bent of the deity or by the way it has been treated by men. These reactions are sometimes capricious, but again, they may be well-adjusted and serious. But along with superhuman power and insight, along with a cosmic immensity, they always manifest something defective and dependent: these gods react. In the last resort, they are almost puppets. They cannot create. They cannot really initiate an enterprise or bring it to a close. The perpetual ups and downs of history are the reflection of their primordial impotence: nothing is settled finally, either in advance or subsequently.

There is no real difference between present history and the mythic history of the beginnings, between the history of men and that of the gods. There is no real history. The same drama is played out throughout the ages, only the personages change.

It is different in Israel. The histories are determined by a definite goal, a single event fixed from the start. The history of David's successors originates in the prophecy of Nathan (2 Sam 7). The history of the settlement in Canaan is based on the promise to Abraham. The historical narratives of the Bible are all the story of a word of God, promise or threat, which has just been fulfilled. This principle is universal, and works at all dimensions, at that of an isolated episode like the victory of Deborah and Barak over Sisera (Jg 4), or at that of a biography like David's, or finally at that of a whole period of the people's existence, from the time it leaves Egypt till it is established in Palestine, or from David's arrival at Jerusalem till the departure of the last of his successors into captivity. This is real history because there is unity of design, and because this design, though formed and realized by God, is still carried out in the real world, through the play of natural forces, human passions and contrivances, and indeed of chance encounters, in a succession of episodes which unquestionably form part of human history. This history is our history and we see ourselves reflected there: but it is at the same time and indeed primarily the history of him who guides it and brings it to its goal, the sacred history of the true God.

At the basis of this authentically historical view of things lies the fundamental religious experience of Israel, that of the covenant. The most ancient historical accounts in the Bible, the professions of faith at Jos 24:2–13 or Deut 26:5–9, are liturgical confessions, incorporated into sacred gestures, pronounced in sacred places, founded on the decisive act of God, the covenant. But this act is essentially historical, not only because it was accomplished at a given place and date, being linked to the historical figure of Moses, but because it is itself the culminating point of a previous history, that of the election, and the starting-point of a further stage of history, the definitive establishment of Israel in the promised land. The experience of the covenant is not only the experience of a fact that was to remain without parallel; it is also the experience of a directed movement which has a beginning, a continued existence and a perfect achievement in time and in the general existence of the world. There is history, because there is an experience destined to be perceived and understood, to be recounted and fixed for ever, and because this experience is a decisive event in the evolution of the world. Something happened which the Bible was composed to express.

3. *From the history of the covenant to the history of the world*. Historical from its beginnings, the experience of the covenant led naturally to the great historical compilations of the Bible. It is almost impossible to reconstruct the stages of this process. It was certainly gradual, and it probably consisted of grouping and combining along a continuous thread memories and traditions which were originally independent, attached to individual groups and scattered shrines. There is no doubt a certain amount of artificiality in the continuous narrative which the hexateuch now offers. The artificial element is particularly noticeable in the book of Judges, but it is not confined to it. Throughout it all, the narrative remains fundamentally historical and interprets the real process which gave birth to the people of Israel and established it in its land.

But the history of Israel is wider than Israel, and goes beyond it in all directions. It goes back not only to the history of Abraham but to the origin of the world. The procedure seems to resemble what went on in Sumer, where the annalists were led to prolong the lists of reigns and royal cities back beyond the deluge, to the times when the gods reigned on earth. But in reality, the motives at work were completely different. In Sumer it was a matter of legitimating the ruling authority by showing that it went back without interruption to the primordial rulers. The histories of Israel, those of the Yahwist or those which told of the succession to David, also aimed at legitimating either the throne of Solomon or the possession of Palestine by Israel. But this legitimacy does not rest on the primordial order of things, on something which is in the end only the recognition of a divine value in the destiny of empires. On the contrary, it rests on an initial fact without anterior explanation and without precedent, on a purely divine initiative which intervened to shatter the normal course of events: the historical fact of the divine election. History up to Abraham was not for Genesis a course of events which led up naturally to Abraham, making what happened to Abraham a repetition of the primordial mythic event. On the contrary, history is built up round Abraham, and it makes the world the framework and the setting in which God raised up Abraham. This framework has the same human and historical consistency as the call of Israel and the covenant.

The description of the world and man presented in the first eleven chapters of Genesis does not offer any historical data which the historian can really make use of. It is not based on documents miraculously preserved, or even on privileged traditions. It puts before us an artificial picture, composed on the model of images furnished by oriental myths. But this picture is no longer mythic. It does not describe an unreal world, half human and half divine. It depicts the real framework of a true history, and this framework is the mankind of history.

4. *The prophets and the history of the world.* Situated in the real history of humanity, the

history of Israel also rejoins it at its end. This encounter was envisaged from the time of the first promise to Abraham, a promise destined to embrace "all the families of the earth" (Gen 12:3). The encounter is proclaimed by the prophets as a certain historical event of the future. The culmination of the history of Israel is also to be that of the history of the peoples. The prophets are constantly pre-occupied with history, which interests them from two points of view, different and complementary. On the one hand, they are very well informed of the past history of their people, very attentive to the religious traditions concerning the patriarchs, the exodus from Egypt and the conquest of Palestine. They consider these facts as fundamental. On the other hand, they are very alert to the events of their own day and strive hard to clarify their immediate significance for Israel. But this double direction of their attention is not based on the conviction that the lessons of the past are bound to furnish them with the interpretation of the present, as if the present action of God was simply the prolongation of what he had done in the past. On the contrary, there is often a profound breach of continuity between God's past actions and his present decisions: "Remember not the former things . . . Behold, I am doing a new thing" (Is 43:18f.). The past will not return again: it has been abolished both by the sins of Israel and by the inventive power of God. But there remains an absolute certainty with regard to the past, an unshakeable conviction with regard to its meaningful historicity: and this is the faith of the prophets. Once it is certain that God never ceases to govern the destiny of Israel, he must be present throughout all its history: and it is in the actual events of the present day that he pursues his purpose and brings it to its goal. The historicity of the original experience of Israel makes the prophets attentive to the religious meaning of each historic moment. They are certain that God will not abandon the work which he has undertaken. They feel themselves gripped by God and constrained to live out their lives under his hand (Jer 15:17). So they know that the history of their people cannot slip from his grasp and that the decisive event, the reign of God over the world, must surely come, in a way of which they can have only very remote conceptions.

5. *The history of Jesus Christ.* The story of Jesus Christ is completely in line with the writing and interpretation of history as done by the chroniclers and prophets of the OT. But it claims at the same time to make a completely fresh start, which both leaves behind and uniquely fulfils the previous history of the people. It is akin to the royal annals of the ancient Orient and to Israelite histories in its intention of legitimating the actual authority. From the very start, the object of the preaching of the gospel is to show how God gave to Jesus his due sovereignty over all flesh, accrediting him by signs during his life, delivering him from death and giving him possession of the Holy Spirit (Acts 2:29–36 and parr.). It is a question of giving the meaning of a series of historical events. But in this case the sequence of events, crowded though it is, is a matter of a few years, and its historical attestation does not rest on more or less ancient memories, on more or less tendentious archives, but on the testimony of disciples who know that they are bound to tell the truth, both out of fidelity to their Lord, and by reason of watchful adversaries always ready to pounce upon error. Of course, we must also remind ourselves that the writers of the gospels did not start from the concept of history which we have today, as produced in the 19th century. Their history writing is determined by the kerygma. The hearer of the message is presented with the historical processes as they are brought to life in faith in the "Pneumatic" Christ living on in his Church. The plane of the purely historical is left behind. The tendency to overcome and eliminate myth which is characteristic of all biblical history is brought to its highest degree in the history of Jesus Christ. The legitimation of Christ is based on the series of events which make up his existence, and this in turn gives meaning and consistency to all the history of Israel and to its prophecies.

The history of Jesus Christ is likewise a perfect example of human history. No other shows so clearly the forces at work in history, the conflict of passions, the import of decisions, the responsibilities of man in face of his destiny. And no other reveals more unmistakably that the history of men, precisely where it is most self-assured and most deliberately willed, remains entirely in the hands of God and accomplishes his design.

213

This history is definitive: it is the stamp of approval on all the prophecies and their final fulfilment. The world needs no other key to its meaning. Everything has happened, the Kingdom of God is there, the Spirit of the Lord fills the universe. It is the "end" of history, but so far from destroying the consistency of the history that follows, it gives it its fullness of meaning. From now on, the actions of men take on their full weight, history acquires its supreme dimension, that of the Spirit.

See also *Biblical Chronology, Old Testament Books, New Testament Books.*

BIBLIOGRAPHY. E. Jacob, *La tradition historique en Israel* (1946); H. U. von Balthasar, *Theologie der Geschichte* (1950), E. T.: *A Theology of History* (1964); E. Otto, *Die biographischen Inschriften der ägyptischen Spätzeit* (1954); J. B. Pritchard, *Ancient Near Eastern Texts relating to the Old Testament* (2nd ed., 1955); R. C. Dentan, ed., *The Idea of History in the Ancient Near East* (1955); G. Goossens, *La philosophie de l'histoire dans l'Ancien Orient* (1959); S. Moscati, *The Face of the Ancient Orient* (1960); M. Noth, *The History of Israel* (2nd ed., 1960); J. J. Finkelstein, "Mesopotamian Historiography", *Proceedings of the American Philosophical Society* 107 (1963), pp. 461–72; H. Gunkel, *Legends of Genesis* (1964); E. Otto, *Gott und Mensch nach den ägyptischen Tempelinschriften der griechisch-römischen Zeit* (1964); P. Ricœur, *History and Truth* (1965); G. von Rad, *Old Testament Theology*, II (1966).

Jacques Guillet

BIBLICAL MOVEMENT

At the same time as the liturgical movement, and no doubt in consequence of it, there arose in the Church a movement whose object was to bring the Bible back into Catholic life and thought. This movement did not originate from the higher institutions of the Church. As a *movement,* it came "from below", that is, from the vital instinct of faith working in the Church as a whole. The biblical movement of the 20th century, starting in Germany at the time of the First World War, has several sources:

1. *Preaching.* In connection with the liturgical renewal of the Eucharist, the importance of the Word of God in Christian worship came to be recognized once more. It was also found necessary to adapt the themes and style of preaching to the high place of Scripture in Christian worship. The ancient patristic tradition of the biblical homily underwent a renewal in keeping with the times.

2. *Awakening of the sense for the historical.* Part of the heritage of the 19th century, which the Church too received, was a new interest in the historical origins of Christianity. To a great extent this had apologetic motives at first, namely to counteract liberal criticism of the historical truth of the Christian faith.

3. *Discussions with Protestants.* Catholic thought had hitherto been rigidly fixed in Counter-Reformation attitudes. As it began to reflect on the Catholicity of the Church, it likewise sought contact with Protestant biblical research. The Reformed tradition, with its intimate knowledge of the Bible and its biblical scholarship, also helped to stimulate the biblical movement in the Catholic Church.

From its beginnings to the present day, the biblical movement has led to new departures in individual piety, in the liturgical life of the community, and in theological studies. Individual piety received a new impulse from being confronted with the Bible, for example when the psalms were used as a personal "prayer book". New possibilities were opened up to the liturgical life of the community, when, for instance, the word of God in Christian worship was revived as an independent element. Thus ensued a new concept of "devotions", which could be composed of Scripture reading and commentary, recitation or chanting of psalms, and prayers of intercession. Systematic theology too was set new tasks by the biblical movement, but it also received a new basis. An exegesis which had been to a great extent uncritical and fundamentalist was enabled to reach a deeper understanding of the revealed word by using modern critical and historical methods and by reflecting on its own principles. Hence arose biblical theology, which in turn occasioned new efforts on the part of fundamental theology, dogmatic theology, and ethics, in face of the fresh problems put to them. Pastoral theology and homiletics also received new sets of problems and new impulses from the study of their biblical sources. Thus the biblical movement stands at the centre of the renewal of the Church in our time. The efforts of the biblical movement received official confirmation from the encyclical published in 1920 by Benedict XV to commemorate St. Jerome (*AAS* 12 [1920], pp. 385–422), and above all from the directives and encouragement given by the encyclical *Divino afflante Spiritu* of Pius XII (*AAS* 35 [1943], pp. 297–325).

The actual development in various countries has taken very different forms, but a definite level of achievement can be recognized in the Church as a whole. It has been true for many years that one may speak of a biblical movement in Germany and the English-speaking countries, in the sense that popular editions of the Old and New Testaments, biblical periodicals, and books on the Bible have reached high figures of circulation. In the Latin countries, however, with the exception of France, interest in the Bible is only growing very slowly.

In England the Catholic biblical movement has been almost entirely the work of the "Catholic Biblical Association" (founded in 1940), and its periodical, *Scripture*. The movement is gradually gaining ground by means of editions of texts for Catholic schools and small-scale commentaries. In the U.S.A. there are far greater possibilities, which are being used by the "Catholic Biblical Association of America" (founded in 1936), whose organ is the predominantly scholarly *Catholic Biblical Quarterly*. With the means of publicity offered by press, radio and television, the biblical movement has a great future in the U.S.A. In Canada the movement has its own organization, the "Catholic Biblical Society" (founded in 1940), to which the bishops have adjoined the "Association catholique des études bibliques au Canada" for scientific research into the Bible. In Germany, the "Katholisches Bibelwerk" (Stuttgart) has been at work since 1933, with its periodical, *Bibel und Kirche*. In 1960 another biblical periodical for wider circles was founded by voluntary initiative, *Bibel und Leben* (Düsseldorf). In Austria the biblical movement is carried on by the "Volksliturgisches Apostolat", the "Klosterneuburger Bibelapostolat" (founded in 1951 by P. Parsch), and the periodical, *Bibel und Liturgie* (founded in 1926). For the German-speaking parts of Switzerland the "Schweizer Katholisches Bibelwerk" (founded in 1935) has published several series of books aimed at spreading the Bible and theological writing connected with the Bible. Though France has strictly

speaking no organized "Bible Society", one may still speak of a biblical movement in France. Leading exegetes have formed the "Association Catholique Française pour les Études Bibliques", and there are several popularizing periodicals. In Italy the biblical movement is being carried on by the "Associazione Biblica Italiana" (founded in 1953). Characteristic of the Italian movement is its close co-operation with Catholic Action and other lay movements such as the "Focolarini". In Spain, in spite of the work of the "Asociación para el Fomento de los Estudios en Espagna", with its periodical, *Boletin Biblico*, the biblical movement is still in its infancy, as it is in Portugal and South America.

A survey of the biblical movement in the Church in various countries thus shows that with few exceptions the biblical movement is still in its very first stages, which is not surprising in view of the relatively short period of its existence.

See also *Liturgical Movement*.

BIBLIOGRAPHY. Benedict XV, "Spiritus Paraclitus", *AAS* 12 (1920), pp. 385–422; Pius XII, "Divino afflante Spiritu", *AAS* 35 (1943), pp. 297–325; "Initiatives du Mouvement Biblique en divers pays", *Lumen Vitae* 10 (1955), pp. 215–55; *The Catholic Biblical Association of America*, supplement to *CBQ* 19 (1957).

Ingo Hermann

BIRTH CONTROL

1. *The general problem.* Birth control and regulation of births are expressions which are sometimes used synonymously, and sometimes to designate morally acceptable or unacceptable means of regulating the number of births. Regulation of births can mean promotion of births (which may mean artificial insemination), though it is usually used to restrict the number of births. Birth control can be attained by abstinence from sexual intercourse, abortion, or by the use of contraceptives. Limitation of births has always been practised, usually consciously, but sometimes unwittingly, as when infanticide was practised for religious reasons, sometimes on a large scale. Birth control is practised today to an alarming extent by means of abortion and infanticide as well as by the use of contraceptives. Since there can be no doubt as to the immorality of abortion or infanticide, the following considerations will be

concerned with preventives of contraception. The methods are numerous and their full range would demand a specialist survey; even the exact way in which some of them work is not yet scientifically established. At any rate, one can no longer speak of contraception if the interference expels the fertilized ovum. Often ineffectual methods are used, and some even of a magical nature among primitives. It is only since the 19th century that knowledge of contraceptives has been systematically and generally propagated.

Reasons for birth control are various: economic, social, eugenic, medical, personal, and even religious. The problem of birth control is now acute as never before. The first main reason is the "population explosion". The population of the world is increasing at a hitherto unthinkable rate. This is due to medical progress, with a fall in child-birth and infant mortality, a longer expectation of life, a longer fertility period in women, and the growing number of mothers (natural increase). Another reason is the demand for a higher standard of living, often under the growing pressure of social and economic relationships. Then, children today are a greater burden. They are not economically useful as in underdeveloped agricultural lands, and they require a more extensive education than before. A further reason is the greater stress now laid on subjective factors in sexuality, the widespread cult of sex, and the systematic propaganda for birth control. Finally, because natural selection is being reduced and the rate of mutation is growing, there are also eugenic reasons. As these reasons are for the most part not based on the intimate life of married couples or on the desire to avoid procreation, but on the inadequacy of social conditions, the solution must also be sought in terms of social reforms which will allow parents the greatest possible freedom of decision. It is the serious duty of the pastors of the Church to arouse the consciences of those responsible, and it is a pressing duty of the faithful in the world to work for conditions favourable to family life.

2. *Tradition*. The attitude of the Church towards contraception has always been — as far back as it can be traced — negative. The Church has never expressly proclaimed the ideal of having as many children as possible; on the contrary, we have witnesses from the time of the ancient Church that it has always understood the need of limiting births for various reasons. Nevertheless, in such cases the Church has up to the present century always rejected the use of contraceptives and has recommended abstinence. But one cannot simply speak of a theological tradition in this matter, especially as recent theologians have shown more and more clearly that revelation does not give a clear answer on the point. Discussion mostly started from a contemporary interpretation of the nature of sexuality and marriage, and hence from a limited perspective. The result is that the real kernel of the theological tradition is difficult to determine. As regards our present question, it seems to be that the exclusion of children on principle would frustrate the marriage consent as much as the fundamental exclusion of marital intercourse (Schillebeeckx).

a) According to the Fathers and especially Augustine, who became the great authority, sexual intercourse was to be kept to a minimum and tolerated, rather than permitted, for the sake of procreation. They held that the original purpose of sexuality was only procreation and that because of the sin of Adam it was so dominated by concupiscence that in fact sin always accompanied sexual intercourse. Only the actual desire for children was thought to justify the act; the accompanying pleasure could not be directly intended, because it was disordered by concupiscence. Augustine went so far in this direction against the Pelagians as to claim that, if there were another possible manner of procreation, sexual intercourse would always be a sinful surrender to lust. Consequently, Augustine held that true married chastity would avoid intercourse when there was no prospect of conception. But on the basis of the apostolic permission expressed in 1 Cor 7, the payment of the "marriage debt" was excused from sin for the sake of marital fidelity. But the husband committed venial sin if he demanded his rights to protect himself from the temptation of unchastity. Because the affection was centred on the marriage partner, grave sin was, as it were, pardoned or avoided in such a case. Such views make the complete rejection of any form of contraception an obvious consequence.

b) In the early Scholastic period, the norm of matrimonial ethics was whether one was yielding to sexual lust or not. Intercourse was only lawful if not solely determined by pleasure. Here too, all contraception had to be rejected.

c) In the classical period of Scholasticism it became clearer that the natural purpose of sexuality — and not just by reason of the Fall or an apostolic indult — was mutual aid, though in dependence on procreation and subordinated to it. Sexual pleasure was clearly seen to have been created by God, but it was not to be directly intended, because, on account of the harm done to nature by original sin, it was not subject to spirit. Hence theologians held that intercourse was only lawful when conception was possible. Contraceptive means and intentions were forbidden. Indeed, they were considered to be greater sins against nature than even incest, since this would at least preserve the natural purpose of sexuality. But there were signs of a new attitude, inasmuch as it was admitted that sexual pleasure was a creation of God and that it would have been even greater in Paradise, though of course subject to the spirit.

d) Since the 16th and 17th centuries, in opposition to the rigorism of the Fathers and the Scholastics which was taken up by the Jansenists in an extreme form, the attempt was made on pastoral grounds to overcome the strongly negative matrimonial ethics and to justify sexual intercourse when it was for the sake of married love (*voluptatis causa,* as the terminology had it). But this attempt was doomed to failure insofar as it considered the *copula per se apta ad generationem* in isolation. It did not question the basic presupposition that the original and fundamental purpose of sexuality was exclusively procreation. Thus, after long deliberation, the view prevailed that the pleasure accompanying the sexual act could rightly be aimed at, provided one did not interfere with the intrinsic ordination to conception. In this way the function of sexuality which justified the pleasure was thought to be sufficiently protected. The decisive criterion was thus a negative one. A positive personalist sexual ethic was subordinated to the formal and objective structure of the act, and hence to an ethic which determined the morality of human actions in the light of objects, instead of the other way round.

The most consistent expression of this tendency is to be found in Pius XI's encyclical *Casti Connubii,* with its solemn condemnation of contraceptives: "Any use of the marriage act, in the exercise of which it is designedly deprived of its natural power of procreating life, infringes on the law of God and of nature, and those who have committed any such act are stained with the guilt of serious sin." (*D* 2240.)

At the same time — and this is the other side of this actualistic as well as pastoral approach — the door was opened for the personal interpretation of sexuality. For the positive norm of intercourse, that it should be an expression of love, becomes clearer and clearer. It was stressed more and more that the *finis operantis* in intercourse could be the attestation of love and must not necessarily be the desire for offspring. Because of these considerations, Pius XI then allowed the choice of suitable times and thus justified the intention of avoiding conception where there were sufficient reasons, though he thereby directly opposed "tradition".

Pius XII went even further, when he gave the following reason for rejecting artificial insemination: "The marriage act is, in its natural use, a personal activity, a simultaneous and direct co-operation of both partners which, by the nature of the agents and of the act, is an expression of mutual self-surrender and according to the words of Scripture is the union of two 'in one flesh'." (Address of 29 Oct. 1951, *AAS* 43 [1951], pp. 835–54.)

Thus it was recognized by the pastoral office that the *finis operis* of the marriage act is to be an expression of love. It is obvious that against this background the conviction of the lawfulness and even the duty of the regulation of births would be better grounded and more widely extended than before. Thus Pius XI expressly emphasized the right to limit the number of children under certain circumstances, and Pius XII even asserted that for adequate reasons married couples could be released from the duty of procreation "for long periods of time and even for the entire duration of the marriage". Further, Pius XII, Paul VI, and Vatican II have unmistakably asserted the obligation of regulating births in responsible parenthood. However, Pius XII himself did not go so far as to recognize the lawfulness of contraceptives, evidently under the impression that the physiological structure of the sexual act could be altered by human intervention in case of need, in the physiological interests of those concerned but not for the sake of other values, even the persons involved. The justification of this principle is disputed by theologians and scientists, so that Paul VI thought it necessary to set up a commission for the study of the problem of regulation of births.

In view of these unresolved problems, Vatican II, in the Pastoral Constitution on the Church in the Modern World, contented itself with the assertion that the marriage act by which the partners are intimately and chastely united is good and right, and when it is performed in a manner worthy of the dignity of man, expresses and arouses the mutual gift of love (art. 49). It also affirmed that marriage and married love are by their nature ordained towards the procreation and education of children (art. 50). Thus the married pair should generously carry out this charge of having and educating children, and as parents with human and Christian responsibilities, determine themselves the number of children. They were also to remember that the omission of intercourse often endangered fidelity and injured the interests of the children (art. 51).

3. *Systematic theological considerations.* Against such a background the problem may be approached as follows.

a) Today the deliberate regulation and even the limitation of births is in many instances a serious moral duty for parents, for otherwise serious harm is done to marriage and the family and the greater social order.

b) Sexual intercourse has a moral value beyond and independent of procreation when it is the chaste expression of the total dedication of love.

The problem of the morality of the regulation of births can thus be precisely formulated in the question: in what circumstances can the sexual union be the expression of love even when fertility is excluded? The usual answer is: when it is sought as dedication and when there is no intervention to deprive it of its intrinsic ordination to fertility (unless intervention is necessary for the health of the person in question). Intervention would be an effort to take back the total gift of self and its intrinsic dynamism. The act would be a self-contradiction and hence nugatory. The practice of rhythm is considered acceptable because it does not interfere with the biological act and remains ordained to the established order of things. But it should be remembered that the history of married love does not simply run parallel to the biological cycle of the woman. Hence intercourse can be very suitable at the very moment when it does not suit the calendar (Beirnaert). If intervention occurs for the sake of health, it makes further giving of self possible. It has thus a simultaneous double effect and is therefore justified. Consequently the use of contraceptive methods is always allowable when, along with their contraceptive effect, they have at the same time a medical purpose and when this purpose, which justifies the intervention, is intended.

Recently, the main discussion centred on the circumstances in which such curative effects can be ascribed to medicaments that hinder ovulation. The particular point was how far regulation of the cycle is medically desirable. The main cases envisaged were the first months after childbirth, the menopause, and irregular cycles. Obviously, only medical indications can decide when medical measures are to be taken. Nevertheless, one may say that as a consequence of medical progress, indirect assistance can be given in a number of cases in which regulation of births is particularly urgent, though application, from the traditional view-point of moral theology, was formerly hard to justify. The principle of the double effect has been given wider application by the authors who allow contraceptive methods not only where both contraception and protection of health actually coincide, but also where the contraceptive effect is directly intended as a means to a greater end (or the interests of the subject). This is the case, for example, when sterilization is allowed, because on medical grounds there is no possibility of child-bearing, though there is the possibility of conception, which, however, in this case has lost its intrinsic finality. A still larger view allows temporary contraceptives to overcome psychosomatic anomalies. This is meant, with the help of therapy, to bring the patient to the stage of accepting normally a possible conception.

A growing number of moral theologians go even further. They suggest that the final criterion for judging the lawfulness of contraceptives should be still more generally and formally the good of the family and the marriage and indeed the good of mankind, according to the good or bad effects of prevention of births. They arrive at this view on the basis of the conviction that contraception in itself is neither morally good nor evil, and that the moral value of concrete actions is to be judged by whether or not they serve the moral developments of human dignity in the free and responsible person, that is, whether they serve or hinder the total fulfillment of man or only a certain dimension of his being. This cannot be determined from the objective end of the action as such, but only from the end which it is given by man in regard to man as such. If one accepts these principles, contraception would always be permitted when it promotes love between married couples and other persons indirectly concerned, and when a new conception could not be responsibly allowed in the concrete situation of those concerned. The question, how far certain contraceptives correspond to the dignity of the sexual union, depends upon how the method employed, with its psycho-physiological effects, can be integrated within the ever-changing relationships which constitute the good of the persons involved. Whether such an integration is possible in a given case is to be determined by the relevant sciences such as medicine, eugenics, psychology, sociology, etc., and, where these are insufficient, by the prudent judgment of those concerned. In this view, the lawfulness of a given means cannot be determined *a priori*, but only *a posteriori* and in the concrete. *A priori* one could only determine in a formal way (as in a model case) under what circumstances the use of contraceptives would be justified; the actual process would depend upon the concrete situation and must be determined with the help of the pertinent sciences and by the exercise of prudent judgment. A number of the authors who think along these lines proceed, nevertheless, from the *a priori* assumption that the dignity of intercourse demands the integrity of the act itself, and only permit contraceptives which leave the actual act unchanged. These are the authors who gave the first and strongest impulse to the personalist approach to birth regulation (L. Janssens, van der Marck).

4. *Pastoral theology*. Pastoral theology, according to various needs, must alert consciences to the possible duty of family planning as part of the divine charge laid upon man, of shaping his destiny and not simply submitting to nature but controlling it to create human culture even in the realms of procreation. It must further explain that the integration of sexuality into self-command is a slow struggle including setbacks, and depends on many factors outside the moral sphere. Its dynamism must be inspired by a view of marriage which sees it as a sacred state in which both partners strive for perfection. Offences against this ideal, departures from the way leading to it, defects in its realization, must be judged according to the extent to which that ideal is known and willed. If the married couple makes this basic attitude their own, they can simply act according to Augustine's principle, *ama et fac quod vis* — "love and do what you will". Their decisions will be guided more and more by the optimum, and less by the defective element possibly included in a given realization of the act (Böckle). Offences against this more or less clear and unprejudiced ideal must be judged according to the extent to which they depart from the basic attitude. When forming consciences, pastors may confidently take the married couple's own verdict as the basis of their own. Those who are conscious of no serious sin should be encouraged to partake of the sacraments and from that living source to receive new strength and hope in their effort at perfection.

See also *Ethics, Man* I–III, *Moral Theology* I, *Morality, Concupiscence, Pastoral Theology, Human Act*.

BIBLIOGRAPHY. Pius XI, "Casti connubii", *AAS* 22 (1930), pp. 539–92; Pius XII, "Addresses", *AAS* 36 (1944), p. 103; 43 (1951), pp. 835–60; 44 (1952), p. 546; 45 (1953), pp. 278–86; 48 (1956), pp. 467–74; R. M. Fagley, *The Population Explosion and Christian Responsibility* (1960); A. Zimmermann, *Catholic Viewpoint on Population* (1961); L. J. Suenens, *Love and Control* (1961); S. de Lestapis, *Family Planning and Modern Problems. A Catholic Analysis* (1961); A. Suavy, *Fertility and Survival* (1961); J. Rock, *The Time Has Come* (1963); L. Janssens, "Morale conjugale et progestogène", *ETL* 39 (1963), pp. 787–826; N. E. Himes, *Medical History of Contraception* (2nd ed., 1963); D. N. Barrett, ed., *The Problem of Population* (1964); T. D. Roberts and others, *Contraception and Holiness* (1964); L. Dupré, *Contraception and Catholics* (1964); W. Birmingham, ed., *What Modern Catholics Think About Birth Control* (1964); M. Novak, ed., *The Experience of*

Marriage (1964); G. G. Grisez, *Contraception and the Natural Law* (1964); F. Böckle, "Bibliographical Survey on the Question of Birth Control", *Concilium* 5, no. 1 (1965); E. McDonagh, "The Moral Theology of Marriage: Recent Literature in English", *Concilium* 5, no. 1 (1965); L. Janssens, "Moral Problems Involved in Responsible Parenthood", *One in Christ* (1965), no. 3; W. van der Marck, *Love and Fertility* (1965); J. T. Noonan, *Contraception. A History of Its Treatment by the Catholic Theologians and Canonists* (1965); L. M. Weber, *On Marriage, Sex and Virginity,* Quaestiones Disputatae 16 (1966); Vatican II, *Pastoral Constitution on the Church in the Modern World*.

Waldemar Molinski

BISHOP

I. New Testament. II. Church History. III. Theology. IV Canon Law.

I. New Testament

The Christian episcopate is a blend of two different systems: episcopal order and presbyterial order, these in turn being based on two different conceptions of apostleship, two different ways of being Jesus' representative. In the synoptics the apostle is one of a college, not tied to one place, but working solely within Israel as a representative of the earthly Jesus. The Twelve preach as Jesus does. This Jewish-Christian, collegiate apostolate continues in the council of presbyters which we find in the local Christian community at the period of Luke's gospel (transposed into Acts), in James, 1 Peter, Titus, 1 Timothy, and Revelation.

Contrasted with it we have the Pauline concept of apostleship, which 2 Cor 8:23 shows must have prevailed in other gentile churches as well. Here the risen Lord is represented by a single apostle, later by a single *episkopos*. There is no presbyter. Whereas the pre-NT *episkopos* was a secular official with limited duties, in the NT he is generally associated with deacons (Phil 1:1; 1 Tim 3:2, 8; cf. *Didache,* 15, 1) and much is made of the connection between *episkopos* and "shepherd" of the flock, intimated in the Septuagint: see 1 Pet 2:25; 5:2, 4; Acts 20:28; cf. Num 27:16. We may gather from 1 Pet 2:15, where ἐπισκοπή is used in the non-technical sense of "visitation", that office is primarily a matter of juridical supervision, whereas the parallel shepherding

of the flock positively leads them to salvation (cf. Ecclus 18:13); so that the two functions of the episcopal office are conveyed by combining the two terms.

Our oldest text is Phil 1:1, according to which there are still several bishops in the local community, presumably the heads of largish families who also have supervisory duties in the Church (cf. Tit 1:6ff.; 1 Tim 3:4–5). On the other hand, we are already on the road to the monarchical episcopate with Timothy's mission as Paul's representative (Phil 2:19). As the apostles disappeared, representatives of this kind gathered the episcopal duties into the hands of one individual. Thus the local character and the duties of the episcopal office derive from the "collective" episcopate, whereas its monarchical character derives from the apostolic office. If we compare the theological concept of the apostle in 2 Cor with 1 Pet, we shall perceive the theological relevance of the monarchical element. According to 2 Cor there can be only one apostle for the community, because he alone represents and communicates with the one Lord Jesus Christ in a communion of suffering and labour in the domain (κανών) that is his responsibility. 1 Pet shows how the idea of the highest local authority as an image of Christ also colours the concept of the *episkopos:* Christ is the *episkopos* of the community (2:25) and its supreme shepherd (5:4); the rulers of the community are presbyters (5:1), but their work too is ἐπίσκοπος, parallel to Christ's "shepherding" the flock. So the presbyters' episcopal work parallels that of Christ the *episkopos.* Here the presbyters represent the glorified Lord, and he is pictured in their image. Several presbyters exercise the function of the supreme shepherd. In this way 1 Pet combines the idea of an *episkopos* with presbyterial order. The monarchical episcopate arises from the image of Christ the one *episkopos,* blended with the Pauline idea of one apostle in each community. Thus the germ of the monarchical episcopate is found in the Hellenistic area which St. Paul evangelized, in the mission of Timothy, in 1 Pet and the pastoral letters. On the other hand, by way of contrast with the synagogue, the Law, and traditional Jewish thought, Paul had no trace of presbyterial order in his communities. True, that order soon penetrated the Pauline churches: by the time Acts was written the churches in Lycaonia and Pisidia had elders, like Corinth when *1 Clem* was written. (Here the Hellenistic term *episkopoi* is used.)

Acts and the Pastoral Letters show us the blending of Hellenistic episcopal order with Jewish presbyterial order. In Acts 20 the presbyters (v. 17) are called *episkopoi* (v. 28). Possession of the Holy Spirit is the decisive criterion of their vocation and authority. We may not suppose from Acts 1:20 that the episcopate is equivalent to the apostolate, since ἐπισκοπή in this text is taken from Ps 108:8. Acts 6:3 uses ἐπισκέπτεσθαι for the institution of the seven deacons. So the language of Acts shows that the word was still taken in the general sense of ruling the community and could therefore be applied to a presbyterial system as well.

Tit 1:6–9 and 1 Tim 3:1–13 belong to the same literary genre as Acts 20:18–38 (the ideal *episkopos*). According to 1 Tim 3:1 ἐπισκοπή is a permanent office which one may aspire to. The qualities necessary in the candidate are described, not the duties of the office: probity, good management of his own family, an aptitude for preaching, modesty. We have a basically presbyterial system crowned by episcopal order: in 1 Tim 5:17 the καλῶς προεστῶτες are obviously the *episkopoi* worthy of double honour. They represent the development which underlies the pre-eminence of the episcopate.

According to Tit 1:5–9 Titus is to appoint elders in Crete (which Paul himself had done: see Acts 14:23), but in v. 7 they are also called *episkopoi*. 1 Tim 3:2 and Tit 1:7, however, already speak of the *episkopos* — "a bishop" (RSV) — in the singular. Even supposing that this is a merely generic singular, the duties which Timothy and Titus had with regard to several communities soon pass to the individual *episkopos*.

See also *Apostle*.

BIBLIOGRAPHY. F. C. Baur, *Über den Ursprung des Episcopats in der christlichen Kirche* (1838); A. von Harnack, *Die Lehre der zwölf Apostel nebst Untersuchungen zur ältesten Geschichte der Kirchenverfassung und des Kirchenrechts* (1884); J. Réville, *Les origines de l'épiscopat. Étude sur la formation du Gouvernement ecclésiastique au sens de l'Église chrétienne dans l'empire romain* (1894); C. von Weizsäcker, *Apostolic Age,* 2 vols. (1894–95); A. von Harnack, *The Constitution and Law of the Church in the First Two Centuries* (1910); H. W. Beyer, "ἐπίσκοπος", *TWNT,* II (1935), pp. 595–619; K. E. Kirk, ed., *The Apostolic Ministry. Essays on the History and Doctrine of the Episcopacy* (1946); J. Colson, *L'Évêque dans les communautés primitives. Tradition paulinienne et tradition johannique de l'épiscopat des origines à S. Irénée* (1951); H. von Campenhausen, *Kirchliches Amt und geistliche Vollmacht in den ersten drei Jahrhunderten* (1953), E. T.: *Ecclesiastical Authority and Spiritual Power in the Church of the First Three Centuries* (1967); J. B. Lightfoot, *The Christian Ministry. Saint Paul's Epistle to the Philippians* (2nd ed., 1956); G. Bornkamm, "πρέσβυς", *TWNT,* VI (1959), pp. 651–83; E. Schweizer, *Church Order in the New Testament* (1961).

Klaus Berger

II. Church History

The episcopate is among those structural elements in the Church which go back to Christ. Nevertheless its precise shape and function were left to be worked out by the Church in the course of time. From the point of view of emphasis we can distinguish three major periods in that process, of which the earlier periods point to the problems of the later and vice versa.

1. *Material and formal development of the episcopal office (1st to 9th century).* At first both forms of Church government found in the NT exist side by side. *1 Clement* still recognizes the collegiate system, with presbyteral *episkopoi* whom "other eminent men" (44:3) appoint after the death of the apostles. Other successors of the apostles are itinerant missionaries (*Didache:* ἀπόστολοι). We have the transition to the monarchical episcopate towards the end of the 1st century, when a single superintendent or *episkopos* takes over in each local church. About the year 110 the letters of St. Ignatius of Antioch, with their theology of the episcopate, show us the fully developed monarchical episcopate. It is the bishop, the representative of Christ and image of the Father, who makes celebration of the Eucharist lawful, thereby guaranteeing unity in the local church; and he ensures the catholicity of that church because of his (necessary) union with the bishops of the Church universal (*Letter to the Smyrneans,* 8, 2). The *Didascalia Apostolorum* provides the canonical elaboration of this model.

By the middle of the 2nd century Ignatius's Christocentric theology of the episcopate yields to the more general notion that the bishop is a successor of the apostles. This doctrine finds classic expression in the anti-Gnostic arguments of St. Irenaeus of Lyons. The bishop is the living witness to tradition because his ancestry in office (recorded in the lists of bishops given by Irenaeus, Epiphanius and Eusebius) goes back to the apostles (*Adv. haer.*, III, 2, 1; later in Tertullian, *De praescr.*, 20, 2–4; St. Augustine, *De civitate Dei,* 18, 50). This rather juridical view is complemented by theological elements: the bishop is full of the Holy Spirit (Hippolytus). Now the episcopate is seen as linked with the historical Jesus by the Apostolic Succession and with the glorified Christ by consecration (holy orders). This twofold bond with Christ guarantees the Church's faith: παράδοσις κατὰ διαδοχήν.

As early as Ignatius we find the threefold division of office (bishop, priest, deacon). Priests and deacons are closely connected with the bishop, but the layman too plays an important part as the bishop's helper, especially in preaching (Origen, St. Cyprian, St. John Chrysostom). Laymen are likewise essentially involved in electing the bishop (St. Leo the Great, *Ep.,* 16, 10: "Qui praefuturus est omnibus, ab omnibus eligatur"), though once elected he is not the delegate of the people but *Dei episcopus.* When the Fathers work out a lofty ideal of the episcopate (St. Gregory the Great), exempting the bishop from all accountability to men because of his commission from God but at the same time binding him to perfection, they do not always escape the temptation of making the legitimacy of office depend on personal holiness (Origen, for example). A bishop's duties, according to the Fathers, include preaching the gospel (in catechesis and missions), conducting worship (where he has certain prerogatives, especially that of ordaining priests), exercising discipline (excommunicating and reconciling), and legislative and executive functions. These duties are regarded as essentially a matter of service, a charism for building up the Church (St. Augustine, *Sermo,* 46, 2: "Christiani propter nos, praepositi propter vos").

On theological foundations laid by St. Ignatius and St. Cyprian an effective ecclesiology of the *communio* is reared, especially from the fourth century onward, which dwells upon the individual bishop's responsibility for the whole Church (several bishops at a consecration, the sending of the *eulogia* [blessed bread] and the *fermentum* [consecrated hosts], bishops' encyclicals; above all, synods and councils). Under the later empire it leads to a firmer concentration (and centralization) of dioceses into units on a higher level (provinces; patriarchates). The Roman See acts as the guardian of Church unity in this process, guiding it, by the exercise of its jurisdiction, for the good of the whole Church.

2. *Relations with State, papacy, and priesthood (10th to 15th century).* Because of the various cultures in that region, several patriarchates grow up in the East. The position of the bishop (as established in the first centuries) is not challenged here; the only real controversy concerns the place of the patriarchates in the complex of the Churches. But in the West, a social and cultural unity, the Roman See remains the only centre to claim special authority over the whole Church as the See of Peter. This claim, together with political and theological developments, brings the episcopate into three magnetic fields:

a) *The State.* From the Constantinian age onwards, in accordance with the unity of the State as conceived of in antiquity, the bishops are assimilated into the hierarchy of secular dignitaries. Very soon the rulers of the empire and of the successor States claim the right to appoint bishops, a right acknowledged in 921 by Pope John X (no bishop to be consecrated *absque jussione regis*). More and more the episcopate becomes a fixed part of the feudal system; as princes of the empire the bishops are pillars of the medieval State. Their consequent involvement in the narrow selfish interests of temporal rulers (lay investiture) meant a secularization of the episcopate which was very dangerous for the Church.

b) *The papacy.* In this respect the struggle of the 11th century reforming Popes to separate the two powers, Church and State, was primarily a struggle to safeguard episcopal autonomy. But it was not long before the tension between Pope and bishops inherent in the Church's structure led to a struggle for supremacy between the two hierarchical powers, which notably enhanced the might of the papacy. Thanks mainly to the theological influence of the mendicant orders (St. Thomas Aquinas, Thomas of York, St. Bonaventure) an unduly papalist theory grew up which made the Bishop of Rome a universal bishop, concluding that the Church as one society must be subject to a single jurisdiction ("unus grex sub uno pastore"). Now the bishops figured as papal officials (Bernold of Constance, *Apol.*, 23, in *PL,* 148, 783). By way of reaction another school (Henry of Ghent, Godfrey de Fontaine, Jean de Pouilly) harked back to the ecclesiology of *communio* in the early Church and sought to make the bishops preponderant in ecclesiastical government. Owing to the weakness of the papacy during the 14th century this episcopalianism placed the bishops in a dominant position which was translated into terms of canon law in the 15th century by Conciliarism (Constance, Basle) and into terms of constitutional law by Gallicanism (Pragmatic Sanction of Bourges). But under both these headings fall a wide variety of views, ranging from repudiation of the Church's structure to justifiable defence of that same structure against papal encroachment. And apart from these controversies we find the beginnings of a collegiate interpretation of the episcopate quite consistent with the papal primacy (Ivo of Chartres, Gratian).

c) *The priesthood.* Following St. Jerome and Ambrosiaster, medieval theologians concentrated the powers of order on the *corpus Christi eucharisticum.* Since priests possess such powers no less than bishops do, practically all the Schoolmen (except William of Auxerre, Durandus, Duns Scotus, and Gabriel Biel) denied the episcopate a separate sacramental dignity, so that there seemed to be little difference between bishop and priest. The "parochialism" which some deduced from this view (parish priests are an institution of divine right) was countered by the theologians of the mendicant orders, who explained the bishop's juridical authority as a power to organize the Church (St. Thomas).

3. *Explanation of the nature of the episcopate (16th to 20th century).* The Reformation of the 16th century attempted to resolve these conflicts over the episcopate, whose representatives had become a source of scandal owing to their worldly manner of life, by casting aside the office itself or treating it as a purely human expedient in the Church. The episcopal structure, variously interpreted, is preserved in the Lutheran Churches of Scandinavia, the Reformed Church of Hungary, among the Moravian Brethren and American Methodists, since 1918 in many territorial Lutheran Churches of Germany, and in the Church of South India. The Churches of the Anglican Communion regard the historic episcopate as part of the Church's *plenum esse.*

Catholic theologians, drawing on patristic tradition, are now working out a new and largely pastoral conception of the episcopate. The Council of Trent clearly distinguished the episcopate from the priesthood (*D* 967) but without specifying how it is related to the primacy, so that much discussion ensued as to whether bishops receive their jurisdiction directly from God or through the Pope. Bishops were exhorted to care for their flocks in an apostolic spirit (duty of residence). 16th-century writers inspired by the Council (Contarini, Giberti, Bartholomew of the Martyrs, L. Abelly) described the ideal bishop as a likeness of the Good Shepherd, a likeness that became flesh and blood in such men as St. Charles Borromeo, St. Francis de Sales, St. Robert Bellarmine, Fénelon and Bossuet. While the papal system grew towards its climax in the tight centralization of the 19th century (concordats, struggle over nunciatures, Joseph de Maistre), and a new episcopal particularism arose in the form of Febronianism, the collapse of the Catholic bishops' power through secularization led men to ponder the spiritual function and autonomy of the bishops under the primacy (J. A. Möhler). Defining the Pope's universal episcopate, Vatican I condemned extreme episcopalianism (*D* 1831), but at the same time rejected extreme papalism by stressing the inherent rights of the bishops (*D* 1828; cf. *DS* 3112–3117). Because the Council was prematurely broken off, there was no time to work out a more thorough theology of the episcopate, a task which remained for Vatican II.

The ground having been prepared by historical and systematic studies of the main issues involved (Bertrams, Botte, Colson, Congar, Dejaive, Küng, Lécuyer, Karl Rahner, Ratzinger), this Council dwelt particularly on the sacramental character of episcopal consecration, the derivation of all episcopal powers from *ordo,* the collegiality of the episcopate under the primacy, the importance of local Churches, and their communion with the Church universal. In the changed conditions of today, when the centrifugal tendencies of earlier episcopalianism are no longer to be feared, the Council wished to do justice to the plurality of cultures by strengthening the Church's peripheral structures in a spirit of true Catholicity. But the heritage of history demands that we further explore certain problems, particularly the practical relations between the primacy and the episcopate (the function of episcopal synods), the bishops' power of jurisdiction, the relations between bishops and priests, and the exercise of collegiality (episcopal conferences).

See also *Apostolic Succession, Episcopalism, Gallicanism, Conciliarism, Patriarchate.*

BIBLIOGRAPHY. K. E. Kirk, ed., *The Apostolic Ministry. Essays on the History and Doctrine of the Episcopacy* (1946); *Episcopus. Studien über das Bischofsamt* (1949); M.-J. le Guillou, *Mission et unité* (1950); H. Jedin, *Il tipo ideale di vescovo secondo la Riforma cattolica* (1950); M. Jourson, *L'Évêque comme membre du peuple de Dieu selon St. Augustine* (1951); J. Colson, *L'évêque dans les communautés primitives* (1951); H. von Campenhausen, *Kirchliches Amt und geistliche Vollmacht in den ersten drei Jahrhunderten* (1953), E. T.: *Ecclesiastical Authority and Spiritual Power in the Church of the First Three Centuries* (1967); P. Bronlin, *L'évêque dans la tradition pastorale du seizième siècle* (1953); *Études sur le sacrement del'ordre* (1957); K. M. Carey, ed., *The Historic Episcopate* (2nd ed., 1960); D. Dejaifve, *Pape et Evêques au Premier Concile du Vatican* (1961); J.-P. Torrell, *La théologie de l'Épiscopat au Premier Concile du Vatican* (1961); G. Alberigo, *Lo sviluppo della dottrina sui poteri nella chiesa universale. Momenti essenziali tra il XVI ed il XIX secolo* (1964); H. Küng, *Structures of the Church* (1965); G. Baraúna, ed., *De Ecclesia,* II (1967).
Wolfgang Beinert

III. Theology

1. *Successors of the apostles.* The institution of the episcopate is to be understood only in relation to the institution of the apostles by Christ. Examination of the texts in the NT permits one to make the following observations:

a) The apostles are called to the *service* of the whole Church, a *diakonia* which finds its most perfect exemplar in Christ, who came not to be served but to serve (Mk 10:42–45; Mt 20:25–28).

b) According to Mt 28:19–20, their mission is to teach all men, to sanctify them

by the sacraments, and to bring the faithful to obey the commands of the Lord.

c) In order to accomplish this mission, the apostles receive a special gift of the Holy Spirit (Jn 20:21–23; Acts 1:8; 2:2–5).

d) Each of the apostles receives this mission and this grace in union with the other apostles. Together they form a whole, a well-defined body to which the NT often applies the expression: *The Twelve* (Mk 3:14–16, etc.). It is to this group, reduced to eleven by the defection of Judas, that Matthias is admitted, to become *with them* a witness of the Resurrection (Acts 1:26).

e) To this group, the unity of which is so manifest, one can apply the title "college", provided that one does not take it to mean that all the members of it are equal. Peter occupies a special place and is endowed with a higher authority which no one contests, founded as it is on the words of Christ himself (Mt 16:16ff.; Lk 22:31ff.).

But the office of the apostles was not to cease with them. We know from Acts and the epistles that they chose helpers in their tasks of preaching and governing the communities (Phil 2:25; Col 4:11). These helpers shared the apostles' authority: "The Holy Spirit has made you guardians, to feed the church of the Lord." (Acts 20:28.) The faithful are to recognize them as their rulers (cf. Heb. 13:7, 13, 24). It is not always possible to distinguish between "elders" (Acts 11:30; 14:23 and *passim*) and "bishops" (Phil 1:1; Acts 20:28, etc.). The fellow-workers of the apostles are warned not to try to lord it over the faithful (1 Pet 5:3). Their office, like that of the apostles, is a ministry, a service for the good of the community.

According to Clement of Rome, the apostles "having received a perfect foreknowledge, appointed the above-mentioned bishops and deacons, and afterwards they made a law according to which other tried men were to succeed to their ministry after their own death" (*1 Clem,* 44). The expression "successors of the apostles" was a common way of designating bishops from the time of St. Irenaeus; cf. First Vatican Council, *D* 3061.

The third chapter of Vatican II's Dogmatic Constitution on the Church bases the connection between the apostles and the bishops on Scripture. The existence of the episcopate is explained by the character of the gospel message: "... since the gospel which was to be handed down by them (the apostles) is for all time the source of all life in the Church. For this reason the apostles took care to appoint successors in this hierarchically structured society." (Art. 20.) More precisely, the Council affirms that the college of the apostles with and under Peter corresponds to the college of bishops with and under the Roman Pontiff, the holder of the Petrine office. "Just as by the Lord's will, St. Peter and the other apostles constituted one apostolic college, so in a similar way *(pari ratione)* the Roman Pontiff as the successor of Peter, and the bishops as the successors of the apostles are joined together." (Art. 22.)

2. *Sacramentality of the episcopate.* To aid them in their task, the apostles received a special gift of the Holy Spirit. Hence from the beginning, in appointing collaborators, they used a liturgical rite consisting of prayer and the imposition of hands, signifying the gift of a special grace in view of the task to be fulfilled. A similar rite was used for the appointment of the first deacons (Acts 6:6), and of the presbyters in the course of the journeys of St. Paul (Acts 14:28). In the case of Timothy (1 Tim 4:4; 2 Tim 1:6), the imposition of hands conferred a special spiritual gift, that of "power, love and self-control", like that which St. Paul himself was conscious of having received (2 Tim 1:7, 11).

Christian tradition has understood episcopal consecration to be the continuation of this rite. It is a sacramental rite, composed of external signs and liturgical words, which confers a grace. An attentive study of liturgical documents, beginning with those of the greatest antiquity, reveals that the Church has always considered this rite to be a sacrament which confers the fullness of the priesthood and bestows a grace enabling the bishop to carry out his own special duties. Doubt could arise on this point only when theology, instead of beginning with the bishop, began with the priest in order to ask what the episcopate could add to his dignity. But episcopal consecration is not something added to one who has previously been ordained a priest. When conferred on one simply baptized, it at once bestows the

fullness of priestly power, enrolling him in the ranks of the supreme pastors of the Church. Before receiving this sacramental rite, a layman can already have authority over other Christians, even over the faithful as a whole. Such would be the case of a layman who is elected Pope. From the time of entering upon office he would enjoy jurisdiction (i.e., every Christian would owe him obedience) as well as personal infallibility (i.e., God would not allow him to affirm an error if he decided to make a definition *ex cathedra*). But even in this case such a possibility is linked to consecration. A layman called to the episcopate must not only have himself consecrated, but any authority he may have depends on his intention of receiving the sacrament. In the Apostolic Constitution *Sacramentum ordinis* of 1947 (*D* 2301) it is assumed that episcopal consecration is a sacrament and not just a sacramental, though this is not formally decided.

Episcopal consecration, therefore, confers a grace which is ordained to the service of the faithful. Liturgical and patristic documents refer to it as the office of pastor, witness, and high priest. By virtue of it the bishops, in carrying out their duties, become the official representatives, the vicars, of the one high priest Jesus Christ. And as, according to the Council of Trent (*D* 964), the sacrament of orders confers a character, the episcopate marks him who receives it with an indelible spiritual sign for the exercise of the *magisterium,* of the priesthood, and of authority in the Church in such a manner that, by means of the bishops, the glorified Christ continues visibly to teach, to sanctify, and to govern his flock. Vatican II developed further the theology of Trent. Christ himself is present and active in the bishops. "In the bishops ... our Lord Jesus Christ the supreme High Priest is present in the midst of those who believe." (Dogmatic Constitution on the Church, art. 21.) The authority and dignity of the office is conferred by the sacrament of episcopal consecration. "This sacred Synod teaches that by episcopal consecration is conferred the fullness of the sacrament of orders." *(Ibid.)* Thus the bishops are entrusted with "the apex of the sacred ministry" *(ibid.),* that of the ministerial or hierarchical priesthood, which presupposes the common priesthood of all the faithful (art. 10).

3. *Ordo Episcoporum*. Just as Peter and the other apostles constitute a community, an established group or body, so the successor of Peter forms with the other bishops an episcopal body *(ordo episcoporum)* which offers many signs of the unity and solidarity which reign among its members. The terms employed, *ordo* (Tertullian), *corpus* (Cyprian), *collegium* (Cyprian, Optatus of Milevis), ought not, however, to lead one to imagine — what the word *collegium* can mean in certain cases — an established group in which all are equal and in which the only authority is that which results from the agreement of all its members (or at least the majority). In the body or college formed by the bishops there is one supreme authority — that of the Bishop of Rome, the Pope, whose prerogatives have been defined by Vatican I. Without him the body of bishops would lose its unity and its stability.

Episcopal consecration manifests and brings about the adoption of a new member into the episcopal college. The most ancient prayers (Apostolic Tradition, *Canones Hippolyti,* Apostolic Constitutions) ask for the new bishop the power of the Spirit, which Christ had given to his apostles. These prayers ask for him the grace necessary to guide the Church of God. Here it is not merely authority over a particular region of the Church (for some bishops have no diocese) but "ad regendam ecclesiam tuam et plebem universam" *(Sacramentarium Leonianum)*. In other words, he is to take a certain part in the government of the universal Church: the sacred rite incorporates him into the episcopal order (Roman Pontifical). An extremely ancient tradition requires all the bishops present, or at least three of them, to impose their hands on the newly elected bishop. It is not merely that a bishop consecrates a successor: the consecration of a new member is the concern of the entire episcopal body, represented by several members.

The doctrine of the *ordo episcoporum* has been re-formulated to some extent by Vatican II, inasmuch as it lays stress on the collegiality which we have mentioned above. The college is not just the sum of its members. It is something prior to the individuals, and as such, goes back to the will of the Lord in instituting it. The individual must be incorporated into the college if he is to become a bishop. "Hence, one is constituted a member of the episcopal body by virtue of sacramental consecration and by hierarchical communion with the head and members of the body." (Dogmatic Constitution on the Church, art. 22.) In this college, the members are united to their head, the Roman Pontiff, and to the other members of the hierarchy. The structure of the Church has therefore two aspects. One is that the bishops of the whole world remain "linked with one another and with the Bishop of Rome by the bonds of unity, charity, and peace" *(ibid.)*. The other is that the monarchical principle is combined with the synodal. "The Roman Pontiff, as the successor of Peter, is the perpetual and visible source and foundation of the unity of the bishops and of the multitude of the faithful. The individual bishop, however, is the visible principle and foundation of unity in his particular church, fashioned after the model of the universal Church. In and from such individual churches there comes into being the one and only Catholic Church." (Art. 23.)

4. *Duties and powers.* As with the apostles, one may readily distinguish three forms of episcopal service or ministry: doctrinal, priestly (administration of sacraments), and pastoral.

a) *The teaching office.* The first duty of the apostles was to teach all nations (Mt 28:19). That mission of teaching all men has passed to the successors of the apostles, and they have received that inheritance in common according to the expression used by Pope Celestine to the Council of Ephesus in 431. Therefore, from the very fact of his incorporation into the episcopal body, each bishop is responsible for the preaching of the gospel, not only to the faithful of his diocese, but to all mankind. Each of the faithful is obliged to participate in the diffusion of the word of God, but the mission of the bishops remains a very special one. Consecration confers a "special charism of truth" (Irenaeus, *Adv. Haer.,* IV, 26, 2), an illumination and force often compared with that which the apostles received at Pentecost. Hence in the bishops as a body, the assistance of the Spirit makes this *magisterium* infallible. The individual bishop is not infallible, but the episcopal body is. Here the collective or collegial character of the episcopate appears. Infallibility belongs to the body of bishops with and under the Bishop of Rome. It is guaranteed to the teaching body united with its head, and in a special way to the latter as leader of this body and centre of the unity of the Church. This infallibility is one of the concrete forms taken by that of the Church itself (First Vatican Council, *D* 1839). When the Pope defines alone a question of faith, the whole fellowship of the bishops which speaks through him, is included.

But it would be wrong to reduce the episcopal magisterium to infallibility, which is a negative notion. The power of the Spirit helps positively to preach the truths of faith so that they correspond to each new situation of the faithful. The bishops are responsible for the study of the word of God, and must be vigilant to exclude all error. "Keep watch, you have received a Pneuma which does not sleep." (Ignatius, *Ad Polycarp.,* I, 3.)

b) *The priestly office.* By his consecration, the bishop receives the fullness of the priesthood. The whole people of God is priestly and royal through baptism, but the one high priest, Jesus Christ, consecrates in a special manner to his service those whom he has chosen for the episcopate, in order that they may be the visible representatives of his sovereign priesthood (cf. Cyprian, *Epistolae,* 63, 14). Because it is especially by the sacraments that the priestly action of Jesus extends to us, the bishops are the principal ministers of the sacraments. If, in this ministry, they provide themselves with helpers who participate in their priesthood, the entire sacramental order still remains under their authority and dependent upon them. There is no legitimate Eucharist, says Ignatius of Antioch, save that "which is celebrated under the presidency of the bishop or of him whom the bishop shall have charged with it" (*Smyrn.,* 8, 1). Likewise St. Thomas teaches, "It pertains to the bishop to give simple priests what is necessary for the fulfilment of their proper function. That is why the blessing of the holy chrism, of the oil of catechumens, of altars, of churches, of vestments, and of sacred vessels . . . is reserved to the bishop as head of the whole *ordo ecclesiae.*" (*Summa Theologica,* III, q. 82, a. 1, ad 4.) Besides, the bishop is the ordinary minister of certain sacraments: such is the case with confirmation and holy orders.

If we prescind from the restrictions in canon law (*CIC,* can. 337), which do not affect the validity but the lawfulness, the power conferred by consecration on the bishop is not restricted to one diocese. It is universal. This means that through consecration each bishop receives a clearly-defined power over the whole Church, for the unity and growth of the mystical body, through the sacraments.

c) *The pastoral office.* Episcopal consecration confers a charism which enables the bishop to govern the people of God. Like the power to consecrate, the pastoral office is for the whole Church. However, for reasons of order and convenience (of which the head of the body of bishops is the judge) the exercise of the individual bishop's power can be (and is) limited. It can only be exercised (with corresponding jurisdiction) over a limited portion of the Church. Yet the bishops remain jointly responsible for the general good of the Church, whose unity and progress in charity they ought to promote, not only by obeying their head, but also by active co-operation with the Pope and with each other. The more fully the local Church is the Church of God, the more fully does it embody the whole Church. This solidarity of pastoral rule is particularly evident when all the bishops are united in Council under the presidency of the successor of Peter. They form with their head, the successor of Peter, the supreme and sovereign authority. Hence as representatives and interpreters of the law of Christ, the law of love, the bishops merit the title which Augustine gave the bishop: "Servant of the servants of God" (*Ep.,* 217; *PL,* XXXIII, col. 978).

On the authority conferred by consecration, Vatican II teaches that the one sacramental power is divided into three offices. The first to be named is the office of preaching the gospel. "Among the principal duties of bishops, the preaching of the gospel occupies an eminent place." (Dogmatic Constitution on the Church, art. 25.) Then comes the office of mediating salvation through the sacraments. The bishop is the "steward of the grace of the supreme priesthood", especially in the Eucharist, which he himself offers or causes to be offered (art. 26). "Through the sacraments, the regular and fruitful distribution of which they direct by their authority, they sanctify the faithful." (*Ibid.*) Thirdly, the bishop is pastor of his Church, governing the local Church entrusted to him as "vicar" and "ambassador" of Christ (art. 27). The word "entrusted" points to the fact that the sacramental-ontological office, which is to be distinguished from the canonical-juridical aspect, cannot be exercised without an act of the Roman Pontiff, however this takes place (N.B. to the *Nota praevia* on ch. 3 of the Constitution on the Church).

See also *Apostolic Succession, Charisms, Orders and Ordination, Magisterium, Council.*

BIBLIOGRAPHY. J. Lécuyer, *Le sacerdoce dans le Mystère du Christ* (1957); K. Rahner and J. Ratzinger, *The Episcopate and the Primacy,* Quaestiones Disputatae 4 (1962); M. Wilks, "The Apostolicus and the Bishop of Rome", *JTS* 13 (1962), pp. 290–317; 14 (1963), pp. 311–54; Y. Congar, *Wide World, My Parish* (1961); W. Bertrams, *De relatione inter episcopatum et primatum* (1963); P. Benoît, M.-D. Chenu and L. M. Orrieux, *L'Évêque dans l'Église du Christ* (1963); J. Lécuyer, *Études sur la collegialité épiscopale* (1964); P. Anciaux, *Episcopate in the Church* (1965); J. Hamer, *Church is a Communion* (1965).

Joseph Lécuyer

IV. Canon Law

1. *Meaning of episcopate.* The episcopate is that ministry established in the Church of Jesus Christ which bestows a share in the Church's office of teaching, sanctifying, and governing. Those called to it are successors of the apostles and consequently exercise their ministry as vicars and envoys of Christ, individually as the head, bishop, of a particular Church, as a collegiate body of several bishops serving a group of particular Churches, and as the collegiate body of all the bishops, united in serving the Church universal. The ministry carries with it a sacred authority which arises from episcopal consecration and becomes an exercisable power through canonical mission from the competent ecclesiastical superior. Catholic tradition regards the bishop as the shepherd of his flock, sometimes expressed in the image of the spiritual marriage. The essential relationship is noted as early as Ignatius of Antioch: "Wherever the bishop appears let the congregation be present; just as wherever Jesus Christ is, there is the Catholic Church." (*Letter to the Smyrnaeans,* 8, 2.) The bishop presides over a component Church which in its own field represents the whole Church — is part of a whole in the sense that the whole works through the part. This presiding ministry is the episcopal office in the juridical sense.

In the *CIC* the term episcopate is always used in this restricted sense (can. 108, § 3; 332, § 1; 333, 334, § 2; 629, § 1; 2398). The Pope's office of supreme jurisdiction and this episcopal office which is subordinated to it, are the two offices of divine institution. They have been supplemented by other ranks by virtue of ecclesiastical institution (can. 108 § 3). Here we have the framework of the Church's constitution so far as the *CIC* is concerned (lib. II, tit. VII and VIII). In canonical parlance the episcopate also means all the bishops or a body of bishops, for example the bishops of a country, but the collegiate aspect of the episcopate is not brought out. Attributive adjectives are generally used to indicate the whole episcopate: thus *universus episcopatus* in the motu proprio *Arduum sane munus* of 19 March 1904, calling on all bishops to collaborate in codifying the canon law, and *totus catholicus episcopatus,* which the episcopal synod created by Pope Paul VI (motu proprio *Apostolica Sollicitudo,* 15 Sept. 1965, no. 1, b) is now to represent. Though this document avoids making any reference to the principle of collegiality, in the light of the doctrine on the episcopal college set forth by Vatican II the word episcopate doubtless includes the collegiate element of the bishops' ministry.

2. *Nature and purpose of the episcopate.* All members of the new people of God share in the mission of the Church. When treating of laymen the Council repeatedly declares that all members share, each in his own way, in the threefold office of Christ and the Church — the office of teaching, sanctification, and governing — and carry out the mission of the whole Christian people in the Church and the world (Vatican II, *De Ecclesia,* art. 31; see *De Ap. Laic.,* art. 2). Without prejudice to this share that all have in the Church's mission, there is a diversity of ministry, for Christ instituted an authority in his Church which does not fall to every member of the Church, but only to those who are called in tangible, juridical form to govern God's people in the name of the Lord. Ecclesiastical authority exists only in order to serve; it is part of the Church's nature, the foundation of its hierarchical structure, of which the Church as a sacramental sign is the theological setting. As a visible society rooted in Christ

and ordained to him, the Church is the sign of salvation, raised up for all men by the Lord, "a kind of sacrament or sign of intimate union with God, and of the unity of all mankind" (Vatican II, *De Ecclesia,* art. 1). Because the divine element proper to the Church shows through its human element and becomes tangible in it, and because the Lord, the invisible Head of the Church, is visibly represented in it by men, the Church is a sign of salvation, something analogous to the mystery of God's Son made flesh, as Vatican II teaches (*De Ecclesia,* art. 8). Without a visible head the Church cannot visibly represent the body of the Lord. And therefore the Lord appointed the twelve apostles, making them, as the word indicates, his representatives in the juridical sense, and set Peter at their head. Peter's successor is the Pope, and the successors of the apostles are the bishops, who are called to represent the Lord in collegiate union with the Pope — he too is a bishop — and in subordination to him. "He who hears them hears Christ, while he who rejects them, rejects Christ and Him who sent Christ." (Lk 10:16 and Vatican II, *De Ecclesia,* art. 20.) The image of the mystical body shows us that the Church is structurally one as head and members are: the invisible Lord is represented for the universal Church by the Pope, and for each particular Church by a bishop.

In this connection the Council observes: "The Roman Pontiff, as the successor of Peter, is the perpetual and visible source and foundation of the unity of the bishops and of the multitude of the faithful. The individual bishop, however, is the visible principle and foundation of unity in his particular church, fashioned after the model of the universal Church. In and from such individual churches there comes into being the one and only Catholic Church. For this reason each individual bishop represents his own church, but all of them together in union with the Pope represent the entire Church joined in the bond of peace, love, and unity." (Vatican II, *De Ecclesia,* art. 23.) This text occurs at the point of transition in the Council's thought from the doctrine of the episcopal college to the doctrine of the bishop as ruler of a local Church and enables us to grasp the inward coherence of the bishop's two roles, the personal and the collegiate. At the head of the whole Church and of each particular Church respectively, we have a personal ruler, and all the heads of the particular Churches, in union with the Pope, represent the universal Church. It is not simply a matter of parts joining to form a whole; at the same time, though we are not expressly told so here, the whole Church is present in the particular Church, and through his hierarchical communion with head and members of the episcopal college each bishop represents the universal Church, present in his particular Church, for the flock that is entrusted to him. Accordingly the bishops have a twofold representative function. They represent the universal Church consisting of many particular Churches, and the particular Churches in which the universal Church is present. In the one case the parts must be integrated into the unity of the whole, while in the other the particular Church must be capable of that integration. There is a reciprocal connection between the personal and collegiate elements, each as it were becoming operative in the other; it would be wrong to play off one element against the other.

3. *Gradations in the episcopal ministry.* Besides the ministry of sanctification, episcopal consecration bestows the ministries of teaching and governing, which by their nature can only be exercised in hierarchical communion with the head and members of the episcopal college (Vatican II, *De Ecclesia,* art. 21). Though all bishops have this same sacramental power, there are nevertheless many gradations within the episcopal ministry which cannot be accounted for in terms of order but only in terms of office. Pope, patriarch, metropolitan, and diocesan bishop are all in the same episcopal orders, but in respect of office they form a hierarchical pyramid for the sake of the unity of God's people. Apart from the office of the Pope and that of the episcopal college, which concretely exist in the Church by divine institution, so that the Church can neither bring them into being nor do away with them, all other episcopal offices, relating as they do to particular societies in the Church, need to be fixed by the appropriate ecclesiastical authority. Law or custom must establish particular forms of episcopal office and then concretely set up a given office. In these two respects the gradations of the episcopal ministry flow from the Church's power to organize itself, but the content of the concrete ministries that are to

be exercised remains of divine right because the episcopate is of divine institution.

The major gradations are the following:

a) The office of diocesan bishop, of prime importance among the episcopal ministries because the organization into episcopal Churches is an essential part of the Church's constitution. The diocesan bishop presides over part of the people of God (diocese) in such a way that he possesses, as a successor of the apostles, all ordinary, proper, and immediate authority necessary for discharging his pastoral duties (Vatican II, Decree on the Bishops' Pastoral Office in the Church, art. 8a). To the flock allotted him he represents the invisible Lord; and working with his priests he so binds the individual faithful into union with Christ and for Christ that "the one, holy, catholic, and apostolic Church of Christ is truly present and operative" in this particular Church (*ibid.*, art. 11). His proper power of jurisdiction extends to legislation, judgment, and administration. So widely may the duties of a diocesan bishop vary, according to the size of his diocese, that without any change in his juridical position one bishop may find himself doing some of the work of a parish priest and another bishop some of the work of a metropolitan.

b) The office of metropolitan, who as an archbishop presides over an ecclesiastical province and has a certain superiority over the diocesan bishops of that province (called his suffragans) — much less in the Latin Church than used to be the case. The metropolitan cannot legislate, but has the right to convoke and preside over provincial synods (*CIC*, can. 284). As to administration he has certain supervisory and supplementary rights (*CIC*, can. 274, nn. 1–5). He is the ordinary court of appeal at common law from judgments pronounced by his suffragans (*CIC*, can. 274, n. 8, 1594, § 1), but for his own part must allow appeals to the court of one of his suffragan bishops (*CIC*, can. 1594, § 2). A metropolitan wears the pallium in token of his metropolitan power and his communion with the Pope. The Eastern Churches in communion with Rome distinguish between a metropolitan within a patriarchate and one outside. The former is immediately subject to the patriarch, the latter immediately to the Pope. Both were given the right by the First Council of Nicaea (can. 4) to consecrate and enthrone the bishops of their province (*CIO*,

can. 319, n. 1, 320 § 1, n. 4). Where metropolitan organization has not yet been restored, the duties of the metropolitan fall to the patriarch (*CIO*, can. 242). Vatican II directed that the boundaries of the ecclesiastical provinces be duly reconsidered and the rights and privileges of metropolitans set down in appropriate new rules (Decree on the Bishops' Pastoral Office, art. 40). In future all dioceses and similar local Churches will be assigned to an ecclesiastical province; and so dioceses now directly subject to the Apostolic See are to form a new ecclesiastical province or to be joined with a neighbouring province and placed under the metropolitan jurisdiction of the archbishop *(ibid.)*. Obviously there is an effort to enhance the dignity of the metropolitan office.

c) The office of patriarch, which has remained intact in the Eastern Churches united with Rome, is absorbed by the papal primacy in the Latin Church, whose patriarch is the Bishop of Rome. The new Oriental Canon Law of persons, codified by Pius XII's motu proprio *Clerici Sanctitati*, 2 June 1957, devotes nearly 100 canons to the patriarch (can. 216–314). In the East the patriarch is the hierarchical head of his patriarchate, that is, a group of episcopal Churches of the same rite. "Father and head" of his patriarchate, the patriarch has ordinary jurisdiction over all the bishops (including metropolitans), clergy, and people of his territory or rite; but besides the link with the supreme pastor of the Church, the patriarch's jurisdiction must often be exercised conjointly with synodal bodies (patriarchal synods and standing synods). The patriarchal territories of various rites overlap, so that several patriarchs have (a basically territorial) jurisdiction over the same area, but each only in respect of members of his own rite. Outside the patriarchate Eastern patriarchs still have jurisdiction over the faithful of their rite insofar as this is expressly affirmed by the common law or local canons (*CIO*, can. 216). Patriarchs are elected by the bishops of the patriarchate assembled in the electoral synod. Papal confirmation is required only if the patriarch-elect is not yet a bishop. A bishop who is elected patriarch takes office by accepting his election; he is then proclaimed patriarch by the electoral synod and enthroned, but must inform the Pope that the election has taken place and ask for the pallium in token of communion with the Pope, before either calling a patriarchal synod or holding episcopal elections or ordinations (*CIO,* can. 221 ff.).

Vatican II speaks with high esteem of certain ancient patriarchal Churches, which have engendered "daughter" Churches in the faith (*De Ecclesia,* art. 23), and rules that the rights and privileges of patriarchs shall be restored in accordance with the ancient traditions of each Church and the decrees of the ecumenical councils, as they stood when East and West were still united, though a certain adjustment to present day conditions is in order (*De Eccles. Orient.,* art. 9). Since the patriarchate is the traditional form of ecclesiastical polity in the Eastern Churches, the Council wishes that new patriarchates be set up where necessary. This is the business of the ecumenical synod or of the Pope (*De Eccles. Orient.,* art. 11). The constitution of the Church provides that the supreme jurisdiction of the Pope and all higher episcopal office, like that of patriarchs or metropolitans, shall be connected with a particular see: that is, Pope, patriarch, and metropolitan also rule a particular diocese, just as any other diocesan bishop does. This feature of the Church's constitution, which has hardly any parallel in secular society, draws attention to the collegiate aspect of the episcopate and at the same time to the inner bond between episcopal orders and episcopal office. Only in the case of the titular (arch-) bishop, who is consecrated for an abandoned see but receives no power of jurisdiction over his fictitious Church, do order and office not go together. He bears the personal character of a bishop but has no episcopal office. The forerunner of the titular bishop was the bishop who had been driven from his homeland, whose right to his lost see it was important to uphold. Titular bishops are employed in many ways: as auxiliaries to a diocesan bishop, as coadjutors with the right of succession, as interim rulers of a diocese (apostolic administrators), as heads of a local Church which is not yet ready to become a diocese (usually as episcopal vicars-general and, in mission territories, vicars or prefects apostolic), and above all in the upper ranks of the Roman Curia.

4. *Collegiate aspect of the episcopate.* The collegiate aspect of the episcopate is no novelty in the ecclesiastical constitution. It is found at lower levels no less than at the level of the Church universal, and to the eye of a historian comes into play mainly in non-ecumenical synods. Many of these, it must be observed, have exerted an influence far beyond their own sphere, affecting the general juridical evolution of the Church quite as much as the decrees of ecumenical councils have done. We must also note that the principle of collegiality is better seen in its purity below ecumenical level, because the fact that these collegiate organs do not have the Pope at their head decisively affects the formation of policy.

At the ecumenical level. With its doctrine of the episcopal college Vatican II settled the question, left open by Vatican I, of the relationship between Pope and bishops. According to this doctrine the bishops form a college which succeeds the apostolic college in the office of teaching and governing, and has the Pope, the successor of Peter, for its head (*De Ecclesia,* arts. 19–22). Just as the apostolic college represented the unity of the twelve tribes of Israel (Mt 19:28), so the bishops united with the Pope represent the unity of the new people of God. Here the word college must not be taken to mean a body of men equal in rank, with a head who is but *primus inter pares* and who derives his authority from the college; rather it means a permanent body whose structure and authority derive from revelation. It is a unique sort of college, whose composition and work are largely determined by its head. "One is constituted a member of the episcopal body by virtue of sacramental consecration and by hierarchical communion with the head and members of the body." (*De Ecclesia,* art. 22.) Consecration as a bishop imprints an indelible character. Hierarchical communion is a thing that is given and may be withdrawn from one who proves unworthy of it. The two elements, that which cannot be forfeited and that which can, are equally necessary for reception into the college; the latter element shows us at once that membership of the college ceases when hierarchical communion is lost. In order to become and remain a member of the bishops' college it is absolutely necessary to be received into communion by the Pope, whereas communion with the members of the college depends on communion with its head and plays no separate part in making one a member.

This fact would seem to be contradicted

by the statement that bishops receive the newly elect into membership by episcopal consecration (*ibid.,* art. 21); but the statement simply means that only a bishop can consecrate a bishop and leaves open the disputed question of whether a priest can validly ordain a priest in certain circumstances. In its character as a juridical person the episcopal college always exists and is always active as the body responsible for the whole Church, even though there are certain limits to its juridical activities. It possesses "supreme authority" over the whole Church (*ibid.,* art. 22), but must scrupulously respect its own hierarchical structure in wielding that power. It solemnly exercises its supreme power at an ecumenical council, and possibly outside a council as well if the Pope calls on the bishops throughout the world to act in concert, or at least sanctions or freely accepts a concerted act by the bishops dispersed throughout the world. Whether the supreme power of the college be used in the one way or the other, the Pope's consent is not added to the collegiate act as from outside but forms a constituent element of that act. In practice the exercise of the supreme power of the college is restricted to an ecumenical council, and therefore it would have been well to give such councils a more flexible form, so that ecumenical councils could be held at frequent intervals, attended by a representative body. Vatican II could not bring itself to do this. Meantime, by creating the Synod of Bishops, although its technical functions are purely advisory, Paul VI has provided an organ through which the representatives of the episcopate — some *ex officio* and some elected — and also the representatives of the religious communities, can have a voice in weighty matters of Church government. The Synod of Bishops is a flexible affair. Basically, as a general assembly, it is something like what an ecumenical council of representative composition would be. As an extraordinary assembly it can be called on at practically any time, and as a special assembly it has a very wide field of operation.

By putting forward the doctrine of the episcopal college Vatican II has in no way retreated from what Vatican I defined as to the Pope's primacy of jurisdiction. In practice it only says about the episcopal college what has long been held about an ecumenical council (*CIC,* can. 229, § 1). There is a difference from the law we have known in that an ecumenical council only comes into being when the bishops assemble, whereas the episcopal college is always there. Thus we have two organs of supreme power, the Pope and the college of bishops, but the distinction between them is not an adequate one, since the Pope is the head of the college. A recent doctrine affirms that there is only one organ, the episcopal college, which wields power in two different ways: through the head alone and through a collegiate act. But one can object that the episcopal college is confined to "teaching authority and pastoral rule" (*De Ecclesia,* art. 22) and that only a physical person is able to represent the Church's invisible Lord in every respect.

At the sub-ecumenical level. As a rule, particular Churches are not integrated directly into the unity of the Church universal but through certain larger ecclesiastical entities, among which the Eastern patriarchates with their special autonomy, and lately in the West the episcopal conferences, play the leading part. Vatican II points out that episcopal conferences can help in the most various and fruitful ways to make the collegiate outlook a concrete reality of our time (*De Ecclesia,* art. 23). Besides fostering the collegiate outlook, of course, they must also bring into effective play that collegiality which, below ecumenical level, is normally active in synodal affairs. Synods of their nature involve the assembling of their members in a given place. The members of a synod, once they are assembled and while they remain so, form a college which takes common counsel and reaches common decisions. The acts of a synod, in the sphere of its own competence, are collegiate acts in the strict sense of the word; and the same is true of an episcopal conference when as a hierarchical authority it takes decisions within its own appointed sphere that juridically bind the dioceses within the territory of the conference. One advantage the bishops' conference has over sub-ecumenical synods is that it is not tied to particular forms: thus it can more readily and more effectively foster and co-ordinate Church work over a largish area (*regio ecclesiastica*). In the Latin Church it assumes the function of the Eastern patriarchal synod, differing from it chiefly in that it is conducted by an elected president instead of by a patriarch.

See also *Apostolic Succession, Charisms, Orders and Ordination, Magisterium, Council.*

BIBLIOGRAPHY. Y. Congar, *Wide World, My Parish* (1961); W. Bertrams, *Vicarius Christi — Vicarii Christi* (1964); J. Lécuyer, *Études sur la collégialité épiscopale* (1964); P. Card. Marella, K. Mörsdorf, W. Müller and K. Rahner, *Über das bischöfliche Amt* (1967); G. Baraúna, ed., *De Ecclesia*, 2 vols. (1967).

Klaus Mörsdorf

BODY

1. *The phenomenon.* The body is the most immediate and proximate object of our experience. It is always with us, inseparable from us, the means whereby alone, along the "ways" of its senses, we attain the world in its manifold aspects and dimensions. But before this, and concurrently, the body is not merely an object with which man is confronted, it is something which he himself *is:* the pleasure and the pain of the body are his own pain and pleasure. The world too is not just opposed to the body as the space outside it: it is rather its and hence our "extension", and is only there insofar as it is seen, heard, and so on — down to the atmosphere which is our breath. Therefore, just as there is a distinction between the self and the body, as between the body and the world (man is not simply body [alone]), so too there is such a unity that we must affirm: man is really and truly *corporeal* in all his dimensions.

It is only through this actual bodily quality that the spiritual nature really comes to be: in the work and the action (instead of the mere potentiality of thought and will) where alone it has actuality and efficacy and concrete expression. But it is likewise this bodily nature which sets limits to the self-realization of man: outwardly, it limits him in space and time; inwardly, it prevents him expressing himself fully, as every thinker, lover and artist has experienced. It cannot but offer resistance to the will, it must absorb energies in the effort to speak which should really be devoted to the actual statement, and thus it clouds the purity of all assertion.

This dialectical situation affects every happening of everyday life, but is most apparent in the supreme events of eros and death. At these pre-eminent moments too the temptation to which man is exposed by this tension is displayed most clearly. It is the temptation, first of all, to give up the effort of unification and to live on two different planes, which would therefore cease to be human and so to be themselves. It is, secondly, the temptation to restrict oneself to any one of the two regions, either a corporeal existence hostile to the spirit, or a spiritual existence filled with hatred of the body — an effort which always destroys the object of its choice and is soon followed by a revulsion which leads to the other extreme. Finally, it is the temptation to try to set up an undialectical unity, either that of a bodily entity simply accepted by the soul ("the soul is just an element of the body"), or that of a spiritual entity accepting the body without discernment ("mens sana in corpore sano"). The truth is that the fluid dialectical relationship of unity and opposition between body and soul can neither be transcended nor dissolved. And no completely satisfactory solution has been found for it in the whole history of thought.

2. *The history of the problem.* The dualism of body and soul is a tenet of Orphism and the Pythagoreans in Greek philosophy (in contrast to the delight in the body displayed by Homer, who uses σῶμα only for a corpse and considers the after-life as a shadowy existence, which Achilles would gladly exchange for the hardships of a drayman). The body is the garment, ship, prison and tomb of the soul ("σῶμα – σῆμα"), which is hindered and thwarted by the body, where it is in exile, banished "from above", and from which it frees itself by detachment and philosophical effort and finally by death (through a series of re-births, metempsychosis). So above all — as in Indian thought — Plato. Aristotle opposes to this purely accidental body-soul relationship the substantial concept of hylemorphism, in which the soul is essentially the form of the body and constitutes with it the one concrete subsistent. But no explanation is offered for the relationship between (immortal) spirit-soul and (mortal) body-soul and hence the primordial unity of man remains obscure.

The Semitic thinking of the Bible contributes a completely different perspective to this tradition. The OT has no special word for the body. The whole man is "flesh" *(bāśār)*, but also soul *(nefeš,* i.e., life). And in death the whole man loses his life (in Sheol, there is no thought of God, nor does God think of it, Ps 88). A stronger distinction between body and soul appears only in late Judaism, under the influence of Hellenism.

The real survival of the soul is taught, and the doctrine of the resurrection of the flesh is developed from some hints in the later books of the OT.

The doctrine of body and soul in the NT is especially noteworthy in St. Paul. It would be wrong to interpret him dualistically (in a Hellenistic or Gnostic way), even though his assertions are not completely clear and cannot be fully harmonized. The σάρξ (flesh) constitutes the nature of sinful, doomed man after Adam (e.g., Rom 8:12f.). But it is not simply identical with σῶμα, even though the fleshly condition is most clearly embodied and active in the body (Rom 6:6; 7:23; Col 3:5), which is the visibility of man himself (1 Cor 5:3; 7:15f., see 1). Hence the redemption which St. Paul preaches and hopes for is not liberation from the σῶμα but its transformation into a "pneumatic" body (1 Cor 15:36ff.), into the likeness of the resplendent body of Christ (Phil 3:21).

When the two streams of tradition meet in the Fathers and in Christian philosophy, however, the more highly developed Greek line of thought, in its Platonic form, is preponderant at first, especially in the conflict with Gnosticism. The Aristotelian concept only penetrates the scholastic discussion gradually from Arab tradition and is finally given its Christian form in the teaching of St. Thomas Aquinas. His explanation is that the soul is the "unica forma corporis", which is not therefore contrasted with an already existing ("informed") body which would be a partial component of the whole along with it; the soul manifests and effectuates itself in the purely potential medium of "materia prima". The (permanent) duality of body and soul is not to be understood as a merely ontic fact, but as an ontological actualization; the body is wholly the body of the soul, while the soul is essentially embodied (and yet immortal – with a permanent relationship to the body and matter).

Later, this ontological view of the way soul and body "participate" in each other recedes into the background, and the relationship is considered more ontically, so that it is seen from either a monist or a dualist point of view. The dualism of modern times was founded by Descartes, who separated soul and body as *res extensa* and *res cogitans*, which were supposed to preside over the central organ of the pineal gland in a sort of mutual causality. But even in Descartes it is really God, and fully and expressly so in the occasionalism of N. Malebranche and in Leibniz, who closes the unbridgeable gulf between the two fields, either by a constant intervention or by the basic institution of the *harmonia praestabilita*. Later, as in modern vitalism, the doctrine of mutual causality found supporters again (H. Lotze, E. Becher), though the difficulties of this theory could not be satisfactorily answered.

Monism is represented by Spinoza, who regards body and soul as merely two modes of existence of the same thing; so too the psycho-physical parallelism of G. T. Fechner, who understands the body-soul relationship as the convex and concave sides of a single spherical surface. And while spiritualism takes the body to be merely the appearance of the soul, which alone is real and true (G. Berkeley, W. Wundt), materialistic monism maintains on the contrary that everything mental and spiritual is a bodily (and glandular) function (C. Vogt, J. Moleschott, L. Büchner).

In the light of psychology as well as of biology, man is now seen again more explicitly as a unity of soul and body, which does not allow of a clear division between the two components, though the presence of both is recognized; psychotherapy and psychosomatic medicine above all try to meet the demands of this more primordial view.

3. *Philosophical and theological explanation.* The magisterium of the Church has defined the unity of man (primarily in view of Christological controversy), having recourse when doing so to the philosophical position of hylemorphism, though without giving a decision on the system or any precise form of its exposition (*D* 481, 1914). As phenomenological considerations show, man is as a whole and essentially a bodily entity. He *has* a body and at the same time he *is* his body in a true sense. He can never distinguish himself adequately from his body; on the contrary, he is the particular man he is precisely on account of his body (individuation). So too the upsurge of his enthusiasm in work and love does not lift him above and out of his body, nor is death simply the separation of body and soul. In each case the one, whole man is wholly involved and challenged, and summoned precisely to accept and take over his spirit-body, which, in keeping with what has been said, calls for a submissive as well as an active Yes, and a

submissive as well as an active No to the body. In his body, man is opened out to his environment and the exterior world, becomes accessible, attackable (Sartre, *La Nausée*) and vulnerable; his body disturbs and hinders his development. But it is in the body and its activity that man shows himself and sees himself: there the "invisible soul" becomes visible (art of self-expression). In the body, man "knows" man (Gen 4:1 — sexuality), and man comes to be by means of this fully human event (generation). In the body he is bound up with and allied to the sub-human — he is "dust" (needs, instinct); but in the body (as in itself something spiritual, and not merely because his spirit is in it) he is also higher than the sub-human ("visage", "look", "posture", speech). The body is man's "primordial activity" (G. Siewerth), the "symbolic reality" of man (K. Rahner), his "medium of being" (B. Welte), in which he lives and "is there" and is present — precisely insofar as it is not the body itself which is intended (e.g., pleasure, the voice) but the essence and its reality (love, the song). The traditional clear-cut pattern is replaced by a multi-dimensional one, in which the person "expounds" itself. And the isolated individualistic view of the body is merged into the dimensions of society, history and historicity, to which it essentially belongs, and in which alone the tension of openness and hiddenness can make the person a "countenance" and a reality.

This unity in duality which can never be fully perspicuous and amenable to philosophical thought is seen at the height of its tension when theology considers the bodily nature of man. The guiding principle of a theology of the body is given in the expression of Tertullian: "caro salutis est cardo" (*De carnis resurrectione,* 8). God, the Logos, becomes "flesh" and true man and redeems the human race by his obedience unto death, in the body. And hence the order of grace which he set up has also an "incarnational" structure. If it seems at first only to affect the soul, this is precisely a symptom of the untoward condition resulting from the loss of the grace of bodily and spiritual integrity in the state of original justice. Thus though sin is manifested precisely in the body (see St. Paul, above), the body is still already sanctified here and now, and is the temple of the Holy Spirit; it is called to the work of co-redemption (1 Cor 6:15; Col 1:24; 1 Cor

6:19) and above all to the glory of the resurrection, in which the very spatio-corporal reality here achieved — and not just a reward for it — will be transformed and be man's definitive state and his eternity. Since this eternity is characterized as conformity to the body of Christ (1 Cor 15:49) and fellowship with it (2 Cor 5:8), it implies that the humanity and the bodily nature of Christ (and hence of man in general) play a role of permanent and indispensable importance. And since finally man's body implies his openness to personal confrontation with others, makes him present to them and constitutes him in an essential relation to his environment, the same will be true in a perfect way, with all obscurity and ambiguity abolished, of the heavenly body: fellowship is of its essence. Hence the ascension of Christ, "the first-fruit of those that slept" (1 Cor 15:20), demands the corporal fulfilment of his brothers, indeed, it calls for and implies "even now" at least a partial realization of this extension of his own definitive state, "in due order" (1 Cor 15:23) (Mt 27:52f.; Eph 4:8–10; the Assumption of the Blessed Virgin). This final, definitive stage is already proclaimed visibly on earth in the sacramental reality and practice of the Church, the "body of Christ" (1 Cor 12:27; Eph 1:23), and in its worship. And we can also begin to understand on the same principle that the fulfilment of the body is not confined to the body. Just as its glorification is not merely an addition appended to the redemption of the soul, but the fulfilment and completion of the soul, so too its fulfilment extends into the world and transforms the whole cosmos along with it (Rom 8:19–23; Rev 21), as the completion of the incarnation in the pneumatic unity where all differences are preserved but where God is "all in all' (1 Cor 15:28).

See also *Soul, Spirit, Spiritualism, Man, Evolution, Death, Resurrection* II.

BIBLIOGRAPHY. G. Marcel, *Être et avoir* (1935), E. T.: *Being and Having;* J.-P. Sartre, *L'Être et le Néant* (1943), E. T.: *Being and Nothingness* (1957); V. E. Frankl, *Doctor and the Soul* (1955); C. Tresmontant, *Study of Hebrew Thought* (1960); M. Merleau-Ponty, *Phenomenology of Perception* (1962); id., *Structure of Behavior* (1963); C. A. van Peursen, *Body, Soul, Spirit. A Survey of the Body-Mind Problem* (1966).

Jörg Splett

BREVIARY

1. *Scope.* The term "Breviary" is derived from the book which, since the Middle Ages, "briefly" comprises, for practical use, the texts from various sources (the Psalter, the holy Scriptures, the Hymnal, the Antiphonary, the Lectionary, the Sacramentary), which make up the "canonical hours"; the entire Office soon began to be described as the "Breviary". It is not the purpose of this article to present the history and structure of the Breviary, but rather to give an indication of the theological meaning of the official and canonical services of the Church, which are today summarily understood by the term "Breviary". The term also indicates that the article will confine itself to the Latin Church. Within the Latin Church the very complex historical development, many details of which have not yet been clarified, was on the whole completed in the early Middle Ages. All components, the principles of the structure and the form, to a large extent even the texts, as well as the theological meaning of the Office have remained basically unaltered since that time. In spite of a relatively large diversity in detail, a fairly uniform order (that of the Roman-Frankish Church) was fixed at that time. The period of reforms after the Council of Trent brought about only a restoration (abandonment of the votive Offices), centralization (1568: the *Breviarium Romanum* of Pius V) and juridical systematization. It was only in recent times that, as a result of the newly-won insights into the history of liturgy, as well as of the pressure of circumstances which have made recitation burdensome, the function of the Office in the life of the Church as a whole has been reflected upon and its individual elements critically examined. Since it is still unclear what shape the reform of the Breviary demanded by the Second Vatican Council (Constitution on the Sacred Liturgy, arts. 83–101) will take, it is impossible to give a systematic and comprehensive presentation, because it could very soon be superseded by the reform. We shall only touch upon a few themes, the clarification of which — irrespective of the future form — is indispensable to a meaningful and responsible recitation of an official "prayer of the Church".

2. *Structure.* The Breviary is in many respects a complex structure with many layers, the components of which are by no means of equal importance, either historically or theologically. This is even true of the individual Offices appointed for the different times of the day ("hours") as such. The morning and evening Office ("Lauds" and "Vespers") must, according to their origin, be regarded as an act of worship of the whole (local) Church, at which the clergy and laity assembled together and which, in the view of the primitive Church, belonged to the indispensable elements of Church life. In contrast, the regular celebration of the "vigils" was not part of community worship, but appears to have been initially a private exercise of ascetic circles, who perhaps copied the Easter vigil before Sundays and feast days, and subsequently every day. (Researches have, however, not yet shown a clear-cut result here.) It was only on the eve of saints' feasts at the tomb of the saint that such vigils were "official", i.e., that the community was invited to participate; this often meant a *duplex officium* for the ascetics (at prayer). It was, however, undoubtedly due to private initiative that the so-called "minor hours" (Terce, Sext, None, and then Prime and Compline as Offices following Lauds and Vespers) were inserted into the cycle of the Office: they were the pious exercises of those who did not wish to let any time of day pass without prayer. It may be true that the synagogue or even the Temple service furnished impulses for the programme of the daily prayer of hours; however, a causal connection does not exist. Compared with the above-mentioned cycle of hours, as it finally came to prevail in the Western Church, the Eastern Church possesses a slightly different order; but even here, as a result of the common tradition of the earliest times, the morning and evening service (Orthros and Hesperinon) are the main official hours.

3. *Individual elements.* The individual components of the various hours are, however, also of varying grades of importance and different origins. Unfortunately, the silent private recitation of the Office, which has become customary in the West, reduces to one level the strikingly different types of prayer, which, as it is, take on a slightly new meaning because of their stylized and solemn utterance. There are direct appeals to God ("Deus in adjutorium ...") and

summary priestly prayers *(Orationes)*, meditative recitation of the psalms and hymns of praise, intercessions (unfortunately almost exclusively as rudiments of the Litany), instructive lessons from Scripture and the Fathers (the latter perhaps as substitutes for a sermon), and finally also solemn readings from the NT, especially the gospels (as is still done at Lauds and Vespers, though it is here attached to the antiphonal chant of the canticles in Lk 1:68–79 [Benedictus] or 46–55 [Magnificat]). Thus monastic and community worship, perhaps even the tradition of the synagogue, have created a rich and artistic structure. It is not unimportant today to note that most of the above-named elements were conceived as chants, while all of them have their function only as parts of community service. A knowledge of the differentiated structure is essential for the understanding and proper recitation of the Breviary — not only in order to have any grasp at all of the Breviary, which is even today basically a community prayer, but also because this is the only way to attain the attitude which the individual elements aim at: recollection, attentiveness, receptivity to instruction, reflection on the saving act of Jesus inspired by the accounts of the old and new saving events, the elevation of the heart called for by the hymn of praise, participation in the prayer of intercession for the Church and its needs in the menacing world in which the suppliant also lives, and finally surrender to the mystery of this "prayer of the Church".

4. *The psalms.* Among the individual elements the psalms deserve special attention. In the Office the recitation of the Psalter is not only quantitatively striking (and will probably remain so), but because of its origin in the primitive Church's understanding of Scripture and the psalms, it has a special significance. In the songs of the Psalter the Church found a compendium of the entire OT, seen as the past and preparatory history of salvation.

And above all it saw there the prophetic prayer which divine inspiration directed so intensely towards the Messiah, by means of David and other OT prefigurations of salvation, that it became Jesus' own prayer in the strictest sense. The Psalter can only be properly recited as Jesus' prayer to the Father, and as the Church's prayer echoing that of Jesus — prayer with Jesus to the Father, and also prayer of the Church to Jesus himself, the historical image of the invisible God and the divine head of the Church. To justify the Church's view theologically, suffice it here to point to the fact that there is only one salvation, which has never been other than Jesus Christ. Even the salvific events "before Christ" are part of the salvation brought by Christ, just as there is no salvation since Christ except as the anamnesis which re-enacts his mystery. In the light of the unity of salvation the ancient Church — like the Church today — had no hesitation in using the psalms christologically in its canonical hours. This was one of the reasons why it was thought well to hear the message of the whole psalter each day, or at least in the course of each week.

5. *Some traditional views.* The Office also appears as the anamnesis of the mystery of Jesus when various hours are considered to be memorials of various phases and acts in the history of salvation. Lauds, for instance, corresponded to the Passover mystery of Christ, the passage to the Resurrection. Terce to the sending of the Spirit or the Crucifixion, None to the death of Jesus on the cross. There is considerable divergence in the detailed application of this line of thought, but in general it is so ancient — it is already found in Tertullian at the end of the 2nd century — that it seems to be basic to the understanding of the Office. The view that the command of the Lord and of the apostles to "pray always" (Lk 18:1; cf. 21:36; 1 Thess 5:17; cf. Eph 6:18; Col 4:2) could (only) be fulfilled in regular prayer which embraced to some extent each hour of the day is probably still more ancient. See also Vatican II's Constitution on the Sacred Liturgy (art. 86). On this point the apostles themselves were faithful to a practice of the synagogue; cf. Acts 3:1; 10:30, the prayer in the Temple at the ninth hour.

6. *"The prayer of the Church".* In contrast to these older interpretations, the special characteristic of the Office is now usually seen in the fact that it is the (official) prayer of the Church. It was not so explicitly emphasized as such in earlier times. Hence this view must be examined dispassionately. The liturgy of prayer would be discredited by being made unduly mysterious. The truth

is that the life of the Church, the basic sacrament of the signs of Christ's salvation, consists to some extent of continuing Christ's prayer to his Father and of making it its own (Constitution on the Liturgy, arts. 83, 85). The visible Church must also be visible as the Church that prays. Wherever the Church claims to exist in a relative fullness (in the diocese or the parish) or wherever an essential characteristic of the Church is expressed in a life of intenser piety (in the clergy as holders of the apostolic office, in monastic orders and so on), the community at prayer must be part of the Church's testimony. The form which such prayer must take can hardly be determined from first principles. It must in any case contain the traits which the invocation of God in Christ and the grace of fellowship in the Church demand from attentive and docile man: steadfast hope, attentive response, thanksgiving, praise and petition, all of which means keeping in mind the salvation which is Jesus Christ. (We need not here ask how deeply man is penetrated by prayer, that is, how much more it is than mere noncommittal "thinking of God" or mere words of praise and petition.) The formation of the Office was determined in the concrete by the forms in use around the Church, which were also the forms used by the members of the Church. These became traditional and were finally regulated by Church authority — with too much rigidity and uniformity, no doubt, in the Roman Church, especially since the setting up of the Congregation of Rites in 1588.

The prescribed form of the Office only really presents a problem where "private" prayer and popular piety have departed from the "liturgical". But even here the "official prayer" still has the rank of an essential note. It is so much the prayer of a given Church (diocesan or regular) that this Church cannot be fully what it ought to be without it. Hence this liturgical prayer forbids the individual to count himself as member of this Church or even to live in it unless he joins in such prayer — or is ready on principle to join in it. This means that Christians must make this "official" prayer (as it is generally but unfortunately called) their own (cf. Constitution on the Liturgy, art. 90), which does not mean that the public manifestation of the Church at prayer could or should absorb and replace all private prayer. The latter continues to be right and necessary

(cf. *ibid.*, art. 12). Hence the same relationship obtains between prayer "in choir" and prayer "in secret" as between sacrament and faith. Both are salvific, but they are not separable, nor is one surer or better than the other. The sacraments as acts of worship are so truly efficacious signs, posited by the Church where Christ is unfailingly present, that normally faith is only authentic and hence acceptable to God when it comes about in the acceptance of these signs. Similarly, a believing Christian, whose "heart watches" in the Church, only prays in keeping with his faith when he prays with the Church and makes the structure of the "prayer of the Church" his own.

Hence it is easy to answer the question of the spiritual value of the Breviary. Just as frequent reception of the sacraments does not automatically increase grace and give still more glory to God if not accompanied by a profounder dedication in faith, so too the Breviary is not "better" just because it is the "prayer of the Church" and is performed by "official mandate". It is only (and always) better when it is a sign of profounder dedication to the Lord — who of course prepares for himself a praying Church and not just individuals at prayer. Conversely, the intelligent participation of those free from the obligation of the canonical hours is urgently desired (cf. Constitution on the Liturgy, art. 100), not because this form is better of itself, but to enable the Church to display itself as the praying community in as many members as possible, and thus to be a more impressive sign of the salvific presence of Christ.

7. *The present situation.* In the light of the above sketch, grave misgivings must be aroused by the situation of Western Christendom, the result of a long development which must be pronounced to be faulty. The feeling that it is indispensable to show the Church, as it exists in the local Churches, as a set of communities which prays regularly, has been lost. The early Middle Ages still took it for granted that every Church worthy of the name (cathedral, parish, monastery or place of pilgrimage) chanted the canonical hours. No doubt the Office was practically an affair of the clergy. Clergy and people could not be regularly assembled even for Vespers. In modern times, the substitute "evening devotions" are often threatened by evening Masses, which are undoubtedly

justified. Thus in fact, in spite of occasional efforts in the opposite direction, the Office is almost exclusively the affair of the clergy and some (not all) orders in the Catholic Church. Further, the obligation in general for the clergy is a personal one, imposed with the sub-diaconate, and no longer attached to the (local) Church primarily and only secondarily to those responsible for its testimony. The Office is totally a clerical liturgy. But even so the principle is asserted that no one can be a leader in the Church except as a participant in the structured prayer which is the sign of the praying Church. The Churches of the Reformation also failed to correct the clericalization of the Office. Efforts to the contrary were ultimately confined to the family prayers of pious households. The Anglican Church alone has provided, in the Book of Common Prayer, a regular order of prayer for the whole Church in the form of (the newly conceived) Morning and Evening Prayer.

8. *The Office as mystery.* An essential aspect must now be mentioned in conclusion, the "mystery" of the Office. Being a "sign" of the Church it is in fact part of the sacramental order. Salvation always comes as the anamnesis which re-enacts the mystery of Jesus Christ — whatever particular theological explanation of this be adopted. The Church is charged with the sanctification of human life by re-enacting the mystery in the liturgy (cf. Constitution on the Liturgy, arts. 2, 7 and *passim*). It must so "celebrate" Christ that his salvation is there present in the faith and active testimony of his own. Insofar as the liturgy has to discharge this task, it is done to a great extent by the Office in the arrangement of each day and season. For the solemnity of the feasts of the liturgical year owes much to the Office, as the natural cycle becomes a sacred memorial; so too the days of the week as they follow the Sunday. But the real work of the Office is to charge each day with the memory of the redemption, so that this primordial unit of natural time may be an offered grace. Independently of the Eucharist (which is not necessarily celebrated every day), and not just as a preparation for it, the Office has a value of its own as a celebration of the unique redemption in Jesus Christ. (Historically, this was recognized by linking various canonical hours with

the salvific acts of Christ; see above, no. 5.) Details in the structure of the Office as it has been built up historically and regulated by authority can and ought to be changed. But the Church will always have to live (and will in fact live, through the promised presence of Christ) in daily memory of its Lord, persevering in prayer, listening to him and turning to him, till salvation is fully revealed and this provisional sign of the Church's remembrance of Christ, the Breviary, is superseded.

See also *Liturgy, Prayer.*

BIBLIOGRAPHY. S. Bäumer, *Geschichte des Breviers* (1895), French translation with additions by R. Biron, 2 vols. (1905); J. Pascher, *Das Stundengebet der römischen Kirche* (1954); A. Baumstark, *Nocturna Laus* (1957); A.-G. Martimort, ed., *L'Église en prière* (1961), pp. 787–876; L. Eisenhofer and J. Lechner, *The Liturgy of the Roman Rite* (1961), pp. 438–75; E. Kassian and B. Botte, eds., *La prière des heures,* Lex orandi 35 (1963).

Angelus Häussling

BURIAL

In composing its burial service, the early Church borrowed extensively from customs of the time, but freed them from a pagan and too materialistic interpretation of life beyond the grave. Ancient burial rites became symbols of the life of the spirit, and the biblical hope of the resurrection of the body is from the very beginning the most striking characteristic of Christian burial. It was customary to visit graves and, while the deceased attended the meal in his wreathed *cathedra,* to celebrate the *agape,* especially on the *dies natalis;* the Eucharist was celebrated chiefly on the anniversary. Such rites were permitted only at the graves of those who had died in the communion of the Church. The excommunicated were denied both *agape* and the Eucharist.

Since the revision of the burial service called for by Vatican II has not yet been executed, the present *Ordo exsequiarum* of the Roman Ritual must be used as the basis for the following presentation. Despite the later liturgical elements which overstress the thought of the inevitable judgment, the themes of hope from the early Christian rites and the theme of Christian fellowship as an assurance of final glory are clearly present in this rite. The official ceremonies of the Roman liturgy — in contrast to the truncated rite common today especially in city parishes — begin in the home of the deceased, where priest and faithful gather to escort the remains from the world of sin to the other world. The opening antiphon is charged with humble confidence in the absolute power of God's grace: "If thou, O Lord, shouldst mark iniquities, Lord, who could stand?" The moving *De profundis* which follows took on in the Middle Ages the character of a penitential psalm. Previously it had been thanksgiving for redemption, as at Christmas Vespers in the early Middle Ages. It was given this sense again in the recent Office of the Sacred Heart, which was composed on classical lines. We can therefore restore to the *De profundis* in the burial rite its Easter character and sing in the name of the dead the mercy and grace of our God, in whom superabundant redemption is found. Next, the corpse of the deceased is carried to the Church, the earthly image of heaven. The anthems accompanying the Christian's last visit to the church explain this procession as the passage from the world to heaven: the antiphon, "The bones that lie in the dust shall thrill with joy before the Lord", and the psalm *Miserere*. Though the obviously penitential character of this psalm need not be denied, its earlier use as an Easter psalm, due above all to its final verse, should not be overlooked in the burial service. We should note, therefore, that the psalm ends with the reassuring vision of God's triumph and the restoration of Jerusalem, and that the antiphon colours the whole psalm with the certainty of resurrection. The "answer", as it were, is the resounding *Subvenite* at the entrance to the church: "Come to his aid, O saints of God; go out to meet him, O angels of the Lord. Take his soul and bring it into the presence of the Most High. May Christ, who called thee, receive thee, and may angels lead thee into Abraham's bosom." The Church on earth submits its power to celestial power. It gives over one of its members to the definitive community. In this connection it is significant that the prayers of the saints are not invoked, but that the saints themselves are summoned together. The burial service continually goes beyond the death of the individual, to become an eschatological celebration of the entire Church.

The petition of the *Subvenite* that Christ take the deceased to himself is urgently stressed when the corpse is placed before the altar, on which Christ makes his redemptive sacrifice present and bids the living and deceased members of the Church to share in it. The sacramental event is prepared for and explained by the texts of the Requiem Mass, especially the word of God in the epistle and gospel. In the epistle (1 Thess 4, 13–18) Paul warns us that we should not grieve like the others "who have no hope". The phrase, applicable to unbelievers, does not refer to survival in a general sense, but to the resurrection and glorious union with Christ. "For since we believe that Jesus died and rose again, even so, through Jesus, God will bring with him those who have fallen asleep." In the gospel, narrating Jesus' conversation with Martha on the death of Lazarus, the necessity of faith in Christ as a precondition of the certainty of resurrection is likewise emphasized. For the believer, union with Christ is a fountain of life which cannot be stopped by bodily death. Faith gives eternal life from God, so powerful that it can draw the body into its life-giving sphere. Because true divine life has appeared in Christ, it triumphs over death and burial. Without Christ there is no life, no resurrection. By faith in him eternal life is transmitted to man. This new life is in fact immunity from death, for he who believes in the Lord "shall never die". In the epistle and gospel the liturgy of the Requiem Mass reveals to us the joyful, hopeful vision of a new world where the agonizing fear of death is overcome by divine life.

The deep union of the faithful with Christ as source of all life is actualized in the sacrifice of the Lord made present on the altar. The Church's celebration of the Mass for its dead is a true Easter event, a *mysterium paschale,* a pledge of resurrection. The singing of the alleluia verse, discontinued only in the Middle Ages, emphasized the Easter character of the Mass. With the reception of Communion during his life on earth the deceased received also a pledge of bodily immortality. By reason of this "medicine of immortality" the Church can sing in the Communion verse of the Requiem Mass: "Eternal light shine upon them, Lord, with thy saints forever: for thou art merciful. Lord, grant them eternal rest; and let perpetual light shine upon them; with thy saints forever, for thou art merciful."

Supported by the word of God in the scriptural readings and by the redemptive sacrifice of Christ, the prayers of the Requiem Mass, and the canon of every Mass, beg for the faithful departed eternal delight and eternal life, eternal light and eternal peace. To be taken up by Christ *(Subvenite)*, to be always with the Lord (epistle of the Requiem Mass), means never-ending delight, life, light and peace. The expectation of immortality recorded in Rev and reflected in the primitive Church lives on in the imagery of the burial service. According to Rev 21:6, in the new world God will give to the thirsty water from the fountain of life, and Rev 22:3 promises that the blessed in heaven will drink from the river of life, i.e., from the stream of unending joy.

The thought that the death of the believer means elevation to true, eternal life is particularly evident in the Preface, which comes from the old Spanish liturgical texts: "In him [Christ] there has dawned for us the hope of a blessed resurrection, heartening with a promise of immortality to come those of us who are saddened by the certainty of dying. The life of those who are faithful to thee, Lord, is but changed, not ended; and when their earthly dwelling-place decays, an everlasting mansion stands prepared for them in heaven."

The petition for eternal light refers to the beatific radiance of God, God's illumination, by which alone man can know him. Again we recall the words of Rev (22:5): "And night shall be no more; they need no light of lamp or sun, for the Lord God will be their light." The meaning of *pax* in liturgical usage with reference to the dead is not a matter of "peace of mind"; the original Latin meaning must be consulted. The deceased has departed in union with Christ and the Church. Everything that could disturb this fellowship is for him definitively eliminated, and heaven is for him not only the place of delight, life and light, but also of peace.

In the rites and prayers that follow the celebration of Mass, the Church's great reverence for the human body is again expressed. The previous course of the rite has already manifested the Church's respect for the body fashioned after the image of God and destined for glorification in Christ. The reproach often levelled against Christianity that it disparages the human body, has no place here. The Church is aware of the frailty of the body, but is equally sure of the final triumph of life, and of the victory of Christ over the weakness and sinfulness of the flesh. Hence the rites after the Mass are also to be seen in the light of the triumphant: "The bones that lie in the dust shall thrill with joy before the Lord." Before the corpse is brought to the grave the priest sprinkles the coffin with holy water, which symbolizes cleansing in the liturgy, but is also a reminder of the baptismal water blessed on the vigil of Easter. The priest then envelops the coffin with incense to symbolize the expected transfiguration of the deceased. In the medieval prayers and hymns accompanying the sprinkling with holy water and the incensation the thought of judgment and the prayer of petition are prominent, as in the *Dies irae*. Both were part of the burial service from the earliest times, but in these later texts (10th to 13th century), they are unmistakably stressed. But even these later texts retain the theme of the Easter mystery. The antiphon *Non intres* before the *Libera* may be cited as an example: the prayer of faith looks to eternal rest and eternal light, beyond the fear of the day of judgment. In the burial service, judge and redeemer are seen as one, and judgment is not severed from the Easter mystery present in the Eucharist. In the prayer that closes the absolutions the assurance of the victory of faith is strong, despite the dark clouds of judgment: "O God, whose nature it is ever to have mercy and to spare, we humbly entreat thee on behalf of the soul of thy servant, whom thou hast this day bid to pass out of this life; deliver him not, we beseech thee, into the hands of the enemy, nor be thou unmindful of him for ever, but command that he be taken up by holy angels, and borne to our home in heaven, that having put his faith and trust in thee, he may not undergo the pains of hell, but obtain the joys of everlasting life. Through Christ our Lord."

For the subsequent procession to the cemetery the Roman Ritual provides only the short antiphon: "May the angels lead thee into Paradise; at thy coming may the martyrs receive thee, and bring thee into the holy city, Jerusalem. May the choir of angels receive thee, and with Lazarus, once a beggar, mayest thou have eternal rest." The short antiphon presumes a short procession. The rite foresees a situation which no longer obtains in large cities, where cemetery and church formed a unit and the cemetery was considered a part of the church.

When the coffin is set down at the side of the grave, the priest sprinkles it with holy water and incenses it. Then he intones the antiphon to the canticle of Zachariah: "I am the resurrectiom and the life; he who believes in me, though he die, yet shall he live, and whoever lives and believes in me, shall never die." At the open grave, faced with the evidence of transitoriness and extinction, the Christian thought of resurrection appears particularly clearly in these words of Christ. Christ is the life. He has passed over from death to life and draws after him those who have believed in him and have eaten his body. So too the *Benedictus,* framed by this antiphon, is to be understood in an Easter context. The aged Zachariah sings the wonder of redemption: "Blessed be the Lord God of Israel; for he has visited and redeemed his people . . . that we should be saved from our enemies . . . in holiness and righteousness before him all the days of our life . . . To give light to those who sit in darkness and in the shadow of death, to guide our feet into the way of peace." The point may be made that the *Benedictus,* certainly not easy to interpret, forms the solemn climax of Lauds, i.e., the "paschal" hour of the Breviary. And it is noteworthy that this canticle is sung as the closing hymn in the restored Easter vigil, the service most replete with the hope of resurrection in the whole liturgical year. While the antiphon, "I am the resurrection and the life . . .", is repeated, the grave is filled in.

Vatican II's Constitution on the Liturgy states in art. 81: "The rite for the burial of the dead should evidence more clearly the paschal character of Christian death, and should correspond more closely to the circumstances and traditions in various regions." In doing so, the Easter themes of the *Ordo exsequiarum* now in use can be retained, but in adaptation to local customs less emphasis should be laid on the theme of judgment, certain expressions that savour of disdain of the human body must be eliminated and Christian death more clearly displayed as participation in the Pasch of the Lord. A new rite is needed in particular where cremation is the practice.

See also *Death, Body, Soul, Spirit, Eternity, Resurrection.*

BIBLIOGRAPHY. *Le mystère de la mort et sa célébration,* Lex orandi 12 (1956); H. Dettori, *L'officio dei Defunti* (1960); L. Eisenhofer and J. Lechner, *The Liturgy of the Roman Rite* (1961), pp. 422–8.

Walter Dürig

BYZANTINE EMPIRE

A. Characteristics

The rise of the Byzantine world was neither the awakening of a mindless people to historical self-consciousness nor the entry of a new "barbarian" nation into the old Graeco-Roman civilization of the Mediterranean. Byzantium was, in fact, a late form of Mediterranean civilization itself with all its distinctive features, a late form of the Roman Empire, of the ancient Hellenistic mentality and the characteristic Mediterranean way of life. Byzantium regarded its inherited forms as classical, without qualification, and from the time of its emergence felt itself bound to this classical past. This explains its frequently rigid and unfruitful conservatism, its tendency to slavish imitation, the dissipation of its creative literary power in a game of variations on traditional elements, and its lack of realism in facing contemporary situations. Its evolution with regard to antiquity took place unseen and without major upheavals, the difference emerging in this process consisting not so much in a complete reversal of traditional values as in a shift of emphasis and the introduction of new ones of which the most important was Christianity.

Geographically, the transfer of the imperial capital from Rome to Constantinople was of fundamental importance. The East, which for religious reasons as well as on the ground of intellectual self-esteem had found it difficult to disguise its contempt for pagan Rome, acquired a new non-suspect centre of gravity which was seen to bring within its orbit every aspect of life in the Eastern part of the Empire and, at the same time, to become fertile soil for animosities against the new Christianized Rome in the West. The second Rome on the Bosporus was new and young primarily because it had from the very beginning been conceived as a Christian city with no memorable pagan past. It was also new because the Roman Emperor who made it his residence regarded himself emphatically as Christian and, as such, possessing a special position in the Church, one which no one there had ever claimed before. This exceptional position was retained by the Byzantine Emperor till the break-up of the Empire in the 15th century. It can only be accounted for by the special character of the "conversion" of Constantine the Great, the first "Byzantine" Emperor. Constantine had not been instructed and converted by men of the Church in the ordinary way. In his own view, which in spite of his unquestionable sincerity he made acceptable to the Christian world by deliberate propaganda, he had been directly called by God, led to Christianity by a special election of grace and by a unique act of divine providence, not only and not primarily for the sake of his own personal salvation but in order that Christendom might receive the divine gift of an enlightened protector, a leader-figure directly inspired by God. Because the Church did not reject the Emperor's propaganda — Eastern theology tends to set a higher value on the extraordinary means of grace than on its fixed sacramental modes of operation — and because it was not long before the distinction between Constantine and his successors was abandoned, the Emperor's position in the Church came to be proof against canonistic analysis. It was and remained charismatic and therefore unassailable; it merely denied the Emperor what had already been amenable to canonical definition in the Church itself, namely, the sacramental authority of the higher *ordines*. So too, the Emperor respected authoritative dogmatic decisions, even non-conciliar, the exceptions to this rule being far fewer than has been generally supposed. This did not, however, exclude the Emperor's participation in theological discussion.

This essentially Constantinian concept of the Church continued to operate throughout the whole Byzantine epoch. Only in extremely critical situations were there attempts to oppose it and even these were rare and without far-reaching consequences. Thus the Byzantine Church never came to regard itself as a *societas perfecta,* nor to construct a complete systematic ecclesiology focused on a hierarchical head; it never maintained any effective distinction between itself and the State as such. The real life of the Byzantine Church is seen, at best, by contrast with other religions or with other Christian denominations on the fringe of the Empire or outside it. Within, it appears at its best in its liturgy and devotional life, in its art, devotional literature and poetry. It is here and not in the field of Church politics that its positive contributions are to be sought; not even in the field of scientific theology, which was the possession of every educated Byzantine, the natural corollary of a broad humanistic general education and not the specialist equipment of one class or a professional occupation. Within the Byzantine area the self-understanding of the Church, along dogmatic lines, had to be a reflection of the philosophical syncretism of late antiquity. The Church adopted the thought-forms of this culture, its basic approach to the problem of the conceptual analysis and definition of religious experiences and affirmations. Out of this encounter emerged the concept of "orthodoxy", chiefly meaning correct intellectual belief, though it also included a right hope and a right love. Within this monolithic society, the exclusive force of this concept and the formalistic application which the time demanded made it the hallmark of Byzantine man, and therefore also of membership of the Empire, at least in the ideal realm. Its disturbing consequence was a growing merger and indeed equation of politics with religion and of expansion with mission. Political self-assertion included the effort to erect into dogma the infrastructure of the world of faith, even where the religious elements of this infrastructure were mere reflections of the dominant culture.

B. DIVISION INTO PERIODS

1. *The early Byzantine epoch (c. 330 – c. 650)* already shows signs of how the whole Empire was to be affected by the principles on which Byzantium was set up. The ever-narrowing concept of orthodoxy, a notion still foreign to Constantine the Great when he first appeared in the Eastern world, brought about a change from the principle of equality and tolerance (to which Constantine himself consistently adhered) to a State-directed policy of religious unity. The result, however, was not the conversion of the main heretical groups, such as the

Nestorians or Monophysites, but rather their alienation from the imperial regime which demanded orthodoxy. A further consequence was the rise of a "national" confessionalism, prepared to abandon loyalty to Emperor and Empire in favour of its own confessional interests on the ground that this Empire had already committed itself confessionally. Further, as orthodox theology became more and more a department of the State, free-ranging speculation gave way, about the middle of the 5th century, to catenae of proofs and texts from the Fathers, and an increasingly sterile variation on individual dogmatic formulas, which then began to lose touch with the native soil of their religious source. Obviously the Christian ethic could not keep pace with developments in the public and private life of Christians in a society where there was no longer a form of Christianity intent on its independence. In consequence, the surviving elements of paganism which hitherto had merely sulked now conquered their inferiority complex and sought to present their ideals persuasively once more, especially in literary form. A radical reversion to paganism such as that attempted by the Emperor Julian (361–363) was doomed to failure, firstly because his enthusiastic neo-Platonism indulged in too many esoteric concepts, then because ordinary Christian life had already in large measure absorbed and neutralized the religious infrastructure of the past, and finally because with the decline in education in late antiquity, the public for heathen missionary literature of a high quality was too small.

The religious reaction to the shortcoming of early Byzantine society was monasticism which, characteristically, arose in the deserts of Egypt, Syria and Palestine where the imperial theology of high society was something quite remote. It is also significant that it was only later that monasticism could establish a real foothold in the imperial capital. It developed not as the fulfilment of strivings within contemporary Christian society, but in opposition to it. It tended to regard itself, therefore, not as the following out of a "supererogatory" evangelical counsel, but rather as the only legitimate form of Christianity as such. This inevitably introduced into early Byzantine Christianity an attitude to the world which did not think in terms of fulfilment and sublimation but

derived its strength from negation of the world, even though here and there the extremes began to level out. In principle it could only seek to influence the world by an introvert spirituality: Simeon Stylites once on his pillar never quit it, and only from this place of withdrawal did he commend his earth-bound admirers to the grace of the last days! In these monastic circles a literature grew up free from the artificiality of dogmatic writings, in some degree original, in some degree based on the spirituality of Origen, stressing the charismatic nature of the monastic calling, resisting not unsuccessfully the hierarchy's attempts to bring it under control, though sometimes falling instead into the hands of heresy-hunting magistrates, but representative on the whole of the spirituality of Byzantine theology for many centuries. Biographies of monks set the standard for all saintly living and hence provided models of unattainable perfection to Byzantine Christians living in the world.

2. *The middle period* (*c.* 650–1204) began with the loss to Islam of great parts of the Empire (Syria, Palestine, Egypt, and Africa). To counterbalance this loss what was left of the Empire tightened up its administration, its economy and cultural forms. Its territorial losses relieved it of the burden of the heterodox groups of Monophysites. Smaller but more homogeneous than ever, it now consolidated its own way of life, even in the Church, sealing itself off increasingly in dogma and ritual. In the great Iconoclastic Controversy (726–787 and 815–842), by surrendering all puritan survivals from the early Church, Orthodoxy discovered a congenial form of worship without having to pay for the bitter controversies by the secession of any group. Earlier still, at the Trullan Synod (691), the Church had secured a privileged position for itself legally and ritually, thereby preparing the way for its loss of contact with the Roman Church in liturgy and dogma. Conflict with the latter could not be avoided, not merely because of ritual and doctrinal problems but still more because the Roman primacy, now increasingly and inevitably stressed, could not penetrate the armour of the East, that complex but well-knit Empire, State, Church, ritual and cultural life. The peaceful periods in the relationship between Rome and Byzantium were always those in which they had nothing

to say to each other. This dangerous calm was disturbed by the struggle under Patriarch Photius and also by the so-called schism of Cerularius (1054), though without a definitive breach, because no one wanted out and out schism. The Eastern schism may be regarded more as a continuing state of hostility than as a formal final rupture — in this period at least.

The more Byzantium shut itself off from Rome, the more intensively it devoted itself to winning the Slav people in the Balkans and in Russia. The result was the creation of an Orthodox block of extreme durability whose ideological basis is even today almost indistinguishable from that of the Byzantine Empire and on whose loyalty in face of the outside world Byzantium could almost always count in spite of all internal friction.

By its misguided policy in relation to the Roman See, Byzantium had, however, manoeuvred the Papacy out of the ancient Mediterranean unity and driven it into the arms of the Germans. This new alliance was consolidated and gradually the whole of the West was drawn into the Church conflict between Constantinople and Rome, naturally on the side of Rome. The political West, as little pluralistic as Byzantium, widened the conflict into a political one. The economic and intellectual awakening of the West in the Middle Ages gave it, in addition, a self-assurance which recognized no claims to monopoly in the East. But in the 11th and 12th centuries, Byzantium, exposed to fresh migrations of peoples, found itself dependent upon Western aid, for which it paid by abandoning its economic self-sufficiency and closed political system. In face of these political concessions the Byzantine hierarchy closed its ranks and for the first time appeared as a class distinct from the imperial court. The result was the disintegration of the uniform imperial policy, particularly in relation to the West. When for political reasons the Emperor sought union, it was now the Church's turn to object. The Middle Byzantine Empire was already breaking up long before Constantinople fell an easy prey to the Crusaders in 1204.

3. *The late Byzantine epoch* (1204–1453). The Empire tried vainly to deal with the legacies of the last decades of the 12th century. Owing to the hopeless divisions between the Crusader States on ancient

Byzantine territory, it did manage, as early as 1261, to recapture the ancient capital, Constantinople. But this solved neither the economic nor the ecclesiastical problems. The capacity of the new Empire was unequal to the demands involved in the possession of Constantinople. Union became a political weapon, but was not seriously sought on a profound religious level. The Council of Lyons (1274) remained a mere episode. The more urgent the Emperor's need of the support of the Papacy became, the more fiercely did the clergy, chiefly supported by the militant monks, oppose it. The development was not, however, uniform. The intellectual élite gradually lost interest in the dogmatic controversy; Orthodoxy in the specific sense became a formality. Men preferred to turn to esoteric cultural values derived from classical antiquity and prepared the ground hopefully for a Renaissance which, however, no longer had any future on Greek soil. Some, like Georgius Gemistos (Plethon), were not content merely to revive classical studies but even went as far as to commend the spirit of classical paganism in preference to Church Christianity, as the means of regenerating the Empire. Others took seriously the intellectual confrontation with the West; they learned Latin, read Augustine, Thomas Aquinas and Anselm, and even translated them into Greek. But none of these groups gained the ascendancy.

While not opposed to these "friends of the Latins", though helped in the long run by this challenge, a mystical current emerged within the framework of strict Orthodox theology, namely, the Hesychastic movement of Archbishop Gregory Palamas (14th century). Orthodoxy was to be freed from the dangers of the Western scholastic dialectic by categorically denying any place at all to dialectic within theology and by locating the source of all theology in immediate religious experience and in a mystical vision of God. Logical objections to this system, however, convincingly presented, proved unavailing in the face of the underlying lack of realism in theology — a facet of the whole Byzantine mentality, which had always dreamt of the present in terms of the classical past.

The conclusion, in Florence in 1439, of a union between Constantinople and Rome which did not involve coercive measures on the part of the Byzantine Emperor but was arrived at on the basis of conviction, made it possible even at that late date to hope that reason would triumph and East and West agree. But the euphoria of the Greek Council fathers faded the moment they arrived back in Constantinople, the only part of their country still unoccupied by the Turks, only to be received there as traitors. In this situation the overwhelming majority of them opted in favour of the "tradition of the Fathers" as interpreted by the Constantinopolitans who had remained behind in the city. They sacrificed their conviction to a desperate loyalty. No Emperor could, at this stage, allow the union to be imposed against the wishes of the inhabitants of Constantinople upon whom, for better or worse, he had now to rely if he were to entertain any hope at all of defending the city against the final onslaught of the Turks.

See also *Hellenism and Christianity, Constan-* *tinian Era, Schism* III, *Middle Ages, Eastern Churches.*

BIBLIOGRAPHY. J. Pargoire, *L'Église byzantine de 527 à 847* (1905); E. J. Martin, *A History of the Iconoclastic Controversy* (1930); J. M. Hussey, *Church and Learning in the Byzantine Empire, 867–1185* (1937); J. Gill, *The Council of Florence* (1939); M. Jugie, *Le schisme byzantin* (1941); F. Dvornik, *The Photian Schism* (1948); S. Runciman, *A History of the Crusades,* 3 vols. (1951–55); G. Zananiri, *Histoire de l'église byzantine* (1954); G. Ostrogorsky, *History of the Byzantine State* (1957); F. Dvornik, *The Idea of Apostolicity in Byzantium and the Legend of the Apostle Andrew* (1958); H.-G. Beck, *Kirche und theologische Literatur im byzantinischen Reich* (1959); A.-J. Festugière, *Les moines d'Orient* (1961 ff.); P. Joannon, *Papes, conciles et patriarches dans la tradition canonique de l'église orientale jusqu'au neuvième siècle* (1962); A. H. H. Jones, *The Later Roman Empire* (1964); S. Runciman, *The Fall of Constantinople, 1453* (1965); J. M. Hussey, ed., *The Byzantine Empire,* part 1 of *The Cambridge Medieval History,* vol. IV (1966).

Hans-Georg Beck

C

CALVINISM

A. CALVINISM AND CALVIN

Calvinism is the name given to that form of Protestantism which had its origin, either directly or indirectly, in the reforming activity of John Calvin (1509–1564). The name itself was introduced by the Lutherans against Calvin's wish. Calvinism took root in the French and Swiss humanism of the early 16th century and, accordingly, it cannot be considered merely as a variant of Lutheranism, though it is true that "the basic teaching of Luther is also that of Calvin" (E. Tröltsch). The influence of Bucer, Melanchthon and Bullinger upon Calvin effected further modifications of Calvinism. Calvin's "conversion" (between 1530 and 1533) was occasioned by his readings of Scripture, chiefly the OT. He read it as the word of God spoken to him personally, and he considered it to be the one source and norm of the Christian faith. This principle that Scripture is not only the one source but also the one norm whereby the faithful can attain to certitude with regard to the content of revelation without the need of an infallible ecclesiastical interpretation, is a basic tenet of the whole Reformation. In this sense, Calvinism always understands itself to be a Church reformed by the word of God and to be corrected by each of the faithful according to the Scriptures. The intention of founding a new Church was as far from Calvin's mind as it was from Luther's. The purpose of Calvin was to affirm the transcendence of revelation in which man could share through grace alone. This basic intention does not contradict Catholic teaching. The criticism that he directed against the Roman Catholic Church, however, was not limited to the elimination of abuses, but aimed at a radical recasting of the whole structure and function of the Church. The reason for this drastic criticism lay in Calvin's repudiation of a mediation of salvation where the Church, by virtue of the Holy Spirit animating it, is a supernatural instrument.

To avoid the danger of presenting as Calvinist teaching something that would not be applicable to every form and stage of its development, we limit ourselves in B) to Calvin's teaching, and then in C) to a brief description of the development in the later and variant forms of Calvinism.

B. CALVIN'S TEACHING AND REFORMS

Calvin's main work, the *Institutio Religionis Christianae,* underwent a series of editions from 1536 to 1560 in which the author further elaborated this handbook of biblical theology and completed his synthesis of Christian teaching. Its final form was the Latin edition of 1559, divided into four books (the French translation followed in 1560). The following references will be to the edition of 1559, indicated by *Inst.* followed by book and chapter number. Calvin presents an orthodox interpretation of the teaching on the Trinity (*Inst.,* I, 13) and makes it clear that there is no basis for the charge that his teaching is Arian in tendency. His Christology (*ibid.,* II, 12–17) is likewise orthodox, though an occasional tendency toward Nestorianism is unmistakable. The role of the Holy Spirit is stressed: his activity in the creation and the conservation of the cosmos, his general providence with regard to man, and his special activity in the individual believer and in the Church (*Corpus Reformatorum,* 36, 349). The significance of the humanity of Christ suffers a corresponding diminution. Calvin's doctrine and later Calvinism are strongly theocentric. Calvin is always preoccupied by the sovereignty of God, his absolute freedom, his omnipotence with a tendency to making him the sole agent, his providence and (only as a consequence of that) the double predestination of man, his election and damnation. That man can remain human and that he can accomplish anything in the realms of art and science, is only to be attributed to the intervention of God through the Holy Spirit, through whom he sustains will and understanding as human functions and even produces relatively good and noble deeds. Yet this remains, as it were, between brackets, the brackets of sin (*Inst.,* II,1,7–12). It is the same with what is relatively good in the social order: human laws, the capacity for rule, and indeed for accomplishment in any sort of vocation. All is the gift of the general activity of the Holy Spirit through which the profound corruption of man is confined within certain bounds (*ibid.,* IV, 20 2). This pessimism is the consequence of Calvin's doctrine of the total corruption of human nature.

Like Luther, Calvin is convinced that man, since the fall of Adam, is born with a nature vitiated at its root. Man is not a sinner because he commits sins, but he commits sins because he is essentially a sinner. Luther and Calvin rightly consider that in the actual order of salvation all man's acts must be at least implicitly performed out of love of God, the supernatural end, and that man is impotent to do this by reason of original sin (Luther: cf. *Confessio Augustana,* art. 2; Calvin: *Inst.,* II, 1, 8–9), but in this they limit unwarrantably the action of the grace of Christ. They do not see that Christ's universally active grace makes an initial ordination towards God, as the supernatural end, possible even in unregenerated man (contrast *Summa Theologica,* II, II, q. 83, art. 16; I, II, 112, art. 2).

1. *The activity of the Holy Spirit in the individual believer.* The "special activity" of the Holy Spirit, for Calvin, is accomplished primarily in the individual believer (in the form of a strictly individual *testimonium Spiritus Sancti*) and only secondarily in comparison in the Church as a whole.

This testimony of the Holy Spirit is an assurance both of the divine truth of sacred Scripture and of the promise of God for the individual in question. The outward testimony of the Spirit in the Scriptures concerning the unshakable fidelity of God to his promises is confirmed by the inner testimony in the heart and from this proceeds the certitude of eternal salvation (*Inst.,* I, 9,3). Calvin gradually came to consider, more properly, that this *testimonium Spiritus Sancti* is only one aspect of the special activity of the Holy Spirit in applying to the individual the salvation won by Christ (*ibid.,* III, 1, 3–4).

This application takes place in justification and sanctification. Calvin, like Luther, teaches that justification comes through faith alone. Not only can man in no way prepare himself by his own strength for justification (which is also Catholic teaching), but in justification itself his grace-inspired Yes to the revelation of faith does not make him co-active with God's saving act. It is the same in all further sanctification, which Calvin stresses more than Luther. The Holy Spirit remains the sole supernatural agent. He accomplishes everything alone (though he also makes use of certain instruments) and asks for obedience freely proffered. This means also the "absolute sovereignty" of the Holy Spirit. He not only needs no mediation in applying the salvation achieved by Christ, but he can also withhold his activity when men use correctly the means given and prescribed by Christ, so that some of those who rely on the sacraments do not escape their (well-merited) damnation (*ibid.,* III, 2, 11; III, 24, 8). The spiritual life of Calvinists is largely determined by the notion of the activity of the Holy Spirit which has been briefly sketched. Together with the consciousness of the radical depravity of man, one finds a steadfast trust in the promises of God, and from this there issues not infrequently a vigorous life of virtue, inspired by thankfulness for salvation received and obedience to the Lord of the covenant. It is this which gives Calvinist piety its sturdy character. The word of God is not only the good news of salvation, but also *law.* "God is the Lord; I am the servant." This rigour in theology and piety is, nevertheless, tempered by what may be called an almost mystical trait (though mysticism is abhorred by Calvinism as a confusion of the divine with the human). It has found beautiful expression in the *Heidelberg Catechism* (question 1): "That I belong, body and soul, both in life and in death, not to myself but to my true saviour Jesus Christ", this is "my one consolation." Fellowship with Christ is, therefore, a feature of Calvinist piety (*Inst.,* III, 1, 1; III, 11, 10).

2. *The Christology and ecclesiology of Calvin.* Almost from the beginning, Calvin had to fight on two fronts: against the Roman Catholic Church, and against the "Libertinists" who rejected fundamental articles of faith, sometimes even the doctrine of the Trinity, and claimed to be led individually by the Spirit, while maintaining very tenuous links with Scripture.

In opposition to the Roman Catholic Church, Calvin based on his Christology his repudiation of the papacy and the Church as a supernaturally effective medium of salvation. For him Christ is the Son of God who had become a man to reconcile the predestined to God. As mediator, he then sent the Holy Spirit after his ascension, to apply fully to the predestined alone the fruits of his work. Calvin thought that the glorified body of Christ remained subject to the spatial limits of this old aeon (*ibid.,* IV, 17, 12). That is why he stressed that the glorified body of Christ remains locally in heaven, and the Church, visible and invisible, of sinful men, is confined to earth. It is only the "power of the Holy Spirit" that bridges this gap, which will endure till the last day. This "power of the Holy Spirit" does not effect an ontological relation to the glorified Lord, who would thereby be present and active in his Church, as Catholic teaching asserts. For Calvin, the power of the Spirit brings about a link with the power of the glorified body of Christ, whereby Christ exercises his lordship over the Church (*ibid.,* II, 15, 3; 75). It is then understandable that Calvin, in his teaching on the Eucharist, explains the presence of Christ in terms of his power and not of his glorified body as such (*ibid.,* IV, 17, 26). Calvin's vigorous affirmations on fellowship with Christ must always be understood within these bounds. Thus the activity of the Holy Spirit extends to the realization of salvation, to the detriment of the Incarnation and consequently of the place of the Church. But if Christ is not present with his glorified body in the Eucharist, and, analogously, in the Church, the Church would not be inwardly sanctified through the sacred humanity and hence cannot effectively co-operate in salvation by its own God-given activity. But this does not prevent Calvin from calling the Church "the mother of the faithful" (*ibid.,* IV, 1, 4), and by this he refers not merely to the invisible (the *universus electorum numerus*) but also to the visible Church. However, the Church is only "mother" insofar as the Holy Spirit exercises in her that activity which is exclusively his own.

But Calvin is equally opposed to the "Libertinists" who tried to separate radically the work of the Spirit from the function of the Church. This cannot be, he says, for divine providence has established an extrinsic link between them. In this way, the activity of the Holy Spirit is bound first to the word of Scripture, then to the word preached by the Church (*ibid.,* IV, 1, 4), and finally also to the sacraments. Hence, Calvin can also say: where the Gospel is preached in its purity and the sacraments rightly administered, the Holy Spirit is active and there the true Church of Christ is to be found (there is, as has been indicated, a discrepancy between this and the absolute "sovereignty" of the Holy Spirit). To these two characteristics, already cited by the *Confession of Augsburg,* Calvin frequently added "proper Church discipline". He was convinced that Church discipline should be dictated not only by historical circumstances and freely adopted measures, but primarily by biblical directives. He maintained the same with regard to liturgical forms. Consequently, he attempted, from the few basic characteristics given in Scripture, to develop a Church order (his *ordinances ecclésiastiques*), and a liturgy reformed according to the word of God ("la forme de prières et chants ecclésiastiques"). Thus Calvin gave to his Church not only its own creed, but also a very characteristic Church order. He based this order on the general priesthood of all the faithful. Then he found in Scripture that for the proper structure of the community four functions were indicated: that of ministers, doctors, elders, and deacons. All the faithful are priests through the "spirit of sonship" in which they are all reborn. The offices are based only upon the "charismata" of the

Holy Spirit which are necessary for the right ordering of the Church, but which do not establish a special priesthood.

And so the aristocratic Calvin was able to build up a "democratically" structured, visible Church by the practical application of the doctrine of the general priesthood. There are a number of levels. Each community is a Church in the full sense, led by a "consistory" formed from the ministers and elders (these "elders" were to guard especially the purity of teaching and Church discipline within the community — whence later the name "Presbyterian Church"). It is the task of doctors to explain the Scriptures and so to preserve the authentic teaching among the faithful. The deacons should fulfil the function of service in the Church and manifest it to those without. The communities together form the national or regional Church (usually there is also an intermediary level in the "presbytery", *classis*). The national Church is governed by a synod or general assembly composed of pastors (ministers) and elders. Calvin recognizes, however, not only the national Church, but also the universality of the visible Church; and hence he constantly strove for the union of all Christians (in practice, only of Protestants). He still strove to discover this unity in the divisions of Christianity.

Calvin's emphasis upon outward structure does not indicate a lack of consideration for the inner bonds of the living organism. He repeatedly stresses that all the gifts of those in official positions as well as of the ordinary faithful are given for the building up of the "body of Christ" (*Inst.*, IV, 3, 2). But in this regard it must be added that this building up of the body of Christ, and growth in fellowship with Christ, takes place "in the power of his Spirit and not in the substance of his body" (*Corpus Reformatorum*, 79, 768). The Church, as the *corpus Christi mysticum*, has no ontological bond with the personal, glorified body of Christ and consequently has no "pneumatic" reality of its own. And so also the leaders of the Church cannot interpret Scripture infallibly, though the charisms of the officials give a certain authority to the Church's preaching. The "presumption" is in favour of the interpretation of the Church, until the contrary becomes clear to the individual from the Scriptures themselves. Councils, such as

were held in earlier times, still have a special authority for Calvin, though not an infallible one. He can find nothing good to say of the Pope, who is only an "unsightly hump on the back" which disfigures the symmetry of the body of the Church (*ibid.*, 202), or, in a word, the Antichrist (*ibid.*, 29, 624). One valuable and practical application of the general priesthood is the stress on professional activity as service and praise of God.

C. The Development of Calvinism

This vigorous ecclesiastical structure with its emphasis on the lay element has given proof of its quality in the course of history, though history has also shown its defects. Along with the confession of faith worked out by Calvin (*Confessio Gallicana*), it was ratified in 1559 at the First National Synod of France and introduced, with some variations, in all Presbyterian Churches. Since *c.* 1550 Calvinism spread swiftly, particularly in many European countries. The international academy founded in 1559 by Calvin in Geneva had no little part to play in that development. After Calvin's agreement with Bullinger, the successor to Zwingli (in the *Consensus Tigurinus* of 1549, the "Zurich Agreement"), Calvinism swiftly spread in Switzerland. At the same time it took root in France, where it has maintained itself to the present day in spite of many persecutions and religious wars. It then established itself in the Netherlands, which in the 17th century was the intellectual centre of Calvinism (cf. the Dordrecht Synod 1618/19). It came to England under Edward VI, 1547-53, where under Cromwell (1649–59) the Calvinist Puritans came to power, though later they migrated in great part, under pressure, to Holland and North America. In Scotland John Knox introduced Calvinism in the second half of the 16th century with lasting success. In Germany Calvinism only took permanent root in a few provinces (the Palatinate, 1563: the Heidelberg Catechism). In Hungary it developed into a strong "Reformed Hungarian Church" and in Poland it took hold swiftly but was then almost fully repelled by the Counter-Reformation. In the United States and in Canada, Calvinism developed strongly and combined into the large "Presbyterian Churches" and also the smaller Free Churches of the same type (usually "fundamentalist" in their creeds). Besides this, the Presbyterians (called the Reformed in Continental Europe, and numbering altogether *c.* 45 million) have been very active in various mission areas where they founded Presbyterian Churches (which have now become independent). Since 1875 most Presbyterians have united in the "Presbyterian World Alliance".

In order to understand the world-wide impact of Calvinism, it is necessary to take account of the large groups which branched out and separated from the body of the Anglican Church in the course of history and adopted Calvinist teaching and Church organization in various forms. In chronological order, after the "Puritans", the first to be mentioned are the Congregationalists, who broke with the Anglican Church in the 17th century and then applied Calvin's notion of the community in its most extreme form: every local Church is a Church in the full sense and hence they are an association of fully independent local Churches (today Congregationalists number *c.* 5 million). In the 18th century the Methodists, under the leadership of John Wesley, broke away from the Anglican Church under pietistic and Calvinistic influence, and took up a more or less pure form (varying according to countries) of Calvinist teaching and Church organization (they number today *c.* 40 million). Also in the 17th century, the Baptists who had left the Anglican Church came more and more under the influence of Calvinism; their Church organization is that of Congregationalism (today they are *c.* 55 million). All these groups are especially well represented in the United States and in the former mission countries.

It is understandable that in the present strong ecumenical movement among Calvinists, most efforts at union concern Presbyterians and the groups just mentioned. But Anglicans are also envisaged.

In Calvinistic doctrine developments have taken place parallel to general currents of thought in Europe and America, and these trends still continue in the various Churches. In the 17th century, the successors of the Reformers developed an orthodox theology which was often scholastic in type. It often lost itself in over-subtle disputes with Lutherans about the Real Presence in the Eucharist and led in general to a narrowing of theology and a desiccation of the spiritual life.

The pietist reaction followed in the 18th century, though spirituality remained orientated to action and averse to mysticism, true to the character given it by Calvin. Calvinistic trends in Anglican pietism found expression in the ethical activities of Methodism. As elsewhere, pietism brought with it into Calvinism an anti-intellectual and anti-orthodox trend which led on occasion to schisms. The rationalism of the 18th and 19th centuries often wrought havoc in theology and spirituality. Christ was reduced to a moral exemplar. The Holy Spirit was understood not as a person but as "divine force" and replaced more and more by human reason. The Lutheran Schleiermacher likewise had a marked influence on Calvinist theology in the 19th century, with his immanentist and anthropocentric theology, which was clearly opposed to Calvin's. Similarly, his relativizing of the concept of Church ("each Church is a unique creation of the Christian spirit") was taken over by the Calvinist theology of his time. Already in the 19th century there set in, more as a reaction to extreme rationalism, a pietistic yet orthodox *réveil* (starting from Geneva). Rationalism was finally overcome only after the end of the First World War, with the rise of "dialectical theology", especially that of Karl Barth. It defended in an extreme way, especially at the beginning, the transcendence of revelation ("God, the wholly Other"), and succeeded in re-introducing the orthodox teaching on the Trinity and Christology in practically all Calvinist Churches. At the same time, Calvinists in general became more conscious of the Church, and this, along with the re-vitalized orthodoxy created in large part the possibility of dialogue with the Catholic Church. On the Catholic side, it is becoming clear that the picture of Calvin was often distorted in polemics. Similarly, among many Calvinists, there is a new awareness of the nature of the papacy and of the Church as a whole, especially since Vatican II has shown that many of Calvin's objections were groundless. But the fundamental opposition unfortunately remains.

See also *Ecumenism* VI, *Protestantism, Reformation, Presbyterian Churches, Predestination.*

BIBLIOGRAPHY. J. Calvin, *Opera*, Corpus reformatorum, vols. 29–87, ed. by G. Baum and others (1863–1900); id., *Opera Selecta*, ed. by

P. Barth and others (1926–36); id., *Commentaries on the New Testament*, 14 vols.; id., *Commentaries on the Old Testament*, 30 vols.; id., *Institutes of the Christian Religion*, 2 vols., ed. by J. T. McNeill (1960); E. Doumergue, *Jean Calvin, les hommes et les choses de son temps*, 7 vols. (1899–1927); T. M. Lindsay, *A History of the Reformation*, II (1907); E. Troeltsch, *Social Teachings of the Christian Church*, I (1931); B. B. Warfield, *Calvin and Calvinism* (1931); C. L. Warr, *The Presbyterian Tradition* (1933); J. Mackinnon, *Calvin and the Reformation* (1934); P. Imbart de la Tour, *Les origines de la Réforme*, IV: *Calvin et l'institution chrétienne* (1935); W. Niesel, ed., *Bekenntnisschriften und Kirchenordnungen der nach Gottes Wort reformierten Kirche* (3rd ed.), 1948); T. F. Torrance, *Calvin's Doctrine of Man* (1949); J. L. Witte, *Het probleem individugemeenschap in Calvijns geloofsnorm*, 2 vols. (1949); E. A. Dowey, *The Knowledge of God in Calvin's Theology* (1952); A. Maxwell, *History and Charakter of Calvinism* (1954); K. Barth, *Knowledge of God and the Service of God* (1955); W. Niesel, *Theology of Calvin* (1956); G. C. Berkouwer, *The Conflict with Rome* (1958); id., *Divine Election* (1960); W. Niesel, *Gospel and the Churches* (1962); F. Wendel, *Calvin* (1963); W. H. van de Pol, *World Protestantism* (1964); A. Gonaezy, *Calvin, Théologien de l'Élise et du ministère* (1964).

Johannes Witte

CANON OF SCRIPTURE

1. *Significance and problem.* Vatican II has called attention in various documents to the greater esteem for Scripture which has characterized theology for some years, and which should also mark Christian life. Not only are the Council texts themselves highly biblical in their language, but in ch. 2 of the Constitution on Revelation, where sacred tradition is discussed (art. 8), the apostolic preaching, "which is expressed in a special way in the inspired books (of sacred Scripture)" is explicitly accorded priority. This should not be lost sight of, even though the statement of the preliminary draft on the sufficiency of Scripture in contrast to oral tradition was not adopted into the constitution. All those whose office it is to serve the word must deepen their knowledge of sacred Scripture by diligent reading and thorough study (art. 25), since "theology rests on the written word of God . . . the sacred Scriptures contain the word of God . . . and so the study of the sacred page is, as it were, the soul of sacred theology" (art. 24). Further, the Decree on Ecumenism pays special attention to the sacred books of

Scripture as "precious instruments in the hands of God", especially in the dialogue, "for obtaining that unity which the Saviour holds out to all men" (art. 21). "Like the Christian religion itself, all the preaching of the Church must be nourished and ruled by sacred Scripture." (Constitution on Revelation, art. 21.)

Hence in spite of the formal equality between Scripture and tradition which appears in the decisions of the Council, the material priority which is in fact accorded to Scripture should not be overlooked. Yet in view of the Council's alertness to change, manifested, for instance, in the fact that the historical character of the gospels is understood in terms of the development of tradition, the manner in which inspiration (Constitution on Revelation, art. 11) and the canon are treated of is surprisingly traditional, the actual criterion of the canonicity of Scripture being left undefined. It is indeed stated (art. 8) that through the Church's tradition the full canon of sacred books is known. The "Church's tradition" here implies, however, that the recognition of the canonical status of the books of Scripture was arrived at progressively and presupposed a series of preliminary stages in the history of dogma, above all during the first four centuries of the Christian era. This is a factor of the highest importance in the process by which the Church determined its own definitive form. Historically inexplicable, it must be ascribed to the mysterious guidance of the divine Spirit in the Church. Its importance has, however, been emphasized more by the non-Catholic than the Catholic theologians of our time. These latter, at least since the Council of Trent (*D* 783 ff.), have regarded the discussion of the canon as closed. However, one decisive exception to this has recently appeared: Whereas Trent (*D* 783) and Vatican I (*D* 1787) require *all* the books of the Old and New Testaments to be recognized and honoured with equal devotion and reverence, Vatican II refers *expressis verbis* to differences between them, notably to a priority of the gospels (Constitution as Revelation, art. 18). This means that the discussion of whether some books take precedence over others in the canon is reopened. The same question regarded from the aspect of fundamental theology or hermeneutics might be expressed as "is there a canon within the canon?" From the outset it is hardly possible to doubt where the answer to such a question would lie: in the priority of the gospels. This in turn throws new light upon the question of what kind of authority is implied when we call the Scriptures canonical.

The difficulty of the question of canonicity lies in the historical disparity between the fundamentally inspired nature of the OT and NT writings on the one hand, a factor which is presupposed by their canonical status, and the progressive circumscribing of the (NT) canon on the other, a process which continued until the 4th century. The explicitation of an authoritative revelation, which must have been already implicitly present in the apostolic age, is therefore completed at a far later stage. Indeed the hagiographers themselves were generally unaware of the fact that their writings were inspired and that their significance extended far beyond the particular occasions for which they were composed. The earliest stages in the history of the Christian Church make this clear.

From the outset a different meaning was ascribed to the word κανών from that which it bore in non-biblical Greek, namely "series", "list" or "chronological table". As used in Christian circles it acquired the fundamental meaning of "rule of right conduct", "reliable standard", "norm" of behaviour or of teaching. Thus Gal 6:16 speaks of the rule of true Christianity as opposed to the standards of the old world. And *1 Clem,* 7, 2 refers clearly to the norms contained in tradition as the guiding rule for Christian preaching and ethics. In the first three centuries of the Christian era the canon designates the *regula fidei,* all therefore that was already in existence as the guiding rule of truth and as the norm of faith prior to the biblical writings. In the second place (since Nicaea, 325) the canon meant the decisions of synods, and finally, from the 4th century onwards, it meant the list of biblical books which are to be used in the Church. This double meaning of the canon as guiding rule and as list or series in which the books of the Bible are enumerated has set the terms for the discussion of the canon by historians of theology to the present day. Hence, ever since the scholastic definition of the doctrine of inspiration, the canon of Scripture — as distinct from ecclesiastical law — has come to be understood more and more simply as "list" or "inventory" of the books of the Bible.

2. *History of the canon.* In spite of the legal prescription directing that the books of the OT canon were to be preserved unaltered in the temple (Deut 31:26), at the time when these books were adopted by the Christian Church the limits of that canon were still far from finally determined. The first group of OT writings, the Pentateuch, had undergone substantial additions in the shape of Deuteronomy in the 7th century and the priestly source at the beginning of the 4th century. With the writing of the Books of Chronicles, and the translation of the Septuagint (*c.* 350), the five books of the Pentateuch had acquired the force of law. At a later date the Sadducees and Samaritans actually held that these books alone constituted sacred Scripture.

The second group of OT writings, namely the books of the prophets, is already recognized as a distinct collection *c.* 190 B.C. (Ecclus 48:22—49:12). The threefold division of the OT canon as attested in Lk 24:44 presupposes the existence of the third group, the *Writings* or *hagiographa.* It should be noticed that with the exception of the psalms these were not intended to be read publicly in the course of liturgical ceremonies. To a large extent these *Writings* owe their inclusion in the canon to the supposition that they derive from Solomon or Jeremiah, or that they originally belonged to one or other of the key festivals of the temple. The theory of canonicity upheld by the Pharisees is explained for the first time by Flavius Josephus *c.* A.D. 95. According to him (cf. *Contr. Apion,* I, 8) the distinctive characteristics of this theory were as follows: divine inspiration, the holiness of their content, the idea that the books were twenty-two in number, the unalterable nature of the text, and the supposition that the books were composed between the time of Moses and that of Artaxerxes I (d. 424), whose death, according to Josephus, marked the close of the period of the prophets. The theory of the canon put forward in *4 Esdras,* 14, 8–48, is based on the supposition that in 557 Ezra, guided by the Holy Spirit, dictated within the space of forty days the writings of the OT which had been destroyed. Thereby, with the help of a direct intervention of God (verbal inspiration) the canon of 24 books was completed in the shortest possible time. This theory of the canon, later adopted by the Jewish Synod of Jamnia (Jabneh) *c.* A.D. 100, also provides the basis for the Christian notion. In spite of this it was precisely in the early Christian period that the writings of later Judaism, which had been rejected as apocryphal, had considerable influence. The Alexandrine canon was wider, and included certain additional books or parts of books which were known as deuterocanonical. Through the Septuagint it became the basis of the Vulgate. Hence this Alexandrine canon was declared binding for the OT both at the Council of Florence (*D* 706) and again at Trent. It comprises twenty-one historical books, seventeen prophetic books and seven wisdom books. Of these forty-five documents Catholic theologians designate eight as deuterocanonical (= apocrypha for Protestants), while the apocalyptic writings of later Judaism are designated as apocryphal (= Protestant pseudepigrapha).

For the community of the faithful of NT times these same books of the OT were at first considered to be the only books of sacred Scripture. Jesus had come to fulfil the promises contained in them (Lk 4:15 ff.; 24:44 ff.), and the community had no intention of challenging their canonical authority (Mt 5:17 f.) or of replacing them with canonical writings of its own (cf. 2 Pet 1:20 f.). The expectation of a return of Christ in the near future at first ruled out any notion of a new canon of Scripture corresponding to the new covenant. The occasional writings of the apostles and their disciples rather sought to show that the salvific event of Christ was "according to the Scriptures" of the OT. And in the light of the same event, they sought to interpret the OT books in such a way as to show that fulfilment of the law had come (2 Cor 3:6, 15 ff.). But with the delay of the parousia, it was only a matter of time till such "comments" took on an independent value. "The idea of setting new canonical books alongside those handed down by ancient tradition is wholly out of place in the apostolic age. The abundance of living canonical authorities, a multitude of prophets, charismatics and teachers, made any further additions to sacred Scripture . . . completely superfluous. The need to create a canon belongs to less privileged times." (A. Jülicher and F. Fascher.)

While continuing to accept the authority of the OT canon, the early Christians regard Jesus Christ the Saviour as the ultimate and supreme authority. In virtue of the fact that he is the divine son of the God of the OT and that his saving work has its origin in the eternal decree of Yahweh's own will to bestow salvation on mankind, his own person becomes the canon and the norm of interpretation for the OT writings (Jn 14:10, 24; 10:30). Christ's deed of salvation, as expressed in the kerygma of the death and resurrection of Jesus Christ, is itself this norm; but the early Christian community also hands down individual sayings from the preaching of Jesus while still on earth, for he, as the exalted Kyrios, is at once the subject of the early apostolic tradition (Col 2:6), its origin (1 Cor 11:23), and in the abiding work of the Holy Spirit (2 Cor 3:17 ff.) its author and guarantor (cf. Jn 14:26; 16:13). After his resurrection the Lord transmits to his apostles (Jn 17:18; 20:21; 2 Pet 3:2) the authoritative power of his own word and deed of salvation. Since the fate of the disciples is the same as that of their Lord, and since their word is accepted or rejected as that of their Lord (Lk 10:16; Jn 15:20), their claim to announce God's salvific will is also the same. Thus they constitute the third element in the unfolding of revelation as set forth in *2 Clem,* 14, 2: OT — Jesus Christ — apostolic preaching (cf. also *Ign. Magn.,* 7, 1; *Polyc.,* 6, 3). The idea of the NT canon as a list or collection of writings constituting an authoritative rule of faith develops independently of this principle of canonicity based on christological or apostolic origin. As the primary preachers of the Christian message and the eye-witnesses of Jesus' life and resurrection died out, their writings, which had often been composed for particular occasions, and sayings from their sermons which had been handed down by word of mouth acquired increasing authority for Christians of the second generation onwards. Thus 2 Pet 3:15 f. already refers to a collection of the Pauline letters, and Polycarp seems already to know of nine of the canonical letters of Paul. The gospels, which were composed in the second half of the 1st century, were initially written for the inhabitants of particular regions, but as early as *c.* 130 in the reign of Hadrian they were assembled into a single collection (A. von Harnack), and Justin (*1 Apol.,* 6, 6 f.) recommends them to be used in the liturgy alongside the OT prophets. The fact that they were four in number did, however, constitute a problem from the outset. Hence *c.* A.D. 170 Tatian composed a harmony of the gospels, the Diatessaron, corresponding to the one Pauline εὐαγγέλιον, taking the four gospels as the basis. Finally, Irenaeus explained the four forms of the one gospel by the significance of the number four in the vision of Ezekiel (Ezek 1:10; Rev 4:7; *Adv. Haer.,* III, 18, 8; Tertullian, *Adv. Marc.,* IV, 2; Clement of Alexandria, *Strom.,* III, 13, 93; I, 21, 136). The third group of NT writings, the Catholic letters, the Acts of the Apostles, Revelation and Hebrews, first acquired canonical authority in the second half of the 2nd century. Even then the degree of authority attached to individual writings varied considerably.

The excommunication of Marcion for his Gnostic and anti-Jewish ideas, which took place at Rome about the middle of the 2nd century, provided a decisive stimulus for the formation of the Church's canon. Marcion rejected the entire OT on the ground that it portrayed a vengeful God. He admitted only ten Pauline letters, as well as a version of Luke's gospel which had been purged of its OT citations and also of the infancy narrative. This Marcionite canon represents a first attempt to provide a substitute for the OT. To guard against the Marcionite heresy the Church provided a prologue to all four of the gospels to show that they were authentic and, in addition to the ten Pauline letters of the Marcionite canon, pronounced the pastoral letters, Acts of the Apostles and Revelation to be canonical. An official expression of this measure is found towards the end of the 2nd century in the Muratorian fragment, which enumerates twenty-two NT writings: the four gospels, Acts, thirteen Pauline letters, three Catholic letters, Revelation and the Apocalypse of Peter, this last not being universally recognized. Thus about 200 the formation of the canon in the Western Church was completed with the exception of Hebrews, which was declared not to be of Pauline provenance, and with some uncertainty still remaining as to the number of the Catholic letters. In the Greek Church Hebrews was recognized, but not Revelation, which was only able to gain a place in the canon gradually from the 6th century onwards. Here too the number of the Catholic letters remained in dispute. In 367, Athanasius (*Festal Letter* 39) designated the twenty-seven books of the NT in addition to the books of the OT, as together comprising a firmly established canon. ("Let no one add anything to these or take anything away from them"; cf. Rev 22:18.) At the anti-Arian synods in the middle of the 4th century the Eastern and Western canons were brought into closer agreement. In the second chapter of the *Decree of Gelasius,* going back to the Synod of Rome of 382 the canon of the twenty-seven writings of the NT was defined, and this was confirmed at the latest in 405 by a letter of Pope Innocent I as well as by the African synods of Hippo Regius (393) and Carthage (297, 419).

After the 5th century no new decrees on the canon are found. Nevertheless the canonical validity and rank of individual NT writings were constantly discussed in connection with the question of their authorship, except during the brief interval of Pietism in the 18th and 19th centuries. In 1546 Trent defined the canon of the Old and New Testaments once and for all, joining its decree to that of Florence and also maintaining the idea of canonicity upheld in the 4th century. Nevertheless it did not decide the question of the authenticity of individual NT writings. Theologians are unanimous in holding that the Council only defined that the books enumerated belonged to the canon. It had no intention of giving an authoritative decision on the historical problems concerning the authors of these books or the authenticity of disputed sections in them. Authenticity and canonicity are notions which must be kept clearly apart.

In so-called "liberal theology" and in the methods of historical criticism of the 20th century the question of the "necessity and limit of the NT canon" (W. G. Kümmel) becomes once more a crucial problem of Protestant theology, which turns upon the unity of the canon of the Bible and the Reformation principle of *sola scriptura.* Thereby a discussion has recently been revived on how Scripture can provide a basis for mutual understanding between the Churches on the principle of Christian theology.

3. *A theological solution of the problem.* We are here concerned with the question of how the biblical writings, especially those of the NT, came increasingly to be regarded as authoritative norms. The history of the canon makes it clear that the theory of inspiration, as developed in later Judaism, and then in the history of dogma, has little

light to throw upon this unless inspiration is taken in the widest possible sense, as the sum of all those criteria which led the Church of the first four centuries to define and evaluate its written sources. This is not to say that canonicity is the result of purely historical circumstances. The writings of the NT were used for liturgical reading and hence undoubtedly became the basis of a living experience of faith. Moreover, being in the broader sense of apostolic origin, they were a radiation of that authoritative revelation which was in principle deemed to be closed with the death of the last apostle. Prior to the point at which the canon was closed these writings had entered into the history of the Church. In the course of that history they had proved to be a norm which stimulated, sustained and tested critically the faith of the Church.

In spite of this it would be inadequate to describe the formation of the canon purely as a process of human history or as an official measure or measures taken by the Church. We should rather accept the judgment of faith and acknowledge with it that the canon is a special gift of God to the Church, and that in its efficacy we can see the special working of the Holy Spirit which was promised to the Church (W. Joest, K. Aland). This might be described as inspiration in the broader sense, but perhaps it should more correctly be called canonicity.

Strathmann (p. 295) speaks of "the creeping sickness of Protestant theology, and so of the Protestant Church; the obscurity of its relationship to the letters patent of its origins, that is, to the canon of the Bible". Perhaps this creeping sickness could be arrested if Protestant exegesis could bring itself to accept this criterion, which goes beyond the methods of historical criticism, and if it could add it to the Lutheran "Urgemus Christum contra scripturam" (*Weimarer Ausgabe*, xxxix, 1, 47). Protestants would have to bring themselves to suppose a decision which partook of the nature of revelation, part of the history of salvation and hence not amenable to historical criticism — a decision which was to bind the whole Church of the future (cf. Cullmann, pp. 45 ff.).

As expounded in Catholic theology the principle of canonicity is decisively affected not only by the doctrine of inspiration but by the idea of the Church. For although Augustine (*Contra Epistolam Manichaei,* 5, 6) held that sacred Scripture was to be believed because it belonged to the Church, today a distinction which does not belong merely to the history of dogma is drawn between the initial composition of the canonical writings (inspiration) and the subsequent recognition of them as canonical by the Church (the definition of the canon). For with regard to their original formation Scripture and the Church are on the same level and cannot, in the last analysis, provide a mutual basis for each other. To suggest this would be to fall into the circle of "Church — canon — Church". Hence what is treated in the history of the canon in the subsequent recognition of original revelation. It is all the more important to notice this since when the Church distinguished the canonical writings both from Gnostic and other heretical writings and also from the writings of the early Fathers, it can have been no part of its intention to set later tradition side by side with this canon as of equal value with it. Thus too today the Church must regard itself as in a pre-eminent manner tied to the canon. Qualitatively speaking, this canon is what it brought forth from within itself in the period of its origin. Quantitatively speaking, it consists of those books which it subsequently set apart as sacred from all other writings. The canon of Scripture is the real *norma non normata* of the Church for all time. Implicitly revealed in the apostolic age, it was explicitly defined and delimited in the decrees produced by the Church under the guidance of the Holy Spirit in the first four centuries of its existence.

See also *Bible* I B, *Apocrypha, Inspiration.*

BIBLIOGRAPHY. B. F. Westcott, *A General Survey of the Canon of the New Testament* (1855; 4th ed., 1875); T. Zahn, *Forschungen zur Geschichte des neutestamentlichen Kanons und der altchristlichen Literatur,* 10 vols. (1881–1929); id., *Geschichte des neutestamentlichen Kanons,* 2 vols. in 3 parts (1888–92); A. Souter, *The Text and Canon of the New Testament* (1913; rev. ed., 1954); A. Harnack, *The Origin of the New Testament and the Most Important Consequences of the New Creation* (1925); M.-J. Lagrange, *Introduction à l'étude du NT,* I: *Histoire ancienne du canon du NT* (1935); H. Strathmann, "Die Krisis des Kanons in der Kirche", *Theologische Blätter* 20 (1941), pp. 295–310; O. Cullmann, "The Tradition. The Exegetical, Historical and Theological Problem", in A. J. B. Higgins, ed., *The Early Church. Historical and Theological Studies* (1956), pp. 57–99; H. Braun,

W. Adresen, W. Maurer and O. Perels, *Die Verbindlichkeit des Kanons* (1960); K. Rahner, *Inspiration in the Bible,* Quaestiones Disputatae 1 (1961); R. M. Grant, *The Formation of the New Testament* (1965); W. G. Kümmel, *Introduction to the NT* (1965), pp. 334–57.

Paul Neuenzeit

CAPPADOCIAN FATHERS

Cappadocia, the most easterly district of Asia Minor, was early taught the Christian message (cf. 1 Pet 1:1), and at the Council of Nicaea was represented by seven bishops. There was no Cappadocian school of theology in the sense of the schools of Alexandria and Antioch. The unity of thought among the "Cappadocian" Fathers derives ultimately from Basil of Caesarea. It is Basil whom Gregory of Nazianzus and his younger brother Gregory of Nyssa recognize as teacher, and from Basil a line can be traced back to Origen through Gregory Thaumaturgus, and thereby to the Alexandrian tradition.

1. *Pagan and Christian culture.* According to the testimony of their many letters, the three great Cappadocians were strongly marked and very different personalities. Despite their differences, however, they were largely stamped by that common milieu from which they sprang. Their aristocratic families lived in a land in which Christianity had long been established and which for its part must have promoted the progressive Hellenization of the Persian Province. The higher culture of Hellenism was as natural to them as a Christian education loyal to Nicaea. Their family wealth made it possible for them to enjoy a thorough and broad education in the best schools of the time. Thus Basil and Gregory of Nazianzus met as students in 351 in Athens, and there began a life-long friendship. Thanks to their social status and the superiority of their culture, they were perfectly at ease in the presence of such pagan intellectuals as the famous rhetorician Libanius. Basil was one of the first to fashion his sermons deliberately according to the rules of rhetoric, though he did not thereby abandon the language of the Scriptures. Gregory of Nazianzus was so highly cultured that he could even adopt the artistic methods of the "Asiatic" style of Late Antiquity. The younger Gregory of Nyssa

performed for a time the secular office of lecturer and gained vast knowledge by independent study, especially through the works of Plotinus, Philo and Origen. Long overshadowed by the two older men, his writings came to the fore only relatively late. While the younger Gregory, as well as Basil himself, shows himself to be surprisingly well versed in the natural sciences and medicine, Gregory of Nazianzus's works reveal a lyrical nature to which poetry was more congenial. From the manner in which the Cappadocians used the classical culture of their day, it is clear that the Church responded to official recognition and aid by according due status to pagan culture, and that it had integrated the wisdom of the world with its own biblical and theological thought. In the work dedicated to his nephew *On the Profitable Use of Pagan Literature,* Basil shows that as a Christian one need not deny oneself the treasure of classical culture. Similarly, Gregory of Nazianzus denounces the Emperor Julian (the Apostate) as the "greatest of tyrants", because he wanted to hinder the development of Christianity by forbidding classical studies to its adherents.

2. *The monastic ideal.* But Basil and his friends feel the distance between the Church of their day and the early Church. The desire for the monastic life which animated each of the Cappadocians is as much an expression of longing for the life of the early Church as it is of the desire to transcend the present world in order to win a future one. Upon his return from Athens, Basil had himself baptized and chose, in place of a brilliant worldly career, the ascetic life. Basil and his friend Gregory joined themselves at first to that monastic movement which had found a wide response in their country under the leadership of Eustatius of Sebaste. It was at this time that they compiled together the *Philocalia,* selections from the writings of Origen. But contrary to Eustatius, Basil was concerned to keep the monastic life from becoming too exclusively ascetical and to give it a function in the Church. Whereas Gregory of Nazianzus preferred an individualistic form of asceticism, Basil formulated "Rules" which bound the monks to a life in community, where the daily demands of fraternal concern would be joined to the love of God exercised in contemplation. Gregory of

Nyssa married in his youth, but it did not hinder him from praising the monastic life in his early work *On Virginity*. His close ties with his sister Macrina, superior of a group of nuns, showed how greatly he himself was influenced by the monastic ideal of their great family.

3. *Their significance for Church policies*. The episcopal office was accepted and carried out by each of the Cappadocians more in compliance with the needs of the Church and the times than out of any personal inclination. Yet Basil proved himself to be an exceptional bishop, guiding the ecclesiastical life of his province with a firm hand, and making Cappadocia a cornerstone of orthodoxy. Though a loyal ally of Athanasius, in the Antiochene schism between Paulinus and Meletius he took the side of the "Neo-Nicenes". Concerned for the unity of the Church, he appealed in this conflict to the Bishop of Rome, Pope Damasus, though without success as Rome did not want to abandon the "Nicene" Paulinus. Both Gregories clearly had little desire for the episcopal office but they were consecrated by Basil to strengthen his own position in Church policy. After Basil's early death (379) they proved their worth at the Council of Constantinople. Gregory of Nazianzus could only retain for a short time the episcopal see of the new imperial city in the face of ecclesiastical intrigues. Gregory of Nyssa, after a few early setbacks, became the trusted agent of the government among the bishops, and in the course of long travels carried out the re-apportionment of episcopal sees according to the newly-established unity of the Churches.

4. *Cappadocian theology*. The theological works of the Cappadocians successfully terminated the disputes following upon Nicaea and promoted the development of the doctrine of the Trinity and Christology, so much so that the decrees of Constantinople and Chalcedon depended largely upon their works. Adopting the Origenist tradition of the "older" Nicenes, Basil went beyond Athanasius in stressing the trinity of the "hypostases" but defended against Eunomius and the Anomoeans the unity of the divine being (οὐσία) as well as the ὁμοούσιος, seeking to win over the more moderate Sabellianists under Basil of Ancyra. He used

philosophical terms only with reluctance, and kept deliberately to the language of the Bible.

Gregory of Nazianzus did not contribute much that was original to the trinitarian discussion, but he strengthened the position of Basil by formulating it in a more balanced and subtle way. While Basil hesitated, for pastoral reasons, to call the Holy Spirit "God", Gregory readily did so. Gregory of Nyssa represents the extreme form of the development whereby the Cappadocians, because of their stress upon the difference between the divine persons, seemed to accept only a unity of the abstract substance and thereby rather a similarity than a unity of nature (hence the reproach of "tritheism"). Gregory of Nyssa, under the influence of the Platonic doctrine of the "forms", conceived of the unity of the divine nature in the manner of a universal concept endowed with reality. On the other hand, the conflict with Eunomius led him to bring out more strongly the inner unity of being and of action in the divine hypostases.

The difference between the divine persons was based for him solely on their relations, so that every activity of God *ad extra* is common to all. In Christological questions Basil recognized the anti-Arian interests of Apollinaris of Laodicaea and avoided stirring up new disputes by the discussion of "superfluous questions". Gregory of Nazianzus, however, found himself compelled by the development of dogma to employ all his mastery of language in the struggle against the Apollinarists. True to the anti-Arian tradition, he proceeded from the divinity of Christ; but he saw the human νοῦς which Apollinaris denied, as assumed into the divine nature, so that the spirit of every man united to Christ could be transformed and divinized. His formulations of this teaching foreshadowed the later position of the orthodox neo-Chalcedonians. Following Origen, Gregory of Nyssa taught the mutual exchange of the attributes of the two natures in Christ *(communicatio idiomatum)*, though he sharply distinguished the divine and human nature in the one person and thus came close to the later Antiochene conception. Similarly, with regard to the anthropology which is at the centre of Gregory of Nyssa's interests, all the Cappadocians have the same point of departure which is finally determined by their ascetical and monastic orientation. Basil had already equated man to the "soul", to which the body is only accidently united. Since for Gregory of Nyssa death was the inexorable end of all joys of the sense, he was intensely concerned to find a reason for our corporality. Without being itself sinful, it must necessarily be connected with sin. Hence he comes finally to the conclusion that we are to assume a purely spiritual heavenly body, thus falling into the error of Origen in spite of his many efforts to counteract that tendency. In his homilies on the Song of Solomon, he describes the bride as the human soul alone, which seeks for the divine bridegroom in progressive mortification of the body.

His theological method corresponds in general to the thought of Origen. The search for a system is more important than the proof from Scripture. He is more interested in endless allegory than in the literal sense of the Scripture. Like the elaborate constructions of the Gnostics, his conception of the creation and redemption is that of a gigantic cosmic theatre in which everything strives painfully to re-mount to its original place. Because of his exceptional speculative gifts it was he more than other Cappadocians who won the title of " the theologian". Gregory of Nazianzus excelled in aptness of formulation rather than in any originality of thought. Basil, for his part, gave the original intellectual impulse to his friends and led them along the orthodox way amidst the doctrinal confusion of their day, by his adherence to Scripture and his grasp of the traditional teaching. In his concern for the Church as a "universal brotherhood" he showed also a truly ecumenical spirit and attitude, as his correspondence with the bishops of many provinces reveals.

See also *Origenism, Alexandrian School of Theology, Antiochene School of Theology, Gnosticism.*

BIBLIOGRAPHY. W. K. L. Clarke, *St. Basil the Great. A Study in Monasticism* (1913); H. U. von Balthasar, *Présence et pensée. Essai sur la philosophie religieuse de Grégoire de Nysse* (1942); P. Gallay, *La vie de s. Grégoire de Nazianze* (1943); J. Daniélou, *Platonisme et théologie mystique. Essai sur la doctrine spirituelle de St. Grégoire de Nysse* (1944); D. Amand, *L'Ascèse monastique de Saint Basile* (1949); L. Vischer, *Basilius der Grosse* (1953); B. Altaner, *Patrology* (1960), pp. 335–57.

Friedrich Normann

CARDINAL

Since the 16th century "Cardinal" has been an exclusive designation for the members of the College of Cardinals, also called the *Sacrum Collegium,* which consists of three classes (cardinal bishops, cardinal priests, and cardinal deacons).

1. *History.* The historical roots of the College of Cardinals go back to the presbyterate of the Bishops of Rome. According to an old custom, which held fast to the memory of the eucharistic celebration by the bishop together with his presbyterate, the heads of the Roman titular churches, whose number rose from eighteen in the pre-Constantinian era to twenty-five in the 6th century and then to twenty-eight in the mid-11th century, were called in weekly rotation, as "hebdomadaries", to the main celebrations of the liturgy in the five patriarchal basilicas. Until the 8th century there were most likely five titular churches assigned in each area to every patriarchal church. A new arrangement was probably made in the 8th century, according to which the seven heads of the neighbouring episcopal churches were called to the liturgy in the Lateran basilica, the old diocesan church of the Pope, and the heads of the titular churches took part in the liturgy of the four other patriarchal basilicas. In any case the designations *diaconus* or *presbyterus cardinalis* and *episcopi cardinales* (*PL,* CXXVIII, arts. 278, 283, cols. 1155 ff.) are to be found first in the *Liber Pontificalis,* in the *Vita* of Stephan III (768–772), whereby deacons and priests of Roman deaconates or titular churches and seven bishops in the vicinity of Rome were meant. The word *cardinalis* means here, according to a usage in existence since Gregory I, a cleric who has been accepted for service in a church which is not the one for which he was consecrated. The cardinal bishops and cardinal priests (together with an archpriest *cardinalium* at the head) were individual groups and pursued their own interests.

In the decree of Nicolas II, 1059, for the election of the Pope, the cardinal bishops became a sort of electoral college at the election of a Pope, and the cardinal priests, under Alexander III (1061–1073) attained a position in their titular churches similar to that of the bishops. The origin of the cardinal deacons is even more obscure.

Besides the "Palatine deacons" (*diaconi pala-tini*), who doubtless go back to the seven original deacons of the Roman community, and who, together with the cardinal bishops, took part in the liturgy of the Lateran basilicas, there were twelve regional deacons, who participated in the liturgy of the Stations. Since the time of Hadrian I there had been eighteen "deaneries", i.e., welfare agencies with a church as the main point of activity; since the 12th century a cardinal deacon headed each of these deaneries, where-upon the former differentiation between the Palatine and regional deacons was done away with. With the rise of this third group the College of Cardinals began to take form in the 11th century, and it was firmly established by the beginning of the 12th century; it was given its juridical organization in the same century and since that time takes part in the guidance of the Church as the senate of the Pope.

The liturgical order from which the College of Cardinals sprang reflects, according to ancient Christian understanding, the order of the Church. The leading role which accrued to the cardinals is shown in the right of papal election, which was granted exclusively to the College of Cardinals by Alexander III (1179); it is also to be seen in the fact that, as the Roman Synod lost in importance, the consistory, i.e., the assembly of the car-dinals, became the most important collegial organ of the Pope, with an advisory function, at times attempting — and this was sup-ported also by election stipulations — to bind the Pope to the consent of the college. With the erection of the Roman Congrega-tions by Sixtus V (1588), in which the activities of the earlier commissions of car-dinals were institutionalized, the consistory lost increasingly in meaning, and in the same measure the influence of those cardinals rose who were active in the courts and adminis-trative offices of the Roman Curia. Cardinals were also preferably chosen for important foreign affairs; since Eugene IV (1431–1447), as a rule only cardinals were sent out as *legati de latere*. In the Middle Ages cardinal bishops had precedence before kings; later the cardinals were also accorded the honours belonging to princes of noble birth. They have had the right to the title of "eminence" since 1630.

The cardinal's leading role made member-ship of the Sacred College desirable. Alex-ander III named a foreign bishop to the College of Cardinals for the first time; it was the Archbishop of Mainz, Conrad von Wittelsbach. This ended the former con-formity of degree of consecration with rank within the College of Cardinals, and the differentiation between the cardinals in the Curia and those *extra curiam* began. From the pontificate of Clement V (1305–1314) on, the creation of the favourites of secular princes as cardinals increased; out of this grew the acknowleged right (since the 15th century) of the Emperor and the Kings of France, Spain and Portugal to name "crown cardinals", who frequently became more or less the diplomatic representatives of their princes at the Apostolic See (cardinal pro-tectors). Under Honorius III a cardinal was appointed for the first time (1218) as pro-tector of an order (Franciscans); from this developed the system of cardinal protec-tors for orders and congregations, which continued right up to the present time, but which, from 1964 on, is being brought to an end.

The number of cardinals was limited to seventy by Sixtus V (1586), on the model of the seventy elders of Israel (Num 11:16): six cardinal bishops, fifty cardinal priests, and fourteen cardinal deacons. Until the middle of the 14th century merely the number of the six cardinal bishops had been fixed. During the Middle Ages, an average of twenty cardinals belonged to the college. The reforming Council of Basle (1436) stipulated a maximum number of twenty-four, which was to be drawn from all areas of Christianity ("de omnibus christianitatis regionibus", sess. XXIII). The Council of Trent repeated the demand for universality ("ex omnibus christianitatis nationibus", sess. XXIV, *de ref.*, ch. 1), but this was subsequently disregarded. A turning point first came under Pius XII at the consistory of 18 February 1946; after regression under John XXIII, who created those members of the Curia cardinals who had been passed over by his predecessor, the endeavour of Paul VI has been directed towards making the College of Cardinals representative of the whole Church.

2. *Current law and notions of reform.* The *CIC*'s law, can. 230–41 (also *CIO,* can. 175–87), has been decisively changed by the legislative measures of John XXIII (motu

proprio of 11 and 15 April 1962: *AAS* 54 [1962], pp. 253 ff.) and Paul VI (motu proprio of 11 and 26 February 1965: *AAS* 57 [1965], pp. 295 ff.). The number of cardinals is no longer legally fixed; at the moment it is about one hundred. In future cardinals are to be bishops. The division into three classes was retained. The class of cardinal bishop, which until now consisted of the ordinaries of the suburbicarian dioceses (Ostia, Albano, Porto-Santa Rufina, Palestrina, Sabina-Poggio Mirteto, Frascati, Velletri, Ostia being ruled in personal union with the diocese of the senior in rank) is made up now of the titular heads of these dioceses, and, following these in rank, the patriarchs of the Eastern Church who have been called to the College of Cardinals. The former retain certain honorary rights in their titular churches; the latter receive no Roman titular churches and are not counted as belonging to the *clerus Urbis*. The cardinal priests, of whom some are active in the Roman Curia (so-called Curia cardinals), but most of whom govern sees outside Rome, receive a Roman parish church as a titular church, while the cardinal deacons, who as a rule are Curia cardinals, receive as their title a "deanery". Cardinal priests and cardinal deacons have a position at their titular churches, or "deaneries", similar to that of a bishop; it does not, however, have any practical effect. The College of Cardinals is a juridical person, which is presided over by a dean as *primus inter pares*. In case of his being hindered he is represented by a subdean. The suburbicarian cardinal bishops elect the dean as well as the sub-dean from among their number; the election requires papal confirmation. The College of Cardinals elects a chamberlain *(camerlengo)* as a trustee, and a secretary.

The Pope names the cardinals at will; however, he considers the tradition that the occupants of certain episcopal sees are to be raised to the cardinalate. The nomination takes place in a secret consistory; the question which is at that time directed to the cardinals who are present has no legal importance ("quid vobis videtur?"). When it does not seem apposite to publish a new appointment, it can take place without the specific name being mentioned ("nomen reservamus in pectore", whence the name: cardinal *in petto*). A cardinal so named first attains to the rights of the cardinalate with the later announcement, but his seniority is reckoned from the day of his nomination. One speaks of the nomination of a cardinal as a creation, the cardinal is a *creatura papae;* the bond is thereby designated which binds the Cardinal to the Pope; this is often portrayed as that of a son, but brother would be more correct (in any case the old formula has it so: "de fratrum nostrorum consilio").

As hitherto, the most important right of the College of Cardinals is that of papal election. Considerations which would transfer this right to the Synod of Bishops erected by Paul VI could not be implemented in view of the present structure of this synod: it is only constituted by papal convocation. During the vacancy of the Roman See, the College of Cardinals has a right to govern, but this is limited to urgent matters. During the life of the Pope the chief importance of the cardinalate's activity does not lie in the College of Cardinals, but in the individual cardinals, who, as directors or members of administrative boards and tribunals in the Curia, hold important positions and who, *extra curiam,* by virtue of their great prestige and especially as presidents of episcopal conferences, promote the connection with the Supreme Pontiff.

The reconstruction of the College of Cardinals, begun by John XXIII, and cautiously but persistently furthered by Paul VI, is an important step towards the reform of the Curia. That in the future all cardinals will be bishops, and that a way has been opened for patriarchs of the Eastern Church to accept a call to the College of Cardinals, signifies a break with its historical past and in the same measure an orientation to the whole Church. Even though the enrolment of the patriarchs of the Eastern Churches is not yet satisfactory — they would need to have special rank —, the conditions have been created to make it possible for the College of Cardinals to represent the whole Church. In order to allow the Sacred College to achieve also a collegial function, the consistory, which at the moment in its three forms (secret, semi-public and public) can scarcely be considered as really functioning, should be revived. Thus the College of Cardinals could supply an important complement to the Synod of Bishops which is only to be called together for particular cases, and together with this synod could be a guarantee that the principle of collegiality would become operative and efficacious.

See also *Curia, Bishop* II, III, *Church* III.

BIBLIOGRAPHY. J. B. Sägmuller, *Die Tätigkeit und Stellung der Kardinäle bis Papst Bonifaz VIII.* (1896); S. Kuttner, "Cardinalis. The History of a Canonical Concept", *Tradition* 3 (1945), pp. 129–214; H. G. Hynes, *The Privileges of Cardinals* (1945); M. Andrieu, "L'origine du titre de Cardinal dans l'Église Romaine", *Miscellanea Giovanni Mercati* 5 (1946), pp. 113–44; H.-W. Klewitz, *Reformpapsttum und Kardinälekolleg* (1957); A. de la Hera, "La reforma del colegio cardinalicio bajo el pontificado de Juan XXIII", *Ius Canonicum* 2 (1962), pp. 677–716; P. C. van Lierde and A. Giraud, *What is a Cardinal?* (1964).

Klaus Mörsdorf

CARTESIANISM

The influence of Descartes on the history of human thought cannot be restricted to the philosophy fashionable in France in the 17th century. Cartesianism is rather one of the sources and norms for the modern mentality in general. Today as in the past its assessment can vary between two extremes, according to whether one sees the basic tendencies of modern thought one-sidedly as either promise or decay. This is a sign of the perpetual relevance of Cartesianism, since it calls for a new estimation of it from each generation. At the same time, it makes this assessment more difficult. Further, the actual effects of Cartesianism on the history of thought do not fully coincide with the original intuitions and intentions of Descartes. The mask which the twenty-three year old Descartes professed to wear ("larvatus prodeo", *Œuvres*, X, p. 213) has never ·been completely stripped from him by research. E. Gilson has disclosed the multiple dependence of the great innovator on tradition, including the scholastic in particular. Much more decisive than any particular element, however, is the efficacy which Descartes imparted to some few principles of method and system, by using them as the focus, as it were, of the progressive lines of scientific and general thinking in his day, to which he thereby gave new strength. It was in this undoubtedly that he showed his greatness and his limits as a thinker. A critical sifting and examination of these principles is for the reasons given above an undertaking which calls for constant revision.

The 16th century, with its bent for methodology, found its authoritative theorist in Descartes. In his *Regulae ad directionem ingenii* (1628, published posthumously) and his famous essay, *Discours de la méthode,* he gives one single programmatic method, modelled predominantly on the deductive processes of mathematical knowledge, which proceeds step by step in logical continuity from analysis to synthesis. Modern science found in this concentrated methodology a source of strength for its sharp and successful climb. But the Cartesian approach also shows the dangers of monism in method (it was already reproached with dogmatism by the Enlightenment of the 18th century), though such dangers are by no means to be laid to the charge of Cartesianism alone, since they are a threat wherever any science is wholeheartedly pursued. The provisional validity which Descartes allowed to traditional Christian morality was in any case too weak a barrier against the totalitarian claims of his own rationalistic type of method.

The scepticism of which Montaigne and the free-thinkers of the age remained prisoners was organized by Descartes (in his chief work, *Meditationes,* 1641) into the methodical destruction of all apparent or insufficiently founded certainties — till doubt eliminated itself in the certainty which the doubter has of his own existence: *cogito-existo.* (In the *Discours,* this is found with the misleading 'therefore' — 'I think, therefore I am'). This way of basing knowledge on the self-consciousness of man is rightly taken to be, in spite of some similar formulations in St. Augustine and medieval philosophers, the guiding principle of the philosophy of the 'subjectivity', which reached its highest points in the transcendental method of Kant and especially in the universal metaphysic of the spirit elaborated by German idealism.

The widespread but superficial view which restricted Descartes's starting-point to an autonomist principle should have been avoided by noting its background: certainty of self is rooted in the vital knowledge of the idea of God. The anthropocentrism is relative, corresponding to its degree of being; human autonomy *is* at once subjection to divine law. The idea of the infinite God is not merely impressed on the human spirit from outside. "Innate", it brings about the dynamism of its nature which is most strictly proper to it (cf. *Meditationes* 3, in *Œuvres,* VII, pp. 51 f.). A primordial, valid, spiritual experience of being is also at the base of the other, "ontological" proof of the existence of God (cf. *Meditationes* 5, *loc. cit.,* pp. 115–120) — in spite of Descartes himself (and later Kant) mistakenly explicitating this experience as a purely *a priori* conceptual knowledge. Jaspers, however, is right in objecting that Descartes abandoned almost unconsciously the profound meaning and the rich possibilities contained in the first certainty; and Heidegger is right in saying that truth is far too easily reduced to correctness. These are the objections, and not that of the much-debated, apparently illegitimate "circle", which must be made to the criterion of truth as offered in fact in Descartes's "clear and distinct idea". Descartes was already too much of a rationalist — Cartesian.

The *Meditationes,* and later (1644) the *Principia,* develop a sharp opposition between spirit and matter, between *res cogitans* and *res extensa.* These are complete substances, which exist in man without any ontological connection, being combined merely in their activity (the theory of psycho-physical interaction), while animals are merely very well-engineered automata. It was this dualism above all, on account of the difficulties which it gave rise to, which caused the Cartesian problem in the 18th century. It led to contrasting systems which took its logic further, the occasionalism of Malebranche with its dualism of parallels, and the "neutralist" monism of Spinoza. But Descartes had a far wider effect in the long run on the modern mentality. Thinking predominantly in terms of existing things, to the complete disregard of the ontological principles whereby, according to the Aristotelian tradition, things are constituted in existence (such as the "substantial forms"), he furthered the levelling out of the differentiated reality of the world, in the sense of materialistic monism, contrary to the original impulses given by his philosophy.

His complete system of mechanics for the world, which he constructed in his *Principia,* is, however, an expressive example of an essay in research which is constantly necessary in all branches of science. The one-sidedness of the method is compensated for by its pioneer work in opening up new paths, though its concrete elements, such as the seven laws of dynamics, have not survived the test of empirical investigation even in classical physics. The equation of matter with extension in the system agitated the theologians of Descartes's time, on account of its consequences for the doctrine of the Eucharist.

It can hardly be said that Descartes made any more fuss about his faith in Christian revelation than scholars of his day were accustomed to do in general. If perhaps he did, this is to be primarily attributed to his irenic nature. That he did in fact succeed in reconciling his continued faith in revelation with very logical and indeed extreme philosophical positions and many kinds of scientific research, is a testimony to a manifold elasticity of mind, which will be credited perhaps in days to come with more objective Christianity than was actually possible in the past.

See also *Kantianism, Transcendental Philosophy, Monism, Spinozism.*

BIBLIOGRAPHY. R. Descartes, *Œuvres,* ed. by C. Adam and P. Tannery, 12 vols. (1897–1910), vol. XIII: Supplement and General Index (1913); id., *The Philosophical Works,* rendered into English by E. S. Haldane and G. R. T. Ross, 2 vols. (1911–12); J. Maritain, *Three Reformers: Luther, Descartes, Rousseau* (1928); A. B. Gibson, *The Philosophy of Descartes* (1932); J. Laporte, *Le rationalisme de Descartes* (2nd ed., 1950); L. J. Beck, *The Method of Descartes* (1952); H. Gouhier, *La pensée métaphysique de Descartes* (1962); K. Jaspers, *Three Essays: Leonardo, Descartes, Max Weber* (1964); G. Schmidt, *Aufklärung und Metaphysik. Die Neubegründung des Wissens durch Descartes* (1965); L. J. Beck, *Metaphysics of Descartes. A Study of the Meditations* (1965).

Walter Kern

CATECHESIS

A. HISTORICAL REVIEW

The noun "catechesis" (κατήχησις) does not occur in the NT; only the verbal form (κατηχεῖν) is to be found there, though not in the technical sense it was later to acquire, being taken rather by the NT authors in the current sense of "recount" or "give *viva voce* instruction". (This is a transferred sense, derived from the physical which was to "echo" or "resound".) It is so used in Acts 21:21, 24: "they [the Jews] have been told [concerning Paul]".

In other contexts the word χατηχεῖν takes on a religious colouring. The reason for this is that the object to which it applies is itself something religious. This is so, for example, when it is a question of the Jews being instructed in the Law (Rom 2:17–21), the Christian in the inspired word (Gal 6:6; 1 Cor 14:19), or in the way of the Lord (Acts 18:25), or yet again in the events of his life (Lk 1:4).

The NT has nothing to say about the *forms* of this teaching. The choice of the word merely emphasizes that it is oral and that it is the handing on of what has been received. The NT itself is a catechesis. The specifically Christian teaching which it contains is designated by a variety of words (ὁδός, διδαχή, παράδοσις, λόγος: way, doctrine, tradition, word). Certain passages suggest different kinds of teaching. Thus Heb 6:1 distinguishes elementary teaching from that reserved for the proficient, and gives the content of the first instruction about Christ: conversion, faith, resurrection from the dead, eternal sanctions, baptism. In the same way the NT accords special treatment to the "kerygma", the unfolding of the Good News to the heathen for the first time (Lk 24:47, Acts 10:42).

In the course of the 2nd and 3rd centuries the vocabulary of our subject became more exact and gradually took on a technical meaning. Derivatives appeared, such as χατηχίζειν , "Catechizare", "Catechisatio", neither standard Greek nor classical Latin.

Hippolytus makes use of the word "catechesis" in its precise sense of teaching given to someone preparing for baptism, in other words to a catechumen, as the candidate came to be termed. (*Traditio Apostolica,* 17; cf. *Constitutiones Apostolicae Lib.,* VIII.)

As the catechumenate developed, the word "catechesis" and its derivatives took on specific meanings. These were the instructions given in the framework of the catechumenate, this being either preparatory to baptism — baptismal catechesis — or subsequent to it — the mystagogical catechesis of the neophytes. The great catechetical works of the 3rd and 4th centuries illustrate this latter kind abundantly, those of Tertullian, St. Ambrose, St. Cyril of Jerusalem, St. John Chrysostom, Theodore of Mopsuestia, St. Augustine.

From the beginning the catechesis preserved its character of oral teaching. The catechumenate took on fixed forms: instruction for the *rudes, competentes,* or *illuminati* as the case may be. The content was at once doctrinal — centred on the Creed — and moral — a study of the Two Ways, i.e., of Life and Death and the Decalogue. The context in which this whole teaching was situated was the liturgy.

Catechesis and catechumenate are so intimately linked that the disappearance of one means the disappearance of the other. The term "catechesis" vanished with the catechumenate in the 8th and 9th centuries. With it there passed away a primordial form of Christian teaching.

Other forms succeeded it, with a new terminology. The Middle Ages spoke of "catechismus", "catechizare", "catechizatus" (cf. St. Thomas, *Summa Theologica*, III, 71, 1), meaning the elementary teaching given by parents or sponsors to the baptized child. The message of the faith is thus passed on inside the Christian community, the liturgy and the accompanying preaching playing a decisive role.

Later ages re-discovered the need for some institution specifically designed for basic instruction in the faith. The pupils, however, were no longer adult converts but baptized children and adults only exceptionally. Consequently, the term "catechesis" was not revived, and the institution which emerged instead was called "Catechism", the name being then applied to the book, which was the prime source of that form of teaching.

In 1529 Luther published his own "Catechism". Among the Reformers, as in the Catholic Church, catechisms multiplied. Prominent examples were those of Canisius (1556), Bellarmine (1598), and the *Catechismus Romanus* of the Council of Trent (1566).

These pioneers were intent on the living word of God and a Christocentric approach. "The important thing is that pastors should never forget that the whole science of Christian living — ot rather as our Lord says, eternal life itself — consists in this, that they know him, the one true God, and Jesus Christ whom he has sent." So runs the preface to the Catechism of the Council of Trent.

In the course of the three centuries which followed, however, the trend of the catechisms was away from the living word of God. Catechism as an institution, no less than the study of the catechism-book, proved inadequate to maintain the living word in the Christian community.

That is why the word "catechesis" has been rehabilitated these latter years. The change of vocabulary indicates that the teaching of the faith cannot be reduced to the provision for a "catechism class" for children. There is also the catechesis of adolescents, youths and adults. Neither is the passing on of the faith a simple memorizing of the catechism. Both in its content and in its form, the catechesis should present the word of God as a living thing. The whole contemporary effort in catechetics is an attempt to restore its due place to the *catechesis* in the life of the Church.

B. Present-Day Problems

1. *Uses of the word "catechesis"*. The word "Catechesis" is now used habitually in two senses.

In the restricted sense catechesis means "the passing on of the deposit of faith to the new members acquired by the Church" (J. Daniélou). This is the technical, historical sense of the word. As in the early centuries of Christianity, it denotes the elementary teaching given to the convert with a view to baptism. Catechesis in this sense differs from the antecedent evangelization and the proclamation of the "kerygma"; it differs also from subsequent higher forms of teaching designed for the baptized — preaching, Church discipline, etc. In this sense we speak of catechesis with reference to an adult catechumen. Similarly, the term is used of the first rudimentary teaching given to baptized children.

In a wider sense, the word "catechesis" is co-extensive with the teaching of the faith, from the first announcement of the kerygma to the higher forms of "scientific" theology. This definition underlines the unity between the various stages: the initial hearing of the Good News, or the preparation for baptism, and the more advanced teaching designed to nourish the Christian life. Hence some writers designate the instruction before conversion as "pre-catechesis". This word, in the context of an adult catechumenate, brings out the point of this time of preparation, namely to provide for a fitting reception of the gospel message. It is not unlike "evangelization", which, however, rather indicates the nature of the preaching.

Both usages serve to clarify each other. The narrower sense emphasizes the formal aspect of the catechesis. It is by analysing the elements of this primary teaching of the faith that we are enabled to determine the content and modes of the catechesis as such, i.e., those things that are necessary for every baptized person. The wider sense, on the other hand, ensures that attention is paid, under pain of imprecision and error, to the time-sequence involved, especially in the case of evangelization and religious instruction. In this larger sense the word "catechesis" may apply legitimately to every form of religious teaching subsequent to evangelization and conversion.

2. *Towards a definition*. Catechesis can be defined in terms of its origin. Seen thus, it is simply the transmission of the word of God, which is the source of the catechesis in two ways.

To begin with, the word of God determines the *content* of the catechesis, which must present the word of God in a well-balanced way. Accordingly, the mystery of Jesus Christ must be central, i.e., his saving death and resurrection, and the whole history of salvation as referred to him. The content of the catechesis is not therefore in the first place a system of ideas or a set of precepts; it is the proclamation of events in which God revealed himself and continues to reveal himself today. In the faith of the Church and its members these events become present once more and hence the catechesis has various stages: Bible history, the world of the liturgy, and finally doctrinal syntheses.

The word of God also determines the *form* of the catechesis. It is "revelation", "good news". It is the present echo of what was accomplished "once upon a time". Consequently, it must preserve the dynamic and joyful character which was intrinsic to the original message of salvation.

From another standpoint, we could define catechesis in terms of the word itself. The word of God is addressed to someone, who is called to accept it. Hence catechesis is the education of the baptized in the faith. Its ultimate aim is that the whole man should experience conversion and salvation through the word of God. The word penetrates man's heart — in the biblical sense — as well as his mind, and thus transforms him, giving him a new understanding of himself and the world, giving him a new place and attitude in society, making him live as he is and as he must be in the kingdom of God, in the fellowship of the people of God. Hence the various forms of catechesis, trying to embrace all the conditions of human life, age, milieu and culture, striving to make man once more at one with himself. The catechesis helps the individual and society to recognize and accept the signs and promises of salvation and to make the *one* word of God the dominant factor in all dimensions of life.

When all aspects are taken into account, catechesis must be defined as "the proclamation of the word of God in view of the education of man to faith". This avoids the danger of immanentism, which might sacrifice the character and originality of the gospel to a wrongly-conceived adaptation. And it avoids the danger of a wrongly-conceived transcendence, which ignores the real conditions under which God reveals himself. But the catechesis must be the privileged place for the encounter of the initiative of God's revelation and man's response in faith. All the efforts of Church preaching aim at this encounter. Biblical events, liturgical signs, dogmatic formulas, the testimony of sanctity — all are revelation made concrete. They are answers to the great questions of man. Thus the catechesis is centred on the relationship between God and man, as it is actualized in the redemptive incarnation.

3. *Catechesis and theology.* Reflection on the revelation received by the Church gives rise to the sacred sciences. Theology, exegesis, biblical theology and liturgy are the sources of the catechesis, which finds in them the content of its message and the criteria which are a guarantee of its soundness and precision.

Still, catechesis is different from theology or exegesis or liturgy. "Applied" catechesis makes use of the data supplied by these sciences, but refers them to their source and their end, namely the word of God and the faith of man respectively. And the manner in which catechesis uses the materials of theological sciences differs from the method which constitutes the latter as sciences. Catechesis presupposes these sciences, but it is not instruction in them. It goes beyond the technical aspects to embrace the living man and the active initiative of God as he turns to man. The theological sciences provide catechesis with its matter and the norms for judging its methods. But it is in itself the living word of God addressed to the man of today.

4. *Catechesis and the human sciences.* In the last hundred years the sciences of the human spirit have made undreamt-of progress. An anthropology has been worked out which is the indispensable prerequisite for catechesis, and it cannot do without the findings of psychology, sociology and pedagogics, though it must avoid superficial adaptations. This means in fact that these sciences help insofar as they are related to an understanding of man which can be orientated to the end of man. This is the real task of a "Christian anthropology". It has to explain what present-day man is in the light of revelation, and how he can do justice to his revelation. And to do this it must take tradition and Scripture into account as well as modern science. It asks how present-day man can accept the word of God, and hence enquires into his understanding of the world and of himself. Here the human sciences can further a catechesis which takes account of the various ages and mentalities of cultural and national groups — always mindful of putting the actual individual into contact with the living God.

C. IMPLEMENTATION OF THE CATECHESIS

This involves a number of aspects, all of which we cannot enumerate here. We can, however, indicate the principal forms of the catechesis or rather the principal domains in which it is operative in the Church.

1. *The degrees of Christian catechesis.* Père Liégé makes the following distinctions:

a) *Catechesis of initiation or fundamental catechesis.* This is the catechumen's first contact with the teaching of the faith during his preparation for baptism. The same term could be applied to the teaching a baptized child receives when preparing for first confession and Communion. It conveys the message of salvation in its entirety, though in an elementary manner, with special attention to a proper balance of the various factors involved — doctrine, liturgy, life. On the quality of this first-stage catechesis all subsequent development depends.

b) *Permanent catechesis.* The essentials acquired during the initiation period grow and develop in the course of life. The function of "permanent catechesis" is to draw out the implications of the gospel in the various situations of life, as far as is possible and practical. Preaching aside, this can assume a variety of forms, courses for adolescents or adults, study-circles, conferences and so forth.

c) *Perfective catechesis* (also called Sapiential) is directed to those whom a special mission or vocation impels to a deeper penetration of their faith. It can mean "wisdom" in the theological sense, mysticism or contemplation.

2. *Catechesis and catechism.* Catechism for the young remains a privileged instrument of the catechesis as a whole. It makes use of suitable pedagogical devices, always with an eye on the goal of catechesis, that is, to make the child receptive to the word of God. Its originality, as compared with other forms of teaching, consists in that. It is with that in mind, too, that any "manual of Catechism" is to be judged. A privileged instrument of the catechesis unquestionably, it is nevertheless not the sole one. One could conceivably make use instead of other methods, Scripture classes with suitably detailed commentaries and the like.

3. *Catechesis and the pastoral ministry.* The word of God is propagated not only through the medium of catechetical institutions, but also in a more diffuse way by means of the whole life of the Church itself. The child is taught the faith in the family circle. The adolescent and the grown-up encounter the gospel in educational or apostolic groups, in community life — here the liturgy comes in — as well as by way of the different mass-media, press, radio and so on. These unlimited possibilities in the means of communication are from one point of view a great advantage, but some additional unifying force is called for. This is the work of God's grace in the mystery of each one's faith, but it will display itself in the various forms of the Church's activity. There will be a unity of goal, which keeps the mystery of Easter at the heart of faith and life; a unity of language, which will ease the difficulties of those who find it hard to connect the older, more analytic form of catechesis with the newer and more living forms. The task of those who have the care of souls is to show the convergence between the various kinds of language used in the Church.

This of course is only another way of saying that the catechesis and the pastoral ministry constantly interact on each other.

4. *Catechetical studies.* Reflection on the teaching of the faith and its place in the Church is the specific object of "catechetics". Catechetical studies have of late seen a renewal, in the light of the comparable developments in the theological and biblical areas, not to mention the advances in anthropology and scientific method. The Munich School must take much of the credit for this. If one were to draw up an ideal syllabus of catechetical studies, it would include: a) The theology of the word of God, its place in the Church, the instruments it uses, the laws of its transmission (formal catechesis); its content (material catechesis) in general or under individual aspects such as biblical or liturgical catechesis. b) Man as a believer, that is to say, Christian anthropology, which would have to face the problem as to how the various natural sciences, psychology, sociology, etc., could be integrated and pressed into the service of the catechesis. c) Catechesis proper, the act by which the word of God is conveyed to man either in a general way or with an eye to actual conditions of age, milieu, or special circumstances. The former could be called general, the latter special catechetical pedagogy. d) Finally the connection between the catechesis itself and other forms of Church apostolate should be studied, in particular the mutual relations between catechetical activities and the various forms of the ministry.

BIBLIOGRAPHY. J. A. Jungmann, *Handing on the Faith. A Manual of Catechetics* (1959); F. H. Drinkwater, *Telling the Good News* (1960); J. Hofinger, ed., *Teaching All Nations. A Symposium on Modern Catechetics* (1961); J. Jungmann, *The Good News Yesterday and Today* (1962); P. Babin, *Crisis of Faith. The Religious Psychology of Adolescence* (1963); G. S. Sloyan, ed., *Modern Catechetics* (1963); J. Hofinger and T. C. Stone, eds., *Pastoral Catechetics* (1964); M. van Caster, *The Structure of Catechetics* (1965); J. Goldbrunner, ed., *New Catechetical Methods* (1965); P. A. Liégé, *Consider Christian Maturity* (1965); M. van Caster, *Themes of Catechetics* (1966); G. Moran, *Catechesis of Revelation* (1966).

Jacques Audinet

CATEGORIES

1. *Concept.* The basic mode of human knowledge is the act of integration accomplished by the judgment, in which the multiplicity

of the data is reduced to synthetic unity. The word synthetic here indicates that this unity is not the first moment in the whole act of knowledge. It is based on the indistinct unity of simple intuition, which for its part is articulated by concepts. In the concept, therefore, the immediate unity is dissolved, but dissolved into unities (of distinct components). This process reaches its goal in the judgment where the conceptual units are united. Being a unity on a higher level, the judgment is not a return to the indistinct beginning, but the functional unity of order.

But the unity of order is not sufficiently described by naming the units *from* which it is composed. It is essentially determined by the principles of unity *by virtue of* which it comprises and orders its parts. Hence we must consider in the judgment not only the concepts which are synthetized, but the concepts which perform the synthesis. The modes of the assertion must be considered along with the objects of it. Since the *Categoriae* of Aristotle these modes have been called categories (from κατηγορεῖν, accuse, affirm), in Latin *praedicamenta* (from *praedicare*, affirm).

2. *History*. Since philosophy tries to grasp reality as order, it strives on principle to reduce its affirmations on reality to order. In the West, after the series of opposites drawn up by the Pythagoreans, Plato designated in the *Theaetetus* as κοινὰ περὶ πάντων the common determinations which are found in all the various orders (called the transcendentals by the Scholastics). These determinations are known by the soul itself and not by any particular organ (*Theaetetus*, 185 Cff.). In contrast to these, he designated as μέγιστα τῶν πάντων (*Sophistes*, 254 Cf.) the basic concepts on which various distinct orders are founded, and which are not, therefore, common to all. But he did not systematize these concepts or enumerate them exactly.

The comprehensive list of the highest classes under which the assertions of philosophy can be arranged is due to Aristotle. It is to be found in its most complete form in the *Categoriae* (4; 1b, 25–27) and in the *Topica* (I, 9; 103b, 20–23). Here ten categories are enumerated, with substance opposed to the nine accidents of quality, quantity, relation, action, passion, where, when, position, possession. In spite of the modifications attempted by the Stoics and Plotinus, this list was adopted as authoritative by the Scholastics, and an attempt was made by Thomas Aquinas to demonstrate its intrinsic necessity (*Comment. in Phys.*, III, 1, 5).

Modern philosophy has devised its own lists of categories. Kant deduced from the forms of the judgment twelve categories which he held to be the transcendental structures of all possible experience. Fichte found fault with the stringency of the deduction, and tried to use his dialectical method to reach a complete classification of the basic determinations, beginning with the notion of deed or action. The most comprehensive effort in this direction is found in the Logic of Hegel, which tries to depict the necessary dialectical stages in the development of the absolute Idea from the indeterminateness of being. In recent years, N. Hartmann has produced detailed analyses of categories. Heidegger, emphasizing that the categories change with each level of reality, restricts the term to the realms of reality comprising what is present outside man. He gives the name of existentials to the basic determinations of human "existence".

3. *The problems*. The analysis of the categories and their systematic and exhaustive enunciation are not, however, the main problem. The basic question is the origin of the categories, which is not enquired into in most "lists". They cannot simply be derived from intuition, since their function is only to unite its elements. And they are not already present in the intellect — "innate", so to speak. They stem rather from the act of knowledge itself. This is not to reduce them to something "merely subjective", since the *cognoscens* and the *cognitum* are the same *in actu*.

In the intuition of the data of experience, the conscious transcendental experience of the self enables the finite mind to determine itself, and so displays to the mind in determinable order the objects of intuition. The categories, therefore, are determinations common to the knower and the known, or more precisely, the self-determination of each in the one act of knowledge. "Just as the I 'comes to itself' and is itself in determinate selfhood in the transcendence of knowing, wherein it actuates what beings themselves are, so too the object attains its formal substance there, formerly undisclosed, but now actuated in the I." (Krings.) The structure common to both is the category.

But this makes it clear that in the nature of things it is impossible to draw up an exhaustive list of categories. This is because the transcendence, the act of knowledge, from which the categories derive, is a free and hence a historical event. Not all thought sees the world in terms of causality, for instance. In aesthetic thought the category of presence more or less takes the place of cause. Certain concepts of knowledge must be presupposed (such as the "scientific", the technical, etc.), before definite systems of categories can be worked out.

Thus the human mind recognizes that it thinks in categories: it is faced with the multiplicity of beings, through which alone it realizes itself in action *(actu)*, so that they too can attain their actuality. But apart from the most general and formal determinations, nothing can be said *a priori* as to the substantial structures which are brought about in the act of knowledge, the categories to which the mind attains.

See also *Aristotelianism* I, *Kantianism, Transcendental Theology, Existence* II.

BIBLIOGRAPHY. E. Lask, *Die Logik der Philosophie und die Kategorienlehre* (1911); R. Guardini, *Der Gegensatz* (1925); A. Marc, *Dialectique de l'affirmation* (1952); N. Hartmann, *New Ways of Ontology* (1953); M. Heidegger, *Being and Time* (1962); *Categories and De Interpretatione*, Clarendon Aristotle Series, tr. and notes by J. L. Ackrill (1963); K. Rahner, *Geist in Welt* (3rd ed., 1964); H. Krings, *Transzendentalelogik* (1964); H. G. Godamer, *Wahrheit und Methode* (2nd ed., 1965); M. Heidegger, *Kant and the Problem of Metaphysics* (1966).

Jörg Splett

CATHARISTS

"Catharists" (from the Greek word καθαροί, pure) has been, since 1163, the most common and apt name for the largest of medieval sects; its own names (Christiani, boni homines), and the names coined by its opponents (Manichaeans, Patarines, Albigenses, also neo-Manichaeans) are scientifically unsuitable.

1. *History.* The first Catharists appeared in Cologne in 1143, having come from the Balkans together with merchants and crusaders; they spread quickly to England and Spain, and particularly to southern France and northern Italy. They combined the heritage of the early heretical poverty-movements (Peter of Bruys, Henry of Lausanne, Arnold of Brescia) with the dualism of the Bogomiles to form a dogmatically and organizationally established sect, which taught and practised itinerant preaching like the apostles along with the severest asceticism as the Christian and evangelical norm. This exemplary life soon made the Catharists well loved among the laity of Western Europe, especially as they called themselves "Christians". Their dualistic doctrine remained in the background until, in 1167, the Bogomile Nicetas held a council of Catharists in St.-Felix-de-Caraman near Toulouse, and thereby convinced all the Catharists of his doctrine of two gods; at the same time he expanded and developed the diocesan organization of the Catharists. They experienced further popularity after this, but changed their countenance; the demand for evangelical poverty receded into the background, was taken up by the Waldenses, Humiliati and others, and in part turned against the Catharists. For these had become rigid in their dogmatic doctrines, which were disputed, however, within the sect itself; furthermore, they separated the real members *(perfecti)* from the associates *(credentes)* and laid great weight upon hierarchy and liturgy.

In this process of ecclesiasticism it was only the group in southern France, the Albigenses, which remained unified in dogma and organization; it became in fact politically very influential in the struggle of the earldom of Toulouse against the Crusaders and the French king in the Albigensian wars. In Italy, on the other hand, differences in doctrine among the Bogomiles led, before 1190, to a splitting-up into six Catharist dioceses with three different "confessions": Albanenses, Bagnolenses and Cocorezzians. The Catholic reaction through crusades and missions was unsuccessful, as long as it relied upon secular power; Innocent III, who in 1215 impressively summarized Catholic doctrine against the Catharists (*D* 428ff.), was the first to achieve a revival of Catholic religious zeal and earnestness of life within the laity, especially through Dominic and Francis of Assisi. The Mendicant Orders soon deprived the Catharists of their best followers. The Inquisition failed to wipe out the Catharists; they themselves, however, began about 1230 to modify their doctrines in a scholastic sense and to assimilate their practices to Catholic tradition. The sect, which had been losing caste socially, thus lost its distinctiveness and from 1250 on its general influence. It still survived in small, out-of-the-way assemblies, in southern France till 1330, in Sicily and north-west Italy till 1442; by then the Inquisition had triumphed.

2. *Doctrine.* The basic thought is the irreconcilable antithesis between the soul of the pure and the evil world, which has fallen away from God. The Catharists took over this Gnostic teaching from the Bogomiles, in the beginning, however, with a more ethical than dogmatic tendency: they considered themselves to be the souls of those angels who fell with Lucifer, who now, through a metempsychosis, were doing penance in this diabolical world in order to return to their original condition. From 1167 on this penitential asceticism was to a great extent dogmatically grounded: Satan, the "God" of the OT, created the world and subjugated the pure souls at creation; he was the enemy of the good God and equal to him in power. The latter spoke in the NT and sent Christ, one of his angels, that he might teach the imprisoned brothers of their homeland. Christ's passion contributed nothing; the enlightened souls of the angels redeem themselves by entering into the sect of the Catharists and by absolute abstention from the world. Every contact with the world (marriage, sexual intercourse, eating of meat, taking of oaths, work, war, murder) is equally sinful, and every sinner shows himself as a creature of Satan. Only the pure *perfecti* are certain of salvation; every relapse is irreparable and is even sometimes hindered by suicide *(endura)*. The *perfecti,* who worked among the still diabolical associates rather to recruit than instruct, were at the same time the sect's members and hierarchs; above them stood elected bishops with coadjutors *(filius maior* and *minor)*. There was never a pope of the Catharists, though the attempts to gain supremacy did not cease; the highest authority was the council of the *perfecti* as the "community of the saints". There were rites for reception and worship: reception through a laying on of hands (called *consolamentum*) and a liturgy (a type of breaking of bread with thanksgiving). Catholic elements, how-ever, penetrated: confession, penitential regulations, rites similar to baptism and the anointing of the sick, which contradicted the dualistic self-redemption. Nevertheless the Catholic Church always remained for the Catharists the diabolical anti-church of this world; its sacraments, Mass, holy days, the sign of the cross, church edifices, prayers for the dead, the cult of saints and relics were rejected as useless materialistic rites, its priests as hypocritical sinners.

3. *Importance.* The Catharists took advantage of the defects in the early medieval Catholic pastoral ministry and of the reformers' call to the Church of poverty, to put forward their dogmatic self-redemption and contempt of the world as Christian asceticism; because every sin meant eternal ruin, dualistic doctrine and ascetical life harmonized together exactly; many were misled by this reasoning. It forced Catholics to take up a double defence: a dogmatic formulation of the Christian understanding of the world (exegesis of the OT, philosophical argumentation, Scholasticism) and an ascetical realization of the evangelical life (apostolate of the laity, parochial pastoral ministry, Mendicant Orders). When the Church had realized both of these demands in an occidental sense, the non-Christian doctrines of the Catharists ceased to be effective. To later heretics, however, they bequeathed arguments and forms of an anti-ecclesiastical sectarian church, an unconditional severity and the dream of self-liberation.

BIBLIOGRAPHY. S. Runciman, *The Medieval Manichee* (1947); A. Borst, *Die Katharer* (1953); R. Nelli and others, *Spiritualité de l'hérésie; le Catharisme* (1953); C. Thouzellier, *Catharisme et Valdéisme en Languedoc à la fin du XIIe et au début du XIIIe Siècle* (1966).
                                                    Arno Borst

CAUSALITY

A. PRELIMINARY NOTE ON PHILOSOPHICAL USAGE

Causality, as the relationship between cause and effect, is treated in various ways. Since modern subjectivism, with its cleavage between subject and object, followed by an emancipation of "thought" from "language", constant efforts have been made to reduce causality to an external phenomenon proper to objects, to be understood as a pure association of ideas or category of thought. But the ancient Greek concept itself (αἰτία, cause, as moral responsibility) points to the original situation embracing both "subject" and "object", by virtue of which the concepts of subjective responsibility and objective causality could be gradually distinguished.

The anthropomorphic — not necessarily subjectivist — notion of causality still reflects the primordial experience of the oneness of man and being. In the Indo-European field of languages, the connection appears first in Greek, in the relationship of φύσις and λόγος. The causal connection between "being" and "language" is consciously envisaged. The "pre-phenomenon" (πρόφασις, "occasion", a concept of causality used by Greek medicine and history) spoken of in this epoch-making distinction between Physis and Logos is the difference between "being" and "becoming", which only exists in the Greek language, and made it possible to distinguish cause and effect. "Greek was the only language where the concept of 'being' was not confused with that of 'becoming' as elsewhere. The distinction left room for an antinomics which was to be the main dynamism of Greek philosophy. Before Parmenides, in the philosophy of the Milesian Pythagoreans and of Heraclitus, the being of the world was described as a 'becoming' (φύσις). Then, with Parmenides, Melissos, Empedocles, the Atomist, Anaxagoras and Plato, this becoming is declared to be an outward appearance, which does not affect the reality of being." (J. Lohmann.) Thus Greek alone succeeded in differentiating what had still been a unity in the nomenclature of myth: the multiplicity of "thing" (ὄν, φυσικόν), "language" and "thought" (λόγος, λεκτόν) and also the equally primordial experience of "being" and "time". While, for instance, the ancient Indian and Chinese cultures, where Brahma or Tao corresponded to the Greek Logos, did not succeed in dissociating the mythic unity of being and language, the Greeks anticipated a universal development. This was the "a priori synthesis" of "being" and "time", one of the constitutive experiences of man, whose self-understanding in the process of change depends on common language. The synthesis was first consciously enunciated by the Greeks in the form of the tension between group-consciousness and the individual (cf.

Heraclitus). It was to present itself as a recurring problem throughout the history of humanity. The self-understanding of man in time and history expressed through the medium of language is in fact the manifestation — at various stages of reflection — of the grasp of causality. It is giving an account of (λόγον διδόναι, later rationem reddere, explaining) and seeking the sufficient reason (αἰτία, ἀρχή, later principium, principle or ultimate ground) for all that is.

With the growth of insight into causality came the progressive self-discovery of European man (now re-acting on non-European man through science and technology). It took many forms, from the sublime "transcendental subjectivism" of Kant to the "production of man by man's work" in the sense of Marx. But it was mostly done at the expense of the original bond (including the obligatory historical links of re-ligio) by which man is referred back to the historically — and not merely logically — primordial totality of being and language. The intellectualization of being and language was followed by the isolation of "being" from "time" in Western metaphysics, in spite of the fact that collective and individual linguistic usage, as the primordial mediation of "being" and "time" which takes place in the existence of man, is prior to any derivative intellectualization of either. It is this process of isolation which explains the question posed since Kant as to whether the principle of causality is "analytic", that is, only justifiable by the analysis of the concepts, or "synthetic a priori", that is, justifiable by the irreducible intellectual processes of the transcendental Ego. In this a priori synthesis, whereby "phenomenon A is regularly associated with a quite different phenomenon B", only the category of causality, as condition of possible experience, gives an objective unity to the multiplicity of stimuli received, by virtue of "consciousness in general". But latent throughout is the forgotten problem of time and its mediation along with being in a process involving not merely consciousness but "logos".

The notion of causality immanent to the Greek logos (as the human effectuation of the incoming reality), first elaborated in the pre-Socratics, was developed in the Analytica Posteriora of Aristotle, in the quest of the principles of the demonstrative science which looks for the "why" of things. It produced the Aristotelian doctrine of the "four causes" which was henceforth to determine the thought of the West. The intellectualization of causality led to its disjunction from time. Ἀρχή, "beginning" became "principle", τέλος, "end" became "aim". The "reason", the "analytical" moment of time-centred and history-centred discourse, had been integrated into the Greek *logos* which was being and language as a historical totality. This conceptual element became more and more independent in Stoic logic, and then led in modern times, through exaggeration of the "logical" function of language in isolation from the historical logos, to the question of the *a priori* synthesis. This appears in Kant as a synthesis of pure concepts (e.g., cause and effect), which is no longer based on the logos-reality of historical speech as the strict condition of possibility of all propositions, but on a regulatory "subjectivity" of man which is constricted to pure consciousness. Thus Kant says (*Critique of Pure Reason,* A 598, B 626), "being is clearly not a real predicate" (cf. Aristotle, *De Anima,* 3, 6; 430a, 27 s). Thus in the course of European thought the understanding of being and causality in Indo-European and Greek was obscured. A disjunction ensued between analytical categories and the supra-categorial synthesis wherein being and time were originally mediated together by the logos of language. Though given in ordinary speech, the analytical ("meta-linguistic") aspect even of the logical nexus of causality was isolated. And Kant's problem of the *a priori* synthesis appeared as the strait-jacket of the pure intellect when separated from the original logos of language. Semantic atomization and objectivation of language proceeded as if its sole function was to describe and designate "beings" as objects. Its universal openness and plasticity — which expresses "being" in its endless outgoing into beings *prior* to any outgoing of object from object — the synthetic function of (human) language, was almost forgotten. There was a one-sided meta-linguistic hypostatization of being, of which the roots were already present in the Platonic εἶδος and the Aristotelian "form". It led to a one-sided posing of even the biblical and Christian problem of creation in terms of a derivative causality, on the pattern of "beings", of which "God" was considered the supreme, instead of the primordial causality between the logos-being

of man in action and all other kinds of beings. Here, of course, the biblical and Christian concept of Logos provides the most vital corrective of the one-sided concept of causality spoken of above. The search which went on in human history for reasons and causes is now enabled to turn to the "Word of God", which cannot be subsumed under causality by human thought. Another one-sided objectivation of causal thinking was responsible for the ostensible dilemma which opposed (Christian) belief in creation and (scientific) notions of natural evolution.

B. Causality in Philosophy and Science

With the early Greek thinkers' quest for principles and causes came the first differentiation in the content and language of causality. The word ἀρχή (from ἀρχεῖν, to be first, in the sense of beginning, ruling) changed in meaning from "beginning" to "principle" (first cause), as may be first seen in Anaximander, where the ἀρχή is the ἄπειρον, indeterminate (boundless) being as the ground of all beings. The change underlines the distinction between "time" and "being" discussed above, which was proper to the Greek concept of being, and characterized Western metaphysics since Plato. It was this distinction which then brought with it the separation of relationships between beings into "causal" and "spatio-temporal", as in the modern discussion between rationalism and empiricism about the demarcation of temporal and causal sequence (*post hoc* or *propter hoc*). It is probable that ἀρχή as a technical term (first verified in Aristotle, *Metaphysics,* D 1, 1012b, 34 ff.) has been pre-dated to the pre-Socratics. Thus Thales is supposed to have seen water as the principle of all things, while for Heraclitus it was fire; for Parmenides, for the first time, it was being, while Empedocles had his four elements. Anaxagoras was the first to consider spirit (νοῦς) as efficient and final cause, while for Democritus the atoms and the void were the ἀρχαί. In Plato there is a clear distinction between the temporal and the causal sense of ἀρχή. The self-moved soul (*Phaedrus,* 245c), the demiurge and the world-soul (*Timaeus*) are causes in the strict sense. Here too we have the first reflections on the principle of causality (*Timaeus,* 28a), as linked with the problem of God. Aristotle starts with the possible questions and answers of dialogue — what a thing "is", what it is made of, how it came to be and what it is for (*Physics,* 194b, 16ff.; *Meta.*, A 3, 983a, 26ff.) — to define his four causes, formal, material, efficient and final, distinguishing between principles of knowledge and of being, though still referring them back to language, unlike later thought, especially in its modern form. And Aristotle stresses the solidarity of all "grounds of being" in the oneness of *physis* (*Meta.*, 1103a, 27f.) and the semantic connection between causality and the problem of movement (*Physics,* 202b, 19ff.). Nonetheless, in the twelfth book of the *Metaphysics* there is an outline of a "first unmoved mover" (*Meta.*, 1072a, 19ff.) in the sense of "a being" which as the final cause is the explanation of movement in finite things. This obscures the causality of "being" — now buried in the unsolved problem of an eternal *materia prima* — and we have a metaphysical notion of God as a "supreme being" exerting causality with respect to movement but not with respect to being.

In the discussion of act and potency, Aristotle puts forward, as a special case of the principle of causality, the famous "anything that moves is moved by another" (*Meta.*, L 8, 1073a, 26; *Physics,* H 1, 241b, 24) which is taken up by Aquinas (*Summa Theologica,* I, q. 2, a. 3c, etc.). In keeping with the intellectualization of the Greek logos, that is, the compartmentalization of language, thought and reality, Stoicism also transformed the ancient notion of physis into a strictly causal concatenation in nature *(series causarum)*. Medieval thought, with its theological perspectives, tried to harmonize the ancient notion of causality with the Christian notion of creation, and encountered the intrinsic difficulties of the attempt (cf. Thomas, *Summa contra Gentiles,* I and II), which were felt most sharply in the late Middle Ages. "The *causa efficiens* of Aristotle — ultimately identical with the *causa finalis* — can explain beings in their *actus* but not in their *potentia,* it induces *ad esse hoc,* not *ad esse simpliciter* (*ibid.,* II, 6). A God proved to be *causa efficiens (= finalis),* as in the first book of the *Summa contra Gentiles,* cannot vice versa be proved to be creator *ex nihilo. Movere,* in fact, in the sense of Aristotle, means no more than *facere aliquid ex materia.* It does not mean *producere res in esse* in the radical sense of the *ex nihilo* (*ibid.,* II, 16, arg. 3 and 4). Thomas surmounts the difficulty with a sort of

theory of the infinitesimally small, which ostensibly bridges the gap by assigning to *materia prima* the value of zero (1. c., arg. 5) and thus making the efficient cause absolute. But one cannot begin by affirming that the *primum movens immobile* is the absolute ground of being (creator), and then affirming — what is certainly legitimate in theology — that 'creatio non est motus' (*ibid.,* II, 17). This is precisely where Aristotelian metaphysics and theology come into conflict. This is the genesis of all the other difficulties, such as the refusal of Christian thought to accept the mechanism of individuation in Aristotle or the indifference of the unmoved mover with regard to the world." (Blumenberg, p. 201.)

In the nominalism of the late Middle Ages, which posed once more the problem of the linguistic and empirical foundation of the "universal concept", against a realism of universals which was often uncritically tributary to Plato, the ancient problem of causality was examined by William of Occam in particular, on the basis of linguistic analysis ("ordinatio verborum", *Summa Logicae,* c. 57, 3ff.). Such criticism aimed at the separation of the theological and the scientific understanding of causality, in a way which was to bear fruit in modern science. And by emphasizing the Christian notion of creation in particular, it demythologized "nature" more and more, and threw it open to empirical investigation of causes (*Quodl.,* 2, q. 1). But the great breakthrough only came with modern science and its increasing reliance on mathematics. This too had its distant roots in the Greek concept of logos (λόγος, also for mathematical proportion) and was connected with the revival of Platonism in the 15th and 16th centuries (the explanation of phenomena by mathematical laws being part of the Pythagorean and Platonic tradition). The first effect was loss of interest in scholastic matter and form and theology, and the concentration on the *causa efficiens* (working universally as pressure and impetus) which gave rise to 17th-century cosmology. The decisive step in the period between Copernicus and Newton was taken by Galileo, who replaced the concept of "efficient cause" (which remained in later materialism and vitalism) by that of unchangeable necessary "laws" which could be formulated mathematically. The exact description of the "how" of measurable phenomena had taken the place of the "why" of explanations in terms of causality. This was a process adumbrated in the Greek logos (Heraclitus spoke of "the self-increasing logos", fr. 115) and which had developed throughout the various changes in the notion of causality. Ultimately, it was the formal "meta-linguistic" affirmation of the copula (the human "is-so" assertion), which in Aristotle had still been restricted to "the language of objects". But meta-linguistic objectivation never ceases to point back to the total human understanding of being and the world, which it both presupposes and corrects in the "hermeneutic circle" (M. Heidegger). This was understood by G. W. von Leibniz, who refused to see in mechanistic causality a contradiction of a precisely enunciated teleology. Nonetheless, Leibniz the philosopher, by reducing causality to the "principle of sufficient reason", that is, by unduly identifying the logic of principle and consequence with the reality of cause and effect, merely intensified the priority of "thought" over "being" underlying modern philosophy (since Descartes's *Discours de la méthode* and Spinoza's *Ethica ordine geometrico demonstrata*).

David Hume was in the old tradition of English philosophy, with its critical attitude to all (metaphysical) rationalism. He rejected the deduction of causality and the principle of causality either from reason or from objective experience. It reposed only on the long observations of custom — "the great guide of human life" — whereby images or ideas were constantly associated. Probably Hume's concept of causality should now be re-considered in the light of the philosophy of language ("custom" as connection of actions, determined by language; the "operative" element prior to any realism or idealism of causality). In the 19th century came Kant's *a priori* justification of causality; then a growing obtuseness to the problems of idealism; finally Schopenhauer's criticism of the traditional concept of causality (*Über die vierfache Wurzel des Satzes vom zureichenden Grunde*, i.e., the four sources of the principle of sufficient reason). The concept of causality and law was replaced more and more by that of "function" (the interdependence of two variable quantities). Then, at the beginning of the 20th century came the great crisis for the classical concept of cause in philosophy and physics, brought about above all by Planck's quantum theory, Einstein's theory of relativity and Heisenberg's indetermination principle.

"If the principle of causality in classical physics is formulated as follows: Once the state of a closed physical system at a given period t_1 is known, its state at any other period t_2 can be strictly calculated, the principle remains unassailable even in the quantum theory. Determinism fails at two different points, according to the way in which the concept of state is defined. If it is understood as the registration of the factors according to the principles of classical physics, the principle of indetermination means that laws of nature make it impossible to give a definite value at one time to all the requisite factors. The protasis of the principle given above cannot be verified. If one understands by state the 'pure' case envisaged by the quantum theory (that which can be ascertained by measurement at its real maximum), the Schrödinger equation does in fact determine with mathematical exactness the change of this state from t_1 to t_2. But the state so defined only gives a statistical indication of the discrepancy which a measurement will display when it is applied to a quantity other than that defined in the state in question. Hence the inapplicability of determinism does not mean a contradiction of the law of causality, but simply the impossibility of fulfilling the conditions which it presupposes. The 'Copenhagen' interpretation of the quantum theory, introduced by Bohr and Heisenberg, understands this restriction not as a consequence of subjective human ignorance, but as the sign that natural processes can never be fully amenable to objective laws. The inapplicability of the classical principle of causality then appears merely as a consequence of the inapplicability of classical ontology." (C. F. von Weizsäcker.)

This new situation, where classical ontology is said to be inapplicable, shows clearly the implications of the notion of "thing in itself" or "properties in themselves" (e.g., space, time, situation and charge of electrons), such as had become dominant since Plato, in its "idealist" or "realist" interpretation. It ultimately means the disregard of the back-reference of all knowledge of objects to the more comprehensive context of human language and action. But the early Greek discussion of the λόγος had had the insight that human knowledge (in the measure in which it is constitutive of objects) stems from the total human situation of language and action, and hence is not primarily an equation (detached from this context) between theoretical knowledge in the subject and the brute fact of the object. This is the insight which has been re-discovered in modern science. The "subjective" aspect of knowledge, related to the observer and processes of measurement, cannot be cleanly separated from the "objective". The two spheres must be understood simply as moments which condition each other in the one experience of reality.

One may compare the statement of Heisenberg in which he refutes all one-sidedly realistic or idealistic "objectivism" even in causal relationships: "If one wishes to be clear about the meaning of the words, 'the position of the object' in a given frame of reference, one must indicate the actual experiments by which one hopes to measure the 'position of the electron'; otherwise the phrase has no meaning." Similarly, the question of the divine "cause" as posed in metaphysical theology must be detached from a one-sided process of objectivation (God as the ultimate ground of "things") or subjectivation (God as the condition of possibility of human knowledge of things). It must be transformed into the "results of certain experiments" in which man as a totality in his endless experience of self and the world (in freedom and in death) finds himself in face of God who is less a definable first cause than the unfathomable abyss from which the mystery wells up.

C. PRINCIPLE OF CAUSALITY

This is understood in scholastic philosophy (in contrast to the laws of causality applicable to natural events), as the supreme law of thought and being according to which all contingent beings necessarily presuppose a cause which is ultimately the absolute being or God. In connection with the acceptance of Kant in neo-Scholasticism, the question arose as to whether this principle was "analytical" (perspicuous because reducible to the principle of non-contradiction) or "synthetic *a priori*" (known along with direct knowledge of being). The question was mostly answered in the latter sense, but it depends, as we have seen above, on the whole problem of the "*a priori* synthesis",

that is, on whether it is derived from the "transcendental consciousness" or from the primordial relationship to reality possessed by man as endowed with and intrinsically linked to language, that is, as active in the I-world relationship.

BIBLIOGRAPHY. T. de Règnon, *La métaphysique des causes* (1906); E. Wentscher, *Geschichte des Kausalproblems in der neueren Philosophie* (1921); L. Brunschvicg, *L'expérience humaine et la causalité physique* (1922); W. Heisenberg, *Physical Principles of the Quantum Theory* (1930); H. Weiss, *Kausalität und Zufall in der Philosophie des Aristoteles* (1942); M. Heidegger, *Der Satz vom Grund* (2nd ed., 1958); C. F. von Weizsäcker and J. Juifs, *Contemporary Physics* (1962).

Franz Karl Mayr

CELIBACY

Celibacy here means not simply the fact of not being married, though such a state can be of theological and pastoral relevance when it serves to promote certain ends. Celibacy is here understood as the unmarried state chosen in the light of the Christian faith, and in particular as one of the duties of the state in life of the clergy of the Latin Church, by which they are forbidden to marry and obliged to live in total continence.

A. HISTORY

1. The biblical foundations for celibacy are taken to be the saying of the Lord about not marrying ("becoming a eunuch") for the sake of the kingdom of heaven (Mt 19:10 ff.); also the saying about leaving one's wife for the sake of Jesus and the gospel (Mk 10:29) or for the sake of the reign of God (Lk 18:29); and also the saying which affirms that in the resurrection there will be no marriage (Mt 22:30; Mk 12:25). Paul wished all men to be in the same state as himself (1 Cor 7:7). The unmarried is devoted to the things of the Lord, while the attention of the married is divided (1 Cor 7:32f.). These texts, however, do not link celibacy directly to the priestly ministry. In early Christianity, they were rather connected with baptism and looked on as counsels which many in fact followed. Support for this tendency was found in such biblical parables as Mt 9:15; 22:1–14; Mk 2:19; Lk 5:34; 12:35ff.; 14:15–24; Jn 3:29.

Celibacy as a duty of the priestly state was introduced only gradually. It derived from the high value attached to virginity (cf. 2 Cor 11:2; Eph 5:25ff., 30ff.; Acts 21:9), the perspective of the final consummation (Rev 14:3f.; 19:7ff.; 21:2, 9) and the way of life of ascetics and monks with their recourse to the OT laws of purity. The evolution of the law of celibacy was greatly influenced by the precept laid down in the Pastoral Letters, that bishops, priests and deacons should be "husband of only one wife" (1 Tim 3:2, 12; Tit 1:6f.), though the precise meaning of the principle was debated.

2. Laws dealing with celibacy are found as early as the beginning of the 4th century. Inspired by the desire for total dedication and also to some extent under the influence of dualistic Gnostic tendencies of a Manichaean type, many priests felt bound to discontinue marriage relationships after their ordination. In the Eastern Churches celibacy prevailed only for those who were equipped with the fullness of the priesthood, the bishops, and was given force of law in the 7th century by the Emperor Justinian and the second Trullan Synod. But in the West the decrees of the Synod of Elvira were widely imposed by Pope Siricius (*DS* 118f.; 185). An effort to prescribe celibacy as a universal Church law was made at the First Council of Nicaea (325), but did not meet with success. Leo I and Gregory I extended the law to include sub-deacons. Since what was forbidden was not so much marriage as the continuation of married life, promises of continence were often demanded of candidates for the priesthood (and their wives) between the 5th and 7th centuries. From the 6th century on, separation of the spouses was also demanded. The constant necessity of synodal intervention in this matter shows how much practical difficulty was involved. A historical factor in the promotion of celibacy in the Middle Ages was the problem which had already exercised minds in the 5th and 6th centuries — the effort to prevent the alienation of Church property, which might otherwise pass into the possession of the priest's family. This gave rise in the 12th century to the statutory declaration of the nullity of the marriage of those in major orders. In spite of sharp controversy at the time of the Reformation, the Council of Trent re-affirmed the principle that clerics in

major orders were incapable of contracting matrimony (*DS* 1809). In the form already laid down by the Council of Nicaea "by virtue of ancient tradition" — that there should be no marriage after the reception of a major order — the magisterium held fast to this law, as though it were an apostolic regulation, even in Vatican II and the documents which have appeared since then.

3. According to the law in force in the Latin Church, as laid down by the *CIC*, clerics in minor orders lose their clerical status by contracting matrimony (can. 132, § 2). Clerics in major orders are forbidden to marry. They are obliged in a special way to preserve chastity. A sin against chastity is a sacrilege (can. 132, § 1) and if it involves an external breach of the law (can. 2195) incurs sanctions (can. 2325). All attempts to contract matrimony are null and void (can. 1072) and to presume to enter even upon a civil form of marriage involves irregularity (can. 985, § 3), loss of ecclesiastical office (can. 188, § 5) and excommunication (can. 2388). The laws concerning absolution from excommunication (can. 2252; Decree of the Sacred Penitentiary of 18 April 1936 and 14 May 1937), dispensation from the impediment to marriage for deacons and sub-deacons in danger of death (can. 1043), laicization with release from the obligation of celibacy (can. 214, 1993–8) have been eased and complemented by various acts of "grace and favour" on the part of the Holy See and above all by the documents of Vatican II (*Lumen Gentium*, art. 29; *Presbyterorum Ordinis*, art. 16), the motu proprio *Sacrum Diaconatus Ordinem* (nos. 4, 11–13, 16) and the encyclical *Sacerdotalis Caelibatus* (nos. 42, 84f., 87f.). Thus pleas of lack of freedom and proper qualification which were formerly (can. 214) not provided for may now be put forward in cases of ordination, and dispensation from all obligations may be obtained on other grounds as well. Married men, with the consent of their wives, may now be ordained deacons, if — according to the conditions laid down in 1 Tim 3:10ff. — they have been married for some years and are over thirty-five years of age. But those who have been ordained deacons while unmarried may no longer contract matrimony. That married men should become priests (cf. can. 132,

§ 3; 987, § 2) is foreseen only in the case of ministers of other Churches or Christian communities who desire unity with the Catholic Church and wish to exercise their sacred ministry.

B. The Doctrine of the Magisterium

1. A characteristic of the doctrine of the magisterium on celibacy is that it sees itself bound by the canonical prescriptions while taking an intermediate position between these and theological reflection on them. There is also the point that the law of celibacy has not lacked opponents in the Church. The constantly recurring trend away from celibacy which has been manifested throughout the centuries has influenced the magisterium in the choice and presentation of the themes concerning celibacy, according to the various types of attack made upon it and the various reasons which they invoked. Hence the documents of the magisterium have often taken the form of apologetics, polemics or exhortation. Celibacy is mostly discussed from the point of view of chastity and placed on the same level as virginity.

2. Though the Council of Trent emphasized very strongly the dignity of sacramental matrimony, it condemned those who maintained that "the married state is preferable to that of virginity or celibacy and that it is not better and more blessed to continue in the state of virginity or celibacy than to enter on the state of matrimony" (*DS* 1810). This verdict, however, which considers the various states of life, does not deny that many married persons can be closer to God than those obliged to celibacy. In the encyclical *Sacra Virginitas,* which also dealt with celibacy, Pius XII rejected the opinion that "only marriage guarantees a natural development of the human person" and that the sacrament "sanctifies married life to such a degree that it becomes a more effective means of union with God than virginity itself" (*DS* 3911 f.). This way of putting things, which is a variation on the Council of Trent, is an indirect invitation to work out the manifold relationships between marriage and celibacy, which may be evaluated from more than one standpoint.

3. A new field is opened up in the development of the doctrine by Vatican II, in as much as the dogmatic constitution *Lumen Gentium* does not restrict the undivided heart to such Christians as remain unmarried (art. 42). The call to supreme holiness, such as that of "your Father who is in heaven" (Mt 5:48) is understood as directed to all Christian believers and not merely to those who remain unmarried for religious reasons (art. 40). Nonetheless, the conciliar decree *Optatam Totius,* on priestly formation, demands that candidates for the priesthood should clearly recognize the precedence of virginity consecrated to Christ over marriage (art. 10). According to *Lumen Gentium,* the holiness of the Church is advanced by the observation of the many counsels which our Lord proposed to his disciples in the gospel. A pre-eminent place is held by the precious gift of divine grace which the Father gives to some, so that they may *more easily* devote themselves whole-heartedly to God in the state of virginity or celibacy. Thus celibacy is a sign of love and an impulse towards it (art. 42). Practically the same terms are used in the decrees *Optatam Totius* (art. 10) and *Perfectae Caritatis* (art. 12) to re-affirm for priests and for religious the law of celibacy "for the sake of the kingdom of heaven". According to *Presbyterorum Ordinis,* art. 16, celibacy is not demanded by the nature of the priesthood, but is appropriate for many reasons and is founded on the mystery of Christ and his mission. Hence the law of celibacy in the Latin Church is re-affirmed for those who have been marked out for the priesthood. This formulation, which in comparison with earlier ones is reserved, allows for married deacons.

4. The encyclical *Sacerdotalis Caelibatus* develops the notion of celibacy with reference to Christ, the Church and the consummation of all things, stressing anthropological viewpoints with an emphasis hitherto unknown in documents of the supreme magisterium. While rejecting all changes in the law of celibacy and adhering unmistakably to the legislation of the Latin Church, the encyclical still raises the question of whether this "difficult law" should not be left to the free choice of the individual (art. 3) and whether candidates should not be admitted who feel the call to the priesthood but not to celibacy (art. 7). When choosing the Twelve, Jesus did not demand celibacy (art. 5). The charism of priestly ministry is

distinct from that of celibacy, the law of celibacy is historically conditioned (art. 14, 17) and the way of life of the Eastern Churches is likewise the work of the Spirit (art. 38). Nonetheless, the encyclical expects that insight into a priestly ministry wholly united to Christ will throw ever greater light on the bond between the priesthood and celibacy (art. 25). Marriage and the family are not the only possibilities of total maturity (art. 56). Bishops must extend their tender care in particular towards those of their brothers who suffer under the burden of celibacy or have come to grief thereby (arts. 87, 91–94).

C. The Present Situation

1. Celibacy is at present a subject of discussion inside and outside the Church. The substance and the actual framing of the arguments may be gathered from the encyclical *Sacerdotalis Caelibatus,* which is attentive to present-day questions without actually answering them, preferring to present copious doctrinal matter from various theological approaches. The encyclical also adopts traditional themes which Vatican II passed over or at least tried to present more moderately: thus for instance the encyclical speaks of *castitas perfecta* (nos. 6 f., 13) and suggests a mystical identification of the priest with Christ, giving the priest a specially exalted place which almost makes him an exceptional type (nos. 13, 24 f., 31 f., 56). Was it perhaps the intention of the encyclical to show that religious and Christian truth is always too great to be fully grasped by any given age? It calls, in any case, for careful study of unresolved problems and provides valuable impulses for such study, which include the recognition of important historical facts and of new pastoral methods.

2. Objective theological discussion, neither aggressive nor defensive but simply bent on the truth, has become difficult at the present day. Two fronts have been formed even within the Church, and the extreme wings either treat the subject as taboo or consider celibacy as disposed of. But no party can register real gains at the cost of objectiveness. Honest expression of opinion is desirable, but lyrical panegyrics and one-sidedly negative criticism merely arouse opposition which obscures the essential values of celibacy. Comprehension is still far from being magnanimous, as may be seen from the un-Christian attitude towards married converts to Catholicism. And those who point to the milder rule of the Eastern Churches as regards celibacy often forget that it can demand considerable sacrifices, especially from priests who are widowers.

3. On theological grounds, the present problems concerning celibacy arise from a new understanding of marriage and of the priestly ministry. In the past marriage was at times considered as something just permissible. But the pastoral constitution *Gaudium et Spes* affirms that it is a union which our Lord has dignified, healed, perfected and exalted by special gifts of his grace and love (art. 49); that he himself dwells with the spouses, who by the help of his Spirit attain their own perfection, sanctify each other and glorify God together (art. 48). Priests, who are so often looked upon as a sort of higher beings, are said in the decree *Presbyterorum Ordinis* to remain disciples of our Lord along with the other faithful, in spite of their lofty and necessary office. Along with all those who were re-born in the fountain of baptism, they remain brothers among brothers, members of the one and the same body of Christ, the building up of which is entrusted to all. Under these circumstances the traditional conventional arguments for celibacy no longer seem conclusive. Where they are still used, they meet with justifiable objections from those who welcome the ideas put forward by the Council. Then, on social grounds, problems arise from the fact that today in practically all walks of life marriage is left to the private judgment of the individuals. The contrast in the ecclesiastical law of celibacy appears to be a relic of former ages. The problem has become more acute with the emphasis on marriage as a partnership, the social equality of women, the new appreciation of the body, and the positive value attributed to sexual relationship in the self-realization, development and maturity of all men, and not merely of that of married people. New answers are called for to meet the demands of the times. On the other hand, no reasonable judgment can be passed on celibacy as a special form of Christian life, except by those who have the Christian faith.

D. PASTORAL TASKS

1. Pastoral considerations are urgent. Celibacy is a gift of grace. Whether it is given to few or to many is outside human control. But if, as is the case today, it becomes a problem for debate within the Church, pastoral theology must try to determine the obstacles to its realization in the life of faith. Has the divine seed of celibacy been choked by the weeds of too purely human motivations? Or has the wheat also been plucked up in the effort to remove the weeds? One of the inspirations of priestly celibacy was the example of the apostolic Church, where many of the faithful experienced the overwhelming surge of the grace of the kingdom of God so strongly that they simply "could" not marry, but "had" to remain completely free for the building up of the community for the sake of the Lord. Is this still really true of the official ministers of the Church who are celibate today?

2. To be effective in the ministry of salvation, celibacy must be lived simply and spontaneously. It is this sense of the normal which needs to be renewed about celibacy. It grows, no one knows how, in stillness (cf. Mk 4:27), being one of the *magnalia Dei* and not one of man's achievements. All the noisy and excited discussion of celibacy will prove to be harmful. And the persistance of talk about the impurity of the body and sexual activity on the one hand, and of "perfect" chastity on the other, not only gives rise to misunderstandings today but is regarded as arrogant and as telling against celibacy. It is best to take a very sober view of celibacy. To remain unmarried for the sake of important tasks which claim one's whole attention can be seen to be rational even in terms of purely human experience, and can be recognized as a way of personal self-realization which is naturally possible. Hence the saying of our Lord that it can be good to remain unmarried for the sake of the kingdom of God can be made quite intelligible to the faithful. There is no need to deny that continence is a source of power which has constantly proved itself to be creative. But the point is secondary, and indeed irrelevant, as regards celibacy for the sake of the kingdom of God. Nonetheless, it does not follow at once from the fact that the priest is unmarried that he is fully at the disposition of the reign of God. But celibacy remains appropriate for the priest, because it is a typical way of achieving full freedom for the kingdom and because those who serve in the priestly ministry should in fact be wholly at the disposition of the kingdom. It remains true, however, that there are married people who show themselves to be wholly responsive and open to the demands of Christ and of the kingship of God.

3. According to the ecclesiastical magisterium, the law of celibacy now in force must remain a strict condition for the priestly ministry. Hence (apart from special exceptions) it regards as suitable for the priesthood only those to whom God has granted the gift of celibacy, along with the other signs of vocation (*Sacerdotalis Caelibatus,* nos. 14f., 62). In spite of this rule, pastoral considerations must include the fact that the canonical precept does not only strengthen the charism of celibacy (no. 62). It may also obscure its effectiveness, since there is a tension between law and charism. The law being what it is, celibacy is often merely endured as a necessary condition of the priesthood, and then it loses the convincing quality of sign which it should have as the expression of a really existential inability to marry for the sake of Christ and his kingdom. Has not this charism also come to light once more within the Protestant Churches without any law which imposes it? But there is another side to the problem, which makes it possible to understand celibacy as a law. The biblical term χωρεῖν need not be translated as "grasp" or "understand", which gives for Mt 19:11 the translation, "Not all men understand this, but only those to whom it is given . . . He who is able to understand this, let him understand it." The term can also mean "receive", "make room for", "adopt", "achieve", "dare". And something of universally human appeal is thereby expressed: "Not all can do this. But if you can summon up the strength, then dare it!" Hence celibacy is probably not one of the charisms which is either there or not, but one of those which may also be striven for, according to the counsel of the Apostle Paul (1 Cor 12:31). This is important to note for the preaching of celibacy.

4. In the formation of priests and in their further development, many of the supports of celibacy which were hitherto relied on will all away, having proved themselves unreal or erroneous. They must no longer be

appealed to. In their place theologically valid arguments must be used, and new aids which correspond to present realities. The celibacy of the contemplative monk and that of the priest engaged directly in the ministry of salvation will develop differently. But both will need not only a personally responsible decision with the will to persevere, but also an effective maturity and growth which corresponds to each phase of age and development. Since the sexuality of the celibate should not remain an isolated element, and since integration is only possible in a genuine relationship between the sexes, appropriate means for such integration must be sought for and provided. Just as celibacy has undergone different developments in various nations (some spiritualizing it, others accepting it simply as law or institution), so too it can have various degrees of realization in the life of individual priests. Here it may range from a loving loneliness with Christ to a highly individual type of friendship with the other sex. Now that women have been recognized as fully qualified lay people in their own right in the Church, dialogue and pastoral co-operation between priests and women can no longer be evaded, but must be boldly undertaken and brought to perfection. A brotherly relationship between the priests and a well-ordered *vita communis* will be a safeguard in such matters. But celibacy is never merely a precept to be fulfilled. It must also remain a cherished goal.

5. Meanwhile new pastoral tasks are taking shape. When the motives of a vocation are being examined to see whether a candidate is fitted or not for priestly celibacy, the encyclical *Sacerdotalis Caelibatus* lays it down that the services of a doctor or psychologist must be availed of (nos. 63 ff.). For the formation of character and for the counselling of priests undergoing mental or moral strain or finding themselves in difficulties with their vocation, the help of a suitable team of professionals will also be necessary. Apart from private circles which voluntarily assist, there are organizations for this purpose in France and other countries. It will be especially important to maintain contact with all who have left the priestly ministry and are more or less happily married. They must be kept at work in the Church in an appropriate way, where they are willing to undertake such tasks. This should be done even at the cost of financial sacrifices. Against the background of the new possibilities, those who contemplate the present crisis of celibacy in the light of faith will be able to welcome it as a work of purification and grace in the service of the kingdom of God.

See also *Marriage, Priesthood, Sex* I, *Virginity*.

BIBLIOGRAPHY. DOCUMENTS: Pius X, Exhortatio *Haerent Animo,* 4 August 1908, *AAS* 41 (1908), pp. 555–77; Benedict XV, Consistorial Allocution of 16 December 1920, *AAS* 12 (1920), pp. 585–8; Pius XI, *Ad Catholici Sacerdotii,* 20 December 1935, *AAS* 28 (1936), pp. 24–30; S. Paenitentiaria, Decrees of 18 April 1936 and 4 May 1937, *AAS* 28 (1936), pp. 242 f., and *ibid.* 29 (1937), pp. 283 ff.; Pius XII, Exhortatio *Menti Nostro,* 23 September 1950, *AAS* 42 (1950), pp. 657–702; id., Encyclical *Sacra Virginitas,* 25 March 1954, *AAS* 46 (1954), pp. 161–91; John XXIII, Encyclical *Sacerdotii Nostri Primordia,* 1 August 1959, *AAS* 51 (1959), pp. 554–6; Vatican II, Constitutions and Decrees, *Lumen Gentium,* 21 November 1964, *Perfectae Caritatis,* and *Optatam Totius,* 28 October 1965, *Presbyterorum Ordinis* and *Gaudium et Spes,* 7 December 1965, *AAS* 57 (1965), pp. 5–75, *ibid.* 58 (1966), pp. 702–12 and 713–27, and *ibid.* 58 (1966), pp. 991–1024 and 1025–1120; Paul VI, Motu proprio *Sacrum Diaconatus Ordinem,* 18 June 1967, *AAS* 59 (1967), pp. 697–704; id., Encyclical *Sacerdotalis Caelibatus,* 24 June 1967, *AAS* 59 (1967), pp. 657–97. BOOKS AND ARTICLES: H. Doms, *Vom Sinn des Zölibats* (1954); O. Mosshamer, *Priester und Frau* (1958); W. Bertrams, *Der Zölibat des Priesters* (2nd ed., 1962); I. F. Görres, *Laiengedanken zum Zölibat* (1962); P. Hermand, *Condition du Prêtre, mariage ou célibat* (1963), E. T.: *The Priest: Celibate or Married* (1965); J. Hünermann, *Freisein und Dienen* (1963); R. Egenter and others, *Jungfräulichkeit und Zölibat* (1964); R. Hostie, *Kriterien geistlicher Berufung* (1964); L. M. Weber, *Mysterium Magnum* (2nd ed., 1965), E. T.: *On Marriage, Sex and Virginity,* Quaestiones Disputatae 16 (1966); K. Mörsdorf and L. Weber, "Zölibat", *LTK,* X, cols. 1395–1401; R. Egenter, "Virginity. Some Ethical and Ascetical Aspects", *The Furrow* 16 (1965), pp. 731–49; M. Pfliegler, *Der Zölibat* (2nd ed., 1966); A. Müller, "Der ehelose Priester", *Diakonia* 1 (1966), pp. 316–28; G. Griesl, *Berufung und Lebensform des Priesters* (1967); K. Rahner, "Der Zölibat des Weltpriesters im heutigen Gespräch", *Geist und Leben* 40 (1967), pp. 122–38; E. Schillebeeckx, *Der Amtszölibat* (1967).

Leonhard M. Weber

CENSORSHIP OF BOOKS

The First Council of Nicaea, safeguarding the teachings of the Church, already thought it necessary to condemn the *Thalia* of Arius, while the Third Council of Constantinople and the Second Council of Nicaea condemned other heretical writings and ordered them to be burnt or withdrawn. In the Middle Ages such books were frequently not only condemned, but forbidden to be read or even possessed, and sometimes they were ordered to be burnt, as in the case of the Apologia for Abaelard written by Berengarius of Poitiers in 1059, and various writings of Abaelard in 1141. Gregory XI had the books of Raymond Lull confiscated in 1376, and the Council of Constance ordered all the writings of John Huss to be burnt. After the invention of printing, the Fifth Lateran Council made general the pre-publication censorship which had already been introduced in four German ecclesiastical provinces. The Council of Trent in its 18th session set up an episcopal commission whose work led to the publication on 24 March 1584 of the Tridentine Index. The *Decem Regulae* of the first part were to be the basis of law up to the end of the 19th century. Thus the censorship of books came into being, and in the modern sense it is therefore ecclesiastical supervision of publications in order to protect the faithful from harmful writings. Toleration then must not hinder this work in principle.

There are two kinds of censorship: pre-censorship, which examines, before publication, all works with theological content, and a ban on books which have already been published. The length of the work and the method of publication, by printing or otherwise, are immaterial.

1. *Pre-censorship* is designed to prevent the publication of writings inimical to faith or morals. A work, subject to censorship, may not be printed without ecclesiastical permission — the imprimatur — and this can only be given if the result of the official examination proves favourable. Permission can be withdrawn at any time if it is later seen to have been granted on erroneous grounds. It can therefore happen that works which were at one time published with an imprimatur are later forbidden.

Subject to censorship in this sense are: a) editions of the Bible, as well as notes and comments included therein; b) writings on the Bible or on theological disciplines; c) prayerbooks, books of devotion or instruction, or containing ascetic, mystic or similar subject matter, in fact any books which have

a special bearing on the truths of faith or morals, and d) holy pictures, with or without prayers, no matter how they are reproduced (*CIC,* can. 1385, § 1).

The authorities competent to grant an imprimatur are the local ordinary of the author, or of the printer or of the publisher, but any refusal by one bishop must be mentioned if another is approached. Religious need the permission of their superiors as well (can. 1385, §§ 2, 3).

There are special regulations regarding documents concerning beatifications and canonizations (can. 1387), indulgences and collections of indulgences (can. 1388), collections of decrees of the Roman Congregations (can. 1389), editions of liturgical books and litanies approved by the Holy See (can. 1390). Translations of the Bible without notes into the local language may only be published with the permission of the Holy See; if they do have notes (taken from the writings of the Fathers of the Church and Catholic scholars), they need episcopal approval (can. 1391). New editions and translations of a work which had already been published with an imprimatur are subject to pre-censorship once more (though not reprints from periodicals (can. 1392).

In order to ensure full freedom of judgment, the names of the official examiners of books, appointed by the bishop from secular and regular clergy, must not be given to the author before a favourable decision has been reached. The examiners must submit a strictly objective, unprejudiced report *(nihil obstat),* taking a safe moderate line, as to whether the views expressed in the book accord with the dogmas and general teaching of the Church. Disagreement with a mere school of thought or a personal opinion of the censor does not justify rejection (can. 1393). The imprimatur which is granted in writing, but which should never be regarded as a recommendation, must be mentioned at the beginning or the end of the book (unless a special dispensation has been granted), giving the place and date, and the name of the bishop concerned. In case of refusal the author may ask for the reasons (perhaps with a view to emendation) which must be given to him (can. 1394) unless there is a very serious reason against it.

The imprimatur, based on an examination of a book, is quite different from *permission to publish secular writings* (can. 1386). Secular clergy who wish to publish non-religious books or write for papers or periodicals need permission from their bishop, and regular clergy must have their own superior's permission as well. Laymen are forbidden to write for papers and periodicals inimical to faith or morals, unless the bishop has granted permission for a just and sensible reason.

2. The *ban on books* condemns works already published which are harmful to the soul either in themselves or because of certain circumstances. Condemned by the *natural law* because the evil in them is intrinsic and inseparable, and because they are liable to corrupt faith or morals, they are also forbidden by a direct divine prohibition in Mt 5:29; 7:15; 18:7 (cf. Acts 19:19 and Rom 16:17). Although one must respect the right to personal information, it is the duty of the individual conscience to decide logically, without self-delusion and after honest self-examination, whether a book is fit to read. It is hardly feasible to make out a list of books giving the precise "degree of danger" for all. The reader himself must work out his own method of defence, taking into account his own instability and vulnerability. This is why few books have been included in the Index because of gross obscenity or immorality. A special condemnation is superfluous because such a book is already sufficiently condemned by the general moral law. The canonical prohibition, now formulated in the *CIC,* stresses the general danger (exceptions are given in can. 1400ff.), so that the law still applies even if in a particular case there really is no foreseeable actual danger. A prohibition may be imposed for the whole Church by the highest ecclesiastical authority, while synods, local ordinaries, abbots and superiors-general and, if necessary, other high superiors may impose it within their own sphere (can. 1395f.). All the faithful, and in particular holders of an ecclesiastical office, have a duty to report pernicious books (can. 1397). Leo XIII's guiding Constitution, *Officiorum ac Munerum,* of 25 January 1897 has been replaced by the new legislation of the *CIC* which stresses prevention rather than the punitive aspect (the latter is dealt with in can. 2318).

There are twelve categories of books which may not be published, read, owned, sold, translated or in any way made accessible to others without permission (can. 1398): i) Non-Catholic editions of the Bible, including translations; ii) books by all authors which defend heresy or schism or seek to undermine the bases of religion; iii) books attacking religion and good morals; iv) books of mainly religious content by non-Catholic authors, unless it is certain that they contain nothing against the Catholic faith; v) editions of the Bible published without pre-censorship (cf. can. 1395, § 1, nos. 1, 2) and books on apparitions and new devotions; vi) books attacking Catholic dogma, liturgy, hierarchy and discipline; vii) books recommending or teaching superstition in any form; viii) books recommending duelling, suicide, divorce, or representing freemasonry and similar movements as harmless; ix) books with an explicitly obscene aim; x) liturgical books containing unauthorized changes; xi) books spreading false indulgences; xii) pictures of our Lord and the saints which do not accord with Catholic teaching (can. 1399).

The motu proprio, *Alloquentes,* of Benedict XV of 25 March 1917 abolished the Congregation of the Index which had been set up by Pius V in March 1571, and transferred its activities to the Holy Office. There was to be a special *Sezione della censura dei libri* which was to examine books (cf. can. 1397) and prohibit them if necessary, i.e., include them in the official list, the procedure being that indicated by the Constitution of Benedict XIV, *Sollicita ac Provida,* of 9 July 1753. The Index had its last official re-issue in 1948.

As a result of Vatican II — Cardinal Frings, in his speech of 8 November 1963, summed up the objections against the Index as administered hitherto — Paul VI issued his motu proprio, *Integrae Servandae,* on 7 December 1965, altering the structure of the Holy Office, changing its name to "Congregation for the Doctrine of the Faith", and giving it a different standing. Under the presidency of the Pope and a Cardinal-Secretary it is to safeguard the doctrines of faith and morals for the whole Catholic world. This task includes examination of any book brought to their notice and, if necessary, condemnation. But the author must be heard and given the opportunity to defend his views in writing. His ordinary is to be informed. In an official *notificatio* of 14 June 1966, signed by a pro-prefect, it was declared furthermore that the Index is no longer to have the force of a law of the

Church: it is to be a moral guide for the conscience of the faithful to help them defend themselves in accordance with the natural law against writings endangering faith or morals. Any condemnation of writings should, where necessary, be made known to the faithful by suitable means. The Congregation for the Doctrine of the Faith declared in an official statement on 15 November 1966 that can. 1399 and 2318, pertaining respectively to the Index and to the penalties for the breach of the hitherto existing stipulations, had lost their validity.

See also *Natural Law, Curia.*

BIBLIOGRAPHY. F. H. Reusch, *Der Index der verbotenen Bücher,* 2 vols. (1883–85); L. Petit, *L'Index, son histoire, ses lois, sa force obligatoire* (1886); J. Hilgers, *Der Index der verbotenen Bücher in seiner neuen Fassung dargelegt und rechtlich-historisch gewürdigt* (1904); A. Bondinhon, *La nouvelle législation de l'Index* (2nd ed., 1925); H. J. T. Johnson, "The Roman Index of Prohibited Books", *Downside Review* 73 (1955), pp. 160–73; G. H. Putnam, *Censorship of the Church of Rome and Its Influence upon the Production and Distribution of Literature,* 2 vols. (1966).

Othmar Heggelbacher

CHARISMS

1. *Biblical.* The word χάρισμα was introduced into theological terminology by Paul. The synoptics, John and Acts are familiar with the phenomenon but have not the term, which is found in Rom, 1 and 2 Cor, 1 and 2 Tim and 1 Pet. Paul created a definite terminology to speak of the charisms, though for the spiritual gifts of grace described as χαρίσματα he also uses πνευματικά, διακονίαι and ἐνεργήματα (1 Cor 12). Paul's approach is characterized by the effort, particularly visible in 1 Cor 12–14, to dislodge the charisms from the region of mere "enthusiasm" and strange ecstatic phenomena and replace them in the ordered life of the community, and finally to understand them as characteristic of the baptized in general (Rom 12:6; 1 Cor 7:7). In the lists enumerating the charisms (Rom 12:6ff.; 1 Cor 12:8ff., 28ff.) the decisive viewpoint is the service of the community. The charisms are bestowed for the general good (1 Cor 12:7) and hence Paul prefers the prophetic discourse, which can be understood by all and serves to build up the community, to the gift of tongues which contributes only to personal piety and edification (1 Cor 14). In the list given in 1 Cor 12:28ff. (cf. also Eph 4:11) he first mentions the charismatic service done for the community by apostles, prophets and teachers, and after that, along with ecstatic and extraordinary charisms like working miracles, special gifts of healing and speaking in tongues, such well-tested charisms as power to help or govern others (1 Cor 12:8ff. adds discourses full of wisdom, discourses full of knowledge, faith and the discernment of spirits; Rom 12:8 liberality and clemency). To describe the purpose and function of the various charisms in their service of the whole Paul uses the image of the body (1 Cor 12:12–26; cf. Rom 12:4ff.). Since ecstatic utterances, as the charisms are to a great extent, can exist outside the Church, and can exist even inside the Church without any legitimation from the faith, Paul affirms that the Spirit is the decisive criterion. Only in the Spirit is it possible to say "Kyrios Jesus"; this Kyrios is the Lord of the gifts of the spirit (1 Cor 12:3ff.) and from him comes the love which must sustain and surpass all the charisms, if they are to be duly integrated into the whole (1 Cor 13).

In contrast to this special notion of charism, with its fixed terminology, Rom 5:16 and 6:23 use the term in the very general sense of God's gratuitous saving gift; in 1 Tim 4:14 and 2 Tim 1:6 charism means the grace of state or of office, while the meaning in 1 Pet 4:10 is close to the Pauline usage outlined above.

2. *The meaning of charisms for the life of the Church.* The scholastic definition of charisms, "privilegia peculiaria Ecclesiae apostolicae et primitivae", cannot seriously claim to derive from Paul, who sees them to a great extent as ecstatic phenomena, corresponding to the eschatological situation of the Church, but in whatever form they take (ecstatic or domesticated), as part of Church life, because the justification of baptism and the living Spirit are ordained to one another. Hence a charism should be called a sign of the triumph of grace (non-sacramental and "disposing" grace), a sign which can at times appear as an extraordinary phenomenon, close to the miraculous, but which can also simply appear as the fortitude given by grace to bear oneself well in ordinary life, and hence as virtue. It is characteristic of the work of the Spirit in the

justified and hence is always part of the image of the Church, and not merely during, say, the foundation period or times of extraordinary movements of enthusiastic piety.

The Pastoral Letters already signal a development, which was to prevail in post-apostolic times. The charism is linked with the office and its regulations. Further, obviously charismatic and ecstatic phenomena grow rarer. Montanism, Messalianism and Donatism provide typical instances of the critical view taken of charisms by office-holders in subsequent times. But the tension between the two never led to so totally exaggerated a view of the office that charismatic gifts and phenomena were completely extinguished. Monasticism (especially where not rigidly institutionalized), asceticism, virginity, martyrdom, poverty and movements favouring poverty, mysticism, social virtues and also theological science have been and can be ways in which charisms are manifested. Finally, the pastoral office is unthinkable without the charism, if it is not to be reduced to something profane. The ministries listed in Rom and 1 Cor, which tend to become an office and were in fact later institutionalized (cf. the pastoral letters) continued to be charismatic even after Paul's time. The statements of Scripture about the general priesthood (Rev 1:6; 5:9f.), the call of all in the Church to the royal priesthood and to the holy people of God (1 Pet 2:9, etc.; cf. Vatican II, Dogmatic Constitution on the Church, art. 11) and the NT understanding of the Church as the eschatological community of the time of salvation which has already dawned (cf. *ibid.*, art. 48) call logically for a high estimation and cherishing of the charismatic gifts in all the members of the Church and on all levels. It is, of course, for the hierarchy to give the final assessment and verdict on charisms, but the hierarchy must also be prepared to be corrected by the charismatic element and to be aware of the protest against rigid institutionalism which is inherent in all charisms. As a testimony to the Spirit, the charisms, beside and along with the sacraments, go to make up the many-sided life of the Church. Their absence or suppression casts a shadow on the title-deeds of the Church, leads to conformism and inhibits all dynamism.

In the Constitution on the Church, Vatican II pays special attention to the charismatic or pneumatic element (especially in art. 12; also arts. 4, 34f., 40f., etc.). The way had been prepared to some extent for this new appreciation by the encyclical *Mystici Corporis* (*D* 2288), though here the charisms were still primarily regarded as "marvellous gifts", that is, as rare and marginal phenomena. Since Vatican II acknowledges the activity of the Spirit outside the visible Catholic Church as well, it allows for the possibility of charisms there (Constitution on the Church, art. 15, Decree on Ecumenism, art. 3), and understands the ecumenical movement itself as an expression of the charismatic element in the Church (Decree on Ecumenism, arts. 1, 4, etc.). For only the Spirit gives the Church its diversity and bases unity on it.

See also *Holy Spirit, Early Church, Ecclesiastical Office.*

BIBLIOGRAPHY. B. Maréchaux, *Les charismes du St. Esprit* (1921); F. Büchsel, *Der Geist Gottes im Neuen Testament* (1926); A. Lemonnyer, "Charismes", *DBS,* I (1928), cols. 1223–43; J. Brosch, *Charisma und Ämter in der Urkirche* (1951); H. von Campenhausen, *Kirchliches Amt und geistliche Vollmacht in den ersten drei Jahrhunderten* (1953; 2nd ed., 1963), E. T.: *Ecclesiastical Authority and Spiritual Power in the Church of the First Three Centuries* (1967); E. Käsemann, *Die Legitimität des Apostels* (1959); E. Schweizer, *Church Order in the New Testament* (1961); G. Delling, *Worship in the New Testament* (1962); K. Rahner, *The Dynamic Element in the Church,* Quaestiones Disputatae 12 (1964); Vatican II, *Dogmatic Constitution on the Church* (21 November 1964); H. Küng, "The Charismatic Structure of the Church", *Concilium* 4 (1965), pp. 23–33; R. Schnackenburg, *The Church in the New Testament* (1965).

Estevao Bettencourt

CHARITY

I. Virtue of Charity. II. Love of Neighbour. III. Charitable Organizations.

I. Virtue of Charity

The Christian value *par excellence,* charity in the sense of supernatural love should be the soul of all apostolic work. This will be the main theme of the present article. At the same time natural love, in its various aspects, plays an essential role. Natural love would not be a sound enough methodical basis: wounded by sin, that is, by egotism, which is the corruption of love, it is mingled with instinctive libido. This article will start from the historic encounter of God, who is charity, with his "beloved children" (Eph 5:1) and our experience of "the love of Christ which surpasses knowledge" (Eph 3:19).

In this complex subject, three strands will constantly interweave: "God's *agape*" (Rom 5:5), our *agape* (Phil 1:9), and our natural love, either voluntary or instinctive, which underlies the workings of our *agape*. The "human act" of love, for our neighbour or for God, combines the great mysteries which the divine *agape* effects in us, the conscious responses of our love and the vigour of all our human life. This article will try to sift out this conscious response to the infinite gift, to the astonishing intimacy God offers us.

Beginning with the message of the NT, the only full light shed on the OT, this article will proceed on the basis of revelation, which gradually initiates us into the conscious life of children before communicating the fullness of life to us. Then in view of certain difficulties the theological interpretation of this "[revealed] life in *agape*" will be set forth, as well as the spontaneous awareness which the faithful have of it, which will be the rediscovery, in the light of revelation, of the part love plays as the human support of charity. It can then be explained how all pastoral teaching may be centred on *agape*: the doctrine of "God's works" — dogma; the doctrine of man's response — morals; and the doctrine of the last things — eschatology.

1. *An eternal meeting in agape, God's one design.* No doubt reason could adequately show that love is the fountain-head of God's works. But the Bible discovers in love "the mystery of God", "the riches of his mercy" and "of his glory" (Eph 2:4; 3:16; Col 1:25–27), which is altogether gratuitous (Rom 9:25). For a love that is literally divine chooses to call creatures to a real dialogue: *admirabile commercium*. God's intention is shown by the mysterious freedom of his election (Rom 9:11); by his gratuitous covenant, a growing intimacy beginning in the OT, in which God tirelessly seeks out his people after their sin (Exod 34:6f.; Is 54: 4–10; Hos 11:8–9; 1 Jn 4:10), as the shepherd his flock and the bridegroom his bride; by creation as it is revealed to us, that is, in the context of the covenant: it is a word (Ps 148:5), a personal, free, loving presence (Ps 18; Col 1:16–17; 2 Cor 13:13), which produces a "very good" work (Gen 1:31; 1 Tim 4:4) and centres on man the "re-

spondent", the confidant, an "image" of God (Gen 1:26–27); and finally by the advent of Jesus. The beloved Son himself has visited us (Lk 1:68, 78; Mt 3:17; Jn 1:18), the incomparable witness to *agape,* its envoy and its healer (Mt 12:18–21). He sacrifices himself even unto death, for sinners, in token of redemptive love (Rom 8:32; Phil 2:18; Jn 15:13). He sums up the call to love in the intimacy of his Eucharist and, on Calvary, in the mystery of his open heart (Jn 19:37). This call, St. Paul and St. John teach, is the central purpose of God's works: "God is love *(agape)*", which means that love is what God wishes to reveal of his infinite riches (1 Jn 4; Eph 3:9, 18, 19; Jn 1:14, 17, 21–23). Only the desire to reveal a perfect love explains the plan of salvation (Rom 11:32; Lk 19:10; Jn 13:1). So God's last word is that we have only to build up the fraternal people, the subject of his promises, and to that end to love, forgive, and serve. This is the crowning glory of God's *agape*.

2. *God has taught us to love.* Man was able to embark on this dialogue of transcendent *agape,* the chief aim of our pastoral efforts, only after a long and gradual education which began with God's revelation of love, fully clarified in the NT.

a) *New Testament.* Living in God's friendship rests upon faith in four basic truths: the adoption of sons in Jesus, introduction into the life of the Trinity, Christ's union, even to death, with our sufferings, and salvation by belonging to the community of brethren, the mystical body of Christ. These revealed truths are meant to teach us in our turn to love "perfectly" (Jn 13:2), with a love that is generous and spontaneous (Gal 2:20), efficacious and active (Eph 1:3–14), and brotherly towards all (Jn 13:34; Mt 5:45–48).

Here are some practical rules for "living in *agape*":

(i) The basic thing is to think, will, act and even feel as sons and brothers, that is, "in love": such is the Christian mind (Jn 13:34; 17:21; Rom 13:8–10; Gal 5:14; Eph 5:1). Love is essentially centred on Christ: *Sequere me.* Everything comes down to adhering to Jesus (Mt 8:19–22; 10:38; 19:27; Phil 2:5), suffering and rising from the dead with him, preaching only him (1 Cor 2:2), loving all men like him; and so brotherly love, creative *agape,* wishes to unite men through us and thus unite us, one in Christ, with God (1 Cor 3:23). Love is incomprehensibly intimate, in response to suffering *agape,* penetrating all within us (2 Cor 5:17). Love, then, is not simply a "virtue" but the very "life" of our good life.

(ii) Mt 22:37–39: Proclaimed by Jesus, echoing Deuteronomy, as "the great and first commandment", love must direct all the activity of man's "heart and soul and mind and strength"; that is, his whole moral life. Love demands the complete fulfilment of the law and the prophets but it must be their one soul, their life. Therefore the whole of "Christian activity" (and human activity) is intrinsically "religious" — tends, that is, to oneness in adoration — and "moral": to do wrong is to violate this bond of love.

(iii) 1 Cor 12:31 – 14:1. Here St. Paul proclaims this revolution of Christian activity in a classical text. Brotherly love is the creative, unique, and universal force behind worthwhile actions. Contrary to Gnostic ideas about the value of knowledge, only charity can and must give our conscious actions their Christian existence (13:2; see 1 Cor 1:30) and their value (13:31).

(iv) Practical formulae in St. Paul and St. John. "Walk in love" (Eph 5:1); let all your earthly journey be directed by this *agape* infused by God — a practical definition of the "morality of sons". Other texts mean the same: love satisfies the whole law, is the fulfilling of the law, binds everything together in perfect harmony (Gal 5:14; Rom 13:8–10; Col 3:12–15). That is to say, where a man acts according to the law or in view of perfection, there *agape* is at work; it makes the action holy. We are not far from the theological thesis that charity is the form of the virtues. In St. John (fraternal) *agape* appears as the only virtue (1 Jn). The discourse after the Last Supper identifies the object of Christian conscience with the new commandment and perfect unity. On the other hand, "if a man loves me he will keep my word" (Jn 14:15f.; 15:10, 14). "This is the commandment ... that you follow (this mutual) love." (2 Jn 6)

b) *Old Testament.* Six themes sum up the touching proofs of *agape* whereby God gradually engages his people in a dialogue of love: (i) Love as a gratuitous choice (Abraham: Gen 12:1–3; 17:1–8; Moses: Exod 2 and 3. See Amos 2:6–12; Is 54:4, 10, etc.). Deuteronomy, "the great biblical document of *agape*", sets this absolute gratuitousness in a magnificent light (4:20, 32–49; 7:6–8; 9:4–6, etc.). (ii) *Agape* proves to be an astonishing intimacy with the "friends" of God (Is 41:8; Jas 2:23; Exod 33:11): there are friendly exchanges, confidences, even argument (Gen 15:13, etc.; 18:1–16; 20:14; Exod 17:4; 33:16), "face to face" (Exod 33:12–23; 34:6–9; Num 7:89; 1 Kg 19:11), God's name is imparted — that is, his power (Exod 3 and 4), and the prophets commune with him. (iii) *Agape* proves itself efficacious. All its creative power is bent on furthering man's good (Gen 1:28–31). It is faithful to its people and its deeds and promises are more and more impressive (for example, Exod 19:5–6; Is 55:3–5; Deut 4:32–40; 5:3–4). (iv) By degrees *agape* calls on the chosen people to love in return: God has always required loving deeds (Gen 17:1; Exod 20:1–6; Hos 6:6); they lead to friendship, the tenderness of a father, even of a bridegroom (Exod 33:16; Hos 2:21–25; 11:1–9; Is 54:4–19; 62:2–5, etc.), to the most ardent exchanges. (v) Above all *agape* enunciates the great commandment which lays claim to a man's every act (Deut 6:4–9) for God alone: "The Lord is a devouring fire" (Deut 4:24; 11:1–8). (vi) Already, though without making it love of God, *agape* demands love of one's racial brother (Lev 19:17f. and 34) and, within the framework of the nation, love of the stranger (Deut 10:18f.), the weak, the poor, the afflicted (Is 58:6; cf. 59:2f.; Jer 22:14).

Thoroughly transforming our consciously sinful life, this personal relationship of love, revealed to us by God, demands of us an essentially active, creative idea of love as obedience. A Christian united with Christ tends to prolong God's creative *agape* by his life, thereby living in faith and hope: to make charity the driving force behind all his moral life; and to build a new mankind, the brotherly people, the mystical Christ. Another demand made on us is that of a new frame of mind, at least an incipient generosity. Ceasing to look on divine law as constraint, since it comes from the Father I yield to the supernatural attraction of the filial love (Rom 8:14) which God pours forth in me, for all his "laws" — which henceforth extend to the whole of his good pleasure: "mandata mea" (Jn 14:23; 15:10; Rom 6:14; Gal 5:18, 23; 1 Tim 1:9; 1 Jn 4:18). Where duties are categorical, love is categorically demanded; but love must always be generous. Instead of calculating the exact limits of duty, as sinful man is prone to do, love is responsive to the "counsels" in their wide diversity and freely chooses among them according to a man's vocation in love. The "spirit of the counsels", which includes the love of strict duties, is the new "law", freely loved and ever more perfectly observed, of filial ethics.

3. *God gives us his agape through the incarnate Word and the Church.* The whole effort and hope of the Church's pastoral life is to diffuse *agape* in abundance.

The NT teaches that charity is a wholly gratuitous gift but one given with the lavishness of Pentecost: the Spirit pours it forth into our hearts (Rom 5:5); a real gift (Eph 1:4–6; 1 Cor 13:1 f.) of God's "great love" and the fruit of his election (Eph 1:4–6; 2:4–8), it is revealed by "the spirit of sonship" (Rom 8:15) which leads us to direct communion with the Trinity (Jn 17:23; see 14:20–24; 17:27) in Jesus.

Theology distinguishes (sanctifying) grace from charity (Eph 2:4–8) without separating them. Charity is the real power to love God as his children and entails a supernatural inclination to do so. Loving me unutterably, *agape* creates in me my *agape*, a kind of echo of itself — a created gift that enables me to respond to it, an infused virtue whereby I can produce acts both conscious and supra-conscious which are of divine worth. In my act of charity what I do is exalted above itself by God's doing: the mystery of holiness in *agape "before him"* (Eph 1:4). An "infused virtue", charity is at the same time "the virtue of the other virtues" as the driving force behind them. So I shall make an act of charity: either explicitly, for its own sake, at least often enough to keep the virtue fervent; or else implicitly, within any good human act which is willed for a particular reason — an act of penance, or justice, or daily duty. My charity is "perfect" as soon as I love God personally, for himself; it is "imperfect" if filial love is still motivated by fear of losing my divine inheritance (*D* 818, 898). Justification begins with a beginning of faith (*D* 798), hope, and then charity (*ibid.*) and is completed by the infusion of grace and charity. The latter dwells in the soul along with grace (*D* 800, 821).

All Christ's activity in the Church shows that the gift of love is necessary and that by it God trains us to conscious dialogue with him. Sacramental life, culminating in the daily Eucharist, expresses and brings about in love our personal encounter with God in Jesus the Redeemer and in ecclesial communion. The Church itself, the mystical bride, is the sacrament of the gift of merciful love and of our loving response, which rises to God in the liturgy (Vatican II: Constitution on the Sacred Liturgy, art. 2). It witnesses to love through its eucharistic communities; through the sacramental encounters of the faithful with the minister, God's instrument, through the love Christians show day by day towards everyone in social life, and their repentance for often not showing it. The three indelible sacramental characters in particular show the unutterable love of God, who wishes to make every Christian conformable to the likeness of his beloved Son, so that each may perform the saving acts of the eternal high priest. For all who are joined with him in his mysteries — his cross, his resurrection, his sacraments, his mystical body — Christ remains the "bright epiphany" (Mt 11:25–30; Tit 2:11; Col 1:13) of encounter with God in the bosom of the Church. His Sacred Heart is the well and supreme disclosure of unfathomable love, whence all his members draw sanctifying grace, life in the God of love, constant actual encounter with him.

4. *Hindrances to "living in charity".* Whereas simple souls find it no problem (Mt 11:25), the primacy of charity poses difficulties in practice and theory which often are hardly adverted to.

a) *The difficulty of loving.* Scripture says that opposing fraternal love is the great social evil: because of original sin, man has been set against man since the beginning (Gen 4; 6:3–11); if he rejects his salvation, says John (17:14; see 15:22–25), it is because he refuses to love; the Apocalypse pictures history as a remorseless battle against the Lamb. Therefore — and the fact is too often overlooked — the new evangelical order, the world's only salvation, is a social order based on love, which means that there the justice of strict rights is all the more necessary (Acts 2:44; 4:32). If the "acquisitive" instincts of human sexuality are not to falsify love, they should evolve into "oblativity"; and that is what God's gratuitous charity aims to do by supernatural means. Where property is concerned the "possessive" instinct, reinforced by an agonizing insecurity, turns "justice" into a defence of selfish interests. These two rooted egotisms, to which people are all but blind, constantly attack love between husband and wife, in the family, and in society, paralyzing even the minimal alms of compassion, not to mention "the alms of sharing" (2 Cor 8:13), begetting enmity, aggression, and war. So a vital part of our pastoral work must be to convert society to love.

b) *The difficulty of explaining in adequate language how charity is the "supreme value".* Deviations here have been too frequent to be allowed to pass without warning. Generally speaking, they see (infused) charity as an activity or virtue separate from human activity or the other virtues. Hence, though charity is the "supreme" virtue, it is allowed to diminish or even displace the human moral values with which it is wrongly compared, whereas the Fathers unanimously teach that charity is the soul of the virtues, that it gives all "duties" a higher value from within but without destroying the particular nature of each. In former times there were the moral systems of Baianism (*D* 1016, 1025, 1036, 1038) and rigorism (*D* 1297, 1394f., 1416, 1523); and on the other side quietism (*D* 1327, 1349) and laxism (*D* 1155, 1157). Nowadays certain people make charity the "concrete" value which properly constitutes the inspiration of the "lived personal moment"; the "only vocation", which transcends or even displaces divine law; that law being an "abstract universal", sound in itself but not applicable to "concrete" life, as in "situation ethics". It has already been seen above that a charity which more or less competes with God's laws is a contradiction in terms. According to the Fathers, charity is an infused dynamism which wills all laws and all our human acts but transmutes them (charity as a "form") into love.

5. *Theology of the primacy of charity.* We must have a theological synthesis for the following reasons: Our "moral theologies", composed as they are on the basis of the mercy to be shown in the confessional, concentrate too much on the minimum of duty. It would be unwise to attempt new formulations until we

have a theological structure wholly acceptable to the Church. We must be able to think correctly about revealed morals, integrating into them all undoubted human values.

St. Thomas's doctrine provides us with one of the most modern elements for our synthesis. Our foundation is an "existential" structure of the "moral object", that is, of any concept which our practical reason declares relevant to morality (for example: this or that "just" deed, or the human act as such; this or that moral law, or "law"; "conscience"). There are two elements in any moral object: one, peculiar to each concept (for instance, payment of this debt), is the complex of "determinations" which arises from my experience of the outside world in relation to this "object". The other, common to all moral objects, is the judgment which gathers together these experiential data and affirms this object as a good in relation to my last end — the beatitude towards which I tend. I affirm this good because I observe that it attracts me (that it is good) or even forces itself upon me (is obligatory; that is, is a necessary good) in view of the end. The affirmation shows that my basic tendency has come into play in the formation of the moral object in my consciousness and that existentially and implicitly I have taken up an attitude towards the end — beatitude — God (St. Thomas's fundamental thesis: *Summa Theologica*, I, II, q. 1, 2, 3). This adoption of an attitude is implicit but actual and efficacious: without it there is no moral knowledge, no responsibility, no awareness that an act is good or bad. The "determinations" of any moral object detail, specify, or "determine" our tendency towards the end.

Now this actuation of my basic tendency, which necessarily enters into every moral affirmation, is the (implicit) actuation of my will — an "existential" act, therefore, of love for God the last end. It is in this act of love that I make moral judgments, perceive (implicitly) before God the attraction, and sometimes also the necessity, of a particular good (mandatory love). It should be noted that it is "natural" for the will to tend towards God, but the concrete (implicit) actuation of the will in moral affirmations, that taking up of an attitude towards the end — beatitude — God, is spiritual (not instinctive) and free in the two senses of the word: (ontologically) the will's desire for good is spiritually spontaneous (in this sense to tend towards evil is to violate freedom); (psychologically) the will can choose indifferently, while we are on earth, either to act or not to act and therefore either to do good or ill.

Once having taken up my attitude before God, I perceive it: my conscience distinguishes the moral object from any other.

By raising it to the supernatural plane, the revelation of the primacy of "charity" has reminded us of this presence of the "love" of God throughout moral life. But whereas the implicit act of love arises from the depths of my will, charity descends into me from the *agape* of God which unites me with him. Frail, sinful man must learn to rouse his conscience and follow it. He can do so by meditating on the call of love that can be heard at the heart of every moral object (paying one's just debts, observing conjugal chastity).

In short, every "object" which is thought of in moral (and Christian) terms comprises two closely interwoven elements: certain "determinations" are affirmed as moral (and Christian) values because love (charity) "informs" them. In an explicit act of charity the "determination" is the present sense (better or less good) that I can give it at this moment.

Thus we have vindicated the intellectual method which will enable us to set forth in *practical* terms what the NT says about morals. Speaking technically, love-charity is the existential "form" (not the "formal cause") of Christian conduct and therefore of every Christian moral "object" rightly conceived. We must recognize that charity informs the virtues not only on the plane of conduct itself but also on the plane of the moral object: effort is called for here. In the moral idea of "law", for example, I must see the divine lawgiver revealing his love to me, the love I shall find by keeping his law for the sake of love. Then law will no longer seem constraint. It will be easy to keep once it has become an exchange of love. The primacy of (natural) love gives us immediately apostolic contact with all men: for they all yearn to love.

6. *Agape in the spontaneous conscience of Christians.* If scholastic language often rendered it unsatisfactorily, the Church has always been keenly aware of the primacy of love-charity. It is implicit in the leitmotivs of the devout life, especially in the ardent love of Jesus (Jn, discourse after the Last Supper), whence it is readily deduced. It is explicit in the Fathers. St. Augustine in particular enlarges on the Pauline themes: "Humble love" is the soul of goodness; virtue and the virtues are "nothing but supreme love of God" (*De Mor. Eccl. Cath.*, XV, 25; *PL*, XXXII, 1322; cf. St. Gregory, *Hom. in Ev.*, XXVII, 1; *PL*, LXX, 1205: Breviary, vigils of apostles). All the "moral theologies" echo the thesis that "charity is the form of the virtues" but they do not use it to *formulate* Christian morals.

7. *The psychology of love.* Acts of love are the human support of our conscious life of *agape*. It has been seen above how St. Thomas bases his metaphysic of the primacy of love on the psychological structure which the moral object derives from love's deep tendency towards the end. A psychology of love may now be sketched. Love is ambiguous to the extent that man himself is divided. As an instinct, love in man arises from the dynamism of growth and, eventually, from an "affective" desire for completion, which must blossom into a personal gift of self to a person; so it is the need and the power to be united with the other. This intra-personal gift of spirit, in which sensibility plays more or less of a part, has to be discovered and achieved by each individual. All mankind has attempted it, ever since the first attempt, which was the first failure — original sin. Were instinct to dominate, it would not get beyond "acquisitive love". It is for the spirit to recognize the *person* of the other and beyond that, if we are dealing with conjugal love, the new person, the child, lasting fruit of a transitory union, where each of the two persons finds himself given anew to the other. Our moral effort must be to grow on both levels, that of respect for the person and that of creativity. In marriage or outside it, love tends towards friendship, the spiritual reciprocity of communion between two persons. Even in marriage love tends to free itself, if not from the union of the sexes as such — which may remain a duty of love —, then from egotistic compulsions. Were our flesh perfectly docile, love would no longer have to force itself upon another person; rather, it would freely give itself. This is the ideal that *agape*

works towards in the sacrament of marriage. As for creativity in friendship, with or without marriage, it is the noblest gift of love. Birth control, if it is to be moral in marriage, must never foster carnal impulses but the esteem of the partners for each other. Thus we return to the philosophic principle: love is "willing the good of another": it is "benevolence", which when mutual becomes friendship. The "love of concupiscence" (which is not "concupiscence") is not opposed to this benevolence unless it remains a solitary thing, a matter of satisfying oneself. In wishing for himself the gift of another, a person in fact wishes the good of the other; for in welcoming the other he opens and gives himself. Similarly *amor complacentiae* ("enjoyment") does not conflict with benevolence, unless it degenerates into a mere selfish will to enjoy the other.

Love as a basic tendency solves many problems. It implicitly unites love of the end, of God, with love of oneself, beatitude. Even by nature man loves God, his total good. This truth is not obvious and will need to be demonstrated; it may be neglected or forgotten when immediate attractions hold the field — the passions of sense, the purely experimental sciences, outward activities. The twofold love of self and God corresponds to the twofold love of self and others in the world, because the self only perceives itself through its existential tendency to love another and the world. Directed to its end, our love of God is not "interested"; with its two complementary aspects, gift and desire, it denies neither the divine transcendence — "God is for me" — nor my personality — "I am for God" — but works for a communion of "me in God and God in me", a communion where the egotism of mine and thine is gradually unlearnt under the instruction of *agape*. "True love seeks to enrich itself only so as to give more to the communion which it begets." (Cf. Eph 5:1–2.)

The formation of human love in any person presupposes a psychical evolution, which depends on heredity and the human and "affective" climate of early childhood, and the formation of a "psychical love", that is, an instinctive "sympathy" which will vary in quality. Higher love (human, and especially infused love) will do much to foster this evolution but will not, in the case of unbalanced psychical impulses, be able to dispense with the help of a psychiatrist. A pastoral approach judiciously informed by love, especially in moral matters, must also further this evolution.

Deviations of instinctive love affect Christian conduct all the more because love is the "form" of the whole virtuous life.

8. *Agape at the heart of teaching the faith.* The Creator has made love-charity the substance of the redeemed world. All things tend towards God (cf. Rom 8:19–22). It remains for us to propose, as a practical means of centring religious teaching on love-charity, the method of "mediation" which Christian truth has in fact always used. Jesus himself teaches as a Mediator: "He is the image of the invisible God" (Col 1:15). First we speak of teaching (as dogma) the works of God, natural and supernatural. We must practise seeing them as "objective mediations" of *agape*. It is a fundamental truth that every work of God bears the mark of *agape* in its intelligible being. Scripture identifies the word of love with creative energy. In us love is weak and energy is harsh. In God all creative energy is loving and beneficent. So the natural (moral) law is the creative word which inscribes on every intelligible being the rules for the human acts that have to do with that being. To follow these rules, even at the cost of pain, is to commune with the benevolent presence, with beatitude (Wis 11:24–25; 13:1–5; Col 1:15–20).

To declare the works of God, then, one must see in them — above all in Jesus (Jn 1:18) and supernatural encounters with him (sacraments, Church, etc.) — the reality which reveals God and brings him to us, the herald of benevolence sent to men. A mere "means" would be of no use. "Mediation" bears its source within it — the *agape* which it proclaims. Thus everything is divinely lovable (Gen 1:4, 10, 31) except sin; indeed everything is grace (Rom 8:28); everything invites us to the dialogue of love: this is the source of gratitude, respect and love for "earthly values".

It is the privilege of the baptized to "consecrate the world" in response to this progressive discovery — that is, to offer to God, efficaciously thanks to Christ, all their activity in the world. See the "contemplation for obtaining love" (St. Ignatius, *Spiritual Exercises*), which invites us to contemplate four progressive encounters with *agape* coming to us through and in all God's works, where one experiences gifts — presences — influences — and finally direct emanations of *agape*. So all creation sets the scene for love's dialogue.

9. *Agape at the heart of moral teaching.* The dialogue of love in every good act, the only Christian morality which hopefully promises the grace of progressive faithfulness, must be capable of formulation. If it seems too lofty, that is only because people do not realize how simple it is in practice (Mt 11:25): the spirit of love-*agape* makes our living and preaching efficacious. Love-charity must recover its status as the universal source and end of all conscious morality, of strict commandments and "counsels" — of every "moral object". We do nothing unless we already convey the atmosphere of our Father's house: "Live as well-beloved sons" (Eph 5:1).

Every moral value, particular or general, good "object" or bad (this or that just act, justice, virtue, law; this or that injustice, sensual indulgence), must be looked on as a "subjective mediation" of love-charity, whereby I adopt a concrete (existential) attitude and by experiencing it experience the tendency of love-charity, obeyed or rejected.

To teach mere "commandments" (not as "mandatory love") would be to ignore the dynamism of conscience, which is love of beatitude — the last end — God — Jesus Christ. We must recognize the commandment as the rudimentary requirement, the "minimum" of love-charity, where love-charity therefore already tends to rise above itself to better things, that is, to the counsels. The object of Christian morality (even of human morality) is "the good which God gives me to love", which despite my sins I already love through my basic orientation, unaltered thanks to *agape*. So in a steadily advancing conversion *(metanoia)* the moral object is the good which the beloved person "wants", in other words it is everything that Christ "advises", which *a fortiori* includes what is of obligation. However we look at it, we are dealing with the Good News, where, going beyond strict duty, generosity has the last word. To start talking again of "venial sin" in connection with choosing what is more perfect would be to relapse, subconsciously anxious, into the "minimizing spirit" which is precisely what we are meant to escape by striving (in serenity of mind) for the more perfect.

Thus all Christian morality is "paschal" longing, a confident longing to "pass over" to better things through Christ suffering and risen — the very definition of tending towards perfection.

Dynamic and progressive, Christian morality is altogether "objective". To declare "charity the most perfect virtue" without qualification is to risk a misunderstanding which prejudices "objective" morality. Charity is most perfect as the existential form which enriches all particular moral "objects". Here is the cure for an inconsistent existentialism or unbridled "facticity".

As subjective mediations of love-charity, all moral ideas gradually bring us into the presence of God and Christ. This is what the forming of conscience consists of. A "doubtful conscience" — and the Christian doubts so as to love the better — will not agree to choose between "the law of God" and "my freedom" (which would oppose the two from the start); it seeks out some "good that is freely loved", that is, a human act that is really justifiable. Love-charity regards law not as an impersonal pronouncement but as the palpable, beloved presence of that Lawgiver who is always kind.

Every virtue, looked on as a mediation of love-charity, will be given a Christian definition which inwardly directs its particular qualities, including its *natural* morality, towards a deepening communion with Christ and the society of the brethren.

In short, Christian morals must be taught in terms of the striving for perfection — and of a spontaneous advance without rigorist tensions, so that the law of liberty shall not be twisted into a "law of constraint".

10. *Agape the substance of the kingdom of heaven.* In scriptural eschatology "the perfect" which will not pass away is *agape* (1 Cor 13:9). Paul speaks in these terms of *fraternal agape:* so it is no evasion, here and now we are building the eternal *koinônia* (Acts 2:42f.; 4:32f.) — the present embodiments of which (family, community, in *agape*) are our great apostolic strength (1 Pet 2:9), the sure hope of which opens us to charity-sharing (2 Cor 8:13; Heb 13:16) — while we await the vision (1 Cor 13:12). *Agape* binds earth to heaven.

Agape alone sheds light on our ultimate purposes: we are expected (Jn 14:2), we are to be with him (1 Thess 4:17), we shall see him "face to face" (1 Cor 13:12); eucharistic communion, viaticum, transmits us at once to eternal life. In purgatory *agape* adjusts us to it. In hell a will which bears the stamp of *agape's* last call refuses itself its own life irremediably. To the extent that the primacy of love-charity is obscured, hell will bewilder men on earth.

The essence of beatitude: Even on earth (fraternal) *agape,* beyond faith and hope, ushers men into a real beatitude (1 Cor 13), a fellowship which opens our eyes to the inadequacy of all earthly ties. Intellectual vision is certainly the essence of heavenly beatitude since it puts us into possession of God; but that possession is inadequate, it is a possession "consummated" by love (Aquinas, *Summa Theologica,* I, II, q. 3, a. 4c), by the perfect intimacy and communion of friendship with God.

Conclusion. Even on the natural plane man would be invited to love God and man, to make a loving home for his family, the foundation of the universal family. The only law of all human advance — in science, technology, thought, or politics — is a growing "amorization" in the Spirit, as Teilhard de Chardin puts it. Supernatural salvation delivers us from sin and its consequences — that is, from "unlove", so that we have "access" (Eph 3:12) in Christ to "life in charity". *Agape* in man, therefore, is an infused dynamism which desires everything good, above all the eternal structure of brotherhood. This brotherly communion, anticipated in our union here below with Jesus and the eucharistic gathering, becomes perfect "thanksgiving" even on earth, surrendering all things to the Father who loved us first. This return to the Father in the *agape* of Jesus is our revealed last end, the "fulfilment of beatitude".

See also *Morality* III, *Situation, Evangelical Counsels, Existence* II, III, *Grace* I, II, *Justification, Order* IV, *Moral Theology* III, *Morality* II, *Natural Law, Nature* III, *Metanoia,* Sex I, III, *Value, Concupiscence, Spirituality* III D.

BIBLIOGRAPHY. P. Rousselot, *Pour l'histoire du problème de l'amour au Moyen Âge* (1933); R. Carpentier, "Mirabilius reformasti", *NRT* (1934), pp. 338 ff.; É. Gilson, *La Théologie mystique de S. Bernard* (1934); M. D'Arcy, *The Mind and Heart of Love* (1945); E. Mersch, "Le plus grand des commandements", *NRT* (1947), pp. 1009–29; A. Viller and P. de Broglie, "Charité", *Dictionnaire de la Spiritualité;* E. Greeff, *Les instincts de défense et de sympathie* (1947); A. Falanga, *Charity, the Form of the Virtues according to St. Thomas* (1948); R. Balducelli, *Il concetto teologico di carità attraverso le maggiori interpretazione patristiche medievali di 1 Cor 13* (1950); V. Warnach, *Agape. Die Liebe als Grundmotiv der neutestamentlichen Theologie* (1951); E. Stauffer, "ἀγάπη", *TWNT,* I, pp. 34–55; C. V. Héris, *La Spiritualité de l'Amour* (1952); A. Nygren, *Agape and Eros* (new ed., 1953); C. Spicq, *Agape: Prolégomènes à une Étude de théologie néotestamentaire* (1955); id., *Agape dans le NT,* 3 vols. (1958–59); S. Lyonnet, "Liberté chrétienne et loi nouvelle", *Christus,* no. 4; G. Gilleman, *The Primacy of Charity in Moral Theology* (1959); R. Carpentier, "Le Primat de l'Amour-Charité", *NRT* (1961), pp. 1 ff., 255 ff., 492 ff.; id., "Conscience", *Dictionnaire de la Spiritualité;* P. Grelot, *Sens chrétien de l'AT* (1962); E. Schillebeeckx, *Christ the Sacrament* (1963); R. Schnackenburg, *The Moral Teaching of the NT* (1965); G. Martelet, "Morale conjugale et vie chrétienne", *NRT* (1965), pp. 245–55.

René Carpentier

II. Love of Neighbour

1. *Concept and problems.* The love which is open to and interested in those close to us is universally recognized as a noble form of moral action. But the question arises as to who are our "neighbours" and how far should charity towards them go. The spontaneous answer of natural ethics is to distinguish between love of those nearest and dearest to us and readiness to help those outside this circle. Men feel bound to love others in proportion to their "social proximity". In the Greek city-state this attitude was deliberately extended to take in the commonwealth of free citizens as a sort of enlarged family, which meant a certain exclusion of those outside the city. The OT also contains an ethics of special charity towards fellow-believers. But since love of the neighbour is based on the fatherhood of God, and since the God of Israel is the God of all men, this love is ready in principle to regard all men as neighbours. But since Israel considered itself a chosen people in a special way, with a special relationship to the fatherhood of God, there was a feeling of a special obligation of love towards the members of the chosen people, which led to a strong tendency to exclude foreigners, especially in late Judaism. Nonetheless, the duty of love went beyond the community

to take in foreigners, because they were also creatures of God and descendants of the fathers of the race of man, Adam and Noah (Exod 22:20; 23:9; Deut 14:29, etc.; Lev 19:33 f.; 19:10; 23:22; Num 9:14; 15:14 ff.; 35:15; see the concordances under the word "stranger"). But while in some cases late Judaism linked love of God and of the neighbour, the main foundation of Jewish ethics was justice.

A different type of love of the neighbour is found in the mystery religions. Entry into an esoteric community made men neighbours. These communities arose from the wish to find closer fellowship, and hence sometimes developed a hostile attitude to those outside the group. But the political unification of the Hellenistic world brought with it, especially in Stoic philosophy, a cosmopolitan ethics, so that Epictetus, for instance, could regard all men as brothers since they all had their origin in God. Thus the one basic attitude of love of the neighbour embraced all men. In the Enlightenment, universal brotherhood and the resulting duty of equal love for all was based on the oneness of nature in all men. The habit of making distinctions was to be overcome, as an irrational atavism. This unrealistic ethics of universal love was abandoned by Marxism in favour of love of one's own class. Those who love the proletariat must be enemies of the capitalists. The division is due to the historical process of the self-alienation of man, which can only be eliminated in the classless society. Dialogical existence-philosophy stresses the I-Thou relationship and communication in contrast to generalizing thought-forms and hence does more justice to the primordially personal and historical in each man. The neighbour is he with whom we are confronted in each unique and incalculable situation. Jaspers, for instance, holds that love is directed to the individual as he appears in his uniqueness. One is not urged to help him by virtue of general ethical principles and duties, but because in the encounter with him, the situation forms a decisive challenge for our destiny. Here love comes to the aid of the neighbour as the situation demands and without conditions. There is no objective absolute ethical duty, but only the summons to personal communication with this unique individual, of which the nature and limits can never be fully fathomed.

In all these ethics, the love of the neighbour is limited by love of self, in the sense of the "golden rule" (Mt 7:12; Lk 6:31), that one should love one's neighbour as oneself. Or again, society is given priority over the individual in the sense of an absolute precedence; or finally, no attempt is made to assess objectively the measure of love of the neighbour. The Christian notion of charity, however, is based on the union of love of God and love of the neighbour. They are linked significantly by Jesus in the "great commandment" (Mk 12:28–31 parr.). Then love of the neighbour appears more precisely as the one norm according to which man will be judged (Mt 25:34–46). No bounds are set to loving the neighbour as oneself: the highest form of love is love of enemies (Mt 5:43 ff.; Lk 6:27 ff.) and giving one's life for one's friends (Jn 15:13). Thus love is the sum-total of the law (Mk 12:31; cf. 3:1–7; Mt 5:23 f.; 9:13). Its motive and its model is the all-embracing love of God (Lk 6:36) and the service rendered by Jesus himself (Mk 10:44 f.; Lk 22:26; Jn 13:14 f.). In Paul, love of the neighbour is the fulfilment of the whole law (Rom 13:8–10; Gal 5:14), and the perfection of Christian life (Col 3:1). Love of God and of the neighbour are seen as unity (1 Cor 13). In James, love is seen as the royal commandment (Jas 2:8). According to John, love of the neighbour is a new commandment (Jn 13:34; 1 Jn 2:8), motivated by the love with which God first loved men (Jn 3:16; 16:27; 1 Jn 4:11), and by the love with which the Son chose the disciples (Jn 15:9 f., 12).

2. *The theology of love of the neighbour.* Love of the neighbour determines the basic structure of the moral act, inasmuch as we cannot turn to God without turning to our neighbour. We can only be with God insofar as we are with our fellowmen. It is only through love of the neighbour that we can find fulfilment in the love of God. Our relationship to transcendence can only come about through our concrete, historical relationship to our fellowmen. The "transcendental depth" of man in the encounter with the "other" always points beyond itself, at least implicitly, to God and at the same time back to him who loves also, since it is only in such encounters that he really possesses his own identity. For it is only when man is materially and implicitly in face of being,

while formally and consciously in face of objectivated reality, that he can be consciously and truly himself. So too, man can only see himself distinct, as person, from the objective reality of the world when at least materially and implicitly he refers himself to God as the personal being as such, and to his fellowmen formally and explicitly. Hence the explicit and formal reference to God is only possible insofar as there is ordination towards man. This is the kernel of truth in the position of the modern non-Catholic theologians who maintain that God is only a "mode of being fellowman". The more we welcome our fellowmen in their uniqueness and their openness to God, the more we surrender ourselves to God without reserve. This openness need not be conscious and explicit, but it is at least materially there. Hence every act of neighbourly charity is materially an act of the love of God. If this love of God is made explicit, it is formally an act of the love of God. Hence our neighbour is every man potentially, and actually every man who meets us in his subjective uniqueness and in the measure in which he does so. He may be someone sought out by me, or one who irrupts unasked into my personal existence. That we can attain through love of the neighbour a fulfilment which surpasses all human understanding, and that we are called to an unconditional love of others, are truths which can only be lived in faith.

Faith reveals the call of all men to sonship of God in the Son, according to God's universal salvific will. It follows that every moral act is in principle ordained through grace to salvation. Justification makes all the justified brothers of one another in Christ by grace (Mk 3:31–35; Jn 14:21; 15:14f.), so that they can love one another in a supernatural way. Only those justified in Christ are brothers in the strict sense. The others are "those outside" (1 Thess 4:10–12; cf. 1 Cor 5:12, 13; Col 4:5). Accordingly, the attitudes prescribed in the Pauline letters for conduct towards those outside are sometimes outgoing (Rom 13:8; 1 Thess 3:12; 5:15; Tit 3:2; also 1 Cor 9:19; 1 Tim 2:1; Rom 13:1; Tit 3:1; Phil 2:15; Rom 12:17; 2 Cor 8:21; 1 Thess 4:12; 5:22; Rom 15:2; 1 Tim 4:12), sometimes deliberately restrictive (Col 4:5; cf. 2 Cor 6:15; Eph 4:28; 1 Thess 4:11–12; Eph 5:6–7; 2 Cor 6:17). But the demarcation of the Christian

fellowship is not aimed at producing an esoteric coterie. It is in the service of the whole, as is particularly clear from Rom 5:12–21. Since Jesus died for all men and since all are therefore called to this supernatural brotherhood, the supernatural love of the neighbour must embrace all men, and in the concrete those who are in need, spiritually or materially (Lk 10:30–37; Mt 25:31–46), especially as the justified are called for the non-elect. For there is a mystery of substitution which was instituted in Christ and which forms the basis of all election, and according to the will of God it continues from Christ on in an economy of salvation which is a series of substitutions. This is in fact the structural law of the history of salvation itself.

Election is always ultimately election on behalf of others. This is true of individuals as of the Church, and hence election is none other than the missionary mandate. This means that Christianity recognizes the existence of various spheres of neighbourly charity, while confining the name of "brother" to fellow-believers. But there is no desire of exclusivity for its own sake. The ultimate meaning of the demarcation is simply to perform the due service for all men. Love of the neighbour is most fully expressed in substitutional or vicarious suffering along with the Lord, in the martyrdom of total dedication in love of the neighbour, since ultimately a parousia of God in Christ takes place in him. Where there is genuine love of the neighbour, the totality of Christianity is presence in substance and in germ, and needs only to be explicitly unfolded.

See also *Justice, Law and Gospel, Human Act, Salvation* I, *Justification, Sacrifice* II, *Church, Salvation* III, *Martyrdom.*

BIBLIOGRAPHY. B. Valuy, *Fraternal Charity* (1948); L. Colin, *Love One Another* (1958); R. O. Johann, *The Meaning of Love* (1959); B. Häring, *Law of Christ,* II (1963); J. Ratzinger, *The Open Circle. The Meaning of Christian Brotherhood* (1966); C. van Ouwerkerk, "Secularism and Christian Ethics", *Concilium* 5, no. 3 (1967), pp. 47–67.

Waldemar Molinski

III. Charitable Organizations

The word "charity", in this article, has the common meaning of Christian brotherly love towards the needy and the suffering. It is not only a sacred duty and the characteristic of every true Christian, but also the characteristic and expression of the life of the Church and the essential reality of every community inspired by the spirit of Christ.

1. *The Church as ecclesia caritatis.* The Second Vatican Council has brought charity with great emphasis into the centre of theological speculation and of Christian consciousness. For the first time in the history of conciliar declarations, place is given to the works of charity of the Church and the faithful, and not merely to charity as a Christian attitude. This is a very clear indication that the apostolic initiative of the people of God on the threshold of a new epoch in the world's history should make itself powerfully felt, in thought and attitude as well as in action, in that practical Christian love which ever since the Church was founded has been the great force transforming the world.

The *ecclesia caritatis,* the basic motive running through the entire Dogmatic Constitution on the Church, is, according to the address of Pope Paul VI at the opening of the second session, the point of unity of all the efforts of the Council. The Church, according to the Constitution, "the sacrament as it were in Christ, i.e., the sign and instrument for the inmost union with God as well as for the unity of all mankind", is not only the Christ living on but that same Christ "qui pertransiit benefaciendo" (Acts 10:38) continuing to love too. Since all the members of this body make up the Church, the entire body of Christ must make this a reality, above all in the charity exercised in common and in community "works", especially where they can be achieved and given secure permanency only through the work of the community.

2. *Misunderstandings of charity.* Three misinterpretations of charity which are unfortunately widespread and to be found even among the clergy are therefore to be guarded against: a) The merely individualistic, ethical understanding of charity; b) the spiritualistic interpretation, according to which charity is present in the Church inasmuch as it is the body of Christ, in the liturgical sphere as its essence by grace, and as well continually active in the pastoral work, as through institutions and organizations of charitable action, insofar at any rate as they are not established in the domain of the religious

orders with a vow of poverty, are a mere second-best, a monetary substitute for truly Christian works of mercy; c) the idea arising out of a critical attitude towards the present, in itself anthropologically and ecclesiologically incorrect, that Church charity in former times and situations of need has achieved very much and indeed today too has obligations in countries whose populations lack the minimum necessary for subsistence, but that it has scarcely any justification in an industrially developed affluent society with a well-established system of social welfare, so that it would be more reasonable and more to the purpose for the Church to leave any remaining cases of need to the care of the State or the general charitable institutions, in which capable Catholics should be active; meanwhile the Church should devote itself to its more important and proper tasks: Mass and administration of the sacraments, preaching, care of souls and apostolic work.

3. *Essential nature of Christian charity.* As against this we must stress that the charitable activity of the Church must not be given up. This follows precisely from the way the emphasis falls in modern theology as a result of the present-day situation. The other chief functions of the Church — celebration of the liturgical mysteries, preaching the word of God, pastoral effort and eagerness for the apostolate will appear unconvincing if it does not also act as refuge for the afflicted, the abandoned and those in distress. The place and form of charity and the method of approach to people in suffering and distress change with the changing forms of society. The transition from a society of peasants and artisans to an industrial society puts charity in a different position, but basically it gives it a more important role: the sick, and especially the incurable and chronically ill need nursing and assistance. The handicapped and especially mental defectives need Christian care. Families with special needs should meet with an understanding that will help them to overcome their difficulties; the perplexed need counselling, youth in a difficult transition period need sympathetic direction; workers far from home, especially emigrants, need friendly interest and welfare arrangements adapted to their needs; addicts and those in danger of addiction must be helped out of danger; former prisoners need to be helped to rehabilitate, and their relatives who

often suffer much without being in any way guilty need relief; children, old people and those who by special circumstances are victims of isolation, loneliness, abandonment or those who are perhaps being badly treated need a renewal of their security. Hospitals, sanatoria, convalescent homes, kindergartens, creches, old people's homes with geriatric departments, advisory bureaus, places of work for those needing special conditions, clubs open to all, training places for difficult problem children and young people, residential institutions for physically and mentally defective children and young people, homes for defective adults, schools above all and institutes for training the many types of social welfare workers and educators (welfare workers, almoners, teachers for physical and mental defectives, children's nurses, kindergarten teachers, directors of youth clubs, nurses for the home whether in the city or in the country, nurses for the aged, general nurses, specialist nurses and ward sisters); finally centres and secretariats are to be established and maintained.

4. *Charity and welfare.* The relation of charity to welfare has been well described as follows: Just as the Church is the "sacramental sign of the world's salvation", so charity as the diaconal function of this Church is the sacramental sign of the sanctification of the social welfare system. Social welfare is a manifold expression of modern society's will to help. Never have there been so many helping hands and hearts, never has help been so well ordered and so firmly based on expert knowledge. This will to help is, consciously or unconsciously, the gospel in action and is valued and rewarded by Christ as service done to himself. Within this general will to help, the presence of the Church through the charity, of individual members or of the entire community, is indispensable. It radiates in this way the power of the words and the sacraments of Christ into the general will to help, sanctifying, strengthening, encouraging, providing a model and guide. Just as the Church takes the world seriously and regards its values as God's creation, so too it takes modern social welfare with its experience, its nature and possibilities seriously. The Church must as a consequence very conscientiously ensure that its help will be technically sound, irreproachable in its motives and attitude, a genuine assistance

corresponding to the true nature of man, so wonderfully created to the likeness of the triune God and still more wonderfully recreated.

5. *Direction and organization of charity.* In principle the direction and organization of charity in a diocese rests with the bishop who, together with the other serious tasks of his office, promises to attend with goodness and mercy to all poor people, strangers and those in need. The Middle Ages, from which this phrase comes down to us, understood by the poor those who had no property, the daily wage earners in the insecurity of their existence, and by the needy all those who could not help themselves: widows, orphans, the chronically ill, the delicate and sickly. The stranger, the person outside his own country and therefore without security was "wretchedness" personified. Just as the bishop in his diocese, so too the parish priest in his parish has an official duty of charity (*CIC*, can. 467). More independent, yet still pertaining with their charitable works and institutions to the charity of the Church, are religious orders, brotherhoods, secular institutes, as well as charitable institutions and professional welfare societies, when they work expressly in the spirit of Christian charity and are in practice approved by the hierarchy. The Spirit breathes where he will. The charismatic, no less than the official and organized, has a great significance, often insufficiently valued and exploited by the community.

6. *The ecclesia caritatis in history.* One of the things that points to the divine origin of the Church is the fact that it has always fulfilled the mission authoritatively entrusted to it by Christ, of bearing witness to his goodness and benevolence and his desire for our salvation. It has done this in a way that corresponds with its visible nature in the structures of the world and of every age, in the life of every country, every race and form of society. It has been always ready not to dwell in complete satisfaction on what had already been accomplished, but rather to move on the unknown territory, to the land that God is to show it. In the history of charity, every period stands expressly in line with all the effort that has gone before, but every period too relates immediately to God. In works of charity there is not only the admirable solidarity of those who work side

by side, but also successive solidarity where temporal has become eternal and the past remains forever present. The charitable activity of the apostolic Church, being the charity of the local community, was closely connected with the celebration of the Eucharist. For this work deacons were chosen and widows invited to help. It was embodied as the word of God into the sacred Scriptures, the reading of which has rightly been called "the eighth sacrament", and as a result it has continued to serve under the influence of grace as a unique source of strength and example. So too the well-organized collection of St. Paul whereby well-off communities helped those who were poor and, in the joy of giving, not only gave according to their means but beyond. Almshouses and hospices which were founded in the times of the earliest Fathers of the Church, especially in cathedral towns, and similar foundations of the monasteries in East and West, were taken in the *communio sanctorum* as models to be imitated and were so regarded by the saints. The first parochial systems of charity in Gaul in the 5th century encouraged similar developments elsewhere. A veritable *connubium* came into being in the cities of the Middle Ages between the charity of Church corporations and the temporal administration, showing us how manifold the forms of true co-operation can be, but reminding us too of the ever-lurking threat of secularism, whether politically or in the general approach and attitude.

7. *Developments in the 19th century.* Time and again, however, there arise in the Church, in answer to God's call, teachers and leaders. To mention but one, St. Vincent de Paul stands out "unequalled in any country", according to Wichern, himself a shining example of charity. Doubtless there were other influences, as for example the beginnings of philanthropic effort in Switzerland, the work of the diaconate in the Inner Mission of the German Lutheran Church, as well as the spontaneous rise of other groups devoted to charity. Yet in post-Napoleonic Germany as elsewhere in Europe where public relief for the poor had sunk to a shamefully low level and where the Church through the sequestration of its property saw itself robbed of the great works of charity, many of which had been carried on since the Middle Ages, it was the example

and direct influence of the movement stemming from St. Vincent de Paul that gave life and new impulse to the charitable work of the religious orders and charitable associations. This activity is naturally to be judged in the light of the limited capabilities of the rural and artisan way of life, not in terms of modern industrial conditions. The rise of great numbers of religious congregation of nuns, who devoted themselves with great self-sacrifice under the hardest conditions to the works of charity, was typical of 19th-century Church activity in this field. Among the more striking we may mention the service given by the Irish Sisters of Mercy in unspeakable conditions to the sick and wounded on the battlefield of the Crimean War. Lay associations too in great variety came into being in response to the growing proletarianization of large masses of the population in the wake of the Industrial Revolution. The founding in 1833 by Frederick Ozanam in Paris of the Conferences of St. Vincent de Paul and their rapid spread made it possible for the Church to meet the growing need in a way adapted to the new conditions. Through these developments it became possible for all groups in the Church, clerical, religious and lay, to participate in charitable activity in a way without which its present position in the sphere of social and charitable help would be unthinkable.

8. *Modern demands.* Changed social attitudes and the increasing ability to provide for the community led in a few decades from a system of Poor Law relief supplemented by private philanthropy to a system of statutory and voluntary welfare and social services, stemming from a widened sense of social responsibility on the part of the community towards the socially dependent groups. This culminated in social legislation on a broad scale especially since World War II, beginning with the "Beveridge Plan" in Britain, leading to a fully fledged universal system of social services, and in other countries to a variety of health and welfare services. In the U.S.A. there has been less tendency to rely on centralized federal aid and more reliance on individual, voluntary and State agencies to meet social welfare needs. In the U.S.A. too the tradition of organized Catholic charity has a long history. The initiative of the hierarchy, chiefly expressed through the National Catholic Welfare Conference, finds

a response in a great variety of organizations such as the National Conference of Catholic Charities. Yet whatever form the help of the neighbour in any country may take, once the principle of community responsibility has been generally accepted, State social services have been in a position to provide finance, equipment and trained personnel on a scale hitherto scarcely considered feasible. Insofar as the Church is engaged in similar work, it will be essential to ensure that hospitals, reform schools, orphanages, etc., under the care of Church organizations, are modernized, extended, and provided with qualified personnel and up-to-date equipment to meet the requirements of a modern social service system. Not everything is possible, but as far as may be the great needs of welfare services in such areas as care of spastics, mentally handicapped, drug and alcohol addicts, etc., must be met. Even in the age of extended State services there is a great, perhaps even an expanding place for the work of Church organizations and for co-operation by the Church with State and local authorities. A co-operative attitude is very helpful here and should stem from the realization that State and voluntary welfare services can often complement one another, providing a service to the community that is, in different ways, the responsibility of both. It is essential to carry on in a new way the great tradition of the Church.

Three factors are decisive here: first, the training and provision of a great number of social workers. This is a real vocation and must be fostered just as carefully as vocations to the priesthood or to religion. Secondly, there is need of a great number of voluntary helpers whose activity is a genuine charism given by God to the community to be recognized, fostered and developed. Finally, the provision of the necessary financial means; and here one must remember that the thousands of individual contributions, which number among them the mites of the poor, are to be reckoned of more value than a single large offering. The voluntary contributions ensure the independence and freedom the Church enjoys and make it clear that the financial contributions become part of the "sacramental cosmos" if only it is reflected on in this way and deeply believed in. *Collecta* signifies first the assembly of the faithful for the celebration of the Eucharist and the penitential procession, then the summary of the prayers of the faithful by the priest during the sacrifice of the Mass, as also the sum-total of all individual money offerings whereby money (for which Christ was betrayed) becomes now in a new form the symbol of the blood of Christ which should penetrate to where it can serve the poor. In this sense Pope Paul VI makes the earnest appeal: "It is absolutely necessary that the faithful make greater offerings than before for the poor. This demand is also an earnest appeal not to forget the spirit of poverty, mortification, fasting, restraint in personal claims, so as to help the brothers in need out of what is saved." The Pope expressly emphasized that it is the earnest wish of the Church to make every effort to inflame the faithful with a great love of their neighbour.

9. *Charity and pastoral care*. For this purpose it is essential to make use of parish groups and to work through parish organizations. Such a form of charity is marked especially by being of a personal nature. Here the personal and the institutional can work together in perfect harmony. Central to the parish charity is the notion of the *conference* as St. Vincent thought of it and as Frederick Ozanam renewed it and as it has been realized in innumerable parish groups. A conference worthy of the name will exemplify the need for unity in freedom as well as freedom in unity. In this connection the Pope has declared it to be very important that Christian parents should lead children at an early age with patience and in a practical way to help their fellowmen. Therefore they must ensure that the family become a source of charity. When as many of the faithful as possible belong to the parish group and express this by a subscription or by helping, this strengthens the resolution of all.

10. *International charity*. The Pope emphatically declared it to be absolutely essential that "the modern means of organization and other technical helps be put to increased use in charitable institutions so as to be able to meet quickly and effectively the great needs and distress of the modern world as soon as they arise" (address to the delegates of Caritas Internationalis). Montini himself contributed to the effective operation of Caritas Internationalis which has been active since 1924, largely through the initiative of Cuno

Jörger, Secretary General of the German Caritas Organization, and which has been centred in Rome since 1951. It includes today the national Caritas organizations in all continents and has also been able to found Caritas organizations in the missions and the developing countries. In Europe the German Caritas Organization and the organizations in Switzerland, Austria, Luxembourg, etc., which are along the same lines, form to some extent a contrast in organization and methods of work to the Secours Catholique in France. The former is organized federally and permanently, the latter centrally and is constantly engaged in new projects. The Italian Pontificia Opera di Assistenza is also centrally organized, partly because of the political structure of the country, the importance of Rome and the presence of the Pope. It arose as a result of the problems of distress following on World War II. The Caritas Catholica Belgica is the fruit of vigorous activity of the Belgian Catholics with considerable co-operation on the part of the laity. The Netherlands Caritas is organized in a way corresponding to their conditions:

The works of Christian charity are not only of primary importance, they are called for, as the Pope says, with an urgency that allows of no delay. Therefore he asks that we set to work with new vigour. "Caritas Christi urget nos" (2 Cor 5:14). The sufferings of the Church are great. Thus it is certain too, according to the words of St. Paul to the Philippians, that since it shares in the sufferings of Christ, there will come about an overflowing of love in the entire Church.

BIBLIOGRAPHY. L. Lallemand, *Histoire de la charité*, 5 vols. (1902–12); W. Liese, *Geschichte der Caritas* (1922); E. Reisch, ed., *An der Aufgabe gewachsen, zum 60jährigen Bestehen des deutschen Caritasverbandes, 1897–1957* (1957); Abbé Pierre, *Man is Your Brother* (1958); B. Ward, *The Rich Nations and the Poor Nations* (1962); M. Harrington, *The Other America* (1962); *International Yearbook of Catholic Charities*.

Erich Reisch

CHRISTIANITY

I. The Essence of Christianity

A. Preliminary Observations on Method

1. The question what Christianity "really" is in "essence", is not one which arises only when doubt is thrown on the unique character of Christianity, its absolute claim. Since the beginning of modern times the question has of course been raised in that way in ever more insistent and explicit terms. As a consequence, the question has been misconstrued. Contrary to the nature of a unique concrete historical personal event based on God's historical act of self-communication, the inquiry has been taken to concern a criterion which is applicable by the individual from "outside", and which would entitle him to distinguish between essentials and merely incidental historical accessories. In fact, however, the question was always present, and indeed belongs to the very nature of Christianity, because Christianity does not regard itself as something simply to be taken for granted. It has its historical development from one starting-point, only gradually reaches individuals, and it always solicits their individual, free and yet rational decision of faith. In doing this it has first to say what it is and why it demands faith. Its view of itself is, therefore, an intrinsic element of Christianity. The reality which is aware of itself in this way regards itself as not comprised within any pre-existing system of spiritual co-ordinates which would permit it adequately to be described and critically evaluated.

2. Nevertheless, according to the Catholic conception of faith, it is possible to speak of Christianity in two ways, both legitimate. The authentically Christian conception can be stated (i.e., the dogmatic teaching of the Roman Catholic Church about itself and about Christianity generally). And it is possible to say what, at least in principle, can be perceived of Christianity "from outside", i.e., by those who do not yet believe (but who are necessarily always placed in the light of the grace of potential belief). There is, therefore, a dogmatic account of the Church and one that belongs to fundamental theology (apologetics), and the latter includes

the relevant religious phenomenology and general historical and sociological considerations. In the Catholic view of the relations between faith and reason and of the rational possibility of recognizing the fact of revelation, such an account "from outside" need not necessarily fail to correspond to Christianity, even though the innermost nature of the latter can only be grasped in the light of faith from the message of faith itself and in the obedience of faith.

3. It is legitimate not simply to identify Christianity and the Catholic Church. This is shown by Catholic doctrine, which recognizes certain non-Catholics as Christians (*CIC*, can. 1325, § 2), regards grace and justification to be possible even outside actual membership of the Church (baptism of desire), teaches the validity of (correctly administered) sacraments outside the Church and acknowledges a sacred Scripture which in itself is the Word of God and does not only become the Word of God when actually (and rightly) preached. An account of Christianity need not, therefore, simply coincide with an account of the Church. Yet, theologically speaking, Christianity is not the sum of empirically observable Christians and their opinions. Even a correct external point of view in apologetics does not permit such a detached summary treatment of all as on an equal footing. The saving act of God in Christ which founded Christianity is present, with the full embodiment (in principle) which it implies, in the one Catholic Church. Consequently an account of Christianity must ultimately find its completion in an account of the one actual Church. And this of course will conceive the Church as constituting the sole salvation of all in such a way that the salvation of all who live outside the Church and yet by the Church, is regarded as possible.

4. A critical account of the actual realization of the nature of Christianity and of its history is, in the Catholic view, quite legitimate and indeed necessary, despite Christianity's claims to possess absolute character. But it is ultimately a function of the Church itself, not of a critic standing "outside" it. For Catholicism holds a rational justification of faith to be possible, in the sense of a demonstration of the credibility of revelation and the obligation to believe, in ways and within

limits which cannot be gone into further here. Ultimately it regards Christianity as a reality which integrates everything into itself, including therefore all intellectual activities. It therefore claims that the critical function belongs to its own nature, that is, the function of discriminating between the nature of what ought to be and what in fact externally is the case.

5. It is not to be expected that there is a formula, an abstract essential definition so expressive of the nature of Christianity that everything essential can be deduced from it in such a way that what cannot be so deduced is thereby to be eliminated as a mere historical accessory. For what is concrete and historical necessarily possesses intrinsic pre-eminence over human reflection about it in the philosophy of religion and in theology, and reflection can never entirely exhaust it. This applies to Christianity which was founded by God's saving action and rests on the real person of Jesus Christ and which conceives itself to be the total integration of all reality (God — salvation — world-history) into its own reality, though in various degrees.

6. An attempt at a relatively brief statement of the nature of Christianity is of some practical importance for the proclamation of the faith. Short syntheses of this kind are necessary for preaching Christianity to non-Christians and have always existed, starting with the Apostles' Creed, but those handed down by tradition are not of a kind to be easily assimilable in the intellectual and cultural situation of the present day. If an almost hazardous attempt is risked here to formulate a brief synthesis, it obviously can only have "Western" (European and American) civilization in mind. For other cultures a different standpoint would have to be chosen, because the rationalized technical one-world civilization has not yet produced such a unified concept of man for this to be yet capable of providing a possible universal basis, and a universal public, for a statement about the nature of Christianity.

B. History of Definitions of Christianity

1. There is such a history, of course, which coincides with the history of Christianity itself and its dogmatic theology (cf. A, 1), but it is only possible to speak of such a

history in a special sense since the beginning of "modern times", from the moment when as a result of the influence of Christianity itself on the history of ideas, man consciously directed his attention to himself in his radical subjectivity. Then Christianity ceased to be simply the sum-total of the religious environment as it in fact existed, with the demands it made. The question had to be raised of its one essential nature in relation to man's own subjectivity. This question, which was and could only be formulated explicitly and consciously in modern times, has probably not yet been sufficiently understood by orthodox Christianity and even less worked out. Catholic dogmatic theology does not raise the question. Yet there "must" be heresies (in the biblical sense of "must", in which in the actual history of salvation what ought not to be becomes, beyond men's plans, a positive means for realizing God's intentions). And heresies, which never draw their vitality from mere negation, may in fact contain in a more explicit way, and earlier, much that is Christian but which in Catholic Christianity remains latent, more unarticulated, less conscious. Moreover, to the extent that heresies derive from Christianity itself, they belong to its own "image". Consequently we have to include in the distinct new history constituted in this way those interpretations of Christianity with which that history chiefly began, and in which a comprehensive normative definition permitting a positive evaluation was attempted. This was done on a basis which on principle lay outside Christian faith (which is an unconditional readiness to hear the historical revelation of the Word), but there was no intention on that account to reject Christianity outright.

2. It is possible to speak of such a history, one which in fact was influenced by heresy, from the 18th century Enlightenment onwards, though signs of it appeared in post-Tridentine scholastic theology, particularly in the *analysis fidei* and cognate themes. The non-Christian criterion and starting-point, from which the nature of Christianity was to be determined and evaluated and by which its historical manifestation was to be subjected to critical discrimination, has since that time either been human nature (either as "universally valid" or as existentially unique), or the phenomenon of religion in general as such, and the latter can ultimately be reduced to the former starting-point. At first, then, all kinds of attempts were made to interpret the essence of Christianity as the perfect representative of "natural religion" or of religion as such. In this respect it is quite immaterial in principle that with the Enlightenment it was thought possible to trace the outlines of this natural religion by pure reason, independently of "truths of fact" and of any encounter with Christianity, as the universal element which, attained by reason, can then be found in all religions, even if in differing degrees of purity, whereas with the Romantic movement and German Idealism, it was detected in the historical phenomenon of Christianity itself. In this case the "mediation" imposed by Christianity on the individual is a mere historical contingency in relation to a universal nature (of man, of religion, of the relation to the Absolute), which with equal justification can make use of other intermediaries. Similarly, the "illustrative material" may from the start be the totality of religions presented by the history and psychology of religions, among which Christianity is inserted (W. Dilthey, E. Troeltsch, G. Mensching, etc.). Finally, it makes no difference in that respect whether on the basis of an autonomously ascertained "nature", the historical manifestation of Christianity in dogma and theology, in ecclesiastical and sociological form, is given positive evaluation as the unimportant though inevitable husk of what is really in question (something chiefly inward and individual), or whether the attempt is made to disentangle the "pure essence" from its previous concrete embodiments (as in Modernism). According to the way man himself and the nature of religion in general are understood (but always as ultimately independent of the historical factual contingency of a free act of revelation by God), the nature of Christianity is differently understood: as pious inwardness (Pietism), freedom of the moral conscience before God, contemplation of the "universe" (in a special sense of the religious act as "feeling" or as "intellectual intuition"), as a sentiment of absolute dependence, as the numinous value feeling for the holy, and so on. If the "nature" of man is posited as absolutely unique and incommensurable, ever in radical solitude, freedom and responsibility, then his religion can only consist in the obedient and therefore

liberating acceptance of that existence, and Christianity will have to be the "religion" in which, in contrast to the illusions of mythologically objectivating statements, man is summoned to have the courage to assume his existence in that way. And this initial position will again become the criterion, applicable only by the individual himself, of what is really meant by Christianity, that is to say, of what it must conceive itself to be. Once the ground of the authentic theology of revelation is abandoned in one of these ways, it is no longer of particular Christian or theological importance which fundamental philosophical views are preferred as the basis for the inquiry into the nature of Christianity. They may involve, for example, the question of what in principle is the relation of the universal and the historical, and whether a permanently valid, regulative essence of the kind postulated is possible at all, and whether it is knowable, or whether anything of that kind is to be denied from the start out of historicist and relativist scepticism. It may be urged that only a knowledge of historical phenomena can be admitted, the subjective conditions of which remain entirely closed to rational justification.

3. From a really Christian standpoint such analyses are questionable for two reasons. The first is that the really concrete religion, which is still universal because founded by God, can only be known and judged by itself. There is no external standpoint from which such a judgment is possible, though there is an access from outside which does not destroy the non-derivative character of faith. But in the second place it is possible that in such an attempt to interpret Christianity from outside, the interpreter may unwittingly and unintentionally, but in fact, be judging from a standpoint which is not really external to Christianity at all. The inner life of the person who is putting forward the interpretation and evaluation itself bears the stamp of grace, of the interior light of faith and of an unconsciously Christian conception of life. Consequently he may give objective expression to more of Christianity than the standpoint explicitly adopted would of itself permit. And Christianity's own understanding of itself may find in this apparently non-Christian interpretation of its nature more that is genuinely Christian than at first sight

might be expected in view of the objectively incorrect or inadequate starting-point.

C. Christianity in Relation to Other Religions

What are in question here are actual features observable from outside which make it possible to compare Christianity with other religions. The common elements which can be perceived in such a comparison only prove that Christianity can be the universal religion without losing its historical character. Precisely such a comparison, however, reveals decisive differences between Christianity and other religions, such as the successful synthesis of elements otherwise divergent, the actual convergence of tendencies of themselves historically independent into a genuine unity; a pure exemplification of the nature of religion in contrast to other religions which are always in fact in decay and which can never critically dissociate themselves on principle by an official authority from their inner decadence, though some noble individual representatives may seek reform. It is at least relatively the best actual concrete religion. This observation can be made by means of objective verifiable standards, partly *a priori,* partly derived from comparative religion and from the phenomenology of religion. Once made, it presents the possibility and the obligation of an absolute affirmation of Christianity, as soon as it is realized on the one hand that in the concrete it is only possible to live, religiously speaking, in absolute affirmation, and on the other hand that among all religions only Christianity has the courage seriously to make an absolute claim and not one that is simply justified by pointing to the universal element found in the particular religion in question.

1. Christianity regards itself as the universal religion of mankind. Not every religion and religious community does this, and therefore it is not to be taken as a matter of course. Although it spread from one particular point in history, and regards itself not as having always existed but as deriving its existence from that point, and although it has a pre-history which it acknowledges and appropriates, nevertheless it ascribed to itself from the start a universal mission. It does not

view itself as a relative, particular manifestation of religion, side by side with which other concrete forms of expression of religion are to be found, differing from region to region, culturally, ethnically or in some other mere matter of degree. It holds that it is the only valid relation of man to God, because founded by God himself for all. In contrast, other religions are to be regarded only as previous stages in sacred history, produced by God's action in historical revelation but now superseded. They were "precursors" or independent, human and of themselves empty adumbrations of the true religion, or apostasy from the possibility of that relation with God which God intends and offers by his saving action, or as effects as yet imperfectly developed, or already curtailed by men, of God's salvific will operative, because of Christ, in all men everywhere, and impelling towards tangible revelation. Christianity therefore regards absolutely every human being of whatever race and culture as called to receive its message, gifts and promises, as a "potential Christian", however much it is aware even apart from sin, the realization of this possibility demands time and conditions which are not equally present everywhere *(anima naturaliter christiana)*. Christianity has never even in fact (and to a Christian this appears providential) belonged to a single closed homogeneous civilization. It arose on the frontier between East and West, so that its roots penetrate directly into almost all the earlier higher civilizations. In the course of history it has in fact become a world religion, even more patently than all other religions, which have scarcely extended beyond the civilization of their origin. Eastern Buddhism is no parallel, partly because of the ethical atheism, and partly because of the radical difference of the religious forms in which it has appeared. Moreover, Christianity spread in the course of that European history which produced the modern planetary unification of the whole of mankind into a single history. But since that unifying force did not operate without Christianity, which in fact was actively at work through missionary enterprises and did not simply spread over the globe through the spread of Western civilization, Christianity alone among religions really did make itself a world religion in fact. It is universal in time and space.

2. Christianity is a higher religion. Though it traces its presuppositions and pre-history, even as divinely effected sacred history, to the very beginnings of mankind (as appears from its notion of primitive revelation, of the universal grace of Christ and from its Old Testament), and deliberately holds fast to what belongs to ancient tradition and to what is fundamental in humanity, it is nevertheless a higher religion which includes elements which are only possible on a higher level of civilization. It therefore comprises the entire intrinsic range of human possibilities as the material in which to embody the religious factor. Consequently in regard to the future also it has a universal perspective and is in no danger of being dismissed at some point as belonging to a superseded stage of civilization.

3. Christianity is a historical, revealed religion. It is of course true that it includes valid statements about God, the world and man which in themselves and in principle are attainable by reason at any point of history. Nevertheless Christianity conceives itself essentially as a historical, revealed religion. It shares this claim of course with Judaism and Islam, so that this aspect too belongs to its "external" phenomenology, but in such a way that the three claims are not simply juxtaposed without relation; it is therefore simply a question which of the three religions can rightly claim to possess the one revelation occurrence in its entirety and without adulteration. Christianity as a historically revealed religion means that the reality which it brings, the truth it proclaims, are in the world because at quite precisely located points of space and time the action of revelation by the living God distinct from the world occurred freely and grace-given in the prophets and in Christ. It occurred "within" the world, therefore, and not merely by means of it. It therefore demands a retrospective link between human beings who inevitably exist in history and not in the abstract, and those distinctive points, by means of Church and tradition, anamnesis and succession, so that men may fully accomplish their union with God. But this corresponds precisely to man's nature which in decisive matters has always to exist in a historical mode, for he will always have an ancestry. The claim of Christianity to be such a historical revealed religion is incom-

patible with a syncretist account of its origins, which in actual fact breaks down at least at the underivative immediacy of the person of Jesus and his claims. We have already pointed out the positive importance for fundamental theology of this claim to be God's historical revelation and moreover the absolute and eschatological one. Since this revelation occurrence as a factual event is not only the object of faith but also a reason for faith, which presents itself as credible to the mind of a person willing to believe, this is also a feature which belongs to the marks of Christianity which can be observed "from outside". But according to Catholic doctrine what is most central and ultimate in this revelation occurrence, despite its historical concentration in one point of space and time, can reach every human being in grace and faith, because of God's universal salvific will. Moreover, the actual concrete elements of Christianity in sacrament and word (when both are understood correctly in a Christian way) can and are intended to be the most direct and most actual encounter with God in the life of each individual. Consequently the historical character of revealed religion does not involve an anthropomorphic restriction of the God who really rules everywhere and in everything, for the very concreteness of this rule, penetrating by its universality every dimension of man, can, and wills to, comprise man's concrete historical nature. It would be an anthropomorphism to think of God as having exclusively one sole relation to a single potentiality of man (his abstract mind, his "inwardness", etc.) as "absolute", to the exclusion of others.

4. Christianity knows itself to be a dogmatic religion. Though the reality which Christianity brings is God's action in man, and transcends all definitive, exhaustive comprehension, for it is God's self-communication to what is not God, nevertheless precisely this incomprehensibility is expressed in words, and can be so stated, for all understanding of man himself is based precisely on his transcendent dynamic ordination towards the holy mystery of God. Since this statement takes place in human terms which already have a long history behind them, it is effected only in analogy, imperfectly, as a provisional stage towards the direct vision of God. For all that, it is absolute truth, because the statement is true and not false, its truth is guaranteed by the God who speaks, and it brings with it over and above the analogous conceptual statement the very reality which it signifies: the self-communication in grace of God forgiving and divinizing his creatures. And this truth has remained unchanged in the authentic Christianity of the Church despite and throughout historical change. This is itself a fact which is empirically verifiable and yet significant for the rational basis of faith. The development of dogma displays beyond human design and control an intrinsic pattern and a convergence of the various lines of development and trends which was not intended by men and manifests the operation of a transcendent power. Christianity therefore possesses a formulated doctrine as well as a teaching authority in the Church's hierarchical leaders and this distinguishes it from religions which do not aim at doing more than producing a numinous experience by means of their rites, and from religious and philosophical interpretations of human life (and from Christian sects), which in sceptical resignation falsely hold that the Absolute impinges on human existence and disposes over a human being's whole actual concrete reality when it is simply "honoured" in mute remoteness and awe of its ineffability. Views of that kind reduce the religion of man in his whole nature to an ethereal "otherworldliness".

5. The Christian religion views itself as eschatological, that is to say, Christianity takes history and man's historical character and its own with profound seriousness. Nevertheless it considers itself to be absolute. This involves three things:

a) Despite its own origin in history, it is not a phase of a process leading to the future history of religion within the world in the course of which it may be superseded by another religion. The legitimate future of religion is its own future, because it is the last, irreplaceable and definitive religion for this world-epoch, which is itself judged and limited. That is also so because in principle it has room within it for all genuine religious creativity and for the possible dispensation of grace by the one God outside Christianity. For it is only finding itself when, through adaptation, it integrates into its abiding nature the intellectual and religious experience of mankind.

b) It regards itself as provisional and

304

conditional, to the extent that, as the "pilgrim" Church, it is dynamically directed towards that end in which the revelation of the glory of God will definitively conclude time and history and therefore the Church as well.

c) Christianity inevitably reduces what surrounds it, i.e., the world, history, civilization and progress, to merely relative importance, for as a permanent "thorn in the flesh" to the world, it opposes any attribution of absolute value to any power of this passing world. It leaves all these things their real validity and does not merely tolerate them, for they all belong to the divinely created world, whereas Christianity is God's eternity in time and is therefore not called either absolutely to affirm the world or to negate it, but to "wait" and "hope" until God is manifest and the final yield of the transitory world is harvested. Precisely as eschatological, supernatural, revealed religion, Christianity leaves earthly realities their relative independence and is not of itself (unlike other religions) confronted with the dilemma either of administering and controlling everything or of abdicating even as a religion. The historical process of the progressive emancipation of an independent secular civilization is therefore in principle an effect of Christianity itself, not the beginning of its death, even though the realization of that independence often, but wrongly, took place at the expense of the enduring historical presence of Christianity in the world.

6. Christianity is integral (not integralist) religion. Produced by the Creator of all earthly realities, Christianity has a doctrine and a summons valid for all domains of human life, but does not on that account seek to deprive man of his own responsibility and historical nature in the perspectives which open out onto an unknown world future. It speaks equally to person and to society and with equal independence of each. Because Christianity is salvation for the individual before God in grace and personal decision, it can never be merely a cultural arrangement in the public life of society. Yet because God in his Word addresses himself to all in a historically tangible form, Christianity by the will of its founder is only wholly present in the one visible Church. This represents the full historical

and tangible reality of God's saving act in Christ for all ages and peoples. Constituted as a society, organized in offices and functions, it extends to all times and places in uninterrupted historical continuity, the Apostolic succession, the self-manifestation of God's saving action to men in its sacraments and doctrinal teaching. Comprehending all dimensions of man, Christianity is a rational religion, i.e., it can never wish to impose itself by excluding from its religious activity rational and critical self-reflection, in order to achieve immunity from such reflection (contrast fideism and modernism).

D. Dogmatic Self-Expression of Christianity "from Within"

With the proviso already made (A, 5), Christianity may be defined as the occurrence of God's free communication of himself to what is created and distinct (and in itself remote) from himself, revealing itself as such and effecting its own acceptance on the part of man. This occurrence has in Jesus Christ its ultimate ground, its highest realization and its unsurpassable historical manifestation. From the human side it may be regarded as the event in which man by faith in Christ accepts the sacred mystery, called God, as absolutely and intimately present and freely pardoning him, whereas humanly speaking that mystery entirely rules his existence as the remote ground and judge of being and spiritual consciousness.

1. In Christianity as a historical revealed religion, the infinite, personal, holy God acts in man and with man. He is utterly distinct from the world and from man as their Creator who posits what he freely creates from nothing as other than himself, in such a way that *a priori* and in every respect it is relative to and oriented towards him as the infinite mystery, but cannot determine purely by itself what its precise relation to God will be, but must remain open for God to dispose of it.

2. By grace God has freely admitted the world created by him, and in particular spiritual creatures, to a share in his own divine life. He is, therefore, not only the efficient cause of the world creating things other than himself, but freely, in grace, he communicates himself in his own being, and

so reveals and manifests his own glory and innermost life (in the Trinity of persons) as the grace-given goal of spiritual creatures, angels and men. As a consequence, the ultimate meaning and goal of man in the concrete is transferred to the infinite mystery both absolute in kind and at the same time radically close and intimate. Every earthly self-development of man and every such "evolution" is surpassed and at the same time opened out towards its infinite fulfilment. Because what is involved is a true communication of God to the world, it is plain that the structure of the relation of God to his created world based on this supernatural communication is God's inner reality itself. The unoriginated who communicates himself ("Father"), the uttered "Word", who enduringly possesses the plenitude of his source ("Son"), and the loving affirmation of the unity of originating source with uttered Word in the enduring presence of the divine plenitude in the term of the procession ("Holy Spirit") form the Trinity of Persons of the one God in himself.

3. God's free and grace-given orientation of man towards his own communication of himself, which everywhere and always determines man's nature and through him, the world (the supernatural existential), is the transcendental ground and the enduring dynamism of the individual and collective history of salvation and revelation. Just as the nature of man, although the ground permanently presupposed by history, finds its accomplishment *in* history itself (and the latter is not merely an incidental which leaves the nature itself untouched), and is given to man himself as a task *in* history, so too with the supernatural existential. That existential is never a datum for man apart from a historical concrete form (of a changing and growing kind), and these concrete forms — worship, human speech, miracles, etc. — constitute the sacred history of salvation and revelation only to the extent that they are accomplished and are understood expressly or implicitly in virtue of that *a priori* supernatural existential.

4. The history of the free acceptance or rejection by man of God's self-communication takes place in every human life which attains the exercise of its freedom. It is

per se possible at all times and in all the changing historical situations of man. Where that history of grace by God's will and attestation becomes a *datum* consciously known, with a tangible social form, an accredited, formulated doctrine and institutional embodiment, which themselves become factors in the situation of that general history of grace, we have the history of revelation and salvation in the narrower sense. These historical, objective expressions (in doctrine, worship, religious institutions) of the supernatural existential are found tacitly and implicitly throughout the individual and collective course of history (particularly in its moral aspect), and explicitly in all religions. But they are present inextricably combined with what is purely natural to man, with erroneous conceptions of man and with morally reprehensible behaviour. Everywhere and always, however, by virtue of God's universal salvific will, the historical situation of man is such that it can enable him to work out in faith his supernatural existential, providing he does not culpably shut himself to God's transcendental self-communication.

5. To distinguish and discern history of salvation from history of perdition, history of revelation from history of religious decadence, is ultimately only possible with Christ as criterion. In that perspective, the immediate and very brief pre-history which Jesus and the apostles recognized in the "Old Testament" as legitimately their own, acquires in a special degree the character of history of revelation and salvation. It was so objectively, because it was monotheism, which interpreted its own course as a history of salvation and perdition in living partnership with God, was oriented towards the coming of the historical manifestation of *universal* salvation in the Messiah and in fact did prepare the coming of the Word of God in the flesh. It can be evaluated with discernment by the help of the Christian Scriptures if these are read in the light of Christ.

6. a) God wills to be man's fulfilment directly himself, not merely through something created. His self-communication as offered is called grace; as accepted, justification; and the actual acceptance in the concrete, faith, hope, love. It exhibits man as *capax infiniti*, as absolutely open (both

ontologically and existentially), to the holy mystery which is the ground of all and itself incomprehensible and which we call God. That mystery is then in itself not only the aloof horizon and unfathomable ground of knowledge and freedom and their predicamental objects, but gives itself in its very self to the spiritual creatures.

b) This receptivity to God's own self-communication has its absolute culmination in what we call the hypostatic union, though this does not mean that we are able, even supposing the possibility of grace is known, to perceive with certainty for ourselves the possibility of this kind of divine self-giving previous to its actual occurrence. But at least it lies in the hypothetical "extension" of grace in its own line: as the actuation of the potentiality of a creature by a supervening act inserted in it, as the rendering possible of the possession of God and of the acceptance of God, by God himself as the quasi-formal principle of that very act itself. If grace is an interior, supernatural determinant of man's personal life, it provides an immanent principle for forming some idea of the Incarnation. This then appears from within, as it were, as the qualitatively unique culmination of God's self-communication. In it God's offer of himself, and its acceptance by man in virtue of this offer itself, absolutely coincide, are realized in the most radical way and at the same time are historically manifested. Consequently it is the culmination of God's communication of himself to the world, and the foundation of the whole of his self-communication and its historical manifestation, as the goal is the cause of the movement towards it.

c) Christianity acknowledges this unique perfection of divine self-communication to the creature to have occurred in Jesus Christ. It recognizes this, because man in grace is open to the expectation of that culmination, and is oriented towards it; because Jesus credibly testified to himself as exemplifying it, if by nothing else than by his awareness that he was the absolute, unsurpassable bringer of salvation, an awareness which implies that of the Incarnation; because he showed himself as the beginning of definitive salvation by the Resurrection; because in actual historical effect he met with such belief in his reality and mission that faith cannot justly be rejected as an illusion by someone who is judging on real historical grounds, i.e., who is not in the grip of a quite unhistorical rationalism.

d) This God-man by his existence, his human acceptance of it in the death of the Cross and by the divine and perfect acceptance of that acceptance (the Resurrection), is the guarantor, the ultimate purpose, the historical manifestation and the revelation, of God's salvific will in regard to the world, divinizing and forgiving; he is the mediator absolutely. When man recognizes Jesus (by explicit faith), or implicitly (by accepting in faith his own life from God's free disposition which in fact has its purpose in Christ), as the man whose existence is that of God living as man with us, and in whose life, fate, death and victory over death, God himself has shared our existence and so accepted it and given it validity, man knows that his own reality is revealed to him, interpreted and given ultimate validity.

7. The history of grace and salvation not only means the communication of God to the world and its spiritual creatures and the revelation of that communication, but an ever more radical experience of what its recipient is, not only the recipient of God's freely bestowed communication of himself (grace as supernatural gift), but one who by his own sin is positively unworthy of the gift. He is the sinner who himself produces alienation from God in condemnation, affirms it as definitive, and in this attitude wills death as the earthly manifestation of his sin. In the unconditionally radical quality of his salvific will, God in view of Christ has both permitted the mystery of sin as the creature's refusal, irretrievable by the creature itself, and at the same time encompassed it in his mercy in Christ and repaired it. Of himself man would be lost, if God — of himself without repentance, and absolute — in the sharing in the death of the sinner by the sinless Mediator obedient to the death of the Cross, did not offer his grace as forgiveness of guilt and in it the actual free acceptance of the offer.

8. Christ willed the foundation of a visible, socially organized embodiment of the fellowship of those who are redeemed in Christ and share in the divine life and who publicly profess themselves to be such. This is the Church. With an organic structure, led by its hierarchy, it is the definitive

307

eschatological manifestation of God's grace, "without repentance", and preserves Christ's truth in this infallible proclamation of the faith, transmits his grace efficaciously in visible and tangible form in the sacraments. It continues the worship of its founder in the sacrifice of the Mass, in which he is present in holy anamnesis, binding the Church into unity, with the power of his redemptive act and in the anticipation of the fulfilment. It rules its members through its precepts, instructions and the charismata bestowed by the Spirit along the way of salvation. The Church is the mystical body of Christ.

9. Christianity views every individual human being as a corporeal spirit of absolute dignity who, in intellectual knowledge and free choice, in his one life on earth within Christ's domain, makes an irrevocable decision for or against God (explicitly known as 'such or unnamed but implied), and so involves his salvation or final loss. The content of this action that constitutes his life is supplied and regulated by the three theological virtues of faith, hope and charity, which also include the fulfilment of the natural moral law and the positive commandments of God which are implied in the foundation of the Church, its authority and sacraments.

10. The Church and with it the world in its history, in individuals and as a unity, is on pilgrimage towards God's final revelation. In this, God's self-communication, which in a hidden way is the ground of the creation and of history, will be made manifest. God, no longer mediated by human signs that conceal him, will give himself to his creatures unveiled and face to face, and God, himself all in all, will have what is created and other than himself, spirit and world, in bliss with himself.

E. On the History of Christianity

1. *Principles*. a) As a historical revealed religion, Christianity is not only historical, but is aware of its own history and historical character. This knowledge belongs to its nature, in anamnesis directed towards its beginning and in expectation looking forward to its end, which is to be the complete revelation of the beginning, the second coming of Christ. It is therefore itself essentially a theology of history, possessing a theology of its own history and preserving in the history of the Church its own past as the permanently binding basis of its present.

b) As a consequence the fundamental aspects of its own historical view of itself are themselves data of revelation. The historical Word of God intrinsically includes the concrete perspectives which interpret the history of the hearing it obtains, and the provision of its own understanding is itself a historical process. The history of revelation known in this way, and Church history, are therefore not homogeneous portions of the universal history of religions, but a theological branch of study indispensable to the Church's actual understanding of itself. The Church is Christianity in its entirety, historically existing, on pilgrimage in faith, and presents a lasting and perpetually changing enigma in its own concrete form and that of its historical situation determined by the mutual relation of what ought to be (deriving from God), and what, through human guilt, is merely what "must" be. Precisely on account of this historical character and despite the fact, essential to its nature, that its gaze is turned towards the ultimate fulfilment, the Church in principle cannot derive any practical temporal prognosis regarding its future from its historical self-awareness. On the contrary, the interpretation, in faith and hope, of its situation at any moment in terms of God's victory (which cannot be deduced from the situation in question), is an essential feature of the Church and its historical situation, which the Church masters through its genuine faith that God alone is the master of history.

c) The following factors present fundamental aspects of the history of Christianity. That history is ultimately the history of the word of God, which creates for itself and for its own history, both in advance and subsequently, the appropriate environment in nature and world history; with the Christ-event the eschatological phase of this whole history has even now begun (cf. C, 5); in it God intervenes repeatedly as ever present and forgiving, despite what "must" be in human contradiction and failure, because the Church is both the invincible Church, even in its historical concrete form, because it is the sign of the victory of God's grace over man's obstinacy, as well as the Church of sinners, which cannot but involve miscalculation and failure. The Church is necessarily in distress. Where it is not, it is not as it should be. This is so because despite and transcending its sinfulness, it must always share in the life of the Logos, the life of Jesus, which the Church continues to live. The Church in its history as a whole clearly bears the mark, for any person who regards it with the free assent of the grace of faith, of its having been effected by God's saving action (*D* 1794). Nevertheless, within that history the individual and his action taken in themselves are ambiguous, and only the further history of the Church will reveal to some degree, and the "day of Christ" plainly, whether the individual was a positive factor in the whole history under God's guidance or a factor in man's resistance in spite of which God remains victorious. The relation of Christianity to its milieu (world, culture) is discussed in the article "Occident".

2. *Aspects and divisions of this history.* There can, of course, be no question here of presenting this history itself; at most a few indications of its content can be given and a division into phases for which some theological basis can be provided.

a) This history is a history of what is "subjective" and enduring. Christianity is not merely a phenomenon belonging to external history and civilization, so that a description of the development and structure of its spatio-temporal and factual objective expressions would itself be a statement about Christianity itself. Christianity by its very nature is the interior life of the human being endowed with grace from God with God as his end, though indeed this interior life provides for the believer, in its manifestations, an unambiguous motive for faith, and hence for theological Church history. For that reason the history of dogma, for example, belongs to this history, for it is the history of faith interpreted in faith, and is therefore a summons and a binding criterion of life in faith. The same is true of the lives of the saints, of the history of charismata and miracles in the Church. This is the appropriate place for the "history of souls", of the complete redemption of Christian persons, each of them unique, to the extent that such history is possible by reason of the faith of the Church (in canonizations); it is the perpetual story of conversion, martyrdom, the evangelical counsels, of service to the

poor, perseverance in resisting the idolatry of the world, and so on. That history takes precedence of the other kind which can describe on a natural basis the development of the social organization and cultural achievements of the Church, its relation to the State, to civilization and to the community of nations. Though accounts of sources and history of development are of no avail in the former, the more important kind of history, the perpetually renewed contemplation in every age of the fact that God was present, is in the most eminent Christian sense historiography, for the apparently identical in this case is a free historical act of the God whose gifts are without repentance for the Church.

b) Christianity as the historical and yet universal religion of all nations is only fully itself when it is in actual fact the universal Church, i.e., when it has a tangible and historical reality among all nations and civilizations. Because it starts from a point located historically in time and space, the entire first phase of the achievement of this world-wide mode forms its first great period. The second period, the concrete form of which is not yet clear, that of global Christianity in a globally united (not necessarily peacefully reconciled) history of humanity, is only now beginning. The first period is usually and rightly taken (even from the theological point of view) as falling into the following phases: i) the foundation of the Church (age of the generation of the apostles; the primitive Church); ii) the assimilation of the cultural and political environment of that Church, an environment which also constituted the pre-history of the future West (i.e., the Church in the world of Greco-Roman civilization in its first hostile encounter — until Constantine — and then in positive relationship with the Empire, the Constantinian era); iii) preparation of a world-wide mission by the Church through the formation of the West as the cause of the one unified history of mankind as it has now become (Church of the Middle Ages); iv) transition from what was in fact the regional Church of the West to the world-wide Church (from the beginning of "modern times" down to the present day).

This assimilation (by content and by regions) of the surrounding world in which and for which the Church has to develop its own proper mission is, however, also a period of growing detachment in which Christianity becomes more and more conscious of its "ontological difference" from its environment, though of course it always knew of it. Ultimately it is Christianity which separates itself in order to be able genuinely to take its environment for granted as fully developed; it is not really forced out of the world by the latter's growth. In this reverse movement, perhaps two great phases can be distinguished, first the Church of the Empire which, viewed theologically, extends from Constantine at least to the Investiture Dispute, a period in which the Church, viewed from outside, though remaining an independent entity, lived as it were in the bosom of political society, and second, the phase of polar opposition between a consciously Christian *imperium* and a *sacerdotium* which, relative to the narrow field involved, was very strongly committed in the secular sphere. This phase ended to all extents and purposes with the French Revolution, but its influence has still been operative down to the present day both in the Catholic Church and among Protestants. It is not easy to say what the new period whose arrival we can foresee will look like. The whole of this first period falls from another point of view into two phases. In both it is again a question of the achievement of full consciouness of the nature of Christianity in the immanence of subjectivity (cf. B, 1, 2). There was first the phase of conceptual development and articulation of the faith in its objective reality (patristic and medieval theology and piety); and second the phase of subjective reflection since the beginning of modern times, the Renaissance and classical humanism and the Reformation (separate rational apologetics; formation of a critical historical self-awareness in biblical criticism and history of dogma; *analysis fidei;* discovery of what is Christian outside Christianity as a social organization; inquiry into the essence of Christianity, etc.). This second phase seems still to have unaccomplished tasks ahead. As the rhythm of history cannot be synchronic in all its dimensions, the variety of these divisions is not surprising. They can, however, be co-ordinated without difficulty. This beginning of the history of Christianity (which came on the scene quite late, at the end of an almost inconceivably long and almost static history of mankind, perhaps extending over a million years),

must nevertheless be the attainment of full self-awareness of the history of salvation of mankind as a whole, for this also belongs to the nature of what is both a historical and yet the universal religion. Consequently the pre-history of Christianity must comprise all history back to its very origins, even if this for technical reasons is omitted in practice in the writing of Church history. Since the history of Christianity is the history of the dialogue between God and man, it has its own centre and real beginning (as opposed to its pre-history) in the absolute and enduring intimacy of the dialogue between God and humanity in Jesus Christ, in whom word and answer of that dialogue are one person. On the other hand, since the dialogue takes place, as human dialogue, by affirmation and denial, it always involves the other partner outside (mankind called by God) and the refusal and failure within (Christians themselves). In this connection it is to be noted that the Church's own genuine theological and historical conception of itself as the society which must understand itself on the basis of the promised future, must be formed on the basis of that future. Theological Church history must look into the future in order to be able correctly to perceive the past. Otherwise it inevitably becomes simply a part of the general history of the world and of religions.

See also *History* I, *Existence* III, *Occident, Church, Church and World, Church and State, Church History.*

BIBLIOGRAPHY. A. von Harnack, *What is Christianity?* (1901); E. Troeltsch, "Was heisst 'Wesen des Christentums'?", *Gesammelte Schriften,* II (1913), pp. 386–451; F. Schleiermacher, *The Christian Faith* (1928); L. de Grandmaison, *Jesus Christ. His Person, His Message, His Credentials,* 3 vols. (1930–35); E. Brunner, *The Word and the World* (1931); K. Barth, *Theological Existence Today* (1933); N. Söderblom, *The Living God. Basal Forms of Personal Religion* (1933); K. Adam, *The Spirit of Catholicism* (rev. ed., 1934); R. Bultmann, *Jesus and the Word* (1935); K. Heim, *Spirit and Truth. The Nature of Evangelical Christianity* (1935); K. S. Latourette, *A Study of the Expansion of Christianism,* 7 vols. (1937–45); R. Guardini, *Das Wesen des Christentums* (1938); R. Otto, *The Kingdom of God and the Son of Man* (1938); S. A. Kierkegaard, *Training in Christianity* (1941); E. Rosenstock-Huessy, *The Christian Future or the Modern Mind Outrun* (1946); H. de Lubac, *Catholicism. A Study of Dogma in Relation to the Corporate Destiny of Mankind* (1950); R. Guardini, *Faith and Modern Man* (1952); J. Mouroux,

The Christian Experience. An Introduction to a Theology (1955); P. Tillich, *Biblical Religion and the Search for Ultimate Reality* (1955); R. Bultmann, *Primitive Christianity in its Contemporary Setting* (1956); K. Löwith, *Meaning in History. The Theological Implications of the Philosophy of History* (1957); A. J. Toynbee, *Christianity among the Religions of the World* (1957); H. U. von Balthasar, *Science, Religion and Christianity* (1958); F. Gogarten, *Reality of Faith* (1959); T. Ohm, *Asia Looks at Western Christianity* (1959); G. Bornkamm, *Jesus of Nazareth* (1960); H. de Lubac, *The Discovery of God* (1960); H. Bouillard, *Blondel et le christianisme* (1961); G. Ebeling, *The Nature of Faith* (1961; new ed., 1966); M. Schmaus, *The Essence of Christianity* (1962); M. Dibelius, *Jesus* (1963); K. Rahner, *Christian Commitment* (1963); O. Karrer, *The Kingdom of God Today* (1964); H. Lilje, *Atheism, Humanism, and Christianity* (1964); H. Gollwitzer, *Existence of God as Confessed by Faith* (1965); H. de Lubac, *The Supernatural* (1967).

Karl Rahner

II. Absoluteness of Christianity

A. Notion and Problem

The notion of the absoluteness of Christianity derives from the philosophy of German Idealism, not from theology itself. From the outset, therefore, theology must beware lest an inappropriate attitude should be thrust upon it from without. Christianity is based on a historical revelation and therefore implies history and historicity, which cannot simply be disposed of by speculating about the Absolute. On the other hand the attempt of Ernst Troeltsch to establish the absolute character of Christianity by proofs drawn from comparative religion was doomed from the start. All that could be shown in such a way was that the world's religions converge to some extent upon Christianity; and that approach, by reducing Christianity to the level of historical phenomena — that is, to the relative — necessarily emptied Christianity's absolute claim of all real content. Dialectical theology (Karl Barth), therefore, chose a third approach. God in his otherness was so remote from history that Christianity, far from fulfilling human religion and culture, judged and abrogated both.

Catholic theologians as a rule take the absoluteness of Christianity to mean that Christianity is not only *de facto* the noblest of all living religions but is God's one ultimate self-disclosure, completely valid for all men in whatever age they may be living, essentially definitive, never to be superseded. A great many modern people consider this claim not only insufferably offensive but inconsistent with the known facts of comparative religion as well as with the fundamental historicity of all things human. It strikes them as unloving and intolerant, as a rupture of communication and a source of fanaticism. Moreover, it seems plainly contradicted by the sinfulness of Christian history. Finally, it seems to belittle all human efforts at progress and to make any theology of earthly things impossible. A purely apologetical or dogmatic response to these objections serves little purpose; what we must do is to consider with more care than before what we really mean, and then point out that the absolute claim is not advanced on behalf of a particular religious body but on behalf of the gospel of grace; its necessity for all men is what we affirm.

B. Theological Argument

If we are to see clearly in this matter we must remember that the absolute claim of Christianity is a strictly theological proposition, which consequently cannot be established by evidence drawn from either comparative religion or the philosophy of religion. Neither, of course, can faith simply contradict facts that have been verified by human reason. Instead, faith recognizes such facts, but interprets them anew in its own light.

What the absolute claim of Christianity means in theological terms is that Christianity is an eschatological religion. The kerygma of Scripture declares as much when it says that with Christ's coming the fullness of time has come (Mk 1:15; Gal 4:4; Eph 1:16, and *passim*); Christianity must be something absolute, because we believe that Jesus is the Χριστός (Messiah), the Lord, the Son of God, the only Mediator between God and men (1 Tim 2:5). He fulfils the promises of salvation made to the people of the Old Covenant and to all mankind (Gen 3:15; 8:21f.; 9:1ff.; 12:3; 2 Cor 1:19f.). By hypostatically assuming a concrete human nature, God has uttered himself, and communicated himself to his creation, once for all in a way that can never be superseded, and this act of God's is also the one supreme and incalculable fulfilment of man. For it is not a neutral openness that fulfils our nature but only free adherence to the absolute mystery of human existence. Thus the event

311

of Christ and faith in him, far from doing violence to man, perfect him at every level.

The absolute character of Christianity means an absolute acceptance and affirmation of man and the world because in Christ God has absolutely and irrevocably assumed a concrete human nature, yet in such a way as to preserve its native character intact and unalloyed (*D* 302). The absoluteness of Christianity is less a claim than the "good news" that the world is not ultimately hollow and worthless, or absurd and insane, because God has accepted it, because he cherishes it with the absolute love of which only God is capable (Jn 3:16).

C. Evolution of the Claim

If we consider the eschatological character of Christianity, we shall find that it offers six insights into our problem:

1. Fullness and fulfilment, in theology, are dialectical notions. On the one hand fulfilment realizes and seals a promise. In this sense Christianity is less an exclusive than an inclusive religion; instead of repudiating other religions and other efforts to discover truth it embraces them, and therefore its very nature disposes it to dialogue with the religions of the world and with philosophy. On the other hand Christ the fulfilment of the law is also its end (Rom 10:4); he fulfils the law by annulling it (Eph 2:15; Col 2:14); because fulfilment here is the wonderful doing of God, it is something creatively and incalculably new. Thus Christianity must always seem a paradox in this world; it can never renounce its character of "scandal". It must both affirm and negate, fulfil the religions and culture of mankind and sit in judgment on them.

2. In the biblical view, the fullness of time comes about in the concrete where the proclamation of it summons it forth, makes it present and bestows it. Word and sacrament make the unique event an event for all times. Only when a concrete individual, or religion, or culture, hears Christianity preached — which is essentially more than an audible phenomenon —, when the absolute claim is perceived as such and not misunderstood (as colonialism, for example, or cultural imperialism, or camouflage for

vested interests, or as a historical curiosity), only then will the fullness of time have come upon that man, or religion, or culture. Accordingly it is clear that in fact a great many people even today are still living in a pre-Christian era.

3. Eschatological fulfilment hovers between what has already happened and what is yet to come. Our present situation as Christians is governed by a conflict between saving history and secular history, the Church and the world, nature and grace, creation and the covenant, the law and the gospel. Only at the end will "God be everything to everyone" (1 Cor 15:28). The absolute claim of Christianity, therefore, is not a claim advanced on behalf of Christendom and the Church. The Church too has its eschatological judgment to undergo (Mt 19:28). A certain *intégrisme* that would do away with this dualism, in effect denying the relative autonomy of the world and its structures, clashes with this situation of the Church in history, where it can never be *ecclesia gloriae*. Error, indeed, has not the same objective rights as truth; but given the continuance in history of this aeon, the time of error persists until the eschatological harvest (Mt 13:30). Thus Christianity's absolute claim, rightly understood, is not only quite consistent with freedom of conscience and religion but forbids the use of any kind of coercion in the service of the gospel.

4. For our sake Jesus Christ assumed our concrete human nature — subject as it is to the consequences of sin — even unto death on the cross, thus redeeming it once for all. Christ's vicarious obedience drew together in his person the unique and the universal. Being a Christian is imitating this representative obedience, sharing in it. What really shows the absolute character of Christianity, then, is this representation in faith, hope, and love that unites the particular with the universal. The Church's mission, which is rooted in the absolute claim of Christianity, is not so much to save the individual — who in principle can be saved outside its visible communion — as to represent and proclaim the love of God, to give testimony to hope, and so to be a sign among the nations (*D* 3014). What Christianity affirms, with its absolute claim, is not its dominion but its vicarious service of all mankind.

5. The eschatological character and absolute claim of Christianity, however, do not make genuine historicity impossible for the Church; quite the contrary. As has been observed, if Christianity is something absolute, the Church is not. Like the individual Christian, the Church too must grow until it attains the full measure of Christ (Eph 4:13; Col 2:2). For the Church as it actually exists, the fullness of Christ is always both a gift and a goal. It has yet to be guided by the Spirit of Christ to all truth (Jn 14:26; 16:13). The gospel is not perfectible, but the Church's love and its understanding of the faith are. That is why a genuine development of theology and of dogma can exist. The historicity of the Church is also evident from the fact that in this aeon its grasp of faith and dogma always remains "imperfect" (1 Cor 13:9) and that it always remains a sinful Church on pilgrimage.

6. For the same reasons Christianity as an eschatological and absolute religion does not deny but rather affirms the theological significance of human progress. True though it be that the last day is known to the Father alone (Mk 13:32), we need not think of it as bursting upon us like a *deus ex machina*. God's revelation is always uttered in human language and through human organs. Consequently, it is theologically possible to suppose that just as the whole Graeco-Roman culture of Christ's day (what Karl Jaspers calls the pivotal period) was a *praeparatio evangelica,* so the powerful modern trend towards the amalgamation of mankind in the fields of technology, economics, and science may be paving the way, under God, for a response of all the human race to the increasingly actual universality of the Christian religion which technical advances will have made possible. Not that we are preaching a foolish optimism and naively assume all secular progress to be the equivalent of religious progress. Secular progress, we must realize, makes it possible for mankind to react to the gospel either with a collective Yes or a collective No. When we say, then, that Christianity is an absolute religion, we mean that grace has been absolutely promised to all, and that it demands of all an absolute decision.

See also *Idealism, Eschatology, Tolerance, History* I.

BIBLIOGRAPHY. E. Troeltsch, *Die Absolutheit des Christentums und die Religionsgeschichte* (1902); H. de Lubac, *Aspects of Buddhism* (1954); J. Daniélou, *Holy Pagans of the Old Testament* (1957); A. C. Bouquet, *Christian Faith and Non-Christian Religions* (1958); R. C. Zaehner, *At Sundry Times* (1958); J. A. Cuttat, *Encounter of Religions* (1960); S. Neill, *Christian Faith and Other Faiths* (1961); J. Daniélou, *Salvation of the Nations* (1962); H. Kraemer, *Why Christianity of all Religions* (1962); G. F. Vicedom, *Challenge of the World Religions* (1963); K. Rahner, "Christianity and the Non-Christian Religions", *Theological Investigations,* V (1966), pp. 115–34; H. R. Schlette, *Towards a Theology of Religions,* Quaestiones Disputatae 14 (1966).

Walter Kasper

CHURCH

I. History of Ecclesiology: A. From the Fathers to the Middle Ages. B. The Formation of the Treatise on the Church. C. Theological Progress. II. Ecclesiology: A. The Teaching of the Church. B. The Place of Ecclesiology. C. The Theology of the Church. D. The Catholic Church and the Other Communions. E. The Church and the Mission. F. The Church and the World. G. The Deficiencies of the Church and Reform. H. Outside the Church No Salvation. III. Constitution of the Church. IV. Universality of the Church. V. Membership

I. History of Ecclesiology

The treatise on the Church appeared late in the history of Christian thought. It began towards the end of the Middle Ages and reached its culmination at Vatican II. In this development of ecclesiological thought we can distinguish three phases which are essentially interrelated: (i) the Fathers and the theologians of the Middle Ages, (ii) the formation of the treatise on the Church, (iii) contemporary theological progress.

A. FROM THE FATHERS TO THE MIDDLE AGES

The Fathers and the theologians of the Middle Ages never composed a treatise on the Church. This is a consequence of the nature of both revelation and of dogmatic development. Prior to its appearance as a subject of teaching, the reality of the Church is presupposed in the proclamation of the gospel and cannot be separated from the whole dogmatic structure of which it forms the existential foundation. Because of this, the experience of the Church regenerated by the Spirit (given as a gift of the Father by the risen Son) conditions the whole of Christian reflection. The Church is built upon the "foundation of the apostles and prophets" (with a special role for Peter) and gathers together in Christ all his disciples. It must be understood in the light of the whole of revelation, and especially of the life and work of Christ which are once more called to mind by the Holy Spirit who makes of the community of believers the dwelling-place of a completely new existence and the sign of the accomplishment of God's plan for the world.

As early as the time of the Apologists, the Church was presented to the world as the proclamation and the presence of the salvation brought by Jesus Christ. In it the new life in the Spirit is imparted, and the apostolic faith is preserved in its memory. As the effective sign of the resurrection of Christ, the Church sees its relationship with God as the principle of salvation through the sending of his Son and as the goal of salvation through the gift of the Spirit. Its position in relation to the Jews and pagans was clarified by its proclamation that in the Spirit it had the power of interpreting the Scriptures in a Christological sense and could communicate the Spirit to all men. The whole of Catholic dogma takes its rise from reflection on the salvation communicated by the Spirit in the Church. To defend its own mystery the Church explicitated its faith: ecclesiology is thus a presupposition of formal Christology and the theology of the Trinity. Starting from the experience of the Church's life, patristic theology paid close attention to the history of salvation as based on the dynamic presence of the Word through the signs of his humanity, and recognized the movement of the economy of salvation which proceeds from the Father through Christ to the Church. The Church sprang from the preaching of the Word, which is achieved in the sacraments, especially the Eucharist and, as the primordial Sacrament of *divinisatio*, was seen as fellowship of those called to Wisdom in the Spirit whilst awaiting the manifestation of glory. The Church came into view, like the Incarnation and Pentecost, as the unfolding of the paschal mystery. It was seen to be constituted by the sacraments (points of contact with the death and resurrection of Christ and conductors of the power of the Spirit), and because of this it empowered the human race to pass from its fragmentary

existence into the unity of Jesus Christ in God. Since it was the human race itself insofar as it must eventually come to Christ and be vivified by his Spirit, the Church was no stranger to the life of the world. It is the human race existing in Christ and already saved in hope.

For the Fathers the whole of Scripture spoke of Christ and the Church: they saw it through the imagery of the Bible (people, body, temple, house, spouse, flock, vineyard, kingdom, field, and net) and the typological interpretation of the OT. Because they were conscious of the eternal and eschatological reality of salvation already present and active in the local Churches, the Fathers insisted upon: a) the Holy Spirit and the Eucharist; b) the spiritual maternity of the whole Church through faith, love, prayer, penance and witness; c) charity, peace and concord between the local churches; d) the collegiality of the episcopate; e) the Pope as the guardian of the charity of the universal Church. Several important ecclesiological ideas emerge: apostolicity and the apostolic succession (Irenaeus); the episcopate (Cyprian); catholicity, the validity of sacramental acts independently of the personal holiness of the minister, the sacramental character (Augustine), etc. And again as early as the 3rd to the 5th centuries the Popes asserted their role as bishop of the Church and their prerogatives of magisterium and jurisdiction (cf. Leo the Great, d. 461).

The theologians of the Middle Ages remained faithful to the vision of the Fathers which was centred on the history of salvation and the Eucharist. St. Thomas treats of the Church within the mystery of Christ. The Church is participation in the mystery of the Trinity, bringing about in us the image of God through the Incarnation and the Resurrection, in the Spirit. Using the theory of the instrumental causality of the humanity of Christ, St. Thomas developed a theology of Christ as Head and of the Church as Body of Christ. In this way ecclesiology was always envisaged in a theological and christological perspective against the background of Easter and the eschaton. Though the primary conception of the Church in the minds of the theologians of the Middle Ages was that of a spiritual society of communion with God in Christ, vivified by the Spirit, a *congregatio fidelium,* they did not ignore the visible institution, the actual shape taken by this spiritual society, its sacrament and its ministry. But various indications, such as the formation of the treatises on the sacraments and the priesthood show that the need was felt for a more exact analysis of the channels of grace. This whole patristic and theological conception signified for ecclesiology the primacy of the Spirit and of the ontology of grace. The Church proceeds from the eternal plan of the Father, from the mission of the Son and of the Holy Spirit and is meant for the whole of the human race.

B. The Formation of the Treatise on the Church

Because the Church was for them salvation itself and because the universal Church appeared to them as a communion of local Churches, the Fathers placed comparatively little emphasis on its structure as a universal body. This was certainly not ignored: the Second Council of Nicaea (787) declared that an ecumenical council could not be assembled without the consent of the Pope and evidence from the East leaves no doubt as to the impossibility of legislating in ecclesiastical matters without the agreement of the Pope.

But the Gregorian reform, which was bound up with the critical struggle for freedom between the Church and the world, and also with the breach with the East, brought out the fact that the universal Church is divinely endowed with a supreme ecumenical authority. The Church depends immediately not only on charity, but on the authority and sacred power of the Church of Rome. It is united to the successors of St. Peter and its first rule is to be "unius sententiae cum Apostolico" (John VIII to his legates — *Mansi*, XVII, p. 469). The Church of Rome represents in a way the whole Church. It is the *ecclesia universalis, ecclesia mater, fons, origo, cardo, fundamentum,* and the Pope is the *vicarius Christi*. Here we have dogmatic teaching on the constitution of the Church as a society under the monarchical rule of the successor of Peter and founded on the *soliditas* of the *princeps apostolorum*. The first treatises on the Church, which were entitled *De Ecclesia Catholica Romana, De Primatu Romanae Ecclesiae,* bear witness to this.

Favoured by the canon law which was worked out to serve the papal authority and so promote the liberation of the Church from lay control and its independence in regard to the secular power, even that of the Emperor, there emerged, at least in germ, the conception of the Church as a *societas perfecta:* this meant that the unity of the Church was now conceived as being like that of a city or a kingdom, and in this way juridical and sociological categories were introduced into ecclesiological thought. Its main principles having originated in the ideas which dominated the Gregorian reform, the treatise on the Church gradually took shape under the pressure of two series of events which directly affected one another: a) the struggle between the Church and the political powers (starting with Philip the Fair and reaching its climax in the 19th and 20th centuries) forcing the Church to define itself as a free agent; b) the critical questionings of the whole charter of the Church and of the way in which man is related to God. The spiritualistic and dualistic heresies of the 12th century, those of the Waldenses, the Albigenses and the Poor Men of Lyons attacked the Church for its worldly interests and political power, and questioned the mediation of the Church in the most radical fashion. (The theme of the Pope as Antichrist dates from the 12th century; the rejection of the hierarchical priesthood by the Waldenses was given its most extreme form at the Reformation and then later in rationalism.)

In his *Adversus Catharos et Valdenses,* Moneta of Cremona was the first to show the impossibility of discussing the Church while abstracting from the concrete forms of its existence on this earth. The study of the actual economy of divine grace was the beginning of a development which with Canisius and Bellarmine was to lead to the inclusion in the definition of the Church of its Roman character. The treatises on the sacraments and the priesthood had already taken shape by the 12th century, but it was the rise of Gallicanism (the struggle between Philip the Fair and Boniface VIII, and then between John XXII and the protégés of Philip the Bavarian) which led to the writing of the first treatises on the Church, which were really treatises about the *potestas papalis,* the authority and rights of the Church: the *De Regimine Christiano* of James of Viterbo (1301–1302), called "the oldest treatise on the Church"; the *De Ecclesiastica Potestate* of Giles of Rome; the *De Potestate*

Regia et Papali of John of Paris and finally the *De Potestate Papae* directed against the claims of the lower clergy.

The denial of the absolute character of the ecclesiastical and social fabric of Christianity by the extreme spiritualistic teaching of Huss and Wycliffe, based on a distorted interpretation of the Augustinian themes of the *ecclesia praedestinatorum, electorum* or *sanctorum* and of grace, attenuated the necessity of belonging to the visible and historical body of the Church and showed the need for a better analysis of what ecclesiastical life meant for membership of the Body of Christ. The development of conciliarist ideas, interpreting the definition of the Church as a *congregatio fidelium* from the viewpoint of individualistic and representative theories about the Church, prompted John of Turrecramata (*Summa de Ecclesia,* 1436) and John of Ragusa to compose their great works. These were the first *systematic* treatises on the Church, with a pronounced emphasis on the notions of kingdom and power. The year 1440 was a sort of solstice (M. Ourliac), a turning point in the history of ecclesiological thought.

The Reformers questioned the whole system of ecclesial mediation (the primacy of the Pope, the powers of bishops and priests, the authority of tradition, the magisterium, the priesthood and the sacraments). This led theologians to concentrate in the definition of the Church on its juridical and visible reality and to give less prominence to the reality of grace. With Bellarmine the juridical power of the Pope enters into the definition of the Church, as does the magisterium into that of tradition. But there is no longer any mention of the relation of the Eucharist to the Church. Jansenism led to a further accentuation of the power and rights of the Roman Pontiff; Febronianism and secularism necessitated the development of the idea of the Church as a perfect society fully equipped with rights and resources, with a hierarchy and powers of jurisdiction, legislation and administration. Liberal Protestantism and Modernism obliged the theologians to insist on Christ's foundation of a visible "society", hierarchically organized and juridically instituted.

Of the notion of the mystical body there remained above all the external and socially organized aspect of the Church. Compared with the patristic and medieval tradition this was a theologically impoverished treatise, for *De Ecclesia* had become for all practical purposes an appendix to the commentary on the *Summa Theologica,* II, IIae, q. 1, a. 10, that is, to the question of the magisterium. The pneumatological aspects, the life of the faithful, the Eucharist and the communion between the local Churches were passed over practically in silence.

C. Theological Progress

In the 19th century, after the upheavals of the 18th century and the French Revolution, along with a movement for renewal which was centred on authority and which was to lead to the First Vatican Council, there developed a movement for the restoration of ecclesiology through a return to the patristic and medieval sources. It originated with the Tübingen school (Sailer, Drey, Möhler, Kuhn) which brought out once again the notion of the Body of Christ animated by the Spirit, in the perspective of a "kingdom of God" theology. The Church was not primarily a visible and hierarchical society endowed with a magisterium, but an organic fellowship with Christ. In spite of the influence of Romanticism, their ideas of "the people" and "organic life", the Church in all its fullness, became once more the object of theology. Through the efforts of Passaglia, who was much influenced by these ideas, and of his disciples, Franzelin and Schrader, the theology of the mystical body found new vigour. It was introduced into the first schema of *De Ecclesia* at Vatican I, but to most of the Fathers it appeared too romantic a notion. Following Franzelin, M. J. Scheeben developed a theology whose inspiration was basically sacramental, and which sought to bring together the aspects of authority and of the organic and vital. The result of these efforts was that the theology of the mystical body was taken up by the encyclical of Leo XIII, *Satis Cognitum,* which depicted the Church from the viewpoint of the saving action of God and Christ. It was to come to full flower in the theological renewal of postwar years. The Church appeared as essentially the *congregatio fidelium,* the Body of Christ, completely permeated by the divine life which issues from the Trinity.

The encyclical *Mystici Corporis,* which saw in the Church — with Christ as its

Head, constituting it in existence, sustaining and ruling it — a social, visible and living reality whose ultimate principle of action is the Holy Spirit, gave the stamp of official approval to this fundamental rediscovery of the vision of the Church. From then on theological studies developed in complementary directions: the Church as sacrament, the Church as fellowship, the Church as mystery. And this development of ecclesiology took place under the combined influence of the biblical and liturgical revivals, the ecumenical movement, lay action, the mission, a new understanding of development (J. H. Newman) and of the historical nature of the Church. All this led to the restoration of the notion of the "People of God", the realization of the dynamic nature of missionary activity, eschatological tension, a new understanding of the community as a fellowship, collegiality etc. Through the work of contemporary theologians a synthesis of ecclesiological thought is being formed, which is totally centred on the mystery of Christ and totally open to the world. Vatican II came to crown this great ecclesiological renewal and to re-establish the links with the broad stream of patristic and theological tradition, whilst preserving all that has been learned from the controversies of the past. The time is now ripe for the construction of a harmonious synthesis of ecclesiological thought.

BIBLIOGRAPHY. E. Hofmann, *Der Kirchenbegriff beim heiligen Augustinus* (1933); J. Leclercq, *Jean de Paris et l'ecclésiologie* (1940); J. C. Plumpe, *Mater Ecclesia. An Enquiry into the Concept of the Church as Mother in Early Christianity* (1943); G. Bardy, *La théologie de l'Église de S. Clément de Rome à S. Irénée* (1945); G. Bardy, *La Théologie de l'Église de S. Irénée au Concile de Nicée* (1957); E. Mersch, *The Theology of the Mystical Body* (1951); J. Ratzinger, *Volk und Haus Gottes in Augustins Lehre von der Kirche* (1954); B. Tierney, *Foundations of the Conciliar Theory. The Contribution of the Medieval Canonists from Gratian to the Great Schism* (1955); W. Ullmann, *The Growth of Papal Government in the Middle Ages* (1955); S. Jaki, *Les tendances nouvelles de l'Ecclésiologie* (1957); Y. Congar, *The Mystery of the Church* (1960); M.-J. le Guillou, *Mission et Unité* (1960); N. Nédoncelle and others, *L'Ecclésiologie au XIXe siècle* (1960); K. Delahaye, *Ecclesia Mater chez les Pères des trois premiers siècles* (1964); H. Küng, *Structures of the Church* (1965); M.-J. le Guillou, *Christ and Church* (1967); G. Baraúna, ed., *De Ecclesia*, 2 vols. (1967).

Marie-Joseph le Guillou

A. The Teaching of the Church

If in the future Vatican II will stand as a synthesis of the teaching of the magisterium on the Church, three important documents of relatively recent date should not be forgotten: *Pastor Aeternus* of Vatican I; *Satis Cognitum* (Leo XIII); *Mystici Corporis* (Pius XII). Formerly the declarations of the magisterium dealt only with particular points (cf. Cavallera, pp. 149–284). An explanation of the teaching of the Church on "outside the Church no salvation" was given by the Holy Office in 1949 (*DS* 3869–80). The primacy of the Pope was asserted at the Councils of Lyons (*D* 466) and Florence (*D* 694), and Vatican I confirmed his universal jurisdiction and doctrinal infallibility. The ecclesiological heresies which overspiritualized the Church were rejected at Constance (*D* 627 ff.); conciliarism was condemned (*D* 740) and the hierarchical structure of the Church vindicated (*D* 666) at the Council of Trent. In papal documents from the time of Pius XI and Leo XIII to the present day we find a detailed examination of the relations of the Church with the State, culture, etc.

B. The Place of Ecclesiology

Under the guidance of the magisterium and in particular of the teaching of Vatican II, the development of ecclesiology today is marked by a return to the sources: Scripture, patristics, liturgy, tradition and the life of the Church (consciousness of the pastoral situation, the sense of mission, relations with the world). Ecclesiology endeavours to combine the different elements which go to make up the mystery of the Church in a living unity whose intelligibility stems from the mystery of God as he has revealed himself. In this way it brings out very clearly the relation of the mysteries between themselves, as was recommended by the First Vatican Council.

As a specifically theological treatise standing in its own right, ecclesiology, being essentially dependent on trinitarian theology, Christology, Mariology and anthropology, appears as a synthesis of the other treatises. But this was not always so. For a very long time ecclesiology had no special place: it was often developed as a mere appendix to Christology or in one or other of the treatises because of its connections with them. Above all it became the object of fundamental theology and apologetics.

Fundamental theology considers the Church as the foundation and necessary condition of theology and of the disciplines which depend upon it, and it analyses its significance as *ministra objecti,* as the permanent mediator of revelation and the subject of faith (the connection between faith and the Church appears clearly in the sacrament of baptism). It shows the credibility of the Church in its role of transmitting revelation by an analysis of the different forms this transmission takes (mediation, ministry, witness, mission), so as to prove the continuity of the Catholic Church with the Church of the early centuries. This involves a detailed examination of the relation between revelation, Scripture and the Church to show in what sense the Church is the normative interpreter of revelation. Fundamental theology also studies the foundation of the Church by Jesus Christ and its identification with the Roman Church, concentrating on the Church as an institution, and characteristics which are externally verifiable and intelligible. Finally, it treats of the Church as a sign recognizable from the outside by every man. The *admirabilis propagatio,* the *eximia sanctitas,* the *inexhausta in omnibus bonis fecunditas* are, according to Vatican I, the irrefutable signs of the mission of the Church and motives of credibility in regard to the Church itself and the revelation it transmits. Taking into account its objective validity, which in principle always remains the same, this type of apologetic must be adapted to the needs of the contemporary mind.

Strictly theological ecclesiology always presupposes a theology of revelation and of the word of God, and its starting point must always be the growing consciousness that the Church, in faith, has of itself (Vatican II: discourse of John XXIII at the opening of the first session; discourse of Paul VI at the opening of the second session; *Ecclesiam suam*). Besides the development and the actual historical forms of the Church, this consciousness also necessarily includes the facts of revelation.

C. The Theology of the Church

The Church is first of all a concrete and tangible reality whose meaning is revealed only to the eyes of faith. "The mystery of the Church is not just an object of theological knowledge, it must be a reality lived by the faithful soul, who has, as it were, a connatural experience of it, even before he has a clear idea of it." *(Ecclesiam Suam.)*

The word of God helps us to understand the Church through a multiplicity of concepts and images. After a period which concentrated too much on concepts, Vatican II restored the biblical imagery through which the mystery of the Church was first revealed: body, spouse, temple, city, vineyard, house, flock; all these words, as Y. Congar has remarked, express collective realities whose gradual realization — in which all are concerned, but some with a special position and responsibility — is part of a great design.

We shall now see what concepts and images should form the basis for a treatise on the Church by a critical analysis of each.

1. *The Church as mystery and sacrament of salvation.* In Eph 3:4 the Church is seen as the "mystery of Christ", because in it is realized the eternal plan of the Father, inaugurating on the cross the union of humanity, Jews and Gentiles, in the Church, and leading it to the consummation where "God will be everything to everyone" (1 Cor 15:28). The word "mystery" comes from Jewish apocalyptic (Dan 2:18 f.), and now means the act whereby God manifests his love in the wisdom incarnate of Jesus Christ, to bring mankind to glory. It is the word of God as the fullness of revelation and it is the accomplishment of the "secret" hidden for ages in God (Col 1:16; Eph 3:3–9; 1 Cor 2:6–10). Hence the mystery implies that the saving incarnation takes effect in the Church through the preaching of the word and through the sacraments, thus leading it to the glory of heaven. The redemption of Christ calls the Church into being (Eph 2:13–16; 5:25 ff.; Col 1:20–22) and there achieves its fulfilment, as all mankind is assembled in the Church.

Hence ecclesiology is to be conceived in terms of the mission of the Son and the Holy Spirit (*Lumen Gentium,* art. 14; *Ad Gentes,* arts. 2–5). The idea of the Church as sacrament takes on its full meaning within the trinitarian perspective in which God's plan is revealed: "The Church is in Christ the sacrament or sacramental sign of intimate union with God and of unity for the whole human race." (*Lumen Gentium,* art. 1.) Or even more explicitly, in a line of thought which stresses the place of the Resurrection and the Holy Spirit in the constitution of the Church: "Lifted up from the earth, Christ draws all men to himself (cf. Jn 12:32); risen from the dead, he has sent his life-giving Spirit upon the disciples; through the Spirit he has established his body, which is the Church, as *the universal sacrament of salvation;* sitting at the right hand of the Father, he is at work in the world without ceasing, to bring men to the Church, to join them more closely to himself through her." (*Ibid.,* art. 48; see also *Ad Gentes,* arts. 2–5; *Gaudium et Spes,* art. 45; Constitution on the Liturgy.)

As the dwelling place of the Christian sacraments or the "sacrament of sacraments" (τελετῶν τελετή, Pseudo-Dionysius, *Hier. Ec.,* III; see *PG,* III, 424 c), the Church is the sacrament of Jesus Christ, just as Jesus Christ himself in his humanity is the sacrament of God, according to the words of Augustine: "Non est enim aliud Dei mysterium, nisi Christus" (*PL,* XXXVIII, 845). So to define the Church as sacrament is to see it in the context of the mystery which binds it closely to Christ and to return to the fundamental, generic meaning of the word sacrament. It is to place it in the line of the economy of salvation, understanding it in terms of the sacrament *par excellence,* which is the humanity of Christ, and as the subject of all the sacraments. The Church is thus the assembly in which, through the action of the Holy Spirit, the past, Jesus Christ in his Passover of salvation, becomes present in view of the eschatological future of the world (cf. Constitution on the Liturgy). Called to "reveal to the world the mystery of the Lord" (*Lumen Gentium,* art. 8), the Church is word and sign for the whole world (*ibid.,* art. 17). Because its vocation is to place the world in the presence of the mystery of Christ in the Spirit, all its structures are completely subordinated to the mystery of Christ. The visible and social structure of the Church is thus only the sign and means of the action of Jesus Christ in the Spirit. As the great theologians of the Middle Ages used to say (St. Thomas, *Summa Theologica,* I, IIae, q. 106, a. 1), what principally constitutes the Church is the Holy Spirit in men's hearts, all the rest (hierarchy, papacy, Eucharist, sacraments) are in the service of this inner transformation.

Such statements do not mean that the social institution of the Church is indifferent. They merely underline that an understanding of the true nature of the Church as a sign presupposes that it is seen in all its spiritual dimensions. In itself and by itself it has no consistency, but draws all its substance from its relationship to Christ, in whom, through whom and for whom it is a sign. It is completely relative to the spiritual reality which it signifies; namely, the whole Christ, head and members, in the Holy Spirit and growing in grace. It stands for ever in dependence on the free saving act of Jesus Christ and thus, in the Spirit, the Church is the place of the theophanic manifestation of the Lord. It is only truly a sign when it allows the Holy Spirit to centre it upon Christ and not upon itself.

As mystery and sacrament the Church is always to be seen as proceeding from its source, which is the Trinity. It appears in the divine thought which establishes it in Jesus Christ and it descends from God's presence to become the "messianic" people of God (*Lumen Gentium,* art. 9). It is sent to the scattered, imperfect and potential people of God, the human race called to the salvation already purchased by the blood of Jesus Christ and even now permeated by the action of grace. As the bearer of the gift made to the world by God in Jesus Christ, the Church thus draws the principle of its universal dynamism from the Trinity.

This mystical and sacramental vision of the Church (that of the Fathers and the theologians of the Middle Ages) indicates that all theological thinking about the Church must be based on this communion with the mystery of the Trinity as well as on a real understanding of the history of salvation.

2. *The Church as the fullness of Christ and of fellowship.* The sacramental conception of the Church could, in fact, present a danger if one was tempted to separate in the Church the sign from the reality which is signified. To think of the Church as purely a sign and cause would be to forget that it is already the reality that it serves and signifies. The true notion of the Church as mystery or sacrament necessarily implies — as shown by our insistence above on its spiritual truth in the Spirit — the notion of the fullness of Christ and of fellowship.

The Church derives its intelligibility from

its end which is the entry of all men into "the fullness of God" (Eph 3:19).

In dependence on Christ in whom is given the fullness of revelation and of God's communication to the human race (Col 2:9), the Church is the fullness of Christ. It is "the fullness of Him who fills all in all" (Eph 1:23), because in it is revealed and realized the mystery of God's own life, giving men fellowship in his charity. This idea of fullness has an essentially eschatological value and is connected with the theme of the spouse sharing the life of her husband. In this way the Church is defined as an extension to the human race of the life of the Trinity through the mystery of the Incarnation, or again, as fellowship in the Holy Spirit (the patristic tradition; St. Thomas; *Lumen Gentium*, art. 8). As a consequence of the communication of the Holy Spirit, the Church is thus defined by its relation to the communion between the persons of the Trinity, the source and exemplar of ecclesial communion (*ibid.,* art. 4).

This eschatological fellowship realized through the Spirit gathering the Church into unity through the diffusion of charity, a fellowship in life, love and truth (*ibid.,* art. 9) is brought to fruition here below through a sacramental communion. The NT describes the Church in terms of fellowship (Acts 2:42) which is at the same time an agreement of minds in the faith, a sharing in the Eucharist and the same prayer, fellowship with the hierarchy (1 Jn 1:4; Gal 2:9) and the service and care of the poor (2 Cor 9:13).

So the Church can be described as the fellowship in the Spirit which is manifested sacramentally. It is the temple of the Spirit, an organic whole constituted by spiritual bonds (faith, hope, charity) and the bonds of visible structures (profession of faith, the sacramental economy, the pastoral ministry) and which is continually developing and moving towards its eschatological completion.

3. *The Church as the Body of Christ.* In St. Paul the idea of the Body of Christ can be understood only through the notions of *mystery, fullness* and *sacrament.*

The Fathers of Vatican I were afraid of using the idea of the Body of Christ because they saw in it the danger of a metaphorical expression which was too vague and imprecise. The German bishops reacted in a similar way in 1940. But the Fathers of

Vatican II finally gave it an important place in association with other biblical images. The idea of the Body of Christ had been developed at length by the encyclicals *Satis Cognitum* and above all *Mystici Corporis.*

In St. Paul the notion of the "Body of Christ" means the actual being of the Lord, the personal body of the dead and risen Christ, the beginning of a new creation.

Thus when St. Paul applies the expression of Body of Christ to the Church, he means the one body which gathers together within it, in the Spirit, the whole assembly of believers by means of the sacraments, and principally the Eucharist. So it is God himself who calls the faithful together in Christ, and it is he who unites them in one body through the Holy Spirit. And that is why the unity binding them together, whilst dwelling within them, does not derive from them, being of the divine order. It is based essentially on the unity of the Body of the Lord who died and rose again.

The Church is thus the Body of Christ, because once brought into existence through the fellowship of the faith professed in baptism — *congregatio fidelium* — it is perfected through communion in the same eucharistic bread which puts Christians in contact with the risen body of the Saviour, drawing those who believe in him into his own body. Ecclesial unity then is something spiritual and real and quite unique (involving even the bodies of the faithful), and clearly showing the connection between the Eucharist and the Church.

The eschatological reality of the Church is thus brought out through this incorporation into Christ who exercises absolute authority over his Body and who, in the Spirit, is the vital principle of the organic union of the whole body. The Church now appears as a visible body made up of men in whom are manifested all the different graces given by the one Spirit who animates and governs the Church. In the texts of the Council which speak about the Church, the role of the Spirit is rightly stressed: "When he provides his brethren with his own Spirit, after assembling them from all the nations, he is making them, as it were, his own body in a mystical fashion." (*Lumen Gentium,* arts. 7, 48; *Orientalium Ecclesiarum,* art. 2) For it was at Pentecost that the Church was born: "The apostles were thus the seeds of the new Israel, and, at the same time, the origin of the sacred hierarchy." (*Ad Gentes,* art. 5.) So the foundation of the Church as fellowship and sacrament is the Holy Spirit, which presupposes an analysis of the relations between ministries and charismatic gifts and between institution and event.

The building up of the Church in time by means of the ministries and charismatic gifts established by Christ tends towards perfect spiritual unity in the eschatological Christ (Eph 4:11–16). Through the will of Christ, its head, and through his permanent action within it, the Church, which is both fellowship with Christ and an institution of salvation, bears within itself all that it needs to complete its construction.

The ministry entrusted to the Church as a gift to be used is also an essential part of its make-up, because the ministry is charged with the preaching of the gospel and celebrating the Eucharist which together build up and develop the Body of Christ. The Church is conceived in the same line as the sacramental mission of Christ, as part of a whole conception which affirms that the whole work of the Church is a continuation of that of Christ.

This means that a sound ecclesiology involves a study of the relations between the Church as a whole and the hierarchy, between the primacy and episcopal collegiality, as well as a study of the theology of the episcopal ministry, the relation between prophecy and authority and of the exercise of authority in the Church, etc.

4. *The Church as the people of God.* Because they involve the unfolding of God's plan of salvation, the notions that we have examined so far are bound up with that of the People of God. The Church must certainly be seen from the point of view of the mystery of God, but the historical process which brought it into existence must also be given its due weight. The Church is the people of God established by the Spirit as the Body of Christ.

The notion of the people of God originally expressed the national and religious unity of Israel (cf. Exod 6:6b), and the covenant that God established with it (cf. Lev 26:9–12). It was used in the NT to give vivid expression to the eschatological consciousness of the Church. It thus brings out the *continuity* of the Church with the people of the old covenant and, even more, it stresses with the liturgy that the Church is a growing community, involved in history and affected by the weakness of its members which always stands in need of the mercy of God. But this notion has the serious drawback that it expresses only those characteristics which are common to the peoples of the old and new covenants. It gives no direct intimation of the overwhelming change brought about by Christ (eternal life in the fellowship of the Father and the Holy Spirit). It can be an excellent description of the Church, and because of its involvement in history and real life can even act as a safeguard against a too abstract treatment of the notion of the mystical body. But to become a definition of the Church, it needs to be completed by the notion of the Body of Christ.

The Church ('Ἐκκλησία, the Septuagint translation of the word *qahal*) understood itself originally in terms of the people of God. The ancient people of God was an assembly established by the summons of the divine word which gathered it together, taught it and created the covenant sealed in the offering of sacrifice (cf. the proclamation of the law on Sinai, Exod 19 ff.; the promulgation of Deuteronomy, 2 Kgs 23; the return from the exile, Neh 8–10).

This call placed the people of God under a system of election which was worked out through a gradual process of segregation: the escape from Egypt, the separation from the tribes of Canaan, the formation of a faithful "remnant" (Amos 5:15; Is 4:2–3 and 11–16; Jer 23:3; Ezek 9:8 and 11:13), and the final reduction to the one faithful servant who is charged with bringing about the final gathering of all the nations.

The Church was foreshadowed in the twelve gathered around the suffering servant, the tiny elected remnant destined to spread out over the whole world. It was then born on the cross and at Pentecost as the people of God of the new and eternal covenant. From then on it is constituted by the preaching of the gospel, by baptism and the response of faith, and is established in unity through fellowship with the dead and risen Christ (1 Cor 10:16, 17; Col 3:11; Gal: 3, 28), as it awaits his return.

The newly-born Church was thus conscious of living in continuity with Israel, whose history was interpreted in the light of the central event of the coming, death and resurrection of Christ Jesus. According to Eph 2, henceforward the Gentiles share, in

Jesus Christ, in the grace and the good news promised to Israel (cf. also Acts 15:8; 15:24). The phrase used in 1 Peter: "You (the believers) . . . are God's own people" (1 Pet 2:9) — a translation of the "'am segulah" describing Israel in its historical and spiritual relationship with God — expresses the mystery of the Church's belonging to the God of Israel because of its "election" in, through and for Jesus Christ. The faith expressed through baptism and the Eucharist is the conclusive mark of belonging to this people authenticated by the seal of the Spirit.

So it is in Christ, "over God's house as a Son" (Heb. 3:6; 1:2), the first-born embodying the complete loyalty of God to his people, that the unique people of God, from now on to be the bearer and witness of salvation, is brought into existence. The theology of the Church as the people of God finds its true basis only in Christology. This people in virtue of its re-creation in Christ is a free people. "The condition of this people is the dignity and freedom of God's sons, whose hearts are like a temple, the dwelling place of the Holy Spirit" (*Lumen Gentium,* art. 9), and so it must live in a spirit of freedom (2 Cor 3:17), as a witness to eschatological hope. This is a point on which the great tradition of the Fathers and Scholasticism, and in particular St. Thomas (*Summa Theologica,* I, IIae, 106a), especially insisted.

So the notion of the people of God by itself is not capable of expressing the whole reality of the Church. Under the new dispensation the people of God has a Christological and pneumatological connotation which can only be expressed through the notion of fellowship in the mystery and the Body of Christ. M. Schmaus writes: "The Church is the people of God of the New Testament, established by Jesus Christ, hierarchically constituted, serving to promote the reign of God and the salvation of men, and this people exists as the mystical body of Christ" (*Katholische Dogmatik,* III/1, p. 48).

5. *The Church as a society.* This idea of people, as the whole ancient tradition saw (cf. St. Thomas, *Com. in Hebr.,* ch. viii, no. 3), immediately suggests that of society and kingdom. But we must say a few words about the limitations of the application of the notion of society to the Church.

Since the 16th century at least, treatises on the Church, which were principally composed as answers to attacks on the concept of the Church's structure as a social body, made great use of the philosophical concept of society as "a stable union of human beings with a view to attaining an end by action pursued in common". It affirms that the Church is a perfect society, i.e., self-sufficient and independent; unequal, i.e., organized hierarchically, and supernatural, by reason of its efficient and final causes. "The Catholic Church instituted by Jesus Christ is a visible society, composed of men who have received baptism and who, united amongst themselves by the profession of the same faith and the bonds of mutual communion, strive for the same supernatural end, under the authority of the Roman Pontiff and the bishops in communion with him." (Catechism of Cardinal Gasparri.)

This concept has had the advantage of bringing out to a certain extent the *sui juris* character of the Church in relation to other societies: a new community, independent of every human factor of race, culture and power, affirming also the true and proper subsistence of temporal society.

But because of a one-sided development which led to the underestimation of almost all the expressions used to describe the Church in the Bible (except those of kingdom and mystical body, which, however, were understood from a predominantly sociological point of view), the notion of society obscured to some extent the specifically Christian character of the common good, authority, obedience, of the relations between communities and their heads and between the Church and temporal society, and also led to a neglect of the importance of the personal element as well as of the anthropological values contained within the Christian community. It also led to a static conception of the Church as a fully-formed juridical institution, standing outside time, and resulted in the practical disappearance of the whole dynamic vision of the Church as the instrument of a plan of universal and cosmic dimensions.

However, the new appreciation of the whole range of biblical expression does not mean the complete elimination of the concept of society, which is to be found on many occasions in *Lumen Gentium*. The Church, the presence of the mystery, appears then under the form of a social body. It is concrete society raised up to the divine level. The full analogical value should be restored to the idea of society, so that all the different ecclesiological themes presented above can be brought harmoniously together. The people of God, the body of Christ and the temple of the Holy Spirit will then be seen as the society (or fellowship) of Christian grace; a truly supernatural and Christ-engendered society, not only in its purpose, but also in its very make-up. A community of men, visibly structured and gathered together, it has an inner principle of fellowship of a supernatural and divine character which makes it the body of Christ. In its complex nature it comprises its sociological aspects, now essentially supernaturalized.

6. *The Church and the kingdom*. The heavenly Church will be still an actual society living in glory, but the make-up of the Church here below is marked by the tension between the Church and the kingdom, by reason of its sacramental structure. The NT shows the connection existing between the Church and the kingdom, but does not authorize a complete identification. The Church will become the perfect divine community of the kingdom only after the proving and sifting time of the judgment. Vatican II sees in the Church the seed and the beginning of the kingdom (*Lumen Gentium,* arts. 3, 5, 9). In the past theologians have sometimes stressed the distance between the Church and the kingdom, and at other times brought out their continuity. This can be easily understood if it is true that the Church is already in substance the kingdom of God, but in a state of pilgrimage in the obscurity of faith. The Church is in a sense the *eschaton* already present and realized, appearing now in what are the last days (Mk 1:14; Acts 2:17; 1 Pet 1:20); it is the anticipated but only partial realization of the kingdom. The benefits of the kingdom (the inheritance) which are the fruits of the Spirit, knowledge and glory, are possessed by the Church individually and collectively, in an imperfect manner (1 Cor 13:2), in "mystery", but really and truly.

But if the kingdom denotes consummation and fullness, there is even now in the Church a clear and growing sense of the distance which still separates it from that glorious consummation and which explains the growing tension which must dominate it in its yearning for the return of the Saviour.

This mid-way situation, standing between what is come and what is yet to come, has a profound effect on the whole nature of the Church and explains a great number of its characteristics, in particular its crucified state. The Church is the realm of the king who is the suffering servant. Just like its Lord, it must suffer to enter into its glory (cf. Lk 24:26). That is why the Church is here below a pilgrim Church (2 Cor 8:6, etc.; cf. 1 Pet 2:11, "aliens and exiles"; the superscription of the letter of Polycarp to the Philippians: "The Church which is on pilgrimage", etc.).

The tension between the kingdom and the Church which, we repeat, results from the sacramental structure of the Church, can also be understood as a consequence of the divine action which involves the whole process of salvation — summons, justification, glorification — and whose final goal is the glory to be revealed (Rom 8:18–30).

All the images and concepts which depict the Church are thus seen to be mutually complementary. They must all be interpreted in the light of the mystery of God whose purpose is to establish men in the fellowship of his Son. One of the fruits of the constitution *Lumen Gentium* has been a deeper theological understanding of the Church. Now, in the light of revelation, the Church is recognized as a society of fellowship with God, the sacrament of salvation, the people of God established as the body of Christ and the temple of the Holy Spirit.

D. The Catholic Church and the Other Communions

The sacramental structure of the Church is also the foundation of ecumenism as well as of mission, of the relations between the Church and the world and of renewal of the Church.

In fact all Christians owe their Christianity to the mediation of the ecclesiastical structure of their own community, or at least to that of baptism. Baptism, with its act of faith, is the primary element of the visible unity which still remains between Christians and is the basis for their search for a more visible unity. Between Christians (not only on the individual but also on the community level), there thus exists an elementary visibility which is at once an imperative, a motive for hope and the seed of ultimate unity, since it is a common sharing in the death and resurrection, the sacrifice and victory of Christ, a common indwelling by the Spirit, a common divine sonship. It all calls to be expanded and developed into the fullness of eucharistic Church unity. And so the relations of Christians between themselves is to be defined as a sacramental fellowship, which is admittedly imperfect, but nonetheless real, while the common desire of all Christians for the full manifestation of this sign of Christ, which is the Church, is the heart of ecumenism.

But then arises the problem of the relations of the Catholic Church with the other communions. In the first chapter of *Lumen Gentium,* after having clearly asserted the unity of the hierarchically organized Church with the mystical body of Christ, the Council goes on: "This Church (the one Church of Christ), founded and organized in this world as a society, subsists in the Catholic Church *(subsistit in)* . . . although outside its framework there are found many elements of holiness and truth, and they give an impetus to universal unity, inasmuch as they are gifts which belong to Christ's Church." (Art. 8.) It would be a false interpretation of the expression *subsistit in* to read into it some sort of ecclesial Platonism, as if the Church had a kind of super-self which pre-exists its tangible manifestation, and as if this manifestation was never adequate to its original archetype. Certainly the Church is never fully itself, and of its very nature there is in it a movement towards its full realization that we must accept and will, so that we can work for its fulfilment. But the starting point for any true conception of the Church is of necessity the risen Christ himself in the historical growth of his Body. There is no place for a kind of universal essence of the Church, of which the real world contains only vestiges or drafts, even if one goes on to say that there is one particular and privileged place, namely the Catholic Church, where this mystery, although never completely realized, really does "subsist".

In the text quoted above, the Roman Catholic Church expresses essentially the belief it has of being the realization as a society (and of being the only one to do so completely) of the form of visible communion that God desires for his Church. But we should notice the difference between the text above, as eventually promulgated, and what appeared in the preliminary draft: "that is why rightly *(iure)* only the Catholic Church is called (the) Church". The expression used in the definitive text has the advantage of suggesting that there is a relation between the Catholic Church and non-Roman Christians not only as individuals, but by reason of the different Christian groups and communities through which these Christians receive faith and are sanctified. *Lumen Gentium,* art. 15 (to be taken with *Unitatis Redintegratio,* art. 3) goes into further detail: the spiritual blessings which constitute the Church of Christ are not present only in the Roman Catholic Church as it is defined through its structure. In different degrees they are also present in other Christian communities which thus partly share in the reality of the mystery of the Church. This recognition includes the assertion of the ecclesial character of these communities. The name of Church, in the proper sense of individual Church, that is to say, as realizing the mystery of the Church, even if only imperfectly and incompletely in a particular place, will, however, be given to them only by reason of the presence in them of the essential hierarchical structures (a ministry of priesthood understood in the same way as, and in continuity with, the ministry of priesthood exercised by the apostles). So there is a distinction to be made between Churches and ecclesial communities by reason of the presence or absence of an espiscopal priesthood.

However, *Unitatis Redintegratio* makes it clear that the whole power of the blessings present in the other Churches flows from the fullness of grace and truth entrusted to the Catholic Church (art. 3), and that the separated brethren — whether we are talking of them as individuals or of their communities and Churches — do not enjoy that unity which Jesus Christ wished to bestow upon all whom he has regenerated and vivified to form a single body with a view to a new life *(ibid.).*

At the same time that it defines its relation to other communions the Catholic Church becomes more and more conscious of the distance there is between the demands that Christ makes upon its life and the actual reality of the empirical communities (art. 4). From this comes its consciousness of the need for renewal. One could also say that the Roman Catholic Church judges itself and other Christian communities and Churches in relation to the eschatological reality that its own sacramental structure reveals and signifies, but which always transcends the Church as it actually exists now in the world and passes judgment upon it.

E. THE CHURCH AND THE MISSION

The sacramental structure of the Church is also the foundation of the mission of the Church. The first two words of the constitution *Lumen Gentium* (taken from Is 49:6; cf. Lk 2:32 and Acts 13:47) present the Church as entrusted with a mission of salvation for the world by reason of its sacramental nature. This vivid realization that the Church has of its own unique character is the basis for the absolute necessity of missionary activity (*Lumen Gentium,* art. 17; *Ad Gentes,* art. 2). "Sent by God to the Gentiles to be 'the universal sacrament of salvation', the Church . . . strives with all its might to preach the gospel to all men" (*ibid.*, art. 1). Thus "of its nature, the Church, during the time of its earthly pilgrimage, is a missionary Church because it derives its origin from the mission of the Son and from the mission of the Holy Spirit according to the design of God the Father" *(ibid.,* art. 2). At the same time the nature of missionary activity is defined as being completely directed to the fullness of the *eschaton.* "Missionary activity is nothing less than the manifestation of God's plan, its presence and realization in the world and its history, in which God guides the whole history of salvation to its appointed end by means of the mission" (*ibid.*, art. 9). So the Church is a wholly missionary Church, for if a commandment, in the true sense of the world, was given to the apostles and after them to their successors, then the whole Church must co-operate in carrying it out (see *Ad Gentes,* art. 5, *Lumen Gentium,* art. 17).

The mission of the Church, which involves the recognition of the sacramental nature of the ministry as seen in *Lumen Gentium*, art. 3, is the foundation of the missions properly so called. The eschatological vision dominating all missionary activity regulates the relations of the Church with others in respect of what they are. The Church strongly asserts that accepting the faith presupposes complete religious freedom. Preparing thus for a new style of relations between the Church, Christian communities and secular States, the Church shows itself in favour of genuine inter-confessional dialogue as a function of the mission of the Church. But general statements are not enough. The Church proclaims not only its connections with Israel (connections based on divine revelation itself), but also with the other religions. It recognizes all the spiritual, moral and socio-cultural values of other religions (*Nostra Aetate,* art. 2) and affirms strongly that a convert from one of these religions to Christianity does not betray the religious and cultural genius of his own people. Like the whole of ancient tradition, the Church sees there "a preparation for the gospel" (*Ad Gentes,* art. 8). This is not the recognition of an economy of salvation parallel to Christ, for the Council solemnly delcares that it is in Christ alone, who is made present for us in his body which is the Church, that men are called to find the fullness of religious life: all authentic religious experience tends towards the fundamental structure willed by God: its Catholic ecclesial form (*Nostra Aetate,* art. 2). The human race, which in its entirety is ordained to salvation in Christ, is therefore no stranger to the Church, but is bound close to it by many different bonds (*Lumen Gentium,* arts. 14–15).

F. THE CHURCH AND THE WORLD

Relations between the Church and the world are also ultimately based on the sacramental character of the Church. "All the good that the people of God, during the time of its earthly pilgrimage, can bring to the human family derives from this fact that the Church is 'the universal sacrament of salvation'" (*Lumen Gentium,* art. 48), at the same time both showing forth and actualizing the mystery of God's love for man. Through becoming more conscious of itself in its missionary function, the Church has realized that it must proclaim salvation to a human race which is real, personal, social and historical reality reborn in every generation, and to a world which is in process of being completely transformed — and also that it has much to learn from mankind.

Henceforward a new solidarity of the Church in regard to the world is proclaimed in the name of the freedom and dignity of man: "The Church is both the sign and the safeguard of the transcendent character of the human person." (*Gaudium et Spes,* art. 76.)

The People of God must thus appear to the world as the eschatological and seminal realization of the urgent desire for unity, peace, justice, liberty and love which dominates all mankind (*Lumen Gentium,* art. 9).

This means that the Church is obliged to take seriously the problems of mankind throughout history, its objections and refusals (atheism). This does not prevent the Church from exercising its function of prophetic judgment or condemnation with regard to certain tendencies which jeopardize man's full development.

G. The Deficiencies of the Church and Reform

The eschatological and sacramental structure of the Church enables us to see in proper perspective the historical nature of a Church now conscious of its own deficiencies: "Although the Church, through the power of the Holy Spirit, has never ceased to be in the world the sign of salvation, it knows only too well that during the course of its long history, amongst its members, both clerical and lay, there have not been lacking those who showed themselves unfaithful to the Spirit of God." (*Gaudium et Spes,* art. 44.) This text takes up a similar statement in the decree *Unitatis Redintegratio* (art. 4). So we see that the very foundation of the ceaseless reform of the Church is the sacramental structure of the Church: in it there is a continuous struggle to be faithful to the Spirit. "The Church, in the course of its earthly pilgrimage, is called by Christ to this continual reform of which it always stands in need as a human and earthly institution." (*Ibid.,* art. 6.)

Recognition of the deficiencies of the Church throughout the course of history stands out very clearly. In the Declaration on Religious Freedom, for instance, mention is made of the unchristian attitudes which have marked the behaviour of Catholics at different times in history (*Dignitatis humanae,* art. 12). *Gaudium et Spes* declares: "In the rise of atheism believers also can have a not inconsiderable part, insofar as through negligence in their own education in the faith, through fallacious presentations of doctrine and also through the short-comings of their religious, moral and social life one might say that they distort the true appearance of God and of religion rather more than they reveal it." (Art. 19; cf. also arts. 21; 36; 43.) And again the common declaration of Paul VI and Patriarch Athenagoras about the excommunications of 1054 (7 December 1965) ratifies solemnly, so to speak, this confession of the historical deficiencies of the Church.

So the Church, which includes sinners within its fold, has need of incessant renewal and purification (cf. *Lumen Gentium,* art. 8; taken up in *Gaudium et Spes,* art. 44, and in *Unitatis Redintegratio,* art. 6), and through its encounter with the world it discovers the full implications of our redemption in Jesus Christ. It learns from human history, which enables it to appreciate better the riches of its faith.

By recognizing its weaknesses the Church, the effective sign of the encounter with God which transforms mankind and of the new creation of all in Christ, knows that it must imitate more closely the self-emptying of Christ who became poor. The foundation of the Church's poverty is also to be sought in its sacramental nature which refers it entirely to Christ in the Spirit.

With this renewed desire to be faithful to Christ and the resolution to be of service to the world, the Church is exploring its own mystery. In the light of events which impose new demands upon the Christian life and call for a more profound understanding of the word of God under pressure of the trials of history, the Church discovers the unsuspected depths of the mystery and contemplates in the light of faith with a growing love the wonderful guidance of God, seeking to conform it to his own death and resurrection.

H. Outside the Church No Salvation

The Church is for the world the universal and efficacious sign of salvation. No one can be saved apart from the efficacy of this sign.

It is, however, important to add that its invisible action infinitely surpasses its visible effectiveness. As the sacrament of salvation, the Church brings about invisibly what it signifies visibly: universal salvation. This means that the axiom, "Outside the Church no salvation", must be interpreted in the light of the sacramental nature of the Church.

In the course of history the magisterium has put forward two series of apparently contradictory statements: the necessity of belonging to the Church for salvation and the condemnation of those who maintain that grace confines its action to the visible boundaries of the Church.

a) The formula of St. Cyprian, "extra ecclesiam nulla salus", is to be found in a profession of faith imposed upon the Waldenses by Innocent III (*DS* 792, 802) and its clearest statement is in the Bull *Unam Sanctam* of Boniface VIII (*DS* 875).

b) But there have also been constant statements that the action of grace is not restricted to the visible boundaries of the Church alone (cf. *DS* 1305, 2429; 2304; and above all 3860, 3872).

A reconciliation between these two contradictory positions was effected through the use of the idea of "error in good faith". Pius IX was the first to refer to invincible error in explaining the axiom "outside the Church no salvation" (*Singulari quadam*). In the same line it is interesting to consult one of the chapters of the schema *De Ecclesia* of Vatican I where it was proposed to define "outside the Church no salvation" as a dogma of faith. But the most important text is the letter of the Holy Office to the Archbishop of Boston (*DS* 3869–80). It recalls first of all that "incorporation through baptism into the Body of Christ, which is the Church, is a very strict commandment of Jesus Christ" (*DS* 3867). "The Saviour has not only ordained that all men and all peoples should enter into the Church, but he has also established that there is a means of salvation without which no one can enter into the kingdom of heavenly glory." (*DS* 3868.) But the necessity of the Church as a means of salvation is explained more fully: there is no question of a necessity of means, that is to say, of an intrinsic necessity bound up with the nature of things, which as absolutely indispensable, would have to be really and effectively employed. Such would be the necessity of the interior disposition of faith and love of God for salvation. The necessity of the Church is that of a precept. It corresponds to a positive institution, and the effect to which such a means is ordered can be obtained even where the means itself cannot be effectively employed. "For someone to obtain eternal salvation, it is not always required that he be in fact incorporated into the Church as a member, but it is at least required that he be united to it by desire or wish." (*DS* 3870.)

There is clear progress in this document

beyond the preparatory project of Vatican I, which still spoke of a necessity of means. Vatican II confirms this by alluding to the document of the Holy Office: "Those also can attain to everlasting salvation who through no fault of their own do not know the gospel of Christ or his Church, yet sincerely seek God and, moved by grace, strive by their deeds to do his will as it is known to them through the dictates of conscience." (*Lumen Gentium,* art. 16.) In short, to be saved, every man, at least by an act of implicit faith and theological desire for salvation, must become a son of the Church. The axiom "Outside the Church no salvation" is only a way of expressing the ecclesiological truth: the Church is the sacrament of salvation.

BIBLIOGRAPHY. K. Adam, *The Spirit of Catholicism* (1929); H. de Lubac, *Catholicism. A Study of Dogma in Relation to the Corporate Destiny of Mankind* (1950); C. Journet, *L' Église du Verbe Incarné,* 2 vols. (1951); H. de Lubac, *The Splendour of the Church* (1956); Y. Congar, *Lay People in the Church. A Study for a Theology of Laity* (1957); L. Cerfaux, *The Church in the Theology of St. Paul* (1959); Y. Congar, *The Mystery of the Church* (1960); M.-J. le Guillou, *Mission et Unité* (1960); H. Fries, *Aspects of the Church* (1965); J. Hamer, *Church is a Communion* (1965); O. Semmelroth, *Church and Sacrament* (1965); id., *The Church and Christian Belief* (1966); H. U. von Balthasar, *Church and World* (1967); G. Baraúna, ed., *De Ecclesia,* 2 vols. (1967); Y. Congar, *Ecumenism and the Future of the Church* (1967); M.-J. le Guillou, *Christ and Church* (1967).

Marie-Joseph le Guillou

III. Constitution of the Church

1. If one wishes to speak in terms of sacred law of a "constitution" of the Catholic Church on the grounds that it is a *societas perfecta,* then the actual details of such a constitution have already been dealt with in other articles. The Church is, among other things, a social reality, a juridically constituted society, the highest governing body of which is the universal episcopate which has as its head the Roman Pontiff with his primatial authority. Here the Pope is not merely a representative commissioned by the college of bishops and the executor of the collegiate will. He is their head in the sense that he always acts as their head, just as of course he only is Pope and only acts as such as the head of the Church, not as an entity

separate from and in contrast to the Church. But he acts with an authority which is given him as his own by Christ and which embraces every individual bishop and the entire Church with truly sovereign power *(potestas iurisdictionis plena et universalis)*. As regards the function of individuals in the Church, there is a distinction *iuris divini* between clergy (hierarchy) and laity. The clergy itself is graded in respect of the sacramentally conferred *potestas ordinis* as well as the *potestas iurisdictionis*. There are bishops, priests and deacons; there is clergy with actual jurisdiction or without it, although its ontological basis is conferred in the sacrament of holy orders itself. There exist two fundamental powers *(potestas ordinis, potestas iurisdictionis)* which are neither unrelated nor simply identical. The Church is divided territorially into dioceses, but these must not be regarded as merely administrative districts (of the papal primatial authority). They are themselves truly "the Church", governed by the bishop in the name of Christ, not of the Pope. They are *sui iuris,* with their own traditions and an independent function in the Church as a whole. Corresponding to its social nature, the Church has a sacred law which in part belongs to its immutable essence, in part is created by the Church itself, as in canon law. By this law other institutions, offices, regions, etc. are set up in the Church which belong to its concrete nature, to its actual historical condition and partly to its constitution, as far as the norms of their existence and function are concerned. To this extent, therefore, the "constitution" of the Church has in fact been dealt with under these other headings.

All that remains, therefore, is a fundamental theological reflection on the constitution of the Church. The question is a topical one because there is a general demand nowadays that larger societies of longer duration should be juridically organized. A State today must live by the "rule of law", have a juridical organization and therefore a written constitution which can be legally invoked even against the authorities of the State (separation of powers, supreme court, etc.). In our democratic age, therefore, a similar question also arises for the Church, for the Church also sees itself as a "perfect society" and Catholic ecclesiology does not hesitate to use the analogy between Church and State, despite the radical differences between them.

2. The first striking fact is that in the Catholic Church there is no actual *written* constitution (of divine or human right). There are statements in the doctrine of faith, even defined ones, regarding the Church, but they are not gathered into a single corpus in a written constitution. Even now that for the first time in the *Lumen Gentium* of Vatican II there is a sort of summary of Catholic ecclesiology (though without any new definitions), this is not a constitution. Most of what it says does not involve juridical norms, but consists almost entirely of the statements of revelation. Consequently, it passes over the *ius humanum* which after all belongs to the Church's concrete structure and therefore offers in regard to the concrete condition of the Church practically only the basic rights, the ultimate constitutional norms, an extensive constitutional preamble. Similarly, the code of canon law is not a written constitution, although it contains numerous juridical constitutional norms. It corresponds rather to the civil, criminal and administrative law of a modern State. There is the further point that, whereas in the modern State the constitution has a higher validity and dignity than the rest of the law, it is not possible in the Church to distinguish divinely established constitutional elements from other juridical norms which are also divinely established, or between humanly established constitutional elements and other norms of humanly established canon law as regards their formal aspects — validity, mutability, authority to change them, etc.

3. Considering the liking of the *Roman* Church for law, this is a surprising fact. Its explanation is not ultimately that juridical development has not yet for historical reasons advanced so far and that the mentality of the Church delays this development (just as, for example, in England there is not really a written constitution). The deepest reason lies in the nature of the Church itself. The legal element in the Church cannot be distinguished from the rest of what it is in other respects and what it does precisely as Church, in the way this can be done in secular society and in the State. Ultimately this derives from the religious character of

the Church on the one hand and from its sacramental and eschatological character on the other. The *ius divinum* which forms the basis of its constitution is religious, revealed truth. To this, however, there belongs (even in respect to the *ius divinum*) not only what has been formulated by explicit reflection at a certain point of time but also, and equally essentially, what has (temporarily or permanently) only been grasped and lived implicitly, what is still only unfolding historically in the Church's consciousness of its faith. This alone shows that a written constitution, with its restrictions and definitions, excluding the unwritten as legally invalid, would be of doubtful value to the Church, even though to a certain extent there is something analogous in the constitution of the State — the living criticism of the written constitution through the unwritten meta-juridical basic rights of man, etc. Furthermore, it is not possible wholly to distinguish in the Church between the *forum internum* and the *forum externum*, for example in the sacrament of penance. The very fact that in ecclesiology and canon law recourse must be had to the paradoxical concept of *forum internum* shows the strange combination which prevails in the Church between what can be comprised in legal terms and what as an individual religious saving event cannot wholly be given juridical form. All the sacraments involve the union of an institutional element (as the social, and therefore juridically regulated, efficacious sign of grace) and grace itself, which can never be controlled but always remains at the sole disposition of God, since, for instance, efficacious grace is needed for the disposition for fruitful reception of a sacrament. The entire guarantee of the indestructibility of the institutional (and only as such is it really ecclesiastically institutional) and every "guarantee" of its producing its genuine effect (infallible teaching, fruitful administration of the sacraments, permanent apostolic succession, etc.) resides in the power of the Spirit, not in the social and legal element as such, and its victory has always to be believed and hoped for anew.

We can therefore only speak of the constitution of the Church if and where it is something more than what is merely juridical in the social domain as such, just as a sacrament is only an effective and fruitful sacrament if it is more than a sacrament (in the sense of a sign with juridical efficacy of a social kind), namely, grace. The Spirit of the Church does not belong to the constitution, but without it this constitution would cease to be itself. To the extent that the Spirit itself belongs to the essence of the Church, just as "uncreated grace" belongs to the justified person, there is in the Church itself a critical principle, a dynamism directed towards the further development of its constitution and a perpetually renewed criticism of the concrete application of this "constitution" which always lags behind the task it imposes. To the extent that the Church knows itself to be a pilgrim, still making its way towards the kingdom of God, its constitution with office and sacrament is something that the Church itself regards as part of the pattern of this "aeon" in which the Church still shares. It is something that the Church knows to be not only historically conditioned by the age (as everyone knows a secular constitution to be): it is that whose end it prays for in its impatient eschatological longing (cf. *Lumen Gentium*, art. 48).

The absence of a really closed, rounded, self-sufficient written constitution of the Church is an expression of the fact that it does not live by the letter, but by the Spirit, that the Church is not law but gospel, however much the letter is the embodiment of the Spirit, of order, of freedom from the arbitrary and the mark of the historical Incarnation.

4. On the other hand this "written" and "unwritten" constitution of the Church is not a mere human, everyday necessity, imperative just because human beings happen to want social organization even in their religious needs and this is not possible without order and regulation. Of course man's social character is an essential factor, and as confirmed and consecrated by the Incarnation is the ultimate reason why there is such a thing as a constitution even in the Church. But the consequence following from this, namely the constitution of the Church by the will of the Father and of Christ made flesh and history, is an element in the Church itself precisely as such. Faith is always the faith of a community confessing its faith under authoritative decision; in virtue of what it is, grace takes concrete form in sacraments "necessary for salvation" (*D* 847, etc.). Salvation takes place in history, in

the covenant, in the Church, whose visible social constitution belongs to the occurrence of grace itself, without being identical with it.

5. The "constitution" of the Church in the concrete can still develop further even today, even if the whole of changing canon law cannot be counted as part of its constitution. Some things which even at the present time are clearly in process of historical change can be reckoned as belonging to the concrete constitution of the Church *(iuris humani)*: the division between the Eastern and the Latin parts of the Church and their mutual relations, the coexistence of an Eastern and a Latin canon law; the renewed tendency in the Latin Church to form large regional Churches (of a new type however), corresponding to the old patriarchates of the East; the tendency towards a clearer institutional form of the rights and duties of the laity in the Church, and to a clearer institutional form of the collaboration between Pope and the college of bishops (the "Synod of Bishops"); the duty of internationalizing the Roman Curia; a better determination of the relation between the episcopate of a country and the papal nuncio; the revival of the synodal principle within the individual dioceses; the statutory definition of episcopal conferences; the enhancement of the function and importance of auxiliary bishops and coadjutors where these are needed; the possibility of bishops with supra-diocesan functions; the speedy establishment of a native episcopate in the Churches of the missionary countries as local Churches with their own character and equal rights. These and similar matters after all belong to some extent to the domain of constitutional law and show that this constitution is involved in historical change. Because, however, there is no definite written constitution in the Church, this change does not mean "revolution", "change of constitution", or "constitutional legislation" which would have to be enacted in the Church in a different way from other ecclesiastical laws, *juris humani*.

BIBLIOGRAPHY. W. M. Plöchl, *Geschichte des Kirchenrechts,* 3 vols. (2nd ed., 1959–62); Y. Congar, *The Mystery of the Church* (1960); id., *The Wide World, My Parish* (1961); U. Valeske, *Votum Ecclesiae,* 2 vols. (1962); R. Schnackenburg, *God's Rule and Kingdom* (1963); K. Rahner, ed., *Church in Action,* Studies in Pastoral Theology 1 (1968).

Karl Rahner

IV. Universality of the Church

1. This article should be regarded as supplementary to the articles *Church* II (Ecclesiology) and *Church and World*. To some extent it stands midway between them. Its theme is a topical one, for it is only at the present time that the Church has manifestly and in historical fact become approximately a world-wide Church, as was clearly shown by Vatican II. Quite considerable consequences follow from this fact for the Church's action.

2. In a first, purely dogmatic and always valid sense, the Church can be called worldwide or universal because it is intended for all men whether or not they belong or will belong to the Church (since Pentecost) in the sense of full membership of the Church in its existence as a social institution. This sense of universality (Church as universal *potentia et destinatione*) implies two facts. In the first place the Church is for *all* men the *sacramentum salutis,* whether they belong actually and fully to the visible unity of the Church or not. In other words, the grace of God in Christ, without which absolutely no one finds supernatural salvation in God's triune life, has its historical and eschatological manifestation (even for the unbaptized) in the Church. Secondly, no human being can in principle be exempted from the obligation of belonging to the visible unity of the Church. This second point follows immediately from the necessity of the Church and of baptism for salvation. We had, however, to formulate this second sense of the universal necessity of the Church for salvation in this way, because theologically it is no longer possible, at any rate at the present time, to affirm that all men receive by the saving providence of God such an actual possibility of recognizing the Church as necessary for salvation and of entering it that they can only miss this opportunity by their own fault. If, however, many individual human beings inculpably until their death fail to belong in an actual visible way to the Church, it is impossible to say that in regard to *every* single human being God has a will which *directly* imposes an *actual* obligation upon this human being of visible membership of the Church. Otherwise God would have to give him such a possibility of fulfilling this will that he could only fail to do so by his own fault. Consequently the necessity of the Church for salvation and the obligation of

Church membership (over and above the Church as *sacramentum salutis omnium*) can only be formulated as we have done. No one can justifiably affirm *a priori* that visible membership of the Church does not enter into the question as a concrete possibility for him personally and therefore as an actual duty, and cannot be *the* chance of salvation by which in fact his salvation is decided.

3. The Church today, however, can and must be called universal or world-wide in a narrower historical and real sense. The Church today has become world-wide in its actual empirical reality, a Church for the whole world. This of course does not mean that all men are Christians (baptized persons) and Catholics. Nor does it mean that the Church, at least today, is so actually present, as the call of God's grace, that this summons can go unheeded through personal guilt alone. Nor does it mean that the Church is already so well-established in all nations and civilizations that it has already ceased to be a missionary Church anywhere in the sense of Vatican II's Decree on the Church's Missionary Activity (cf. art. 19). It cannot in fact even be disputed that there are still regions in the world in which the Catholic Church (which means more than "Christianity") is in practice not yet present at all, e.g., certain parts of Asia. At all events the Church in large parts of Asia (China, Siberia, etc.), in the domain of Islam and in many parts of Africa, is still a mission Church. In other words, the community of the faithful is not yet rooted in the social life of that country and not yet adapted to its civilization, the number of priests, religious and laity is still very small, organization is still on a very modest scale, there is no native bishop and so it is not yet possible to say that missionary activity has to a certain extent come to an end. Yet it is already possible to speak of a world-wide Church at the present time. What could still not be said even 150 years ago can be said today. The Church is almost everywhere present in some way. At least if we leave out of account the very large area under the domination of militant Communism, the Church possesses local Churches or missions throughout the world. Its doctrine and existence are among the things which are known to public opinion and with which people reckon. Its highest governing body includes representatives from all the important nations, racial groups,

etc. Furthermore — and this is perhaps the decisive factor, although primarily determined by profane history — the peoples and their histories which were formerly almost totally separated by historical no man's land, have now grown together into an actual family of nations and a single world history, largely as a result of European colonialism since the 16th century. This process is of course still going on and its consequences are becoming more marked.

At the present time, therefore, every particular history of a nation, a civilization, a continent, has become an empirically contributory factor in every other (as Vatican II's Pastoral Constitution on the Church in the Modern World frequently emphasizes). It follows immediately that the major higher religions, even though they originated at a particular place in history which continues to be the root of their life and influence, have become a contributory factor in the history of the world generally, even if their physical presence (constituted by their institutions and greater numbers of their adherents) is in certain places very slight or even absent. That, however, also holds good of Christianity because of the relatively large number of its adherents and because it is the religion of the civilization from which the unification of the one world-history of today proceeded. It therefore also applies to the largest Church of Christendom. It must be noted that the unification of world-history did not just in fact contribute to the actual universality of the Church. It is true that European expansion and the world-wide mission have interacted since the 16th century, though sometimes to the detriment of the mission because it roused the suspicion that it was a piece of European imperialism. There is a more fundamental connection. The European, rational attitude to the world which aims at its active transformation, and European technology, were the condition and foundations of the European expansion which created world-history. Now these sprang from a radically Christian attitude to the world, for which the world has no numinous character but instead is a created reality, the environment and the material for man's self-realization. This is so despite the deformations of rationalism and technocracy, and despite even the profanation of the world under practical or militant atheism.

4. Universality involves consequences for the Church itself and its action, only a few of which can be indicated here. In a world-wide Church contained within the unity of a single world-history, the mutual importance, duties and interdependence of all the regional Churches are greater. When old regional Churches found young Churches in non-Christian countries, the destiny of the latter reacts upon the mother Churches themselves. This in fact increases the missionary obligation, because it has now become even empirically a part of the duty of self-preservation of the ancient Churches themselves, whose own fate is partly determined by that of Christianity throughout the world. In this situation of a universal world-history in which all nations are simultaneously becoming independent, the Church has clearly to manifest its character as a world-Church to all the nations, which have equal rights in it. This is done by creating as rapidly as possible a native clergy and episcopate, the incorporation of all civilizations and national mentalities on an equal basis into the Church's life, the removal of the earlier European features from the missions, internationalization of the Roman Curia, the "naturalization" of the liturgy, whereby it will have to be a world-liturgy varying in form, not a Latin liturgy (in fact almost that of the city of Rome). As a world-Church in a unified world-history the Church will have more clearly to show itself acting as a single whole, not only in the action of the Pope as highest guarantor and representative of the visible unity of the Church, but also through the universal episcopate as highest collegiate presiding body of the universal Church; by the distribution of priests throughout the whole world out of wider concern than the sectional interest of a regional Church; by ecclesiastical "help for underdeveloped countries" — the missions and South America; by each bishop's (and even each Christian's) coming to take a share of practical responsibility for the Church as a whole in all its parts, though not for its government. Over and above national concordats etc., the world-Church will have to discover and develop a relation of dialogue and collaboration with other institutions which represent in a social form the unity of the human family and its history — UNO, UNESCO, the World Council of Churches, etc.

5. The unification of mankind is a *process,* which is not yet at an end. For that reason alone, apart from properly and directly theological grounds, the one world-wide Church is still in process of realization, and forms part of the responsibility of all Christians.

BIBLIOGRAPHY. N. Söderblom, *Pater Max Pribilla und die ökumenische Erweckung* (1931); *The Church and the International Disorder.* An ecumenical study prepared under the auspices of the World Council of Churches (1948); H. S. John, *Essays in Christian Unity, 1928–1954* (1955); G. Thils, *Histoire doctrinale du mouvement œcuménique* (1955); B. Leeming, *The Churches and the Church* (1960); S. Neill, *Christian Faiths and Other Faiths* (1961); R. J. W. Bevan, ed., *The Churches and Christian Unity* (1963); T. Sartory, *Ecumenical Movement and the Unity of the Church* (1963); Y. Congar, *Chrétiens en dialogue. Contributions catholiques à l'œcuménisme,* Unam Sanctam 50 (1964); C. O'Neill, ed., *Ecumenism and Vatican II* (1964); H. Roux, *Le concile et le dialogue œcuménique* (1964); M.-J. le Guillou, *Mission et Unité,* 2 vols. (1966); B. Lambert, *Ecumenism. Theology and History* (1967).

Karl Rahner

V. Membership of the Church

The word "Church" does not always bear the same meaning in Scripture. It sometimes means the people of Israel, wandering in the wilderness (Acts 7:38). On other occasions it means a Christian society, either a household (Rom 16:4–5) or throughout a city (Acts 8:1) or a district (Acts 9:31; 1 Cor 16:9). Sometimes it means the society which comprises all the sons of God, redeemed by Jesus Christ and built upon the foundation of the apostles (Acts 20:28; 1 Cor 12:28). Moreover, Scripture uses a good deal of metaphor in referring to what we call the Church: the flock (Jn 10:9), the vine (Jn 16:1–6), the house of God (1 Pet 2:26–31; 1 Tim 3:15), the heavenly Jerusalem (Gal 4:26–31), the bride (Eph 5:25–27), a nation (1 Pet 2:10). Now simply to call the Church by all these names would be to lapse into real theological nominalism. For they are all comparisons or metaphors, and a metaphor is like the reality only in certain respects (*Summa Theologica,* I, 33, 3; III, 8, 1, ad 2). Each metaphor stresses one particular feature of the true Church.

The first schema of the Dogmatic Constitution on the Church, presented to the Fathers of Vatican II on 10 November 1962, listed some of these metaphors in arts. 3–4. And the definitive constitution, promulgated on

19 November 1964 *(Lumen Gentium)*, also contains them in arts. 5–6. The whole of art. 7 is a fairly complete treatise on the Church considered under the metaphor of a *body*. And the whole of chapter ii expounds the doctrine of the Church considered under the metaphor of a *people*.

The metaphor of the body involves several subordinate figures — such as head, life, and members. It occurs most often in St. Paul. Those who are united with Christ form a body, of which he is the head and they are the members. Here we are already speaking the language of the title of this article. To speak of members of the Church is to speak of those of whom it is composed, who are part of it insofar as it is a body. And since the Church is a mystical and social body, it follows that to do our subject justice we shall have to speak of those who belong to the Church insofar as it is a mystical body and insofar as it is a social body.

But we must be still more precise. The term mystical body, which at present means, as noted above, a mystical and social body, a body which on the one hand has an interior life and on the other is external and visible, is also applied to the Church in a different sense by patristic and theological tradition. So when we speak of members we must determine what sort of body they are thought of as composing.

In the first place, before the Incarnation the mystical body had only an inward, secret existence on earth, just as it still has beyond the earth. It is the body made up of all who today are vitally joined with Christ by the grace that comes from and through him, without the mediating agency of any institution. This mystical body, on earth then and beyond the earth now, was and is an ampler thing than the Church of Peter.

And in the second place there is the mystical body bounded by space and time — the space that is the earth and the time that stretches from Jesus Christ to the end of time. This body, besides being inward and secret — supernaturally alive — is visible and social. And to belong to it something more is required than union with Christ by grace. Here it is through ecclesial society that one must be incorporated with Christ. Accordingly no one can be a member of this latter mystical body without also being a member of the society in which it is so to speak incarnate.

So much having been said, it is clear that there are two different approaches to the problem of membership of the Church, or mystical body of Christ, and therefore two different solutions according as we take one approach or the other.

Members of the mystical body in the first sense. If we are to pose and duly solve the problem of who these members are, we must bear three points in mind: First, that the redemption Christ has wrought is universal, extending to all men from Adam down to the last of his descendants. Second, that in the present dispensation no grace comes from heaven to men that is not Christian grace, that men do not derive from Christ and owe to him. Third, that in a certain sense all grace is sanctifying grace, grace which imparts supernatural life. Some graces are in the nature of preparation. They do not sanctify but pave the way for others that do sanctify. We refer to charismata, *gratiae gratis datae,* and actual graces. Then other graces actually sanctify — habitual grace, the infused virtues, the gifts of the Holy Spirit.

If we owe all this supernatural equipment to Christ and it all sanctifies or vivifies, enabling us therefore to be vitally incorporated; if in some degree or other such grace reached all the just of the OT and now reaches all who today are beyond the earth — then it is easy to account for the statements cited below from Scripture, patristic and theological tradition, and the common language of the faithful. St. Paul speaks of Christ being head not only of the just who are now on earth but of all men in whatever place or age they may live — their head not only as ordering and perfecting them but also as bestowing on them the grace of redemption (Col 1:18). The Apostle also compares the second Adam with the first and declares the grace of Christ to be superabundant (Rom 5). In the same vein the Fathers speak of the Church *universal,* or the Church which begins in Abel (St. Gregory, *PL,* LXXVI, col. 1154). From the beginning all mankind has belonged to it. And the theologians say the same thing: "The patriarchs belonged to the body of the Church just as we do" (*Summa Theologica,* III, 8, 3, ad 3). The language of the faithful knows of more than the one Church here on earth, founded by Christ, which we call the Church militant and today is often

333

called the pilgrim Church. They also speak of the Church suffering and triumphant — the Church in purgatory and the Church in heaven. There is grace in purgatory and it comes from Christ. In both places there is vital incorporation in him. The souls in purgatory and the blessed in heaven are members of Christ.

Such being the case we must affirm that all men who lived on earth before the present Church was founded were members of this *universal* Church, this mystical body, whose members are now incorporated in Christ without the mediating agency of the institutional Church which is the Church on earth, and that everyone in purgatory and in heaven is also a member of it.

To make this point clear it will be well to turn to classical theology, to what St. Thomas says in *Summa Theologica,* III, 8, 3. His doctrine, solid and profound, is as pertinent today as ever. He distinguishes between members *in actu* and members *in potentia.* Let us begin by explaining what theologians mean by a member *in potentia.* They do not mean that a person has a mere logical or objective potentiality, simply that his becoming a member is not a contradiction in terms, that by grace it is not impossible. They mean that the person already possesses a real principle ordered to that in respect of which it is still potential. To say that a person is a member *in potentia* means that although he does not yet have the supernatural life which vitally incorporates one in the Church, he does have *something* which, if made good use of, will lead to his incorporation. That something is what the potentiality gives; for St. Thomas it is many things that will be noted below.

Now, the blessed are members *in actu* of this universal Church; they are united most intimately of all with Christ. They draw from him everything supernatural that makes them blessed. The souls in purgatory are also members *in actu.* So were the just on earth who lived before Christ; all others were members *in potentia.* All had at least a juridical title, a moral title, and an ontic title orientating them to the possession of sanctifying grace which would make them members *in actu* and which they would attain if they made good use of what they had already. This means the right to grace which all had in virtue of being redeemed (in God's eyes they already were, though

Christ had not yet come). This also means the orientation to the supernatural end — salvation — which characterized all their morally good acts (St. Thomas, *In I Sent. dist.,* 46, q. 1, a. 1). They were ignorant of that destiny, but God was not. And since in the present dispensation there is no natural last end, only a supernatural one, and since God never abstracts from the last end, it follows that he ordered all the good acts of pagans to that end. And finally we mean the divine impulse which moved them to perform those morally good acts; an impulse which was actual grace, proportionate to the end to which God ordered them. Here we have our three titles — the juridical, which we have called a right; the moral, which we have called an orientation; and the ontic, which we have called an impulse. All these things were genuine realities which were able, if properly used, to lead their possessors to the possession of habitual or sanctifying grace. That was a membership *in potentia.*

What we have said of pagans who lived before Christ, in whom we have found three positive realities that made them members *in potentia,* can be said of pagans who lived and live since Christ and since he attached salvation to the institutional Church of which he is the founder. They too have the three realities and are accordingly members of the Church *in potentia.* The dogmatic constitution *Lumen Gentium* refers to those positive elements: "Nor does divine Providence deny the help necessary for salvation to those who, without blame on their part, have not yet arrived at an explicit knowledge of God, but who strive to live a good life, thanks to his grace. Whatever goodness or truth is found among them is looked upon by the Church as a preparation for the gospel. It regards such qualities as given by him who enlightens all men so that they may finally have life." (*Lumen Gentium,* art. 16.) "The Catholic Church rejects nothing which is true and holy in these (non-Christian) religions. It looks with sincere respect upon those ways of conduct and of life, those rules and teachings which, though differing in many particulars from what it holds and sets forth, nevertheless often reflect a ray of that Truth which enlightens all men." (Declaration *Nostra Aetate,* on the Relationship of the Church to Non-Christian Religions, art. 2.)

Now we have shown in the light of theology and the teaching of Vatican II how all the redeemed possess potential realities of the supernatural order, which can lead them to be actually incorporated in Christ and make them his living members; and that while they possess them these elements make them members *in potentia* of the secret body he has formed.

Members of the mystical body in the second sense. But the term "mystical body" and its correlative, "members of the mystical body", have another meaning since the Church was founded as an institution. It is not now simply a question of being a member of a secret, invisible body; one belongs to it by the mediating agency of another body which is social and institutional. Concretely, one is incorporated in Christ by becoming a member of the Church. Now that the Church exists man needs it in order to be incorporated into the Lord. Direct contact with him is not sufficient. The contact must be made through the mediating agency of ecclesial society, of which one has to be a member in some sense. Such is the positive will of the Church's founder. From its foundation onward, Christ willed that the Church be the custodian and dispenser of those divine elements which make up supernatural life for us who dwell on earth. God's truth and grace are in the Church and the Church dispenses them. And so, in order to be incorporated in Christ we must belong to it. This is a tremendous claim, but there is no doubting it. It is rooted in the gospel, affirmed by an unvarying tradition, and insistently taught by the magisterium.

Peter (Mt 16:18) and the apostles with Peter (Eph 2:20) are the rock on which the Church is built. The Lord says that this Church enjoys his assistance so that it can be sure of God's truth (Lk 22:32), that it possesses and dispenses grace (Mt 16:19; Lk 10:15) — which is equivalent to saying that without it there is no mystical body, since the substance of that body is union with Christ through the *sensus* (knowledge) and *motus* (grace) which flow down from the head into the members.

We have recently been reminded of this truth of revelation and tradition by papal utterances and the dogmatic constitution *Lumen Gentium*. "To define and describe this true Church of Christ, which is the holy, Catholic, Apostolic, Roman Church, there is nothing nobler, nothing more excel-lent, nothing more divine than that term which describes it as the mystical body of Christ; a term which derives, as it were springs forth, from what holy Scripture and the writings of the Fathers teach time and again." (*Mystici Corporis: AAS* 35 [1943], p. 199.) This is what the encyclical *Mystici Corporis* has to say. And the encyclical *Humani Generis* confirms it, for among the inadmissable theological positions we find the position of those who "judge that they are under no obligation to accept the doctrine we set forth in an encyclical a few years ago, which is based on the sources of revela-tion and affirms that the mystical body of Christ and the Catholic, Roman Church are one and the same thing" (*AAS* 42 [1950], p. 571). And the dogmatic constitution *Lumen Gentium* likewise identifies the mystical body of Christ with the Roman Church: "This Church, constituted and organized in the world as a society, subsists in the Catho-lic Church, which is governed by the succes-sor of Peter and by the bishops in union with that successor." (*Lumen Gentium,* art. 8.)

But in what sense is the mystical body said to be the same thing as the Church of Peter? Obviously the identification is not a formal but a material one. It is a question of what we normally call the co-existence of two things (in our case the mystical and the social) in a single subject. In other words, the inward, vital elements in the Church, which are the graces of Christ, and the social elements in the Church, which are its structure and organiza-tion as an institution, are not in themselves the same thing. Obviously they are not. But they exist inseparably in a single collective subject, the Catholic Church. It is an excellent thing that a single Church should possess the two characters we have mentioned; for the result is that the two things are materially identical (identical in their subject) but formally distinct (distinct in their values). The very theological data involved force this interpretation upon us: graces, the mystical element; and institutional structure, the social element. Plainly they are two different things. Our view is upheld, moreover, by the doctrinal arrangement of the first two sections of the encyclical *Mystici Corporis,* and by the very words of Pius XII, where he rejects a distinction of opposition between the two but not a distinction of coincidence (*AAS* 35 [1943], p. 224). And art. 8 of *Lumen Gentium* suggests the same view by rendering "are the same thing" in *Humani Generis* as "*subsists in* the Catholic Church".

Having explained all this, we can now say that the problem of who the members of the mystical body on earth are may be approached from two points of view. Since that body on earth is mystical or secret as possessing grace, and social and visible as being an institution, it follows that incorporation in it can be defined either in terms of grace, the first point of view, or in social terms, the second point of view. We do not propose to solve the problem by saying that some are members of the soul of this body while others are members of its body. We are considering members of the mystical body of Christ which exists on earth. And that body is the Church as the Lord founded it. He made it mystical and social, and whoever does not belong to the Church as mystical and social does not belong to the Church Christ founded. Accordingly, those who become incorporated in it in the mystical, secret way also belong to it as a society; otherwise they would not be members of the Lord's mystical body, which today, here on earth, is a social entity by his own express will. And since this body is the only one possessed of grace, it would follow that a person who did not belong to it as a social thing could not belong to it as a mystical, secret thing either. And those who become incorporated in the Church in the institutional way will somehow or other belong to it as a mystical thing. In short, either one is simultaneously a member of the mystical and the visible Church, or one is not a member of it in either respect.

Here we must recall the theological doctrine of the *votum,* the desire, tendency, or orientation. The doctrine has a number of applications in theology. This desire or orientation is sometimes personal, because it is an explicit act of the will or because it is implicit in some other act of the will. The catechumen who wishes to be baptized has an explicit personal desire for baptism. The pagan who wants to do God's will in all things has a personal implicit desire for baptism, because it is God's will that he be saved and salvation comes by that sacrament.

In other cases the desire or orientation is "real". It is not part of the personal will of the man to whom we attribute it; it is part of

things. For things also have an orientation, a tendency towards something or a "desire" for something.

After these preliminary explanations we can now classify the members of Christ's mystical body on earth — the members of the Church.

Some are real and perfect members of the mystical body by the two titles we have spoken of. They have been perfectly incorporated in Christ, are his living members, because they live in grace. And they have been so by a real and perfect incorporation in the social body which here on earth possesses and dispenses grace, for they profess the faith, receive the sacraments, and obey the hierarchy. Some are real members of the mystical body in the first respect, because they have grace, and are intentional members, members *in voto,* in the second respect, because they belong to the society only by desire. With some the desire is personal — catechumens. With others it is "real" — pagans who keep the natural law and are disposed to obey God in all things, and have therefore received sanctifying grace from God (*D* 1677; *Mystici Corporis: AAS* 35 [1943], p. 243; *Lumen Gentium,* arts. 9, 16). The dogmatic constitution *Lumen Gentium* points out that there are elements of sanctity outside the visible structure of the Church — elements, however, which unite a man with the Church in a certain way. "Many elements of sanctification and of truth can be found outside of its visible structure. These elements, however, as gifts properly belonging to the Church of Christ, possess an inner dynamism toward Catholic unity." (Art. 8.)

Some are real members of the mystical body in its social aspect and intentional members, members *in voto,* of the body in its mystical, vital, or secret aspect. Others are possessed of supernatural gifts which have a native tendency or *votum* or inclination towards sanctifying grace. For instance, the sacramental character in baptized persons who live in mortal sin makes them members of the Church as a society but does not make them live by grace; still it is a supernatural reality which calls upon grace to become active in its own rightful domain.

Some are real and perfect members of the mystical body in its vital aspect because they live by grace, and imperfect members of the mystical body in its social aspect, with which they have a certain connection but an incomplete one. Through what they have they really belong to the institutional Church; by baptism, for example, by obeying the hierarchy, by sharing in the Church's worship, or the like. In respect of what they lack they belong to the Church only *in voto*. We mean our separated brethren, who may be perfect members of the Church in its mystical or secret aspect by possessing grace; they are members of the Church in its social aspect insofar as they agree in belief and practice with the Catholic Church (*Lumen Gentium*, art. 15; *Unitatis Redintegratio*, art. 3). Finally they are members *in voto*, or by intention, in respect of what they do not have in common with the Catholic Church. The sound elements of religion which they do possess have a tendency, a real, objective instinct, to seek completion in what they lack.

To sum up: The Church of Christ is the one built on Peter and the apostles. There is no other mystical body on earth but that Church. It is the custodian and dispenser of grace. But grace lives in many who have not yet entered the Church. It lives in them because they are connected with it in one way or another, in one degree or another, consciously or by a purely objective bond.

See also *Ecumenism* III, IV, *Atheism, Grace* I, II, *Communion of Saints, Purgatory*.

BIBLIOGRAPHY. OFFICIAL DOCUMENTS: Pius XII, Encyclical *Mystici Corporis Christi*, 29 June 1943 (*AAS* 35 [1943], pp. 193–248); Vatican II, Dogmatic Constitution on the Church, *Lumen Gentium*, and Decree on Ecumenism, *Unitatis Redintegratio*. LITERATURE: H. de Lubac, *Catholicism* (1943); F. X. Lawlor, "Occult Heresy and Membership in the Church", *Theological Studies* 10 (1949), pp. 541–54; T. Sartory, *Kirche und Kirchen: Fragen der Theologie heute* (1957); P. Hamell, "Membership of the Mystical Body", *Irish Ecclesiastical Record* 89 (1958), pp. 393–411; C. O'Neill, "Members of the Church", *ibid.* 92 (1959), pp. 312–22; Y. Congar, *The Mystery of the Church* (1960); H. U. von Balthasar, "Wer ist die Kirche? Sponsa Verbi", *Skizzen zur Theologie,* II (1961); K. McNamara, "The Theology of Christian Unity", *Irish Theological Quarterly* 28 (1961), pp. 255–77; K. Mörsdorf, "Persona in Ecclesia Christi", *Archiv für Katholisches Kirchenrecht* 131 (1962), pp. 345–93; U. Valeske, *Votum Ecclesiae* (1962), biblio.; K. McNamara, "The Theology of Christian Unity", *Christian Unity* (1962), pp. 158–82; C. O'Neill, "St. Thomas on Membership of the Church", *The Thomist* 27 (1963), pp. 88–140; id., "Members of the Church", *American Ecclesiastical Review* 148 (1963), pp. 113–28, 167–84; E. Sauras, "The Members of the Church", *The Thomist* 27 (1963), pp. 86 ff.; J. Ratzinger, *Wesen und Grenzen der Kirche: Das Zweite Vatikanische Konzil* (1963); Y. Congar, *Sainte Église. Études et approches ecclésiologiques* (1963); K. Rahner, *Theological Investigations,* II (1963), V (1966); H. Heinemann, *Die rechtliche Stellung der nichtkatholischen Christen* (1964); E. Lamirande, "La signification ecclésiologique des communautés dissidentes et la doctrine des 'vestigia ecclesiae'", *Istina* 10 (1964), pp. 25–58; G. Lafont, "L'Appartenance fondamentale à l'Église catholique", in M.-J. le Guillou and G. Lafont, *L'Église en Marche* (1964); B. Willems, "Who Belongs to the Church?", *Concilium* 1, no. 1 (1965), pp. 62–71; G. Baum, *De Ecclesia. The Constitution on the Church with Commentary* (1965); D. Flanagan, ed., *The Meaning of the Church* (1966); H. Küng, *Die Kirche* (1967); contributions by K. Rahner, A. Grillmeier and H. Vorgrimler in H. Vorgrimler, ed., *Commentary on the Documents of Vatican II*, vol. I (1967), pp. 138–226.

Emilio Sauras

CHURCH AND STATE

Because Church and State essentially differ, the relationship between them is always a dialectical one. Though with different ends in view, each claims the allegiance of the same person. The State's business is to defend and promote the natural goods of its citizens on earth, whereas the Church is called upon to continue the redemptive work of its founder on earth and lead men by word and sacrament to their eternal salvation. Church and State being composed of the same members, the relations between them must be regulated in accordance with historical evolution and the concrete situation at a given time. All attempts to fix the relations between Church and State in the abstract are foredoomed, because they ignore the historicity of both Church and State. In the West the many forms of relationship between Church and State over the centuries reflect varying political situations but even more the ideas men had of Church and State from time to time.

A. IN THE NEW TESTAMENT

While the NT contains no doctrine or explicit statement on the concrete relationship between Church and State, it does have something to say about the State. It teaches that the Christian is not excused from obeying civil authority and it sets forth the meaning and measure of that obedience. The biblical view of the Christian's position vis-à-vis civil authority — as found in the logion on paying taxes (Mk 12:13–17 and parr.), in Rom 13:1 ff.; 1 Pet 2:13; 1 Tim 2:2; Tit 3:1; but also in Rev 13:1 ff. — must be compared with what natural theology and natural law tell us of Church and State, before the Catholic Church can find a basis for its relations with the State. The variety of statements on the civil power which are encountered in the NT (compare Rom 13:1 ff. with Rev 13:1 ff.) shows us the dialectical position of the Christian and the Church vis-à-vis secular rulers; at the same time it shows that the attitude of the Church towards the State must be governed not only by the possible abuse of the State's authority (with which the Church always has to reckon) but also by the dignity of the State, which the Church recognizes as a power different from and completely independent of itself. At the same time the NT constantly reminds the Church that its normal lot in this world is not tranquillity and peace but persecution (see Mt 10:17 f.; Rev 13:1 ff.), persecution meaning not only attacks on the Church but the temptation, in an over-friendly State, for the Church to try to do its work through the State and in the State's interest. Two NT themes govern the relationship between Church and State: on the one hand the affirmation of civil authority because it comes from God, and on the other the rejection of the State's claim to complete dominion. The State is not the supreme and ultimate value; being an element of order in this aeon, it is finite and provisional (see Phil 3:20) and its business differs from the business of the Church.

Any identification of the State with the Church (even *de facto*) is repugnant to the nature of Church and State alike. But this does not mean that the two exist side by side without any sort of connection between them. Each is an enterprise of God in the world and each has its service to render man, which can best be done through peaceful co-operation with the other, each retaining its own nature, independence, and inviolable sphere of competence. A sound scriptural idea of the Christian's position vis-à-vis the State cannot have us ignore the institutions and affairs of this world; rather it will move us to play a responsible and serviceable part in both; for where the NT speaks of civil authorities it calls on the Christian to obey them and pray for them, whether they be Christian or not. Indeed the religion of the ruler presents no problem at all to the NT: we must remember that Rom 13:1f. was written while Nero governed the Roman Empire. Nevertheless, Scripture takes a more personal view than the abstract, institutional one which is deduced from natural theology and natural law. Foreshortening the biblical view has had the most harmful effect on relations between Church and State over the centuries; and it is also foreshortening the biblical view to interpret certain texts (that on paying taxes, for example, Mk 12:13–17 and parr., or Rom 13:1f. in particular) as enunciations of natural law, so that their meaning for redemptive history, eschatology, and concrete life is lost from sight. The deliberations and pronouncements of Vatican II have clearly shown that today the question of the relations between Church and State is deeply embedded in the broader question of the Church's relations with the world at large. Vatican II certainly seems to mark a break with the past, when the question of the Church's relations with the world and human society was often reduced to the question of Church and State. (Leo XIII's encyclicals on civil society still reflect that view.)

But once we are clear that the relationship between Church and State is only one element, though a very important one, in the total problem of "the Church and the world", then the purely juridical approach to the problem of Church and State is seen to be quite inadequate. Not as though it were irrelevant to inquire what the legitimate relationship between Church and State may be (trying to work out, for instance, how far they are independent and how they should co-operate), or as though we would ignore those matters in favour of a purely sociological approach. We only wish to fit them into a wider context which future juridical arrangements will also have to take into account.

B. Autonomy of Church and State

The modern Catholic view of the autonomy of Church and State undoubtedly reflects a notion of the State which has only developed in modern times, and also a new self-consciousness of the Church, as totally different from the State, which the Church has acquired by meditating on its nature as the "mystical body", the "people of God", the "primordial sacrament" (all of which it is, of course, as the institutional, hierarchical, official Church) and its mission of ministering to human society. True, since later antiquity the Church has stressed its independence of the State, but the principle has been interpreted and applied in a great variety of ways. Since the competence of the Church derives from the authority of God, not that of the State, and the competence of the State likewise derives from the authority of God, not that of the Church, the State is independent in its own temporal, political domain, in pursuing its natural end, which is the defence and promotion of its citizens' temporal well-being; and the Church is independent in performing its supernatural tasks (teaching faith and morals, celebrating the liturgy, preaching the word, administering the sacraments, in all that concerns the structure and administration of the Church). The many attempts that the State has made in the past and in our own day to control the inner or outer order of the Church (various kinds of State Church, Gallicanism, Febronianism, Josephinism) are inconsistent with this independence; but so are the claims of the Church (mainly in the Middle Ages) to supremacy over the State and the attempt to enforce them when the Church was able (papal institution and deposition of princes and attempts to subject the State to canon law).

Following the doctrine of the "two swords", which Pope Gelasius I propounded against Byzantium, medieval theories of Church and State sometimes went to extremes (like the hierocratic doctrine of the *potestas ecclesiae directa in temporalibus*). But in evaluating them we must remember that the historical background and the philosophico-theological idea of a single Christendom — *ecclesia universalis* — embracing crown and clergy, the spiritual and the temporal power, in one metaphysical sweep, meant that Church and State were closely interwoven. Given the idea that the society which pursues the nobler end is the nobler society, men compared the two powers to gold and lead or sun and moon. (Unlike the State, the Church works for our supernatural, eternal good and so its end is the higher. We find the Fathers themselves, St. Gregory of Nazianzus, for instance, and St. John Chrysostom, comparing Church and State to soul and body or heaven and earth.) This meant that the Church was regarded as essentially superior to the State. In the investiture controversy Gregory VII fought not only for the freedom of the Church (*libertas ecclesiae*) but also for its supremacy within the total *Corpus Christianum* which embraced both Church and State; and his attitude develops logically, by way of Innocent III and Innocent IV, to Boniface VIII and the bull *Unam Sanctam* (18 November 1302). This bull presents the Pope as the source of both powers, though it recognizes that Church and State differ in their general nature. The hierocratic theory itself affirmed the autonomous jurisdiction of the State and the Pope's duty to pass on the temporal sword. Papal intervention in temporal affairs was considered legitimate only *ratione peccati*, that is, if the salvation of souls were at stake. But since the Pope was sole judge of whether a given case involved the salvation of souls, the formula *ratione peccati* could in fact be used to justify any political move on the Pope's part.

St. Thomas Aquinas considered the State an institution of natural law, and, therefore, part of the natural order, whereas the Church belonged to the supernatural order of revelation and grace. His doctrine combined scriptural and Augustinian thought with Aristotle and stressed the origin of both powers in God: "Both powers derive from God, the spiritual and the temporal. Temporal authority, therefore, is subject to the spiritual insofar as God has subordinated it, namely in matters concerning the salvation of souls; so in these matters a man must obey the spiritual power rather than the temporal." (*II Sent.* d. 44, q. 2, a. 3 and 4.) In accordance with the Aristotelian teleology of his thought, St. Thomas affirms the superiority of the spiritual power, but not without qualification: "Civil authority is subject to ecclesiastical authority only where the exigencies of our supernatural end — eternal life — are involved; in its own sphere the civil power enjoys ample independence." (M. Grabmann.) In St. Thomas we already have a sharper distinction of the ends of Church and State which Bellarmine accentuates and which produces the doctrine of the Church's indirect power *in temporalibus*.

On Thomistic foundations Leo XIII constructed a doctrine of Church and State which has prevailed down to the present time. Leo also proceeds on the assumption that the State, being an institution of natural right, comes directly from God. "Like civil society, the civil power has its source in nature and therefore in God himself. Whence it follows that civil authority as such is from God alone." (*Immortale Dei,* 1 November 1885.) Church and State are autonomous societies, each with its own native right; each is a *societas perfecta,* each sovereign in its own sphere. "God has divided the care of the human race between two powers, the ecclesiastical and the civil. One is in charge of divine concerns, the other of human concerns. Each is supreme in its own sphere, each is confined within certain limits which follow from its nature and proximate goal." (*Ibid.*) And *Sapientiae Christianae* (10 January 1890) says: "Since Church and State each has its own authority, neither of the two societies is subject to the other in the ordering and conduct of its own affairs — within the limits, of course, that each is assigned by its proximate goal." Just as the Church acknowledges the independence of the State in all purely civil matters, so the State must also acknowledge the sovereignty of the Church in her own sphere: "Whatever, therefore, in human affairs is in any way sacred, whatever concerns the salvation of souls or the worship of God, either by its own nature or by reason of the end to which it is referred — all this is subject to the authority and judgment of the Church. On the other hand civil and political matters are quite rightly subject to the authority of the State." (*Immortale Dei.*) It is still disputed whether Leo XIII teaches a *potestas indirecta* or only a *potestas directiva.* His utterances certainly advance no explicit claim to jurisdiction; but since he does not discuss what power, if any, the Church can have over temporal things (much less over the State) and what means it can use to give its principles effect in the world, his teaching will not tell us the nature of the Church's power *in temporalibus.*

On the other hand it is increasingly recognized today that the independence of Church and State ultimately depends on the nature and origin of each one's authority; these also determine the means which Church and State may use in pursuance of their various ends. The spiritual nature and the spiritual authority entrusted to it determine the nature and scope of the Church's work in the world.

C. Co-operation between Church and State

Though Church and State pursue two different ends, they are composed of the same members. The same individuals are expected to satisfy the requirements of both powers, and so those requirements must be attuned as far as possible. This is particularly necessary in "mixed matters", which concern Church law under one aspect and State law under another (for instance, marriage, education, schools, appointments to ecclesiastical office [insofar as they may affect the State], establishing Church holidays, Sunday work, the legal position of Church property, and the like). If there is to be lasting agreement on such matters, which the Church has traditionally preferred to settle by concordat, each side must be prepared to meet the other half-way and accept a solution that takes account of all citizens, not only of the Church's members. As the champion of personal freedom the Church must take care that no agreement it makes with the State shall prejudice the rights of third parties who are not Catholics. In such arrangements the Church seeks first of all recognition and contractual guarantees of its independence. Its chief requirement is always that the State allow it to carry out its mission without hindrance, that the citizens of the State shall be free to discharge their supernatural duties, and that the State's demands within its own sphere shall not conflict with the natural moral law or the revealed law of God.

Here most Catholic canonists and moral theologians warn us not to conclude, from the sovereignty of the two powers, that their respective goals and purposes are equal in rank; because, they say, the Church firmly maintains that its supernatural end is higher than the purely natural end of the State (and therefore it must take precedence over the State). This point has relevance for the individual in a concrete case of conflict; but it is quite irrelevant to the legitimate relations of Church and State nowadays when the State, indifferent to all Churches and religions, would reject any such argument simply on the grounds of civil liberty, so that in any case of conflict between itself and the State it would be futile for the Church to argue the subordination of ends.

Even in the case of an individual, the

theoretical superiority of the Church will not mean that its law must always be obeyed in preference to the law of the State if the two happen to conflict. For the principle that the Church's law takes precedence rests on the assumption that a man is faced with a choice between supernatural duty (represented by the Church) and natural, earthly duty (represented by the State). If the case is otherwise, then the principle cannot apply. The fact that the Syllabus condemned the proposition (no. 42), "In conflictu legum utriusque potestatis ius civile praevalet", does not mean that the Church claims precedence for its law over the law of the State in every case; it means that the law of the State does not take precedence in every case. If the civil law conflicts with the natural moral law or God's revealed law, then it is equally wrong to impose or to obey such a law (see the relevant passages in the encyclicals *Diuturnum Illud* and *Sapientiae Christianae*). In every age the Church proclaims with St. Peter: "We must obey God rather than men" (Acts 5:29; see also Acts 4:19).

The right and duty which the Church has to declare with binding authority what is contained in divine revelation and to condemn such doctrines and practices as offend against revelation, extends to the civil and political sphere, which is subject to God's commandments like every other sphere of human life. The State is no less bound to obey God than the Church is. But this right of the Church implies no coercive power over the State. The history of theory about Church and State reflects the many forms which actual relations between them have taken down the ages. Yves Congar rightly warns against overlooking this variety: "Let us not turn the law and arrangements of one period into an absolute, but recognize that the three successive theories of the *potestas directa, indirecta,* and *directiva* reflect a historical evolution which is normal but irreversible." Decisions that the Church makes in virtue of its *potestas spiritualis directa* are not acts of civil jurisdiction. At the same time it would be an error to regard them as mere exhortations that oblige no one; they are commands which bind members of the Church in conscience, and the Church can demand that they be strictly obeyed (for example, forbidding Catholics to be members of a given political party under pain of excommunication).

D. SEPARATION OF CHURCH AND STATE

New thinking about the relationship between the two powers also affects our ideas about the separation of Church and State. The complete separation championed by liberals and socialists was meant to deprive the Church of all influence in public life. The demand was used as a weapon in a struggle to destroy the Church completely, and as such the Church could not and cannot accept it. This is the sense in which we must interpret the many condemnations by 19th- and 20th-century Popes (see especially Gregory XVI against Lamennais, encyclical *Mirari Vos,* 15 August 1832; Pius IX, *Syllabus of Errors,* 8 December 1864; Leo XIII, encyclicals *Immortale Dei,* 1 November 1885, and *Libertas Praestantissimum,* 28 June 1888; Pius X against the French law separating Church and State, encyclicals *Vehementer Nos,* 11 February 1906, *Gravissimo Officii,* 10 August 1906, *Une fois encore,* 6 January 1907, and the similar Portuguese law, *Iamdudum,* 24 May 1911; Benedict XV, encyclical *Ad Beatissimi,* 1 November 1914; Pius XII, various addresses after 1945).

If the separation of Church and State is designed to treat the Church as though it were non-existent or a mere private concern of individual citizens, who are even denied the right to organize as a religious body (as happened in France in 1905), then the modern State is not simply affirming its neutrality towards all religions, it is attacking the very existence of religion. But a constitutional separation of the two powers which recognizes the public existence of the Church or at least allows it to work unhampered, is another matter. Thus separation in the U.S.A., for example, has benefited the Church, allowing it to flourish in the public sphere free of any State tutelage. In the libertarian democracies today the old idea of separation is increasingly yielding to the idea of partnership between Church and State, and it is not felt to be a major concern whether this new partnership is secured by a concordat or results from the State's acceptance of a plurality of social forces. A constitutional separation of the two powers which does not interfere with the Church's free growth in social life but guarantees it the area of freedom necessary for carrying out its saving mission can do justice to the nature of Church and State alike. A. Hartmann pertinently observes that for the State to bear its own limited competence in mind does not make it a laicized State. The *État laïque* is not an *État laïcisé,* and confining the State to its proper domain must not be confused with separating State from Church as many 19th-century liberals and socialists wished to do.

So it is inconsistent with the modern view of both powers to maintain traditional rights which the State has had to supervise the Church. These are historical relics from the days of established Churches and are incompatible with the autonomy of the Church. Any future agreement between Church and State must take account of altered circumstances. The problem of the separation of Church and State has entered a new phase, as is clear from the lively discussion of John Courtney Murray's ideas on the subject, and we must ask whether the term "separation", with its many historical overtones, is a suitable term to use at all of the relationship existing between Church and State in the libertarian democracies. More distance between Church and State does not mean that the Church renounces any attempt to influence public life; rather, "being henceforth wholly independent of the State, the Church can and must take that much closer an interest in the world and the State" (R. Smend).

E. The Church and the Secularized State

The altered conception which modern democracy has of itself has made it possible for the Church to establish a positive relationship with the "neutral" State (neutral towards all religions and philosophies). On the one hand the Church has to give up a number of privileges in the civil order; it can no longer identify its own work wholly or in part with the work of the State and it acknowledges the State's autonomy in secular affairs. On the other hand the State leaves the Church entirely free to carry out its saving mission in the world, part of which is to preach the truth that is necessary to human dignity rightly understood. Of course before one can approve of the secular State one must realize that religious liberty is a civil right of the individual even according to the Church's doctrine, and that the Church, certain as it is of objective truth, does not merely tolerate the erroneous conscience of the individual but acknowledges it as responsible decision. Only on this basis can the Church not merely tolerate the State's neutrality towards all religions and philosophies but affirm it as consistent with the natural moral order. Vatican II decided in favour of religious liberty thus understood, with its Declaration on Religious Freedom.

The drawing apart of Church and State in democracy means at once an opportunity and a responsibility for the Church. When the State recognizes a plurality of social forces, which often assert a group interest to the prejudice of the national interest, it is the more difficult for the State to ensure the common good; especially since the parties, being dependent on votes, are always tempted to court organized interests. Here the Church is as it were the conscience of the public; it is its business to awaken and fortify in the State and society a sense of their duty to the common good. It is the business of the Church, the guardian of the moral order, to keep that order present to the minds of men, both those who command and those who obey. Even in a pluralistic world the Church can exercise its native right and work for a fair consideration of its interests, so that its adherents may freely cultivate their convictions in contrast to other views within the State.

By using its due freedom to awaken the conscience of all men, proclaiming that they must always observe justice and love in their doings, it makes its contribution to the State and society. This is the real "social mission" of the Church, so much talked of and so much misunderstood. Thus the Church consciously influences the temporal sphere but not in order to rule, to impose its own commands, but to serve, to make known to men that they are subject to God's law individually and as society. True, the Church regards itself as the accredited organ of God's commands, but does not on that account claim that the State is in any way subordinate to it, even in moral or spiritual matters; for the secular State is free to decide which moral values it wishes to make the foundation of the civil order. In the eyes of the Church, moral principles are objective truths; but in the eyes of the State they are subjective value-judgments — except for human rights which exist antecedent to the State. So long as the State is a libertarian democracy the Church has an opportunity to make objective truth prevail in the realm of politics through its faithful. This method of redemptive work necessarily means a further shift from the institutional to the personal approach.

The Pastoral Constitution of Vatican II on the Church in the Modern World confirms the fact that the Church, without succumbing to "progressivism", is moving towards a new view of the world and of its relations with the State; it is prepared to admit that the bond between the State and man is willed by God, at the same time differentiating this bond from man's inalienable status as a son of God and his saving bond with the Church of Jesus Christ. The constitution deliberately places the modern idea of Church and State in the context of the pluralist society and distinguishes what Christians do as citizens, individually or in groups, guided by their own Christian conscience, from activities which they carry on in the name of the Church and in union with their pastors (art. 76, 1). It stresses the point that the Church has no wish whatever to encroach on the business of civil society and is not committed to any political system (art. 76, 2). Henceforth, therefore, there can be no question of identifying the work of the Church with that of the State or at least confounding the two. The activity which the Christian as a citizen chooses to engage in, following his own judgment and inspired by his faith, is differentiated from his activity as a member of the Church, under its authority. The constitution expressly acknowledges the independence of Church and State alike, but points out that both serve the personal and social vocation of man (art. 76, 3). Above all it is the Church's duty to continue fostering justice and love among the nations. A comparison of this declaration with Leo XIII's doctrine of Church and State as the "two powers" will throw into sharp relief the change there has been, from the idea of domination to that of service.

Breaking with the traditional view that the State is to help the Church carry out its mission, the Council concludes: "But it [the Church] does not lodge its hopes in privileges conferred by civil authority. Indeed, it stands ready to renounce the exercise of certain legitimately acquired rights if it becomes clear that their use raises doubts about the sincerity of its witness or that new conditions of life call for some other arrangements." (Art. 76, 5.)

The willingness of the Church to give up outdated privileges and duly acquired rights proves that it accepts the implications of being different from the State as it follows Christ in this world. It now turns to its spiritual mission, which enables and constrains it to undertake a dialogue with the world. This means that the Church in the whole of its life has become an intellectual and spiritual partner indispensable for the State precisely because it is neutral towards all religions and psychologies. It is citizens making their own personal decisions according to their Christian conscience who represent Christian values in the State and ensure the presence of Christ's Church in the secular State. Instead of confronting the State as a kind of outside power, almost another nation, the Church now works and lives its life in the same society which produces the State, though it does not identify itself with society and the State. Co-operation between Church and State is seen in a new light. Now the question is not so much defining each one's rights and sphere of competence as practical adaptation in their joint responsibility for man; for Church and State are both entrusted with the welfare of man, though in two entirely different ways, according to the nature and operation of each. Wherever the Church awakens and sensitizes conscience, wherever it proclaims the gospel and teaches Christian moral principles, wherever it spreads justice and love, it is accomplishing its true mission. Of temporal powers it expects freedom to work without let or hindrance, freedom vis-à-vis the State and other social forces as well.

F. The Present Situation

There are now roughly three types of relationship between Church and State in the West and in the other countries with a Christian background. Certain countries still preserve the old forms of an established Church; most countries have made a separation between Church and State, some enforcing a strict break (with complete religious freedom) and others co-operating with the Church in various ways; and the Communist countries have a separation designed to exclude the Church altogether from public life. This general classification, however, does not tell us how far religious freedom — freedom of conscience for the individual and freedom of worship and witness for religious bodies — is allowed in the libertarian democracies (even those which maintain a traditional established Church). The practice varies widely and is often of quite recent introduction. On the other hand totalitarian States in the East thwart the practice of religion so far as possible, even when religious freedom is guaranteed in the constitution. Many States regulate their relations with the Churches not only by relevant constitutional provisions but also by concordats and other agreements reached with the religious bodies.

1. *Established Churches.* Originally, the special feature of an established Church was that it relegated to an inferior legal status such citizens as did not belong to it. But today all States which retain an established Church not only allow religious freedom but give all citizens full equality before the law. Only here and there are specially representative State offices reserved to members of the State Church: thus the Sovereign and Lord Chancellor in England, the King and Minister for Worship in Sweden, the King in Denmark, and the Head of State in Spain must belong to the established Church. Even as to purely religious matters, the State shares in the government of modern established Churches. In the United Kingdom only the Church of England (Anglican) and the Church of Scotland (Presbyterian) are still established. The Sovereign is head of the Church of England but not of other Churches of the Anglican Communion.

The British Parliament, where certain bishops are members of the Upper House as Lords Spiritual, maintains in many ways its right to determine the doctrine and liturgy of the Church of England. In Norway and Sweden the Sovereign is also head of the established Lutheran Church. The "Danish National Church" really has no head. Lutheranism is still the official religion of Iceland and Finland. The Finnish President nominates bishops of the Lutheran Church and the Orthodox Church as well. Both these Churches are financially supported by the State and their synodal decrees must be confirmed by Parliament. The only other country which has an established Orthodox Church is Greece. The position in Switzerland is exceptional in a number of respects. Some cantons (Zurich, Waadt) have a Calvinist established Church or, having separated Church and State, only recognize the Calvinist Church as existing at law (Basle Town, Appenzell-Aùsserrhoden). Some recognize only the Catholic Church in the same way (Ticino, Valais). Most cantons recognize both Churches, either as the established Churches of the canton or, where Church and State have been separated (Neuchâtel, Geneva), as the only Churches with a legal existence there. One relic of the past is the express prohibition of the Society of Jesus in the constitution of the Swiss Confederation, and there are still certain other restrictions on religious freedom.

Elsewhere in Europe Catholicism is the State religion only in Italy and Spain. The Lateran Treaty of 1929 established the Church in Italy and was confirmed by the republican constitution (1946), which, however, also guarantees freedom of religion and organization to non-Catholics, reserving their relationship to the State to special agreements. Until recently, non-Catholics in Spain were subject to real disabilities. Now, as a result of the Council's Declaration on Religious Freedom, a law of 1967 has given them a large measure of freedom, as individuals and as religious bodies. It will be necessary to make a corresponding adjustment in the provisions of the fundamental law (1947) and the concordat (1953), which give the Catholic Church a special status.

In Latin America the Catholic Church is the State Church of Argentina, Bolivia, Colombia, Costa Rica, the Dominican Republic, Haiti, and Paraguay. Nevertheless religious freedom is guaranteed by the constitution, although a few years ago the Colombian government took measures against Protestants. Costa Rica and Bolivia still retain the right to nominate bishops which was enjoyed by the Spanish crown; Argentina surrendered the right in 1966 (responding to the desire expressed by the Council in its Decree on the Bishops' Pastoral Office in the Church, art. 20).

2. *Separation of Church and State in the West.* All other States in the West which have a Christian background provide in their constitutions for separation of Church and State and religious freedom. Even where the separation was brought about by secularist, anti-clerical forces, relations have improved. In France, for example, despite the hostile legislation of 1905 and 1914, there was a *rapprochement* of Church and State after the

First World War. In 1921 diplomatic relations were resumed with the Vatican and it was agreed to hold consultations before bishops were appointed (though so far there has been no concordat). Thus the Church is free to expand. Close co-operation has grown up between Church and State in West Germany, on the basis of relevant articles from the Weimar Constitution which are now embodied in the fundamental law of 1949, together with the concordats still in force (those of constituent States of the Federal Republic and the concordat made with Germany in 1933). Legislation envisages the Churches' engaging in public activities, especially social work and relief, and provides them with substantial sums.

In Austria too, religious bodies may be recognized by the State as legal corporations. The ecclesiastical reorganization provided for by the concordat of 1933 has been carried out and ill-feeling about State subsidies to the Churches and religious instruction in State schools has been allayed. The Belgian constitution of 1831, much admired in the last century for the freedom it secured the Church, exempts all recognized religions from State control. But the State pays the salaries of the clergy — Catholic, Protestant and Jewish. In Luxemburg the position is similar. The Netherlands also allows religious bodies to carry on social and political activity without interference from the State; here an extensive school system and broadcasting stations of their own are very useful to them. In the Republic of Ireland the constitution provides for religious liberty and the separation of Church and State, and forbids the State to subsidize any religion. It recognizes that the Catholic religion, for which there is no concordat, is that of the great majority, but also protects the Protestant Churches and Jewish congregations. The constitution of 1933 still separates Church and State in Portugal and the concordat of 1940 accepts that position. Though the Catholic Church is recognized as a corporate body, the State is free to extend the same recognition to other religious bodies; they can, however, worship and organize without such recognition. Portugal still claims and uses the right of patronage in the mission areas of its overseas provinces.

The two powers are completely separate in the U.S.A. There the Supreme Court has ruled that the First Amendment forbids providing a religion with any local or national subsidy, and therefore that no religious instruction can be given in "public" schools. At the same time the separation ensures the widest religious freedom. Churches are free, for instance, to set up schools and even universities — an opportunity of which the Catholic Church has made full use, so that today it has a complete system of independent schools. A similar freedom exists in the Philippines, whose constitution is modelled on the American one. In Canada the separation is not so sharp; Church schools can obtain a degree of State assistance. Even the radical separation in Mexico (constitution of 1917), which was meant to annihilate the influence of the Catholic Church, has been ineffective to that end, despite the persecutions from 1923 to 1928. Today religious liberty prevails, and the anti-Catholic legislation is tending to become a dead letter. Other Latin American countries have various forms of separation. In 1964, even before Argentina, Venezuela gave up the right to nominate bishops, an agreement to that effect being made with the Holy See.

3. *Separation of Church and State in Communist countries.* Modelled on the constitution of the U.S.S.R., the system of separation in Communist countries demands "separation of the State from the Church and of the Church from the schools", so as to deprive religion of all influence whatever, especially over the young. Constitutional texts may proclaim freedom of conscience and worship but the State does everything possible to paralyze the Churches while offering atheist propaganda every facility, for atheism alone is considered scientific and therefore worthy of State patronage. The concrete situation varies a great deal from country to country. In Poland and East Germany pastoral work can be carried on, though often amid difficulties and friction with the authorities. While the Church in Czechoslovakia, strictly supervised by the State, is left with very little scope for its life and work, conditions in Yugoslavia and even in Hungary have begun to improve quite recently.

See also *Church and World, Natural Law, Constantinian Era, Investiture Controversy, Bishop IV, Josephinism, Justice, Occident, Pluralism, Social Movements IV C, Society III, Conscience.*

BIBLIOGRAPHY. F.-J. Moulart, *L'Église et l'État ou les deux Puissances* (4th ed., 1895); O. Schilling, *Die Staat- und Soziallehre des heiligen Augustinus* (1910); W. Müller, *Der Staat in seinen Beziehungen zur sittlichen Ordnung bei Thomas von Aquin* (1916); O. Schilling, *Die Staat- und Soziallehre Leos XIII.* (1925); M. Rommen, *Die Staatslehre des F. Suárez* (1927); A. Farner, *Die Lehre vom Staat bei Kalvin und Zwingli* (1930); O. Schilling, *Die Staat- und Soziallehre des heiligen Thomas von Aquin* (2nd ed., 1930); M. Grabmann, *Studien über den Einfluss der aristotelischen Philosophie auf die mittelalterlichen Themen über das Verhältnis von Kirche und Staat* (1934); F. X. Arnold, *Die Staatslehre des Kardinal Bellarmin* (1934); J. Bohatec, *Calvins Lehre von Staat und Kirche* (1937; repr. 1961); F. Gavin, *Seven Centuries of the Problems of Church and State* (1938); J. Maritain, *Christianity and Democracy* (1945); M. S. Bates, *Religious Liberty. An Inquiry* (2nd ed., 1946); K. Barth, *Community, Church, State* (1946); J. Lecler, *L'Église et la souveraineté de l'État* (1946); J. B. Barron and H. M. Waddams, *Communism and the Churches. A Documentation* (1950); C. Garbett, *Church and State in England* (1950); R. F. Pattee, *The Religious Question in Spain* (1950); A. P. Stocker, *Church and State in the U.S.*, 3 vols. (1950); J. S. Curtiss, *The Russian Church and the Soviet State, 1917–1950* (1953); L. Pfeffer, *Church, State and Freedom* (1953); S. Ehler and J. Morrall, *Church and State through the Centuries,* a collection of documents (1954); W. Gurian and M. A. Fitzsimons, eds., *The Catholic Church in World Affairs* (1954); V. Gsovski, ed., *Church and State behind the Iron Curtain. Czechoslovakia, Hungary, Poland, Rumania, with an Introduction on the Soviet Union* (1955); H. D. Hughey, *Religious Freedom in Spain* (1955); W. Ullmann, *The Growth of Papal Government in the Middle Ages* (1955); J. J. Baierl, *The Catholic Church and the Modern State* (1956); M. Spinka, *The Church in Soviet Russia* (1956); M. P. Fogarty, *Christian Democracy in Western Europe, 1820–1953* (1957); T. Kenny, *The Political Thought of Cardinal Newman* (1957); A. V. Murray, *The State and the Church in a Free Society* (1958); Y. Congar, *The Mystery of the Church* (1960); J. C. Murray, *We Hold These Truths* (1960); O. Cullmann, *The State in the New Testament* (rev. ed., 1963); P. Mikat, *Das Verhältnis von Kirche und Staat in der Bundesrepublik Deutschland* (1964); J. C. Murray, *The Problem of Religious Freedom* (1965).

Paul Mikat

CHURCH AND WORLD

1. *Introduction.* The Church's reflection and teaching on the mutual relation of world and Church have to some extent entered on a new stage with Vatican II. The Church has always of course been concerned with the theme. Scripture itself raises the question of the significance of secular authority and of the obligation and limit of Christians' obedience to it. The patristic period, the Middle Ages and modern times, all dealt in theory and in actual practice which often involved bitter conflicts, with the relation between Sacerdotium and Imperium, the question of the relation between Church and State, the Church's freedom in face of the State, the relative autonomy of the State in face of the Church, the right of the Church to a particular kind of influence on the action of the State, the question of the separation of Church and State, the task of the State in regard to the true religion and the Church. But if we leave aside the perpetually recurring question of the relation between revelation (dogma, magisterium) and secular science and learning (which of course is also an essential portion of the "world"), almost the only question formerly raised was that of Church and State, the latter regarded in terms of authority. Today it is a question of the relation between the Church and the *world*. And the "world" is envisaged as it is experienced at the present time — as a history of humanity as a single whole, and as a world which is not simply an antecedent datum, a situation of interest solely in the perspective of salvation. It is a world planned and produced by man himself and it therefore concerns man even in its own empirically observable importance. This new way of raising the question was plainly seen at Vatican II. The Church deliberately set itself this question. It had been prepared for in the Church's dispute with 19th century Liberalism and with Marxism (chiefly, however, in the economic domain). Marxism was really the first to work out a genuine theory of a world to be constructed by man himself in order to escape his own "self-alienation". Vatican II explicitly took up this comprehensive set of themes in the Pastoral Constitution on the Church in the Modern World. And other texts dealt with other aspects of the same themes. For the Church lives in a divided Christendom, a world of many non-Christian higher religions, a pluralist society in which the State with its authority has a quite different function from its task in an ideologically homogeneous society, or in one which became so after short periods of transition and conflict. Consequently we are certainly justified in understanding the Council's declarations on ecumenism, the non-Christian religions and religious freedom as sympto-

matic and as a partial answer to the frankly stated general question of the relation between the Church and the historical and changing world of the present day.

2. Before anything more precise can be said on this relation, the two concepts must be briefly explained.

a) For theology "the world" in the first place signifies in a neutral sense the whole of creation as a unity (in origin, destiny, goal, general structures, interdependence of part on part). It either includes man, or is distinguished from him as his environment, the stage set by God for the history of his salvation. In this sense world has the same meaning as "heaven and earth", and is a revelation of God, exists for his glory; it is good, meaningful and beautiful, the freely and lovingly created recipient of God's self-communication (Jn 3:16f.; D 428, 1805). It does not separate man from God but mediates between God and man, as is shown above all in the Incarnation. Through guilt in the realm of the angels and by the initial guilt of man in original sin and by his subsequent calamitous history, this world and especially that of man is also deeply affected, even in the material realm, so that it is hostile to God and in conflict with its own ultimate structures and characteristics. The world in this sense (biblically "this" cosmos, "this" aeon) signifies the totality of "principalities and powers" hostile to God, i.e., everything in the world which prompts to new guilt and is the tangible embodiment of this guilt. In this sense the Christian must not be "of the world" (Jn 18:36 and *passim*), even if he must be "in" the world (Jn 17:11). Yet even as this sinful world it is nevertheless loved by God. It is in need of redemption but also capable of it, enveloped by God's grace despite its guilt and in its guilt, and its history will end in the kingdom of God. Consequently, despite its opposition to God it constitutes a task for the Christian, who by the power of grace is to uphold its true order, discern the possibilities of its development, while critically distinguishing the forces present in it and patiently bearing its burden and darkness which will never cease until the end.

This world has a history which has entered on its eschatological stage through the incarnation, cross and resurrection of the eternal Word of God. The outcome of this history in its entirety is already decided by Christ in the depths of reality, even though that outcome is still hidden and is only grasped by faith. Hence the world or aeon "to come" is already present and operative in the present world. It is clear from this that while Christianity recognizes a certain dualism between God and world in redemptive history, a dualism which is already in process of dissolution, it does not acknowledge any radical and insuperable dualism. No such dualism should therefore secretly colour the practical life of Christians.

The various aspects of this theological, many-sided concept of the world can never be wholly separated from one another in practice, and this is what makes the whole problem so difficult. Two things must therefore be borne in mind. The three meanings of the term "world" (the good created world, the sinful world of perdition, the redeemed world orientated supernaturally by grace, which is the situation in which salvation is worked out) are not three simply disparate uses of a single term. They are linked by the fact that this world (as the world of man) is a history which is still in progress. Because the world is history and not merely an unchanging stage on which history unfolds, it has a beginning, presuppositions and a goal towards which it moves in the decisions open to men. This is the world as creation and as partner of God's supernatural self-communication in grace. Because it is a history, the outcome of which remains hidden within it because it is still unfolding, it is possible for this world to form a unity in multiplicity, which we can never fully distinguish. It comprises both personal decision in relation to God, and the external factors which make this possible and fulfil it, yet which also have their own intra-mundane significance. It is a unity in difference of saving action and guilt. This world is not only a history (because changing). It has now become a history which can be planned, actively manipulated and guided by men, even in its empirical space-time reality, and not merely in its transcendent meaning in God's sight for salvation and perdition, in a way which was not possible earlier to any considerable extent.

b) The meaning of the term "Church" need not of course be developed at length here. Only what is of particular importance for the questions which occupy us need be emphasized. The Church is not identical with the kingdom of God. It is the sacrament of the kingdom of God in the eschatological phase of sacred history which began with Christ, the phase which brings about the kingdom of God. As long as history lasts, the Church will not be identical with the kingdom of God, for the latter is only definitively present when history ends with the coming of Christ and the last judgment. Yet the kingdom of God is not simply something due to come later, which later will replace the world, its history and the outcome of its history. The kingdom of God itself is coming to be in the history of the world (not only in that of the Church) wherever obedience to God occurs in grace as the acceptance of God's self-communication. And this does not take place solely in the Church as the socially constituted, historically visible society of the redeemed. It does not take place solely in a secret inwardness of conscience, in meta-historical religious subjectivity, but in the concrete fulfilment of an earthly task, of active love of others, even of collective love of others.

It is of course true that this history remains ambiguous in its empirically observable external expressions, and that the "occurrence" of grace is just as hidden as the material character of its acceptance. The thesis of the kingdom of God as "the world" is fundamentally implied by the Catholic doctrine that grace and justification are in fact to be found outside the visible unity of the Church, so that Church history and the history of salvation are therefore not identical. It follows from Catholic teaching on the inseparable unity of material and formal morality, which demands definite, material, meaningful activities in this world, and cannot be reduced to a purely religious or formally "believing" frame of mind. It also follows from the unity of love of God and the neighbour. For this kingdom of God in the world, which of course can never simply be identified with any particular objective secular phenomenon, the Church is a part, because of course the Church itself is in the world and in its members makes world history (cf. D 1783). Above all, however, the Church is precisely its special fundamental sacrament, i.e., the eschatological and efficacious manifestation (sign) in redemptive history that in the unity, activity, fraternity, etc. of the *world*, the kingdom of

God is at hand. Even here, therefore, as in the various individual sacraments, sign and thing signified can never be separated or identified (cf. Vatican II, *Lumen Gentium*, art. 9).

3. This relation between Church and world has a history. The relation is not and must not always be the same. It is historically changing because the world as an individual and collective history of freedom and also the Church in its official ministry and above all in its members is subject to faults and even succumbs to guilt. This can distort and falsely determine the relation between the two realities through one's trespassing on the domain of the other, through neglect or misinterpretation of the function which each in its own way can and should perform for the other. But this relation is subject to change even prior to such guilt in the course of history, simply because both parts are historical, i.e., changing realities. Their mutual relationship itself changes as a consequence. There is not only a secular history of the world, in its knowledge, culture, self-emancipation from the domination of nature, in its increasingly complex social structures, its whole conception of itself, its attitude to its past and to its open future. The Church itself is only slowly led into the fullness of the truth which it already possesses, in a historical process under the guidance of the Spirit, and this history of the Church's truth as the standard of its action also alters its relation to the world in all its domains. For example, the Church only slowly learns fully to appreciate the freedom of the individual and of human groups, or to value the unity and multiplicity of the many Churches which the one Church comprises and also their basis in national and secular history (cf. Vatican II: Decrees on Eastern Catholic Churches and on Ecumenism). The Church only slowly came to acknowledge the relative autonomy of secular sciences and the potential variety of the social, political and economic organization of human groups (decline of mistrust of democracy or of certain forms of socialization etc.). The Church is slowly attaining a more unconstrained, comprehensive and personal appreciation of human sexuality.

And despite the secular occasions of such growth and change in theory and practice, this alteration in the Church is ultimately regulated by the standard of the Church's own spirit and its own ancient truth. It is not merely a case of enforced adaptation to a historical situation which the Church is powerless to alter. Changes in the Church and in the world mutually interact. The change in the Western mind in modern times ultimately sprang from the spirit of Christianity itself, even though it often rightly or wrongly turned against the actual existing Church and forced it slowly to learn what it really always knew. That change led from a Greek cosmocentrism to anthropocentrism, meant destroying the numinous character of the world and making it the material of human activity. Other aspects were its rationality and technology, conscious reflection on its own historical character with a consequent critical relation to the past and openness to a novel future, and the reduction of human tradition to a merely relative value.

Because the relation between Church and world is really history and has a history, it always has to be determined anew in the concrete, although all its fundamental structures remain. Similarly it retains the unforeseeable and incalculable character of history. It cannot simply be deduced in its entirety from eternal principles capable of concretely determining it once and for all. It is also an original decision of the human beings in the Church and in the world acting in history. It is therefore always a struggle. It is not a matter for doctrinal tribunals alone, but for the Church's pastoral office *and* for the charismatic representatives of a freely adopted attitude towards the world in the dialectical, changing union of flight from the world and affirmation of the world, the relation between which cannot in the concrete be laid down once and for all. Precisely because this history is history, it is difficult to reduce it to a formula, and this cannot be done without express reserves. Yet we might perhaps say that it is the history of the Church's growing self-discovery and of the increasing emancipation of the world into its own secular nature by the Church. The Church comes to know itself more and more as "not of this world" and at the same time as the sacrament of the absolute future of the world, which is not produced by the world by its own power but is given to it by God as a supra-mundane grace, thus relativizing in theory and practice any conception which the world forms of

itself, in other words, opens it out to the absolute future.

4. Two fundamental ways of misconceiving the relation between Church and world can definitely be noted. World in the comprehensive sense which, as we have seen, it now bears, was not a theme of explicit reflection in earlier ages of the Church and consequently these two fundamental heresies concerning this relationship were scarcely constituted consciously and explicitly. As latent but operative, however, they play a part everywhere in history. We may call the one heresy "integrism", the other, for want of a better, current term, "esotericism".

a) Integrism regards the world as mere material for the action and self-manifestation of the Church, and wants to integrate the world into the Church. Even if it is conceded that there are "two swords" in the world, the secular sword is regarded as conferred by the Church to be employed in the service of the Church and its higher purposes. Even a doctrine of the *potestas indirecta* of the Church *ratione peccati* over secular realities can be misconstrued in an integrist way. It is sufficient to start from the false but widespread tacit assumption that the moral principles of human action which are defended by the official Church and applied by its pastoral ministry to men's action are of such a kind that (at least in principle) in each case a concrete prescription can be deduced from them for the particular action in question. Then all earthly action in the history of the world is nothing but the putting into practice of the principles taught, expounded and applied by the Church. The activity of the world in State, history and social life is then simply a realization of the Church's principles, and in fact an embodiment of the Church itself. The world would be the *corpus christianum* and nothing else.

If the Church at some point was not interested in a particular form of the world (and left "worldly business" to the "princes"), this, on the view we are describing, could only be a consequence of the factual impossibility of the Church's permeating the world. It was not an emancipation by the Church of the world into its secular nature. Or else its origin was that such secular action was regarded as without importance for salvation simply because it cannot be fully determined by the explicit principles of the

Church and so, as *adiaphora,* could not be performed by man himself before God with the passion of moral and historical decision. But this tacit assumption of integrism is false. It is not possible wholly to derive from the principles of natural law and the gospel the human action which ought to be done *here and now,* although of course all action must respect those principles. Nor when such action is more than the carrying into effect of those principles and of the official instructions of the Church, does it cease to be morally important from the point of view of God and in relation to him as goal. It still concerns salvation and has to be performed with the absolute earnestness of moral responsibility. It can even be the subject of charismatic inspiration from on high, and, while remaining secular, a factor in the coming of the kingdom of God.

Integrism also overlooks the Catholic doctrine of man's intrinsic pluralism which he can never overcome. Man always finds himself exposed to a multiplicity of experiences (sources of knowledge) and impulses, which are not directly interrelated, and in addition, to a situation of "concupiscence". The will to integrate and synthesize this human plurality is of course justified and is a duty. It can include the will to form a sum of all knowledge in a humane and Christian philosophical view of the world; to action which springs from love of God; to a positive relation between Church and State; to Christian inspiration of culture. But integrism falsely believes that this synthesis can fully succeed, that the secular and the Christian can be wholly interrelated. Above all, it holds that this synthesis can be produced by the official Church precisely because it is the Church, that this total synthesis can be not merely the asymptotic goal of history in the kingdom of God beyond history, but can become an event in history itself.

Integrism is therefore the false opinion that everything has to be given an ecclesiastical stamp because everything of importance for salvation belongs to the official Church, at least in principle, and all that is non-ecclesiastical is merely indifferent secular business which has no serious significance for man as such as a unity and therefore for his salvation and the kingdom of God. What is radically false about this position becomes particularly clear (and dangerous) at a moment when the world is moving from a static condition and a theoretical way of looking at things to one which can be altered and manipulated by man and man's action. For then it becomes palpably evident that the actively created future is no longer wholly to be deduced from eternal principles but, as something really new and the outcome of active decision, stands under the summons of God and the responsibility of man in a way which is not the purely official, ecclesiastical way. As a consequence the Christian himself and above all the layman in his secular task is more than a recipient of orders from the Church's ministry. Yet even where he is not in receipt of them, he does not cease to act as a Christian in responsible historical decision. Action regulated by the Church and Christian action which is genuinely human do not coincide.

b) We might give the name "esotericism" to a false attitude towards the world of the factual Church or of the Christian, in which what is secular is regarded as a matter of indifference for Christianity, for a life directed towards salvation and therefore towards God's absolute future. Here a Christian considers flight from the world as the only genuinely Christian attitude, and therefore regards affirmation of the world, its values, enjoyment, achievement and success as in principle suspect from a Christian point of view, unless it is already directly and explicitly inspired and commanded by a "supernatural", "religious" intention. He cannot see it as merely inevitably interwoven with a world that is also a sinful one.

The sources and varieties of such esotericism are many. It may be based on a latent dualism which simply identifies the empirical aspect of the world with its sinfulness, so that remoteness from the world (its civilization, sexuality, self-development) is identified with detachment from sin and regarded undialectically as identical with greater closeness to God. Esotericism may think itself well-founded because of the NT attitude of the Sermon on the Mount, the recommendation of sexual abstinence, indifference to social conditions, imminent expectation of the end of the world, etc. On that basis it may consider that all Christian life has in this NT attitude not only an ever necessary warning and correction but its total expression, and all that has to be done is simply to maintain and reproduce this.

Such esotericism can in certain circumstances be extended into the doctrine of the invisible Church of the predestined known only to God. It can be based on the view that what is genuinely moral and valid in God's sight is absolutely meta-historical, beyond any concrete material determinable action; that it is purely a disposition, inwardness (faith, a "commitment" which remains purely formal in character); that there is no Christian ethics with positive Christian content; that the "secular" is totally inaccessible to a Christian attitude, remaining indifferent to this or even simply and solely sinful in all its shapes and forms; that it stands only under the law, not under the gospel which redeems and sanctifies the world itself. A Catholic variety of such esotericism may hold, for example, that life according to the evangelical counsels in the religious orders is of itself the sole or self-evidently the higher realization of the Christian spirit from which the many are dispensed only because of their weakness. Integrism and esotericism can form a strange combination in the tendency, e.g., in the Irish monastic Church, to make the world a monastery. The Calvinist conception of the theocracy of the Christian community with its Church discipline has a certain element of such a combination about it.

The decisive feature of esotericism is that the secular is abandoned to itself, as an indifferent or sinful residue in an explicitly religious life which as far as possible is carried on as exclusively as possible in the small circle of religious esoterics. It is not regarded as constituting in itself a positive task for the Christian as such.

5. The true relation of the Christian and the Church to the world lies in the mean between these two extremes. This mean should not be regarded as a facile compromise which is imposed by circumstances and which simply has to be because the world as a matter of unfortunate fact will never allow itself to be wholly integrated into the ecclesiastical and religious domain and because even the exclusively pious person cannot avoid serving the secular necessities of life. It is a question of a mean which, as we shall have to explain, lies above the two extremes as a radical unity, combining on its own basis both the unity and the difference of what is explicitly Christian and ecclesiastical on the one hand, and the world and secular

action on the other. Furthermore, the true relation between Church and world has to be determined in one way when it is a question of the relation of the official Church — the magisterium and pastoral office, the "official" action of the Church engaging the responsibility of the socially constituted Church — to the world, and in another when it is a question of the relation to the world of Christians, especially the laity, for all of them also are, of course, the Church.

The relation to the world of the Christians who form the Church is not identical in all, for each has his own vocation and function in the Body of Christ, and this can and should shape his relation to the world in very different ways, extending, for example, from what is to a certain extent the flight from the world of the contemplative monk to the apparently wholly secular involvement of an ambitious statesman eager to make history. And these manifold aspects of the Church (official Church, Church as people of God) have themselves, as has already been noted, a history which changes them, and so, for example, all these aspects, despite their differences, can have a common "period style". Nowadays, for instance, the contemplative monk will be more explicitly conscious of his apostolic function than formerly, and this will contribute to determine his style of life.

a) For the official Church and its relation to the world at the present time it will be decisive to renounce all integrism even merely in practice. As a concrete, juridically constituted society, it cannot of course renounce having institutionalized relations with the world and its groupings, States, other Churches, etc. and their organizations. Nor should it renounce this in the genuine freedom of a pluralist society. Where it is really possible and useful, concordats, for example, can be concluded, even though the time for regulating relationships between Church and world by such methods is perhaps coming to an end. The Church can have diplomatic representatives, can work for State recognition of its own schools system and itself maintain an educational system if and where a good one is really possible. In this way, it inevitably and quite rightly has a certain social power, even if this is lessening rather than increasing with the growing diaspora status of the Church throughout the world. This in fact is changing the Church even in formerly "Christian nations" from a national Church to a Church of professed believers.

But the official Church has to take care not to turn unconsciously these institutional contacts with the world, and its own social power, into a means of exerting pressure in order to attain its legitimate aims, i.e., the effective proclamation of the gospel and the Christianization of as many human beings as possible. For to do so would mean that the Church was having recourse to something other than men's free, unforced obedience in a faith which has perpetually to be exercised anew. And in this respect, at least in practice and as far as public life is concerned, the difference between baptized and unbaptized on which in former times great stress was laid, is now of little account. Even where it could, the Church may no longer use secular means of coercion, e.g., economic sanctions, against its baptized members who act in an un-Christian way. In its whole attitude it must make it quite clear that the Church is and wills to be nothing but the socially constituted community of those who freely believe in Christ, joined with him and with one another in their love of him; that it is not the religious institution of a State or of a secular society as such. It must radically respect the freedom of conscience and religion of individuals and groups because of its own nature, not simply because in certain circumstances it cannot do otherwise. Precisely as such a free society of those who personally believe, it will no longer give the impression of being a traditional institution, almost a piece of folk-lore, a set of religious trimmings to life for those who were baptized as children of Catholic parents and for that reason have to keep up religious custom. On the other hand the Church can then much more readily be a missionary Church, addressing all, seriously seeking to win serious adults to baptism even in "Christian countries", making room in the Church for "modern" men with their own attitudes to life and their personalities already formed.

The official Church will also have to realize clearly that nowadays in a dynamic, extremely complex world with an extreme man-made abundance of goods, plans and possibilities, it is no longer possible for the Church to give directly concrete prescriptions regarding detailed economic organi-zation, the actual direction of culture, the allocation of revenue for under-developed countries, space travel, regulation of the growth of population, armaments or dis-armament, etc., even if it were in principle able to do so. The Church will proclaim the general principles of the dignity of man, freedom, justice and love, and will certainly not be of the opinion that such proclamation is useless or unimportant, or that it is merely an ideological veneer on a brutal existence which pursues its course by quite different laws. The Church can certainly have the cour-age in certain circumstances like John XXIII, or Paul VI before the United Nations, to come forward as representative spokesman of a Christian feeling for history or a Chris-tian decision, even when the latter is "charis-matic" rather than purely and simply a deduction from Christian principles, pro-vided the distinction between the two is not obscured. But the Church must also really make clear the difference between Christian principles and the concrete decision which cannot be deduced from them alone, so that the limits of the possibilities open to the official Church (free of integrist claims) are plain. This problem becomes partic-ularly acute when a statesman who is a Christian must take decisions for the pluralist society itself of which he is the representative.

If the distinction in question is made clear, it is then possible really to fight against the misconception which is still very prevalent among Christians, that the Christian can be assured of the morality of his action, and of its accordance with God's will, by the mere fact that it does not come into clear conflict with the material content of the Church's norms. Then it will also be clear that Chris-tian action as such is possible and obligatory even in the secular domain, even where it is not "ecclesiastical", and that secular action objectively appropriate to the historical moment and situation is Christian action of importance for salvation without ceasing to be secular in character, provided it is per-formed as obligatory in the way indicated and on the basis of an ultimately Christian attitude. This liberating modesty of the official Church in encouraging what is really Christian outside the ecclesiastical sphere, is not a restriction imposed from outside on the Church's power and influence but flows from the Christian conception of the world itself, as will have to be shown even more clearly in a moment.

b) Christians, and therefore the Church as the people of God, stand in a relation to the world which is partly different from that of the official Church. It is in the last resort based on the fact that, as is shown most clearly and in the highest way in the incarnation of the divine Logos, the acceptance of the world by God — that is, grace, the really "Christian" feature — does not involve a destructive, annihilating absorption of the world (as recipient of God's self-communication) into God and the disappearance of the world. It means the setting free of the world into independence, intrinsic significance and autonomy. Closeness to God and the world's own intrinsic reality are not inversely but directly proportionate. Two things which have already been referred to briefly are to be noted in this respect. This acceptance of the world has its own (redemptive) history. Consequently the emancipation of the world into its own secular nature through its acceptance on the part of God can become fuller and clearer, and this has happened in the course of Christian history. This growth of the world's secular character continues to be a Christian phenomenon even where, viewed superficially, it takes place by purely secular means (progress of rational science, technology, the higher stages of human social organization and life) and although it has often taken place under protest from Christians. The emancipation of the world into its growing independence by its acceptance on the part of God, in fact, however, also establishes the world at the same time in a "concupiscent" condition, yet it is not possible for this aspect of the world's secular nature to be grasped as inevitable. Ultimately it is the free disposition of divine love which willed to be triumphant in futility and death.

This means that the liberating acceptance of the world by God is not simply a transparent fact in its secular nature. The secularity is also the veil concealing the acceptance, which is only accessible to faith and hope. For us the world's plurality is not integrated empirically and tangibly into the movement of all reality towards God under the creative and merciful will of God. Man always finds himself from the start exposed to a plurality of factors in his life, of unsynthesized experiences, of contradictory impulses,

in short, the secular world. And these cannot be adequately integrated by him from one ultimate point, that of the love of God. And this world in its development does not simply move in an evolutionary way towards its integration into the love of God, into his epiphany in the world and into the kingdom of God. It moves towards this goal through collapse, futility, the zero of death. This "concupiscent" situation of the world which contributes to its secular nature, is from a Christian point of view (in a way which is never wholly explicable by man within his history) both the manifestation of the "sin of the world" and the mediation and manifestation of the redemptive sharing in Christ's lot, for the salvation of the world and the attainment of its absolute future which is God himself.

For the Christian, therefore, the world is not the "esoterically" indifferent which lies outside his heavenly calling. In its permanent and even increasingly secular character something Christian occurs, even if the latter as such must have an empirical manifestation of a historical and social kind limited and distinct in scope within the world, i.e., an ecclesiastically Christian form. However, for this very reason the secular world as such in its direct secular empirical character (before faith and hope) is not for the Christian the Christian element itself, in such a way that nothing further would be needed except a candid, historically responsible identification with the world experienced in this way alone. Rather its own peculiar dimension of depth, inserted into it by the grace of God, and its ultimate dynamism must be experienced and accepted, for it is in these that it is open towards a direct relation to God. This experience and acceptance, which are significant for salvation, can, of course, where inculpably they have no longer any predicamental and social objective expression — that is, no ecclesiastical element — take place in responsible administration, endurance and obediently trusting acceptance of this world subject to death, in accordance with the judgment of a good conscience. Consequently in certain circumstances this can occur inculpably in purely secular conditions, and may even be done by someone who in the sphere of conceptual reflection is an atheist. This world must furthermore (contrary to all integrism) be accepted as having been accepted by God in Christ precisely in its concupiscent secular nature and therefore as enduring and growing in this form.

The Christian understands this concupiscent secularity from the point of view of the meaning of the saving Cross. He is, therefore, far from thinking that the world is only Christian (and nothing but Christian) where he has mastered it by a successfully religious interpretation and integration and an ecclesiastical one. Therefore, despite his serene endeavour to integrate life into what has explicitly religious motives, he can also calmly be secular, and have earthly wishes and goals and enjoy the empirical world without religious mediation. He may spontaneously understand this as the way in which he obediently submits to God's transcendent decrees, especially if he is also ready to accept the frustration of the world, and death, obediently and with hope against hope. The earthly task and the "heavenly" vocation therefore are different, but this does not destroy their unity (contrary to esotericism) and they form a unity without being identical (as against integrism). This also means that their relation cannot be clearly determined in the concrete. The Church, being on the one hand the people of God and on the other the sacrament of the salvation of the *world,* can and must manifest this relation only in itself as a whole. Individuals in the Church have each a different call and task in this respect. Consequently there are rightly and necessarily found in the Church asceticism, flight from the world, the life of the evangelical counsels as imitation of the Crucified and as inchoative advance towards that renunciation of the world which is demanded of everyone in death, and the life of the religious orders. All this flight from the world is not merely a well-tried method of combating sin and its threat, but is the sign in the Church for the Church and the world that the world is the world of God, of grace, of hope in the absolute future of God, which God himself bestows and which is not simply identical with the autonomous development of the world. Legitimate flight from the world is an exercise of faith and hope in the divinely bestowed fulfilment of the world and consequently a sign of that courage of faith which can serenely allow the world to be world, i.e., finite, and does not need to place a strain on the world it cannot bear by divinizing it. Such a flight from the world would, however, become un-Christian if it were to posit

itself as absolute, overlook its intermediate function of service in the Church, regard itself as the sole truly radical Christian element, viewing itself as the coming of grace.

Grace after all is ultimately given to the growing world (even though it has to pass through death), as the grace of the living Risen Lord. Christian flight from the world cannot therefore in principle, not merely in practice, intend to be complete. It is always a partial factor, even if a very emphatic one, in a Christian life which with thanksgiving also takes the earth seriously, and can enjoy it while acknowledging that God has given himself to the earth so that it may be free and independent and that this gift is the ultimate content of the world's significance. From that point of view alone, not as a concession to human weakness, it is meaningful that there should, for example, exist in the Church more strict and less strict religious orders. And for the same ultimate reason there is in the same Church a ministry to the world, responsibility for the world, real though Christian acceptance of the secular nature of the world, a positive will for its development in all the domains which through man exist in it.

This Christian ministry to the world does not begin only when a worldly task is undertaken from explicitly Christian motives or when the secular is incorporated into Christian theology. It is contained within the secular itself because this itself is opened out towards God by the grace of God. But this must not only be taught theoretically for the life of Christians in the world. It must also be lived in practice. This can of course in certain circumstances take place in an "anonymously" Christian life. And for the same reason there also belong to the life of the Christian, together with joy in the world and secular activity, readiness for death with Christ, the spirit of the Sermon on the Mount, of the evangelical counsels; the practice of readiness for renunciation, for scepticism in regard to any identification with the world which would make an absolute of the world and idolize it, i.e., identify it ultimately with God.

How, in the individual, flight from the world and activity in the world must be united is a matter for the individual, of his vocation and spiritual experience. Only if the Church in multifarious ways and at the service of different vocations is both detached from the world and critical of it and at the same time belongs to the world, is it the sacrament of the salvation of that world which itself has to exist and grow. Provided that the spirit of detachment from the world, of criticism of the world, of penance, contemplation and renunciation (even to a heroic degree in individuals) remains alive in the Church, there need be no mistrust of the present course of the Church in seeking dialogue with the world, in announcing the unity of love of God and the neighbour, in taking up arms on behalf of the social development of society, freedom, racial equality, fraternity, etc. In a world which has itself changed from a static one to a world of man which has still to be created, tasks and modes of Christian existence accrue to the Christian and the Church which simply did not exist earlier but which now must be accepted and mastered by the Church in a *new* spirit and a positive will to affirm the world. Not everything which in this way exists in the Church in contrast to earlier times can be suspected of being a concession to the spirit of the evil world, as worldliness in the bad sense.

6. Particular problems and maxims regarding the relation between Church and world.

a) The world of today has become a single world and its unity is increasing. For the Church this does not simply mean that it is, as it always was, juridically a "perfect society" and that as a *single* community of believers it has to act as a unity in doctrine, liturgy and constitution. It does not simply mean that the Church's world mission receives a new urgency in the situation of universal interdependence of men beyond the range of local groups (nations, states), because now even the fate of Christianity in a "Christian country" is beginning to be dependent on its fate throughout the world, even among the "non-Christian peoples". The new situation also means that the whole Church as such has duties in respect of the shaping and further development of the one world in its unity. The speech of Paul VI before the United Nations is a symbol of this, and the Pastoral Constitution of Vatican II to a certain extent provides a basic programme for it. In spite of the justifiable emphasis on the special character and independence of particular, regional Churches by Vatican II (Decree on the Eastern Churches; bishops'

conferences with greater powers; national liturgies, etc.), the Church as a whole must be in a position to act in regard to the world as a unity, and needs new and appropriate organs and institutions (charitable organization by the Church as a whole, the various new secretariats, help to underdeveloped countries by the Church as a whole, contacts with UNO, UNESCO, etc.).

b) If the Church necessarily has to be everywhere in the unified world of today and is so, though with very different degrees of intensity, and if the Church is always "the sign which is contradicted", then quite apart from any other reasons, the Church will necessarily everywhere, though of course in varying degrees, be a diaspora-Church in a pluralist world. And in practice it will remain so, despite its fundamental claim on all men, in accordance with which it has to undertake an active mission within and without, actively aiming at success. This also means that the Church must have the courage to make the transition from a national Church to a community Church of those who personally believe by their own decision. That is, it may in the concrete lay *more* weight on having communities which, though numerically small in comparison with the total surrounding population, are composed of those who believe seriously and personally and live in a Christian way, rather than on reaching and maintaining "everyone" in traditional Church-membership. This also means that the Church may organize its pastoral strategy and tactics accordingly.

In this way the Church will naturally become a Church of open dialogue with the world, both within and without. Even within itself, for such a community Church, despite its abidingly hierarchical constitution, will be a Church the existence of which is based on the laity as personal believers, and less on the institutional element or on the clergy as the traditional supports and recipients of its social prestige. A laity of that kind, however, by its very nature is the world (in the legitimate sense) in the Church. That laity's culture, mentality, aspirations, etc. (even to the extent that they find expression in the Church) are no longer created solely by the Church as an institution (as was almost entirely the case in earlier times). They are brought into the Church by the laity as part of the already existing world, and also by the clergy themselves as men of our time. In that way there is and must be a dialogue within the Church between Church and world. Outwardly there will be a similar dialogue because a community Church in the diaspora, which also has to be a missionary one, may not and cannot shut itself off in itself in a sectarian way. It must engage openly in dialogue with the world, its civilization, endeavours and creations. For it cannot and may not want to live solely on such culture as it produces within its own circle ("Christian literature", "Christian art"). It cannot have a ghetto-mentality in which people think they can live in social and cultural autarchy. To be able to give, the Church must receive.

c) The forces of the present time (and also of the future) are those without which the realization of the universality of the Church is not conceivable. Precisely for that reason — leaving deeper ones out of account — the Church has the duty of meeting the age as it is openly and with trust, however radically the Church criticizes world-civilization in detail. The Church as Church can neither fall into a reactionary resistance to the approaching future nor into an eschatologism which instead of sober waiting for the Lord would mean a flight forwards impelled by what in fact would be an ideology of this world. Because the Church is the Church, it has to recognize the Cross promised by Christ's coming in the very fact that we have to endure the sober harshness of an unromantic, planned technical world with all the burdens which such a situation brings upon itself and Christianity. No doubt when Christianity finds willing minds and hearts it changes not merely men's dispositions but also their conditions. But the Church cannot think on that account that it can exist, especially in the way incumbent on it today, only if the very elements of the situation which cannot seriously be expected to disappear were other than they are — a mass-society, a secular civilization, the relative lack of distinctive character in the Christianity of the present time, the diaspora situation, etc.

Consequently the smallest victory in this situation and against it is more important than anything else achieved in other situations which still exist but are in process of disappearance, or any success obtained in transitory counter-attempts to restore the past in contradiction to the decisive fundamental trend of history. Wherever a victory is won in the new situation of the unified secular world history, it is a victory for the whole world, and consequently for those non-European non-Christian peoples who to an increasing extent are entering upon this same situation. The Church, therefore, must abandon in its actual attitude to life and not merely in its abstract theory, the medieval ideal of a very direct and universal control of all human realities. Anyone who is a Christian and really intends to be one will of course do all human things differently from non-Christians, or from most of them. But this different manner of doing them will seem to the tolerant non-Christian simply to be one possible conception of human existence and activity side by side with others. And the Christian himself will never be able to say with absolute certainty in regard to his shaping of terrestrial reality, to which he knows himself in duty bound here and now as an individual and as a Christian, that precisely the shape he gives it is the Christian one as such. Even he will not know whether a possibility may not be tested for the first time by the non-Christians around him, which himself will later recognize as possible for him too as a Christian.

d) If despite its enduring ministry to the world and despite its teaching and pastoral office, the Church recognizes in this way that in all its members it commits itself less directly than in former times as regards the concrete shaping of social reality as a whole, this is not a flight into the realm of the utopian or the comfortable and safe, nor into the sacristy. It must be regarded as a more attentive reflection and concentration on its own authentic nature. For the Church is not a world-organization ("moral rearmament") for a better world — on earth. It is the community of believers in that eternal life in God, into which history is raised and transcended. Only in the measure in which the Church is the "kingdom not of this world" does it in the long run hold the promise that it is the blessing of eternity for time.

See also *Church, Christianity* I, *Dualism, Reign of God, Law and Gospel, Marxism, Pluralism, Science* I, *Society* I, II, *World.*

BIBLIOGRAPHY. G. Thils, *Théologie des Réalités terrestres* (1946); R. Guardini, *Faith and Modern Man* (1952); F. Gogarten, *Verhängnis und Hoffnung der Neuzeit. Die Säkularisierung als theologisches Problem* (1953); J. Leclercq, *Christian and World Integra-*

tion (1959); J.-M. Aubert, *Recherche scientifique et foi chrétienne* (1962); J. A. T. Robinson, *Honest to God* (1963); E. Brunner, *Word of God and Modern Man* (1964); A. Dondeyne, *Faith and the World* (1964); J. Lacroix, *Meaning of Modern Atheism* (1965); H. Lübbe, *Säkularisierung. Geschichte eines ideen-politischen Begriffs* (1965); J. Moltmann, *Theologie der Hoffnung* (4th ed., 1965), E. T.: Theology of Hope (1967); B. Welte, *Heilsverständnis* (1966); H. U. von Balthasar, *Church and World* (1967).

Karl Rahner

CHURCH HISTORY

A. Subject-Matter. B. Task and Method. C. Historiography. D. Periodization and Survey.

A. SUBJECT-MATTER

The subject-matter of Church history is the Church's past. As a historical religion of revelation, Christianity originates in the historical person and saving work of Jesus Christ, the God-man. It not only has this local and temporal origin; its historical existence as this original Christianity is also continued in the Church. Its historicity is essential to its existence; it not merely *has* a history, it also *is* historical in its entire self-realization, for it is in and with history that it realizes itself. From this it follows that in order to experience and realize this essential element in its being it must turn its attention to history. Church history as a scientific theological discipline reminds Christianity of its origin and past as the permanently binding basis of its existence.

1. The *character,* and therefore the task and method, of Church history is determined by the view taken of the Church and by the function assigned to it within the history of the world and the history of salvation. In the Christian revelation attested in the NT, the nature of the Church is not expressed in timeless abstract concepts but in metaphors (analogies). The Church is presented as the people of God, the bride of Christ, flock, family, communion of saints, the new Israel. This variety of metaphors and aspects permits a multi-dimensional view. Since for the most part these analogies are employed dynamically rather than statically, stressing the building of the house, the cultivation of the field, and the feeding of the flock, rather than the house itself etc., they allow for the possibility of historical developments and changes in the Church's understanding of itself with the passage of time.

The profoundest theological interpretation of the Church is the concept of the "body of Christ", formulated by Paul. The Church is Christ's body (Col 1:24), the organism in which the believers as the members constitute a living unity with Christ the head (1 Cor 12:12ff.; Rom 12:4f.); Paul can even call the Church simply "Christ", because on the Damascus road Christ revealed himself to Paul as the one whom he had been persecuting in persecuting the Church ("Saul, why do you persecute *me?"*, Acts 9:4). Paul defines the Church unequivocally as "the mystery of Christ" (Eph 3:4) and sees in it the fulfilment of God's eternal plan of salvation for the whole of mankind. The Church continues and brings to fruition among men the saving work of Christ who "reconciled" God and man "in one body through the cross" (Eph 2:16). It is the exalted pneuma-filled Christ who is at work in the Church. His Spirit, the Holy Spirit himself, is its life-principle by whom it is furnished with heavenly powers (Eph 4:4; 1 Cor 12:3ff., 13).

It is significant that when men sought to understand and describe the Church's life and growth, each of these metaphors, and especially that of the "body of Christ", could become historically influential. Augustine defined the Church as the continuing life of Christ, as the *totus Christus,* comprising both head and members. But this notion was most fully developed by J. A. Möhler, who spoke of the continued incarnation of Christ in his Church: "The Church is the Son of God continuing to manifest himself among men in human form, constantly renewing and ever rejuvenating himself, the permanent incarnation of the same Son of God." He regarded the history of the Church as the unfolding of "the principle of light and life imparted to and shared with mankind by Christ in order to reconcile it with God and to make it capable of glorifying him".

While the central mystery of Christianity (the incarnation and the Pauline view of the Church as the continued life of Christ) is rightly taken here as the starting point for the presentation of Church history, it must also be remembered that the metaphor would be distorted were Christ simply to be identified with the Church without qualification. He is its head; it is his body. We should be in danger of "ecclesiological monophysitism" (H. Fries) if we were to obliterate the distinction between Christ and the Church as his body and ignore the distance (not separation) between them. The function and even the existence of the body and its members are not identical with those of its head. Christ is the Lord of the Church; the Church is his bride, the mother who brings forth believers. When we speak of Christ's becoming the body, this must be understood in the sense of a spiritual generation by which believing, hoping, loving and obedient children are born to him in the Church. It is not only Christ's incarnation but also his appointment to suffering, death and resurrection which determine the life and function of the members of his body (*theologia crucis*). Paul exhorts the faithful not just to accept the life, suffering and death of Christ as objective historical facts but also to realize them subjectively after him in order in this way to participate in his grace.

As the community of believers, the Church exhibits a great variety of offices and gifts (1 Cor 12) and also possesses a structure deriving from Christ. This too must be clearly distinguished (though not separated) from the community of persons.

To this divine structure of the Church belongs what was given it by God through Christ for its journey and for the realization of the divine economy of salvation in humanity: the preaching of the word, the sacraments, the missionary task and the fundamental hierarchical order. This structure is unchangeable and partakes of God's perfection and holiness. In word, sacrament, and ministry the *Christus praesens* imparts his invisible grace directly in the Church through the Holy Spirit. God's saving activity is by its very nature structurally supra-historical. But since it is essentially related to men and becomes visible in the Church, it enters history. As the visible form of invisible grace, the Church is the "primordial sacrament" (O. Semmelroth). We describe as sacramental every supernatural saving reality which finds historical expression in our life under some visible sign. The Church is essentially both a divine structure and a visible sign, both a mystery of grace which acts invisibly and also historical human life.

This divine structure is not rigid and immobile but adapted to men, with a genuine evolution and development in history which in no way diminishes its constant and unchanging identity of substance. Itself a *mysterium fidei,* it shares the uniqueness of the divine process of revelation which moves forward under the formative impulse of the Holy Spirit. Just as in the OT God's speech and action find expression in forms and saving events which are embedded in the theological notions of the time and are accommodated to contemporary forms of experience, so too in the NT.

Salvation is a historical event. The Church, having its origin in the fact of Christ — in his incarnation, sacrificial death, and resurrection — stands in direct continuity with the OT history of salvation. With the foundation of the Church by the Holy Spirit at Pentecost, this history entered upon its final phase, the "time of the Church", which lasts until the parousia. As the "pilgrim people of God", journeying in the time between Christ's incarnation and return, the Church watches for the coming of God's kingdom in which salvation is to be achieved and manifested.

In its consummation, the salvation of mankind is an ultimate eschatological mystery of faith, transcending history. As such it is not a moment of history, though it involves the resurrection of the body. Yet salvation is already taking place concretely in history in those to whom God offers his grace. It is within history that God carries out his plan to save mankind, to lead them to salvation; and he does this "in such a way that his intervention on man's behalf is recognizably divine. God's saving activity is history because it is revealed and it is revealed in becoming history" (H. Schillebeeckx).

Thus the very concept of the Church again and again directs us back to history. When we turn to the Church's outward form, the historical element comes even more palpably into view. Church history in fact only comes to be by the interaction and co-operation of the divine and human factors throughout the ages.

The special character of revelation and respect for the Church's incarnational principle require the Church to be embodied in the humanity to which salvation is to be proclaimed and in which Christ is to be born anew. For the Church this adaptation does not involve any relativizing of its divine structure; it means, rather, a progressive self-realization in the direction of its eschatological goal. In this process the Church continually allows fresh aspects of its being to emerge in the course of time and in its confrontation with different peoples and cultures; in its developing doctrine, in its worship, in its preaching and pastoral care, in its constitution and administration. The aid of the Holy Spirit preserves it from fundamental error and guarantees at all times its substantial truth and holiness. This does not, however, exclude the possibility of distortions in the human aspects. Revelation and grace do not work by compulsion but presuppose genuine human partnership. As the meeting point between God and man, the Church stands in the field of tension between divine holiness and human frailty. It is the stage on which the dramatic struggle for the salvation or perdition of mankind is being waged.

On its human side, Church history gives no occasion for pride and boasting; it is on the contrary a depressing story of continual failure and miserable weakness. The moral deficiencies of individuals can operate even in the highest offices and institutions (e.g., Alexander VI). In its first stages, the history of doctrine (development of dogma) seems to be a tangle of conflicting views right up to the very point when by the aid of the Holy Spirit heresy is finally fended off and it is possible for the Church to frame and promulgate a valid formulation of dogma. Yet however true it is that this history is indeed the story of the search for truth and of progress in the victory of the truths of faith, it is also true that it inevitably obscures other aspects of the same truth. In other and less important areas of the Church's life, history corrects the erroneous temporary developments. "One of the finest and most impressive aspects of the history of the Church is the fact that the Church, despite the appalling developments and the many sicknesses through which it has passed, has nevertheless remained true to its nature, infallible at its core and unerringly unchangeable." (J. Lortz.)

Grace alone has saved the Church from being overwhelmed by the human element. In fact its history is in this respect a signal demonstration of the grace which is made perfect in weakness (2 Cor 12:9). It is "holy" Church not only in virtue of the indwelling holiness of God but because in every age it also accomplishes holy things in its members and produces "saints". In the figures of its great saints, the Church demonstrates its salutary force in a pre-eminent way. Though it is never an exclusive "Church of saints" for a few choice souls and always remains a redemptive institution for all who need salvation and are called by God, it is nevertheless in its saints that it continually finds its finest expression as "holy" Church. As long as the Church remains on earth there must and will also always be saints in it. "In the saints Christ himself strides through history and causes something of the light of his own earthly life to shine in our midst." (K. Rahner.)

Human weakness and sinfulness in the Church continually distort the image of Christ in it. Personal guilt, erroneous temporary developments, various failures and deformities obscure its form. Its dealings with the world and its own rapid development bring dangers to which it is not always equal. Instead of forming itself in genuine conformity to Christ and, in the Spirit of Christ, re-shaping this form in the world and in history, adapting itself to men and cultures, i.e., informing them with the image of Christ, the Church becomes "worldly" and by its conformity to the world becomes unfaithful to its destiny. Whenever the *forma Christi* is distorted in the Church, re-form is necessary, a return to conformity to Christ. Christ's image and commission always constitute the centre and focus of its existence. In this sense, reform is of the Church's essence: *ecclesia semper reformanda*.

The call for reform always acquires special urgency whenever wide areas and whole states within the Church become unfaithful to their calling and serious disorders take root in the Church's institutions. Superficial observers usually begin then to talk of decline and fundamental apostasy from Christ, calling for a return to primitive Christian conditions and believing that the purity of the ideal can be restored by copying the forms of primitive Christianity. Such sectarians and heretics lack a genuine feeling for history and in demanding an anachronistic restoration of former conditions are seeking something not merely inherently impossible but also contradictory to the very nature of the Church. The Church which God wills should remain open to all men, to all times and cultures, cannot identify itself with any period or culture, not even with the primitive Church. True reform means recalling Christ as the Church's original form and fulfilling his saving commission, given from the outset and binding on every generation. Certainly we may learn from the primitive Church how genuine conformity to Christ is lived out. But the contemporary expression of this ideal continues to be a task set to each generation afresh. The form of Christ shines out in the saints. They therefore have more justification than anyone else for calling for reform and carrying it out. Reform is a task for saints.

Even the emergence of schisms and heresies seems to be a part of the authentic reality of the Church (1 Cor 11:19) and it would be wrong to misinterpret the moral quality of the conduct of the heretic, springing as this often did from a zealous search for the truth. "No one can establish a heresy unless he has an ardent heart and natural gifts created by the divine Artist", declared Jerome. "Do not imagine, brethren, that heresies can possibly arise from petty minds. Only great men have produced heresies", said Augustine (*In Ps.* 124). Yet both these issue warnings against heresy. Paul regarded heresy as a fearful threat to salvation not just for the individual but still more for the Church, which the devil seeks by heresy to divert from the truth and from its eschatological goal. Augustine calls heresy the Church's excreta ("quos partim digessit ecclesia, tamquam stercora", *Sermo* V). In order to assure the salvation of its children the Church must conquer heresy.

No less dangerous is the narrow-minded truncation of the faith by rigorous encratistic sectarianism such as Montanism, Tertullianism, Jansenism, Integralism. Nothing harms the Church more than anything which makes it narrow.

2. *The function of Church history as a scientific discipline* is already implicit in the concept of the Church. Church history must investigate closely what historically took on various forms; it must test this history for its essential content and measure it against its normative origin. The account of the origin and growth of the Church shows its connection and essential identity with the community founded by Jesus Christ and also serves to sharpen the Church's conscience and to stimulate a true understanding of its history and a better understanding of its own being. The nature of the Church is not grasped by systematic theology alone; it appears only against the background of its total history; only at the end of time, at the parousia, will it be fully revealed.

B. TASK AND METHOD

The task and method of Church history are likewise determined by the concept and nature of the Church. Since the Church historian is dealing with a subject matter which is both visible and invisible, both historical and an object of faith, his thinking about history must be at once factual and theological. It must proceed *a posteriori* by first establishing the historical facts, investigating their contexts and connections and analysing their significance. At the same time, it must proceed on the *a priori* theological assumption that what has taken place in the historically verifiable facts is the revelation of God's saving activity.

As a historical science, Church history continues to depend on the strict scientific investigation of the facts. The demonstration of facts and dates is a primary requisite and, for a historical religion, an indispensable presupposition. Since "the Church itself is not an idea but a fact" (H. Jedin), its history cannot be dissolved into a history of ideas or philosophy. It is "a science of the facts; it is tied to the facts; it respects the facts; it seeks to inculcate reverence for the facts" (H. Jedin). The facts and dates constitute the scaffolding; if these are not known and assured, each further step in the direction of connected argument and theological and philosophical evaluation would be insecure. Nothing is gained by unfounded speculations; they do not advance knowledge. The historian must always start from the sources and treat the facts with respect even when they lead to apparent difficulties with the faith. To clarify the facts he employs all the tools and methods of the secular historian. Only the objective presentation based on the facts ("pragmatic" presentation) does justice to the honour and holiness of the Church. *Ne audeat historia falsa dicere, ne audeat vera non dicere* (Leo XIII). Exaggeration, touching-up, falsification of the facts — these would be a poor apologia for the Church. The only important question is the question of truth.

A purely positivistic historical presentation, limited to the accumulation and listing of facts and dates, cannot, of course, do justice to historical realities of any kind, least of all to a spiritual reality such as the Church. The aim of the Church historian's research must be to see beyond the facts, to grasp the abiding in the changing and temporary, and to press forward to the essence of the Church. It is the synthesis which brings the history alive. The past is connected up and interpreted from certain standpoints in the mind of the historian. Being a mystery of faith, the Church can in the last resort only be understood by faith. Thus even the interpretation of facts, the assessment of religious and intellectual movements and personalities, and the entire inner life of the Church is only accessible to faith. The non-believing historian cannot grasp or present the phenomenon of the Church in its profundity. In his interpretation of the facts and in his arrangement of them into the total picture, the believing historian will take faith and dogma into account, so that real contradictions cannot arise.

Church history is a science of faith; as such it is a part of theology. It not only adopts the theological concept of the Church, but also puts its own historical and theological questions to its subject matter, the Church, and tries to answer them from theological standpoints. It is not satisfied with an analytical description of the form taken by the Church at different periods, among different peoples and cultures; it probes deeper, questions the theological presuppositions and tries to interpret events in the light of revelation.

It has been deplored that "we have never yet had a genuine theology of history or of the Church's historicity" (K. Rahner), although there have been a number of praiseworthy approaches and attempts in this direction. A convincing theology of history would have to begin by explaining, within the framework of dogmatic ecclesiology, "how and why the Church lives historically, changes, must present in ever new forms one and the same Christianity in truth, law and religious life, in order to present the fullness of Christ throughout the totality of all its times" (K. Rahner).

Church history can only be understood as a whole as a theology of history. It is a part of the history of salvation. Imbued with the conviction that the Holy Spirit is the "soul" of the Church, guiding and impelling it to fulfil its task of continuing among men through the centuries Christ's saving work, the Church historian in his capacity as theologian becomes an "interpreter of the activity of the Holy Spirit on earth" (J. Spoerl); indeed, his discipline has been called "an auxiliary science serving the knowledge of God". Yet he never forgets that unlike the systematic theologian he must always start from the facts of human life, from the sober and sobering realities of history. His business is not "dogmatic" historical research in the sense of trying to prove from history the doctrinal theses and ideas of the systematic theologian. He avoids all new style "pragmatism", which scours Church history for illustrations and documents to furnish historical proof of the Church's invisible divine character. He proceeds always from the outward to the inward, from below upwards. He sees the stains and frailties of the pilgrim Church as it follows its Lord along his *via dolorosa*. "Church history is *theologia crucis*" (H. Jedin). In this way Church history tries to assist the Church to understand itself better.

C. Historiography

The changing form and self-understanding of the Church is reflected in the way Church history is written. The distinctive Christian view of history first appears in the NT. Its consistent interpretation of universal history in terms of the history of salvation involved a breach with certain ancient views of history as an unending recurrence, and the replacement of the cyclical view by the linear teleological view according to which history is a development under divine providence from creation to Christ's incarnation and from the incarnation to the final judgment. The incarnation of the Logos in the "fullness of time" is both the centre of universal history and the beginning of a new epoch, the "time of the Church" which lasts until the parousia.

The more unreservedly the early Church knew itself committed to the unique reality of the event of Christ and to the gospel, the more care it felt obliged to take to ensure the unalloyed preservation of what the apostles as eye-witnesses entrusted to it. The "apostolic tradition" became the kernel of belief; to guarantee and establish this tradition the formation of the canon was undertaken

(2nd century). The drawing up of episcopal lists in the apostolic communities and the stress on apostolic succession (Hegesippus, Irenaeus, Tertullian) bear witness to this early Christian awareness of history.

The universal and theological aspects of history were also stressed very early. The chronographers (Theophilus of Antioch, d. after 180; Hippolytus of Rome, d. 235; Sextus Julius Africanus, d. after 240; Eusebius of Caesarea, d. 339) sought to set Christianity in its universal context and in this way to demonstrate its antiquity and priority. Eusebius, "the father of Church history", was the first to synchronize Christian chronology with world history and the history of the Caesars. He already discerned an essential historico-theological connection between the *Imperium Romanum* and the emergence and expansion of Christianity. To Eusebius, not only the OT but also the whole of ancient history seemed to be a preparation for Christ. This positive evaluation provided him with the basis of his later "theology of the Empire", developed in his *Vita Constantini*.

The great value of Eusebius's *Church History* (down to 324) as a source, now generally acknowledged, soon prompted the Greek writers Socrates (d. *c.* 450), Sozomenus (d. after 450) and Theodoret of Cyrrhus (d. after 450) to expand and continue it. They in turn were translated into Latin by Rufinus of Aquileia (403) and Epiphanius (6th century), while Cassiodorus (*c.* 490–583) worked them together into a *Historia Tripartita*. It was in this form that they became known in the West and served the whole medieval period as the principal handbook of Church history. The Chronicles were also continued (Jerome, Sulpicius Severus, Prosper of Aquitaine, Cassiodorus, Isidore of Seville) and frequently imitated in the Middle Ages.

The greatest influence on the understanding of history was that of Augustine (354–430) with his *De Civitate Dei* (413–26). Augustine also left his mark on the Christian view of the State. Deliberately abandoning the Eastern notion of religio-political unity, for which Eusebius provided a basis by his "theology of the Empire", he conceived the relationship between Church and State in dualistic terms. In this respect as in many others he was the teacher of the West. It was a misunderstanding of Augustine when later rulers like Charlemagne, the German Emperors and the French kings used him as an authority for a new "theology of the Empire" in the West.

When in 525 Dionysius Exiguus (*c.* 470–550) transposed the dates of Roman history (reckoned from the foundation of the city of Rome) into a new reckoning from the birth of Christ, he introduced into chronology the "Christian era". He placed Christ's birth 4 or 5 years too late, assigning it to 754 A.U.C. instead of to 749 A.U.C. which would have been the correct date. He thereby introduced an error which has not yet been corrected.

Ancient Christian historians divided the course of history according to one or other of three theologico-historical schemes: a) The *six world-ages,* analogous to the six days of creation, each world-day being equivalent to 1000 years (in accordance with Ps. 90:4; 2 Pet 3:8). The seventh day, the universal sabbath, would bring the "millennium" of divine peace and rest under the rule of Christ (Rev 20:1–6). This "Milleniarism", an interpretation of history which constantly recurred, took on various forms in Cerinthus, Papias, Justin, Irenaeus, Julius Africanus, Tertullian and Hippolytus; in the medieval theologians, the Venerable Bede, Wilfred Strabo, Rupert of Deutz, Richard of St. Victor and many others down to Joachim of Flora (d. 1202) and the Franciscan "Spirituals" of the 14th century. Once this view had been rejected by Thomas Aquinas on theological grounds, it was not long before it was condemned by the Church and, in one precise form, branded as heresy. Right down to modern times it has continued as an "enthusiastic" hope among the sects (Anabaptists, Moravian Brethren, Adventists, Mormons, Jehovah's Witnesses). b) The *four world-empires* (Assyrian-Babylonian, Persian, Macedonian [Alexander the Great], and Roman, an interpretation of Dan 2:36 ff.; 7:3 ff.); the fourth of these empires, the Roman, now Christianized, would last, it was thought, to the end of the world, which is why men clung to it so tenaciously even in the Middle Ages. c) The *threefold scheme* of Augustine: *ante legem, sub lege, post legem.* In the Middle Ages this was varied (Otto of Freising: *ante gratiam, tempore gratiae, post praesentem vitam*) and interpreted in a trinitarian sense (Joachim of Flora).

In the Middle Ages history was seen as the

history of salvation. There is a remarkable change in the picture of the Church. In the early Middle Ages the universal idea was completely eclipsed. The chief interest then was in describing the Christian history of one's own people or of the monastery or diocese. Hagiography occupied much space. It is impossible to speak of this as genuine Church history, for the concept of the Church is absent. Instead, the chronicler or annalist offers us simply Christian historiography, linked to the history of salvation at most by a brief prologue. This was a continuation of the concept of history held by the post-Constantinian imperial Church. In the Carolingian and subsequent period the symbiosis of the secular (or temporal) and the "spiritual" found expression in the casual replacement of the word *mundus* by the word *ecclesia*. Charlemagne called himself *caput ecclesiae;* Church and State merge into one. This notion of unity is echoed in the early medieval chronicles.

It was only with the monastic reform of the 11th century that awareness of the Church as such was quickened. The signs of deterioration in that period (wealth, secularization, feudalism) were opposed by the ideals of the *ecclesia primitiva,* the *imitatio Christi* and the *vita apostolica.* A new self-understanding began to emerge in the Church (Odericus Vitalis, John of Salisbury). The threefold scheme was applied to the history of salvation and interpreted in a trinitarian sense. Rupert of Deutz (d. 1129) distinguished three periods: creation (God the Father), redemption (God the Son), and sanctification (God the Spirit). Joachim of Flora collected triple typological sequences from the OT and the NT (law, grace, love; science, wisdom, full knowledge; slavery, service, freedom; etc.) and from these deduced that succeeding the era of the Father in the OT and the era of the Son in the NT the era of the Holy Spirit in love and freedom would now soon follow. He prophesied that in the year 1260 the present Petrine hierarchical Church would be replaced by the new "Johannine" Church of the Spirit.

The medieval world chronicles quarried from Eusebius and Jerome and for the most part simply revised these writers for purposes of edification (Regino of Prüm, Hermann the Lame, Sigebert of Gembloux). Otto of Freising, the most important historical thinker of the Middle Ages, was the first to link up with Augustine. The annals, unlike the more individualistic chronicles, are completely anonymous and utilitarian. The papal chronicles represented a special class, providing in the *Liber Pontificalis* a pattern for the chronicling of successive "lives". Imperial, diocesan and monastic annals, and lives of saints and bishops multiplied.

From about 1300 on, a slow but steady breakdown in the medieval consciousness of the Church becomes apparent. The struggle between Papacy and Empire, Boniface VIII and Philip the Fair, the Avignon Papacy (1309–78) and finally the great Western Schism (1378–1417) shook men's confidence. Joachim of Flora's criticism of the hierarchical Church, taken further by the Franciscan "Spirituals", favoured the theory of decline, which regarded the post-Constantinian Church as increasingly a victim of decline, and needing to be replaced by the pure, ideal, invisible "Spirit Church" *(ecclesia spiritualis).*

A vigorous theological reflection on the Church began. In strong opposition to the Papal Church, Marsilius of Padua (d. 1343) and William of Occam (d. 1349) developed a new democratic concept of the Church, placing the Council, as representative of the Christian people, above the Pope. A serious ecclesiastical constitutional crisis was precipitated by the conciliarism of the Councils of Constance (1414–18) and Basle (1431–37). Papalism (Jacob of Vitry, Aegidius Romanus, Alvar Pelayo, Augustinus Triumphus) which since Gregory VII had been developed in an increasingly one-sided way by the canonists, was forced into an impasse by the Great Schism. The doctrine of the Church had become the sole concern of the canonists, and this legalism on the eve of the Reformation was to have far-reaching consequences.

By opening up the sources the humanists both extended the knowledge of history and at the same time promoted a critical approach, e.g., to the Donation of Constantine (Nicholas of Cusa, Lorenzo Vally). The new editions of the Fathers (Erasmus of Rotterdam) threw fresh light on the NT and primitive Church. The call for reform which continued throughout the entire 15th century became a call to return to the *ecclesia primitiva.* Luther and the Protestants gave it explosive force.

The Reformation challenged everything which the medieval Church had constructed, and called for a return to the ancient Church. It sought "witnesses of the truth" in primitive times to support its reforms. Matthias Flaccius (1520–75) in his *Catalogus Testium Veritatis* (1556) and in his *Historia Ecclesiastica* ("Magdeburg Centuries", 1559–74) tried to prove from the sources that Lutheranism alone, and not the Papal Church, was in agreement with the ancient Church in doctrine and discipline. In opposition to him Caesar Baronius (1538–1607) produced in Rome (1588–1607) his historical work *Annales Ecclesiastici* (12 vols., down to 1198) which was also quarried wholly from the sources. His work was continued by Abraham Bzovius (d. 1637) down to Pius V; Odorico Rinaldi (d. 1671) and Jacob Laderchi (d. 1738) corrected and expanded it. A new interest in Church History developed.

Melanchthon had in 1520 introduced the study of Church history as part of his reform of the University of Wittenberg, and it became a compulsory subject in 1583 at Frankfurt-am-Oder and soon afterwards at Helmstedt as an independent discipline. Protestant criticism stimulated an intensive study of the sources on the Catholic side, and this led to the development of critical historical methods in the analysis of sources and progress in auxiliary disciplines (chronology, diplomatics, palaeography). For the first time Church history now became a "science". The Bollandists (Jan Bolland, d. 1665, Gottfried Henschen, d. 1681, Daniel Papebroch, d. 1714, and other Jesuits) published the monumental *Acta Sanctorum* from 1643 onwards. The Maurists (Benedictines of St. Maur in France) provided critical editions of the Fathers. Jean Mabillon accomplished astonishing feats (science of documents and editions, the *Acta Sanctorum OSB* and the *Annales OSB*) as did Edmond Martene de Sainte-Marthe (*Gallia Christiana*, 1656), F. Ughelli (*Italia Sacra*, 1644–62), L. Wadding (*Annales Ordinis Minorum*, 1625–54), J. Quétif and J. Echard (*Scriptores Ord. Praedicatorum*, 1719–21), L. A. Muratori (*Rerum Italicarum Scriptores*, 1723–51), E. Florez (*España Sagrada*, 1747–75), D. Farlati (*Illyricum Sacrum*, 1751 ff.), M. Gerbert of St. Blaise (*Germania Sacra*, 1764 ff.). So too the great conciliar collections, the *Collectio Regia* (37 vols., 1644 ff.), that of J. Hardouin (12 vols., 1714/15) and of G. D. Mansi (31 vols., 1759–98), and the narrative histories of Louis Sebastien le Nain de Tillemont, Alexander Natalis and C. Fleury, are all monumental achievements. In his *Discours sur l'histoire universelle* (1681) J. B. Bossuet tried to provide once more a total survey of history from the standpoint of the history of salvation.

Meanwhile the Enlightenment, with its fundamental rejection of theological principles, brought about a complete secularization of Church history. Church history now became in Catholic countries an official subject in the universities (Curriculum of Maria Theresia, 1752); but the Emperor Joseph II described it as the task of Church history (Instruction, 1775) to "discuss" the morality of historical events. His concern was that the relationship between Church and State should be presented as far as possible in accordance with his own view. For this reason the "Dark Middle Ages" were to be ignored as far as possible.

Opposition to the pragmatism of the Enlightenment came from the Catholic Renewal of the 19th century, from Ultramontanism in Italy (M. Cappellari, later Gregory XVI) and Traditionalism in France (J. de Maistre, Lamennais). Neo-Scholasticism was also an influence for renewal both by reason of its origin and because of its fundamental impulse. Its lack of interest in history derived from its philosophical approach. But the real renewal of the Catholic spirit in Church history originated with J. A. Möhler (1796–1838) and the Tübingen School.

The burgeoning of historical sciences in the 19th century had a stimulating influence on Church history. The critical researches of I. Döllinger (1799–1890), C. J. Hefele (1809–93), F. X. Funk and many others elevated Church History in Germany to a high scientific rank. The monumental works, the *Monumenta Germaniae Historica* (from 1819), the *Corpus Scriptorum Eccl. Lat.* (from 1866) and *Die griechischen christlichen Schriftsteller der ersten drei Jahrhunderte* (from 1893) enriched the basic source material. The opening of the Vatican archives by Leo XIII (1884) gave fresh impetus to research. In addition to the newly founded National Historical Institutes in Rome, H. Denifle, F. Ehrle, and Ludwig von Pastor (d. 1928), author of the *History of the Popes*, did outstanding work. The French register of Popes, P. F. Kehr's work on papal documents, the edition of the diplomatic reports and the *Concilium Tridentinum* of the Görres Society are major achievements both in content and form. All periods profited from this upsurge: the early period (archaeological research into the catacombs, by de Rossi, J. Wilpert; history of the early Church, by L. Duchesne, P. Batiffol, Fr. J. Dölger, and the *Reallexikon für Antike und Christentum;* patrology, by A. von Harnack, O. Bardenhewer); the Middle Ages (by A. Hauck and others); history of the Reformation (*Corpus Reformatorum* and the Weimar edition of Luther, *Corpus Catholicorum* and countless studies and accounts — J. Lortz, A. Herte, K. Holl). In France, H. Bremond's *Histoire littéraire du sentiment religieux en France* (12 vols., 1916–36) laid the foundations for the history of spirituality.

Increasing specialization brought greater independence to certain individual disciplines within Church history (hagiography, iconography, liturgics, history of missions, history of dogma, religious anthropology). Numerous specialist journals provided information about the mass of new publications resulting from this research, especially valuable being the Louvain *Revue d'histoire ecclésiastique* (from 1900).

Since the Second World War a new theological emphasis is evident in Church History, turning away from 19th century positivism and towards a theologico-historical and ecclesiological orientation. K. and H. Rahner, H. U. von Balthasar, Y. Congar, H. Lubac, J. Daniélou and others have posed afresh the question of the Church's historicity from the standpoint of its nature and are seeking to develop a new theology of its history. A Church which experiences and progressively realizes itself in its history cannot regard its past as an inert possession. Accordingly, the uniform concern of recent full-scale accounts of Church history is to go beyond the mere presentation of historical facts and to seek to understand the events in terms of the history of ideas and to interpret them theologically: J. Lortz (*Geschichte der Kirche in ideengeschichtlicher Betrachtung,* 21st ed., 2 vols., 1962), H. Jedin and J. Dolan (eds., *Handbook of Church History,* 1965 ff.), R. Aubert, D. Knowles and L. J. Rogier, eds., *Christian Centuries,* 5 vols. (1964 ff.), the recent volumes of Fliche and Martin, *Histoire de l'Église,* 24 vols. (1935 ff.), and K. Bihlmeier and H. Tüchle, *Church History* (15th ed., 1956). This more profound approach to Church History enriches ecclesiology just as it was ecclesiology which first stimulated this new approach.

D. Periodization and Survey

To facilitate a survey of the whole, it is reasonable and necessary to arrange the material into epochs. This often seems quite impossible, however, since every principle of division proves inadequate. The continuous flow of history recognizes no pauses. When changes take place they never involve the whole but only certain partial areas. But because the total history is a confluence of many single forces and various streams, it can nevertheless still be useful to isolate particular aspects which have helped in important respects to shape the total picture.

Down to the 17th century the schema of the history of salvation seemed to be adequate. It was the Protestant historian Christoph Cellarius (1634–1707) in Halle who introduced the division into epochs: ancient, medieval, modern. 15th and 16th century humanists and Protestants had coined the term "Middle Ages" in a pejorative sense because they saw there nothing but a decline in language and religion and wished for that reason to link up again with classical "antiquity", with its pure Latin speech and undefiled Christianity. The 18th century Enlightenment thought even less of the "dark" Middle Ages, the period from about 500 to 1500. The intrinsic value of this period was only rediscovered by Romanticism and the burgeoning science of history in the 19th century which filled it with positive content by intensive research into documents and sources. J. A. Möhler applied the threefold scheme to Catholic Church history, and since then it has dominated historical writing as a whole, although doubts about its objective adequacy are everywhere in evidence. Today in an age of ecumenical thinking, the threefold division, designed mainly to fit the European West, seems doubly inadequate.

Yet it is difficult to replace it. Philosophical interpretations of history (Hegel, Marx, historicism and metaphysical relativism, existentialism) are excluded as alien to the nature of the Church, and the same applies to the purely politico-geographical view of Halecki (Mediterranean, European, Atlantic periods) and to the theories of civilization-cycles (Spengler and Toynbee). But even from the nature of the Church itself no particular division into periods imposes itself, since the biblical revelation nowhere informs us by what stages and in what forms the divine plan of salvation is to be realized; the gracious inner working of the Holy Spirit certainly cannot be measured and defined, even though recognizable by its outward effects.

Thus the only remaining possibility is to seek a theologically practicable division into periods in the context of the "Church and the world", more precisely within the actual way in which the Church has carried out its divine task in the world. We could perhaps start from the expansion of Christianity (history of missions) and distinguish two main periods: a) the period of its growth from Jerusalem over the entire Graeco-Roman world (antiquity) to the Western Church (Middle Ages), and from the *(de facto)* regional Church of the West to the world Church (modern period down to the present day) and b) the period of universal Christianity in an age of universal human history only just beginning (K. Rahner). But this solution would mean adhering to the old threefold division for the early period, and this should surely be corrected. H. Jedin's proposal of four periods is therefore preferable: a) the Church within Graeco-Roman civilization (1st – 7th century); b) the Church as the dominant factor of the Western community of Christian nations (about 700–1300); c) the disintegration of the Christian unity of the West and the transition to the world-mission (1300–1750); d) the Church in the industrialization period (19th and 20th centuries). For a true understanding of the third period (1300–1750) it is important to insist that the period from 1300 to 1500 is no longer "medieval" while that from 1500 to 1750 is not yet "modern". This third period has a pronounced transitional character and is marked by a new self-awareness in the Church and by a struggle for reform.

Whenever an era comes to an end, the Church is summoned to detach itself from the previous environment in which it has made itself at home, and to open itself to new peoples and cultures. For the sake of its divine commission it must not identify itself with any civilization but must "accommodate" itself to the new order in order to assimilate it to itself, i.e., in order to make possible Christ's incorporation into it. Such transitions, which usually take place only to the accompaniment of great upheavals, have always greatly altered the Church's appearance: for example, the change from Judaic to Gentile Christianity (Apostolic Council of Jerusalem), from Graeco-Roman to Western Germanic civilization (between 400 and 700), from the unified religio-political culture of the Middle Ages to the disintegration of the unity of Church and Empire (about 1300), and from the great radical change introduced by revolution and secularization down to the present day (1800–1966). It is clear that once again today an era is ending and a new beginning heralded.

First period: the Church in the world of Graeco-Roman civilization (1st–7th century). The first section, from the time of the Church's foundation at the first Pentecost down to Constantine the Great, is particularly important as the foundation period of the Church. The period of the primitive Church and of the apostles (apostolic age), i.e., the first and second generations of Christians, saw the emergence of the NT writings. As authentic interpreters of the mind of Jesus, the twelve apostles, eye-witnesses of the Word and themselves bearers of Christ's revelation, created "the Church", under the guidance of the Holy Spirit, as a reality which is an integral part of the Christian fact. In the doctrine, worship, order and discipline of the primitive Church the "apostolic tradition" was laid down, to which Christianity in all ages has known itself to be bound as a matter of life and death. It is on this that the normative significance of the first period rests, a significance which has again and again demonstrated itself in the call for reform and for a return to the *ecclesia primitiva* and the *vita apostolica*.

Judaism and the mother Church of Jerusalem greatly influenced the form taken by the life of the early Christian communities. But Christianity was not to enter upon its course through history as a sect of the Jewish religious community, but as an independent universal religion. At the Apostolic Council (*c.* 50) it detached itself from Judaism and soon invaded the world of Graeco-Roman civilization. The "Apostolic Fathers", themselves still pupils of the apostles, and the early Christian "Apologists" developed further the life of the Church and entered into discussion with the intellectual world around them. They unhesitatingly made use of the language and concepts of Hellenism. At the end of the 2nd century the Alexandrian school of theology came into being as a voluntary missionary enterprise on the part of educated Christians (Pantaenus, c. 180; Clement of Alexandria; Origen). About 260 Lucian founded another school of theology, the Antiochene. Greek philosophy, Hellenistic culture and Christian doctrine entered into alliance. From this alliance developed the remarkable Greek patristic writings of the 4th and 5th centuries, upon whose massive theological labour the first "ecumenical" councils depended.

The lofty spirituality and richness of thought of revelation, its genuine historicity and the part played by the human factor in its development are sufficient explanation of the frequent emergence of erroneous views and overt heresies in Christianity. Christian heresy and schism began already in the 1st century: Judaizers, Ebionites, Nazarenes, Elkesites and Cerinthus were contemporary with the apostles. The main threat in the 2nd century was Gnosticism. Because the Christian "Gnostics" were fond of appealing to their private revelations, the Church found itself compelled to establish the canon of Scripture as the sole norm of faith and to develop the Church's teaching office. Bishops standing in the "apostolic succession" were seen as guarantors of the pure apostolic tradition. From the latter half of the 2nd century the bishops met together in synods in order to present a common defence of the true faith against Gnosticism, Montanism, Marcionism and other heresies (Donatism, Manicheism). The more widespread heresy became, the more representative the synods. Local synods were soon replaced by provincial ones. The Church's sense of universality was reinforced; despite persecution and danger, great councils assembled from the middle of the 3rd century on, in the metropolis Rome, in Carthage, Alexandria, Antioch and Caesarea in Asia (later councils of the Patriarchates), and when following the conversion of Constantine, Arianism and Donatism threatened the entire empire (= *oekumene*), the Christian Emperor summoned the first ecumenical imperial council to Nicaea (325). At such councils, the Church acted as a universal community. Heretical opposition also forced it to grapple more closely with the treasure of revelation; the history of the discovery and unfolding of the truth of faith, the development of dogma, is inseparably connected with the continual invasion of heresies and the accompanying discernment of spirits in the Church.

Once Christianity became a historical factor (beginning of the 2nd century) Christians were persecuted in the Roman Empire. This persecution was in three phases. The last and severest of them, under Diocletian, ended in the victory of Christianity with Constantine the Great (306–37). His "conversion" (312/13) gave the Church freedom and brought it to a turning-point. Subsequently the Church was integrated with the State as an "established" religion. This gave rise to many problems and remained an important factor for almost fifteen hundred years of Western history. But it was not long before joy at the "Christianization" of the State was mingled with laments at the secularization of the Church. Many Christians, bishops, priests and laity, failed to maintain the detachment from the world obligatory on all Christians.

It was then that God raised up in the Church the monastic movement, not as a "protest" but as a clearly visible sign of Christian perfection. If in the days of persecution the martyr's death was the supreme form of Christian discipleship, its place was now taken by the supreme spiritual sacrifice, martyrdom according to the spirit. The original Christian *pneuma* was united with an asceticism penetrated by mysticism to form a perfect imitation of the suffering and dying Redeemer (*theologia crucis*) and thus gave expression to an essential aspect of Christian living. The religious dynamism of monasticism saved the Church from becoming mere outward show in the Constantinian era, and also gave it fresh impulses. All the great bishops and theologians of the 4th century were closely connected with monasticism. The strong missionary impetus, the remarkable development of pastoral care, the effort to Christianize the Roman State, and above all the theological work of the great councils of the 4th to the 7th century are inconceivable without monasticism.

In the struggle against Arianism, Subordinationism and Monarchianism, Athanasius and the "three great Cappadocians" — Basil, Gregory of Nazianzus, and Gregory of Nyssa — elaborated the theological doctrine of the Trinity (2nd general council, Constantinople I, 381). In conflict with Monophysitism, Nestorianism and Monothelitism, the theology of the Greek Fathers clarified Christology (Councils of Ephesus, 431, Chalcedon, 451, Constantinople II, 553, Constantinople III, 680/81). All these councils took place in the Greek East.

But Latin patristic theology too attained great heights in Augustine (354–430). It turned more to soteriological problems, to the doctrines of justification and grace. Pelagianism provided a special stimulus here. The West was then caught up in the vortex of the great Germanic invasions (from about the beginning of the 5th century). In the 7th century, the onslaught of the Arabs dealt the Mediterranean world its death blow. For the Church, which had so closely identified itself with this civilization, it was far from certain that it would survive its overthrow and open itself to the newly emerging Germanic Western world.

Second period: the Church as the dominant factor of the Western community of Christian nations (c. 700–1300). The Arianization of the Germans made access to them impossible for a long period. Only with the Catholic baptism of Clovis, king of the Franks (c. 496), did new possibilities arise, though little use was made of them by Rome. Pope Gregory the Great (590–604) finally seized the opportunity when in 596 he inaugurated the Anglo-Saxon mission. The work of Boniface (d. 754), the alliance between Pepin and the papacy (751–54), and the imperial coronation of Charlemagne (Christmas 800) were further steps leading to the establishment of the Western Christian community of nations.

Antiquity, Germanic culture and Christianity were welded into one and the Church itself took on a new form. The "Germanization" of Christianity had far-reaching effects on every aspect of the Church's life.

A profound grasp of the Christian ethos and a naive openness to the world produced in time a genuine organic union of Church and State and, in the early medieval German and French kingdoms, an impressive unified religio-political culture. With the feudalization of the imperial Church and a theocratic concept of the ruler, the boundaries between Church and State disappeared completely. The Emperor took the place of a papacy

which had lapsed into insignificance in the *saeculum obscurum* (10th and 11th centuries). The papacy, renewed by the Gregorian Reform, had to win back the Church's freedom, threatened chiefly by lay investiture, in the course of the Investiture Controversy (Gregory VII, 1073–85; Henry IV, 1056–1106; journey to Canossa, 1077; Concordat of Worms, 1122).

Although in the ensuing struggles for power between the *imperium* and the *sacerdotium* it was ostensibly the restoration of a proper balance between the two powers which was the issue (political dualism of the West), in reality it was a struggle for supremacy. Under Innocent III (1198–1216) the papacy was undisputed leader of the Christian West. But when the Hohenstaufen empire collapsed (1286) the dominant position of the papacy was not long maintained. About 1300 it was subordinated to the national power of Philip the Fair of France.

The renewal which began at Cluny in the 10th century had by the 11th and 12th centuries embraced the entire Western Church. New monastic orders appeared: Camaldolenses (Romuald, d. 1027), Carthusians (Bruno, d. 1101), Cistercians (Robert of Molesme, d. 1111; Bernard of Clairvaux, d. 1153) and the Orders of Chivalry (Johannites, 1099, Templars, 1118, Teutonic Knights, 1189/90). Clergy reform was carried through by the Canons Regular movement (Augustinians, Premonstratensians or White Canons, Norbert of Xanten, d. 1134). The laity formed Bible groups and the Poverty Movement. The Crusades generated tremendous religious energy; they strengthened the consciousness of solidarity in the Western community, widened the European horizon, and assisted the advance of knowledge through the encounter with Byzantine and Islamic culture. The amazing development of Western philosophy and theology in Scholasticism would be inconceivable without this encounter with the Orient.

Critical minds had since the middle of the 11th century ceased to be satisfied with the early medieval scriptural theology of the monastic schools. Independent schools came into being and sought new ways in their theology (Anselm of Canterbury, d. 1109, *theologia scholastica*). When c. 1200 several such schools in Paris united to form a single corporation, the *universitas magistrorum,* the first university, came into existence. Not long after followed Bologna, Padua, Naples, Montpellier, Oxford, Cambridge, Salamanca and Valencia. Germany had to wait until the 14th century for the universities of Prague (1348), Vienna (1365), Heidelberg (1386) and Cologne (1388).

There were new heresies too: Berengarius of Tours (d. 1088), Tanchelm (d. 1115), Arnold of Brescia (d. 1155), Catharists and Waldensians. When to purely spiritual weapons in the struggle against heresy the Inquisition was added, special processes of law were introduced (Innocent III) and torture was used to secure proof; one of the most lamentable chapters in Church history began. Later the Inquisition was used in the service of an insane hunt for witches. But Francis of Assisi (d. 1226) and Dominic (d. 1221) showed that there was another way of combating heresy. The mendicant orders, the Franciscans and Dominicans, were a more persuasive influence by their ideal of voluntary poverty and by their preaching than were weapons and courts. Their pastoral concern and preaching ministry led to a deep interest in theology. Their greatest theologians, the Dominicans Albertus Magnus (d. 1280), Thomas Aquinas (d. 1274) and Master Eckhard (d. 1328), and the Franciscans Alexander of Hales (d. 1245), Bonaventure (d. 1274) and Duns Scotus (d. 1308) were the most brilliant masters of Scholasticism.

The papacy meanwhile, renewed and consolidated by the reform of Gregory VII, rose to the pinnacle of its authority. The proclamation of supreme jurisdiction in the *Dictatus Papae* (1075) and the systematic development of the Roman Curia into the central organ of Church government gave Innocent III (1198–1216) a unique position of authority and leadership among all the Western nations. This found expression in the new Western general councils (Lateran: 1123, 1139, 1179, 1215; Lyons I, 1245; Lyons II, 1274) and was undergirded by the Church's canonists.

Unfortunately, the Christian East was absent from these councils. The growing division had led in this period to ever increasing estrangement (iconoclast controversy, *filioque* clause, problem of the two Emperors, question of primacy) and finally to the Eastern Schism (1054). The Crusades, especially the senseless fourth Crusade and the establishment of the Latin Empire in Constantinople (1204–61), widened the gulf

still more with the result that no union ever materialized again.

Third period: the disintegration of Western Christian unity and the transition to world mission (1300–1750). The unified civilization of the West rested on the two universally recognized authorities, Empire and Papacy. Only together, in an "elliptical" tension, could they fulfill their task. The disintegration of European political unity brought in its train that of the Church. When Boniface VIII (1294–1303) asserted his papal authority over the French national state (Bull *Unam Sanctam*, 1302), he was humiliatingly arrested by Philip the Fair at Anagni (Sept. 1303). The decline of the papal power showed itself in the period following this, in the Avignon Exile (1309–78) and the great Western Schism (1378–1417).

This third period is chiefly characterized by the dissolution of the unified order created by the previous period. The process began in the 14th century, continued in the 15th, and reached its ecclesiastical climax in the great division of the Church in the 16th century. The process was only arrested in the 18th century.

In France, England and Spain, the trend towards national states was at first accompanied by a marked trend towards national churches. In Germany the growing strength of the territorial princedoms already foreshadowed the territorial Churches which would prove so significant for the Reformation of the 16th century. The social order was disturbed by the conflict between princes and nobility, patricians and guilds, a conflict arising from economic changes (transition from an agrarian to a financial economy, early capitalism). The feudal Church was involved in both. Tensions between territorial Church authorities on the one hand, and the nobility and cities on the other, largely prepared the way for the decline of the faith in the 16th century. The fiscal policies of the papacy alienated people from the Church. But still more important was the loss of intellectual unity. The traditional Thomist-Scotist philosophy *(via antiqua)* was superseded by the new Occamist-nominalist philosophy *(via moderna)*. Moreover, humanism provided a new cultural ideal.

In the Great Schism it was ultimately the Church itself which became problematical. As Pope and anti-Popes excommunicated one another, no one knew which of the three was the legitimate one and on which side the true Church was to be found. At the councils (Pisa, 1409; Constance, 1414/15; Basle–Ferrara–Florence, 1431–42) conciliarism provoked the most serious constitutional crisis of the hierarchical Church. Even though it proved possible to avert the catastrophe once again, disquiet nevertheless remained as regards the papacy. The Renaissance Popes soon found fresh burdens adding to their anxiety. *Reformatio in capite et membris* was the most pressing concern of the 15th century. Since the papacy declined this task, reformation came from below.

Considered as a historical process, the 16th century Reformation is an extremely complex event in which almost all the aspirations of the age meet — religious, intellectual, political, and social. As an ecclesiastical process it was a major turning-point which decisively shaped all subsequent developments. With the breach in the Church's unity, even the common basis of faith was shaken. The unified Christian consciousness of the West was fragmented into denominational thinking. Luther (1483–1546), Zwingli (1484–1531) and Calvin (1509–64) created their own Church bodies; these came into vigorous conflict with the papal Church and with one another. The era of the wars of religion began (16th and 17th centuries).

It took the Church far too long to rediscover the way to renewal and self-realization. But once the foundations of faith and discipline had been re-affirmed at the Council of Trent (1545–63) the inner reform of the Church could begin and the progress of Protestantism checked through the Catholic Reform and Counter-Reformation. This work of reconstruction is one of the most astonishing phenomena of Church history. True reform is always the work of saints. The reform of the papacy only became convincing when a saintly Pope appeared in the person of Pius V (1566–72). There were now many saints in all walks of life. The "century of saints" dawned. In these saints the purified "holy" Church found and understood itself once more.

New orders, especially the Jesuits and Capuchins, led the reform. A disabling apathy gave way to a new Catholic vitality which found fresh expression in the art, piety, and theology of the Baroque age (1550–1750). Theological study was stimulated by Protestantism and encouraged by the work of the Council of Trent. Baroque scholasticism dispelled much of the obscurity of pre-Reformation theology. Spanish and Italian theologians distinguished themselves (Bellarmine, Soto, Suárez, Cano and others — mostly Jesuits and Dominicans) and later, French theologians. The main themes treated were the Trinity, Christology and grace. The intellectual movement started by the Jesuit Suárez (1548–1617) influenced every branch of theology (dogmatics, moral theology, canon law) and philosophy. It was his declared aim to penetrate the latter with Christianity. Suarezianism was also fruitful religiously. The Spanish mystics (Theresa of Ávila and John of the Cross) helped forward the deepening of religious life in the Church, influencing France especially. In France P. de Bérulle established a distinctive priestly spirituality which left its mark on the French clergy of the 17th century.

But the dangers also persisted. In the controversy with Calvinism, Michael de Bay of Louvain (1513–89) sought to develop a modern theology closely related to life, but produced instead a doctrine of original sin and grace which was based on a misunderstanding of Augustine and which had to be condemned by the Church. Baianism had fateful consequences through his Louvain pupil Cornelius Jansen (d. 1638) who adopted his ideas and introduced them into Catholic theology and piety. Jansenism's rigoristic doctrine of grace and sacramental practice dealt heavy blows to the French Church in the 17th and 18th centuries.

The other main currents which affected the Church between 1600 and 1800 were also French: Gallicanism, State Absolutism, and Episcopalism. These ideas were transplanted to Germany in the form of the "Febronianism" of Johann Nikolaus von Hontheim, auxiliary bishop of Trier, in the period when the union of Church and State, under the Emperor Joseph II (1780–90), reached its zenith in Austria. The Western mind became increasingly alienated from religion and the Church and intellectual secularization progressed rapidly in the 18th century under the stimulus of the Enlightenment. By the end of the century the papacy had finally lost the leadership of Europe.

One ray of light in this period was the world mission which began with the discovery of new territories by the Spanish and

Portuguese in the early years of the 15th century. It reached its climax in the 16th and 17th centuries but was also to meet with discouraging setbacks in the 18th century. The missionary work, which in any case suffered because of Spanish and Portuguese colonialism, was also hindered by internal disagreements in the Church over missionary methods. The controversy on the Chinese (1645–92, 1704) and Malabar rites brought the promising Jesuit missions in China and India to an end.

Fourth period: the world Church in the industrial age (19th and 20th centuries). The French Revolution (1789) represents the great watershed. The renewal was prepared by the Enlightenment, which brought the Church a long-needed modification of traditional forms and of intellectual rigidity. It was introduced by the great secularization (1803), which liberated the Church from the old feudalism and, while depriving it of its earthly sovereignty, at the same time gave it the "grace of destitution". It proceeded to the accompaniment of a continuous controversy with the new forces of national Churches and movements. Liberalism, Socialism, Communism and Materialism were bitterly hostile. Permeated by an immense faith in progress, modern society turned more and more away from the Church and from every form of positive Christianity. This movement attained the proportions of an organized mass apostasy, involving especially the upper classes and the industrial workers. Yet in all European countries there was a discernible renewal of religious and Church life, and a strengthening of the papacy.

Reconstruction involved a twofold process: on the one hand the material re-ordering of the Church's organization and legal relationships with the civil authorities by means of concordats concluded between the Holy See and the individual countries, and on the other hand the inner renewal of the religious life of the Church. In Germany, the Romantic Movement was an important spiritual factor for the revival of religion in general and for the new respect for Catholicism in particular. Catholic "revival groups" came into existence (J. M. Sailer, Princess Gallitzin, K. M. Hofbauer, Bishop Zirkel) as well as new theological schools. G. Hermes (d. 1831) in Bonn employed the concepts of Kant and of Fichte in an effort to vanquish the rationalism

of the Enlightenment in a positive way; his system was condemned by the Church in 1835 as semi-rationalistic. Similar efforts were made by A. Günther (d. 1863) and J. Frohschammer (d. 1893). The Tübingen School (Drey, Hirscher, Möhler) was influential; it too linked itself to the spirit of the age (Romanticism, German Idealism) but combined it with the tradition of the Church. The common concern of all these was to combat prevailing religious scepticism by a new apologia of religion. Reaction against the Enlightenment led in France to a rigid traditionalism distrustful of human reason in religious matters and denying it any capacity to know God; all order, whether intellectual, ethical, social or political, has its basis and support in revelation and tradition alone (Fideism, Integralism, Supernaturalism); the Church and the papacy are in all such matters the primary authorities (Ultramontanism, de Maistre, de Lamennais, Veuillot).

Supported by ideas of this kind and upheld by the affection of the Catholic people, the papacy became increasingly important for religion and the Church, while it was at the same time vigorously attacked. In 1854 Pius IX proclaimed *ex cathedra* the dogma of the Immaculate Conception; in his *Syllabus* of 1864 he declared war on *Liberalism* as a philosophy of life and on other opinions; at the First Vatican Council (1869/70) he secured the dogmatic definition of the primacy and infallibility of the Pope. At the same time he encountered stiff opposition (Risorgimento, Old Catholicism), was deprived of the Papal States (Sept. 1870) and suffered the loss of political power. Nevertheless the moral prestige of the papacy was on the whole enhanced and under Leo XIII (1878–1903) actually reached great heights.

The 19th century was a time of dramatic struggles. Within the Church the scene in the latter half of the century was dominated by the struggle between the so-called German theology and neo-Scholasticism; this came to a head in the First Vatican Council and ended in the victory of neo-Thomism (Leo XIII in various encyclicals). The encounter with the non-Catholic Churches, favourably influenced by pietism at the beginning of the century, developed on both sides into an aggressive denominationalism; liberal Protestant theology constantly called for an answer. The positive encounter introduced by J. A. Mohler's famous book

Symbolik, which presented a comparison between the dogmatic positions of Catholics and Protestants on the basis of their confessional statements (1832), unfortunately degenerated on both sides by the end of the century into increasingly bitter polemics until finally the alliance of militant Protestantism, Liberalism, and Bismarck's *raison d'état* set in motion the momentous *Kulturkampf* against the Catholic Church in Germany. Nor did the experience of Catholicism with modern industrialism bring much encouragement. Certainly the considerable pastoral efforts to remedy the condition of the workers and the contributions of charitable works to this end represent a glorious chapter and testify, along with the upsurge of the religious orders, to the Church's inner vitality. But the social question itself was recognized as such too late (Leo XIII, 1891). The mass of industrial workers were outside the Church and adopted socialism both as a political party and as a philosophy of life. In the political sphere too, difficulties arose in almost every country.

These experiences produced a certain anxiety and narrowness of view in the Catholic camp. Pius X (1903–14), honoured within the Church as a reforming Pope, conducted a stern fight against Modernism. Ecclesiastical integralism soon began to suspect heresy in anyone who sought an accommodation with modern culture and science. The retreat into the ghetto eliminated Catholicism as a cultural force in public life.

The turning point came with the First World War. The experience of war and revolution summoned Catholics too back to a greater sense of responsibility for the world. At the same time a new awareness of the Church became evident. "The Church awakens in men's souls", wrote R. Guardini in 1922. The liturgical movement, lay action, the encounter between the Churches, the *una sancta* and the ecumenical movement stressed the fellowship of Christians. The juridical picture of the Church determined by the Counter-Reformation (Bellarmine) gave way to a new conception of the *corpus Christi mysticum*. Pius XII summed up this concept in the encyclical *Mystici Corporis* of 29 June 1943: the Church really is the body of Christ, not just in a spiritual, moral or metaphorical sense but as a visible, social, all-embracing hierarchically-ordered corporation. The joint responsibility of the laity in the Church's life was seen in a fresh light. In connection with the liturgical renewal, a new encounter with holy Scripture took place. Theological science, preaching, and Church life came together in the biblical movement. The life of the religious orders also flourished and in conjunction with the new theology and spirituality of the laity brought about the great "secular institutes".

The dialogue (and co-operation) between the Churches developed into a genuine conversation. Instead of denominational quarrels there emerged tolerance, mutual respect and co-operation, particularly during the period of persecution under the Third Reich. The Churches saw their own mistakes and shortcomings and recognized that the desired reunion in faith had to be preceded by profound reflection upon the essentials. This was the thought which made John XXIII convoke a council: the Second Vatican Council (1962–65) was to lay the foundations for the renewal of the Catholic Church with a view to the reunion of divided Christendom. Union was no longer thought of as an unconditional return but prepared for as a real integration. With this intention the Secretariat for the Promotion of Christian Unity was established in 1960 under Cardinal Bea in Rome. The Catholic *oekumene* in alliance with the non-Catholic ecumenical movement was to make the 20th century the "century of the reunited Church". The meeting between Pope Paul VI and the Ecumenical Patriarch Athenagoras in Jerusalem (Jan. 1964), the surrender of the papal tiara, and the conciliar Decree on Ecumenism, all underline the sincere desire of the Catholic Church for reunion.

The Church's openness both internally and externally is the characteristic of our time. John XXIII broke with the centralism of the Curia and re-emphasized the joint collegial responsibility of the bishops in the leadership of the whole Church. The adaptation of the Church to present-day needs *(aggiornamento)* demanded consideration of the Church in the modern world. The Catholic world mission, which had long been coloured by colonialism and Europeanism and had therefore been unable to strike roots in the indigenous cultures, was given its first native bishops in 1926. Pius XII furnished the mission countries with their own hierarchies. But it was John XXIII who first emphasized the Church's duty to go to meet the peoples and not to uproot them from their cultures; the world Church was not European but universal and the continued incarnation of Christ in the Church was not restricted to the Western nations alone but intended for all who come to believe in him. The conversation with the other major religions (Buddhism, Hinduism, Islam) which Paul VI officially endorsed by his journey to India (Eucharistic World Congress, Bombay, 1964) also stands under the sign of this new openness. This visit was intended not as a missionary journey but as a simple pilgrimage. The Pope's large charitable donation to the Hindu people was intended, in his own words, as "the first concrete expression of the brotherly dialogue which the Church desires to enter into with the whole world".

The most stubborn problem is the relationship of the Church to the Communist countries which dominate so much of the world today. Their aggressive atheism and dialectical materialism leave no room for faith and Church, and have therefore been condemned by the Church. In view of the unhappy experience of the Church under totalitarian dictators (Hitler, Mussolini, the party dictatorships in Communist countries), it is not easy to foresee what the future holds, despite the initiative taken here too by John XXIII.

Is one era ending today and a new era dawning? There are many signs pointing in this direction. The global extension of the Church and its world-wide encounter with all nations and cultures made possible by modern means of communication, the process whereby world civilization is being rearranged and standardized, the new picture of the world presented by science and research, and finally the inner secularization of man and growing unbelief, all confront the Church today with new tasks. The need of the hour is not identification with and rigid insistence on what now exists, but rather openness to what is to come. There can, of course, be no progress without constant reference to what is essential. The Church is still bound to maintain the *traditio apostolica* as a matter of life and death.

See also *History, Salvation* III, *Church and State, Church and World, Modern Church History, Apostolic Church, Constantinian Era, Crusades, Middle Ages, Reformation, Enlightenment, Secularization* II.

BIBLIOGRAPHY. F. C. Baur, *Die Epochen der kirchlichen Geschichtsschreibung* (1852; repr. 1962); K. Heussi, *Altertum, Mittelalter und Neuzeit in der Kirchengeschichte* (1921); K. Löwith, *Meaning in History. The Theological Implications of the Philosophy of History* (1949); O. E. Strasser, "Les périodes et les époques de l'histoire de l'Église", *RHPR* 30 (1950), pp. 290–304; W. Kamlah, *Christentum und Geschichtlichkeit* (2nd ed., 1951); Y. Congar, *Vraie et fausse réforme dans l'Église* (1954); J. Daniélou, *The Lord of History. Reflections on the Inner Meaning of History* (1958); P. E. Hübinger, *Spätantike und frühes Mittelalter. Ein Problem historischer Periodenbildung* (1959); H. U. von Balthasar, *A Theology of History* (1964); O. Cullmann, *Christ and Time* (rev. ed., 1964); H. Jedin, "General Introduction to Church History", in H. Jedin and J. Dolan, eds., *Handbook of Church History,* I (1964), pp. 1–56; J. Connolly, *Human History and the Word of God* (1965); H. Küng, *Structures of the Church* (1965); P. Meinhold, *Geschichte der kirchlichen Historiographie* (1966); K. Rahner, "History of the World and Salvation-History", *Theological Investigations,* V (1966), pp. 97–114; O. Chadwick, *The History of the Church. A Select Bibliography* (2nd ed., 1966).

August Franzen

CHURCH ORDERS

Definition. By Church Orders or Constitutions we understand here only those of ancient Christian literature, most of which have only been re-discovered in the 19th and 20th centuries. They are the most ancient surviving records of law, constitution, discipline, liturgy and custom in the Church. The initial stages of such directives, which soon became necessary for the well-being of the community, are to be found in the NT. The ancient collections now known are so disparate in form and content that it was difficult to determine their origin and date, and also mutual relationships and dependence. The following dates may be taken as reliable. The pastoral letters (cf. 1 Tim 2:1–3, 13; 5:1–20; 6:1f.; Tit 1:6–9; 2:2–5, 9f.; [3:1f.]) must be regarded as the first example of a Church Order. The first to exist as an independent document is the "Doctrine of the Twelve Apostles" *(Didache)*, probably from the first half of the 2nd century, which is generally listed among the Apostolic Fathers. It was of enduring influence. The so-called Egyptian Church Order is from the beginning of the 3rd century, and has been identified with great probability with the Apostolic Tradition of Hyppolytus of Rome (with slight revisions). The (Syrian) *Didascalia* is from the second half of the 3rd century. It is notably dependent on the *Didache,* as is the Apostolic Church Order (beginning of the 4th century). This completes the list of the known writings which are behind the large-scale collections which began to be formed in the 4th century, and which were the only form in which they had been preserved. The Verona collection *(Sacramentarium Veronense [Leonianum])* for instance, incorporates the *Didascalia,* the Church Order of Hippolytus and the Apostolic Church Order. The best-known and most comprehensive of these later collections are the Apostolic Constitutions, into which traditions from the *Didache,* the *Didascalia* and Hippolytus have been worked; as an appendix from the same compiler they contain the Apostolic Canons. Other special collections include the *Testamentum Domini,* which is a revision of the Egyptian Church Order in the apocalyptic framework of a dialogue between the risen Lord and his disciples. Some of the Church Orders come from Syria directly, others are influenced by Eastern traditions.

Characteristics and contents. These works repay study in many ways from the point of view of history of theology. Leaving aside individual variations in content, which cannot be gone into in detail here, we may say that they are the documentation of the Church as its constitution, liturgy and customs crystallized. They present a steadily growing mass of regulations on the appointment, rights and duties of office-holders — teachers, apostles, prophets, presbyters, bishops and deacons. They give directives for the arrangement and celebration of the liturgy — baptism, Eucharist, fasting, calendar of feasts and formularies of prayer. They give indications for the right conduct of life in the Church, regulate penitential discipline and the order of rank in the community. Thus they are a revealing reflection of conditions in the Church at a given place and date, though their testimony, copious as it is, is not without gaps. The picture which they thus give of Church life is anything but uniform. Their rites and their paraenetic and liturgical texts show that Jewish material of Eastern origin has been taken over, though decisively reinterpreted in a Christian sense, so that the reaction against Judaism (often the object of polemics) is verified in the very reception of Jewish traits. The general picture is of a

Church which was painfully precise in legislating for the details of its life and in considering local conditions, but was on the whole, in contrast with later attitudes, astonishingly broad-minded and untroubled as regards uniformity in constitution and liturgy. It was convinced that such diversity was the best proof of the unity of faith (Irenaeus, in Eusebius, *Hist. Eccles.,* V, 24, 13).

The strictly local bearings of the Church Orders are displayed in many ways. There is no uniform code of law in the early days of the Church. The Church Orders were conditioned by varying circumstances and grew out of the actual practice of the regional Church in question. They thus paralleled the development of preaching, theology and dogma, with which, of course, the practice of Church life is closely linked. The local Churches developed to a great extent independently and along different lines.

The drawing up of Church Orders to provide permanent rules for the life of the community shows the persistent tendency to stabilization throughout the mobility and spontaneity of development. To endow codified law and custom with the authority necessary if it was to be acknowledged widely and permanently, these works were attributed to the apostles and thus given a rank which could not be challenged. Apostolic authorship (Pastoral Letters, *Didache, Didascalia,* Apostolic Church Order) or at least apostolic tradition is claimed for most of the Church Orders, in their titles. Ultimately, these indications of authorship are neither put forward as scientific history nor as dishonest claims. They simply express the conviction of the ancient Church that its regulations, like its preaching, are of an apostolic and obligatory nature. What the Church does down to the last concrete detail, its changing forms throughout its history, go back in unbroken links to the apostolic age and its permanent norm. That norm was fresh and vigorous enough to do without much codification. Still, it entailed even in its early days a number of regulations and juridical principles of which the NT records only a small part.

Thus the Church Orders are authenticated by apostolic tradition, as is the preaching. It is the same apostolic self-consciousness of the ancient Church which demarcated the canon of apostolic writings from all the "scriptures" that were circulating, fixed the apostolic succession with the help of lists of bishops in spite of the variety of traditions, and had one "Apostles' Creed" from the 4th century on, acknowledged by the manifold Christian groups. The Church Orders are apostolic in the same sense. This tendency to refer all important ecclesiological elements to the solid basis of apostolicity is due in part to the fear of abandoning the preaching, faith and life of the Churches to arbitrary change. But it also denotes a closing of the ranks. Every affirmation of apostolic origin serves directly or indirectly the self-affirmation of the Church against heterodox developments, which for their part mostly claimed apostolic antecedents also. Hence the terminology always has more or less polemical connotations or at least the sense of a demarcation, which is also true of the Church Orders which lay down authoritative rules in controversial questions of offices and ranks, liturgy, discipline and ethics in the Church.

The constant effectiveness of the Church Orders is thereby assured. Their apostolic authority should not be considered just as a *post factum* legitimation of what has been done. It also confers on the codification already performed the right to influence the future. This is clear from the way the earlier Church Orders were taken over, revised, brought up to date and expanded in the later ones. Thus these codes of law and even their literary procedures manifest the conviction of the continuity of apostolic institutions through all the variations of the historical way of the Church.

Editions. There is no single publication which contains them all. Editions of particular works must be looked up in the relevant lexicons; see also Altaner, Quasten and Denzinger-Schönmetzer.

For modern Church Orders see *Church* III.

BIBLIOGRAPHY. R. H. Connolly, *The So-called Egyptian Church Order and Derived Documents* (1916); V. J. Bartlet, *Church-Life and Church-Order during the First Four Centuries* (1943); J. Quasten, *Patrology,* I (1950), pp. 29–39; II (1953), pp. 119f., 147–52, 180–94; A. F. Walls, "A Note on the Apostolic Claim in the Church Order Literature", in K. Aland and F. L. Cross, eds., *Studia Patristica* (1957), pp. 83–92; B. Altaner, *Patrology* (1960), pp. 54–61; W. Bartsch, *Die Anfänge urchristlicher Rechtsbildungen* (1965); G. Dix, ed., *The Apostolic Tradition of St. Hippolytus,* reissued with new introduction by H. Chadwick (1967). *Norbert Brox*

CLERGY

In contrast to the laity, the clergy signify those members of the new people of God who through holy orders have a special ministry in the Church and who form a separate ecclesiastical state *(status clericalis).* Κλῆρος originally meant a lot, the share resulting from a lottery. In 1 Pet 5:3 κλῆρος means the shares which the individual presbyters receive from the whole community. In Acts 1:17 κλῆρος is the share in spiritual service. Clergy was used in this narrower sense by Origen to denote the ministers of the Church, in contrast to the laity. The Latin word *clerus* (the oldest witness is Tertullian, *De Monog.,* 12) takes it in this narrower sense and adds to it that of *sors.* Cf. Jerome, *Ep. ad Nepotianum* (*PL,* XIII, 531): "Si enim κλῆρος Graece, sors Latine appellatur: propterea vocantur Clerici, vel quia de sorte sunt Domini, vel quia ipse Dominus sors, id est, pars Clericorum est."

1. *Concept and constitutional status.* In the legal sense a cleric is one who, having taken at least the first tonsure, has dedicated himself to the divine service (*CIC,* can. 108 § 1); nevertheless, not all clerics are such by divine constitution (can. 107). Since the order of deacon is the first to give an indelible character, it is here that the line between clerics of divine and of ecclesiastical law is to be drawn. The religious state is not a status in between the clerical and the lay state (Vatican II, *De Ecclesia,* art. 43), but is a creation of the Church which encompasses both clergy and laity. A separation within the people of God is accomplished by holy orders which is the basis for the differentiation between clerics and laity which dominates the constitution of the hierarchical Church.

Ordination bestows a personal character which is ordained to the exercise of the sacred ministry and which, in the stages of episcopal and sacerdotal orders, bestows the power visibly to represent the invisible head of the Church and to govern as head an ecclesiastical community. The pre-eminence of the priest is essentially service for the community. He does not win any advantage for himself over the laity, but has a greater obligation and responsibility before the Lord, who has taken him into his special service. In all things which concern his personal

Christian existence, i.e., in all questions concerning his salvation, the cleric remains on the same level as all Christians. Vatican II makes its own the words of Augustine (*De Ecclesia,* art. 23): "Where I am dismayed that I am for you, there I am comforted that I am with you. I am a bishop for you, I am a Christian with you. The former is the name of the office, the latter of grace; the former points towards danger, the latter towards salvation." (*Serm.,* 340, 1) All members of the people of God, clerics and laity, have the same Christian dignity and are engaged in the tasks which are circumscribed by the triad of magisterium, sacerdotal office and pastoral office (Vatican II, Decree on the Apostolate of the Laity, art. 2). The difference between the two is only that the manner of co-operation is different in each case; this is in turn based upon the different orientation of the person in the Church and the ensuing ministry. Thus clerics and laity are intrinsically ordained to one another, and their roles in the service of the people of God are not interchangeable.

2. *Incorporation into a spiritual group.* Every cleric must belong to a spiritual group; the secular cleric to a diocese, or the like; the regular cleric to a religious community. The incorporation (incardination) into the spiritual group takes place at tonsure (*CIC,* can. 111). The cleric performs his sacred ministries at the behest of his ordinary, to whom he is also subject in the conduct of his life. Transfer to another diocese or the equivalent, when not governed by canons 114 and 115, involves unconditional and perpetual release from his previous diocese and similar "incardination" in another (can. 112 and 113). Excardination only takes effect when incardination in another diocese is completed.

Vatican II maintains the principle that each cleric must be incardinated into a diocese; but the link with the diocese must be brought into line with the needs of the universal Church. In keeping with the decree on the bishops (art. 6) and on priests (art. 10), new norms have been laid down by the motu proprio *Ecclesiae Sanctae* (6 August 1966, *AAS* 58 [1966], pp. 759 ff.). These aim at a better distribution of the clergy, especially to meet the needs of undermanned regions and the missions. Priestly formation should strive to inculcate a sense of responsibility

for the whole Church. Ordinaries should provide a suitable training for priests who are ready to serve in foreign dioceses. The ordinary, except when the needs of his own diocese are paramount, must not refuse permission for transfer to regions which are short of priests, where those who request permission are fitted for such duties. Such priests remain incardinated into their own dioceses, and on their return enjoy all the rights that would have been theirs had they remained.

Patriarchal synods and episcopal conferences are enjoined to investigate the possibility of sending clergy into other local Churches, and to issue directions to the bishops in question, though their execution presupposes the willingness of the priests concerned. Priests who have transferred regularly to other dioceses are duly incardinated into such dioceses after five years, if they have indicated their intention to the ordinary of their new diocese and to their own, and neither ordinary has indicated his disagreement, in writing, within four months. To facilitate the movement of diocesan priests, the erection of prelacies is provided for. These are to be composed of diocesan priests, and their aim will be to prepare priests for special pastoral and missionary tasks in regions and social groups which are in special need of help. Such prelacies will not be local Churches, but groups of secular priests with special duties, resembling to some extent the centralized religious communities.

3. *Rights and obligations.* By virtue of his state, the cleric has a sacred authority. Canon 118 affirms that only clerics can have sacerdotal or pastoral authority. In view of the system of purely sacred ordination which prevails in the Latin Church, where the conferring of orders and of jurisdiction are separate processes, the canon means that in spite of such separation the unity of the hierarchy is assured. Priests have precedence over laymen (can. 119). Traditional privileges are the *privilegium canonis,* the *privilegium fori,* the *privilegium competentiae* (can. 120–2). The obligations of the clerical state are in part precepts, in part prohibitions, which seek to guarantee a successful activity in the spiritual ministry (can. 124–44).

4. *Laicization,* reduction to the lay state, abolishes the special status of membership of

the priestly state which was acquired by ordination. This is a juridical change of personal status, and the priest, in spite of his having been and remaining validly ordained, has the juridical status of a layman (can. 211–14). A cleric in minor orders may abandon the clerical state if he wills. He may be dismissed by his ordinary if he does not seem a suitable candidate for major orders. Those in minor orders cease *ipso facto* to be clerics if they enter upon matrimony, lay aside clerical dress, and in certain other cases. Those in major orders cannot abandon the priestly state of their own will. A peaceful exclusion is possible: a) by a gracious rescript of the Holy See; b) by laicization in the course of proceedings for release from the obligation of celibacy (can. 214 with can. 1993–8); c) through marriage where the priest has been released from the obligation of celibacy (cf. can. 1043 f.). Forcible exclusion takes place through the penalty of degradation (can. 298, 12; 2305). Readmission of a laicized priest is made very difficult and is never granted in practice.

See also *Bishop* I–III, *Diocese, Ecclesiastical Authority, Ecclesiastical Office, Hierarchy, Priest, Laity.*

BIBLIOGRAPHY. J. B. Brunini, *The Clerical Obligations of Canons 139 and 142* (1937); J. Donovan, *The Clerical Obligation of Canons 138 and 140* (1948); F. P. Sweeney, *The Reduction of Clerics to the Lay State* (1945); J. C. Fenton, *The Concept of Diocesan Priesthood* (1951); E. Eichmann and K. Mörsdorf, *Lehrbuch des Kirchenrechts auf Grund des Codex Iuris Canonici,* I (11th ed., 1964), pp. 249–72.

Klaus Mörsdorf

COLLECTIVISM

I. Masses and Crowds. II. Nature, History and Forms of Collectivism.

I. Masses and Crowds

1. *The problem of the masses.* Crowd psychology has been seen as a precise problem since the end of the 19th century. The perspectives in which it was seen were determined for some time by the works of G. Le Bon (*Psychologie de foules,* 1895), G. Tarde (*L'opinion et la foule,* 1901) and G. Sighele (*La folla delinquente,* 1891). These analyses were motivated less by scientific objectiveness than by emotional reactions to far-reaching social changes, such as revolutions, restlessness of the middle classes, growth of the workers, urbanization. A sense of isolation among the intellectuals was also a contributory factor. An ideology was invented for the psychology of the masses (Hofstätter), and furthered rather than countered by J. Ortega y Gasset's *La rebelión de las masas* in 1930.

The problem was then taken up more seriously by sociologists (L. von Wiese, W. Vleugels, T. Geiger) and psychologists (S. Freud, W. MacDougall). But it was only after the Second World War that the masses were recognized as an object of the sociology or the social psychology of collective behaviour. The preceding phase of social analysis may have seemed pessimistic and infertile, but the "psychology of the masses" had had a certain result, in the sense that it had been "a self-fulfilling prophecy" (R. K. Merton). "The psychology of the masses must bear part of the blame for turning individuals into mass-phenomena and deepening their anxiety" (Hofstätter). In spite of belonging to a group or fellowship, people felt themselves as part of a mass. The illusion of being lost in the crowd may be a more real characteristic of our times than the mass-society. Hence the problem of the masses is now treated scientifically under the heading of "collective behaviour" (R. E. Park) or "the phenomena of the masses". E. K. Francis places it between "micro-sociology" and "macro-sociology". A severe effort of detachment is needed to arrive at objectiveness here. We distinguish between the masses in motion ("the mob in being"), the hidden masses and mass-society.

2. *The masses in motion.* Le Bon, Tarde and Sighele took as their starting-point the masses "as a mob on the move, before its turbulence is channelled into a series of waves beating on fixed points" (Hofstätter). This is crowd behaviour in the form of panic, revolution, riotous demonstrations and so on. Its causes are infectious social unrest, uncertainty due to lack of planned outlets with its consequent emotional instability. There is a vicious circle of mutual stimulation as the elements identify with each other and highly charged feelings are shared. The inhibitions of normal social behaviour are eliminated as the rules of the groups and their values and norms are brushed aside.

Le Bon proposed suggestibility and conformism as the explanation of the masses in motion and their destructive actions, while Freud attributed it to a regression into an earlier stage of evolution. The processes have not been adequately explained. The "collective subconscious", the "mass mind" and so on remain hypotheses. Hence the evaluation of such phenomena remains doubtful. T. Geiger describes them as "the spirit of society in revolt", since they are anti-social processes. E. K. Francis regards them as "mechanisms of social change". Other problems are the means of manipulating crowds by symbols, chants and so on; the relationship of leaders to the masses in motion — is their influence due to their prestige, or their stronger wills or what?

3. *The hidden masses*. In contrast to the masses in actual movement, the phenomenon of the hidden masses or the latent crowd psychology is even more difficult to grasp. It is considered to be more dangerous because it is less conspicuous. The pre-conditions of a latent mass movement are said to be the presence of a generalized emotional and cultural basis of orientation, and influences at work without direct inter-action of the affected groups. According to H. Blumer, this mass phenomenon takes place where there is a great number of individuals unknown to each other, composed of highly differentiated groups and local cultures, all affected by an emotional and psychical instability which weakens the force of traditional values and the normal attachment to the various social groups, while large-scale organizations are carrying through major operations in the social system.

It was assumed hitherto that definite mass phenomena could be traced, on the basis of similar levels of purchase of consumer goods, and similar attitudes adopted as the result of persuasion by the mass media of communication, as for instance in fashion and public opinion. This assumption was due to the difficulty of a full coverage and anlysis of the complicated chain-reactions in the mass-society, but was not fully justified, as has been shown by recent researches into films (von Hovland), the press (Janowitz) and the other mass media (Riley, Floverman, Lazarsfeld). The behaviour of consumers is due not so much to a uniformly effective stimulus as to structural dispositions of the personality and group relationships. The "hidden per-

suaders" are of varied types (A. Gehlen). The notion of the "mass mind" is accordingly becoming suspect, as the expression of a social pessimism, and it may well be that such slogans stem from our inability to grasp intellectually the essentials of social structures.

4. *The mass-society*. T. Geiger has rejected the notion of the mass-society as a mere slogan, arrived at by the disregard of the dualism of the social spheres (private and public) which is the special characteristic of modern times. E. K. Francis dismisses the term as contradictory, because "the masses" (as an amorphous phenomenon) denies what "society" (as a structured social formation) affirms. But H. Blumer considers that the phenomenon of the mass-society means that sociology as hitherto known has broken down. It lacks, he thinks, the perspectives and schemes of concepts apt to describe the four characteristics of the mass-society: its quality of mass, the heterogeneous development of the structural elements of a society, its unrestricted access to the spheres of public life and its inclusion within a constantly changing society. The disintegration and disorganization which others denounce as decay and disorder are regarded by Blumer as symptoms of the inability of the mass-society to realize the order proper to it. Since sociological concepts are derived from the society of the past, they are inadequate in analyzing the mass-society. Social change, for instance, was formerly considered destructive, but it is the natural condition of the mass-society which is in a constant flux of re-adaptation to new complexes of factors. A revision of such sociological concepts as culture, social system, function, social attitude, conformity and anomaly seems to be called for.

5. *The mass-society and social attitudes*. If the mass-society is not to lead to decay, it must be educated to a dualism of attitudes, according to whether the private or the public sphere is involved, and to flexibility in fulfilling different functions. Hence T. Geiger suggests that all sentimental attitudes be avoided and replaced by an education in mental discipline and an asceticism of the feelings: "There is no need to love one another in order to co-operate." Such an education might well be suspect, as merely

"adjustment" in the worst sense of the word, which indeed it well might be, and hence H. Schelsky, following D. Riesman *(The Lonely Crowd)*, points out that in the mass-society of today, with its pressure to "conform", freedom's only hope is to be found somewhere between anarchy or anomaly and an adaptation combined with a rightly-understood autonomy. This presupposes a willingness to face psychical and social isolation, the force of mind to accept failure, the resolute exclusion of utopianisms. These demands apply, *mutatis mutandis,* to the basic attitudes of the modern Christian if he is to be properly attuned and open to the world, and of the élite who are now so necessary. It is a character and attitude which goes beyond "partial opting-out" (P. Tillich) and "non-conspicuous consumption" to guarantee the survival of the person in spite of all real or alleged conditioning of the mass-mind (for which background see the "Utopian" novels of R. H. Benson, A. Huxley and G. Orwell).

See also *Society* IV, *Communications Media.*

BIBLIOGRAPHY. W. McDougall, *The Group Mind. A Sketch of the Principles of Collective Psychology* (1920); S. Freud, *Group Psychology and Analysis of Ego,* trans. by. J. Strackey (1922); T. Geiger, *Die Masse und ihre Aktion* (1926); J. Ortega y Gasset, *Revolt of the Masses* (1932); D. Riesman, *Lonely Crowd* (1950); R. E. Park, *Society* (1955); P. Hofstätter, *Gruppendynamik* (1957); R. K. Merton, *Social Theory and Social Structure* (rev. ed., 1957); E. K. Francis, *Wissenschaftliche Grundlagen soziologischen Denkens* (1957); H. Blumer, "Collective Behaviour", in J. B. Gittler, ed., *Review of Sociology* (1957); G. Le Bon, *Crowd* (1960); E. Canetti, *Crowds and Power* (1963).

Roman Bleistein

II. Nature, History and Forms of Collectivism

1. *Nature.* Collectivism is the attitude, more or less consciously adopted and practised, that man is merely a collective being. By "collective" is meant the form of social organization in which the individual is robbed of his personal independence and dignity and reduced to a mere functional organ of the community. The importance of social bonds is so exaggerated that the individual no longer seems to have any importance in himself but only in respect of the totality, which is thereby distorted in monistic or pantheistic fashion and given an absolute power of disposal over the individual.

2. *History and forms.* Collectivism is the antithesis to individualism, not only in social theory but historically as well. Individualism in its exaggerated form makes the individual absolute and puts him in the place of God. So as not to allow society as a result of this lack of social bonds to disintegrate into a "war of all against all", society in its turn was made absolute and put in the place of God. Collectivism in this sense originated in the 19th century (Proudhon, Owen, Engels, List), inasmuch as society was declared to be the absolute basis for the understanding of man and man was made its creature. The degradation of personality thus initiated led to a gradual degradation of the concept of the corresponding society, stressing at first the spiritual and idealistic element (idealistic collectivism), going on to the biological (biologistic collectivism) and finally to the material element (materialistic collectivism). Under the influence of romanticism and German idealism the nation saw itself as the direct manifestation of the ideal of the divine and so became the "national collective" (idealistic collectivism). Inasmuch as the individual, as a mere transitory element of the divinized society, was thereby robbed of his individual independence, freedom and responsibility, society became for him the obscure, infra-spiritual ground-force of life (biologistic collectivism or racial collectivism in National Socialism).

In still more radical fashion both individual and society were regarded by Communism as the product and manifestation of absolute, endless matter which produces everything in a dialectical process (the collectivism of dialectical materialism). Since the ideal of social happiness of Communism, a classless society based on "free solidarity", is not capable of being put into effect directly without resistance, it presents itself at first in the form of a State totalitarianism in which the individual must sacrifice all rights to the coercive power of the State (political collectivism). The typical method is the formation of planned collectives which every member must consciously help to carry into effect — collectivism shows itself here in its ultimate radicalism. The people are formed into working groups by the society or its directing functionaries. The composition, purposes and divisions of work are minutely determined and supervised from above, and are expected to be consciously and unconditionally accepted by every individual by way of "collective self-education".

This "conscious collectivism" is paralleled in the West by a more "unconscious" collectivism inasmuch as the members do not have to submit themselves with conscious approval to purposive mass regulation. It is rather a matter of unconscious manipulation (as, for example, in commercial advertising in economic life or election propaganda in political life). And while in the East all partial collectives are planned as part of the total collective which includes everybody and every social sphere (total collectivism), we can speak in the West rather of a chaotic struggle of all collectives against all — collectivism having thus developed into a radicalized form of the individualism from which it originated (individualistic collectivism).

3. *Criticism*. The age of technology demands indeed an ever closer collaboration in rationally planned work, not however a depersonalizing collectivism, but a solidarism which brings into operation the person in its full dignity and powers, the formation, that is, not of collectives but of teams. The difference between a team and a collective is that in the team the individual is not the object of an absolute power planning and disposing of him, but is taken seriously as partner in work and consultation, in his right to free initiative and co-determination of the aim and methods of production and thus called to genuine responsibility. In this way decisive human powers and capabilities can be actuated. If, however, we are to avoid in this way the individualistic extreme of "co-determination without responsibility" as well as the extreme of "responsibility without co-determination" of the collective which tramples on the individual, and to unite the relative elements of truth in both in a demand for the solidarity of "free co-determination in responsibility", the place of absolute value is to be given neither to the individual (individualism) nor to society (collectivism) but to an absolute and personal being (God) who transcends both and whose absolute claim frees the individual *from* himself and from society (i.e., from subjection to both) and thus frees them both *for* themselves. The greatest temptation of collectivism thus lies in removing from the individual the burden of free decision taken on his own responsibility, thus giving the appearance of an unending ("divine") security in the collective.

See also *Marxism* II, III, *Man* I, III, *Social Movements* V, *Society* I–III.

BIBLIOGRAPHY R. T. LaPiere, *Collective Behaviour* (1938); L. Doob, *Public Opinion and Propaganda* (1948); G. Orwell, *Nineteen Eighty-Four* (1949); V. Packard, *The Hidden Persuaders* (1957); E. Strauss, *The Ruling Servants* (1961); C. Argyris, *Integrating the Individual and the Organization* (1961); N. S. Timasheff, *The Sociology of Luigi Sturzo* (1962).

Heinrich Beck

COLONIALISM

Colonization must be distinguished from colonialism. The term colonization is often, though not invariably, applied to the ambitions which Babylonia, Assyria, Persia, Greece, Phoenicia, Macedonia, and Rome had to rule the world, and also to the activities of medieval Christendom in Eastern Europe. Here it is used in a good sense, to mean civilizing and "developing" a territory. But it would be misreading history to ignore the many negative aspects — political, religious, and psychological — of "colonization", which often anticipated later colonialism. So it is difficult to draw the line: where and when does colonization end and colonialism begin?

The notion of colonialism will be most readily grasped if we confine it to the occupation of extra-European territory by what are called the "colonial powers" of Europe — a process which was usually accompanied by racial friction. Thus understood, colonialism begins with the geographical discoveries of the 16th and 17th centuries, follows very different courses in respect of politics, economics, international law, religion, and sociology, and finally leads in the 20th century to the no less variegated process of decolonization.

Colonialism could only arise because of the economic, military, and to a great extent cultural superiority of Europe (the cultural superiority was far from complete). The self-confidence of Europeans, not infrequently taking the form of arrogance, was based on the Graeco-Roman and Christian civilization, but often also on a conviction that they were specially chosen by God. This conviction, which was at first explicit, and later implicit and secularized, they thought they derived from their Hebrew and Christian religious background. Indigenous cultures were generally underestimated, though sometimes appreciated, but in any case often exterminated and blotted from the memory of man for centuries (especially in Africa). Certain individuals held the European wars of conquest overseas to be unjust (Las Casas) and discussed the question of the native rulers' *iustus titulus* (Victoria and others); but on the whole politicians, ethnologists, and even theologians looked on the natives as "primitives" and treated them accordingly.

Where those people had advanced civilizations, as in China, Japan, and India, colonialism evolved various more indirect forms of control. There were always individuals who used their influence in a humane direction and tried to separate the Christian missions (and so the gospel itself) from colonialism. The Church's magisterium often insisted on the dignity and equality of all men before God as a principle plainly taught in Scripture (Deut 10:17; Wis 6:8; Ecclus 35:15; Mt 22:16; Acts 10:34; Rom 2:11; Jas 2:1, 9; 1 Pet 1:17, and other texts), although the NT Church took no stand against the institution of slavery as such. Many persuaded themselves that a highly dubious interpretation of Gen 9:22, 25 and 10:6–20 excused slavery and colonialism. The story of "the missions and slavery" is a sad one (cf. T. Ohm, *Theorie der Mission* [1962], pp. 647–57 [biblio.]). On the whole colonialism and missions went hand in hand among Catholics and equally so among Protestants. Only in the present century have Christians as a body realized the mortal danger this unhappy combination involved not for Europe alone but for the Christian faith itself.

The first great political and historical event in "de-colonization" was the breakaway of the British colonies in America from the mother-country in 1776. Though the slave trade had already grown notorious in the 16th and 17th centuries ("black ivory"), slavery was not abolished in the USA till 1865. But we should note that strenuous and effective efforts were made in the most various quarters, between the 18th and 20th century, to abolish slavery because it betokened a colonialist attitude, even though the struggle did not end colonialism itself. That task was substantially accomplished by the colonized peoples, not by the colonial powers.

The Marxist analysis of capitalism and of its imperialist epiphenomenon at first aimed chiefly at colonialism, but then in its Leninist version was extended into a general theory of emancipation for all the "exploited" and "oppressed". It was a good deal later that Christian or liberal European politicians, theologians, and intellectuals recognized the proportions of the problem. Until well into the 20th century they still thought in terms of "natives", people "from the bush", "savages", and so forth, failing to understand the irreversible process that modern technology, economics, and science had set in motion.

The whole problem of colonialism and decolonization can be rightly seen only in a broad, supra-national perspective of history, but for that very reason was bound to become part of the fierce ideological and political struggle which characterizes the 20th century. So when discussing this vast and complex problem — which involves such subjects as the "evolution of the world", nationalism, racialism, acculturation and pluralism, but also more concrete problems such as starvation, the population explosion, *apartheid,* social and national revolution — we must remember that in practice we are dealing with a political, economic, sociological, and cultural process which, having once been started, continues largely by its own momentum; and that there is violent controversy as to whether this process can or must be fitted into the general scheme of a philosophy of history — the future as seen either by Marxists or by positivists and liberals.

There are various views of the "laws" of the process and hence of the course to be followed: some hold (or held) that the decolonization which can be had here and now — political autonomy for each nation (and entry into UNO) — is indispensable; others consider such decolonization desirable only in circumstances favourable to it; others again seek tolerable economic and political compromises; and some, for the most diverse reasons try to put off decolonization as long as possible. True, political autonomy has now been achieved practically everywhere, but this cannot hide the fact that economic, psychological, and cultural decolonization is far from complete, indeed has hardly begun. Important though it is, political independence is only a first condition for decolonization. Today it is often necessary to thwart a neo-colonialism — a political, economic, cultural, psychological and ideological attitude which accepts the political independence of the "new nations" but tries to maintain or even exploit the various degrees of dependence in which these nations perforce find themselves. The charge of neo-colonialism is bandied to and fro: Communists accuse America and Europe; the "West" accuses communism, especially the pro-Chinese group; the underdeveloped nations accuse now one side, now the other, now both. Occasionally, instead of the traditional classification as colonial powers and colonies, we hear of rich and poor countries, of the northern and southern hemisphere, of white and coloured areas of the globe; but it is the same problem of colonialism and decolonization.

The direction of history should be clear; it is heading for a free world, where national, international, and supra-national bodies — political, economic, cultural, religious, and ideological — will all have their place. A theological attitude to colonialism and decolonization logically presupposes a theological concept of the world-process, of the secular future, especially of the historical cycles, but also of peace, justice, law, toleration, co-operation, and so on. The cruelties of colonialism must be roundly condemned. In principle the missions long ago renounced the support of colonialism, and also the arrogance of "theological colonialism" (Panikkar); cf. the encyclicals *Maximum illud* of Benedict XV and *Evangelii praecones* of Pius XII, and the Declaration on non-Christian Religions of Vatican II; but a special, self-critical declaration on the subject would certainly be salutary. Generally speaking, the Church and theologians must not rest content to discuss these matters in terms of moral theology; they must see matters in the perspective of world-history; and their willingness to do so has been proved by numerous declarations of the Council.

Still, it must be the special task of Christians and the Church to see justice done in the reading of history, and while supporting decolonization, to acknowledge the good in colonialism, which after all has produced the modern situation with all the opportunities it offers. One may also recall certain Popes, like Paul III, Urban VIII, and Benedict XIV, who clearly saw the dangers and gave wise counsel, and mention what the missions have done for colonization in the good sense.

Today in particular the Church must warn against a nationalism which in a fanatical love of country loses sight of the modern State's international and supra-national obligations. The Church has spiritual, cultural, educational, social, and humanitarian services to offer towards the forming of a universal humanism which will transcend traditional but outdated antagonisms, making a theoretical and practical contribution to peace, justice, freedom, racial equality, the feeding of the world, and the solution of the population problem. Thus, precisely as the Church, it must take part in international organizations and also make its presence felt, through the initiative and zeal of individual Christians — in other words, co-operate in the humanization of history. Not the will to direct but the will to co-operate is what the Council would see in the Church; not to "go it alone" or to opt out, but to share and support. Finally, the Church must think out anew the theological problem and the practice of the missions (their nature, goal, and rights) which means devoting new and more thorough reflection to the nature and rights of the Christian religion as it confronts the free, equal men and nations that have arisen out of colonialism.

See also *Missions, Race, Communism, Humanism.*

BIBLIOGRAPHY. J. Höffner, *Christentum und Menschenwürde. Das Anliegen der spanischen Kolonialethik im Goldenen Zeitalter* (1957); E. Sieber, *Kolonialgeschichte der Neuzeit* (1949); K. M. Panikkar, *Asia and Western Dominance* (1953); A. C. Burns, *In Defence of Colonies* (1957); R. Sedillot, *Histoire des colonisations* (1957); H. Labouret, *Africa before the White Man* (1963); R. Delavignette, *Christianity and Colonialism* (1964); F. Fanon, *Wretched of the Earth* (1965); J.-P. Sartre, *Situations* (1965).

Heinz Robert Schlette

COMMANDMENTS, THE TEN

The "ten words" (our "Decalogue") is a term used in the OT to describe a group of divine commandments written down by

Moses on the occasion of the theophany in the desert. In Deuteronomy the term clearly refers to the ten commandments of Horeb (4:13; 10:4), which are quoted at 5:6–21; they are written on tables of stone and preserved in the ark of the covenant (10:6; 31:26; cf. 1 Kg 8:9). In Exod 34:28 the "ten words" seem at first sight to refer to the short code of laws given in the preceding verses 14–27. But since the repetition of the term "words" is awkward, and since it is difficult to form a group of ten from the preceding set of commandments, we are probably dealing here with an addition which refers in reality to the decalogue of Exod 20:1–7. We shall not consider here the "ritual decalogue" of Exod 34.

1. *The Decalogue in the Bible.* Exod 20 and Deut 5 give us two versions which are very close to one another. But a notably different version may be seen in Lev 19:3–4, 11–13, dealing with respect for parents, the sabbath, prohibition of idols, theft, false oaths and covetousness. These commandments are couched in the plural (except from v. 12 b to v. 13), and the list is incomplete, since it does not mention murder and adultery, which, however, are dealt with in other passages of this discourse, the so-called "Law of Holiness". There are difficulties in dividing up the precepts of Exodus and Deuteronomy into "ten words", and this has led to distinguishing covetousness with regard to goods from covetousness with regard to the neighbour's wife, and to assigning the precept about respect for parents to the first part (Origen and especially Augustine).

2. *History of the text.* It was engraved on tablets, perhaps of clay, such as were used in cuneiform writing (cf. Is 30:18; Hab 2:2; these texts are not conclusive). But more probably, according to the text, they were "tables of stone" (Exod 24:12; 34:1 etc.), like the 10th century Gezer Calendar, the most ancient piece of writing in Hebrew. In any case, the text was not a book *(sepher),* as it is described in Deuteronomic and Priestly texts, which, however, may reflect a tradition going back at least to Solomon (1 Kg 8:9). The tablets were destroyed along with the ark of the covenant in which they were kept, but the text was preserved in copies of the Law, in Greek translations and in excerpts from the Bible. Such excerpts are represented in the ancient manuscripts such as the Nash papyrus found in Egypt, texts from Qumran, and Samaritan inscriptions.

3. *Structure and style.* The traces of the Decalogue in the Law of Holiness do not constitute a decalogue. The differences of redaction between Deuteronomy and Exodus allow us to consider that the motivation given to the Sabbath precept is an addition. Other variants of detail have led some authors to take Exod 20 (Elohist) as the most ancient text. The Decalogue presents variations in style which certain scholars have tried to eliminate to restore the primitive form of the Decalogue. It is based on a set of precepts couched in the second person of the imperfect, a form which is used in all the commandments except that of respect for parents, (in the imperative or infinitive). This style has been preserved in its pure state in the first and in the 6th to 9th commandments, but in the others it has been modified by Deuteronomic or pre-Deuteronomic additions (Exod 20), where motivations have been inserted, under the influence of the Wisdom teachers.

If one takes into account that respect for parents is a sapiential theme, and if one relies strictly on literary criteria, the primitive Decalogue could be reconstructed as follows: "You shall have no other gods before me (Exod 20:3). You shall not make yourself a graven image (v. 4). You shall not bow down to them or serve them (v. 5). You shall not take the name of Yahweh your God in vain (v. 7). Six days you shall labour, and do all your work (v. 9). The seventh day you shall not do any work (v. 10). You shall not kill (v. 13). You shall not commit adultery (v. 14). You shall not steal (v. 15). You shall not bear false witness against your neighbour (v. 16). You shall not covet your neighbour's house (v. 17)." But scholars in general are rather doubtful about such reconstructions. It seems certain that the second part of the Decalogue has a more markedly ethical character and deals with relations towards one's neighbour.

4. *The function of the Decalogue in Israel.* The text of the Decalogue is at the base of the legislation in the Book of the Covenant in Exodus and Deuteronomy, and to a lesser degree at the base of the exposition of the Law of Holiness. It is presented as "words",

which are the attribute of the prophet at the time of the redaction of the texts into which it is now inserted. But these same texts regard Moses as a prophet (Num 12; Deut 18; Hos 12:14) and connect the Decalogue with Horeb (Exod 17:6; 33:6; Deut). A prophet like Hosea who connects the covenant with the time of the desert wanderings (2; 11) attributes its rupture and the ensuing disasters to the same faults which are condemned in the Decalogue (4:2 — lack of knowledge of God, perjury, lying, murder, stealing, adultery). Hosea and the prophetical movement are very doubtful of the liturgical worship and the sanctuaries of their day; but these traditions still regard Horeb as the sanctuary in which the people offer worship to God (Exod 3:12; 18:12; cf. 17:6).

Further, in Exod 34:28b the expression "ten words" is referred to a group of prescriptions of a cultic nature. Some scholars therefore hold that the Decalogue was a catalogue of all the prescriptions to be complied with in view of participating in worship. It would thus be a brief and trenchant expression of the moral nature of the God of Israel. It is not unlikely that the Decalogue was preserved in a northern sanctuary like that of Dan which was in the charge of the descendants of Moses through Gershom (Jud 18:30).

5. *Origin of the Decalogue*. The text is presented in an oratorical and imperative style, with hortatory developments which suggest (Stamm, Reventlow etc.) that it used to be proclaimed at a liturgical feast as a commemoration and re-enactment of the ancient theophany. A feast of the covenant has been suggested, and also the feast of Tabernacles, at which the law was to be read out (Deut 31:10f.). Further, the Decalogue is introduced by the formula "I am Yahweh ..." which belongs to the priestly style (Zimmerli), and gives an authentically divine value to the oracle uttered by the priest. A similar formula is used by an Egyptian divinity when manifesting himself to a believer (*Thut-mose* IV) in a theophany (Pritchard, 1st ed., p. 448). Egyptian rituals use a formula of the same type to present the Pharaoh as the son of Re or Osiris, or the priest as Horus, when addressing officials or subjects.

This is not the only contact with the Egypt of the middle of the second millenium B.C. It also provides us with lists of faults which are to be avoided, as in the protestations of innocence in the *Book of the Dead,* and on the stelae of Uriage and Abydos. These texts are at the base of later lists which are more complete (Edfu, Denderah, Jumilhac Papyrus). These lists may be compared with the series of interrogations put by the Babylonian exorcists. They bring up myths along with food taboos and combine the defence of particular interests with the purest of moral prescriptions (with regard to theft, murder and injustice). The Egyptian lists have a special interest inasmuch as they were drawn up in view of entrance to the palace (*Pi-ankhi*), to the necropolis or to the shrine of Osiris, king of the dead. It is quite conceivable that Moses should have drawn up a similar list in view of entrance to the sanctuary and that it should have been preserved by his descendants who were Levites. But the prescriptions include important modifications in which the religion proper to Moses comes to the fore. On the one hand, they are now confined to the moral demands of a God who speaks to man's conscience. On the other hand, they are imperatives by which the God of the fathers, without intermediary, addresses a living people, as directly as he spoke to the patriarchs. The basis is laid down for the covenant of the God of Abraham with the people of Israel.

See also *Old Testament Books* I, *Old Testament Theology, Covenant.*

BIBLIOGRAPHY. S. Mowinckel, *Le Décalogue* (1927); M. Buber, *Moses* (1946); H. H. Rowley, *Moses and the Decalogue* (1951); A. Alt, *Kleine Schriften zur Geschichte des Volkes Israel,* I (1953), pp. 278–332; W. Eichrodt, *Theology of the Old Testament,* 2 vols. (1961–67), see Index; G. von Rad, *Old Testament Theology,* I (1962); H. von Reventlow, *Gebot und Predigt im Dekalog* (1962); G. J. Botterweck, "Form and Growth of the Decalogue", *Concilium* 5, no. 1 (1965), pp. 33–44; E. Gerstenberger, *Wesen und Herkunft des apodiktischen Rechts* (1965); M. Noth, *The Laws in the Pentateuch and other Essays* (1966); J. J. Stamm, *The Ten Commandments in Recent Research* (1967).

Henri Cazelles

COMMANDMENTS OF THE CHURCH

1. *Notion.* In the wider sense one understands under the term "Commandments of the Church" all the general precepts of the

Church's pastoral office which define in the concrete the divine law in view of the salvation of the faithful (canon law). They must be distinguished from the instructions which may be imparted by the ecclesiastical superiors to particular members of the faithful. Taken in the strict sense, however, the commandments of the Church grew up in the Middle Ages, in association with confessional practice, out of obligatory ecclesiastical custom. Under the influence of the *Summa Confessionalis* of Antony of Florence (1389–1459) the teaching on the commandments acquired a clearer form. Since 1444 five commandments can be verified, and the decrees of the Council of Trent on the administration of the sacrament of penance have led to the stronger emphasis subsequently laid on them. In a typical formulation the catechism of Cardinal Gasparri, for example, describes them as those commandments "which are of very great significance for the general spiritual life of the faithful". In their present most widespread form they are derived from the catechism of Peter Canisius (1555): i) observance of particular feastdays; ii) reverent attendance at Mass on Sundays and holy days of obligation; iii) observance of obligatory days of fasting and abstinence; iv) annual confession; v) reception of Holy Communion at Eastertide.

To this catalogue of the commandments of the Church others have been added, such as the duty of supporting the Church, which was adduced under the influence of Bellarmine, or the observance of "forbidden times" regarding marriage and dancing. In many countries the duty of sending children to Catholic schools is counted as one of the Church's commandments, and the censorship of books and the rejection of cremation have also functioned as precepts of the Church. No matter how they have been summed up, the Church has not taken over any of the lists as official. Thus one does not find any special list of the commandments of the Church in the *Catechismus Romanus*.

In the popular conception, the commandments of the Church are a means used by the hierarchy to lead the individual in a fatherly manner to a minimal fulfilment of his religious duties and in this way to safeguard the common good of the Church. Here it is assumed that commandments of the Church are necessary and effective in order to attain the aims envisaged by such means.

2. *Difficulties.* Pastoral practice shows that commandments have in fact contributed in great measure towards sustaining and giving concrete expression to the common life of the Church. It also shows, however, that the interpretation of them as privileged instruments in the moral guidance of the individual believer, and the over-emphasis of obedience lead to a dangerous legalistic morality, which restricts the effort of many too one-sidedly to loyalty to the law and misleads them to equate the observance of the commandments with a life according to Christian morality, or to adhere to them to the detriment of higher values.

Moral handbooks, intended originally as practical guides for confessors, by their undue emphasis on the commandments of the Church, by their methods and their casuistry, have greatly hindered the development of personal responsibility and proper judgment of the situation in moral action. The most obvious abuses of this legalism are gradually being rectified, but it still persists subconsciously in moral thought and attitudes.

The deeper reason for this legalism is no doubt to be found in a false need of religious security. This attachment to the law shuns the responsibility of personal decision and evades God's call in the ever-changing situation of the moral act. As soon as one begins to think legalistically the tendency arises to construct as far as possible a cast-iron system of external laws. Then, out of consideration for real life, enforced by pastoral needs, this tightly-woven legal system is again loosened by an extensive system of dispensation and casuistic interpretations. Thus the impression is established that one need only know sufficient about the matter to be released from following the law or that one need only have oneself dispensed. Then the initial rigorism of the legalistic approach easily switches to laxism. Many of the faithful, then, especially those who are aiming at moral maturity, feel that many commandments of the Church are out of date, arbitrary and superfluous. The severe sanctions which are sometimes attached to them are regarded as paternalistic leading-strings. Further, the duty of obedience with regard to the precepts is often unduly emphasized without corresponding explanation of their meaning. Here one proceeds from the erroneous concept that the human legislator, as God's representative, is able to bind morally — something which God alone can do. The consequence is that obedience for its own sake is juridically overestimated.

3. *Meaning*. Hence arises the question of the meaning and obligatory character of the commandments of the Church. We must start from the premise that all general laws imposed from outside have as their immediate object the safeguarding of the common good, and only serve indirectly the perfection of the individual. The individual is affected only insofar as his rights and duties towards the community and his neighbour are defined. The commandments of the Church, like ecclesiastical law in general, have therefore as their immediate object the preservation of public order in the Church. This must take place of course in view of the end and object of the Church, which is the sacramental re-presentation of Christ and his work in this world as sign and means of salvation for mankind. Therefore, all commandments of the Church are meaningful which promote the common good of the Church under this aspect. Insofar as they are necessary to this end they can be legitimately urged and if need be upheld by appropriate ecclesiastical penalties. Conversely, in conformity with the principle of subsidiarity nothing should be prescribed which is not necessary for the common good of the Church. In adhering to this fundamental principle, no resistance is offered to the free working of the Holy Spirit, room is left for a corresponding initiative in the individual, and ecclesiastical office can perform its allotted task in the service of the Church under the guidance of the Spirit. The question of what is needed for the common spiritual welfare is not always kept clearly enough in mind. Thus, for example, we lack a theory about the extent to which impediments to marriage are possible.

What is necessary for the common good of the Church cannot be laid down *a priori* once and for all, but is dependent on changing ecclesiastical situations and must be worked out *a posteriori*. However, since laws should always have as much permanence as possible for the sake of sureness, it follows that the commandments should be drafted as widely as possible but also with the necessary precision, as they would not otherwise be able to fulfil their purpose. A system of dispensations is always necessary to a certain extent on account of the imperfection of human legislation, but it should be reduced to a minimum. Otherwise there is uncertainty with regard to the law and the danger arises of a paternalist tutelage of the faithful.

4. *Their binding character*. The common good of the Church calls for common and co-ordinated action. The faithful should fulfil the commandments in an obedience which strives to perceive their significance for the welfare of the Church. In this way the faithful will contribute to the building up and preservation of the body of Christ not only by their obedience but also by their exercise of the corresponding virtue. Insofar as the commandments serve this end they transmit the divine law and thus far are morally binding. The binding character of the Church's commandments is, therefore, to be measured according to their function with regard to the common good, and the legislator can only demand obedience insofar as the common good demands it. This means that the legislator in his law does not bring about the will of God as his delegate but manifests the divine will in the exercise of his office.

It is well to bear in mind here that on account of the subjective incertitude of the individual with regard to what is necessary for the common good, the legislator must create through his law the unity of judgment necessary for the common action. The faithful must therefore obey him insofar as a law is necessary for the common good and its observance is required. If a law is unnecessary, then it is unjust; if the observance of a law in a particular case is absurd, then the obligation lapses. If the observance of the spirit and not of the letter of the law is apposite, then one must act according to the virtue of epikeia. In order to have a balanced attitude towards the commandments of the Church, as loyal as it is responsible, the faithful must be equally prepared for obedience to the ecclesiastical legislator and for the service of the common good of the Church which is demanded in the circumstances.

In view of the above, we can now deal with the classical controversy as to whether the ecclesiastical legislator can demand an internal act or merely external acts and the internal act only indirectly. We may say that internal acts necessary for the common good of the Church can also be demanded, for, in contrast to the State, these acts are essential to the ends of the Church. The thesis that the commandments are fulfilled by positing the required external act fails to recognize the spiritual character of canon law. So too the view that a violation of the Church's commandments may be under certain circumstances only an offence against obedience. Rather, if there is any offence at all, it is always also an offence against the virtues demanded by the commandment.

5. *Pastoral requirements.* From such a view of the commandments of the Church it follows that in practice the faithful should always have the significance of the respective precepts explained to them as clearly as possible. It is also fitting that the commandments of the Church and their actual topical relevance be discussed in open dialogue within the Church and that the faithful be duly offered the opportunity of bringing their influence to bear in the shaping of the commandments of the Church to meet the needs of the times. This will always promote a rational observance of the commandments, because in the ecclesiastical sphere, much more than in the secular, it is important that the line of conduct demanded be followed from an internal conviction. For here the salvation of man is at stake which fundamentally demands personal compliance with God's call.

Furthermore, ecclesiastical legislation must not aim at sustaining and assuring as extensively as possible the spiritual life of the faithful. Such a "socialization" of the spiritual life would be opposed to the free working of the Holy Spirit and detrimental to the personal initiative of the faithful. The commandments of the Church must attempt, then, to promote equally the common good of the Church and the possibility of free spiritual development. The present commandments of the Church do not always do justice to the need of developing personal responsibility in keeping with our times. The Pope has therefore set up a commission for the reform of canon law and several changes have already been made, e.g., in respect of fasting and the censorship of books. However, the tension between the common and individual good will never be finally harmonized even in the sphere of spiritual

legislation. Rather, in the end, the individual must bridge this gap by his *sentire cum ecclesia* and interpret the commandments by applying an enlightened epikeia, in keeping with God's will, which is manifested interiorly and which alone imposes an absolute obligation.

Pastoral education should therefore be more concerned with enabling the faithful to observe the precepts in a meaningful way. For this it is necessary that the predominant religious individualism be abandoned in favour of a strong Church consciousness. This will also serve to explain the necessity of appropriate commandments and strengthen the authority of the Church.

See also *Ecclesiastical Law* I, II, *Ecclesiastical Office* I.

BIBLIOGRAPHY. E. Dublanchy, "Commandements de l'Église", *DTC,* III (1908), cols. 388–93; A. Villien, *Histoire des commandements de l'Église* (1936); G. Ebeling, *Kirchenzucht* (1947); B. Schüller, *Gesetz und Freiheit* (1966).

Waldemar Molinski

COMMUNICATIONS MEDIA

What Catholic circles call social communications media are generally known elsewhere as mass media (an expression that has been popularized by the Americans), media of mass communication, collective communication media, modern techniques in publicity, and so forth.

The Catholic expression, coined and spread by the Second Vatican Council in its decree *Inter Mirifica*, highlights the role that these media, ideally, should play. To communicate is to convey and share. By exchanging what they have, men help each other, draw together, and come to resemble each other. Free, orderly communication is the substance of society. The adjective "social" was chosen with great care, on the one hand to eliminate the word "mass" with its overtones of depersonalization, irresponsibility, and levelling, and on the other hand to show that communication reaches great numbers of people, "even the whole of mankind", and that it is one of the operative factors in socialization as defined by the encyclical *Mater et Magistra* (no. 58) and the Pastoral Constitution on the Church in the Modern World (arts. 25 and 75). Still it will be in order to note that in the expression "mass media" the word "mass" refers neither to the conduct of those who use them nor yet to any degrading effect those media may have; it simply indicates the extent, and particularly the diversity, of the public concerned.

Much is made, and rightly so, of the speed, simultaneity, universal reach, and volume of the communication which modern techniques make possible; but the variety of readers, hearers, and spectators involved is perhaps more relevant. People who differ in culture, occupation, income, age, sex, race, and religion, all receive the same messages at the same moment. Here we have one of the hall-marks of our civilization and one full of promise for the future of mankind: the equal opportunities for culture which men of our day enjoy. That equality will be more marked as time goes on.

Even more than the press, which offers an endless variety of reading material and is compelled to adapt itself to the different mental levels of the public, radio and television provide us all day long, at home and at trifling cost, with cultural nourishment which not long ago was hardly to be had at all, or only at great expense, and was therefore the prerequisite of one particular class in society.

Operating in a general context of urbanization and industrialization, communications media express, spread, and shape what is called mass culture. Since cultural material can be manufactured and stored up (tape recordings, gramophone records, etc.), it must be sold on a business basis and it must be consumed. Even where culture is concerned, ours is a consumers' civilization. A need latent in every human being is awakened, stimulated, directed, and sometimes perverted.

This mass culture will be widened and intensified to a degree we can hardly guess, by developments in electronics. An immediate prospect is the transmission from satellites of world television programmes and entire newspapers. The most various messages, constantly multiplying — news, comment, data and doctrine, art and entertainment, dreams and emotions — will rain without warning on a public as huge and heterogeneous as the world itself. It will be real planetary communication.

All mankind will be exposed to the same information and entertainment, but what use will it make of them? The same tidings may provoke different reactions: approval and delight in one quarter, condemnation and grief in another. Far from uniting men, they may have the opposite effect. Yet one likes to think that by degrees men will perceive their common destiny and that a sense of solidarity will mean a common effort for a juster, freer, more brotherly world. It should become an almost biological urge in man.

Each new invention of *homo faber* has given man a new instrument with which to destroy or achieve himself; and despite all the ups and downs, the race has survived and even progressed. In our day we have produced instruments which are so potent over matter and the mind that we now face a basic choice: "Man is becoming aware that it is his responsibility to guide aright the forces which he has unleashed and which can enslave him or minister to him." (*Gaudium et Spes,* art. 9, 4.)

Communications media "directly impinge on our spiritual faculties", and therefore they confront the Christian conscience and the Church, whose mission it is to serve mankind, with nothing less than the human condition and the fate of mankind. The Council itself declares that "the Christian community realizes that it is truly and intimately linked with mankind and its history" (*Gaudium et Spes,* art. 1).

In our day the Church has taken a definitely positive, even optimistic attitude towards communications media (the press, cinema, radio, television, and other techniques). The opening words of the major documents published in the past few years are significant. Pius XII's encyclical on cinema, radio, and television (8 September 1957) begins with the words *Miranda prorsus* ("the marvellous advances") and the conciliar Decree on the Instruments of Social Communication (4 December 1963) begins with *Inter mirifica* ("among the marvellous discoveries"). So the Church is neither suspicious nor indifferent towards science and its techniques; it regards them with admiration. But it sees beyond these achievements of science, and is chiefly concerned with their role in society, the messages they convey.

The decree *Inter Mirifica* was published at the end of the second session of Vatican II. It is the conciliar text about which the Fathers were most hesitant during the discussions in the aula. Thus at the last plenary session there were 503 votes against it. Most of the weaknesses of the document seem to result from the fact that after a preliminary discussion the editors were told to keep to the substance of a text drawn up during preparations for the Council. So they were not able to take account of the different light in which the relationship between the Church and the world, the kingdom of God and earthly realities, the apostolate and one's occupation, was seen by the time the second session closed. Still we must not overlook all the good features and dynamism of the document: the intrinsic importance of communications media for the service of man and the advancement of the race; the right to be informed; the function of the State, which must safeguard and foster freedom as well as morals; the need for personal choice, and therefore for training people up to freedom; respect for the laws of communication proper to each medium; bringing these media into the normal work of the Church's ministry; defining the Catholic press; rejection of amateurism; demanding high standards, etc. Comprising 24 paragraphs, the decree is divided into two sections — the Church's teaching (arts. 3 to 12) and its pastoral work (arts. 13 to 22) — with an introduction, and a conclusion (arts. 23 and 24) which announces that there will be a pastoral instruction on communications media. The motu proprio *In Fructibus Multis,* 2 April 1965, set up the Pontifical Commission on Communications Media envisaged in the Council's decree, art. 19. This commission is attached to the Secretariat of State and includes laymen among its members and consultors.

Is it possible to outline a theology of communications media in themselves and in their human significance, quite apart from the use which the Church makes of them to spread the gospel? We suggest three trains of thought.

Anything that creates, facilitates and improves communication among men causes us to share in the goodness of God, who disseminates his benefits to all the human race. Therefore communication is semireligious by nature. Pius XII enlarges on this doctrine in *Miranda Prorsus:* "God, being the sovereign good, showers his gifts on men, whom he particularly loves . . .

Wishing to see in man the image of his own perfection, God has associated him with the divine largesse: drawing man into his own work, God has made him herald, bearer, and dispenser of these good things to his brethren and society. By his very nature man has learnt from the earliest times to communicate his spiritual possessions to others by signs, found in material things, which he has endeavoured to perfect more and more. And so all means of communication, from the drawings and writings of the remotest ages to the techniques of our own day, must serve the lofty end of helping man to be God's minister." (I, 2, 3; see *AAS* 49 [1957], pp. 771–2.)

Here, then, the nature of God himself is seen as the foundation of the mysterious imperative of communication in man; here we find in God the foundations of professional ethics. For a Christian this is not a categorical imperative secreted by cold, utilitarian reason, it is — or should be — a loving response to Christ's watchword: "You, therefore, must be perfect, as your heavenly Father is perfect." Through the universal communication which modern technology now brings within his reach man can be, more than was ever possible in the past, the minister of a God who generously communicates himself.

Doubtless there will be shortcomings, since we are creatures; there will even be distortions and abuses, since we are sinners. Sometimes one is tempted to think that the enemy mentioned in the gospel (Mt 13:24 to 30) uses these means of communication to sow more weeds than ever in the Lord's field. But no abuse can alter the ontological purpose of communication.

There is another reason for the Christian to welcome the amazing development of communications media. Under the guiding hand of providence and the impulse of the Spirit, mankind advances towards fulfilment. That will certainly be found in the next world; but even here, within time, it is prefigured and we draw near to it. It would be misconceiving God's plan for mankind were we to seek fulfilment exclusively in the supernatural order, on the grounds that man's natural history must lead to ruin as a punishment for sin. Because God loves the whole of man, the powerful communications media we now have and the still more powerful media we shall have tomorrow, are part of his providential plan. They come into it not empty-handed or as makeshifts, but positively, as a sign and an instrument of fulfilment.

If men are reunited even on the physical plane, is that not the doing of redemption, is it not part of the triumph of grace? For sin is refusal, rupture, turning in on self, isolation — which means that it is the antithesis of communication. In the last year of his life, on 19 March 1958, Pius XII spoke of this situation with something very like Teilhardian optimism: "For the first time men are becoming aware not only of their growing interdependence but even more of their astonishing unity; which means that mankind will be more and more disposed to become the mystical body of Christ." Having recovered its unity — by what agonies, with what delays, and how precariously — may not the world be the symbol, the touchstone, even the inspiration of Christian unity, of the *de facto* catholicity of the Church?

We have considered a sign of the times which relates to the nature and role of communications media. There is another, which relates to their use — to the fact that these media are chiefly used in people's spare time. Economically, socially, psychologically, and culturally leisure is one of the acutest problems facing modern society. So we must create a theology of leisure, just as we had to create a theology of work. Leisure is spare time, the time man can use as he pleases. It ought to be a special time when man discovers and realizes himself, instead of time wasted in sloth and self-degradation. Will it be so? That depends less on what communications man is offered than on what communications he chooses for himself. For in the last analysis, at least in democratic, pluralist society, the user chooses his own communications. It is vital to know why he chooses them and how he chooses them, not only so as not to be misled by certain phenomena but especially so as to take the appropriate steps. Here we should recall the importance which the decree *Inter Mirifica* attaches to preparing people morally, technically, and aesthetically — in a word, by a total culture — to use communications media. Since the user chooses according to what he is and what he wants to become, it is important for the Church and society that the man of today, and especially the man of tomorrow, be able and willing to choose among the messages offered him those which will help him realize his ideal of a human being, laboriously but joyfully.

The duty of self-culture, which the Council reminds us of in chapter II of the second part of *Gaudium et Spes* (under the significant heading of "the proper development of culture") is closely bound up in our civilization with the use of communications media in spare time.

In order to form an accurate appreciation of these media in our present context, two observations are called for:

a) If we are primarily interested in what is communicated, we still may not neglect to consider to whom it is communicated, and when and how. Yet it is useless to choose your hour, impose bans, or select an audience: the messages you have sent forth are beyond your control. How can you forbid anyone to pick up a magazine or push a button? Civil authority may and should intervene to control certain excesses and uphold a minimum of public decency; but otherwise no human society can protect the weak against organized corruption, usually carried on out of greed for gain and often hypocritically defended in the name of freedom of expression and the rights of art.

Responsibility here rests primarily on those who (in any sense) produce the material, even if it is often difficult for them to judge how far they can in good conscience invoke the right to information and the laws of artistic creation. In principle the Council has declared: "On these persons (who produce the material), then, will lie the task of regulating the commercial, political, and artistic aspects of these media in ways which will never conflict with the common good." (*Gaudium et Spes*, art. 11.) But who is to judge when and how the common good is threatened? For in our day when communications media have destroyed all closed worlds and speeded up the evolution of society, are not calculated risks often more conducive to the common good than timid precautions? On this matter there will always be disagreement between the moral and political authorities, the guardians of law and order, and the "producers" who have it at heart to defend freedom of expression.

The Church nowadays seems to have more respect for freedom of expression and more confidence in it. One sentence in *Inter Mirifica* well conveys the new attitude. Formerly the Church was mainly concerned that the State should not allow freedom of the press to be abused. Now it reminds the State that it "is duty bound to defend and protect a true and just availability of information; the progress of modern society utterly depends on this, especially as regards freedom of the press" (*ibid., art.* 12).

b) A second observation is in order: communications media differ in their techniques, history, juridical and economic structure, laws, role in society, practices, etc. Indeed some people consider that the medium as such is a message in that it sets different human faculties working and therefore of itself shows reality in a new light. The same message may convey different things to the recipient according as it is set down in a text, or pictured, or spoken. Thus audiovisual techniques have helped man rediscover, express, and communicate reality. In sound, image, and movement we experience concrete, individual, existential being. And so one may ask whether the present formulation of our faith, which relies so much on printing, and especially the catechism, still suits the mental habits and categories of young people more or less formed by audiovisual techniques. The question exercises specialists in catechetics. If the Church wishes to use these modern techniques to convey its message, it must as it were run it through the mould of the form or aesthetic peculiar to each technique. So to convey the message we must invent a new language which will make more use of suggestion, parable, and analogies drawn from our own experience, than of abstract ideas and tidy theses.

If communications media must "be used for making Christian doctrine known" (Decree on the Bishops' Pastoral Office, art. 13), if we must "strive immediately and most energetically to use the instruments of social communication effectively in the many fields of the apostolate, as the circumstances and the times require" (Decree on the Instruments of Social Communication, art. 13), they nevertheless face the Church with an antecedent problem which is even graver than the problem of their use, normal and necessary as that may be. For the Church has to deal with men who, as society and as individuals, are daily marked and transformed by modern communications.

These media are tremendously speeding up the evolution of mankind. They keep everything in a state of flux, and the eternal gospel will have to seek out man in this very situation. The position and role of communications media in the modern world may also mean a new eschatological dimension for the Church, which means reconsidering the truth that seems to have been already established, remaining faithful to it in essentials but investigating, reaching out, and refusing to say "it is enough".

See also *Church and World, Culture* II, *Leisure, Humanism, Work, Society.*

BIBLIOGRAPHY. OFFICIAL DOCUMENTS: Pius XI, Encyclical *Vigilanti Cura,* 29 June 1936; Pius XII, Encyclical *Miranda Prorsus,* 8 September 1957; Vatican II, Decree *Inter Mirifica,* on the Instruments of Social Communication. GENERAL: B. Smith and others, *Propaganda, Communication and Public Opinion* (1946); P. Lazarsfeld and others, *The People's Choice* (1948); P. Hofstätter, *Psychologie der öffentlichen Meinung* (1949); C. Siepmann, *Radio, Television and Society* (1950); UNESCO, *Reports on the Facilities of Mass Communication, Press, Film, Radio* (1951 ff.); C. Siepmann, *Television and Education in the United States,* pub. by UNESCO (1952); D. Riesman, *The Lonely Crowd* (1952); J. Dumazedier, *Les techniques de diffusion dans la civilisation contemporaine, Presse, radio, cinéma, télévision* (1955); L. Engart, *The Age of Television* (1956); V. Packard, *The Hidden Persuaders* (1957); J. Klapper, *The Effects of Mass Communication* (1960); W. Schramm, *Mass Media and National Development. The Role of Information in the Developing Countries* (1964); H. M. McLuhan, *Understanding Media* (1964); H. M. McLuhan and Q. Fioxe, *Medium is the Message* (1967). RELIGIOUS: K. Rahner, *Das freie Wort in der Kirche* (2nd ed., 1954); E. Parker and others, *The Television-Radio Audiences and Religion* (1955); J. Mole, "The Communications Decree of the Second Vatican Council", *Social Justice Review* 40 (1960); U. Bergfried, *Kirche und Massenmedien* (1964). PERIODICALS: *The Christian Broadcaster,* pub. by the World Committee for Christian Broadcasting (1953 ff.); *Rundfunk und Fernsehen* (1953 ff.); *Jahrbuch der christlichen Rundfunkarbeit* (1958 ff.); *Revue catholique de radio et de télévision* (1960 ff.); *I. A. M. C. R. Bulletin,* Quarterly published by the International Association for Mass Communication Research (1962 ff.).

Émile Gabel

COMMUNION OF SAINTS

1. The article of faith asserting the communion of saints is first found in the Western creed at the end of the 5th century in the form given by Nicetas of Remesiana. From the

5th century onwards it is found in the Gallic variations (Faustus of Riez, Caesarius of Arles; DS 26; 27) and later in all the Western forms. Nicetas used the word *sanctorum* as the genetive form of the neuter *sancta,* i.e., a share in the sacred things of the Church, in keeping with the Augustinian concept of the *communio sacramentorum* (*Sermo,* 214, 11). The phrase κοινωνία τῶν ἁγίων was, however, used much earlier in the East, though not as part of the creed; it was used there also in the sense of participation in the blessings of salvation, including therefore the personal element of fellowship. κοινωνία as such is not a share in things or effects but a personal community relationship whose quality is determined by the ἅγια. Although this community of salvation encompasses the entire Church, heavenly and earthly, it was only gradually that the term was expressly used to denote communion between the heavenly and the earthly Church and its members. The insertion of the phrase into the creed was probably meant to emphasize the nature of the Church as a fellowship *(communio)* of persons constituted and determined as such by the blessings of salvation. The limitation of the phrase in modern times to indicate the possibility of a salutary exchange of blessings between the individual members within the *communio* should again be broadened by a re-stressing of the fact that the *communio* represents the *res* of the *sacramentum* which is the Church itself.

2. This *res* of the primordial sacrament, the Church, must be first presented in biblical terms. The theological meaning of the NT fellowship (κοινωνία) is especially developed in the theology of Paul and John. It is significant for the history of religion that the OT does not speak of fellowship with God — in spite of the great stress which it places upon the personal element in the covenant given by God and in spite of the recognition that Israel owes its existence as a people to its covenant with Yahweh. Though Greek philosophy spoke of a fellowship or participation of man in the realm of the "ideas" or with the divine, Paul and John were able to proclaim the unique reality of the mystery of Christ with the help of existing concepts (1 Cor 1:9, etc.; 1 Jn 1:3, etc.)

Our fellowship with Christ presupposes that God has given us his Son as our companion. Fellowship comes about by the Son's participating in our nature (Heb 2:14–17 also Rom 5:8–10; 8:3, 32ff.; Jn 1:14). In this way the fellowship of the Son with us stands in the direct line of sacred history which had its beginning in the first covenant; thus it also includes the OT whose true goal was only to be revealed in Christ: that God wills to be "for us" just as he is "for himself". God's "being-for-us" in Christ is the great liberation. It constitutes the new beginning of salvation within the history of human iniquity, in that it makes human history the sphere of fraternal unity with the Son. Man's nostalgia for the secure and promising unity of a fresh start is consoled, since this yearning is more than satisfied by the brotherliness of the second Adam. For his brotherliness is characterized by the fact that he is the beloved Son. That salvation which is "in Christ" leads in its realization to an existence "with Christ", the realization of the κοινωνία. It is already communion with the body given for our sakes and the blood shed for us (1 Cor 10:16ff.); it leads to full conformity with Christ at the resurrection (Rom 8:21). But it is communion with the body and blood of Christ which first constitutes the Church as a fellowship. Here one sees most clearly the intimate relation between the concept of fellowship with Christ and the designation of the Church as the "body of Christ".

3. Fellowship with Christ is thus the basis for the "two communities" which are implicit in Christian fellowship: fellowship with Christ is also fellowship with the Father. It is true that Paul does not speak explicitly of fellowship with the Father, but the thought is implied in his conception of Christian fellowship as participation in the form of the Son. The thought is explicit in 1 Jn 1:3. Fellowship with Christ is also the basis of the fellowship of the justified, which is not merely the sum total of all individual relationships to Christ.

4. Nevertheless, these two aspects of the Christian fellowship are rooted in the one mystery of Christ which, because of the trinitarian mystery of God and the inclusion of mankind within it, is "many-sided". This unity must be considered in relation to the divine reality which has revealed itself as Spirit and which in the NT is expressly

related to the fellowship (2 Cor 13:13). A developed scriptural doctrine of the Holy Spirit must show that "communion with the Holy Spirit" is communion with Christ and with the Father, because the Holy Spirit is himself this communion. The fellowship between the Father and Son is a divine reality, as is the Father and the Son. As their fellowship it is distinct from them and thus constitutes in the one divine nature the relationship between Father and Son. But as the immanent intercommunication between the Father and the Son, he is nevertheless the same Spirit who as the *Pneuma* from the glorified body of Jesus (Jn 7:37–39) is also the intercommunication of the Church with its Lord. As such the Spirit is also the intercommunication between all members of Christ who are living in grace. Through this trinitarian structure of the divine being, which is in itself fellowship, the doctrine of the communion of saints may be distinguished — in spite of its considering that fellowship with the Father is communicated "through Christ" and "in the Spirit" — from the notion of a participation in the divine on a lower level of emanations, as is found in neo-Platonism.

5. Since intercommunication between Christ and his own is treated of in soteriology, the traditional doctrine of the communion of saints is mostly restricted to the intercommunication between the other members of Christ as it is made manifest in the mystery of salvation. Here it must be noted that the Holy Spirit can bestow his gift of fellowship in such a way that a creaturely and historical crystallization of it is not only not excluded, but quite possible. Just as through the Holy Spirit it was possible for the Son to live his Sonship in a human being, so too the Church is given access to participation in that Sonship. And this is its human realization in the people of Christ. This human manifestation reveals the sacramental character of the communion of saints. The fullness of the *Sacramentum Christi* continues to present and communicate itself through the action of the Spirit, and the Church is led deeper and deeper into the *res* of this *sacramentum,* according to the salvific will of God. The more profoundly it is rooted in Christ, the stronger grows the unity of the communion of saints. At the same time, the fellowship thus constituted by Christ bears the individual along the way to Christ. The signs of Christ's salvation which have been entrusted to the Church, which signify and effect salvation infallibly through the power of Christ, find expression in a Church which as a totality can only pray for the coming of the Spirit (the Epiclesis).

The salutary effect of the activity of the members on behalf of each other is explained by the fact that when the Church prays for its members, or the individual for the Church and for other individuals, this intercession takes place in the medium constituted by the Spirit in the communion of saints. When the Spirit takes up the cry of the Bride, and makes it resound before the Father along with the voice of Christ, Christ is not thereby lessened: "he is glorified in his own" (cf. Jn 17:10). If this supplication takes the form of enterprising and active service, this work of love is also inspired by the Spirit, who gives it the deep conformity to Christ which is proper to such action on behalf of others. Above all, the Spirit brings about in the members of Christ that steadfast conquest of suffering which wrought our salvation in the sacrifice of Christ. The whole Church is to be drawn to share this dedication, and thus the obedient dedication of the one is meaningful for all, because there too the Son is glorified. Nonetheless, Christ's position remains unique, because it is only he, as the man glorified who is also the Son, who sends the Spirit. The fruitfulness of the members for each other is rooted in the same Spirit, but they do not send him, they only receive him. This has been expressed technically by the magisterium, in terms that lack somewhat in expressiveness, by saying that only Christ merits for us *de condigno,* while we may merit for each other *de congruo.*

6. The form of "inter-aid" so far described envisaged the communion of saints more particularly in its state of pilgrimage. But the *status perfectionis,* the consummation, does not interrupt communications. Nothing new accrues to these members, but their having been made perfect is of particular importance, as being not merely an example but also a gift to the people on pilgrimage. The pilgrim is always in danger of feeling constricted and oppressed by his anxiety for his salvation. When the Spirit gives him the perfected angels and saints as brothers in every way close to him, he reveals himself as

the love who gives the one Christ, the life of all, ever more fully as the fellowship grows wider.

7. Finally, there is also the loving care of the pilgrims for the members who must still suffer to attain their consummation. This care does not lead them to bargain with God for what is still wanting to the perfection of the suffering. The pilgrims are only impelled by the conviction that in the Spirit their supplications help those who still suffer on the way to salvation, since even in purgatory "no man is an island". There are no fully isolated individuals even there.

See also *Covenant, People of God, Salvation IV C, Purgatory, Neo-Platonism.*

BIBLIOGRAPHY. J. P. Kirsch, *Die Lehre von der Gemeinschaft der Heiligen im christlichen Altertum* (1900); P. Bernard, "Communion des Saints", *DTC,* III (1908), cols. 429–80; H. B. Swete, *The Holy Catholic Church, the Communion of Saints* (1916); F. J. Badcock, "Sanctorum Communio as an Article in the Creed", *JTS* 21 (1919–20), pp. 106–26; H. Seesemann, *Der Begriff der koinonia im Neuen Testament* (1933); J. de Ghellinck, *Patristique et Moyen-âge,* I (2nd ed., 1949); J. N. Kelly, *Early Christian Creeds* (1950); A. Piolanti, *Il mistero della communione dei Santi nella rivelazione e nella teologia* (1957); D. Bonhoeffer, *Communion of Saints* (1964).

Wilhelm Breuning

COMMUNION UNDER BOTH KINDS

1. Instituted probably within the framework of the paschal meal, the Eucharist has retained the structure of a meal in which Christ gives himself to his own, under the twofold appearances of bread and wine, as their food and drink. By eating his flesh and drinking his blood the faithful attain the unity with him which confers on them eternal life. The eucharistic discourse (Jn 6:51, 53, 54, 56) affirms in realistic terms the necessity of the reception of the Eucharist for salvation. If the matter of the Eucharist is twofold, that is because a meal is only complete if it comprises food and drink. And so Communion under both kinds certainly belongs to the integrity of the sacramental sign, and is in keeping with Christ's institution.

There is also a basis for it in the sacrificial character of the Eucharist. According to the fourth gospel (Jn 6:51) and the accounts of the institution (Mt 26:26–29; Mk 14:22–25; Lk 22:14–20; 1 Cor 11:23–27) Christ's flesh and blood at the Last Supper are directly referred to his sacrifice on the cross, and indeed are identical with the flesh and blood as sacrificed on Golgotha. Thus the Eucharist is a sacrificial meal; to partake sacramentally of the atoning flesh and cleansing blood is to receive the grace of the Redeemer. Sacramentally commemorating the Lord and appropriating his sacrifice on the cross, the sacrificial meal of the Eucharist is to be repeated, according to his commandment, until his eschatological Second Coming (1 Cor 11:26). As often as the words of consecration are pronounced over bread and wine, Christ's sacrificial death becomes present once again in the Church. Now to this end the two species are necessary.

2. So it was only natural for Communion to be given under both kinds from the beginning, as is still done in the Eastern Church to this day. The Western Church continued the practice until the 13th century, or later in special cases (in papal Masses until the 15th century, and in coronation Masses for emperors and kings). The form of administration varied. At first the communicants drank from the chalice (either the consecration chalice or a Communion chalice or a chalice in which the consecrated species was mixed with other wine); then little tubes (pugillaris, calamus, fistula) or spoons were used; or the Host was dipped in the Precious Blood *(intinctio).* There is still an allusion to this form of the Communion of the faithful under both kinds in the prayer "Haec commixtio . . ." of the Latin Mass.

3. At the same time the ancient Church always practised Communion under *one* kind, which it considered a perfectly valid, complete sacrament in the appropriate circumstances (*sub specie panis* for those who communicated at home, for the sick, prisoners, and anchorites; *sub specie vini* for infants and the gravely ill; and also under one kind in the Mass of the Presanctified). It did not hold the form of administration to be fixed by divine law, and altered the Communion rite without misgivings when it seemed necessary or fitting to do so. Recognition of the symbolic character helped to preserve a balanced view. There is only one gift, Christ himself; that gift is received whole and

undivided under each of the two kinds; the grace of salvation is not tied to one or the other. The Schoolmen give the theological reason: *ex vi verborum* or *in virtute sacramenti* each kind contains only what it signifies, either the body or the blood of Christ; but *ex concomitantia* each kind contains the "whole" Christ, with his soul and divinity, present in all the fullness and power of his life, sufferings, and resurrection; the "whole" of him is received.

This doctrine explains how the Church was able to discontinue Communion under both kinds without prejudice to the faithful when it perceived that there were weighty reasons for doing so (danger of contagion in time of pestilence, danger of irreverence and spilling, repugnance of some communicants to drinking from the same chalice as others, the multitude of communicants at Easter and other great feasts, scarcity of wine in northern countries). Without any formal legislation, Communion under one kind became customary throughout the West during the 13th and 14th centuries. This change was the easier because people approached the sacraments very infrequently and, failing to realize sufficiently that sacrifice and sacrificial meal are one in the Mass, regarded Communion as a special act apart from the eucharistic sacrifice.

4. A reaction set in in the 14th century. At first the only aim was to revive eucharistic piety. Then in 1414 Jacob of Mies, citing Jn 6:53, began to preach at Prague that Communion under both kinds was absolutely necessary for salvation and enjoined by a direct commandment of God (Mt 26:27; Lk 22:17ff.). The reactions of the ecclesiastical authorities brought a polemical note into his preaching, which degenerated into propaganda against the Church. By discontinuing Communion under both kinds, he declared, the Church had defrauded the faithful of their eternal salvation. The Council then sitting at Constance rejected the demand for restoration of the chalice to the laity (Session XIII, 15 June 1415) and forbade the practice because of its association with the erroneous view of Jacob of Mies. Full of religious zeal and political passion, the Hussite movement which flared up on the execution of John Huss (6 July 1415) made Communion under both kinds its battle-cry (Calixtines, Utraquists) in an assault on

Church and State (Hussite Wars, 1419–36). Eventually the Council of Basle allowed Communion under both kinds in Bohemia (the "Compactata of Basle", 1436), bringing the wars to an end. But in 1462 Pius II annulled the Compactata. Though many Utraquists returned to the Roman Catholic rite, Utraquism maintained itself in Bohemia until 1629 (Edict of Restitution).

5. Luther originally rejected the Utraquist doctrine, but soon had harsh things to say of the Church for withholding Communion under both kinds ("De captivitate babylonica", *Weimarer Ausgabe,* VI, 501ff.), and in the end that form of Communion became one of the main demands of the Reformers. Recognizing that the question was one of discipline, not dogma, many Catholics at the Diet of Augsburg (1530) advocated admitting the laity to the chalice. Cardinal Cajetan de Vio himself argued in that sense in his report to Clement VII. In Germany the conciliatory Erasmian theologians (von Pflug, Witzel, and also Cochlaeus) and many princes (Bavaria, Austria, Jülich-Cleves) were ardent supporters of Communion under both kinds, which they considered an important defence against the innovators. By the Augsburg Interim of 1548 Charles V admitted German Protestants to the chalice "until the Council decides the matter", which only happened at Trent in the 22nd Session (September 1562).

6. The Council of Constance (*D* 626) having repudiated the Hussite heresy, the Fathers of Trent expressly declared:

a) There is not strict divine commandment for all to receive Communion *sub utraque specie;* besides Jn 6:53f. there are Jn 6:51 and 58, which speak only of receiving the bread; the twofold command is a case of pleonasm, designed to ensure a realist as against a merely allegorical interpretation. As for Mt 26:27 and Lk 22:17ff., they are directly addressed to the apostles alone, and mean that *communio sub utraque* on the part of the *celebrant* is always essential to the Eucharist. Nor does 1 Cor 11:28 say there is a strict divine commandment for all to communicate under both kinds; it is a testimony which is to be read in the light of the other traditions, as already discussed.

b) So long as the substance of the sacraments is safeguarded, it is a matter of Church discipline to determine how they shall be administered.

c) Christ is received whole and entire even under one kind; one who thus communicates receives the complete sacrament and is cheated of no grace necessary for salvation.

Theologians have asked whether *communio sub utraque specie* confers more or specifically different graces than *communio sub una specie*. Soto, Bellarmine, and Suárez answer that the sacrament bestows one and the same Lord whole and entire, and therefore one and the same grace, whether under one kind or both. Others lay more stress on the symbolic character of the species and speak of a two-fold grace imparted by the sacrament received *sub utraque*. The Council of Trent said nothing as to this point. It left the Pope to decide whether laymen should be admitted to the chalice, and in fact on 16 May 1564 Pius IV granted the metropolitan Archbishops of Mainz, Cologne, Trier, Salzburg, and Glan a special indult for Communion *sub utraque* because of the diaspora character of their dioceses. But it now emerged that the Catholic movement in favour of the chalice was a thing of the past. Communion under both kinds, having become the hall-mark of Protestantism, was rejected by the Catholic population (in Bavaria and the lower Rhineland). Albrecht V, Duke of Bavaria, withdrew permission for it in 1571 and in 1584 Gregory XIII suspended the papal indult. In 1604 and 1621 Rome once more directly forbade Communion under both kinds in Hungary and Bohemia.

7. Only with the recent liturgical movement has the question arisen once more. A deeper conception of the sacraments and a better insight into dogma and exegesis, which preclude any risk of heretical misinterpretation, besides an ecumenical spirit transcending the rigid outlook of the Counter-Reformation and anxious to meet Orthodox and Protestants half-way, have set the problem in a new light. Thus the Second Vatican Council's Constitution on the Sacred Liturgy says (art. 55): "Without prejudice to the dogmatic principles laid down by the Council of Trent, the bishops, in cases to be specified by the Apostolic See, may allow clerics, religious, and laypeople to communicate under both kinds . . ." The rite for concelebration and Communion under both kinds, of 7 March 1965, states that the latter can be administered in nuptial Masses at the request of bride and groom. But the Council has not introduced

the practice generally. With all due regard for Communion under both kinds, we must not overvalue it.

See also *Eucharist, Liturgical Movement.*

BIBLIOGRAPHY. J. B. Bossuet, *Traité de la communion sous les deux espèces* (1682); J. Hoffmann, *Geschichte der Laienkommunion* (1891); E. Dublanchy, "Communion eucharistique (sous les deux espèces)", *DTC,* III (1908), cols. 552–72; G. Constant, *Concession à l'Allemagne de la communion sous les deux espèces par Pie IV,* 2 vols. (1922–26); M. Andrieu, *Immixtio et consecratio* (1924); J. Jungmann, *Mass of the Roman Rite, its Origins and Development,* II (1952).

August Franzen

COMMUNISM

1. *Notion.* Communism today — we disregard its older sense — means three things: the philosophical and political theory of the revolutionary workers' movement, this revolutionary (Communist) movement itself, and the (future) society which is the movement's ultimate goal. There have been many ideals of the Communist society in Asian and Western history. They allowed no private property (sometimes not even the private marriage-bond) and had a political organization regarded as ideal, often (as in Thomas More, Campanella and Bacon) based on the rule of an intellectual and moral élite. But whereas these older visions of the future were chiefly meant as critiques of contemporary conditions, Karl Marx believed he had found the way which was sure to bring about the desirable future. He wished to supplant an utopian by a scientific Socialism, comprising a theory of history (historical materialism) and a "critique of political economy" which applied the historical theory to contemporary and prospective developments.

As early as 1848 Marx deliberately used the term "Communist" to describe the manifesto of the revolutionary workers' movement drawn up by himself and Engels. At that time the word "Socialist" meant "bourgeois" and "petty bourgeois" theories and groups of social reformers which contemplated no basic change in the system of ownership. Nonetheless, the revolutionary workers' parties throughout Europe called themselves Socialist or Social Democrat, and it was only after the October Revolution that the Russian Social Democratic Labour Party (Bolsheviks) adopted the name of the Communist Party, to distinguish itself from the parties of the Second International which had betrayed the "principles of internationalism" at the outbreak of war in 1914 and made no effort to stop the conflict. Everywhere extremist revolutionary Communist parties were founded, on the Russian model, demanding the abolition of private ownership of the means of production (land, mineral resources, factories, transport, banks, and so forth). Their outlook was internationalist.

When the European revolution, which Lenin still hoped for in 1923, failed to materialize, and Stalin decreed the "building of Socialism in one country", this internationalism came to mean subordination of Communist parties throughout the world to the interests of the Soviet Union, eulogized as "the vanguard of the world revolutionary movement", the "homeland of all workers". This political change, which manifested itself at the congresses of the "Communist International" (Comintern) during the 1920's, led to splinter movements in many countries. These either expressed the national point of view of the country concerned or "loyalty to internationalism, betrayed" by Stalin's Soviet party (Leon Trotsky).

2. *The Communist movement and its theory.* In order to understand the revolutionary Communist movement and its theory we must examine the historical growth of democracy and industrial society in Russia and other backward agrarian countries. Whereas in the Western democracies the working-class was gradually integrated into society and given the political and social rights of citizens, so that the workers' parties increasingly accepted gradual reforms and finally became nation-wide, the ruling minorities in States like Tsarist Russia clung to their privileges, forcing all democratic and socialist movements to the fringes of society. The "Social Democratic Labour Party", led by an intelligentsia with lofty ideals, was soon committed to radical revolution and internationalism by the efforts of G. V. Plechanov and V. I. Lenin (Ulyanov).

Defeat at the hands of the Japanese (1905) revealed the internal weakness of Tsarist Russia, which tried to be an imperialist great power on an altogether inadequate economic and industrial basis. The new burdens brought by the First World War were too much for the country, and the peasant masses on whom they chiefly bore began to revolt. Trotsky and Lenin were able to mobilize the growing discontent of the army, the peasants, and the industrial workers, who had multiplied rapidly during the War and were strongly concentrated in a few centres. The feeble middle-class parties who had come to power in February 1917 were unable to resist their assault.

In Communist theory as outlined by Lenin and made a dogma by Stalin, the October Revolution in Russia was not only a special form of "proletarian" revolution but an application of Marxist theory as taken further by Lenin. Leninism is still said to be 20th-century Marxism. In support of this view Lenin appealed mainly to the theory of imperialism, according to which in this "most advanced stage of capitalism" the unequal development of different countries, and the existence of an aristocracy of labour, in industrial States, sharing the profits of colonialism, makes socialist revolution break out on the periphery of the capitalist world. No longer is it the highly industrialized countries which, as Marx taught, lead the way to revolution, but relatively backward countries like Russia. Lenin also pointed to a connection between the Marxist workers' revolution and the "movement for national liberation" in the countries of Asia (as well as Africa and Latin America). He saw Russia as the bridge between the European proletarian revolution and the "Asian revolution which would decide the world's destiny". But at all events Lenin never doubted that after a successful revolution in an advanced Western State the working class (and party) of that State would take over leadership of the world revolutionary movement. It was only when revolution in the West had obviously proved a complete failure that Stalin produced the doctrine of "building Socialism in one country".

3. *The Communist Party.* The special role of the Communist movement in backward (under-industrialized) countries was reflected in the special form the Party assumed there. Whereas Marxists in Central and Western Europe held that the Social Democratic Party should provide the working class with leadership, vindicating the real interests of that class — whether by revolutionary or evolutionary means — in Russia (and later

in China), the Communist Party (or rather its predecessor, the Bolshevik section of the Russian Social Democratic Labour Party) was founded before an industrial proletariat of any strength existed. In both cases the Party began as a rigidly disciplined group of intellectuals and organizers, mostly of middle-class or lower middle-class background, who had espoused the "cause of the working class". In reality the Russian Social Democrats depended at least as much on the discontented peasant masses as they did on the small but highly concentrated industrial proletariat, easy to push to revolution. Before the Communists in China became a real revolutionary peasant party, they suffered a crushing defeat in the towns. Given the lack of spontaneous, broadly based organization among the peasantry and the patchwork "masses" that had to be led and, as Lenin said, imbued with revolutionary class-consciousness from without, the Party organization set itself above the people, claiming to represent their true interests. Such being the circumstances, the brilliant strategist and tactician of revolution, V. I. Lenin, demanded the utmost discipline, centralization, striking-power, and cohesion of the Party cadres, which he liked to call the "general staff" of the army he had created for civil war.

If Soviet society became a totalitarian dictatorship, it was largely because this type of organization, justified by the situation in Tsarist Russia, was retained after the revolution had triumphed, although the lack of any firm democratic, libertarian tradition and the inevitable consequences of a centralizing, planned economy were contributory factors. Thus, contrary to the expectations of Marx and Engels, an antinomy grew up between real democracy and Socialist society. Whereas once Marxists — down to Plechanov, Lenin's teacher — had assumed that the proletarian, Socialist revolution would be achieved by the working class in a highly industrialized country (indeed in several highly industrialized countries at once), independent Communist revolutions during the 20th century have been successful only in backward agrarian countries (Russia, Yugoslavia, China, Cuba).

These countries then set themselves what for Marx would be the highly paradoxical task of "catching up with and overtaking the capitalist countries". Historical develop-

ments in the aforesaid countries (as well as in some Communist-occupied ones) can in fact be characterized as variants of capitalist industrialization on a basis of national Communism; and they produce types of friction different from but no less serious than those produced by the capitalist development of industrial society. If the troubles of the liberal economy were mainly impoverishment and mass unemployment due to recurrent economic crises, the troubles of Communist industrialization are of a more political nature. Lack of economic compulsion is made up for by political coercion of various sorts (including physical terror, labour camps, and so forth). Revisionist Communists (including most Yugoslav Communists), however, reject the argument that economic backwardness justifies restriction of freedom. At any rate as Communist countries reach the more advanced stages of industrialization their bureaucratic rulers are forced to modify the pressures of the police-State, offering the people "material inducements" to achieve greater things.

4. *The future Communist society*. Post-revolutionary society, according to Marxist-Leninist doctrine, passes through two stages. The first, lower stage is "Socialist". All important means of production are given over to common ownership (the State or trade unions), but distribution is still governed by the "bourgeois" principle of formal equality: equal pay for equal work (unequal pay for unequal work). At this stage, therefore, a public authority (State) is still necessary to ensure formal equality and material inequality in the distribution of goods. Coercion cannot be done away with as yet: "Whoever will not work shall not eat" (Soviet Constitution). Only at a more advanced stage, when all the "well-springs of social wealth are flowing", can the distribution of goods on the basis of formal justice be abandoned and the needs of all be freely and completely satisfied. Then each man will receive according to his (specific, individual) needs without regard to the amount of work he does or its quality. The work still socially necessary will then be done voluntarily and gladly by all the members of society. Coercion by the State will be unnecessary, either to ensure material inequality in the distribution of goods or to make people work. The State "withers away".

Only in the past ten years has there again been discussion in the Soviet Union of what is actually necessary for the transition to Communism. True, Stalin indicated his own views on the subject in his last book, calling in particular for nationalization of the trade-union sectors of the economy. Here Yugoslav Communist theory contradicts Stalinist theory: it holds that trade union ownership, something tangible for the individual worker, is "superior" to State or national ownership; hence nationalization can never be regarded as a further stage. During the Khruschev era much was heard of the thesis that the Party has an increasing part to play as the Communist age draws near, and his successors have not repudiated it. Here again the Yugoslav Communists dissent: they hold that the Party must wither away along with the State so that society may directly govern itself.

Opinions are as divided about the political shape of the future Communist society as about its social order and the role of ideology. According to Marx the political order would wither away altogether, yielding to a self-administration of society without rulers; the social order would consist in perfect harmony between individual interests and the interests of the community; and there would be no need at all of an ideology to justify political and social conditions. On each of these points Soviet ideology has corrected and revised Marx's view: The Party must be preserved to rule and educate society; harmony of interests will not come about spontaneously (because of the property system) but through intensive education and an ideology which will dominate all minds. A Soviet theoretician of Communism writes that only a person wholly penetrated by the Marxist-Leninist Party's dialectical materialism gives any assurance that he will not "turn criminal".

5. *Evaluation and criticism*. Communist doctrine can be considered to have been empirically refuted by the fate it has undergone in the Soviet Union (and China). The lofty predictions of Marx and Engels have proved false. Instead of complete emancipation, a new and more rigorous type of coercion has come about; instead of equality, a new inequality; instead of deliverance from ideology and "conquest of religion", the rule of a philosophy that is in many ways a counterfeit religion.

These characteristics of the "Socialist society", which the Communists have built up, discredit their criticism — fair in itself — of many features of capitalist industrial society. Open-minded revisionist Communists, however, do not admit that facts have refuted theory. They explain that Marx expected revolutionary upheaval in a highly industrialized, capitalist society which had neither to achieve rapid economic expansion nor to defend, itself against powerful capitalist neighbour-States. If we take this point seriously, it can only mean that no one has yet shown the Communist goal to be attainable and that neither the Soviet Union nor any other "Socialist State" is entitled to be recognized as "Socialist". Marxist-Leninists generally respond to the objection that the individual needs private property for his own proper development and that even in Russia the peasants were not willing to surrender their property freely, with their theory of the "petty bourgeois". The petty bourgeois, they say, leads a typically intermediate sort of existence, sharing manual labour with the proletariat and property (and the possessive instinct) with the bourgeoisie. But only the characteristic which the petty bourgeois share with the proletariat is forward-looking, so that the Party must orientate them (and small farmers) in a progressive direction by appropriate controls and education. Fifty years after the Revolution all traces of attachment to or desire for private property are still described as petty bourgeois survivals in the consciousness of Soviet citizens.

But this argument is convincing only if one accepts its unproved premises. Moreover, Marx himself pointed out the great importance of private property (especially the ownership of land) in fostering an independent mind, and explained the existence of Asiatic despotisms by the fact that they allowed no (or at least no secure) private ownership of land, as well as by the technical necessity for vast irrigation (cf. Wittfogel, *Der orientalische Despotismus*). But these necessary objections by no means imply that arbitrary private control of huge properties on whose right use the weal or woe of many families and even of entire States depends, should go uncriticized and uncontrolled. Now that the great expectations Communists everywhere had of the abolition of private ownership of the means of production have been shattered, most of them recognize that the main problem is to ensure effective control of the means of production and their extensive use for the good of all — a problem which has not been satisfactorily solved by any of the economic systems we have known.

See also *Social Movement* I, II, *Marxism*.

BIBLIOGRAPHY. M. Dobb, *Soviet Economic Development Since 1917* (2nd ed., 1951); H. Marcuse, *Soviet Marxism* (1958); B. Moore, *Soviet Politics, the Dilemma of Power. The Role of Ideas in Social Change* (1959); G. Wetter, *Dialectical Materialism* (1959); L. Trotsky, *Terrorism and Communism* (1961); F. Borkenau, *World Communism* (1962); J. M. Bocheński and G. Niemeyer, *Handbook on Communism* (1962); A. B. Ulam, *The New Face of Soviet Totalitarianism* (1963); I. Fetscher, *Von Marx zur Sowjetideologie* (9th ed., 1963).

Irving Fetscher

CONCEPT

A concept is the representation of an object (a thing or a state of things) in a general way. The general character is not due to a certain obscurity and vagueness, as in "general" sensible representations. It is due to the drawing out (abstraction) by the intellect of something that is common as such to several objects — a "whatness" or essence about the existence of which no affirmation at all is immediately made. Abstraction takes place in the "light" of the "active" intellect *(intellectus agens)* which manifests the intelligible element in the sensible thing present.

Thus the concept lies between the simple apprehension of sensible intuition, and the purely intellectual intuition: its sign in speech is the word. While it does not yet *affirm* any reality, like the proposition or judgment, its object is not just the representation as such, its content. It "means" the transcendent object itself which is independent of consciousness. In this sense the concept (*conceptus*, from *concipere*, to receive) is *intentio* (meaning), something with an aim or purpose.

As a mental, abstract intention, however, the concept does not point to its object without qualification. It always envisages it under a particular aspect (the formal object, in contrast to the material object, the object as such). The poorer and more "abstract" this characteristic is, the more objects there are in which it can be found.

Thus the intension or content of a concept is in inverse proportion to its extension or application. The limit case on one side is the concept of the individual, on the other the notion of being: neither of them concepts in the ordinary sense, but only in a special way (as "names" or "presentiments") since the former signifies nothing universal, the latter no content which could be defined by anything other than itself.

The characteristic intended in the objects in view may be verified in them in the same or in an (essentially) different way. Then we have the distinction between univocal and analogical concepts. A fully uniform or univocal application can only be had by a higher degree of abstraction: by reflecting on the concept as such. The last stage of the reflection which aims at univocal expression is the definition, which determines the concept by setting out its characteristics. (Hence an immediate concept can only be described, but not really defined). But when we are dealing with the concrete reality, not only is the universal present in each object in its own way: the concept too is always determined in its actual formation by its context and immediate use. Here we must first remember the classical doctrine of "supposition". The concept is used in various ways — more or less absolutely, as when we say "man is a rational being", or collectively, as when we say "man peoples the earth", or distributively, as in "(every) man is a liar" (Ps 116:11). And then we must note that even prior to such ways of "supposing for" something, the concept — in any one application — already "lives" by the totality of what is meant in each case, whence it derives its own proper meaning in every judgment, and is coloured to some extent by the other members and elements of the synthesis.

Thus a static consideration sees the concept as the simplest form and hence the primary element of thought, out of which grows the judgment and finally the conclusion. But in a dynamic perspective, the total act of knowledge in the judgment is basic, and it is only as a moment of this knowledge that the concept is comprehensible and its relationship to reality (its finality or direction) understandable. This shows how one-sided are nominalism and conceptualism, as are intuitionism and anti-intellectual life-philosophies, which all treat the concept as a mere label without true value in the order of knowledge. At the same time it helps to avoid the exaggerations of rationalism and absolutist *a priori* systems, which make the concept and the process of discursive thought which forms it the whole or at least the essential element of the life of the spirit.

Concepts without intuition are in fact empty, just as — for man — intuitions without concepts are blind (Kant). If then the concept constitutes the dignity of human intuition and enables man to keep his distance and independence in face of the multiplicity of the world which presses in upon him, it also shows how limited is its grasp of reality. Even while it grasps the spiritual and suprasensible, it remains bound to sense-perception, to space and time.

This brings us to a second meaning of "analogous". It means a concept not as contrasted with a univocal but with a proper concept. The latter arises from intuition and reflects the positive conceptual content of what is known. The analogous concept, however, speaks of the metempirical reality merely on the basis of things experienced which are not perfectly similar to the metempirical reality. In this way the element common to both can be positively expressed. But the proper mode in which this common element exists there can only be designated through the negation of its form of existence as known within the world. Thus, for instance, we possess no proper concept of God, but only an analogous one, though this concept, in terms of the first distinction made above, is by no means equivocal, but a quite definite one. The same use of non-proper concepts is found in dogma to express revelation. The imperfection which the abstract nature of the concept involves from the start becomes qualitatively greater here and thus becomes one of the factors which give rise to the development of dogma.

But the analogous nature of the concept, in the first sense, may now also be seen in a new light. We have already spoken of the concrete analogy of every concept as it is actually formed. We must now note in particular its historical and "epochal" variability, which stems from the fact that the horizon of experience in each case is caught up in the movement of history. (It is only the most formal and abstract concept of the "State", for instance, that remains the same when applied to the city-state of the Greeks,

the medieval empire, the modern nation and the vast organizations of the dawning future.) It is not just a matter of a uniform development and enrichment of the content. It also means a change in the way of conceiving things, which disregards certain elements, just as it also brings new insights.

A rationalism which ignores the historical factor is at fault here as much as relativism and historicism. The first misses the far-reaching difference (which is not just something "accidental", which can be clearly distinguished from the permanent, unchanging content), the others fail to recognize the continuity throughout change which knowledge and intellection make possible in spite of the limiting factors of time and culture. Something similar occurs here as in the relationship between concept and word: the word is not simply an interchangeable shell, which brings with it exactly the same content from one language to another. The key-word for the task thus set, which has only recently come to be recognized as explicitly as it is today, is hermeneutics; and the problem which is decisive in this context is called "the hermeneutic circle". This means that a concept can only be grasped in the light of the total act of knowledge and verbal expression of which it is an element; but this act again can only be known by means of the concept which it involves. The solution of the problem — already solved and always still to be solved because endless — as it is presented by the perceptive spirit, is the theme of the metaphysics of knowledge.

See also *Idea, Nominalism, Rationalism, Transcendental Philosophy, Historicism, Hermeneutics.*

BIBLIOGRAPHY. E. Husserl, *Ideas. General Introduction to Pure Phenomenology* (1931); J. B. Lotz, *Das Urteil und das Sein* (2nd ed., 1957); G. Siewerth, *Das Sein und die Abstraktion* (1958); J. Stenzel, *Sinn, Bedeutung, Begriff, Definition* (1958); G. Frege, *Funktion, Begriff, Bedeutung* (1962); M. Heidegger, *Being and Time* (1962); J. de Vries, *Logica* (2nd ed., 1962); H. Krings, *Transzendentale Logik* (1964); K. Rahner, *Geist in Welt* (3rd ed., 1964).

Jörg Splett

CONCILIARISM

Conciliarism, or the conciliar theory, which was developed in the 14th century and applied to the so-called reform councils of the 15th century, teaches that an ecumenical council is superior to the Pope.

1. Conciliarism was not originally and exclusively the creation of Marsilius of Padua and William of Occam, as has often been supposed.

It had its roots in the discussions on the Church by canonists of the 12th and 13th centuries, resulting from efforts to set juridical limitations to the power of the papacy. According to Huguccio and others, the Pope can fall into error, but not the *Ecclesia Romana,* which many already identified with the *Ecclesia Universalis.* Because a general council was conceived as a "representation" of the whole Church, it followed that a council, together with the Pope, *maior est papa* (Johannes Teutonicus [Zemeckel]), not only in matters of faith, but also whenever the *generalis status Ecclesiae* is endangered; the opinion, common later during the Western Schism, is already found in the *Summa* of Rufinus that a schism, if it persists, inevitably becomes a heresy (*sine comite heresis non permanet*).

Though the discussion was concerned only with possible eventualities, still the corporate theory (head and members as an organic unity and joint bearers of authority) lays the foundation for Conciliarism. It was first developed with reference to local Churches, and then used by Henry of Segusia to provide a basis for the co-regency of the college of cardinals. Finally, in conjunction with the representation theory, it was applied by John (Quidort) of Paris to the whole Church: the Pope is the delegate of the whole Church, which, through designation by the cardinals, entrusts to him its powers and rights. If these are misused they can be revoked, and then the cardinalate or a general council represents the whole Church.

The idea of appealing to a general council against real or alleged abuse of papal power underlay the appeals of Frederick II against Gregory IX, of the Colonnas against Boniface VIII, and of Louis of Bavaria against John XXII. Durandus the Younger of Mende, thinking of a return to the ancient Christian synodal practice, recommended the periodic convocation of general councils. But it was Marsilius of Padua's *Defensor Pacis,* with its rejection of the divine institution of the papal primacy, hitherto never challenged, together with his concept of Church, that gave Conciliarism a revolutionary basis: "ad solum generale concilium fidelium omnium vel eorum, qui omnium fidelium auctoritatem habuerint, determinacionem hanc (i.e., of disputed matters of faith) tantummodo pertinere" (II, 18, 8). Civil authority has the right to summon the participants ("vicem universitatis fidelium repraesentantes", II, 20, 2).

The teaching of Marsilius was immediately condemned, but was maintained in William of Occam's *Dialogus,* though it was not used by Conrad of Gelnhausen and Heinrich Heinbuche of Langenstein to support their suggestion of a council to solve the Western Schism, shortly after its outbreak; only later did it gain ground, when, having been recommended by numerous writers (e.g., Dietrich of Niem), Church unity was pursued by a general council, first unsuccessfully at Pisa, and then successfully at Constance.

2. The decrees *Haec Sancta* (Session V) and *Frequens* (Session XXXIX) of the Council of Constance are considered the classical formulations of Conciliarism. But the first decree, carried through chiefly by the efforts of John Gerson, who strongly emphasized the role of *epikeia* in an emergency, was primarily meant to save the Council of Constance from dissolution after John XXII had fled: it subordinated the three quarrelling Popes to the authority of the assembled council ("Haec sancta synodus Constantiensis . . . ecclesiam catholicam repraesentans, potestatem a Christo immediate habet, cui quilibet, cuiuscumque status vel dignitatis, etiamsi papalis existat, obedire tenetur in his, quae pertinent ad fidem et exstirpationem dicti schismatis et generalem reformationem ecclesiae Dei in capite et in membris"). Although the decree demanded obedience not only to the directives of the Council of Constance, but to those *cuiuscumque alterius concilii legitime congregati,* still its primary concern was the ending of the schism. If Church reform is one of the motives behind this decree, it becomes predominant in the second, which in view of the imminent papal election stipulated periodic general councils as a counter-balance to papal absolutism and a guarantee of Church reform.

The affirmation of the superiority of council over Pope was reiterated at Basle, where it was clearly interpreted as a matter of faith. The decree was indirectly affected by the prohibition of Martin V, repeated by Pius II, Sixtus IV and Julius II, of appeals from the Pope to the council. But even during Eugene IV's conflict with the Council of Basle it was not directly abrogated.

In moulding public opinion conciliarists like Nicolas of Tudeschis were as effective as papalists. Martin V and Eugene IV felt themselves bound by the decree *Frequens;* its non-observance by their successors gave rise to a constant sense of grievance, which signalled the persistence of Conciliarism. Often in a milder form, the doctrine was maintained by universities (Paris, Vienna) and by ecclesiastical writers (G. Gozzadini, M. Ugoni). In politics, it took the practical form of the threat of calling a council (Louis XI of France). It finally bore fruit in the anti-papal *conciliabulum* of Pisa (1511), and was a grave obstacle to the convocation of the Council of Trent, where the discussions about *universalem ecclesiam repraesentans* and the attitude of the Gallicans during the great conciliar crisis of 1562–63 testified to its continued existence. The declaration of Gallican freedoms in 1682 re-affirmed in Thesis 2 the decree *Haec Sancta* of Constance.

Although not all difficulties with regard to the authority of the decrees of Constance have been resolved, it is clear that they must not be detached from their historical context. The historical occasion — the Great Schism — explains how Pope and council could be counter-poised as two separate entities, whereas Vatican II's Constitution on the Church teaches that the Pope as member and head of the college of bishops forms with it at all times an organic unity, especially when the college is assembled in a general council.

See also *Gallicanism, Bishop, Cardinal, Reform* I, *Schism* IV.

BIBLIOGRAPHY. F. Bliemetzrieder, *Das Generalkonzil im grossen abendländischen Schisma* (1904); H. Heimpel, *Dietrich von Niem* (1932); V. Martin, "Comment s'est formée la doctrine de la supériorité du concile sur le pape", *RSR* 17 (1937), pp. 121–43, 261–89, 404–27; C. Hofmann, *Papato, Conciliarismo, Patriarcato* (1940); J. Leclercq, *Jean de Paris et l'ecclésiologie du XIIIe siècle* (1942); J. Klotzner, *Kard. D. Jacobazzi und sein Konzilswerk. Ein Beitrag zur Geschichte der konziliaren Idee* (1948); B. Tierney, *Foundations of the Conciliar Theory* (1955); H. Jedin, *A History of the Council of Trent,* I (1957), pp. 5–61; B. Tierney, "Pope and Council", *Medieval Studies* 19 (1957), pp. 197–218; H. Jedin, *Bischöfliches Konzil oder Kirchenparlament? Ein Beitrag zur Ekklesiologie der Konzilien von Konstanz und Basel* (1963); K. W. Nörr, *Kirche und Konzil bei Nicolaus de Tudeschis* (1964); H. Küng, *Structures of the Church* (1965); P. De Vooght, *Les pouvoirs du concile et l'autorité du pape au concile de Constance* (1965).

Hubert Jedin

CONCUPISCENCE

Concupiscence is a fundamental element of Christian anthropology. This anthropology understands man as a being of finite resources orientated to the infinite, and hence intrinsically affected by an element of resistance and tension (between essence and existence, nature and person). Christian anthropology also sees in man a more profound division resulting from sin (original and actual). The fact of such a division is so obvious and familiar to human experience that it has found a place even in the most diverse philosophies (e.g., in Marxism and existentialism), although its nature and origin are interpreted very differently. But the Christian understanding of concupiscence is not to be deduced from a purely metaphysical concept of man, but from the history of God's involvement with mankind.

In the OT, in passages propounding man's consciousness of sin, a power impelling men to evil is spoken of. It is viewed as an inherent desire which is not itself formally a sin, but which incites man to oppose God (Gen 8:21; Jer 17:9). In the Wisdom literature this thought is further developed as the notion of the "evil urge" (cf. Ecclus 15:14), which then takes on a demonic aspect in rabbinical writings. This evil inclination, not yet deduced from a sin affecting all mankind, is not part of the bodily and sensible nature of man as such, but affects the whole man, in keeping with the Hebrew notion of the unity of man.

So too the NT does not oppose the desires of the flesh and the spirit. Even if Paul occasionally uses a dualistic expression reminiscent of Hellenism, the lust (ἐπιθυμία) of the "flesh" (σάρξ) remains for him an expression of the self-assertion of the whole man against the salvific power of the πνεῦμα (of God). Thus unduly pessimistic views of the body and the senses are avoided, though it is not denied that evil desire can manifest itself especially in man's sensual life (Gal 5:19 ff.; Eph 2:3). When the whole man in his earthly constitution appears as the source of concupiscence, it is in fact a more powerful force than if it were restricted to the area of the sensible. With such emphasis laid on concupiscence as a force hostile to God, the thought of its "naturalness" and of its possibly positive function in the attainment of human salvation was bound to be lost sight of. But the recognition that concupiscence is present even in the redeemed (Rom 7:5; 8:8; 13:14; Gal 5:24), and its link with the sin of Adam in the history of salvation, would eventually raise the question of the relationship of concupiscence to human nature as such and of its concrete manifestations.

Under the influence of Stoic psychology and Platonic dualism, the biblical view of man as a total unity was coloured in patristic thought by an unduly negative attitude to the bodily and sensible aspect of man (though Augustine, for instance, was aware of man as a unity when he characterized *cupiditas* as the selfish striving of the spirit for that which is not God, an interpretation that was to survive into the Middle Ages [Bernard of Clairvaux]). The question was kept alive among the Fathers insofar as the immunity from concupiscence postulated for the original state of man was always considered a preternatural gift of grace and concupiscence was accordingly considered a natural consequence of man's being, which would have obtained in the theoretically possible *status naturae purae*. Yet against Pelagianism it was maintained that concupiscence is not a *vigor naturae,* but a defect of nature.

When the Council of Trent, in apparent contradiction to this "natural" interpretation, declares that concupiscence "comes from sin and induces to sin" (*D* 792), the assertion is made in the perspective of the history of salvation and sees the concrete form and the actual intensity of concupiscence in strict dependence on sin. But because even here, in its clearest expression as a factor in the economy of redemption, concupiscence presupposes a natural condition, it remains possible to maintain its natural structure and at the same time to attribute to it a sort of ethical ambivalence. This leaves room for a positive evaluation of the spontaneous movements of passion and a general rehabilitation of human "sensuality". Nonetheless, the "naturalness" of concupiscence is only

its formal and structural component. The material reality of it comes from the tendencies released by sin.

This reality can only be properly grasped when concupiscence is seen as the dynamism of man's self-assertion against the supernatural. Only thus is concupiscence revealed as it is in the present economy of salvation. It is the rebelliousness of man under sin against his "supernatural" orientation and his infinite destiny. It is then a negative "existential" which prevents man's self-realization in terms of his natural-supernatural fulfilment.

The comprehensiveness of concupiscence which stems from the revolt against the supernatural order has also natural consequences which display the negative character of concupiscence in the whole field of human nature, and not just in sensuality. For when an existence orientated to a supernatural end opposes this tendency and tries to be self-contained, it is frustrated of its ultimate fulfilment and concupiscence has destructive effects in the natural order of the whole human being. This enables us to see concupiscence as a naturally destructive tendency. It is a negative dynamism opposed to each individual goal of human fulfilment. It can appear, for instance, as the will to self-preservation raised to the status of an absolute, or again, as the will to regression, the self-destructive death-wish, various forms of addiction.

But the power of its destructive tendency must not be exaggerated either in the natural or supernatural order. It must always be remembered that concupiscence is not evil in itself (Rom 7:8; *D* 792) and that the sin from which it stems has not corrupted nature intrinsically. As regards its negative dynamism in the supernatural sense, it must be remembered that this is kept in check by an opposing force, the *desiderium naturale,* which includes the permanent affinity of the finite spirit with regard to the absolute God, and of the human will with regard to the absolute good. This confrontation imposes in practice a limit on the concupiscence of man. Hence it cannot be treated as a fixed, objective entity. It is a fluctuating movement which is constantly being thwarted and moderated by the tendency of the will to the good and the realization of this tendency through grace.

This also enables us to see the positive

significance of concupiscence in man's struggle. It offers him the possibility of being conformed to the sufferings of Christ and thus of sharing in the redemption. In the light of the history of salvation, this means that we must strive to overcome concupiscence by progressively integrating it into the ethical order sustained by grace. But it must not be imagined that such an integration can be an evolutionary process within this world. This conquest is not a goal to be attained in this world. The goal can only be attained by the passage through death.

See also *Man* II, III, *Judaism* III, *Pelagianism, Existence* III B, *Grace, Good, Death.*

BIBLIOGRAPHY. J. Fuchs, *Die Sexualethik des heiligen Thomas von Aquin* (1949); C. Bouyer, "La concupiscence est-elle impossible dans un état d'innocence?", *Augustinus Magister,* II (1954), pp. 737–47; M. Müller, *Die Lehre des Augustinus von der Paradiesehe und ihre Auswirkung in der Sexualethik des 12. und 13. Jahrhunderts bis Thomas von Aquin* (1954); B. Stoeckle, *Die Lehre von der erbsündlichen Konkupiscenz in ihrer Bedeutung für das christliche Leibethos* (1954); W. van Roo, *Grace and Original Justice according to St. Thomas* (1955); J. Gross, *Entstehungsgeschichte des Erbsündendogmas,* 2 vols. (1960–63); K. Rahner, "The Theological Concept of Concupiscentia", *Theological Investigations,* I (1961), pp. 347–82; C. Journet, *The Meaning of Evil* (1963); A.-M. Dubarle, *Original Sin in Scripture* (1964); A. Vanneste, "Le décret du Concile de Trente sur le péché originel", *NRT* 86 (1964), pp. 355–68, 490–510; 87 (1965), pp. 688–724; 88 (1966), pp. 581–602; P. Grelot, "Réflexions sur le problème du péché originel", *NRT* 89 (1967), pp. 337–75, 449–84.
Leo Scheffczyk

CONFIRMATION

A. METHODOLOGY

Most studies of confirmation are unconvincing because the problems are envisaged in too narrow a perspective. Since the beginning of the Middle Ages the Scholastics sought, by an analysis of the fruits proper to this sacrament, to define its special nature, in contrast to baptism, or even the Eucharist, on account of Ps 103:3, "panis cor hominis *confirmat*". This method was based on "axioms" of a rather meagre sacramental theology. The sacraments were considered too exclusively as "instruments of grace", and not sufficiently as "mysteries of salvation in the Church". There was too much effort to differentiate the so-called "sacramental graces", with too little attention to the primordial source of all grace, sacramental or otherwise. But once one considers all grace as necessarily implied in the saving presence of the Trinity, as the reality of salvation coming from the Father, in the image of the Son and by the power of the perfecting Spirit, the proper efficacy of the sacraments in general, and of confirmation in particular, is seen to be inseparable from this loving activity of the three divine persons — insofar as it is visibly attested and sacramentally effected in the liturgical prayer of the Church, i.e., in the celebration of the mystery of salvation.

Further, a theology of confirmation must include the fact that confirmation, with baptism and the Eucharist, is one of the three sacraments of Christian initiation, which make up together the fullness of Christian life, by the consecration and mission which they confer. Hence the three sacraments, since they communicate the saving action of the Father in the Son through their Spirit, must necessarily be considered in their organic unity.

Finally, the NT and liturgical and theological tradition reveal a notable accord, too often neglected in technical discussion, with regard to the central fact that confirmation bestows on us above all the "gift of the Holy Spirit". This must guide our reflection above all else, but in the framework of a sacramental, ecclesial and trinitarian theology much broader than before.

B. DATA OF REVELATION

1. *Scripture.* It will not be enough, therefore, to study confirmation on the basis of the few texts of Acts which probably attest the existence of a still very rudimentary rite in apostolic times: prayer, imposition of hands and gift of the Holy Spirit, sometimes manifested by the charismatic character which it took on in the primitive Church (Acts 8:12–17; 19:1–7; Heb 6:2 is less certain). A biblical theology of confirmation must also envisage the salvific action of the Spirit as messianic gift (the OT doctrine), given by the risen Saviour (Jn 19:30), offered to the nascent Church as a body (Acts 2:1–47), to the nations universally (Acts 10; 11; 18 — the Pentecost of the

gentiles) and individually to each of the faithful (e.g., Acts 1:7–8, the general theme of Acts). We must go back with Scripture to the mystery of the incarnation as mission from the Father and prototype of our new life. It was in and by the power of the Spirit (cf. esp. Lk) that Christ was conceived by Mary, and consecrated prophet and Messiah when baptized by John. It was through the same Spirit that he preached, worked miracles, prayed and died (Heb 9:14). Finally, reflection on the rich data of the Bible (that is, theology stemming from the "economy" or dispensation) allows us to recognize the true nature of the Spirit and hence to understand better what the NT means when it says so often that the Spirit has been "given" us, that he is the great gift of the risen Lord.

Clearly, in the NT, the proper activity of the Spirit is to sustain the whole of Christian life from the birth of faith in the heart. I. de la Potterie has shown, after an ancient tradition, that the "anointing of the Christian" (2 Cor 1:21–22; cf. Eph 1:13) or the "chrism" (1 Jn 2:20, 27) was not ritual but spiritual, like the anointing of the prophets in the OT and the prophetic anointing of Christ (Lk 4:18; Acts 4:27; 10:38; Heb 1:9). Paul links it with the seal of baptism, while John sees its influence in the whole development of Christian life through the faith which precedes (1 Jn 5:6), accompanies (Jn 19:34–35) and follows (Jn 3:5) baptism. "This divine anointing signifies the action of God in arousing faith in the hearts of those who listen to the word of truth." (De la Potterie, p. 120.) This faith is "confirmed" by the Spirit. Incidentally, we may note that the notion of *gratia ad robur* is not wholly foreign to apostolic and sub-apostolic tradition, though it is not attributed exclusively to the Spirit (1 Cor 1:6–8; 2 Cor 1:21–22; Col 2:7; Phil 1:7; 1 Clem, 1, 2; Ignatius, *Magn.,* 13, 1; Polycarp, *Phil,* 1, 2). We must be reborn by the water of baptism, but we must also be born again through the Spirit, that is through faith in the word (Jn 3:5; 19:35; 1 Jn 5:6–8). This doctrine corresponds to the synoptic doctrine of the necessity of faith for salvation.

The Spirit is also the source of our charity (Rom 5:5; 1 Cor 13). He inspires our prayer (Rom 8:16; Gal 4:6). He is the source of the charisms (1 Cor 12:4–12), through which he "builds up" the Church (1 Cor 14:4, 12, 26) and consecrates it as the temple of God (1 Cor 3:16; Eph 2:22) in the "communion" (Eph 4:3; Phil 2:1). He is truly the soul of all Christian existence (Gal 5:25; 6:9; Rom 8:9, 13; Eph 4:30). Through faith he is already present at baptism (1 Cor 6:11; 2 Cor 1:22; Tit 3:5) and in the Eucharist (1 Cor 12:13), a tradition retained by the ancient Church in the practice of the epiclesis.

This doctrine of wide and varied perspectives allows the NT to distinguish baptism from confirmation. Baptism is linked only with salvation, the remission of sins, the new creation, entrance into the Church ("circumcision") and above all with belonging to Christ (εἰς τὸ ὄνομα). Confirmation is concerned only with the "gift of the Spirit" defined above all by the experience of the first Pentecost. But it would be wrong to make of them totally separate entities. For the primitive Church they form together one rite of initiation (Acts 10:44–48). Theologically they both derive from the initial mystery of the baptism of Christ in the Jordan (Jn 1:19–34). In any case, especially in Paul, Christian life is indissolubly one in Christ and in the Spirit.

2. *Liturgy.* a) *Confirmation as an integral part of the rite of initiation.* During the first eleven centuries, confirmation, along with baptism, is part of the solemn rite of initiation celebrated at the Easter and the Whit vigils. It is sometimes hard, and possibly incorrect, to allot to one sacrament or the other a given rite, such as the second anointing. The main rites of confirmation are the imposition of hands, with the epiclesis, the anointing and the sign of the cross on the forehead (an allusion to the "Tau" of Ezek 9:4).

The *Apostolic Tradition* of Hippolytus of Rome proves the importance of the imposition of hands in the Roman (and perhaps the Alexandrian) Church in the 3rd century. In the East, the imposition of hands is replaced about this time by the anointing with consecrated oil, the perfumed μύρον, except in Egypt. This also happened in northern Italy, Gaul and Ireland. The imposition of hands is rarely mentioned for Africa and Spain. When the Roman liturgy came into widespread use in Europe, in the era of the "sacramentaries" and the "ordines", Frankish influence seems to have been responsible in some places for the replacement of the imposition of hands by the anointing. In the 11th century, however, a temporary restoration of the ancient rite can be noted, in the form of the laying on of hands over a group or on each individual. The origin of the rite of anointing at confirmation is unknown, but no doubt the biblical texts cited above had something to do with it. The peoples of Europe perhaps found the laying on of hands less meaningful a symbol. In this context it should be noted that the anointing before baptism in the ancient Syrian Church, so close to Palestine, was not an exorcism. It seems to have been regarded as a consecration of the faith of the catechumen by the Spirit.

b) *Confirmation as a separate rite.* Towards the 11th century, confirmation takes on a liturgy of its own, especially in the West, where the bishop remains the ordinary minister. The multiplication of parishes makes it harder to link confirmation with baptism, especially in the case of children. Meanwhile, the anointing of the forehead with chrism is merged into one ritual gesture with the sign of the cross, sometimes combined with the laying on of hands (so in Alcuin, *D* 419, 450). In an effort to unify the liturgy, Innocent VIII in 1485 ordered the use of the Pontifical of Durandus of Mende (1293–95) which was already widespread. After the 1497 edition of this Pontifical the imposition of hands disappears completely, the Council of Florence having ratified the omission (*D* 697), as did the Tridentine reform. The rite of the "alapa", probably of Germanic origin, became general in the West. The imposition of hands at the anointing was re-introduced by Benedict XIV in 1752, in the appendix of his Pontifical. Leo XIII and the *editio typica* of the Pontifical of 1925 give the rite very clearly: "per manus impositionem cum unctione chrismatis in fronte" (cf. *CIC,* can. 780). The laying on of hands now seems to be considered as the principle rite (*AAS* 27 [1935], p. 16). Vatican II ordered the rite of confirmation to be revised so as to bring out its character of Christian initiation, and allowed its conferring during Mass (Constitution on the Sacred Liturgy, art. 71).

The dogmatic import of the liturgy is to be sought above all in the prayers, which according to St. Thomas and the whole medieval tradition are expressions of the faith of the Church. The ancient liturgy indicated the meaning of confirmation chiefly in the epiclesis. Is 11:2 is quoted from the earliest times. The East has preserved a formula of consecration from the 4th century: Σφραγίς δωρέας Πνεύματος 'Αγίου. 'Αμήν. Similar consecratory formulae were used for a time in the West. The one we now use came in about the 10th century: "Signo te signo crucis (the ancient *consignatio*) et confirmo te chrismate salutis in nomine Patris et Filii et Spiritus Sancti. Amen." Various prayers, some of them very ancient, expound the biblical doctrine of the gift of the Spirit.

3. *Doctrinal tradition.* We should not wish to maintain with G. Dix and L. Bouyer that Scholasticism was not in continuity with patristic theology, but it is undeniable that the theology of confirmation presents very different characteristics between one epoch and the other. There are various reasons for this. The Fathers generally give their doctrine during the great catechetical instructions in preparation for the Easter vigil, of which they spontaneously respect the liturgical unity. Their intentions are pastoral and devotional. The central truth that confirmation gives us the Spirit is enough for them, all the more so because their theology of the Trinity brings out more clearly the proprieties of the divine persons. The biblical texts which mention χρῖσμα or σφραγίς are used to elaborate by means of fertile allegories a wide-ranging doctrine of the presence and activity of the Spirit in the soul.

The early Scholastics seem to be at a loss when they find themselves confronted with confirmation as a separate sacrament. Their whole theology is an effort to define the sacramental grace proper to confirmation, in contrast to baptism and the Eucharist. The success of the pseudo-Melchiades tended to underline too strongly a secondary aspect of the ancient tradition, the famous *gratia ad robur.* But sometimes theologians resigned themselves to the simple *augmentum gratiae.* These are the two aspects, unfortunately, which were retained by Peter Lombard, the "Master of the Sentences" in his *IV Sent.,* d. 7.

But it would be incorrect and unjust to reduce scholastic theology to these meagre findings. The more spiritual tradition of the "fullness of the Spirit" (Is 11:2), preserved in any case in the liturgy, never ceased to be influential. The doctrine of the "character" allowed the great Scholastics to develop the ecclesial and cultic aspects of confirmation. The great patristic themes of the royal priesthood (1 Pet 2:5) and of the analogy between the anointing of Christ or the descent of the Spirit at Pentecost, and the anointing of the faithful at confirmation, too frequently omitted in technical theology, come constantly to the fore. This is particularly true of the last fifty years, sometimes, however, because of subsidiary preoccupations, such as Catholic Action or the emancipation of the laity.

4. *The magisterium*. a) *General doctrine*. The magisterium confirmed the theological teaching at the Council of Florence in the Decree for the Armenians (*D* 695, 697, a resumé of the *De Fide et Sacramentis* of St. Thomas) and at the Council of Trent (*D* 844, 852, 871 ff.). This is the doctrine summarized in *CIC*, can. 780–800. Confirmation is one of the seven sacraments (*D* 52 d, 98, 419, 424, 465, 669, 697, 871) and like baptism and orders imparts a sacramental character (*D* 695, 852, 960, 996).

b) *The minister*. In the East, the priest has been the ordinary minister since the 4th century, but the consecration of the μύρον was always reserved to the bishop, preferably to a patriarch. In the West, between the 4th and 8th centuries, delegation to a priest is envisaged in case of necessity or by special decree (*Mansi*, IV, 1002; IX, 856). The Roman Church always considered the bishop as the ordinary minister, and imposed this regulation first in the suburbicarian dioceses (Innocent I, *D* 98; Gregory I, *PL*, LXXVII, 677 and 696; Gelasius I, *PL*, LIX, 51), and then throughout the West, where the *False Decretals* also influenced events. The practice became so common, under the influence of the *Decretum* of Gratian and of Peter Lombard, that the question soon arose of the necessity of papal delegation if confirmation by a priest was to be licit or even valid. The bishop's privilege, confirmed by the Council of Florence (*D* 573, 697), was maintained by the Popes from the 13th century (apropos of the missions in Asia) till Pius XII, when the parish priest was delegated to confirm when there was danger of death (*AAS* 38 [1946], pp. 349–58).

After Trent, theologians even asked whether confirmation by a priest in the East was valid. It was thought to be invalid, especially in countries where papal delegation was not supposed to exist (*D* 1459, n. 2), as in the case of the "Greeks" of Italy (*D* 1086, n. 1; 1458). Benedict XIV recognized the validity of confirmation in the other Oriental jurisdictions "ob tacitum privilegium a Sede Apostolica illis concessum" (*De Syn. Disquis.*, VII, 9). This opinion then became common among theologians (cf. the preliminaries of Vatican I, *Mansi*, IL, 1115–27, 1162–65) and was ratified by Vatican II (Decree on Ecumenism, art. 16; Decree on Eastern Catholic Churches, art. 13). Vatican II gives priests of the Latin rite the privilege of confirming Christians of Oriental rites according to the norms of canon law (*ibid.*, art. 14; *CIC*, can. 782, par. 4; *S. C. pro Eccl. Orient.*, decree of 1 May 1948).

c) *The subject of confirmation* is any baptized Christian in the state of grace (*CIC*, can. 786). The most controversial pastoral question is the age of confirmation. There is no universal practice. In the East, baptism, confirmation and the Eucharist are given to the infant, the unity and structure of the rite of initiation being respected. In Spain, Portugal and their former colonies, confirmation is given a few years after baptism. It was sometimes postponed till the age of fifteen in the Middle Ages (*D* 437), and after the Council of Trent the usual age was from seven to eleven years. In some European countries, after the French Revolution, it was delayed till twelve, and then, after Pius X's decree in 1910 on first Communion about the age of seven, was combined with the so-called "solemn Communion". Rome made discreet efforts through various instructions of the Congregations to re-establish the ancient sequence of initiation, and put confirmation about the age of seven (*CIC*, can. 788).

The whole question is simply a pastoral one. It is important, no doubt, to restore the old order of initiation, and above all, to make the Eucharist the climax of initiation, with the people of God united around their Lord. But it is equally certain that there are grave pastoral reasons in some countries for confirming children only when they are about to become adults. Vatican II wisely refused to impose a uniform rule on all.

d) *The sacramental sign*. In the anointing, the Western Church uses chrism, made of olive oil and balsam (*D* 419, 450, 697, 872, 1458), while the Eastern mixes the μύρον sometimes with as many as forty aromatic substances. The chrism is consecrated only by the bishop (*D* 93*, 98, 450, 571, 697, 1088). We have already discussed the evolution of the rites of the imposition of hands (*D* 424, 1963) and of anointing (*D* 419, 450, 465, 697), as also of the sacramental words, in the East and in the West.

e) *The character and the special grace.* The magisterium has never stated the precise doctrine of the character. As regards the grace, the magisterium followed the fluctuations of the theologians. The Holy Spirit is given in confirmation (*D* 98, 450), which is a new Pentecost (*D* 697) and perfects baptism (*D* 52 d, 695). In the Middle Ages, the magisterium stressed more strongly the increase of grace, and the grace of fortitude (*D* 419, 695) to confess the faith (*D* 697). We may conclude that the magisterium leaves plenty of latitude to theologians as regards the theoretical interpretation of the essence of the sacrament.

C. Theology

1. *Fundamental positions.* We have already stated the fundamental aspects. Confirmation is the "gift of the Spirit" and hence a new Pentecost. As sacrament of consecration in Christian initiation it perfects baptism and is the normal preparation for the full ecclesial communion in the Eucharist. The theology of confirmation must justify and explain these three constitutive elements.

The Spirit revealed himself at Pentecost, when the Church was constituted in its primordial state, and hence as the model for future ages. In the Pentecostal experience, the Spirit made known the nature of his mission of salvation, as "promise of the Father" and "gift of Christ" crucified and risen from the dead; implicitly, the intratrinitarian propriety of his person was revealed. A divine person cannot be revealed in his salvific mission without manifesting in a certain way his proper identity in the mystery of the Trinity. When he reveals himself in his work, in the function which he exercises "for us", he cannot but give a glimpse of what he is "in himself" and "for himself". Formerly, theologians may have spoken with too much assurance of what the divine persons are "in themselves", but today we are inclined to yield to the temptation of considering only their function "for us". The two aspects necessarily exist in a dialectical relationship which must not be lost sight of.

In the apostolic Church, the Spirit is not allotted a work which is exclusively proper to himself. He consummates the work of the Father in Christ. What is this achievement? Primarily, it is to take us *out of ourselves* in the act of bearing witness, which is one of the aspects preserved most clearly in the theological tradition. Such testimony is more than the techniques of the apostolate, of government or organization. It comprises the whole range of mysterious influences (consolation, peace, persuasion, love, etc.), which flow out from the human person in its own authenticity and its profound solidarity with others. These personal relationships are purified, intensified and entirely transformed (in the dialectic of the natural and the supernatural) through the force of the Spirit who unites us all in his "communion". But the dimension of "for others" is dialectically inseparable from that of our being "in ourselves". Hence the Spirit also leads us *into ourselves,* perfecting our participation in the existence of the Son and so directing us to the Father, the transcendent and immanent source of divine life and salvation. For through grace, to be "in ourselves" and "for ourselves" becomes being "in God", the interior source which nourishes perpetually the mystery of our person and its communion with others. In a word, the grace of the Spirit is a constantly growing "interiorization", and an "exteriorization" in testimony and in prophecy, two aspects in which are realized our participation in the existence of Christ and our encounter with the Father.

This is how baptism is completed by confirmation. Baptism unites us to Christ, communicating to us the fundamental grace of being "servants in the Servant and adoptive sons in the Son". Confirmation gives full reality to this act of salvation, in the dialectic of mystical union and testimony. In the history of salvation, baptism applies to us the death and resurrection of the Lord, while confirmation communicates the grace of Pentecost. Basically, the necessity of confirmation is that of the descent of the Holy Spirit with regard to the salvific act of Christ. In other words, the relationship between baptism and confirmation stems from the relationship between the resurrection and

Pentecost in the history of salvation. Thus the two sacraments are truly mysteries and divine acts of salvation, manifested and realized sacramentally in the Church and applied to a given person, who is thereby taken into the community of the people of God. Hence too these sacraments may be termed "constitutive", since the consecration and the mission which they confer constitute men as members of the community of salvation established by Christ and his Spirit.

The doctrine of the sacramental character comes in here. There are various theological explanations of it. The Thomist notion of the *ordinatio ad cultum* remains valid. Theologians have overlooked the fact that the character *(sacramentum et res)* had originally a visible aspect, being in the nature of a "sign". The ontological structures of the character have perhaps been exaggerated. We prefer to restore to the sacramental character its ancient aspect of sign. Existentially, the sacramental character is based on the divine fidelity, which is the basic reason for the sacrament's not being repeated; this fidelity is also manifested visibly and attested by the Church in the sacramental act. The character exists on three levels of growing interiority: a complex of rights and duties in the visible Church; a particular mission, participating in the priesthood of Christ, in the sacerdotal Church (the notion of worship); a consecration to God in the spiritual Church. These three aspects are united to one another and ultimately to the sacramental grace by the dialectic of symbol and its realization *(sacramentum et res)*.

Hence above all, confirmation gives us the full rights of membership in the Church. This juridical status signifies and brings about a real mission which is a participation of the priesthood of Christ (the royal priesthood of the faithful). This mission signifies and brings about a consecration (the anointing by the Spirit). The consecration signifies and brings about our sanctification through the grace of the Spirit. This aspect above all makes it disastrous to separate totally confirmation from baptism. The two make up together the totality of our Christian initiation in the unity of being "in Christ" and "in the Spirit" in the one salvation wrought by the Father.

2. *Comparison with standard opinions.* This truth has been retained by the theological tradition, though often in a too narrow and materialistic formulation. In the wider context of a sound theology of the "gift of the Spirit" we can understand better how confirmation can "increase" the grace of baptism and give us a *gratia ad robur in protestatione fidei.* Some theologians define confirmation as the sacrament of Christian maturity, which is acceptable, provided the term is not taken unwittingly in a biological or psychological sense, but in the dogmatic sense of Christian fullness in the Spirit. In the same order of ideas we can see the importance of confirmation for the spiritual emancipation of the laity, since it completes the consecration of the baptized within the royal priesthood of the faithful. It is just as important for priests and bishops, who remain fundamentally "of the faithful". Orders is not a constitutive sacrament like baptism and confirmation. But it confers on certain of the faithful, hence within the people of God, a consecration and a *functional* mission to exercise prophetic authority and be ministers of sanctification. A priest is not "constituted" in an order superior to that of the faithful, but he is ordained for the service of Christ and the community.

See also *Holy Spirit* II, *Grace, Priest.*

BIBLIOGRAPHY. A. J. Mason, *The Relation of Confirmation to Baptism* (1891); J. Dölger, *Das Sakrament der Firmung, historisch-dogmatisch dargestellt* (1906); J. Coppens, *L'imposition des mains et rites connexes dans le Nouveau Testament et dans l'Église ancienne* (1925); G. Dix, *The Theology of Confirmation in Relation to Baptism* (1946); A. Charasse, *L'initiation à Rome dans l'antiquité et le haut moyen âge, Communion solennelle, profession de foi* (1952); A. Mostaza Rodríguez, *El Sujeto de la Confirmación* (1952); J. Crehan, "Ten Years' Study on Baptism and Confirmation", *Theological Studies* 14 (1953), pp. 273–9; 17 (1956), pp. 494–515; A. Mostaza Rodríguez, *Problema del ministro extraordinario de la Confirmación* (1954); L. Thornton, *Confirmation* (1954); G. W. H. Lampe, *The Seal of the Spirit* (1956); Y.-M. Congar, *Lay People in the Church. A Study for a Theology of Laity* (1957); K. F. Lynch, *The Sacrament of Confirmation in the Early-Middle Scholastic Period,* I (1957); A. Adams, *Das Sakrament der Firmung nach dem heiligen Thomas von Aquin* (1958); R. E. D. White, *The Biblical Doctrine of Initiation* (1960); B. Botte, "La Confirmation", *L'Église en prière* (1961), pp. 551–63; M. Bohen, *The Mystery of Confirmation* (1963); B. Neunheuser, *Baptism and Confirmation,* Herder History of Dogma (1964); I. de la Potterie and S. Lyonnet, *La vie selon l'Esprit, Condition du chrétien* (1965).

Piet Fransen

CONSCIENCE

1. *General description.* The word conscience (the "inwit" of Chaucer and Joyce) derives from *conscientia,* as does this from συνείδησις. While it is used in many senses, both in popular and scientific language, it denotes, in its specifically moral usage (French: *conscience morale*), a series of related phenomena of the soul, the kernel of which is an impressive basic experience reaching deep into personal consciousness. Long familiar, especially in the form of the so-called bad conscience, it has been apprehended and expressed in a variety of ways, and provides an appropriate starting point for a system of empirical, inductive ethics. Because of the present great lack of clarity in the use of the word a scientific description more properly starts, not from the linguistic usage, but from daily experience of conscience.

a) A careful analysis shows that in conscience man has a direct experience in the depths of his personality of the moral quality of a concrete personal decision or act as a call of duty on him, through his awareness of its significance for the ultimate fulfilment of his personal being. "The depths of his personality" means the nucleus, the centre of his integral, personal life, whose powers are first experienced as a unity before the various acts of soul and spirit come to be differentiated. Conscience is distinguished from moral knowledge (consciousness of value) on which it constantly draws and for which it provides the most vital content, by its immediate reference to one's own concrete action. Simplicity of experience — *simplex intuitus* in the scholastic psychology of knowledge — does not connote primitiveness but the intuition of a genuine and most delicate reality of the spirit, namely the moral value of one's own decision. An experience is made, not so much of norms capable of formulation, but of the immediate attraction of value or its opposite, of a richness and fullness encouraging and drawing one on towards what is good or of constriction and threat from evil and its harmful consequences. The basis is a capability in man for the moral, including the ultimate capability of decision about one's personal being. A certain parallel to conscience as a primary disposition may be found in the human power of language, in view of its elemental qualities, its integral and intuitive, at once mental and emotional receptivity for meaning, the general character of its laws of development and formation, and its essentially purposive nature.

b) Conscience is not correctly explained by the assumption of innate moral ideas. Neither does Kant's explanation as a transcendental faculty suffice. Inadequate also are theories which find an explanation of the origin, development and activity of conscience in extra-moral factors, naturalistic and evolutionary doctrines according to which conscience is a development from experiences of its usefulness in the history of the person or the species, of the individual or of society. F. Nietzsche, under the influence of biological evolutionism, regards the bad conscience as a product of human civilization. According to him it reveals a decadent, psychopathological development of man whose thwarted instincts have turned in on themselves. Very widely accepted is the explanation stemming from the depth psychology of S. Freud according to which an imperfectly developed form of conscience (Super Ego) is a product of the unconscious activity of the underlying instinctive reality. Existential philosophy accepts a formal concept of conscience which is not really moral, and which contains substantially the call to existential realization.

c) The primary intellectual and emotional receptivity for moral values, including the ordination to the good, which is present in the structure of conscience, can, through faulty training, not indeed be made false in itself, but weakened to the point of being practically ineffective. This incapability of being falsified, rooted as it is in the ultimate reality of personal existence and of consciousness, ensures the ethical dependability and authority of conscience and points as well to their limitation. The total lack of conscientious response (moral insanity), apart from cases of severe mental deficiency, can be caused by the psychopathic lack of that emotional function which is essential for conscience, even though intelligence remains intact. The development of conscience comes about under the influence of all the morally significant impressions drawn from the human environment, together with one's own life-experience. Beginning with the adoption of external patterns and norms of conduct and the acceptance of moral attitudes and values from others (authoritarian, legal conscience), it progresses to the point where an independent position is adopted as a response to one's appreciation of the claim of moral values (personal conscience). Defects in the normal psychological development frequently result in inhibitions or interferences with the development and functioning of conscience (fixation, regression to earlier stages of development, unhealthy guilt feelings, transference of guilt, compulsion of conscience or scruples).

d) The training of conscience, the aim of which is the fully developed conscience functioning in terms of autonomy (independence), intensity (depth, immediacy, vitality of experience) and extent of moral knowledge at one's command, is only partly the result of moral instruction and incomparably more the result of the encouragement of genuine activity of conscience implemented throughout the entire field of personal experience. Its aim is the fullest possible exercise of conscientious decision, and therefore the opportunity of adopting a personal point of view must not be taken away. Decisions of conscience are necessarily incomplete and partial because of the limiting circumstances of the individual, the time and environment. As a result they can be one-sided and are subject to prejudice and error. Critical examination and continuing formation of conscience are indispensable. As with every genuine appreciation of value, an attitude of reverence and love is an essential precondition both for the development and for the activity of conscience. To be aimed at is the sensitively alert conscience, dependable in every question of moral significance, reacting quickly and weighing accurately all the factors involved (opposite: the slow, dull, lax conscience).

e) In individual judgments of conscience a distinction is to be made between true and false propositions (*conscientia recta—falsa, vera—erronea,* or *error conscientiae*) according to whether the particular judgment agrees with the objective norm or not. The judgment which precedes action (*conscientia antecedens*) includes a warning, restraining from evil or urging to what is good; the latter, as the response to the claim of the good which is never capable of full realization, is a true function of conscience. The judgment of conscience following an action (*conscientia consequens*) is either the bad conscience (condemning and punishing) or the good conscience. This is not, as a mere correlative to bad conscience, a judgment on the goodness of one's own action, but the experience of overcoming an evil which is somehow felt as impending or threatening.

2. *Theology of conscience.* a) *Biblical.* The OT describes experiences of conscience without using the word itself. (The word first occurs, and then only in isolated instances, in the Wisdom books.) Instead it uses "heart" or "reins" or other such images. Conscience is always related to God as the hearing of his word, the acceptance of his will, consciousness of one's own position, one's own responsibility before God, of the divine judgment. In the NT conscience has a central significance (the inward moral attitude). With συνείδησις, a word taken from contemporary popular philosophy and not always given the same meaning, St. Paul indicates the essential functions of conscience in Christian life, without, however, developing a systematic teaching on conscience. The Christian knows himself to be confronted with the demands and judgments of God, which makes him conscious of the commandments and the grace of God (2 Cor 1:12), and is the guiding line for a life lived in the sight of God (Acts 24:16; Rom 13:5; 1 Cor 10:25f.; 1 Tim 1:5, 19), whether as a pure conscience (2 Tim 1:3; Heb 13:18; 1 Pet 2:19), or as a bad conscience (1 Tim 4:2; Tit 1:15; Heb 10:2, 22). As good conscience it makes him free and independent of the judgments of others (Acts 23:1; 1 Cor 10:29; 2 Cor 1:12; 1 Pet 3:16). As a human power it can give no certainty about God's judgment (1 Cor 4:4). It transmits the commandment even outside revelation as a law given by nature (Rom 2:15). Linked to human knowledge, it is subject to deception but remains a moral norm of the individual in this case (1 Cor 8:7f.; 10:25ff.; Rom 14). In the Christian it is active in the Holy Spirit (Rom 9:1), through the power of Christ's resurrection (1 Pet 3:21), cannot be purified and perfected through sacrifice but only through Christ's blood, in the power of the eternal spirit (Heb 9:9, 14). Conscience is also an organ of the religious life to which the apostolic revelation of truth is made (2 Cor 4:2) and which preserves the mysteries of faith in their purity (1 Tim 3:9). It can in fact take on the meaning of the theologically deeper and more precise Pauline term πίστις (Rom 14:23).

b) *History of the doctrine.* The rich foundations in NT for a theological teaching on conscience were not followed up by the Church Fathers. We find numerous single statements and opinions, especially in Tertullian, Origen, Chrysostom, and more details in Augustine, who describes especially the religious functions of conscience. In the Middle Ages, as well as a remarkable practical religious teaching on conscience (Bernard of Clairvaux, Petrus Cellensis, Gerson, etc.), there gradually developed from the 12th century on in relation to a text of St. Jerome (*Commentary on Ezek,* ch. 6), a systematic theological teaching on conscience on the basis of the two terms *synteresis (synderesis)* and *conscientia.* In general *synteresis* was taken as the natural nucleus of the conscience remaining essentially intact even after the fall of man, as the *a priori* intellectual and volitive basis of all activity of conscience. Bonaventure attributes the affective processes in conscience to the *synteresis,* the more intellectual functions both habitual and actual to the *conscientia.* Thomas Aquinas calls the *synteresis* the permanent natural *habitus* of the primary moral principles, *conscientia* the actual judgment of conscience arrived at by way of conclusion. The full recognition of conscience as the valid norm for the individual made much difficulty for the extremely objectively orientated medieval theology. St. Thomas Aquinas was the first to overcome this difficulty in principle and his success had its effect on succeeding generations. The reformers sought a meaning of conscience in line with their theological anthropology and their teaching on justification. In modern times our theological understanding of conscience had to be secured against a secularized notion of conscience with its tendency to absolute moral autonomy.

c) *Modern problems relating to conscience.* Theology must develop the traditional teaching into an understanding which is in the full sense Christian and theological as well as personal, taking cognizance of the insights of psychology and depth psychology, of sociology and ethnology. An intensive study of the teaching of the Bible is essential, as well as a thorough appreciation of the role of conscience in the entire Christian life, especially in its significance for the spiritual life and for the circumstances of the individual Christian. Conscience itself cannot be taken as being equivalent to moral evaluation or moral knowledge. Primarily and directly it applies to the claim on the human ego in a concrete situation of decision as being what is of ultimately radical significance for the person as such. In connection with this there also arises of itself in most cases a new or deeper insight into objective moral value precisely in its relation to the particular circumstances of the individual person and the unique situation of decision. As the faculty for ultimate personal commitment, the conscience of the Christian responds on the basis of the faith to the personal demands made by God's work and word in revelation, having an immediate experience of their significance for personal salvation. Conscience has here become the conscience of the believer. Theology must reject all attempts to restrict the understanding of conscience to the sphere of the moral, even though this can in fact set the limits for the experience of conscience by the unbeliever. The conscience of the Christian will fulfil its function only when every dawning value is deeply experienced as a gracious approach of the divine perfection and every situation of decision as "the fullness of time", as a gift and a call of God, as a possibility of Christian loyalty in the presence of the divine "Thou".

3. *Conscience as moral norm.* Conscience brings to mind the objective moral norm in its relation to the concrete decision to be made in the present situation. Since the role of conscience is thus an intermediary one, it does not set the moral norms itself in an autonomous sense. This is true even though this receptivity of conscience can by no means be regarded as merely passive, and no matter how creatively active in personal reverence and love conscience is in discovering with delicate sensitivity the good that is to be done together with its most minute circumstances, and no matter how much it brings to bear the entire extent of personal knowledge and experience of life in moral matters. It interiorizes, in fact ("autonomizes"), the objective norms. The relation of the objective norms to conscience cannot be understood as the meeting of two competing values. The objective "law" is the will and order of God in his creation and this is made known in the conscience of man who carries on his life within this creation and its plan of salvation. For moral orientation in a

situation where a concrete decision is called for, conscience cannot be dispensed with or bypassed. Its place cannot be taken either by moral knowledge or opinion or by direction from another. The judgment of conscience is the ultimate definitive norm for the individual decision *(regula proxima moralitatis),* but it does not thereby become a general norm for people faced with similar decisions. The moral value of an action is measured exclusively according to the judgment of conscience arrived at after due consideration of all the circumstances.

The judgment of conscience retains its normative value in the case where there is a genuine error of conscience *(error invincibilis),* that is, where in an individual case something that is done in accordance with the dictate of conscience is at variance with the objective norm. As the final subjective norm for moral action the judgment of conscience must be definite and unambiguous so that a well-grounded uncertainty is excluded *(certitudo moralis).* Where certainty cannot be attained there arise doubts of conscience *(dubium practicum conscientiae,* also *error vincibilis).* The actual (practical) doubt of conscience is not a moral defect, but rather a necessary stage especially in cases where a decision is difficult. It can occur over the entire range of moral life in the form of a lack of clarity in respect of moral norms *(dubium iuris)* or their application in a particular situation *(dubium facti);* also in the case of several competing moral claims. Higher experiences of the spiritual life move often at the margin of the certain conscience. The most difficult situation is the conflict of conscience: the conjunction of conflicting obligations, even in the most extreme form, where, in consequence of a life permeated in all its relationships and circumstances with evil, conscience can show no possibility of action that does not entail sin *(conscientia perplexa).* The causes of the individual's doubts of conscience are, apart from the natural limitation of knowledge, ignorance in moral matters and lack of certainty in moral judgment. To act with positive practical doubts of conscience implies indifference to the danger of sin (Rom 14:23). The objectively safest way must be chosen when the attainment of an end is absolutely demanded (e.g., the validity of administration of the sacraments).

Generally speaking, practical certainty in the judgment of conscience must be striven for: a) through clarification of the moral position by personal reflection or with the help of the advice of another *(certitudo directa);* b) when this is impossible, a morally justifiable decision must be arrived at from moral considerations of a general nature *(certitudo indirecta sive reflexa);* c) finally, the Christian must have as his general moral attitude the desire to discover what is good and commit himself to it with all his personal moral power (risk in the positive sense), so as purely out of love of God and loyalty to him to make his way through the darkness which cannot be enlightened. Historically, the attempt to arrive reflexively, with the help of rationally enunciated general principles, at the best possible solution to the most difficult problems arising from doubts of conscience, led to the construction of the so-called moral systems. For the overcoming of doubts of conscience there is need above all of prudence.

See also *Morality* III, *Decision, Value, Psychology, Existence* II, *Good, Illness* II, *Education, Authority, Natural Law.*

BIBLIOGRAPHY. H. Rashdall, *Conscience and Christ. Six Lectures on Christian Ethics* (1916); H. G. Stocker, *Das Gewissen* (1925); J. H. Breasted, *Dawn of Conscience* (1933); O. Lottin, *Psychologie et Morale aux XIIe et XIIIe siècles,* 4 vols. (1942–54); G. Madimer, *La conscience morale* (1954); C. Pierce, *Conscience in the New Testament* (1955); E. D'Arcy, *Conscience and its Right to Freedom* (1961); J. Leclercq, *Christ and the Modern Conscience* (1962); P. Delhaye, *La conscience morale du chrétien* (1964); L. Janssens, *Freedom of Conscience and Religious Freedom* (1966).

Rudolf Hofmann

CONSCIOUSNESS

1. Consciousness, literally the state of knowing, of knowing well in one's own mind, is the spirit's awareness not merely of the objects of its experience, but of this experience as its own and hence of itself. Consciousness includes, as well as the immediate moment of experience, the memory of past experience — based on experience — and a more or less general anticipation of its future. At the most primitive level it is not a matter of two or more different acts, which might then perhaps give rise to the epistemological question about the nature and criteria of their accord, which would

lead to a *regressus in infinitum* without issue. It is a self-luminous state, the spirit's awareness of self in its awareness of the other. It is therefore a matter of identity in the strict sense, which when fully understood involves not only material sameness but "affirmed", "reduplicative" self-hood. In this primitive oneness of the "intentionality" of consciousness (its essential reference to the self, the world and being) is contained the presupposition and possibility of all further explicit reflection.

Reflection can then distinguish and classify the various elements of the single reality of consciousness. These are: the perception of the objects of experience (things and states); knowledge of the act or acts of this perception; of the power and the faculties to produce these acts; knowledge finally of the principle of these faculties, the "I" or the self. This knowledge of the "subjective" conditions of knowledge is accompanied by apprehension of the "objective" elements: objects, and their categories and relationships, without which they would lack form and reality. Finally, as original and originating unity of subjective and objective moments, there is the ontological openness of consciousness for the first principles, of being, truth and goodness.

This reflection makes it possible for the spirit to judge itself in its acts. It can look at them from a distance and determine them as such, examine how "objectively" apt or inapt they are with regard to the object envisaged, and with regard to the intention and the nature of the self in general; how legitimate they are in view of the first principles, at once theoretical and "practical", which call for the true and the good. As knowledge of these first principles of thought and action (which they are because first and fundamentally principles of being), consciousness is called in scholastic tradition *intellectus principiorum* (with regard to theoretical propositions like the principle of contradiction), or *synderesis* (with regard to the basic principles of morality). In the light of such conscious ties to the basic laws of being, man finds himself at a distance from himself and from the reality which confronts him. He is therefore free.

Here, by virtue of the intentionality of consciousness, man's freedom is such that the spirit is all the more with itself the more it is with the other. It is all the more itself, the more the other is there and present as itself in the spirit, and the more the spirit itself, as itself, is that other (in the identity of self-hood and differentiation). But man is finite and corporeal — and, as theology says of man after Adam, subject to concupiscence. Of himself, he is unequal to the tension set up by this unity. Thus he finds the object overpowering as it entices or threatens. Confrontation with it disguises rather than intensifies the presence of self, act and ontological principle. Insofar as the object gains the mastery, consciousness is reduced to what is felt or undergone unconsciously. (Whether one is to ascribe consciousness to animals or not, is primarily a question of terminology. In any case, one is confronted here by the difficult task of how to conceive a consciousness [higher than merely vegetative life] which would still not be *self*-consciousness. This is why the animal is at once what is closest and most foreign to man.)

In fact, even when the mind is fully conscious, all the objects of consciousness are not present with equal clearness. Our field of consciousness is so limited that we can only grasp a small amount at "the centre" with full attentiveness. The rest remains "on the margin of consciousness", as an object or "horizon" which is only sensed along with what is thought of, and can only be brought explicitly to mind by means of further reflection. The region of the unconsciously known is even more mysterious. It was investigated as early as St. Augustine, who studied the phenomenon of forgetting, trying to remember, and remembering.

Here man's consciousness cannot be completely transparent to him in reflection. A particular subject is involved in each act of reflection, which embraces previous decisions which cannot be separated from it. Above all, it is itself an act of free decision, and this is essentially initiative and so cannot be objectivated, that is, grasped in terms of known objects. This is not to deny that the immediate light of consciousness is the norm and legitimation of truth as well as of the good (evidence is the criterion of certainty). But it means that this light is absolutely sovereign. It is authoritative immediately as it falls but it cannot be subsequently accounted for and so brought under control. One can and must think and live by it, but it is equally true that it accords no absolute certainty in explicit reflection. The certainty can never be independent of the personal self-surrender which is constantly called for. Theoretically and practically man can "repress" the truth, and he can never be absolutely sure that that is not what he is doing in the last resort (*D* 802).

2. Consciousness and certainty could be taken as the slogans of modern thought since Descartes, in its effort to dig deeper and deeper for the *fundamentum inconcussum* of the life of the spirit. This is the result of what the Christian experience has contributed to the philosophical tradition of the West. The development of "objective" Greek thought has been balanced by the Christian teaching which affirms that man is personally and historically touched by God at the centre of his being *(cor, mens, anima)* and summoned to make an absolute, eternal decision. The Christian experience acts in a unique manner to take consciousness or man out of the world of created things and confront him with the absolute. The ultimate source of this consciousness and freedom is the creative principle and mystery — as was most keenly felt by the Christian mystics such as Meister Eckhart. If the link with the mystery is lost sight of, consciousness is no longer assured of meaningfulness and is forced to look for its justification in itself. The method of "scepticism" adopted in the search leads to the dilemma of the Enlightenment, rationalism or empiricism. It ends in the dilemma of Kant, who first defines consciousness as "consciousness in general", that is, the transcendental condition of possibility of all knowing, and then goes on to affirm that its unconditioned and infinite nature is merely formal and hence only existing in relation to the finite material endlessly supplied by sense-data: a difficulty from which he can see no escape except by the postulates of his doctrine of the practical reason.

German idealism, on the contrary, seeks to make even matter an element of consciousness and so make consciousness really infinite and absolute. Though Fichte and Schelling abandon this idealism in their later philosophy, Hegel tries to apply it consistently throughout. He frankly accepts the consequence this entails, that such a material consciousness must be thought of as historical (and history — of the world and of God himself — as the gradual growth of consciousness till it reaches the full, liberating knowledge of its own necessary being). With this he prepared the ground for the later reaction to historicism and relativism in the "historical consciousness" upheld in the 19th century. This situation leads, in philosophy as in psychology, to thinking merely in terms of consciousness on the one hand (as in the efforts to find a basis for neo-Kantianism and present-day logistics), and on the other hand, to conjuring up the genies of life, passion, and power in a process hostile to consciousness (life-philosophy).

At present ontology is linking up once more with traditional thought and affirming the precedence of being (truth, goodness) over consciousness (certainty, volition, values) — not, however, in the sense of "immutable essences" but on the basis of the experience of the historical summons. And just as (partly under the influence of ontology) modern psychology and psychotherapy try to grasp human reality at its basic origin (depth-psychology), so ontology also regards man once more in such a light. It sees him as one on whom the unconditioned impinges not just in his consciousness or in the living depths of his subconscious, but in the centre of his person. For there takes place the experience — self-luminous but inexpressible, beyond doubt but without guarantees — from which perpetually stem consciousness and freedom, in their self-determination as in their dependence on their absolute ground.

See also *Spirit, Principle, Transcendentals, Freedom, Decision, Absolute and Contingent, Kantianism.*

BIBLIOGRAPHY. G. Siewerth, *Die Metaphysik der Erkenntnis,* I (1933); J. de Vries, *Denken und Sein* (1937); K. Port, *Die Enge des Bewusstseins* (1955); O. Marquard, *Skeptische Methode im Blick auf Kant* (1958); M. Heidegger, *Nietzsche,* II (1961); id., *Being and Time* (1962); P. Lersch, *Aufbau der Person* (9th ed., 1964); M. Müller, *Existenzphilosophie im geistigen Leben der Gegenwart* (3rd ed., 1964); K. Rahner, *Geist in Welt* (3rd ed., 1964); M. Heidegger, *Discourse and Thinking* (1966).

Jörg Splett

CONSTANTINIAN ERA

In every discussion of the Church in history, the age of Constantine takes pride of place, less in view of a possible division of Church history into periods than in an attempt to assess this encounter of Church and State initiated by the Emperor Constantine (*c.* 285–337), which determined to some extent the outward form of the Christian Church for centuries, and perhaps still does. The "age of Constantine" is a historical category which has become a judgment of value — mostly negative; hence the various meanings of the expression.

If we are to be consistent, the analogy of the "age of Augustus" or the "age of Justinian" suggests that we should restrict it to the three full decades of Constantine's reign at the beginning of the 4th century. This provides research with a definite framework for assessing the significance of the emperor in world history. If, on the other hand, the concept is made wider — as, for instance, in modern comment on the Constantinian era — we get a division of Church history which is as questionable as the over-emphasis on Constantine's policy. As regards the Church, the development in question was clearly adumbrated in the previous period. As regards the State, the contribution of Theodosius I (379–95) or Justinian (527–65) should not be lost sight of. The mutual infiltration of Church and State, which was started by Constantine, which found a comprehensive expression in the *res publica christiana* of the Middle Ages and still influences the modern world in many ways, was not the work of a few years but a lengthy process whose complex character can only be revealed by careful analysis. Then it is clear that the merger between Christianity and Empire in the first half of the 4th century had far-reaching consequences. And these too have to be investigated, even without the aid of global judgments.

1. *The history of the problem.* The importance of Constantine may be seen from the fact that historians have found him a challenge from the start, evoking praise or blame in turn, a symbol of the responsible Christian ruler or of the depravation of the Church. If Constantine has been judged favourably, the reason undoubtedly lies in the *Life of Constantine* by Eusebius of Caesarea (d. 339), who Christianized the notion of emperor and thus impressed on succeeding ages his image of Constantine. In his *City of God* (V, 24 f.), Augustine likewise used Constantine to depict his ideal emperor — a notion which

was to have enormous influence in the Middle Ages. O. Treitinger has convincingly demonstrated the impact of this image in the Byzantine world. The West too was inspired by the Constantinian model. The coronation of Charlemagne implied the acceptance of the tradition. Constantine remained the ideal Christian ruler, and it is significant that the Reformers had hardly any misgivings about "the good Emperor Constantine" (Luther). He was never quite canonized, but the notion of his Christian kingdom has been influential down to the present day, even where the negative elements were recognized.

Criticism was, indeed, never wanting. The basic question was already posed by the African heretic Donatus when he asked Constantine's envoy, "What has the Emperor to do with the Church?" (Optatus of Milevis, *Contra Parm. Don.,* III, 3.) Even Eusebius, for all his admiration, was not blind to the disadvantages of the Emperor's promoting religion; he states bluntly that pagans and secret heretics "crept into the Church for fear of the Emperor's menaces" (*Life,* III, 66). The ambiguity of his personal decision with regard to the faith was clearly felt as a problem by his contemporaries and we can be sure that the joy which greeted his policy of favouring Christianity was not unmixed.

The pagan reaction, of course, as in the case of the Emperor Julian (d. 363) and the Byzantine historian Zosimus (5th century), was to try to blacken the memory of Constantine, by recalling, for instance, his cruelty. But Jerome had already sketched the plan of a history which unfortunately he never carried out, of which decline and fall was to have been the key-note. "If God spares me", he wrote, "and my slanderers stop persecuting me, now that I have fled and hidden myself away, I intend to write a history of the period between the coming of our Redeemer and our own days, that is, from the apostles till the apostasy of our times. It will show how and by whom the Church was founded, how it grew, how it flourished through persecution, how it is glorified by its martyrs, and how it was cherished by Christian princes, gaining thereby in power and riches, but paying for it in the loss of inward strength." (*Vita Malchi,* 1.) This is the view of history which sees in Constantine, even when he is not mentioned, a turning-point in the history of the Church and hence regards the Constantinian age as a particularly grave development. With the complaints of Socrates (d. 439) about a "Hellenizing Christianity" (*Hist. eccles.,* I, 22), the characteristic elements of later polemics have already been voiced.

The Middle Ages too had their reserves about Constantine and his religious policies. Religious movements, sometimes fanatical in type, which broke with the Church also condemned the unity of Church and State of which the first Christian emperor was supposed to be the author. Albigenses and Waldenses, Fraticelli and Hussites pilloried this type of Church, and argued from the *ecclesia primitiva* against the Church of their day. How deeply rooted was this attitude may be seen from the triple "Woe!" of the angel over "King Constantine" in Walter v. d. Vogelweide, or from Dante's complaint about the misery caused by the baptism, "or rather, Donation" of Constantine (*Divina Commedia, Inferno,* XIX, 115–7).

In the controversies which followed the Reformation, the theme was given new emphasis, since the theory of "decline and fall" was invoked to provide historical justification for new departures. The centuriators of Magdeburg wrote their histories from this point of view, which was again taken up by G. Arnold (d. 1714) in his *Dispassionate History of Churches and Heresies* (in German: *Unpartheyische Kirchen- und Ketzer-Historie,* 1699–1700), with Constantine as an Antichrist. His main fault was to have forced the world upon the Church. "The original purity of Christianity was done away with. Constantine tried to mingle the two things that are most opposed to each other. God and the devil were to reign together, Christ and Belial were to be friends." (I, 145.) The space devoted to the theme shows how seriously Arnold took it. His influence on the most diverse religious movements, and especially on the Pietists, is strikingly clear. Polemic against the Church concentrated in a way on Constantine as the first cause of its degeneration. Thus even before J. Burckhardt's influential *Age of Constantine* (in German: *Die Zeit Constantins des Grossen,* first published 1853) there was a long tradition of criticism. A more positive view is making headway at present, thanks to the careful interpretation of the sources by such authors as J. Vogt, H. Dörries, H. Kraft and K. Aland.

But this survey of the problem shows that the first Christian monarch is a key to the interpretation of Church history. He became a symbol which often embodied prejudice rather than scientific historical judgment. Objections to the Constantinian type of Christian State did not die out in the course of time. They are stronger than ever now, with the new reflection on the nature of the Church.

2. *Church and State.* In the first half of the 4th century, Church and State came together, through Constantine, in a way which changed the history of the Church and of the world. This meeting, however, was not entirely novel. Severe as had been the persecutions, the State had, on the whole, attacked only sporadically or at intervals which allowed the Church to consolidate itself. J. Vogt rightly describes the years before the persecution of Diocletian as halcyon days in which the Church was able to form a sort of State within the State. It is still remarkable that Christians on the whole remained well-disposed. Criticism such as that of Rev was not wanting, but from Paul (Rom 13:1–7), Melito of Sardes (in Eusebius, *Hist. Eccles.,* IV, 26), and Origen (*Contra Cels.,* II, 30; VIII, 69), down to Eusebius, there is a positive attitude which almost makes the change under Constantine seem the achievement of a long-desired end. Harmonious co-operation with the State seemed natural to the Church in terms of antique thought, and the expulsion of Paul of Samosata from his bishopric by the Emperor Aurelian (Eusebius, *Hist. Eccles.,* VII, 30) shows how far co-operation could go even before Constantine. Persecutions did not mean the end of contact: the Apologies of these periods show how eager Christians were for dialogue, thus preparing for the great change-over.

When the tetrarchical administration set up (285–305) by Diocletian broke down, Constantine succeeded to the north-western part of the Empire after the death of his father, Constantius Chlorus, in 306. He continued his father's tolerance towards Christians, a policy undoubtedly furthered by the vague monotheism towards which he increasingly inclined (the worship of *Sol Invictus*). His path to Christianity is marked by a series of measures and edicts which are signs of his sincerity. The year 311 saw a notable improvement in the relationship of the Empire to the Church, when the Emperor of the East, Galerius, recognized that persecution had failed and issued an edict of tolerance (Lactantius, *Mort. pers.,* 34; Eusebius, *Hist. Eccles.,* VIII, 17, 3–10) also signed by Constantine, which gave a basically new direction to the religious policies of the Roman State — "the charter of Christianity in the Empire", as J. Vogt has called it.

For a while, East and West were at one, but Maximinus soon turned once more to coercion. Things changed also in the West, when Constantine opened hostilities against Maxentius — for political reasons, not for the sake of Christianity. Nonetheless, the campaign of 312 proved to be, for Christianity, a decisive step, symbolized by tradition in the vision of the cross attributed to Constantine. What happened is difficult to explain, all the more so since the accounts vary (Lactantius, *Mort. pers.,* 44; Eusebius, *Vita Const.,* 1, 27–32), but Constantine's behaviour after the victory of the Milvian Bridge, 28 October 312, shows that he felt himself under an obligation to the God of the Christians.

Then came official favour for Christians and the promotion of Christian worship. The *domus Faustae,* for instance, where the Lateran basilica was built, was assigned to the Bishop of Rome. Before the year was out, Constantine was summoning Maximinus to put an end to the recrudescence of persecution in his territory. Africa received orders to return Church property, and even to provide money for the clergy of "the lawful and most holy Catholic religion" (Eusebius, *Hist. Eccles.,* X, 6, 1–5). These measures expressed the conviction that prohibition of Christian worship had only done damage to the State, while its promotion was a blessing, a view undoubtedly supported by the juridical Roman concept of religion — *do ut des.*

In February 313, Constantine and Licinius came to an accord at Milan which was more liberal towards Christianity than the edict of Galerius. The stress on the freedom of religious decision (Lactantius, *Mort. pers.,* 48, 2. 5. 6) is undoubtedly due to the conqueror who had set his hopes on the sign of Christian salvation. But Constantine had already in fact gone beyond this programme in his policy of furthering Christianity, from the truly Roman conviction that the true

religion (now serving the Christian God) guaranteed the good of the State. It was not just the organization of the Church and its moral authority that made it a decisive factor in Constantine's religious policy, it was also its religious worship. This attitude assured Christianity of precedence as a religion in the age of Constantine, though the quality of religious adherence was often doubtful.

In the Church, the change was greeted with joy. Eusebius undoubtedly expresses the sentiments of Christians when he writes, "More than all others, we who had set our hopes on the Christ of God were filled with inexpressible joy, and a sort of divine bliss radiated from our faces" (*Hist. Eccles.,* X, 2). The memory of the harsh persecution under Diocletian makes it easy to understand this triumphant jubilation.

Constantine was a skilful enough politician to consolidate his rule, taking advantage of the accord with Licinius, who had defeated Maximinus and now ruled the whole of the East. His religious policy, however, brought him into conflict with the Donatists. His efforts to restore unity, either by setting up ecclesiastical courts of arbitration or by applying coercion, met with failure, and he had to acknowledge his limitations, in spite of his sense of mission.

The official favour shown to Christianity did not at once interfere with paganism. Its traditions were upheld by Constantine both in his self-understanding as emperor and in his interest in the official religion — the title of Pontifex Maximus was not laid aside till the reign of Gratian, 379. The coinage in particular demonstrates how the ancient gods still dominated the mentality of the empire. And the prudence of Constantine's own statements show well enough that he did not simply try to abolish the ancient mode of thought. In the transitional period, Christianity and paganism proceeded their separate ways with equal rights. The emperor, from personal conviction, turned more and more to Christianity, and showed his attitude by bestowing privileges and passing Christianized laws. But the freedom of pagans was still fully preserved. Licinius's re-opening of hostilities against Christianity in the East enabled Constantine to add a religious motive to his struggle for supreme power (324). His victory placed the whole empire under his sway, so that his religious policy could be applied everywhere. The feeling that he had come to power under the sign of the saving cross strengthened his sense of mission and his determination to follow this path to the end. The dove-tailing of Church and State went on, as high offices were given to Christians and Christian notions impinged on the idea of emperor, a notable sign being the emperor's conscientious intervention in Church affairs (as ἐπίσκοπος τῶν ἐκτός).

When the East came under his rule, Constantine suddenly found himself faced with the Arian controversy, which he tried to smooth out on his own initiative, in spite of his disheartening experiences with the Donatists. His convocation of the Council of Nicaea shows that he felt he shared the responsibility, certain as he was that the well-being of the empire depended essentially on the unity of the Church. His function at this Council of the Empire shows that he understood himself as a "Vicar of Christ". As such, he sought to have the confusions caused by Arianism dissipated, less for the sake of theological clarity than to guarantee the right worship of God. But in fact the great theological discussions began during the peace of the Constantinian age, and at the same time, the resistance of the Church to State tutelage.

Externally, the change was exemplified in great building activity, not merely in the founding of Constantinople but in the brilliant monuments which the Church could erect in its hour of triumph, thanks to the generosity of the emperor.

Constantine died while preparing for war against the Persians, 337, having been baptized shortly before. His burial in the mausoleum of the Church of the Apostles at Byzantium proclaimed him the equal of the apostles even in death, and hence enshrined the programme of his life.

3. *Structures and consequences.* The reign of Constantine was undoubtedly a turning-point in world history, especially for the development of Christianity. But the shape of the pre-Constantinian Church warns us against exaggerating the change, and so coming too hastily to condemn the age of Constantine. The postulates of antiquity made the meeting of Church and State fruitful and hence legitimate; nonetheless, the structures of this Christian and imperial cosmos pose some questions.

a) Ancient notions of unity forced the identification of Church and State on the religious policies of Constantine. There seemed to be an anticipation of the final reign of Christ. The concept was imposingly realized in the unified cosmos of medieval Christendom. This amalgamation of Church and State, personified in the Christian "King by the grace of God", often hid the differences between the two entities. The Church was sometimes taken in tow by the State, as an established State Church, or indeed was at the mercy of the world.

b) The assimilation of Church and State helped to impose a large measure of profane structures on Christianity. Organizational forms, feudal systems and court ceremonial affected so strongly the outward form of the Church that its spiritual mission was often lost sight of in history.

c) This brought with it the same set of interests in the spiritual, political and geographical spheres. Constantine undoubtedly threw open great possibilities to the Church. But the alliance often brought it into discredit and hindered the prophetic spirit. As long as the citizen was identified with the Christian, the problem was more or less hidden away. But the very fact that unbelievers could be looked on as enemies of the State involved pernicious consequences.

d) The favour shown to Christianity by the State led to conversions in which opportunism was often more strongly at work than faith. The phenomenon of the Church as a national institution ensued, and with it the danger of a paganizing of Christianity, which even the catechumenate could not fully counter. The missionary effort of the Church was to be absorbed in future mostly by mass conversions, while monasticism disengaged itself.

e) Sociological differences then developed in the people of God, as between clergy and laity. As the ecclesiastical hierarchy assimilated itself to the various grades of public office and was granted privileges and titles of nobility, the (higher) clergy stood out in sharp contrast to the people, a fact underlined in Church architecture by the distinction between the choir and the nave. The original tension between the Church and the world was replaced by the difference between clergy and laity. The "churchman" was henceforth the cleric, and not the baptized

Christian as such; and only the cleric was educated.

f) The Christian faith was the bond of union in the Constantinian concept of the empire. Eusebius formulated this ideal more or less as: One God, one emperor, one empire and one faith or creed. Inspired by a sense of universal authority and mission, Christian rulers then intervened in theological debate, to the detriment of the freedom of the Church. This prepared the way for making an ideology of the faith, a temptation which besets all efforts to form a "Christian" State, and makes the genuineness of the decision for God's saving act questionable.

See also *Church History, Early Church, Church and State*.

BIBLIOGRAPHY. N. H. Baynes, *Constantine the Great and the Christian Church* (1929); E. Peterson, *Der Monotheismus als politisches Problem. Ein Beitrag zur Geschichte der politischen Theologie im Imperium Romanum* (1935); A. Alföldi, *The Conversion of Constantine and Pagan Rome* (1948); A. H. Jones, *Constantine the Great and the Conversion of Europe* (1948); S. L. Greenslade, *Church and State from Constantine to Theodosius* (1954); A. A. T. Ehrhardt, *Politische Metaphysik von Solon bis Augustin,* 2 vols. (1959); H. Dörries, *Constantine and Religious Liberty* (1960); H. Rahner, *Kirche und Staat im frühen Christentum. Dokumente aus acht Jahrhunderten und ihre Deutung* (1961); A. Momigliano, ed., *The Conflict between Paganism and Christianity in the Fourth Century* (1967); K. Baus, *From the Apostolic Community to Constantine,* Handbook of Church History, ed. by H. Jedin and J. Dolan, I (1965), pp. 405–32; A. Mirgeler, *Mutation of Western Christianity* (1964).

Peter Stockmeier